# Master Keys to Personal Christhood

# Master Keys to Personal Christhood

Kim Michaels

More to Life Publishing

Master Keys to Personal Christhood
by Kim Michaels.

More to Life Publishing. www.morepublish.com



ISBN: 978-0-9825746-1-4

**Other books by Kim Michaels:**
The Art of Non-war
Master Keys to Spiritual Freedom
I Love Jesus, I Hate Christianity
The Least You Should Know About Life
Master Keys to the Abundant Life
Beyond Religious Conflict
I Am a Thinking Christian
The Secret Coming of Christ
The Jesus Koans
Save Your Planet
Save Yourself!
The Inner Path of Light
The Christ Is Born in You
Master Keys to Personal Wholeness

*Who are you and why are you here?*

*You are here because you know you want MORE.*

*You do not want more of what the material world has to offer.*

*You want MORE than what the material world has to offer.*

*Thus, you are looking for a teacher who can show you how to find the MORE you are seeking. And that is why I have come to offer my services, for did I not say, "I AM come that all might have LIFE and that they might have it MORE abundantly."*

*Thus, let me show you the way to the LIFE that is MORE.*

*Jesus*

# Table of Contents

# Introduction
# The sword of Christ

I AM the Living Christ!

My main purpose for releasing this course in Christhood is to help the most spiritually aware people understand and master the timeless challenges of Christ.

When I walked the Earth 2,000 years ago – as the historical person most people know as Jesus – I made this statement:

> 32 Whosoever therefore shall confess me before men, him will I confess also before my Father which is in heaven.
> 33 But whosoever shall deny me before men, him will I also deny before my Father which is in heaven.
> 34 Think not that I am come to send peace on Earth: I came not to send peace, but a sword. (Mark, Chapter 10)

The role of the Living Christ is to be the open door for the Living Word that divides people into two categories:

- There are those who are willing to let the Word awaken them onto life—meaning spiritual life, eternal life, life beyond time and space.

- There are those who are not willing to be awakened and who are therefore judged for their unwillingness to rise above – to leave behind – the state of spiritual death.

The sword of Christ, the Sacred **WORD** of Christ, divides people into those who confess Christ and those who deny Christ. The mere existence of this course presents people with the first challenge of Christ, the challenge to confess or deny Christ.

There are many who have been brought up – programmed – to reject the Living Christ, and consequently they are predisposed to reject this course. Some will be programmed to reject the course based on the title alone. They have come to accept a graven image of Christ, according to which I, Jesus, was the only person who could possibly attain personal Christhood. Thus, they consider it blasphemous to claim that everyone has the potential to become the Living Christ. Yet in so doing, these people must deny Christ before men, for they must deny one of my pivotal statements:

> Verily, verily, I say unto you, He that believeth on me, the works that I do shall he do also; and greater works than these shall he do; because I go unto my Father. (John 14:12)

How can one claim to be a follower of Christ while ignoring this statement or refusing to seek for a deeper understanding of it? When you seek for such an understanding, you realize that no one can do the same works that I did without attaining the state of consciousness that I demonstrated, namely the Christ consciousness. Thus, those who think the Living Christ can be confined to one historical person – or to a mental image of that person created by a self-serving institution – do not know Christ and have not confessed Christ before men.

There are those who have been programmed to reject this course based on the statement that the course is given directly by me, the ascended Jesus Christ. These people have come to accept another graven image of Christ, namely that I stopped speaking to humankind after I had released the official Christian scriptures. It is as if they think I can no longer bring forth spiritual revelations or that I have nothing to say to today's people. These people also deny Christ before men, for they deny the following statements:

> "All power is given unto me in heaven and in Earth" (Matthew 28:18).
>
> I have yet many things to say unto you, but ye cannot bear them now. (John 16:12)

Those who ignore these statements are in reality saying that they do not want me to speak to humankind today—they do not want me to disturb them in their self-created comfortability, in which they claim to be my followers yet have shut me out of their hearts and their churches. I do indeed have the ability and the will to bring forth new teachings in the modern world, for did I not say that I am with you always (Matthew 28:20)?

It should now be clear for those who have eyes to see that having a graven image of Christ will indeed cause people to deny Christ—while actually believing they are true followers of Christ. It is a fact that many people call themselves Christians, but they have adopted the very same mindset that I challenged many times:

> 1 Judge not, that ye be not judged.
> 2 For with what judgment ye judge, ye shall be judged: and with what measure ye mete, it shall be measured to you again.
> 3 And why beholdest thou the mote that is in thy brother's eye, but considerest not the beam that is in thine own eye?
> 4 Or how wilt thou say to thy brother, Let me pull out the mote out of thine eye; and, behold, a beam is in thine own eye?
> 5 Thou hypocrite, first cast out the beam out of thine own eye; and then shalt thou see clearly to cast out the mote out of thy brother's eye. (Matthew, Chapter 7)

Many people will judge this course based on a graven image, and in so doing they will bring about their own judgment. For you will be judged according to the words that you allow to fill your heart and mind:

> 47 And if any man hear my words, and believe not, I judge him not: for I came not to judge the world, but to save the world.
> 48 He that rejecteth me, and receiveth not my words, hath one that judgeth him: the word that I have spoken, the same shall judge him in the last day. (John, Chapter 12)

Yet many people judge because they simply do not know better, because they have been brought up to believe a false word about me. Thus, I offer this course in order to give people the opportunity to understand the true teachings of Christ. When you – with all your getting – get understanding, you have a free choice to reject the dead doctrines, the graven images, and accept the Living Christ. So the real question is not whether you know better right now, but whether you are willing to get to know better. Are you willing to let the Living Christ take you beyond your current knowledge, beliefs and understanding—your current mental box?

As will become clear in this course, I do indeed have many more things to say to humankind, and in this modern age many people can bear the full explanation of my true teachings. Thus, one of the main purposes of this course is to offer modern spiritual people a full understanding of the real mission of Christ, the mission that most people have never heard about because it has been obscured behind a multitude of graven images.

***

Let it be made clear that this course is indeed a gift directly from the heart of the ascended Jesus Christ. I have all power in heaven and on Earth, yet I have chosen to bring forth this course the same way I brought forth the four gospels that most Christians recognize as being the result of Divine inspiration—or revelation. Over the past 2,000 years I have inspired a number of people to bring forth genuine spiritual teachings, yet in this course I will, for the first time, give the full and unmasked truth about the mission of the Living Christ on Earth.

Those who are willing to look beyond all graven images will then be able to make a free choice as to whether they will confess or deny Christ before men. For let it be made clear that there is hardly anyone on Earth who has not come to accept one or more graven images of Christ. And such images make it impossible for them to choose freely whether to confess or deny Christ. Many do indeed think they confess Christ, but in reality they are confessing a graven image of Christ while denying the living reality of Christ. Take note of what I said to my disciples:

> He that receiveth you receiveth me, and he that receiveth me receiveth him that sent me. (Matthew 10:40)

The same holds true for this course. This course is my wake-up call, sent to people in the modern age. Be careful that you do not allow a graven image of me – or of the message I sent humankind almost 20 centuries ago – to cause you to reject the message I send today. For those who reject this course do indeed deny Christ before men. And then, the law requires that I confirm their own choice before the Father.

> 22 For the Father judgeth no man, but hath committed all judgment unto the Son:
> 23 That all men should honour the Son, even as they honour the Father. He that honoureth not the Son honoureth not the Father which hath sent him.
> 24 Verily, verily, I say unto you, He that heareth my word, and believeth on him that sent me, hath everlasting life, and shall not come into condemnation; but is passed from death unto life. (John, Chapter 5)

You cannot enter the Father's kingdom without going through the Son – the Christ consciousness – and this is precisely why it is such a travesty that I have been elevated to an exception rather than an example for all to follow. For people cannot enter the kingdom by following an *external* Christ. They can enter the kingdom *only* by becoming one with the *internal* Christ, by *becoming* the Living Christ. Thus, in this course I shall explain clearly how to truly honor the Son by letting this mind be in you which was – and *is* – also in Christ Jesus (Galatians 2:5), and I shall offer you a systematic path to personal Christhood.

Let it be made clear that this course is not meant to make people comfortable, but to bring them to face the choice to either accept Christ or deny Christ. Yet I am not insensitive to the fact that so many people will find it difficult to accept this course because they have been brought up to accept a graven image of Christ. Therefore, I shall give the first chapter as a bridge, whereby people can cross the chasm between the graven images of Christ and the living reality of Christ. As I said many times 2,000 years ago, I now say again:

Who hath ears to hear, let them hear.

# PART ONE

# Chapter 1
# Exposing the graven images of Christ

There is a multitude of graven images of Christ, so many that I could not possibly comment on all of them. Neither do I intend to comment on all of them, for it is indeed *your* responsibility to free your mind from false images. My task in this chapter is to give you certain questions and thoughts that can – if you are willing – help you get started on this process. The rest can be accomplished as you apply the remainder of the course.

***

I feel great compassion for the many people who have been brought up with a graven image of Christ. I wish all children had been brought up with a clear understanding of my true teachings, for as the Bible says:

> Train up a child in the way he should go: and when he is old, he will not depart from it. (Proverbs 22:6)

This statement naturally works in reverse also, meaning that when children have been brought up with a graven image of Christ, it is often very difficult for them to question it. I am aware that many people are indeed afraid to question their childhood beliefs about me, and they have either accepted orthodox doctrines or have numbed themselves so they rarely think about deeper questions. I am aware that many of these people feel they have to remain loyal to me, but I ask you to consider whether you are loyal to an outer church and its doctrines or whether you are loyal to *me*, the Living Christ?

Are you loyal to a graven image, often created for political reasons in a past age, or are you loyal to the Living Christ, the reality of what I am? If you find that your loyalty lies with men rather than with me, then I strongly encourage you to redirect it, for you cannot serve two masters (Matthew 6:24). And as I will explain shortly, the outer churches and their doctrines will not get you where you want to go.

I am aware that, in a modern, rational and scientific age, many people can make no sense out of orthodox Christian doctrines because the doctrines insist on upholding a world view that became obsolete centuries ago. Thus, some have rejected Christianity and have rejected me as a spiritual teacher, perhaps looking to other religions or rejecting all religion. I am aware that many people look at the violent and oppressive history of mainstream Christian churches and can see no connection between the fruits of the churches and the teachings of Christ. Some have rejected all organized religion, seeking an inner, universal spirituality or perhaps feeling like no form of spirituality could fulfill their needs.

Yet while I feel compassion for all of these people, the compassion of Christ is not human sympathy. For indeed, I know the basic fact of life, namely that *you* are responsible for what you allow to enter your mind. *You* are responsible for the words you accept, the words and teachings that make up your belief system and world view. As I said:

> 33 Either make the tree good, and his fruit good; or else make the tree corrupt, and his fruit corrupt: for the tree is known by his fruit.
> 34 O generation of vipers, how can ye, being evil, speak good things? for out of the abundance of the heart the mouth speaketh.
> 35 A good man out of the good treasure of the heart bringeth forth good things: and an evil man out of the evil treasure bringeth forth evil things.
> 36 But I say unto you, That every idle word that men shall speak, they shall give account thereof in the day of judgment.
> 37 For by thy words thou shalt be justified, and by thy words thou shalt be condemned. (Matthew, Chapter 12)

Your fruits – including, but not limited to, words and actions – are the products of your belief system, and your world view is made up of the worded teachings and beliefs you have accepted. Certainly, you could not help being programmed during childhood, but you are now an adult, and as such you have the responsibility to examine all of your beliefs and look for a higher understanding. You can follow the Bible's admonition to get understanding before getting anything in this world (Proverbs 4:7). You will be justified or condemned based on the words you believe, for your fruits will be determined by the words that fill your heart.

I know that for people from a traditional Christian background this might sound ominous, perhaps even judgmental and non-loving, and it might remind them of the images of an angry God with which they were brought up. Yet let me give you a different picture. As I have hinted, the real key to salvation is not membership of an outer church but that you attain the Christ consciousness, which is the *only* thing that can give you entry to the spiritual realm. That is why I said:

> I am the way, the truth, and the life: no man cometh unto the Father, but by me. (John 14:6)

Contrary to popular interpretations, I did not speak these words as a historical person. I spoke them in oneness with the Christ mind, and thus it is the universal Christ consciousness that is the *only* way to reach the Father and his kingdom. The main message of my mission was to set forth an example that all can follow, for, truly, all people have the potential to attain the Christ consciousness.

Attaining the Christ consciousness includes purifying your mind and heart of beliefs that are unreal because they are out of alignment with the reality of Christ. So we might say that the door to the spiritual realm is not a traditional door that opens. Instead, it is an opening that is carved like a very intricate pattern, almost like an old-fashioned iron gate with small openings, thus forming a filter. In order for you to pass through the filter, your consciousness must be able to pass through the openings without being held back by anything. And as long as you hold on to beliefs – words – that are out of alignment with the reality of Christ, those false words will not pass through the openings in the gate, and thus they will hold you back. That is why the true disciples of Christ must examine the false words in their hearts and minds and remove that beam from their own eyes.

I am aware that most people go through life without examining the words that fill their hearts, and that is why they indiscriminately allow their mouths to speak from the abundance of their hearts. Yet those who have ears to hear are those who are willing to recognize that becoming a true disciple of Christ means that you accept responsibility for your life—both in this world and beyond this world. This includes examining the words and beliefs that fill your heart – as a symbol for your mind – so you can purify your mind of false beliefs and graven images.

The spiritual law is no respecter of persons (Acts 10:34). *You* are the one who must give account for *your* words. Your entry into heaven will be determined by what *you* have allowed into your mind. That you have been influenced by society and family is a given, but it is still up to *you* to be the master of your own house, meaning your heart and mind. You can begin – right now – a process of re-examining what has accumulated in your mind, deciding what you will allow to remain there. This book will help you go through that process, until – if you are willing to let go – there is nothing left but the reality of Christ.

***

I am quite aware that for some this will sound very different from what they were brought up to believe, but that is because they have been affected by another graven image of Christ. In reality, I am simply telling you a basic fact. I have already given you one analogy to illustrate this, but since it is a crucial point, let me give you another one.

Imagine that you stand in front of a locked door and you have a bundle of keys. There is one key that will open the lock and many keys that will not open the lock. So until you find the right key, how can you realistically expect to open the door? And what good will it do you to blame the door, when you are the one who is not using the right key? The door to the kingdom of God can be opened by all people, but in order to open it, you must find the right key, meaning that you must have the right understanding. And that includes freeing your mind from incorrect beliefs – incorrect words – so that you do not violate God's command to have no other gods before the one true God and to not take unto yourself any graven image (Exodus 20:3-4). As I described it in one of my parables:

> 10 So those servants went out into the highways, and gathered together all as many as they found, both bad and good: and the wedding was furnished with guests.
> 11 And when the king came in to see the guests, he saw there a man which had not on a wedding garment:
> 12 And he saith unto him, Friend, how camest thou in hither not having a wedding garment? And he was speechless.
> 13 Then said the king to the servants, Bind him hand and foot, and take him away, and cast him into outer darkness; there shall be weeping and gnashing of teeth.

> 14 For many are called, but few are chosen. (Matthew, Chapter 22)

Again, this can sound ominous to people from a Christian background, but the real message here is that the wedding garment is a symbol for a state of consciousness in which your mind is free from graven images, so you see the reality of God. When you attain that state of consciousness, you are *inside* the kingdom of God, and until you attain it, you will be *outside* the kingdom, where you will be "bound hand and foot" by your own erroneous beliefs. Many are called to enter the kingdom, but few are "chosen" because few choose to purify their minds from *all* graven images.

How can you change the inner words and teachings that fill your heart and mind? One of the indisputable accomplishments of science is the discovery of universal, natural laws – such as gravity – that work the same no matter what you believe or don't believe. I described one such universal law when I said:

> 7 Ask, and it shall be given you; seek, and ye shall find; knock, and it shall be opened unto you:
> 8 For every one that asketh receiveth; and he that seeketh findeth; and to him that knocketh it shall be opened. (Matthew, Chapter 7)

It is a natural law that if you truly seek a greater understanding of the deeper, spiritual mysteries of life, you *will* be offered such an understanding. However, for this law to be fulfilled, *you* must be willing to do your part. You must be willing to become a chalice into which the elixir of wisdom can be poured, for God will not cast his pearls before the swine of a closed mind, nor will he give that which is holy to the dogs of prejudice (Matthew 7:6). Thus, you must be open to receiving an understanding that goes beyond your present belief system and world view, your present mental box. Did I not say:

> Verily I say unto you, Whosoever shall not receive the kingdom of God as a little child shall in no wise enter therein. (Luke 18:17)

A little child receives understanding with an open and unbiased mind, a mind that is free of prejudice. This is one of the main reasons why so many people reject the Living Christ. They have allowed their minds to calcify around a dead image of Christ, and they are prejudiced against anything that is not in accord with their image. They want the Living Christ to fit into their mental box, and they are not willing to let the Living Christ disturb their sense of stability, security and control.

I feel compassion for the many people who have been brought up with a graven image of Christ. Yet I must also tell you that having been brought up with a false image does not free you from your personal responsibility to seek a higher understanding and to do so with an open mind. Too many people use their upbringing as an excuse for holding on to prejudices that either make them feel comfortable or give them a fragile sense of being in control.

The indisputable fact is that no matter what you may have been programmed to believe, you *can* rise above your past and clear your mind of all graven images. In fact, my entire mission could well be seen as a demonstration of the fact that it is possible to rise above *all* human limitations, even death itself.

So for me, the important question is not what you were conditioned to believe in the past or even what you believe now. It is of no real concern to me whether you believe in the orthodox image of Christ, reject me, reject all religion or reject anything that goes beyond orthodox doctrines. The real question is whether you are willing to look at your beliefs, examine them openly and then reach for a higher understanding that will help you rise above all graven images. I am not concerned about the box in which your mind currently resides; I am only concerned about your willingness to expand that box, eventually coming to the point where you throw away all man-made boxes and follow my command:

> God is a Spirit: and they that worship him must worship him in spirit and in truth. (John 4:24)

I am – among other things – come to teach human beings, and in that respect my primary concern is whether people are teachable. Are they willing to let the Living Christ challenge their existing ideas and help them leave the mental box that makes them think they are human beings? The timeless question is whether you have eyes to see and ears to hear. For those who do not have an open mind will always reject the Living Christ, preferring a "dead" Christ who seemingly confirms what they want to believe.

***

Why did I so often call for those who had ears to hear? Because most people did not have ears to hear the Living Word of the Living Christ! This was the case when I walked the Earth, and it is the case today. Yet in the modern world many more people do actually have ears to hear, and that is why I am bringing forth this course. The problem is that there can be a conflict between your inner being and your outer mind. Many people in today's world do indeed have the inner readiness to receive the Living Word, but their outer minds have been so programmed by graven images – be they of a religious or materialistic nature – that people tend to reject the truth with the outer mind without truly considering it with their hearts, meaning their intuitive faculties. Consider my statement:

> This people draweth nigh unto me with their mouth, and honoureth me with their lips; but their heart is far from me. (Matthew 15:8)

The reverse of that statement is that many people actually do love the Living Christ and the Living Truth with their hearts, but their lips – as a symbol for the outer, analytical mind – have been programmed to reject the Living Word. Many people have been programmed to compare any new idea or teaching to a "database" of their existing beliefs, rejecting anything that contradicts or goes too far beyond what they currently accept. Yet if you reject anything new, you do not receive God's kingdom with the innocent mind of a little child. And then you cannot receive the kingdom at all, for God's kingdom cannot be crammed into any man-made mental box.

The dynamic is simple. If you are not currently experiencing the kingdom of God and the abundant life, it is because there is something you do not know, something you do not understand. And the only way to find what is missing is to look *beyond* the mental box of your current beliefs. Thus, having ears to hear means being willing to look beyond one's current mental box, to think outside the box.

***

What did it take for people to follow the Living Christ when I walked the Earth? After three years of preaching all over Palestine – performing many miracles and healing many people – I had contacted a relatively small number of people and had a limited number of direct followers. For those who have grown up in a culture where Christianity is mainstream, consider that things were very different back then. There was no Christian religion with huge cathedrals, printed Bibles, elaborate rituals and clearly defined doctrines. So following me when I walked the Earth was not for the faint of heart, it was not for those who preferred to follow the crowd.

Who were my early followers? Well, since there was no organized religion, they could not have been those who prefer the safe boundaries of a well-defined religion. Since there was no clearly defined scripture or doctrine, they could not have been those who prefer to feel they are religious but are not willing to think deeply about spiritual matters. Look at the history of my ministry, and you will see that I was ignored by most, rejected by many and persecuted by the elite. There were three main reasons why people rejected me:

- Some felt threatened by the fact that I pointed to a different way to live, a more intense form of life. They were so focused on their daily lives that they were not willing to step back, reevaluate their lives and adopt a more spiritual lifestyle. They simply wanted to continue living as their forefathers had done. They preferred comfortability over any form of change, even a change for the better. They actually preferred to live as the living dead rather than accepting my offer to enter the ranks of the spiritually alive.

- Some felt threatened by the fact that my preaching went far beyond the established religion of their culture. And it truly matters not that it was the Jewish religion, for is not the Christian religion as rigid today as the Jewish religion was back then? You will always find people who want to feel that they are saved by belonging to an outer religion and who do not want to think for themselves about religious matters. They want to be told what to believe so they can believe their salvation is guaranteed. These people felt threatened by my preaching, for I taught that people had to find salvation within themselves. As I said, "The kingdom of God is within you" (Luke 17:21). I also said that you will not be saved simply by belonging to an outer religion and following all its doctrines and rituals:

> For I say unto you, That except your righteousness shall exceed the righteousness of the scribes and Pharisees, ye shall in no case enter into the kingdom of heaven. (Matthew 5:20)

The scribes and Pharisees thought they were sure to be saved, because they followed all of the outer rituals of their religion. However, they were not willing to realize that most of those rituals were defined by men and that they did not "automatically" cause people to put on the wedding garment. Performing outer rituals will not automatically change your state of consciousness, for doing so is an inner process that requires you to understand why and how you need to change. It also requires you to make the conscious decision to change.

- Finally, there were those who felt that their privileged positions in the religious and political establishment – and their control over the population – were being threatened by my "blasphemous" teachings. The leaders of the established institutions did not want to lose their power and privileges, so they had to silence me before I could set the people free from their control. Why did they feel so threatened? Because I preached that the kingdom of God is within you, meaning that you do not need an outer religion – or its priesthood – in order to enter the kingdom. I challenged the very core of what allows oppressive institutions to control people, namely the belief that you need someone or something from outside yourself in order to be saved.

My immediate point here is that in order to be one of my early followers, you could *not* fit into one of these categories. You had to be willing to change your lifestyle and make the spiritual path, the path of discipleship, the primary focus of your life. You had to be willing to look beyond orthodox doctrines and think for yourself—for unless you think for yourself, how can you enter the kingdom that is within you? You also had to be willing to go beyond the dictates of the established religion of your time, even defying its leaders. You had to be willing to no longer follow the blind leaders (Matthew 15:14) but to open your inner eyes and ears and follow the Living Christ—who speaks in the stillness of your own heart.

***

Some Christians have built a habit – for some it was only a short-lived fad – of asking themselves, "What would Jesus do?," "What would Jesus say?," "What would Jesus drive?" and so on. This can potentially be constructive, for all people have experienced being so overwhelmed by the pressures of a situation that they could not think clearly and therefore did something they later regretted. By considering how a being who is not blinded by the situation would respond, people can potentially step back from it and think more clearly. Yet I wish all who call themselves Christians would combine the thought of how I would respond with one particular commandment given by me. After all, I did say:

> If ye love me, keep my commandments. (John 14:15)

Thus, I wish people would combine the thought of "What would Jesus say" with this commandment:

> 3 And why beholdest thou the mote that is in thy brother's eye, but considerest not the beam that is in thine own eye?
> 4 Or how wilt thou say to thy brother, Let me pull out the mote out of thine eye; and, behold, a beam is in thine own eye?
> 5 Thou hypocrite, first cast out the beam out of thine own eye; and then shalt thou see clearly to cast out the mote out of thy brother's eye. (Matthew, Chapter 7)

People could then begin to consider what I, the ascended Jesus Christ, would think or say about the religion that claims to represent me on Earth. Too many people simply assume that if I walked into their church on any given Sunday, I would approve of everything I found. Few have ever truly considered that I might indeed overturn the tables of the money changers (as a symbol for people who seek to manipulate others) who have infiltrated modern Christian churches as they had infiltrated the Jewish religion of old.

For those who are willing to think along these lines, let me assure you that throughout the rest of this course, I will give a clear and detailed view of how you can transcend modern – and ancient – Christianity. Yet for now I want to focus on one particular concern. I wish all who call themselves Christians – and who claim to be my followers – would seriously consider the deeper meaning of what it means to follow this one commandment:

> Let them alone: they be blind leaders of the blind. And if the blind lead the blind, both shall fall into the ditch. (Matthew 15:14)

As I said above, my early followers were not blind followers of the blind leaders. They were willing to think for themselves instead of blindly believing in the doctrines and rules handed down by the established religion. Consider that my disciples had grown up in the Jewish religion, and they had to go far beyond that religion in order to accept my teachings and accept the fact that I often – the scriptures giving only sketchy glimpses – broke the unbreachable rules of that religion. Those who have eyes to see will conclude from this that what I came to start was *not* a rigid religion. On the contrary, I came to start a movement that was diametrically opposed to the rigid Jewish religion, indeed all rigid religions. After all, it was the leaders of such a religion who had me killed in an attempt to silence me.

So how can modern Christians take an honest look at modern Christianity without seeing that their religion has become as rigid and stifled by doctrines and rules as the religion whose priesthood had me killed? How can they fail to see that the universal spiritual movement I came to start was – within a few centuries – turned into the exact same kind of religion as the one that killed the Living Christ? And how can they fail to see that modern Christianity is still a rigid religion that would persecute the Living Christ if I entered their churches and dared to challenge their doctrines? How can modern Christians be so blind that they refuse to look for the beam in their own eyes and see that there is no longer room for the Living Christ in their churches—there is no longer room in the inn for the Living Christ to be born? The response – or non-response – of mainstream churches to this course will surely prove my point for those who have eyes to see.

***

Most Christians assume that if they had been alive 2,000 years ago, they would instantly have recognized me as the Savior. Yet I tell you that the majority of modern Christians would fit into the three categories described above. Many would refuse to change their lifestyle, many would reject me because I would challenge their – supposedly *Christian* – doctrines. And some would persecute me because I would threaten their power over the people.

As I said, there are many who think that if I entered their church today, I would approve of everything. Yet this is a complete fallacy. It is spiritual blindness, caused by two factors. One is the spiritual pride that makes people unwilling to look for the beam in their own eyes. The other is a complete failure to understand the true mission of Christ. That mission will be fully explained later in this course, but for now let it be enough to say that the mission of Christ is *never* to confirm people's beliefs but to challenge people to expand their understanding by reaching beyond *all* man-made beliefs and belief systems. Thus, the Living Christ will *always* challenge the established religion of the time—even if it claims to be a *Christian* religion.

If you are not willing to have your religion and your approach to religion challenged, it proves that you are not a follower of the Living Christ but that you have made yourself a follower of a dead "Christ." You have made yourself a follower of the blind leaders who created the graven image of a dead "Christ" and elevated it to the status of an infallible doctrine.

Again, consider that many Christians think that had they been alive 2,000 years ago, they would have instantly recognized and followed me. Yet there was no Christian church back then, and thus there was nothing outer to confirm me as a spiritual leader of any stature. People had to go beyond outer signs and find the truth in their hearts, which most contemporary Christians simply are not willing to do—preferring a set of doctrines full of dead men's bones. The brutal fact is that if you are not willing to follow me in the form in which I appear today – including, but not limited to, this course – you would not have been willing to follow me back then.

***

What kind of people followed me back then and what kind of people are my true followers today? One thing should be clear from reading the scriptures: *Hypocrites need not apply!*

Look at how many times I challenged the scribes and Pharisees and called them hypocrites. I said that unless your righteousness exceeds that of the scribes and Pharisees, you cannot enter the kingdom. Why is this so? Because the scribes and Pharisees believed they could enter God's kingdom by following the outer doctrines and observances of their religion. Yet where is the kingdom located? It is located within you, so what sense does it make that you will automatically enter an inner kingdom by following an outer religion? Let me give you the entire quote about the inner kingdom:

> 20 And when he was demanded of the Pharisees, when the kingdom of God should come, he answered them and said, The kingdom of God cometh not with observation:
> 21 Neither shall they say, Lo here! or, lo there! for, behold, the kingdom of God is within you. (Luke, Chapter 17)

Take note of what I really said here. The scribes and Pharisees thought they were guaranteed to be saved because they strictly observed all the rules of the outer religion. Yet I made it clear that doing this will not guarantee your salvation. Why did I call them hypocrites? Because they were simply putting on a facade of being good and religious people, and they justified this by their strict observance of the outer rules. They were – essentially – trying to strike a bargain with God, thinking that if they followed the outer rules, they could force God to let them into his kingdom without going through a change of heart. Yet anyone willing to carefully read the scriptures will see that I challenged this approach over and over again:

> 6 ... Thus have ye made the commandment of God of none effect by your tradition.
> 7 Ye hypocrites, well did Esaias prophesy of you, saying,
> 8 This people draweth nigh unto me with their mouth, and honoureth me with their lips; but their heart is far from me.
> 9 But in vain they do worship me, teaching for doctrines the commandments of men. (Matthew, Chapter 15)

Oh how many Christians have read these statements and used them to reinforce their sense of being holier-than-thou, feeling that my words applied only to the scribes and Pharisees – or the members of other religions – and that they – being good Christians – were above my reproach. Even now many who read this will feel that the real Jesus could not possibly say that observing the rules and doctrines of their *Christian* religion is not enough to get them to heaven. Yet that is precisely what the Living Jesus Christ does say—for only a dead "Christ" could claim that blindly following *any* religion will get you to the real kingdom of God that is within you.

Did I not tell my followers to look first for the beam in their own eyes? Then why is it so difficult for Christians to take a critical look at their own religion and their own lives, acknowledging that Christianity has deviated from the true, living teachings of Christ and has become as stifled by doctrines, rules and rituals as the Jewish religion I challenged?

Why do Christians think that because they call themselves Christians – honoring me with their mouth – they are exempt from self-examination or from the chastisement of the Living Christ? This unwillingness to examine yourself can only come from one factor, namely that your heart is far from me. For if you truly love the Living Christ, you are willing to overcome anything in this world – including anything in your own psyche – in order to follow me. If you truly love me, you will spontaneously seek to overcome anything that separates you from me!

Do modern Christians think I am a respecter of men or of the institutions created by men? Do they think I will not challenge those who teach for doctrines the commandments of men? Do they think they can fool me and pretend to be good Christians, and I shall not see that their hearts are far from me? How long can one go on acting like a hypocrite – having the exact same mindset as the scribes and Pharisees – and still call oneself a Christian? Those who have ears had better hear.

***

I am well aware that some who read this will dispute every point I make and that they will do so by referring to certain passages in scripture or certain – literal – interpretations of them. How often did I encounter the scribes, Pharisees and lawyers who took the same approach by seeking to trap or refute me back then? How often did I have to listen to their literal interpretations of the Jewish scriptures, where they cleverly sought to find some scriptural proof that I could not possibly be the promised Messiah. Their reasoning being that the real Messiah could not possibly do or say anything that was contrary to or beyond the scriptures and *their* interpretations of those scriptures.

So I am indeed not surprised that people with the exact same mindset are found in – indeed have come to dominate – the Christian religion. Yet I am somewhat surprised that so many modern Christians accept this state of affairs and fail to see that these blind leaders have taken over Christianity and have attempted to silence any expression of the Living Christ.

Consider the reality of the situation. I had come to save the people in ancient Israel, but why did they need to be saved? If the Jewish religion had been sufficient to ensure their salvation, why would God have needed to send me as the Messiah? Therefore, those who have eyes to see will realize that the Living Christ comes into this world precisely because – as explained earlier – observing an outer religion – *any* outer religion – is not enough to ensure people's salvation. In fact, one might well say that the Living Christ comes to save people from the outer religion, or at least from the blind belief that observing an outer religion will get them to the kingdom.

All who understand this should be able to see the irony that those who need to be saved from following an outer religion will use the scriptures and traditions of that religion to reject the Living Christ—who is sent to awaken them from the folly of their ways and offer them the true – inner – path to salvation.

The basic reality of life is that after the building of the Tower of Babel, God confounded people's speech:

> 4 And they said, Go to, let us build us a city and a tower, whose top may reach unto heaven; and let us make us a name, lest we be scattered abroad upon the face of the whole Earth.
> 5 And the LORD came down to see the city and the tower, which the children of men builded.
> 6 And the LORD said, Behold, the people is one, and they have all one language; and this they begin to do: and now nothing will be restrained from them, which they have imagined to do.
> 7 Go to, let us go down, and there confound their language, that they may not understand one another's speech.
> 8 So the LORD scattered them abroad from thence upon the face of all the Earth: and they left off to build the city.
> 9 Therefore is the name of it called Babel; because the LORD did there confound the language of all the Earth: and from thence did the LORD scatter them abroad upon the face of all the Earth. (Genesis, Chapter 11)

There is – as always – a deeper meaning behind this, which will be discussed later (including that this was not actually done by God but is a result of people's free-will choices to engage in the consciousness of death). Yet this quote is not simply talking about language but about the entire use of words in this world. All words are ambiguous, having more than one meaning, and thus being capable of being interpreted differently by different people. This is the state of duality that makes it possible for two groups of people to come up with mutually exclusive interpretations of the same religious scripture—and even makes them willing to kill each other in the name of the same God.

***

The scribes and the Pharisees sought to set up their particular interpretation of the scriptures as the only true one, and they used it to persecute the Living Christ when I walked among them. This is a misuse of the Word. In fact, it is what I spoke about when I said:

> 31 Wherefore I say unto you, All manner of sin and blasphemy shall be forgiven unto men: but the blasphemy against the Holy Ghost shall not be forgiven unto men.
> 32 And whosoever speaketh a word against the Son of man, it shall be forgiven him: but whosoever speaketh

> against the Holy Ghost, it shall not be forgiven him, neither in this world, neither in the world to come. (Matthew, Chapter 12)

What does it mean to speak against the Holy Ghost? It means to use a man-made interpretation as a justification for rejecting the Living Word spoken by the Living Christ—in whatever form the Living Christ might appear. Therefore, those who use the scriptures of the past to reject new revelation from above are indeed speaking against the Holy Ghost, as the scribes and the Pharisees did repeatedly and as many modern Christian preachers do every Sunday. Who is the Holy Ghost? I said:

> But the Comforter, which is the Holy Ghost, whom the Father will send in my name, he shall teach you all things, and bring all things to your remembrance, whatsoever I have said unto you. (John 14:26)

The Holy Ghost comes as the inner Comforter for each person. The Comforter comes to bring all things to your remembrance that the Living Christ wants you to know, so that you can rise above your old mental box and put on the mind of Christ. Thus, those who refuse to listen to this inner voice – by using an outer scripture to nullify the Living Word from within – are indeed blaspheming against the Holy Ghost.

My point is that too many Christians are caught up in the endless and pointless game of focusing so much attention on the written word, the scriptures of yesterday, that they close their minds to the Living Word that still flows from heaven over the agency of the Holy Spirit. Had they been around back then, these people would have sided with the scribes and the Pharisees and would have used the old scriptures to reject me as the Messiah. And this is truly denying Christ before men.

In reality, being one of my followers is not about interpreting the dead word but about being open to the Living Word. For only through the Living Word can you follow my commandment to worship God through the spirit of the word and not the letter of the word:

> God is a Spirit: and they that worship him must worship him in spirit and in truth. (John 4:24)

Or as Paul put it:

Who also hath made us able ministers of the new testament; not of the letter, but of the spirit: for the letter killeth, but the spirit giveth life. (2Corinthians 3:6)

***

Those who have ears to hear are those who are willing to look beyond the surface appearances, to look for the hidden meaning, for the deeper layers of understanding. Such people are the only ones who were willing to follow me back then, and they are the only ones who will be willing to follow me today. For such people the following statement contains an essential clue:

I have yet many things to say unto you, but ye cannot bear them now. (John 16:12)

A seemingly simple statement, but the implications are profound. There are those who seem to think that the Christ is a constant, and thus the words of Christ should be a constant. In reality, this need for an unchanging foundation in an ever-changing world springs from a particular part of the human psyche, as will be explained later. However, for now my point is that there are those who have reasoned that the word of Christ should not change, and thus nothing new should be added to the scriptures given almost 2,000 years ago. In other words, when I walked the Earth back then, I told Christians everything they will ever need to know in order to attain salvation. These people often reason that because I was the son of God, what I said was perfect and something that is perfect could never change.

On the opposite side of the spectrum, there are those who reason that if I really was the Son of God or the only Savior, I should have been able to foresee the immense changes in society that have occurred over the past 2,000 years. And thus, I should have given people some directions that are more applicable to the modern age.

Based on the quote above, you can gain a deeper understanding. I did indeed have many more things to say to humankind, but as I said, the people of the time were not able to "bear" them. If I had given directions that were too far ahead of the state of consciousness that most people had at the time – and few modern people can imagine the state of consciousness people had back then – then they would have been even more reluctant to accept my words than was already the case.

We now see a truth that should be self-evident for all who are willing to think logically about this. The teachings I gave 2,000 years ago were not meant to be ultimate, absolute, infallible or perfect. They were carefully adapted to the state of consciousness of the intended recipients. They were intended to reach people at *their* level of consciousness and then challenge them to come up higher. Yet because people were in such a low state of consciousness, there was no possibility whatsoever of giving them the highest possible teaching about God. For that matter, as we will discuss later, there is no "highest possible" teaching.

My statement above was meant for those who have ears to hear, so they would realize that the Living Christ has much more to say to those who are open to hearing it. Thus, they should not limit their understanding to the words and scriptures of yesterday but would remain open to the progressive revelation given through the agency of the Holy Spirit. As people – on an individual level but also humankind as a whole – grew in awareness, I fully intended to give people more advanced teachings. For each step people take up the ladder of understanding, the Living Christ has a teaching that can take them higher—if they are willing to let their old understanding be challenged. How did I intend to give people this new understanding? As already mentioned:

> 16 And I will pray the Father, and he shall give you another Comforter, that he may abide with you for ever;
> 17 Even the Spirit of truth; whom the world cannot receive, because it seeth him not, neither knoweth him: but ye know him; for he dwelleth with you, and shall be in you. (John, Chapter 14)

> 25 These things have I spoken unto you, being yet present with you.
> 26 But the Comforter, which is the Holy Ghost, whom the Father will send in my name, he shall teach you all things, and bring all things to your remembrance, whatsoever I have said unto you. (John, Chapter 14)

It was my intention to keep alive an unbroken tradition of giving forth the Living Word through the agency of the Holy Spirit, working through people who had embodied my inner teachings and had therefore made themselves the open doors for the Spirit. Because the Christian religion was turned into a rigid and dogmatic religion, this tradition was broken. Yet over the past 2,000 years a number of people have been used to bring forth new teachings – progressive revelation – and this course is part of that tradition.

***

Another quote is related to this topic, namely:

> 33 And with many such parables spake he the word unto them, as they were able to hear it.
> 34 But without a parable spake he not unto them: and when they were alone, he expounded all things to his disciples. (Mark, Chapter 4)

I spoke to the multitudes in parable because they were not able to "bear" the more advanced teachings I gave to my disciples. Yet in today's age many more people are ready for these direct teachings. Thus, the question you face is simple. Will you settle for the scriptures of yesterday and the doctrines and "literal" interpretations of them? Or will you open your mind and heart to my Living Word, so I can give you both the inner teachings that I gave to my disciples and the more modern teachings that are specifically adapted to the spiritual people of this age? The choice is yours, for I have already decided to offer my inner teachings for all who are willing to receive them. The question is: Will you receive them in the Spirit in which they were given – the Spirit of Truth – or will you want them to fit into your present mental box?

Obviously, much more could be said about the many graven images of Christ that are circulating in this world—and much more will indeed be said throughout this course. Yet if what has been said here is not sufficient to get you to read on, then nothing *will* be sufficient. For the cause is that although you might honor me with your mouth, you are not willing to open your heart to my Living Word. You do not have ears to hear me, for you are denying me before men. Thus, I will move on to the real goal of this course, namely to reach those who have ears to hear the fullness of the teachings of the Living Christ for this age.

# Chapter 2
# The first challenge of Christ

Where shall we begin our journey out of the jungle of graven images and into the clear light of Christ Truth? We shall begin by discussing a topic that few modern people give serious consideration, namely why the Living Christ comes to Earth. The reason why few consider this question with an open mind is that most Christians believe they already know the answer and most non-christians think the answer is not relevant for them. Yet let us consider the real answer—an answer that has implications for *all* people on Earth.

Christians from most denominations have been brought up to believe that I came to Earth in order to save people. They have also been brought up to see this as a passive measure on their part. I am the Savior, so I am the one who saves, and they only need to live up to certain requirements, such as being baptized, verbally confessing me as their Lord and Savior, believing in me, believing in the blood of Christ or other such measures. Despite some individual nuances, the basic image of salvation is the same for most churches:

- Jesus is the only one who can save you. You cannot save yourself.
- Jesus is the external savior; I am portrayed as being somewhere up in heaven, meaning far away from you.
- Although I am the savior, you still need an outer church in order to receive my salvation. The church is the mediator between you and me.

In this course I will explain fully how and why the Living Christ is the key to salvation. Yet this requires me to give you some profound and subtle teachings, and I will do this after we set a better foundation. For now, I want to contrast the popular Christian image of a passive, external salvation with some of my direct words. First of all, we have one of my most pivotal sayings, a saying I have quoted before and will return to again and again—for it is indeed the missing link in Christianity:

> 20 And when he was demanded of the Pharisees, when the kingdom of God should come, he answered them and said, The kingdom of God cometh not with observation:
> 21 Neither shall they say, Lo here! or, lo there! for, behold, the kingdom of God is within you. (Luke, Chapter 17)

What I point to here is not an external salvation, but an internal process. This is precisely why the leaders of the religious establishment of the time decided to kill me. If I had been successful in awakening the people to the reality of the internal salvation, the religious leaders would have lost their power. Thus, any perceptive person should be able to see the irony in the fact that most modern Christian churches preach an external salvation and portray me as the external savior. I gave my life to bring forth the truth that salvation is an internal process, yet the very church that claims to represent me on Earth has done everything in its power to nullify my sacrifice.

Salvation clearly means that you enter the kingdom of God. You will not be saved until you are in the kingdom of God—this is something all Christians should be able to agree upon, although I am well aware that many will question my statement. As I clearly express in the above quote, entering the kingdom of God is *not* an outer, or external, process. It will not happen because you observe the rules and rituals of an outer religion. You will enter the kingdom of God only by finding the kingdom *inside* yourself. You simply will not find the kingdom as long as you are looking for it *outside* yourself—and this includes looking for an external savior or a religion on Earth to save you.

I am not hereby saying that you can save yourself without Christ. What I *am* saying is that you will not find Christ *outside* yourself, not even in a Christian church. You will find me only *inside* yourself. In fact, you will *never* find Christ as long as you look for him *outside* yourself. You will find me *only* when you start looking for me *inside* yourself!

Yet what does it truly mean that the kingdom of God is within you? Some people believe the kingdom of God is a physical kingdom that will descend to Earth and transform the planet, while others believe the Earth will be raised up into the kingdom of God. I am not denying that a planetary transformation can take place, but I am obviously not talking about a world-wide, physical kingdom when I say that the kingdom of God is within you—for how can the material world fit inside of you? So what exactly *did* I mean?

Once again, let me remind you that when I walked the Earth, I was limited by people's understanding, their world view. That is why I spoke in parables and why I made many statements that contain a veiled truth. The purpose was to separate those who took everything literally – looking only at the letter of the word and not the Spirit of the word – from those who were willing to go beyond appearances. Modern people take so much knowledge for granted, knowledge that simply wasn't available 2,000 years ago. Thus, many modern people find it difficult to understand – or have simply never considered – how difficult it was for me to give deeper explanations of my teachings. For example, most modern people find it natural to think about the psyche, yet this concept was virtually unknown to the people in ancient Israel. They had no understanding of the fact that you have a mind that can be independent of the physical body.

Yet when you have the concept of the psyche, it becomes easy to see that when I said that the kingdom of God is within you, I was *not* talking about a physical kingdom. What is inside of you is obviously the psyche, and thus I used the "kingdom of God" as a symbol for a psychological condition, a state of mind, a state of consciousness. Being in the kingdom of God means attaining a state of consciousness that is above and beyond the state of consciousness that most people have and that is considered "normal."

***

Let me ask you to consider a few logical questions:

- Do you think that I am come to save you by doing all the work for you, or do you think you have to do your part?

- Do you think the salvation I offer is automatic, or do you think you have to live up to certain conditions in order to be saved?

- Do you think those conditions are purely outer conditions – such as being baptized or verbally declaring me to be your Lord and Savior – or do you think they are *inner* conditions?

- Do you think salvation is an outer process – you fulfill outer requirements and are allowed into an external kingdom – or do you think it is an inner process, whereby you go through a transformation of consciousness?

If you have been brought up in a mainstream Christian church, you have been conditioned to believe in the external, passive salvation. Yet let me contrast that image with the reality of my own words. There is the story of the woman who anointed my feet and washed them with her tears. When a Pharisee – always a Pharisee – questioned me, I said:

> Wherefore I say unto thee, Her sins, which are many, are forgiven; for she loved much: but to whom little is forgiven, the same loveth little. (Luke 7:47)

What I am truly saying here is that the forgiveness of her sins was not a matter of an *outer* act on her part. It was linked to an *inner* state, the state of her heart because she loved much. Consider this statement:

> 1 Judge not, that ye be not judged.
> 2 For with what judgment ye judge, ye shall be judged: and with what measure ye mete, it shall be measured to you again. (Matthew, Chapter 7)

Is it not clear that there is a direct link between what you do to other people and how you will be judged? And is not the tendency to judge others a psychological condition, an *inner* condition? Now consider the teaching I gave as part of the Our Father:

> 14 For if ye forgive men their trespasses, your heavenly Father will also forgive you:
> 15 But if ye forgive not men their trespasses, neither will your Father forgive your trespasses. (Matthew, Chapter 6)

Again, there is a clear link between your willingness to forgive others and God's willingness to forgive *your* sins. Yet forgiveness is not an outer act; it is an *inner* condition, for to truly forgive, one must have a pure heart. Thus, one must be willing to overcome hardness of heart, the desire for revenge and the anger that feeds it. And once again, these feelings are inner conditions. Hate is not something you can take off, as you shed an old coat. It is a psychological condition, and you can overcome it only by changing something inside your psyche. Going to church and saying the "Our Father" will not automatically change your heart, as millions of so-called "good" Christians prove every Sunday. Use your Bible software to search my words and see how often I talked about the importance of the heart. Here are just a few quotes:

> Blessed are the pure in heart: for they shall see God. (Matthew 5:8)

> 34 O generation of vipers, how can ye, being evil, speak good things? for out of the abundance of the heart the mouth speaketh.
> 35 A good man out of the good treasure of the heart bringeth forth good things: and an evil man out of the evil treasure bringeth forth evil things. (Matthew, Chapter 12)

> This people draweth nigh unto me with their mouth, and honoureth me with their lips; but their heart is far from me. (Matthew 15:8)

> 18 But those things which proceed out of the mouth come forth from the heart; and they defile the man.
> 19 For out of the heart proceed evil thoughts, murders, adulteries, fornications, thefts, false witness, blasphemies:
> 20 These are the things which defile a man: but to eat with unwashen hands defileth not a man. (Matthew, Chapter 15)

Is it not clear from this last quote that I am *not* primarily concerned with people's outer actions but more concerned with their state of consciousness? Then why are most Christians focused on reforming outer actions, rather than looking for the beam in their own eyes and changing their state of consciousness? Now consider how the Pharisees challenged me to say what was the greatest commandment of the law. I answered:

> Jesus said unto him, Thou shalt love the Lord thy God with all thy heart, and with all thy soul, and with all thy mind. (Matthew 22:37)

Do you think this is something that can be faked—do you think you can fool God by taking on an outer appearance and hiding from him the *inner* condition of your heart? Do you think one can *pretend* to love God with ALL one's heart? For if you do, you are spiritually blind. Thus, those who have eyes to see will realize that salvation is not an *external* but an *internal* process. The essential requirement for salvation is *not* some outer measure or observance. The essential requirement for salvation is an inner condition, a purification of the heart, a transformation of one's entire inner condition, one's state of consciousness.

Contrary to what is believed by most people – Christian or not – this is no trivial or simple transformation. It cannot be accomplished simply by declaring me to be your Lord and Savior—potentially honoring me with your mouth while your heart is still far from me. You must be willing to take a look at your own psyche and remove the beam from your own eye. This is a fundamental shift in one's consciousness, and here is how I described it to Nicodemus:

> 1 There was a man of the Pharisees, named Nicodemus, a ruler of the Jews:
> 2 The same came to Jesus by night, and said unto him, Rabbi, we know that thou art a teacher come from God: for no man can do these miracles that thou doest, except God be with him.
> 3 Jesus answered and said unto him, Verily, verily, I say unto thee, Except a man be born again, he cannot see the kingdom of God.

Nicodemus, being a Pharisee, tended to take things literally, so he did not understand:

> 4 Nicodemus saith unto him, How can a man be born when he is old? can he enter the second time into his mother's womb, and be born?

Therefore, I attempted to clear things up:

> 5 Jesus answered, Verily, verily, I say unto thee, Except a man be born of water and of the Spirit, he cannot enter into the kingdom of God.
> 6 That which is born of the flesh is flesh; and that which is born of the Spirit is spirit. (John, Chapter 3)

Obviously, this left Nicodemus none the wiser, and I am aware that these words have confused many sincere Christians. Yet can you begin to see that what I was talking about here was – obviously – not a physical but a spiritual, a *psychological*, rebirth? It was a change so fundamental that it could only be described as a rebirth, as a fresh new start in life. There are deeper layers of meaning, which we will return to later, yet can you begin to see that my words were deliberately meant to confound Nicodemus' literal mind? Can you see that I was actually saying that in order to be reborn, one has to be willing to go beyond the state of consciousness that is normal for human beings? One has to be willing to flow with the Spirit, and the Spirit does not follow human customs, prejudices and traditions:

> 7 Marvel not that I said unto thee, Ye must be born again.
> 8 The wind bloweth where it listeth, and thou hearest the sound thereof, but canst not tell whence it cometh, and whither it goeth: so is every one that is born of the Spirit. (John, Chapter 3)

My point is that in order to receive the kind of salvation that the Living Christ offers, you have to be willing to change your state of consciousness, which means that you must be willing to let go of the old state of mind. In fact, you have to be willing to let your old sense of self, your old sense of identity, *die*.

***

We can learn another important lesson from the story of Nicodemus. When I said that you have to be born again in order to enter the kingdom, Nicodemus' mind could only interpret my words literally. Thus, he struggled to understand how one could be physically born again, which would entail entering your mother's womb a second time, something that is physically impossible. In reality, my words were simply symbols, hiding a deeper meaning. This shows us that there was a fundamental difference between the state of consciousness that Nicodemus had and the state of consciousness I was talking about as the result of a rebirth.

The consequence seems trivial to many, but in reality it is extremely profound. What I was truly telling Nicodemus was that most human beings are trapped in a state of consciousness that does not give them access to the kingdom of God. You literally cannot enter the kingdom – cannot be saved – as long as you are in this state of consciousness, as long as you have not put on the "wedding garment" of a higher state of consciousness. In other words, most people are trapped in a state of consciousness that keeps them outside the kingdom of God, and in order to enter – in order to be saved – they have to rise – be reborn – into a higher state of consciousness. The difference between the two states of consciousness is not a simple matter of degree. The two states are fundamentally different, which is why it requires a dramatic change to rise from one to the other.

You have experienced boiling a pot of water on the stove, and after a time all the water disappears from the pot. In reality, the water is not gone, but it has undergone a phase transition, and the water molecules are now found as steam in the air. The water has been reborn into a new state, and in the process, all the impurities in the liquid water have been left behind. Likewise, you must undergo a rebirth in consciousness, whereby your consciousness is raised to a fundamentally different level, leaving all human impurities behind.

Do you see a connection between this analogy and my words, "Except a man be born of water and of the Spirit, he cannot enter into the kingdom of God?" The words "water" and "Spirit" are symbols that hide a deeper meaning. The salvation offered by the Living Christ is a two-step process. The end goal is a transformation of consciousness, but this takes place in two stages. The first stage is to "be born of water" and the second stage is to be "born of Spirit." Let us consider what that means.

The two stages of being born of water and of Spirit symbolize your relationship with me, with the Living Christ. Water symbolizes what *you* must do as part of that relationship, and Spirit symbolizes what *I* will do. The reason why the Living Christ comes to Earth is that you need to be saved, and you cannot bring about that salvation on your own. The reason is that you are in a state of consciousness that prevents you from entering the kingdom of God, and that state of consciousness forms a closed loop, a trap with no exit—what in modern times is known as a catch-22. As the saying goes, "You can't get there from here," meaning that you can't get to the kingdom of God from your current state of consciousness.

Nicodemus symbolizes a person who is in this state of consciousness, and his inability to understand my statements demonstrates why the human state of consciousness is a closed loop. This frame of mind is so focused on the things of this world, the appearances that can be seen with the senses and grasped by the outer mind, that it cannot see beyond them. It cannot see beyond the words of the Living Christ, and a literal interpretation of them, to the deeper meaning behind them.

The deeper meaning is that most human beings are trapped in a state of consciousness that makes them spiritually blind. There is something they cannot see, and that "something" is what prevents them from entering the kingdom. Thus, the very first task of the Living Christ is to show people that there is something they cannot see, that there is something they need, that they need to change something if they want to be saved.

This is no easy task, for many people are so blinded by the human state of consciousness that they are firmly convinced that they are right, that their state is normal and that they *will* be saved by belonging to an outer religion and observing its rules. When people are in this state, they tend to follow the blind leaders, who are even more trapped in spiritual blindness than the average person—although they are convinced they know all things, as did the scribes and Pharisees. And when people follow the blind leaders, they are obviously not open to following the Living Christ.

So the first step in the process of salvation that is offered by the Living Christ is that you must come to the realization that you need to change something. One of the things you need to change is that you must be willing to change your consciousness, to purify it of all false beliefs. This is symbolized by the baptism by water, and the original intention behind having my disciples baptize people with water was that it symbolizes people's commitment to walking the inner path of purifying their hearts and minds from all human elements.

This is the process I described in one of my most important parables, where I describe how a master leaves his house and gives different numbers of talents to three servants (Matthew 25:14-30). The essence of the story is that two servants multiplied their talents and were given more, whereas one servant buried his talents in the ground and lost what he had. The deeper meaning is that the salvation I offer people is a process that gradually raises their consciousness. I give you something – a catalyst, a certain amount of "talents" – to start the process, and your task is to multiply what I have given you, whereby I can give you more. This creates an upward spiral, whereby you gradually purify your consciousness, until it reaches a state where you can bear a more direct encounter with my Spirit. This encounter is the baptism by fire, whereby you are born of the Spirit and you now take a quantum leap above the human state of consciousness to a higher state of consciousness that will give you entry into the kingdom of God.

Do you see the point? Being born of water means that you consciously recognize the need to change your consciousness and that you decide you are willing to actively pursue this. As you do, you gradually qualify for the next stage, which is the rebirth of Spirit. I also described this process in another parable:

> The kingdom of heaven is like unto leaven, which a woman took, and hid in three measures of meal, till the whole was leavened. (Matthew 13:33)

What I give to those who make a commitment to the inner path is a portion of my Spirit. This portion forms a leaven, and if you are willing, it can raise the whole loaf of your consciousness until you transcend the human state of mind. Yet this is not an outer process, and it is not an automatic or guaranteed process where I will do all the work for you. It is an interactive process, where the Law of God prevents me from doing everything for you. I am allowed to give you the leaven, but from then on I am only allowed to give you more as you multiply your talents.

Can you now begin to see why a passive approach to salvation simply will not work? Can you see that many Christians have been brought up to take an approach to salvation that is suicide in a spiritual sense? They do nothing to multiply my initial offering. By thinking their salvation is guaranteed by outer measures and that no one can be like me, they bury their talents in the ground, and thus I have nothing to multiply. Instead of engaging in an interactive relationship with me, they passively (or by conforming to outer rules of behavior without changing their consciousness) wait for me to do all the work for them, as if I was some kind of genie in a bottle. Many so-called Christians actually *want* me to be like a genie who stays in the bottle and doesn't bother them – so they can live their lives the way they want – until they need me to save them and get them into heaven. They want me to leave them alone while they live life according to their present understanding, and then I am supposed to jump out of the bottle and save them in the end.

Fortunately, there are also many Christians – and many non-christians – who have an inner understanding that they must do something to change themselves, that they must pull the beam from their own eyes. Thus, many people – Christians and non-christians – do indeed have the personal, interactive relationship with me that causes them to grow. However, if these people were to rise above the limits of many official doctrines, they could accelerate that relationship tremendously. And that is one of my hopes for this course.

***

Why does the Living Christ manifest its Presence on Earth? Why does the Living Christ appear in a form that every human being can see—although many do not have eyes to recognize what they see? Let us look at one of my own statements that reveal part of my purpose:

> I am come that they might have life, and that they might have it more abundantly. (John 10:10)

Those who take a literal approach to interpreting scripture – as did the scribes and Pharisees who opposed every aspect of my mission – cannot make sense out of this statement. For as Jesus I did indeed appear to, preach to and minister onto those who were physically alive. So why would I declare that I had come to give life to those who were already alive? This mystery is underscored by another baffling statement:

> 21 And another of his disciples said unto him, Lord, suffer me first to go and bury my father.
> 22 But Jesus said unto him, Follow me; and let the dead bury their dead. (Matthew, Chapter 8)

Since when do those who are physically dead bury others who are dead? Anyone willing to think logically about this will see that either I was not making any sense or I was talking in a coded, symbolic language that can only be understood by those who have ears to hear. By now you should be able to see the logical explanation, namely that I used the word "death" to mean more than physical death. I used it as a symbol with a hidden meaning. What *is* the hidden meaning? Let us first set a proper foundation.

Even a casual knowledge of the scriptures or of the events described in them points to the following facts:

- Many people failed to recognize my outer person as the Living Christ. Some believed in me because of visible miracles, but few saw the deeper purpose of my mission. That is why I so often talked about those who were blind (Matthew 15:14) and why I called for those who had eyes to see (Matthew 13:16) and ears to hear (Matthew 13:9). I even chastised my own disciples for not understanding my teachings (Mark 7:18) or my true mission (Matthew 16:23). It is no straightforward task to recognize and understand the Living Christ. Most modern Christians think that had they been alive back then, they would instantly have recognized me, but this is little more than wishful thinking.

- Some people actively opposed the Living Christ and my mission on Earth. The scribes, the Pharisees, the lawyers and the temple priests opposed me at every turn, for I threatened their control over the population. And when they could not scare or manipulate me into silence, they took my physical life, thinking – blinded by their spiritual pride – that physical death can silence the Living Christ.

> And while this is not true, the blind leaders have so far been remarkably successful in manipulating most people into ignoring the Living Christ and settling for a dead doctrine – a dead image, a graven image – of Christ.

Many modern Christians have been brought up with a romanticized image of me, according to which I always appear with clean clothes, neatly trimmed hair and with a halo that makes it easy to identify me. In reality, recognizing that you are or have been in the Presence of the Living Christ is no easy task, and there is no guarantee that people will recognize Christ. Nor is it easy to accept the challenge that the Living Christ presents to all who encounter him—or her. Yet how can it be that people can fail to recognize the Living Christ? And how is it possible that some can actively oppose the Living Christ, thinking he is the devil and that it is their sacred duty to silence him? Truly, as I exclaimed when I was hanging on the cross:

> Father, forgive them; for they know not what they do. (Luke 23:34)

The immediate cause that prevents people from recognizing the Living Christ is ignorance, lack of vision, spiritual blindness. Yet how can people be so blind that they fail to recognize the very Presence that is sent to save them from a mortal life of suffering by offering them the eternal life, the abundant life? How can people be so blind that they fail to recognize that they lack vision? Most people are so blinded that they neither see that they are blind nor recognize that there is anything they cannot see. They see not, yet they think they see all.

Take note that spiritual blindness is not the same as physical blindness. When you are physically blind, you see nothing, and one might think being spiritually blind means being unable to see that life has a spiritual side. In reality, some of the most spiritually blind people are the ones who claim to be the most religious—such as the scribes and Pharisees. Such people – many modern Christian preachers being among them – think they know everything they need to know about religion, and they base it on their intimate knowledge of the outer scriptures.

Yet precisely because they have so much outer knowledge, they have developed spiritual pride, and this makes them completely closed to the possibility that there might be something they cannot see. They will not even consider that they might be unable to see an entire dimension of spirituality, namely the true, inner teachings of the Living Christ. And thus, when the Living Christ challenges their doctrines – in an attempt to open their eyes to the fact that there is something they cannot see – they reject him. They reject the messenger from God by referring to something in this world—and even a holy scripture is something in this world. Truly, the most blind are they who think they know all.

One reason why the Living Christ manifests its Presence in this world is that people are trapped in this limited state of consciousness, so they need to be awakened to the truth that will make them free. Yet the very fact that people are trapped also prevents people from recognizing the Living Christ, understanding his mission and accepting his call for them to rise above their limitations. It is like the serpent swallowing its own tail. The very condition that makes it necessary for people to be saved also prevents them from recognizing the savior and the true message behind his coming. Their spiritual blindness prevents them from breaking the closed circle of human logic.

Let me repeat this point, for it describes the essence of the problem on planet Earth. The very condition that makes it necessary for people to be saved also prevents them from doing what is necessary for them to attain salvation. The very condition that makes it necessary for the Living Christ to enter this world – in order to bring about people's salvation – also prevents them from recognizing the Living Christ and taking advantage of what is offered to them. The very condition that traps people prevents them from rising above the condition.

Instead of accepting the "body and blood" of the Living Christ, people either ignore, explain away, reject or persecute the very Presence that is sent to save them from the condition they cannot – or *will* not – see. Truly, they know not what they do.

Instead of allowing the Living Christ to take them beyond their state of blindness, people use their blindness to create a graven image of who the Living Christ is and what he will do for them. They do not have eyes to see the reality of the Living Christ nor ears to hear his true, inner message. They will not allow the Living Christ to awaken them to the laws that God has put in their inward parts, for they prefer to remain a law onto themselves.

***

We now see that some people are so blind that they do not see that they need the Living Christ. The first step toward overcoming any problem is to recognize that there is a problem and that you need to do something about it. So no one – not even the Living Christ – can save those who do not acknowledge that they need to be saved.

No one can save those who will not see that they need to change their consciousness – by pulling the beam from their own eye – in order to obtain salvation.

You cannot give something to a person who thinks he or she needs nothing. Take note that it is not only people who are not religious that reject the Living Christ. As the scriptures reveal, many of the most religious people of ancient Israel – the scribes, Pharisees, lawyers and temple priests – rejected me. They thought their salvation was already secured – because of their outer observances – and thus they thought I had nothing to offer them. It is the exact same mindset that causes many modern Christians to cling to a dead image of Christ and reject the Living Christ, whether I appear through this course, my website or in other ways. It should be cause for profound introspection that when I walked the Earth, I had limited success in awakening the scribes and Pharisees. Anyone serious about spiritual growth should consider whether he or she has elements of the very consciousness that causes people to reject the Living Christ.

What shall we call the state of consciousness in which people are so completely blind that they fail to acknowledge that they need the Living Christ? Back then, I chose to refer to it as a state of "death," and I worded certain statements in such a way that people should be able to see I was not talking about physical death. Thus, those who had ears to hear would realize that I used the word with a deeper meaning. And when they contemplated that meaning, I could – through the agency of the Comforter – give them a deeper understanding from within. We can now talk about three states of consciousness – three states of "life" for a human being:

- The lowest state is complete spiritual blindness, spiritual death. You are in a state of mind in which you cannot enter the kingdom of God, but you fail to recognize that you are lacking. Therefore, you are going nowhere, you are moving nowhere closer to salvation, no matter how well you might observe the rules of an outer religion. Take note that this state is characterized by illusion and deception. Many people in this state are absolutely convinced that they will be saved because they belong to an outer religion. They completely fail to recognize the fallacy of this belief—that the belief forms a catch-22. They have not yet recognized the reality that salvation requires an inner transformation, a spiritual rebirth. Such people are physically alive but in a spiritual sense, they are the living dead. They are the ones I talked about when I said:

Verily, verily, I say unto you, Except ye eat the flesh of the Son of man, and drink his blood, ye have no life in you. (John 6:53).

- The interim state is where you have awakened to your need to rise above death, but you have not yet attained the higher state that gives you entry into the inner kingdom. Yet as long as you are committed to following the process of raising your consciousness, you are moving closer to salvation. Thus, you are giving me something to work with, and when you multiply the talents you have been given, I can multiply what you bring to the inner altar of the heart. Take note here that some Christians talk about being awakened onto life, or being "born again," but they often identify it as an outer measure, where you recognize me as your Lord and Savior or are baptized. Yet the true awakening is an inner process. Some Christians are indeed awakened to the need to change their consciousness, while others are not—thinking all that is needed is an outer change. Such people are still spiritually dead, even though they claim to be good Christians.

- The final state is when you are fully awakened, when you have been spiritually reborn, when you have been born of the Spirit, when you have been baptized by fire. It truly is the goal of the Living Christ to raise all people to this state of consciousness, whereby they can enter God's kingdom, even while they are still on Earth. We will talk more about this state as the course progresses, but let us not get ahead of ourselves—or rather, get ahead of your ability to understand and accept.

We can now see that the most important turning point for any human being is to become aware of the state of spiritual death and the need to rise above it, the need to be reborn. Why did I say that I had come to give life to those who were already alive—at least in a physical sense? Because the vast majority of the people on this planet are alive physically, but they are not alive spiritually. They have no – spiritual – life in them.

***

The first major hurdle faced by the Living Christ is that most people do not see that they are spiritually dead, for the very condition of spiritual death makes it impossible for people to see that there is more to life, that there is a state of life that is higher than what they have been conditioned to see as the *only* form of life, the *normal* form of life. Because people have grown up in a society where everyone is spiritually dead, they think this is normal or unavoidable. Once the condition of spiritual death has become the norm in a society, it becomes a self-perpetuating condition, a downward spiral, a self-fulfilling prophecy—for people see no alternative. Once people begin to think spiritual death is normal, how can they even reach for eternal life, spiritual life? How can they know they are spiritually dead, when they have never encountered a person who is spiritually alive?

When people have never seen a person who expresses a higher form of life, they do not realize that there is an alternative to *their* form of "life." They think their condition of spiritual death is the normal state of "life" for a human being. Currently, spiritual death *is* the normal condition for a human being, but you have the potential to be MORE than a human being. You can be spiritually reborn and attain spiritual life, whereby you no longer identify yourself as a human being. You know that you are a spiritual being, and you see that you are only temporarily expressing yourself through a human body.

Because humans have become trapped in this state of spiritual death, the very first task of the Living Christ is to enter this world in a human body in order to demonstrate that there *is* a higher form of life than what people see all around them. The Living Christ comes to demonstrate that it is possible to attain a higher state of life, a higher state of mind. It is possible to go beyond spiritual death and become a whole being rather than a being who is pulled hither and yon by the dualistic forces that – temporarily – rule this world.

The first task of the Living Christ is to awaken people from their sleep, awaken them from the illusion that the life they know is the only or the highest form of life. That is why I said that I am come that all might have life and that they might have it more abundantly. I came to this Earth to demonstrate that there is a spiritual form of life beyond the human form of life – which is spiritual death – and that this is a more abundant form of life. This is the eternal life that will not be lost when the body dies and will not be lost even through the death of what most people call the soul. It is the life of realizing who you truly are, who you were created to be, namely, a spiritual being who is beyond both bodily and spiritual death, beyond both the first death and the second death. You realize that there are two forms of life, namely human, physical, mortal life and spiritual, non-material, eternal LIFE.

***

By reading this, you now face the first challenge of Christ. It has two aspects. The first is the recognition that there is more to life than what people normally call life. There is a spiritual life beyond mere physical or human life. The second aspect is the realization that it is possible to attain, radiate and demonstrate this higher life while being in a physical body on Earth. This is the realization that it is – at least in principle – possible for a person in a physical body to attain the higher form of life, to attain the Christ consciousness. It is the recognition that it is possible for the Living Christ to appear on Earth.

This is no easy challenge, and many people have failed it. Even many who call themselves Christians – and who have been baptized into a Christian church – fail to fully acknowledge what it means that the Christ can appear in this world—thinking it only happened once 2,000 years ago. They fail to see that I came to call them to overcome spiritual death, which means they must be willing to remove the beam in their own eyes—instead of thinking that I will do all the work for them.

There are also those who deny that I ever appeared as a real, physical and historical person. This is not a new phenomenon, as can be seen by the words attributed to John:

> 1 Beloved, believe not every spirit, but try the spirits whether they are of God: because many false prophets are gone out into the world.
> 2 Hereby know ye the Spirit of God: Every spirit that confesseth that Jesus Christ is come in the flesh is of God:
> 3 And every spirit that confesseth not that Jesus Christ is come in the flesh is not of God: and this is that spirit of antichrist, whereof ye have heard that it should come; and even now already is it in the world. (1John 4)

Even in the early days of Christianity, there were those who denied that I had appeared "in the flesh," as a physical person. They promoted the belief that the Christ is a principle, concept or spirit that cannot actually enter this world but can be obtained only after one has passed from this world into the spiritual world. Even today there are those who deny that there ever was a real, historical person who gave rise to the Christian movement.

Certainly, there is much that is questionable about the image of Christ that has been handed down by the official churches. Certainly, it is in order to question this image and go beyond the idol of a dead Christ who is hanging on a cross and will remove all of humankind's sins without requiring people to follow his own commandment to remove the beam in their own eyes.

Yet there is an essential dividing line between questioning the man-made idol, the graven image of Christ, and questioning the reality of Christ appearing in this world. Those who refuse to acknowledge that the Living Christ can indeed appear physically on this planet are trapped in the consciousness of spiritual death—and they want to remain there. Thus, they must refuse to see that there is an alternative, that there is something beyond the human mind.

Truly, there are those who are so trapped in spiritual death that they refuse to go beyond it. To justify this, they must deny that the Living Christ can enter this world, for the Presence of the Living Christ in this world demonstrates that it is possible to go beyond spiritual death and have spiritual life, even the abundant life, *right here on Earth.*

Those who are not willing to change themselves, those who are not willing to see and remove the beam in their own eyes, must of necessity deny that it is even possible to go beyond death. And thus, they must deny the Presence of the Living Christ in this world. They can still acknowledge that the Christ can exist in a higher world or that the Christ is a principle that can be attained in a higher world. Many who call themselves Christians acknowledge that I appeared in the flesh 2,000 years ago as Jesus, but they say that the Living Christ could not possibly appear in any other form, before or after that time. Thus, they too fail the first challenge of Christ while actually believing they are true followers of Christ.

***

The first step in overcoming spiritual death is to recognize that one is spiritually dead and that it is possible to attain a higher form of life, even in this world. The next step is to recognize that in order to escape the state of death, one must reach beyond the human state of consciousness. One must find some immovable foundation, some anchor point, that can give one a defense against the onslaught of the illusions – born from the consciousness of death – that dominate this world. That foundation is the Rock of Christ, which takes the form of the Word of Christ:

> 24 Therefore whosoever heareth these sayings of mine, and doeth them, I will liken him unto a wise man, which built his house upon a rock:
> 25 And the rain descended, and the floods came, and the winds blew, and beat upon that house; and it fell not: for it was founded upon a rock.

> 26 And every one that heareth these sayings of mine, and doeth them not, shall be likened unto a foolish man, which built his house upon the sand:
> 27 And the rain descended, and the floods came, and the winds blew, and beat upon that house; and it fell: and great was the fall of it. (Matthew, Chapter 7)

Spiritual death is like walking in a dense jungle, where one cannot see beyond one's immediate vicinity and therefore cannot see where one came from, where one is now and where one is going. One has lost the way. The Word of Christ is like a lifeline that is lowered through the dense canopy of the jungle trees. By climbing the rope, you can raise yourself, your consciousness, above the jungle of illusions and see clearly the reality of who you are and where you are going. Yet finding the lifeline of Christ – be it in the form of the Christian scriptures or one of the many other valid spiritual teachings found in this world – is one thing, climbing the rope is another.

Many people have found the lifeline of a spiritually inspired outer teaching, but they have not decided to climb that rope. They still stand on the ground, thinking it is sufficient to hold on to the rope and that someone will pull them up with no further effort on their part. Some have engaged in the dualistic struggle of seeking to prove that their rope is better than any of the other ropes that the Living Christ has lowered in order to give people from all backgrounds an opportunity to climb above the blindness of the jungle. Some people have found the lifeline of the Living Christ, but instead of using it to rise above the illusions of death, they have used it to cement the belief that one man-made doctrine is superior to another and that seeking to establish the dominance of *their* belief system will gain them entry into the kingdom. They think they can enter God's kingdom without pulling the beam from their own eye, they think they can enter the undivided kingdom of God without overcoming the division in their own minds.

What will it take to actually use the lifeline of the Living Christ, to be one who "heareth these sayings of mine, and doeth them?" It will take a willingness to go beyond spiritual blindness, a realization that the Word of Christ is not the dead word but the Living Word. This is the realization that it is necessary to absorb and internalize the Word, so that one is profoundly changed by the word—not simply using it as a confirmation of one's outer beliefs and conditions. One must be willing to be fundamentally changed, to be reborn, to leave everything else behind in order to follow the

Living Christ. One must leave behind the kingdom of this world in order to enter the kingdom of God.

***

I ask you to carefully consider whether you have understood – truly understood – the point I am making in this chapter. I did not come to this Earth in order to give humankind a blank check. I did not come to offer people an instant salvation, whereby they could fulfill a few outer requirements, and then I simply *had* to save them. I did not come to take upon myself all of the sins that could ever be committed by humankind. What incentive would there be for people to change their consciousness if I had already done the work for them?

In reality, the instant salvation promised by some Christian churches is what I talked about when I said:

> 12 Therefore all things whatsoever ye would that men should do to you, do ye even so to them: for this is the law and the prophets.
> 13 Enter ye in at the strait gate: for wide is the gate, and broad is the way, that leadeth to destruction, and many there be which go in thereat: (Matthew, Chapter 7)

Can you see that when I told you to do unto others what you want them to do to you, I was referring to a law of God, a law which essentially says that the universe is a mirror? What you do to others, the cosmic mirror will reflect back to you. So the only way to change what comes back is to change what you send out. Yet your actions are a reflection of your state of consciousness, so the only way to truly change your life is to change your consciousness. The only way to change the output – what comes out of your mind and heart – is to change the contents—what is inside your mind and heart. This is a gradual path, whereby you place yourself as a disciple of the Living Christ and make a commitment to following my directions—both inner and outer directions. This is the path I described as follows:

> Because strait is the gate, and narrow is the way, which leadeth unto life, and few there be that find it. (Matthew 7:14)

The broad way that most people follow is the path of thinking you can be saved without changing yourself, without pulling the beam from your own eye, without fundamentally changing your consciousness. People think they can "buy" or force their way into heaven by following outer observances, and since this can never work, it is truly the way that leads to destruction. The true way – the Way of Christ – is the process of pulling the beam from your own eye by allowing the Living Christ to expose that beam until you can see what you cannot see right now. This is the hard path of self-examination that requires you to be willing to look at the things that most people will not look at. It requires you to be willing to let the Living Christ show you what you cannot see on your own.

***

Many of my early followers were following this way of inner transformation. In fact, some modern scholars have realized that my early followers were not called Christians. They were called "Followers of the Way." Once again, we see that there is a deeper meaning behind everything I said (and say). Did I not say:

> I am the way, the truth, and the life: no man cometh unto the Father, but by me. (John 14:6)

Can you see that I was not here talking about an outer religion, partly because no such religion existed when I made that statement, partly because no outer religion can guarantee a change in your consciousness? I was, once again, using the word "way" as a symbol for the inner process of rising above the human state of consciousness. Even the word "I" was used as a symbol with a deeper meaning, for it did not only refer to my outer, historical person but something larger than any one person, namely the universal Christ mind.

No one can come to the Father except by going through the Christ consciousness, which means that no one can be saved, can enter the kingdom of God, without going through the Christ mind, without becoming one with the Christ mind. Paul had understood this, which is why he said:

> Let this mind be in you, which was also in Christ Jesus. (Philippians 2:5)

What I am truly saying here is that the salvation I offer humankind is a path of discipleship under me. Yet the end goal of that path is *not* that you forever remain a disciple of Christ but that you come into a state of oneness with the Living Christ, whereby you *become* the Living Christ. I am well aware that most modern Christians have been brought up to see this as blasphemy, for they have been programmed to think I was the *only* Son of God. Yet in so doing they must deny Christ before men, for they must deny this statement from the Gospel of John:

> But as many as received him, to them gave he power to become the sons of God, even to them that believe on his name. (John 1:12)

And again, in the letter of John:

> 1 Behold, what manner of love the Father hath bestowed upon us, that we should be called the sons of God: therefore the world knoweth us not, because it knew him not.
> 2 Beloved, now are we the sons of God, and it doth not yet appear what we shall be: but we know that, when he shall appear, we shall be like him; for we shall see him as he is. (1John, Chapter 3)

As I have tried to explain, you cannot see the Living Christ "as he is" when you are blinded by the illusions of the consciousness of spiritual death. That is why the world does not know me. You can only see the Living Christ as he is if you are willing to be like Christ by transcending the human condition, by being born of the Spirit. Look again at this quote:

> 5 Let this mind be in you, which was also in Christ Jesus:
> 6 Who, being in the form of God, thought it not robbery to be equal with God. (Philippians, Chapter 2)

Those who are true followers of Christ must begin by not thinking it robbery for them to be equal with Christ. And then they must go beyond and see that they too can become sons and daughters of God—as I am.

The inner reality behind all outer doctrines is that I came to this Earth in order to offer all people a path of direct discipleship under me. Yet that path has an end goal, which is to no longer be a disciple of Christ but to attain oneness with me. Whereby, you can affirm the oneness with your teacher that I affirmed when I said:

> I and my Father are one. (John 10:30)

When I appeared physically 2,000 years ago, only a few people were ready for this direct path. That is why I had only a few disciples to whom I described the path directly and then taught the multitudes in parables. Yet in the modern world the situation has changed dramatically.

There are now many people on Earth who are ready for a path of direct discipleship under me. And since no mainstream Christian churches are open to me teaching this path through them, I have decided to describe this path in a course that will be available to all people. Yet this course is only the first step that can help you discover the inner Way of Christ. In order to follow that way, you must go beyond the outer word and establish a direct, inner, personal relationship with me and with the Comforter who is your personal teacher. This will be described in more detail later, but first we need to take a look at the second challenge of Christ, which we will do in the next chapter.

***

Before we move on, let me make one more attempt to explain the essence of the early stages of the path to Christhood. As the parable with Nicodemus shows, the human consciousness simply cannot fathom the reality of God that is only seen through the Christ consciousness. So as a spiritual teacher, I am fully aware that at your current level of consciousness, you simply cannot fathom every aspect of the path to Christhood—you cannot bear it now.

It is extremely important for you to also come to the realization that you currently cannot understand the fullness of the path. If you do not acknowledge this, you will easily fall into the trap of thinking that you have understood the path because you understand an outer scripture, or even the outer teachings I give in this course. And this form of intellectual or spiritual pride will prevent you from multiplying your talents, thus aborting the gradual process that leads toward the point where the Christ can be born within you.

Let me suggest the following illustration. You know that when you put on a pair of sunglasses, you are seeing the same reality as before, but it appears slightly colored by the lenses. Well, you currently have many imperfect beliefs that have been programmed into your consciousness, and they form a filter through which you see everything—*including my teachings on the path to Christhood*. Thus, even though I can give you a truth, your personal filter may distort that truth and prevent you from grasping the true meaning or at least the full meaning.

If you look at humanity, you will see that most people are wearing certain mental "glasses" that prevent them from seeing the reality of Christ. And on top of that, they are unaware that they are wearing such glasses. They think reality really does conform to their mental box, for they are unaware that they have a mental box that distorts their view of everything. They do not have ears to hear and consequently cannot recognize the Living Christ, instead seeking to make him conform to their mental box.

In contrast, those who are able to follow the path to Christhood have begun to recognize that they are wearing glasses, that the glasses color their vision and that they need to take active measures to remove those glasses—to pull the beam from their own eye. They realize that if they could remove those glasses, they would instantly gain a vastly different perspective on life—even though they cannot currently grasp this perspective (because of the glasses).

The first step toward overcoming spiritual death is to see that there is something you cannot see—even though you cannot currently see what it is you cannot see. The next step is to realize that removing the glasses in order to gain clear vision must – in all practicality – be a gradual process. Yet what is the essence of that process? It is that *you* must be willing to do two things:

- You must be willing to accept the direction from the Living Christ, either through an outer teaching, such as this course, or through the Comforter in your heart.
- You must be willing to follow that direction—even though your outer mind does not currently understand the direction and its purpose!

Do you see the essential point here? I have to give you a direction that will help you take the next step on the path, knowing full well that you cannot fully grasp that direction. Why is this so? Because the path can be seen as a series of steps, where each step represents a certain state of consciousness. You make progress on the path by transcending, going beyond, one state of consciousness and rising to a higher one.

Yet how do you transcend your current state of consciousness? You can do so only by reaching for an understanding that is above and beyond that state of consciousness. In other words, what you can fathom with your current state of consciousness cannot take you beyond that state of consciousness.

The Living Christ comes to you to give you the understanding that can take you to the next level, but in order to make use of it, you must be willing to apply it, even though you cannot – yet – understand it. This is not to say that you must blindly follow the directions of the Living Christ without thinking about them, for this would only make you a blind follower. Instead, you must continually ponder and meditate upon the direction, seeking to grasp a higher, more subtle understanding, until you have internalized the direction. And when the direction is fully internalized, you have made the leap to a higher level of consciousness—at which point the Living Christ will present you with the next challenge that will take you even higher.

My point being that you never allow yourself to think you have fully understood the directions of the Living Christ but always strive to gain a deeper understanding. It is wise to accept the fact that as long as you are in physical embodiment, there will always be deeper layers of understanding for the Christ to unveil—if you are willing to see them.

Some people decide to stop this process at a given level, and I will later explain why and how this happens. Yet for now, I want you to understand the central challenge that is required for the multiplication of the talents. You must ponder a given idea or teaching until it has become internalized and has transformed your consciousness in the process. And you must be willing to start this process even though you do not fully understand it with the outer, analytical mind that so loves to control everything. Doing this is truly receiving the kingdom of God with the innocent mind of a little child—this is having ears to hear and eyes to see. I am always willing to receive a student who decides that he or she is willing to have that openness of mind and heart.

# Chapter 3
# The second challenge of Christ

Have you ever considered how often you force yourself to do, say, feel or think things in order to fit into society, in order to accommodate some kind of standard put upon you from outside yourself? Have you ever considered that as you grow up, you are conditioned – programmed, brainwashed – to accept many things that are norms in your society without ever questioning them? Have you ever considered that you do many things simply because they are a tradition in your society, and perhaps no one has ever considered whether they are actually necessary? Everyone keeps doing them because everyone has always been doing them. Have you ever considered that some people live their entire lives by following the norms of their society – in anything from religion to fashion – and they never actually have an original thought or make their own decisions?

Well, the fact that you are studying this course indicates that you have considered such things and that you are willing to look for a better way of doing things. You have – at some level of your being – realized, at least sensed, that there must be more to life than what you experience right now. You sense that there must be an alternative, a more abundant form of life, and you are reading this book with the hope that it can help you manifest that more abundant life—however you conceive of it right now. This longing for something more, this inability to be satisfied by doing things the way they have always been done, demonstrates something very important. It demonstrates the very mechanism, the saving grace, that makes it possible for people to escape the condition of spiritual death. It also holds the key to understanding how to overcome the second challenge of Christ.

Let us first look at a question that follows my description of the state of spiritual death. I have explained that this condition forms a closed loop, a mental box from which there seems to be no escape, because the box itself prevents people from seeing that there is something outside the box. I have said that the Living Christ comes into this world in order to demonstrate that there is indeed a higher, more spiritual, form of life. Yet I have also said that people who are completely blind cannot recognize the Christ. So if there was no saving grace, if there was no mechanism that provided a way out of the closed box, how could anyone ever escape?

The mechanism that is the saving grace is precisely the inner, intuitive sense that there must be something more to life than what you experience inside the box—be it the box of your society or the box of your own mind. This sense is built into your innermost being, and the reason for this is that your true being is an extension of God's own Being. This is even confirmed by the Bible:

> 26 And God said, Let us make man in our image, after our likeness: and let them have dominion over the fish of the sea, and over the fowl of the air, and over the cattle, and over all the Earth, and over every creeping thing that creepeth upon the Earth.
> 27 So God created man in his own image, in the image of God created he him; male and female created he them.
> 28 And God blessed them, and God said unto them, Be fruitful, and multiply, and replenish the Earth, and subdue it: and have dominion over the fish of the sea, and over the fowl of the air, and over every living thing that moveth upon the Earth. (Genesis, Chapter 1)

The fact that your inner being is created after the image and likeness of your Creator – who is beyond this material world – means that you can never totally lose your longing for something beyond this world. You can forget this longing for a time, either by focusing on the endless pursuit of the things of this world, or because you think you belong to an outer religion and your salvation is guaranteed. Yet at some point you will inevitably feel an inner sense of emptiness, a longing for something more:

> 2 Vanity of vanities, saith the Preacher, vanity of vanities; all is vanity.
> 3 What profit hath a man of all his labour which he taketh under the sun? (Ecclesiastes, Chapter 1)

For a long time, people can fall under the temptation that the devil presented to me after my fasting in the wilderness:

> 8 Again, the devil taketh him up into an exceeding high mountain, and showeth him all the kingdoms of the world, and the glory of them;

> 9 And saith unto him, All these things will I give thee, if thou wilt fall down and worship me.
> 10 Then saith Jesus unto him, Get thee hence, Satan: for it is written, Thou shalt worship the Lord thy God, and him only shalt thou serve. (Matthew, Chapter 4)

The devil can be seen as a symbol for the appearances of this world and the temptation to seek to gain some kind of ultimate state in this world, be it power, possessions, pleasure, fame, security or whatever this world has to offer. For a very long time, people can be completely absorbed by such pursuits, and thus they will reject the Living Christ who comes to show them that there is a more abundant form of life than what this world has to offer. Yet at some point in time, a lifestream will begin to sense that there is something more than what this world has to offer and that this world cannot give you what you long for in your innermost being. You will begin to sense the truth in my words:

> 36 For what shall it profit a man, if he shall gain the whole world, and lose his own soul?
> 37 Or what shall a man give in exchange for his soul? (Mark, Chapter 8)

When a person begins to become aware of this inner longing for something beyond this world, the person now becomes open to passing the first challenge of Christ, namely to consciously recognize that there is a higher form of life. Thus, such a person can now recognize the Living Christ. The recognition that it is possible for the Living Christ to enter this world can give rise to the awareness that:

- I am lacking, there is something I do not have. I do not have the fullness of spiritual life that I see in the Christ, and I want it.
- I need to overcome the state of spiritual death, and I cannot do that on my own. I need something from the Living Christ in order to rise beyond death.

This can then give rise to the desire to follow the Living Christ, to become a disciple of Christ, in order to receive from Christ what you recognize you need. However, here is where we run into an absolutely essential consideration, and unfortunately most people – be they Christians or not – have not understood this problem, which is why it prevents them from truly making spiritual progress, from truly following Christ.

***

As I said in the beginning of this chapter, there are two forces that pull on your conscious mind. One is the force that pulls you into conforming to the conditions in this world and the other is the force that pulls you beyond this world. We might call them the material force and the spiritual force, or, in a traditional Christian vernacular, anti-christ and Christ.

If you are completely blinded by the force of anti-christ, you cannot even recognize the force of Christ. So the fact that you are a religious person or a spiritual seeker shows that you have started escaping the control of the worldly force. Yet this does not mean that you are completely free from its control. It should be a cause of humility for Christians that God allowed me to be tempted by the devil. The lesson is that all people are being tempted by the devil, or rather by the force that seeks to pull you into conforming to this world rather than rising above this world. Thus, you should realize that by facing the temptations of the devil, I demonstrated the temptations all people must face in order to follow Christ and escape the pull of this world. And this temptation will remain – in some form and with varying intensity and subtlety – as long as you are in a physical body.

Do you see what I am saying here? I have said that the condition of spiritual death forms a self-reinforcing condition because it pulls you into conforming to a set of illusions that blind you to the spiritual reality. So the forces of this world – the devil, the consciousness of death, the mass consciousness, your ego – pull you into conforming to a false image, a graven image, of who you are and what you can and cannot be. The very essence of the consciousness of spiritual death is that it has set up a graven image that obscures the one true God, and this image prevents people from seeing beyond the image. As the Bible says, you are created in the image of God and you are here to have dominion over the Earth. Yet the force of anti-christ creates a graven image, which says you are *not* the offspring of God and that you cannot take dominion over this planet—for the devil wants that dominion for himself.

How can you escape the catch-22? By coming to the point of realizing the truth I stated earlier, namely that the things of this world are vanity and that it does you no good to gain the whole world but lose your soul. What will it take for you to come to that point? It can happen through an inner realization – an intuitive or

"Aha experience" – or by attending the school of hard knocks. In this school it is simply a question of how hard the knocks have to become before you begin to consciously acknowledge that there must be a better way to live, that there must be something beyond this world.

When you begin to escape the blinding force of the graven image, you begin to realize that there is something beyond the graven image—and this is what allows you to recognize the Living Christ. Yet this does not mean that you are completely free from the graven image. In fact, the interim period I talked about earlier is precisely a period where you still have graven images in your mind, and you are not completely free of them. The absolutely essential question now becomes whether you will be willing to let the Living Christ pull you – perhaps kicking and screaming if necessary – beyond all of your graven images *or* whether you will seek to impose some of those images upon the Living Christ and the path Christ offers?

In other words, will you follow the true path that is offered by the Living Christ, or will you follow the false path that is offered by the prince of this world and the blind leaders of this world? Take another look at my words:

> 13 Enter ye in at the strait gate: for wide is the gate, and broad is the way, that leadeth to destruction, and many there be which go in thereat:
> 14 Because strait is the gate, and narrow is the way, which leadeth unto life, and few there be that find it. (Matthew, Chapter 7)

The straight and narrow path offered by the Living Christ is the path of overcoming *all* of the graven images – the beams – in your mind. In contrast, the broad way that leads to destruction is the path of recognizing that you have a need for salvation, recognizing the Living Christ, but then imposing a graven image upon the Living Christ and the path he offers. Thus, instead of seeing and following the true path, you enter the false path while actually being convinced that you are following the true path! The true path is about overcoming graven images, the false path is based on graven images and elevates some of them to the status of infallibility, meaning you never question them.

So instead of allowing the Living Christ to take you beyond the consciousness of death, you have used the Living Christ – or rather your dualistic image of the Christ – to create a false path. This false path offers you salvation, but it offers you an external salvation that makes it seem like you do not have to remove the beam in your own eye. In reality, this false path offers you the promise that you can attain eternal life without overcoming the consciousness of death and removing all of the graven images that spring from the consciousness of death. Look at the words that follow the above quote:

> 15 Beware of false prophets, which come to you in sheep's clothing, but inwardly they are ravening wolves.
> 16 Ye shall know them by their fruits. Do men gather grapes of thorns, or figs of thistles?
>
> 20 Wherefore by their fruits ye shall know them.
> 21 Not every one that saith unto me, Lord, Lord, shall enter into the kingdom of heaven; but he that doeth the will of my Father which is in heaven.
> 22 Many will say to me in that day, Lord, Lord, have we not prophesied in thy name? and in thy name have cast out devils? and in thy name done many wonderful works?
> 23 And then will I profess unto them, I never knew you: depart from me, ye that work iniquity. (Matthew, Chapter 7)

Why do you think I found it necessary to be so detailed and direct in warning people about the false path? Could it be because I was well aware that many of the people, who come to the realization that they need to be saved, are misled into following a false path that cannot lead them to salvation? Why do you think I was opposed by the scribes and Pharisees? Why do you think they could not recognize me as the Living Christ? It was because they were following the false path while being completely convinced that they would be saved. In other words, they had passed the first hurdle of recognizing that they needed to be saved, yet they had become trapped by the false path that makes people think they can be saved without truly following the Living Christ all the way, without letting go of their graven images.

Many modern Christians are trapped in the very consciousness I spoke about when I said, "Many will say to me in that day, Lord, Lord, have we not prophesied in thy name? and in thy name have cast out devils? and in thy name done many wonderful works? And then will I profess unto them, I never knew you: depart from me, ye that work iniquity." They claim to be following Christ, but they are following the false path, the outer path, that is based on a graven image of Christ. Although they constantly proclaim my name before men, they are actually denying the Living Christ before men – by professing a dead Christ – and thus I have no other option but to deny them before the Father.

I know that the point I am making here can be quite subtle and difficult to understand for many people. The best proof of this is that I have to make this point and that it has not been preached clearly by a single Christian church over the past 2,000 years. So in order to help people understand this crucial point, I will explain it from several different perspectives. You might think you have understood my point, but I caution you against this idea. Be willing to follow me as I expose the topic from different vantage points.

***

There are many people in the modern world who have come to accept an image of me that portrays me as a very loving, kind and compassionate being who basically included and tolerated everybody. Such people are found in many Christian denominations and they are found in the self-help, personal growth or New Age movements. As I said, I did teach on two different levels, namely one teaching for the multitudes (in parables) and one teaching for my disciples (a more direct teaching). So if you want to hold on to the image of the soft and gentle Jesus, you can keep that image, but then you should be willing to acknowledge that you will not rise beyond the teaching I gave to the multitudes, and you have no opportunity to become my direct disciple.

If, on the other hand, you want to become my direct disciple in this age, you will have to live up to the requirements for being a disciple of the Living Christ. Obviously, some of those requirements were not known publicly, so they are not even described in the Bible. I shall describe these requirements in this course, but I will begin by looking at the requirements that are described in the official scriptures. And those who have ears to hear will realize that I am – back then and today – a very direct and uncompromising teacher. Take for example the description of how I called my disciples:

> 18 And Jesus, walking by the sea of Galilee, saw two brethren, Simon called Peter, and Andrew his brother, casting a net into the sea: for they were fishers.
> 19 And he saith unto them, Follow me, and I will make you fishers of men.
> 20 And they straightway left their nets, and followed him.
> 21 And going on from thence, he saw other two brethren, James the son of Zebedee, and John his brother, in a ship

with Zebedee their father, mending their nets; and he called them.
22 And they immediately left the ship and their father, and followed him. (Matthew, Chapter 4)

What is the essential phrase in the above quote? Most people will say it is "I will make you fishers of men." In reality, the central phrase is "And they straightway left their nets." Many modern people have a highly romanticized view, according to which my disciples where called and then had ample time to get their affairs in order before they followed me. The reality was quite different. I literally walked up to the disciples, called them to follow me, turned around and walked away. The time they had to decide whether or not to follow me was the time it took for me to walk around the next bend in the road. If they had not left everything and followed me at that point, their opportunity was lost. The scriptures mainly describe the disciples who *did* follow me. In reality, I called many who did not leave their nets – as a symbol for their entanglements with the things of this world – and thus remained trapped in those nets. Here is one example of a person who was called but was not willing to leave behind his possessions:

20 The young man saith unto him, All these things have I kept from my youth up: what lack I yet?
21 Jesus said unto him, If thou wilt be perfect, go and sell that thou hast, and give to the poor, and thou shalt have treasure in heaven: and come and follow me.
22 But when the young man heard that saying, he went away sorrowful: for he had great possessions.
23 Then said Jesus unto his disciples, Verily I say unto you, That a rich man shall hardly enter into the kingdom of heaven.
24 And again I say unto you, It is easier for a camel to go through the eye of a needle, than for a rich man to enter into the kingdom of God.
25 When his disciples heard it, they were exceedingly amazed, saying, Who then can be saved? (Matthew, Chapter 19)

I know this can sound harsh, but I had a very specific mission, and I had only a short time to accomplish it. I needed to have disciples who would follow me without compromise, and thus I had a right to test their willingness to leave everything else behind. Today the situation is slightly different. You do not necessarily have to follow me "straightway," but on the other hand, if you are to overcome the consciousness of death before the end of your present lifetime, I recommend that you do not hesitate.

What is the essential test you must pass in order to become a disciple of the Living Christ? I have said that the key to salvation is to rise above the consciousness of death, which means you must leave behind *all* of the graven images that spring from the consciousness of death. Thus, in order to qualify as my direct disciple, you have to demonstrate a willingness to leave behind everything in this world. Did you take note that I said "everything?" Well, I can assure you that I *do* mean *everything*! Yet I am not saying you have to leave behind everything, I am only saying you have to *be willing* to leave behind everything. Let me illustrate that by repeating another quote:

> 21 And another of his disciples said unto him, Lord, suffer me first to go and bury my father.
> 22 But Jesus said unto him, Follow me; and let the dead bury their dead. (Matthew, Chapter 8)

If you have things you absolutely have to do before you feel you can follow the Living Christ, then by all means go do them. But be aware that the prince of this world is extremely subtle and extremely skilled at coming up with things you absolutely have to do before you can follow Christ. You can easily spend the rest of this lifetime doing "one last thing." In fact, the state of mind in which you feel you have one last thing to do will not stop until *you* decide that you do not have to do this last thing—you can let the dead bury their dead. Now for a series of quotes from Matthew, Chapter 10:

> 34 Think not that I am come to send peace on Earth: I came not to send peace, but a sword.
> 35 For I am come to set a man at variance against his father, and the daughter against her mother, and the daughter in law against her mother in law.

As I said earlier, in order to follow Christ you must overcome the pull to conform to the norms and standards of this world, including those of your own family. I am not saying every disciple of Christ will have trouble with his or her family. I am simply saying that if you value conforming to the norms and expectations of others over the need to follow the requirements of the path of Christhood, you are not ready to be my disciple.

> 36 And a man's foes shall be they of his own household.
> 37 He that loveth father or mother more than me is not worthy of me: and he that loveth son or daughter more than me is not worthy of me.

Some people interpret this to mean that I was an egomaniac who wanted my disciples to worship me—much like a modern cult leader. Yet the reality is that if you love anything in this world more than you love following the path, then you will not be able to give up the things of this world in order to follow the Living Christ. Take note that I am not actually saying you cannot love others; I am only saying you cannot love them *more* than you love following the path to Christhood. What does it actually mean to follow the path?

> 38 And he that taketh not his cross, and followeth after me, is not worthy of me.

Taking up your cross has more than one meaning, and I will expound on this later. But for now, suffice it to say that taking up your cross is a symbol for looking at and removing the beam in your own eye. That beam is the consciousness of death and all of the illusions – graven images – that spring from it. The cross is a symbol for something that keeps you paralyzed, and you are literally nailed to your personal cross by the elements of the death consciousness in your own mind. Taking up your cross means being willing to look at and remove the beam in your own eye, not letting any condition – any excuse – in this world prevent you from following me all the way to total freedom from the death consciousness. If you are not willing to do the hard and unpleasant work of removing the beam from your own eye, you cannot even begin to follow the path that I offer. Just how uncompromising *is* that path? Just what do you have to be willing to give up in order to follow that path:

> 24 If any man will come after me, let him deny himself, and take up his cross, and follow me.
> 25 For whosoever will save his life shall lose it: and whosoever will lose his life for my sake shall find it. (Matthew, Chapter 16)

I am not hereby calling you to join some kind of suicide cult. The deeper meaning is that what most people call "life" is actually the identity they have built based on the consciousness of spiritual death. And if you are not willing to give up that sense of "life," if you seek to save that *mortal* life, you will indeed lose the *eternal* life.

In order to take up your cross and follow the Living Christ, you have to deny your "self," meaning the sense of self that is based on the consciousness of death. When you are willing to lose that mortal life – and everything that goes with it – you will indeed gain the eternal life that comes only by following the straight and narrow Way of Christ until you put on the mind of Christ, until you *become one* with Christ.

***

Why is the path to Christhood so uncompromising? I have said that there are three stages on the road to salvation. The first is the state of spiritual death, where you have not yet been awakened to the existence of the path. You have only elements of death in your being and there is no life in you, meaning that you have no elements of the truth of Christ in your being. The second stage is the interim phase, where you have both elements of death and elements of life in your being. The danger at this stage is that if there are elements of death – graven images – that you are not willing to let go of, you can use them to create the image of a false path. I tried to warn people very strongly against this false path, because it is such a subtle temptation.

The reality is that in order to work through the interim stage, you must leave behind *all* graven images, all elements of death. The consciousness of death and the consciousness of life are mutually exclusive. You cannot be in two mutually exclusive states of consciousness at the same time, meaning that you cannot be fully *in* the consciousness of Christ until you have left behind *all* elements of death. This is illustrated in my words:

> No man can serve two masters: for either he will hate the one, and love the other; or else he will hold to the one, and despise the other. Ye cannot serve God and mammon. (Matthew 6:24)

So many people think "mammon" refers only to money. In reality, it is another symbol that refers to anything in this world that you value more than attaining the Christ consciousness. It refers to an attachment to anything in this world. What is an attachment? You might have certain material things that have a sentimental value to you, such as a memento from your childhood or an important event in your life. You find it difficult to let go of these things even though they have no financial or practical value. That unwillingness to let go is a simple – and relatively harmless – example of an emotional attachment.

However, such attachments come in many varied and subtle forms. For example, many people are attached to certain beliefs or a certain belief system. They are attached to a certain way of looking at life and a certain way of looking at themselves. Many Christians cannot let go of the belief that I will save them, and thus they are likely to reject this course. Many people are attached to a certain self-image as being good people, and thus they are not willing to consider that they might have certain flaws that need to be corrected. Such attachments prevent people from even looking for the beam in their own eye, and thus how can they start removing that beam? Thus, an attachment is a reluctance to let of something in this world in order to gain something beyond this world.

The dynamic is quite simple. Your attachments will pull your attention in a certain direction, and wherever you focus your attention, your mental energies will follow. In the modern world, you know that science has proven that everything is energy, so your thoughts and feelings are forms of energy. The more you focus your attention on a certain topic, the more mental energy you will direct there, causing it to accumulate.

When the energy reaches a critical mass, it will begin to pull on your attention, so you concentrate even more energy in that direction. This will become a self-reinforcing spiral that can easily take your attention off the path of Christhood. You have probably experienced facing a difficult situation that causes you to think about a topic over and over again, often with a lot of emotional energy to reinforce the thoughts. This will pull on your mind to where you simply cannot get your mind off the topic, and this is what leads to stress. Thus, you now see a more modern explanation for a truth I expressed in the following way 2,000 years ago:

> 19 Lay not up for yourselves treasures upon Earth, where moth and rust doth corrupt, and where thieves break through and steal:
> 20 But lay up for yourselves treasures in heaven, where neither moth nor rust doth corrupt, and where thieves do not break through nor steal:
> 21 For where your treasure is, there will your heart be also.
> (Matthew, Chapter 6)

The more you focus your attention on something in this world, and the more emotionally attached you are to that something, the more mental energy you concentrate in this world, which obviously pulls you away from focusing on the spiritual path. You only have so much attention and so much mental energy, so you must choose how you spend your investment capital—your talents. As a wise investor, you should invest your capital where you stand to get the best return—rather than burying it in the ground, as a symbol for this world. And the path of Christ will give you a far better return than anything in this world. The prince of peace has infinitely more to offer than the prince of this world:

> Hereafter I will not talk much with you: for the prince of this world cometh, and hath nothing in me. (John 14:30)

A literal person will think I am only talking about myself, but I am describing one of the later stages on the path of Christhood. When you still have attachments to anything in this world, the prince of this world has something in you, whereby he can tempt you into following the false path. What is the essence of the false path? It is the belief that you can enter the kingdom of God without letting go of certain things in this world. More on this later.

You now see why I was tempted by the devil after my fasting in the wilderness. I had to prove how to rise above all of the temptations of the consciousness of death. In order to follow my path to eternal life, you too must overcome all of the temptations of the prince of this world. And you can do that only when the prince finds no attachments whereby he can tempt or manipulate you. Of course, in order to overcome all attachments, you have to *be willing* to let go of *anything* in this world. This is one of the inescapable requirements for being my disciple. Take another look at this story:

> 20 The young man saith unto him, All these things have I kept from my youth up: what lack I yet?
> 21 Jesus said unto him, If thou wilt be perfect, go and sell that thou hast, and give to the poor, and thou shalt have treasure in heaven: and come and follow me.
> 22 But when the young man heard that saying, he went away sorrowful: for he had great possessions.
> 23 Then said Jesus unto his disciples, Verily I say unto you, That a rich man shall hardly enter into the kingdom of heaven.
> 24 And again I say unto you, It is easier for a camel to go through the eye of a needle, than for a rich man to enter into the kingdom of God.

> 25 When his disciples heard it, they were exceedingly amazed, saying, Who then can be saved?
> 26 But Jesus beheld them, and said unto them, With men this is impossible; but with God all things are possible. (Matthew, Chapter 19)

Do you now see beyond the literal interpretation to the deeper meaning? I was not simply talking about people who have money. I was talking about anyone who has something – *anything* – in this world that he or she is not willing to give up in order to follow Christ. Just as a camel cannot go through the eye of a needle, a person cannot enter heaven as long as he or she is attached to anything on Earth. A "rich" person is a person who has accumulated many attachments to the things of this world, thus being unwilling to give them up in order to follow Christ.

Even my disciples did not fully understand this, and my answer to them shows another layer of truth. When I said that with men it is impossible to be saved, I meant that there is nothing from this world that can bring about your salvation. The consciousness of death contains innumerable illusions – graven images – and when people accept them, they think they can force or buy their way into heaven by doing something in this world. The scribes and the Pharisees were sure they would be saved because they followed the observances of the outer religion. Yet the reality is that you need to be saved because you have become blinded by the consciousness of death. Thus, you can be saved only by leaving behind all elements of that consciousness. You cannot *use* the consciousness of death to save yourself *from* the consciousness of death. You cannot overcome a problem through the same state of consciousness that created the problem. You have *done* your way out of heaven by acting through the spiritual blindness of the consciousness of death, so there is nothing you can *do* with that consciousness that will get you back into heaven.

You can be saved only by completely giving up your mortal life and being willing to be reborn into a higher state of consciousness. You can be saved only by leaving behind the human state of consciousness and being reborn into the Christ consciousness. You must leave behind all that is "with men" and trust fully in that which is "with God."

***

We now come to the essential point I want to make in this chapter. To illustrate it, let us look at the following incident:

> 13 When Jesus came into the coasts of Caesarea Philippi, he asked his disciples, saying, Whom do men say that I the Son of man am?
> 14 And they said, Some say that thou art John the Baptist: some, Elias; and others, Jeremias, or one of the prophets.
> 15 He saith unto them, But whom say ye that I am?
> 16 And Simon Peter answered and said, Thou art the Christ, the Son of the living God.
> 17 And Jesus answered and said unto him, Blessed art thou, Simon Barjona: for flesh and blood hath not revealed it unto thee, but my Father which is in heaven.
> 18 And I say also unto thee, That thou art Peter, and upon this rock I will build my church; and the gates of hell shall not prevail against it. (Matthew, Chapter 16)

Many Christians – especially Catholics – love to give this quote and use it as a proof that I intended to build my church upon the person of Peter and his example. Yet by now you should have realized that everything in the scriptures can be interpreted at – at least – two levels. There is the surface level of interpreting everything literally. And then there is the deeper level that I gave to my disciples. So for those who are willing to be my modern-day disciples, let me expound all things about this situation.

The reality is that Peter – although a historical person – was a symbol for the many people in the world who are at a certain level of consciousness. This is the state I described earlier, where you know there is something beyond this world, and thus you are open to recognizing the Living Christ. Because you were created in the image and likeness of God, you have a built-in ability to recognize the Living Christ in this world. You do this by realizing that the Christ stirs something in you. When you encounter the Living Christ, the light he or she radiates literally reactivates something in the core of your being, and you are awakened to the realization that you are more than a human being. You can then recognize the Living Christ and decide to follow him or her, although you still see the Christ as being outside yourself.

So the rock upon which I would build my church back then was people's ability to recognize the Living Christ and their willingness to strive for something more than what is offered by the prince of this world. In an inner sense, the gates of hell will not prevail against this, since you can never completely lose your potential to recognize Christ or your longing for something beyond this world—a longing which Peter had and demonstrated. Yet you can become temporarily blinded by the consciousness of death, so that you cannot or will not use this ability, as was the case with the scribes and Pharisees.

Thus, in a practical sense, it is by no means a given that the gates of hell shall not prevail against my church as an outer institution. The infallibility of any Earthly institution is a graven image, and the reality is that everything in this world is subject to people's free will. If people did not have free will, the Living Christ would not need to come into this world and take on a human form that people can accept or reject.

I came to present people with a choice between Christ and anti-christ. This proves that God has given people free will, meaning that the fate of the Christian church will depend on people's choices. Thus, the fate of my church will depend on whether people are willing to continually follow the Living Christ or whether they will stop following the Christ and instead begin following one of the graven images created by anti-christ. To illustrate this, let us look at the following verses, verses that most Christian preachers conveniently "forget" when they talk about Peter:

> 21 From that time forth began Jesus to show unto his disciples, how that he must go unto Jerusalem, and suffer many things of the elders and chief priests and scribes, and be killed, and be raised again the third day.
> 22 Then Peter took him, and began to rebuke him, saying, Be it far from thee, Lord: this shall not be unto thee.
> 23 But he turned, and said unto Peter, Get thee behind me, Satan: thou art an offence unto me: for thou savourest not the things that be of God, but those that be of men.
> (Matthew, Chapter 16)

Some modern psychologists have looked at this and the preceding quote and concluded that I must have had a bipolar or schizophrenic personality disorder. In one situation I tell Peter he is the rock upon which I will build my church and that the gates of hell shall not prevail against it, and in the next situation I tell Peter that he is Satan himself. We can now understand what was really happening.

Peter represented a person who is in the interim phase that I described earlier. During this phase, you will have elements of life and elements of death in your consciousness, meaning that you can switch between being in alignment with Christ and being in alignment with anti-christ. In the first situation, Peter was in alignment with Christ, and it was this alignment upon which my church is built. As long as he stayed in that state of alignment – seeking for something beyond this world – the gates of hell would not prevail against my church.

In the second situation, Peter had lost the alignment with Christ. The quote reveals that Peter had a graven image of what it meant that the Christ had come into this world and what should happen as a result. As most people in ancient Israel, Peter thought the Messiah would come as a triumphant king who would overthrow the Romans and restore the kingdom of God to Israel, whereby the Jews would be universally recognized as God's chosen people, being exalted above all others. Peter was – as were most Jews and as are most Christians today – very emotionally attached to this graven image. So when I started – deliberately I might say – to challenge his image, he got upset with me and wanted to silence me.

What really happened was that Peter passed the first challenge of Christ but failed the second challenge. As I have explained, the first challenge is to recognize the Living Christ and develop the desire to follow him—to reach for something beyond this world. The second challenge is to continue to follow the Living Christ until you have completely overcome the interim stage—until you have freed your mind from all graven images from this world. This requires you to allow the Living Christ to systematically – and without compromise – expose all of your graven images, so you can see the beams in your own eye and leave them *all* behind.

If you are not willing to take up this cross, you will leave the straight and narrow way of the Christ and step onto the broad way of anti-christ. This is the path where – instead of allowing the Christ to challenge your graven images – you hold on to your mental images and even seek to impose them upon the Living Christ. Instead of letting the Christ challenge your graven images, you seek to force the Christ to conform to those images. You want the Christ to adapt to and fit inside your mental box instead of allowing the Christ to take you beyond the box. Instead of reaching for something *beyond* this world, you are now holding on to something *from* this world.

You essentially think you can force the Living Christ to worship your graven image of a false God. Yet the role of the Living Christ is to *always* maintain the direct connection to the reality of the true God, thus calling people to rise above all graven images and discover the kingdom of God within them—the inner kingdom where no graven images are needed, for you experience God directly. Thus, the role of the Living Christ is to challenge *any* and *all* graven images that people have.

Seeking to impose a graven image upon the Living Christ is the very essence of the consciousness of anti-christ that was embodied by the devil and Satan. Thus, when Peter sought to impose his image of Christ as the triumphant king upon me, he was trapped in the consciousness of anti-christ and was actually acting as an extension of the devil, tempting me one more time.

Would I conform to one of the graven images of this world, or would I refuse to be limited by anything springing from the consciousness of Christ? Thus, the sternness of my rebuke was born of the fact that I was rebuking the entire planetary consciousness of anti-christ, the very consciousness that has kept humankind trapped in the state of spiritual death for thousands of years. I was also aiming to set an obvious example for how those who follow the true path of Christ need to be alert to the very subtle temptation to conform to a graven image—sometimes coming from those from whom you least expect it. Thus, you need to rebuke and challenge that consciousness whenever you encounter it.

***

You may still think I was being unnecessarily harsh toward Peter, but I knew Peter's high potential and his low potential. I knew there was a very fine line – as there is for most people – between Peter taking the high road and the low road. Unfortunately, Peter did indeed take the low road, as evidenced by the following quotes that are also often ignored by Christian preachers:

> 69 Now Peter sat without in the palace: and a damsel came unto him, saying, Thou also wast with Jesus of Galilee.
> 70 But he denied before them all, saying, I know not what thou sayest.
> 71 And when he was gone out into the porch, another maid saw him, and said unto them that were there, This fellow was also with Jesus of Nazareth.
> 72 And again he denied with an oath, I do not know the man.
> 73 And after a while came unto him they that stood by, and said to Peter, Surely thou also art one of them; for thy speech betrayeth thee.
> 74 Then began he to curse and to swear, saying, I know not the man. And immediately the cock crew.
> 75 And Peter remembered the word of Jesus, which said unto him, Before the cock crow, thou shalt deny me thrice. And he went out, and wept bitterly. (Matthew, Chapter 26)

Now compare these actions of Peter to the reality I quoted earlier:

> 32 Whosoever therefore shall confess me before men, him will I confess also before my Father which is in heaven.
> 33 But whosoever shall deny me before men, him will I also deny before my Father which is in heaven. (Matthew, Chapter 10)

The stark reality is that by denying me before men, Peter failed the second challenge of Christ, and thus he truly cannot represent me on Earth. It is thus highly unfortunate that the Catholic Church adopted Peter as their patron saint, for this meant that from its very inception this church has been based on Peter's denial of the Living Christ and the imposing of a graven image upon me. Thus, the very church that claims to represent me on Earth has – from the very beginning – promoted a graven image of Christ that simply cannot lead people to salvation. And since the Catholic church has influenced most succeeding Christian churches, the entire Christian religion is to this day based on a graven image of Christ. It is therefore promoting a false image of salvation, namely the broad way that leads to destruction, the way of imposing your graven images upon Christ instead of letting Christ lead you beyond the consciousness of death.

You might conclude from this that there is a grave need for a complete reform of the Christian religion, which I am not disputing. However, for now I am concerned that you do not fall for the temptation to focus on the mote in the eye of another. For if *you* are to win your personal victory, you have to first look at and remove the beam in your own eye. In the next chapter we will take a very direct look at that beam, for in the modern world you do indeed have a much better foundation for understanding it than what was available 2,000 years ago.

***

Before we leave the topic of Peter and what he symbolizes, I will make one more point. Why did Peter actually follow me? Well, in part out of a pure motivation to work for the cause of God and in part based on a selfish motivation. The latter is exposed by the following quote:

> 27 Then answered Peter and said unto him, Behold, we have forsaken all, and followed thee; what shall we have therefore?

> 28 And Jesus said unto them, Verily I say unto you, That ye which have followed me, in the regeneration when the Son of man shall sit in the throne of his glory, ye also shall sit upon twelve thrones, judging the twelve tribes of Israel.
> 29 And every one that hath forsaken houses, or brethren, or sisters, or father, or mother, or wife, or children, or lands, for my name's sake, shall receive an hundredfold, and shall inherit everlasting life.
> 30 But many that are first shall be last; and the last shall be first. (Matthew, Chapter 19)

Do you see what is behind Peter's request? He feels that he has given up something in this world in order to follow me. He feels he has lost something, and now he wonders what he will receive as a compensation. Truly, this springs from the underlying failure to pass the second challenge of Christ, for if Peter had been willing to let go of his graven images, he would have overcome the sense of loss. Only the graven images make it seem like the transient things of this world have any value and that forsaking them can be a loss. Only the graven images can prevent you from seeing what you get by following the Living Christ, namely that you get LIFE instead of death.

Nevertheless, Peter represents a person who is in the interim phase of having seen the Christ but still being affected by spiritual blindness. Thus, I attempted to give Peter a vision that by forsaking the things in this world, he will receive something more valuable in the next world. This is not invalid, but it is truly a consequence of the fact that Peter still had many graven images left, and thus my vision was adapted to his limited state of consciousness. However, my point here is that people in the interim phase approach spirituality and religion with an – often unrecognized – motivation that is self-centered. They seek to gain something for themselves, either in this world or the next.

I will talk more about this later, but for now I simply want to plant the seed in your mind that in order to work through the interim phase and fully overcome the consciousness of death, you must rise to a higher motivation. You must come to a point where your involvement with spirituality and religion is not self-centered, is not aimed at attaining something for "your self," meaning your separate, mortal self. Instead, you need to understand and integrate the truth hidden in the following quote:

> 34 But when the Pharisees had heard that he had put the Sadducees to silence, they were gathered together.

35 Then one of them, which was a lawyer, asked him a
question, tempting him, and saying,
36 Master, which is the great commandment in the law?
37 Jesus said unto him, Thou shalt love the Lord thy God
with all thy heart, and with all thy soul, and with all thy
mind.
38 This is the first and great commandment.
39 And the second is like unto it, Thou shalt love thy
neighbour as thyself. (Matthew, Chapter 22)

Only when you are motivated exclusively by love for God, love for others and a true love for your real self will you have escaped the consciousness of death that thinks it can own anything for itself, whether in this world or the next.

# Chapter 4 The beam in your own eye

What I have given you in these first few chapters is a new view of the mission and teachings of Christ, and I am aware that for most people this will be a revolutionary view. I am also aware that most Christian preachers will say – if they ever read it – that it is a blasphemous view, and they will use their literal interpretations of the official scriptures to denounce my words. They will say that I could not possibly be the real Jesus Christ, for *he* would never say anything that is contrary to the scriptures or *their* interpretations of them. Thereby, they demonstrate that they have entered into the same mindset as the scribes and Pharisees, who denied the Living Christ because I did and said things that were contrary to *their* interpretations of the Jewish scriptures.

Yet I know those who have open minds and hearts can now see that there is a very logical and practical reason why I will indeed say things today that go far beyond what I said 2,000 years ago. The reason is that humankind has risen in consciousness, both in a spiritual sense and in terms of people's knowledge of the material world. Therefore, I can tell you things today that people could not "bear" – could not accept, could not comprehend – 2,000 years ago. As one obvious example of this, people today have a far greater knowledge of human psychology, and thus I can indeed give you a better understanding of the central factor that prevents you from attaining salvation. Because of the lower consciousness people had 2,000 years ago, I could only describe that factor in parables and hint at its true nature. For example, I described it this way:

> 1 Judge not, that ye be not judged.
> 2 For with what judgment ye judge, ye shall be judged: and with what measure ye mete, it shall be measured to you again.
> 3 And why beholdest thou the mote that is in thy brother's eye, but considerest not the beam that is in thine own eye?

> 4 Or how wilt thou say to thy brother, Let me pull out the mote out of thine eye; and, behold, a beam is in thine own eye?
> 5 Thou hypocrite, first cast out the beam out of thine own eye; and then shalt thou see clearly to cast out the mote out of thy brother's eye. (Matthew, Chapter 7)

Few Christians seriously consider the deeper meaning behind that statement, because they think it doesn't apply to them. They think that because they are "good Christians," they don't need to look for the beam in their own eyes—they just need to follow the outer rules of their religion and then I will do all the work for them. Yet God is no respecter of persons (Acts 10:34), and my statement does indeed apply to all people. Or one might put it this way: not all people need to look for the beam in their own eyes—only those who want to enter the kingdom of God.

Thus, those who want to consider themselves disciples of Christ should be the first to seek a deeper understanding of exactly what hides behind the expression "the beam that is in thine own eye." What exactly is that beam and how does it prevent you from attaining salvation? So far I have said the following:

- The first step toward becoming a true follower of the Living Christ is to realize that you are trapped in a limited state of consciousness, namely what I call spiritual death.

- By acknowledging that the Living Christ can appear in the flesh, you realize that it is possible for you to overcome that state of consciousness, even while you are still here on Earth.

- Yet this is no automatic process because spiritual death forms a closed mental box that prevents you from seeing beyond the graven images that make up the box.

- Therefore, the beam that is in your own eye will prevent you from seeing what you need to overcome. As I said, "first cast out the beam out of thine own eye; and *then* shalt thou see clearly..." In other words, until you remove that beam, you cannot clearly understand the teachings of the Living Christ.

- The beam in your eye is made up of a number of illusions – mental images – that obscure the truth. Many people – even many religions – see these images as absolute and infallible, and this unwillingness to look beyond the mental images is what makes them *graven* images, meaning unchanging images that stand between you and the Living God.

- After you recognize the Living Christ, you enter an interim stage, in which you must systematically purify your consciousness from these graven images.

- The major challenge during this interim stage is to overcome the very subtle temptation to impose your mental images upon the Living Christ and his teachings—thereby preventing Christ from leading you outside your mental box. You can even use the outer teachings of Christ to reinforce your mental box, as Christians have demonstrated for 2,000 years and continue to demonstrate today.

- If you fall prey to this temptation, you will no longer be following the straight and narrow Way of Christ. You will instead be following the broad way of anti-christ, whereby you use your mental images to create the belief that you are guaranteed to be saved.

- The real challenge is whether you will allow the Living Christ to expose all of your graven images or whether you will seek to hold on to some of those images and the sense of identity based upon them.

  Will you be willing to leave behind any and all graven images and the attachments to anything on Earth? Will you seek to save your mortal sense of identity or will you be willing to lose that "life" in order to follow Christ?

  Will you follow the true path of Christ, or will you fall prey to the subtle temptation of anti-christ, namely to think you can enter the kingdom of God while – for any number of subtle, intellectual reasons – maintaining certain dualistic images? Will you believe the lie that you can be saved by doing outer things without removing the beam in your own eye?

The conclusion is that the essential element for any true follower of Christ is the willingness to see something that you cannot see, to allow the Living Christ to expose to you what you cannot see on your own. We now need to add to this that there are things people *do not want to see*, and this is most clearly demonstrated by the scribes and Pharisees who refused to see the shortcomings of their religious world view and their personal psyches. They would not give up their mortal lives in order to follow Christ.

Yet all people have an element in their psyches that will try to prevent them from following Christ. Take note that this is a subtle force—it is hiding behind the beam that you do not see. Thus, it is perfectly possible to be a member of a Christian church – or any spiritual organization for that matter – and follow all of its rules and doctrines while denying the Living Christ. It is possible to be a Christian scribe and Pharisee—dancing around the golden calf of a graven image of Christ instead of looking for the Living Christ beyond all graven images.

During my physical mission on Earth I had limited options for describing the force that resists your freedom. Thus, I had to describe it in veiled, symbolic language in my parables, where I referred to it as the beam in your own eye, the tares among the wheat, the house built on sand, mammon and other such indirect expressions. However, in today's world, most people are aware of a modern name for this force, namely what is commonly known as the ego.

Obviously, there are various definitions of the ego, but in this course I will use the term to refer to a force in your psychology that resists your efforts to rise above the consciousness of spiritual death and follow the Living Christ into the consciousness of eternal life. You may think that definition is too general, but at this point I do not want to give a more specific definition. The reason being that I first want to talk more about the major effect of the ego, namely that is causes spiritual blindness that prevents you from seeing the reality of Christ.

***

A perceptive person will notice that what I have given in these first chapters is a description of salvation that is in stark contrast to the description given by most Christian churches. Christianity generally portrays salvation as something that *I* give to people, and it is an instant, or guaranteed, salvation. It is also a passive salvation, where I do the work for you, and if you live up to certain outer requirements, I simply *have* to save you.

Yet what I am describing here is a form of salvation that is neither instant, nor guaranteed, nor passive. It is a process that requires you to *consciously* and *actively* purify your consciousness of all graven images. And, of course, I trust you can begin to see that when I walked the Earth, I did indeed describe this inner way to salvation. The official churches later created the outer, instant, automatic salvation as a way for them to control people—just as the Jewish priesthood had placed the outer religion between people and salvation.

The stark reality is that I always preached the real salvation, which is indeed a gradual process, whereby you must actively and consciously seek to uncover the beam in your own eye and remove it. This is not to say that you can save yourself entirely by your own power, for as I have described, salvation is an interactive process between you here below and I – or another ascended being – above. What I offer as *my* part of the bargain is a morsel of my Christ consciousness, which is what I often referred to as the kingdom of God or the kingdom of heaven. Take note of how I repeatedly attempted to make people understand that this is a gradual, interactive process:

> 31 Another parable put he forth unto them, saying, The kingdom of heaven is like to a grain of mustard seed, which a man took, and sowed in his field:
> 32 Which indeed is the least of all seeds: but when it is grown, it is the greatest among herbs, and becometh a tree, so that the birds of the air come and lodge in the branches thereof.
> 33 Another parable spake he unto them; The kingdom of heaven is like unto leaven, which a woman took, and hid in three measures of meal, till the whole was leavened. (Matthew, Chapter 13)

Can you see how I made it clear that entering the kingdom of heaven – as a symbol for attaining the Christ consciousness – is a gradual process? The mustard seed takes time to grow, and the leaven takes time to raise the whole loaf. When you have descended into the consciousness of death, you cannot pull yourself up by your own bootstraps. The absolutely only way for you to escape spiritual death is to receive a morsel of spiritual life, which can *only* come from the Christ consciousness. Therefore, you do need an external savior in the form of a representative of the Christ consciousness who descends into this world and becomes the Living Christ—the Word incarnate.

The Living Christ offers you a morsel of spiritual life, a morsel of truth, but this will not automatically save you. You must accept that truth, you must take it into your consciousness, and you must multiply the talents you have been given. Only by watering the mustard seed, only by allowing the leaven of truth to raise your consciousness – by challenging your graven images – will you go through the interim phase and overcome the consciousness of death.

Yet this morsel of truth is offered to *all* people on Earth. Those who met me physically received it directly from me, but because I won a physical victory of being the Living Christ on Earth, it is not necessary to meet a physical person who is the Living Christ. You can now receive a morsel of Christ consciousness through the Comforter, but in order to do so, you must search for that Comforter in the only place it can be found, namely in the kingdom of God that is within you.

***

The important point is to realize that once you accept a morsel of the Christ consciousness, it acts like a catalyst. It starts a chain reaction that will affect every part of your being—if you allow it. Following the path of the Living Christ is not a comfortable process, for it requires you to let go of *all* of your graven images, including the mortal sense of self that has so far given you a sense of security, identity, belonging and comfortability. The Living Christ has no armchair disciples, for *my* way is an all-consuming process.

One might indeed refer to the old saying that ignorance is bliss. As long as you are completely blinded by the consciousness of death, you might experience a certain state of contentment, for you do not see that there is an alternative to your state of "life." Yet once you accept a morsel of the Christ consciousness, you cannot maintain that illusion. The interim phase – in which you have both elements of Christ and anti-christ in your being – is a somewhat schizophrenic stage, because the Living Christ pulls you *up* and your ego and the prince of this world pull you *down*.

You are caught in the middle – between the rock of Christ and the hard spot of this world – where you have a longing for security but you cannot be fully content with anything in this world. This state is not comfortable, but it will not last forever, and the freedom you will experience when overcoming it is well worth the effort. The interim stage will last a finite time – how long is largely up to your willingness to let go of your illusions – and after you have passed it, *you* will last forever. As quoted in the Gospel of Thomas:

> Jesus said, "Those who seek should not stop seeking until they find. When they find, they will be disturbed. When they are disturbed, they will marvel, and will reign over all." (Thomas 1:2)

Once you awaken to what it really means to follow the Way of Christ, your outer sense that you are saved – your sense of security and identity – will indeed be disturbed, for you will see the need to let the Living Christ challenge *all* of your beliefs and assumptions. You will literally go through a period where you will not know what to believe, yet if you are willing to endure – to not stop seeking until you find – you will gradually begin to find a stable foundation—a foundation built on the rock of Christ truth rather than upon the shifting sands of the "truth" from the mind of anti-christ. When you overcome the consciousness of death, you will indeed marvel at the beauty and vastness of the reality of God, and knowing this reality will empower you to attain mastery over your mind and world.

This process will require you to let go of *all* your attachments. Depending on how attached you are to your graven images, it can be both difficult and painful to let them go, and this is what can turn the spiritual path into the Via Dolorosa that has caused many Christians to glorify suffering as the only way to God. Yet did I not say that I had come to give all people life and that more abundantly so? Thus, it is my hope that this course will help you see that following the true Way of Christ is *not* the Via Dolorosa. In fact, it is the way of the spiritually abundant life, where you walk toward greater and greater freedom and take each step with an infinite sense of joy. For I did indeed come to bring joy to the world.

Before you can step on to this straight and narrow way, you need to understand and see the ego – and the forces that pull you onto the broad way that leads to destruction – and this is one of the main purposes of this course. Yet for now let me emphasize the importance of not falling prey to the illusion that because you have done some outer thing, you are now saved and no longer need to look for the beam in your own eye.

The Way of Christ is an ongoing process, a process of perpetual self-transcendence. And there can be no self-transcendence without self-examination, for if you do not examine the self, how can you decide that certain aspects of self need to die, so that the totality of self can be reborn into a higher sense of self? Thus, it is wise to recognize that this process will not stop as long as you are here on Earth. The concept of resting on your laurels simply does not apply to the true disciples of the Living Christ.

The master key to following the Way of Christ is to *always* self-transcend, to *never* stop self-transcendence, to never stop looking for the beam – or even a splinter – in your own eye. As I have explained, the second challenge of Christ is to never allow anything in this world to prevent you from transcending. You always allow the Living Christ to challenge your beliefs and mental images. If there is a mental image that you are not willing to question, then that image has become a graven image, and it will stand between you and the true God.

If you truly want to make it all the way to your father's kingdom, you must never allow any Earthly, man-made image to stand between you and the Living Christ. Seek the Living Christ within you and keep seeking until you not only find Christ but become one with Christ—until *you* become the Living Christ. Peter is an example of a person who is holding on to a graven image and will not let go. That is why he could not confess me before men and denied me three times. I call you to follow my true way and *not* the way of Peter.

***

At this point, we need to consider a logical question. If I truly preached a gradual path to salvation, how come the official Christian churches lost that true teaching and began to preach an instant salvation? And how come most Christians to this day believe in this instant salvation? The reason for this is that the ego itself can never fathom the true way to salvation, and thus it creates a false path to salvation, a path that does not require you to pull the beam from your own eye and let the ego die. This counterfeit path is precisely what I called the broad way that leads to destruction—even though many Christians think I was talking about any religion besides their particular branch of Christianity.

This is the path that makes people fully convinced that they are on the only true path to salvation, while in reality they are getting no closer to finding the true kingdom inside themselves. The reason being that if you do not pull the beam from your own eye, how can you possibly discover the kingdom of God that is within you? It is the ego – and the spiritual blindness it produces – that causes people to follow the false path and deny or overlook the true, inner way. Yet in order to fully realize this, you need to have a deeper understanding of your own being and the origin of the ego.

I have said that the consciousness of death – which I will hereafter refer to as the ego – forms a closed box that prevents you from seeing beyond the box. You are spiritually dead, but you do not see that you are lacking. From a certain perspective it would seem that once you are in this closed box, there is no way out. Once you are blind, you cannot recognize the Living Christ and cannot understand his true teachings.

Yet I have also said that the Living Christ comes to Earth to demonstrate to people that there is a higher form of life, a more abundant form of life. So if the ego really *was* a closed box – and if people had no way of recognizing the Living Christ – what would be the point in the Living Christ coming to Earth? Thus, there is clearly some mechanism whereby people can escape the closed box of the ego, and it is important for you to understand that mechanism.

To demonstrate the mechanism, let me ask you to consider what you are doing right now. You are able to mentally step away from your situation and be aware that you are reading this book. Up until I asked you to do this, you might have been absorbed in reading the book, but now you are aware that there is a "you" which is reading this book. There is a subject – you – and an object – the book – and the subject is perceiving – experiencing – the object.

This might seem so simple that there is nothing remarkable about it, and indeed most people hardly give it a second thought. Yet what you have just done is something that no other kind of creature on this planet is capable of doing. A cow grazing in the field is not able to see itself as a cow eating grass, nor can a bird be conscious of itself gliding through the air. No animal has the faculty that you just exercised, namely the faculty of self-awareness. This is a fundamental difference between animals and humans. As a side note, this in itself proves that humans are not merely highly evolved animals. The fact that scientists can deny that they are more than animals proves that they are more than animals.

Why do you have self-awareness? Because God created you that way! This is even described in the limited language that could be used in the – very distant – time when Genesis was given to human beings:

> And God said, Let us make man in our image, after our likeness. (Genesis 1:26)

You are literally made in the image and likeness of your Creator. Obviously, I am not here talking in literal terms, so I am not saying God has a physical body and resembles an old man with a long, white beard—for the true God is beyond any image in this world. I am talking about your mind, your consciousness, which has the same basic capabilities as the consciousness of your Creator. We will later explore in greater depth what this means, but for now I want to stay with one capability that you share with your God, namely self-awareness. The very fact that God could decide to create humans in his own image shows that he was aware of his own existence. Look at the following quote:

> 3 And God said, Let there be light: and there was light.

> 4 And God saw the light, that it was good: and God divided the light from the darkness. (Genesis, Chapter 1)

The Creator was conscious of its own existence and had the awareness to consciously create something and to evaluate what it had created. This clearly shows self-awareness, for unless you are aware that you exist, how can you know that you have created something? And unless you are aware that you exist, how can you evaluate what you just created? These are abilities that you use every day, although you might not be aware of what you are doing.

We now see that the very core of your ability to escape the spiritual blindness of the ego is your self-awareness. I realize that most people are not aware that they are *self*-aware. In fact, the state of spiritual death can be described as a state in which people are not exercising their self-awareness, even a state in which they have completely forgotten that they have this ability.

Yet the fact that you have *forgotten* that you have a certain ability does not mean that you have actually *lost* that ability. When you forget where you put your car keys, the keys are still in existence. So your ability still exists as a potential—you are simply not exercising it right now. One might say that if you are completely unaware that you have self-awareness, then the ability is, for all practical purposes, lost. However, the essential difference is that you can recover the ability, and you do so by simply becoming aware that you have it and by beginning to consciously make use of it. A human can recover self-awareness, whereas an animal cannot attain it.

***

Do you now begin to see part of the reason why the Living Christ comes to Earth? The Christ comes first and foremost to awaken people to the fact that they have self-awareness, so that they can begin to consciously use this ability—they can begin to look for the beam in their own eyes. Can you also see that this is not something that comes automatically from being baptized or joining an outer organization? Do you see why I said:

> Thou hypocrite, first cast out the beam out of thine own eye; (Matthew 7:5)

There are millions of people who think they are true followers of Christ, yet they have not even awakened to the very first condition you must meet in order to become a disciple of the Living Christ. They have not become aware that they have self-awareness and that they can use it to discover the beam in their own eyes, namely the very conditions that they need to overcome in order to find the kingdom of God—which is within them. They still think that blindly following the outer rules – following the blind leaders of the outer churches – will get them to heaven without exercising their self-awareness. They have not decided to take responsibility for using their self-awareness to examine themselves and their own state of consciousness. Take another look at my words:

> And why beholdest thou the mote that is in thy brother's eye. (Matthew 7:3)

Can you see that looking for the mote in the eye of another means that your attention is focused *outside* yourself on the appearances of this world? And if you are always looking *outside* yourself, how can you possibly discover the kingdom of God which is – as I might have mentioned – *within* you? It simply is not possible for you to find the kingdom until you redirect your attention. Only by looking at and dissolving your own illusions, will you gradually uncover the reality of the inner kingdom. Thus, self-awareness is the foundation for discovering the beam that prevents you from entering the inner kingdom. Which means that entering the kingdom of God is a process of using your self-awareness to attain a higher sense of self, a higher awareness of your true identity and origin.

One might say that because the kingdom of God is *within* you, you can find it only by looking *inside* yourself. Yet as you start using your self-awareness, your vision will be obstructed by the beam in your own eye, meaning the conditions in your psyche that stand between you and the inner kingdom. You must then go through a – somewhat difficult and subtle – process of removing those conditions until nothing obscures your entry into the higher state of consciousness, where there is nothing in your psyche that divides you, that separates you from the kingdom. Obviously, the key to completing this process is to use your self-awareness, your ability to look at yourself and realize that certain things must be left behind because they are unreal, they are illusions springing from the mind of anti-christ—the mind based on the illusion that you are separated from your source.

The broad way that leads to destruction is the way of thinking you can be saved by following outer rules and that you do not need to exercise your self-awareness. The strait and narrow way is the process of using your self-awareness to remove the beam in your own eye by engaging in a constant, life-long process of self-examination. Being a true disciple of the Living Christ means that you are willing to examine yourself, and we will now move on to consider what exactly that means.

***

The concept of self-awareness has two components, namely *awareness* and *self*. You have a pure state of awareness, which gives you the ability to recognize that you exist, the ability to say, "I am." Then you have the awareness that you are a self and that it has certain characteristics. We might compare "awareness" to an empty container and "self" to the contents in that container. These contents give you a sense of what and who you are, but this sense would not be possible unless you also had a state of pure awareness, a sense of *being*.

I know this is a subtle point that can be difficult to grasp at first, so let me illustrate it with an example. Let me ask you to close your eyes and then open them again. When your eyes were closed, you could see nothing, and now that your eyes are open, you are seeing this book. However, your ability to see is not limited to this book. You know that your eyes have the ability to see many different things. So we might say that there is a distinction between your ability to see and the object you are seeing. Your eyes are more than the object they are actually seeing right now, for they can see other objects than this book. Likewise, there is a distinction between your sense of self and the pure awareness that you exist. Your pure awareness is more than the sense of self upon which it is focused right now. As you can move your eyes from this book and see something different, you can move your pure awareness from your current sense of self and experience something beyond that self.

Let me give you one more illustration. Your pure awareness is like the white light that is emitted from the light bulb in a movie projector. Your sense of self is like the film strip through which the light shines on its way to the movie screen—which represents your conscious mind. The images you see on the screen are obviously shaped by the images on the film strip, but without the white light, there would be no movie. Yet the white light is more than the film strip, and if you change the film strip in the projector, you can fundamentally change the movie. In other words, the white light exists independently of the film strip and can shine through any film strip.

Thus, we might say that the Living Christ comes to tell you that if your life is a horror movie – or if it seems to be the same movie playing over and over again – you can change it by changing your sense of self. Instead of looking for someone or something outside yourself to change your life *for* you, you can engage in a systematic process of changing the contents in your container of self—which will inevitably change your outer life as well. This is a matter of going to the cause instead of trying to change the effects. As I described it 2,000 years ago:

> But seek ye first the kingdom of God, and his righteousness; and all these things shall be added unto you. (Matthew 6:33)

Do you begin to grasp what I am implying here? Right now you have a specific sense of self, a particular sense of identity. Yet the very foundation for this sense of self is that you have pure awareness. This pure awareness is more than the self you have right now, the self that is largely a product of your environment and upbringing. The fact that there is more to *you* than your worldly sense of identity – your mortal self – is what gives you the ability to become aware of the beam in your own eye, to pull that beam and thereby rise above the consciousness of spiritual death. In other words, you can – consciously and deliberately – make your self more than it is right now. You can step outside your current self, look at it objectively, decide that it is *not* the self you want to have for all eternity and then consciously and deliberately expand your self. *This is the Way of Christ!*

I know very well that you have grown up in a world where hardly anyone is aware of what I am telling you here. As people grow up, they build a particular sense of identity, and it is often determined by external factors, such as family and society. You are, so to speak, being told who you are, and you begin to believe what you are told. You are being programmed to follow the norms of your society, and most people step into such a pre-defined role without giving it a second thought—they blindly follow the blind leaders. Therefore, people can live an entire lifetime thinking that they *are* who they were told to *be*, never realizing that there is more to them than this worldly identity. This is what makes it possible that an entire planet can fall under the spell of the death consciousness, so that all people believe they are nothing more than human beings and that they can never go beyond the limitations they have been brought up to see as inescapable for a human being.

Do you now begin to see why the Living Christ comes to Earth? The Living Christ comes to awaken people to the fact that they are *more* than their current sense of identity, that they do indeed have the potential to rise above that sense of self. Yet the very faculty that makes this awakening possible is that the core of your being is a state of pure awareness that is not limited to your current sense of identity. Consider the fact that almost no matter where you have grown up on this planet, you will have been programmed to accept a very limited sense of identity. If you grew up in any mainstream Christian church, you will have been brought up to accept that you are a sinner, possibly a miserable sinner who can never do anything but sin and that you cannot – on your own – escape this condition. If you were brought up in a scientifically minded environment, you will have been programmed to think you are nothing more than a highly evolved monkey, and that all of your thoughts, hopes and dreams are nothing more than the firing of neurons in the machinery of your brain.

Can you see that both of these identities are incredibly limited compared to the reality that you were created in the image and likeness of your God? Your God is *not* a sinner and your God is *not* a highly evolved monkey. Thus, God did not create you as a sinner or as a monkey. God created you as a spiritual being who is far more than the physical body and far more than the limited sense of identity most people currently have on Earth.

We can now see that the first task of the Living Christ is to awaken people to the fact that they are more than human beings. Why do you think I challenged people's concept of reality by my words and actions, including my so-called miracles? Well, if you consider the traditional Christian idolatry of me, you might reason that I was an ego-maniac who wanted to set myself above all (other) people. Certainly, mainstream Christianity has set me above and beyond all people by claiming I was God. And while I am not denying that statement, it must be understood correctly, as I will later explain. My point here being that I did not come to Earth in order to set myself above other people. I came to shatter people's limited sense of identity by demonstrating that *it is possible to go beyond human limitations*. I came to show everyone that they have the potential to be *more* than a mere human being, which is precisely why I said:

> Verily, verily, I say unto you, He that believeth on me, the works that I do shall he do also; and greater works than these shall he do; because I go unto my Father. (John 14:12)

Do you see that the first task of the Living Christ is to challenge people's sense of being so boxed in by limitations that they cannot even conceive of going beyond them? And the reason why it is possible to challenge your sense of identity is that you have a pure state of awareness that is beyond your current sense of identity. Thus, your pure awareness, your pure self, can separate itself from your current sense of identity and can reach for something more.

By using your pure awareness to become conscious of your current sense of self, you can become aware of how limited it is. And then you can decide to pull that beam from your own eye and build a higher sense of self. We might say that your pure self is like the sleeping beauty who has forgotten who it really is, and the Living Christ comes to awaken it. The Christ will do this through a kiss or whatever else is necessary—even allowing people to nail him to a wooden cross if that is what it takes.

***

You can now begin to see that my quote about the beam in your own eye has a deeper meaning than most Christians have ever considered. It says a lot between the lines, and it actually outlines the two components that will determine whether you enter the kingdom of God or remain outside—where there is weeping and gnashing of teeth. What are the two components? Well, one is obviously the beam, which is what I have called the human ego. The other is the "you" who is able to make the choice between looking for that beam or ignoring the beam by focusing its attention outside itself. We will later talk more about both components, for as we build a better foundation, I will reveal deeper layers of understanding. Yet the important point at this stage is that you understand the dynamic between the two.

Obviously, the term "ego" was not known 2,000 years ago, yet I inspired Paul to use another term to describe the same phenomenon. Look at this quote:

> 5 For they that are after the flesh do mind the things of the flesh; but they that are after the Spirit the things of the Spirit.
> 6 For to be carnally minded is death; but to be spiritually minded is life and peace.
> 7 Because the carnal mind is enmity against God: for it is not subject to the law of God, neither indeed can be.
> 8 So then they that are in the flesh cannot please God.
> 9 But ye are not in the flesh, but in the Spirit, if so be that the Spirit of God dwell in you. Now if any man have not the Spirit of Christ, he is none of his. (Romans, Chapter 8)

We can learn many things from these words, but let me stay with the present point. The "carnal mind" is another term for the ego, and Paul clearly describes that this mind is what traps you in the consciousness of death. The reason is that the carnal mind – the ego – is not subject to the law of God and never can be. Yet what exactly does that mean? It means that the ego was not created by God and therefore it can *never* enter the kingdom of God.

This is an essential point, for it means that the ego can never be saved. There is literally nothing you could ever do that would make the ego acceptable in the eyes of God. Yet as we will see later, the ego cannot fathom this truth (if the ego acknowledged this truth, it would realize that it is unreal and thus it would instantly cease to exist. So as a survival mechanism, the ego must always deny this reality, which explains why it is attached to a world view that affirms the external salvation). The ego believes that it can become acceptable in the eyes of God, and *then* it will be allowed to enter heaven. Thus, the ego – assisted by the prince of this world – sets up an entirely false path that is aimed at creating the appearance that the ego has now become acceptable to God. It does so by creating the impression that as long as you do all the outer things right, you – meaning the ego, the mortal self – *will* be saved. This is the outer path, the broad way that leads to destruction, and it can *never* work.

I know this will be difficult to understand or accept for many people, so I will later explain it in greater detail. Yet for now let me return to my previous quote, where I said that unless your righteousness exceeds the righteousness of the scribes and Pharisees you will not enter the kingdom. The reason is that the scribes and Pharisees had become so blinded by their egos that they truly believed in the illusion of the outer path, the path that is based on the things of the flesh. Thus, they were of the flesh, and they were attempting to use the reasoning of the carnal mind to force their way into heaven. Yet because the carnal mind can never be subject to the law of God, it can never enter heaven, it can never enter the wedding feast:

> 11 And when the king came in to see the guests, he saw there a man which had not on a wedding garment:
> 12 And he saith unto him, Friend, how camest thou in hither not having a wedding garment? And he was speechless.
> 13 Then said the king to the servants, Bind him hand and foot, and take him away, and cast him into outer darkness; there shall be weeping and gnashing of teeth.
> 14 For many are called, but few are chosen. (Matthew, Chapter 22)

Do you see the absolutely uncompromising nature of this quote? It makes it very clear that those who do not wear a wedding garment cannot enter the feast. Yet what exactly is a wedding garment? It is, as already mentioned, the Christ consciousness, where you have risen above the carnal mind, the human ego. You have been reborn of water and of Spirit, so that you are now a new person in Christ:

> Therefore if any man be in Christ, he is a new creature: old things are passed away; behold, all things are become new. (2Corinthians 5:17)

What happens in this process is that the old creature – the self you have right now, the self that is based on the carnal mind, the ego – is allowed to die:

> For whosoever will save his life shall lose it: and whosoever will lose his life for my sake shall find it. (Matthew 16:25)

As I said, I was not calling people to commit physical suicide or even spiritual suicide, meaning that *you* will not disappear by letting the mortal self die. Yet what is left when the *mortal* "you" dies? What is left is the *spiritual* you, the conscious self that has now become conscious of its own existence and its true identity.

And what *is* that identity? It is that the core of your being – your conscious self – is not a mortal, human, carnal being – is not of the flesh – but is a spiritual being. Since you are a spiritually interested person, you should already know that "you" are more than your body. Yet you are also more than the mortal self—what many people call the soul. The real you is the offspring of God, for you were created in the image and after the likeness of your Creator.

***

This spiritual part of your being obviously *is* subject to the law of God, which means that it is *not* subject to the laws of mortality. Thus, the real you can awaken to the fact that it is a spiritual being who is only temporarily expressing itself through a vehicle, meaning both the physical body and the outer mind and identity. Yet beyond these outer things, there is the spiritual self which has forgotten its true origin but can be reawakened by fulfilling this requirement, "ye are not in the flesh, but in the Spirit, if so be that the Spirit of God dwell in you." Because the real you was created in the image and likeness of God, you have the potential to let "the Spirit of God dwell in you." And when you do so, you will have overcome the downward pull of the spirits of death.

Yet what will it take to come to this point? It will take more than a simple act of confessing Jesus Christ as your Lord and Savior or allowing some minister to splash water on you. It will take a completely life-altering process, whereby you systematically come to see the beam in your own eye, the beam that is made up of many individual illusions. You must be willing to see these illusions and then consciously realize they did not spring from the Christ mind. And when you see this, you must then be willing to let the sense of self that is based on these illusions die and choose the reality of Christ—so that the Conscious You can be reborn as a new creature in Christ.

Contrary to what the modern consumer culture wants you to believe, this is not an instant process and there is no instant salvation. The dream of an instant salvation is the ego's quintessential dream. Paul had understood this process, which is why he said, "I die daily," (1Corinthians 15:31) meaning that a part of his mortal self died every day as he gave up another illusion.

We can now see the essential dynamic that determines your entry or non-entry into the kingdom of God. As long as you identify yourself as a mortal human being – your identity is based on the flesh, as a symbol for the illusions that spring from the consciousness of death – you simply cannot find the kingdom of God that is within you. Your attention will be focused outside yourself, and you will believe in the lie that you can attain salvation by following the outer path. It is only when you turn your attention *within* that you will begin the true path that leads to salvation, namely the path that is not instant or easy but requires you to do the hard and painful work of looking at yourself and realizing how your beliefs and actions are out of alignment with the reality of Christ.

This is the real path to salvation, and it is a path that cannot be completed by hypocrites because they are not willing to consider that they could be wrong, that they could be out of alignment with the reality of Christ. They want to keep believing in the outer path, so they can use their outer accomplishments as a justification for not looking at the beam in their own eyes. Which leads us to the point where I can explain the central element of the true path.

***

As I have already explained, the central feature of your conscious self is self-awareness, which gives you the ability to mentally step outside of your current situation, even your current sense of identity. You can – so to speak – look at yourself from the outside and thus gain a more neutral and objective perspective on yourself than you have when looking from the inside. The reason why I told people to look for the beam in their own eyes is that I knew the conscious self has the ability to step outside your mortal sense of self and see that beam.

In other words, your conscious self has the ability to perform self-examination. So the central characteristic of a true disciple of the Living Christ is the willingness to examine yourself and see what most people are not willing to see. This is not actually a religious or spiritual characteristic but common sense. Most psychologists and self-help experts know that before you can solve any problem, you have to first be willing to look at the problem. Denying that the problem exists, or refusing to understand it, will get you no closer to solving it.

Yet here we run into a major problem in the sense that too many Christians have been programmed to believe that the purpose of self-examination is for you to acknowledge that you are a sinner who should feel guilty for every wrong thing you have ever done. This is a perfect example of a culture that is completely out of touch with the reality of Christ and springs from the consciousness of death. For did I not say:

> 47 And if any man hear my words, and believe not, I judge him not: for I came not to judge the world, but to save the world.
> 48 He that rejecteth me, and receiveth not my words, hath one that judgeth him: the word that I have spoken, the same shall judge him in the last day. (John, Chapter 12)

Can you see that I am not sitting up here in heaven and judging every little mistake you have ever made? Can you see that I have no interest in making you feel guilty—on the contrary, I am only interested in one thing, namely to save you. Yet in order to be saved, you have to be willing to change. And in order to change, you have to be willing to look at the beam in your psyche. Thus, I want you to examine yourself, but I do not want you to go into the blind alley of guilt, for it only paralyzes people.

To save you truly means to set you free—namely to set you free from the illusions that keep you trapped in the consciousness of death. Thus, I want you to examine yourself for the purpose of discovering that you are not a *mortal* sinner but an *immortal* spiritual being. And as such, you can overcome all sin by letting the mortal sense of self die, so that the Conscious You can be spiritually reborn. In other words, the real purpose of self-examination is *not* to bring yourself *down* but to raise yourself *up*. The real purpose is for you to be free.

Do you see my point? Some people are so blinded by the false path that they truly believe they are already saved. These people *do* need to wake up and realize they are lacking because they have not removed the beam in their own eyes. Yet the purpose of this awakening is *not* to get people to focus on the beam, but to help them see beyond the beam and discover their true, spiritual potential. This is their potential to go beyond the false path to salvation – the broad way offered by the ego and the prince of this world – and instead follow the true path, the narrow way, offered by the Living Christ.

***

So what will it take for you to be free? It will take that you make choices—better choices than you made in the past! Here is another problem, for many Christians have gotten themselves into another catch-22 by subscribing to the belief that God is almighty and thus everything that happens on Earth must be part of God's plan. And because of this belief, most Christians tend to downplay or ignore the importance of free will.

I assume that because you are a more spiritually aware person, you are open to the fact that you have free will—which means that your salvation is *not* predetermined according to some plan made by a remote being up in heaven. Your salvation is determined by the choices *you* make!

Now, I am fully aware that people who are completely blinded by their egos will deny this fact, and I will later explain why they do so. Yet for now I simply want to point out three things about free will:

- No one is forcing you to read this course. You can stop reading any time, and you can accept or deny what I say.
- If everything was determined by God's plan, then all evil occurrences – such as the holocaust or serial murders – would be predetermined by God, which means that God wants you to experience evil.
- If you did not have free will and if your salvation did not depend on your choices, then why would God send Christ to Earth? If everything is predetermined according to God's plan, then the fact that you need to be saved must

> be a condition that is part of God's plan. So why doesn't God simply change the condition so that you are saved? Why go through the trouble of sending me to Earth in a human form, thereby giving people the choice to either accept or reject Christ? The very fact that people can reject Christ proves that you have free will, or you simply would not have that option.

Can you see that denying free will is based on a misunderstanding of the first two challenges of Christ? As I explained earlier, those two challenges require you to first accept that Christ can appear on Earth and then allow the Living Christ to take you beyond the illusions created by your ego. Both require you to make choices, proving that God did indeed give you free will.

We now see a fact that most Christians have failed to understand: Your salvation is determined by the choices *you* make! And I am *not* here talking about the one-time choice to become a Christian in an outer way; I am talking about a life-long process of learning to make choices based on Christ truth. Certain choices bring you closer to salvation and certain choices take you further away from salvation. In a traditional vernacular, one might talk about right and wrong choices, but what does that really mean?

This topic has confused many religious people, and it has often been defined by religious authorities in such a way that "right" choices are what is in alignment with official church doctrines and "wrong" choices are anything beyond doctrine. Yet we can now see the real difference.

What we have discussed so far leads up to a very important conclusion. There is such a thing as reality, yet you can know reality *only* through the mind of Christ, which is always one with the Father. That is why I stated:

> All things are delivered unto me of my Father: and no man knoweth the Son, but the Father; neither knoweth any man the Father, save the Son, and he to whomsoever the Son will reveal him. (John 11:7)

The challenge here is to see beyond the official idolatry of my person and realize that the "Son" is the universal Christ mind. I had attained complete union with that Christ mind, and that is the ultimate goal for any true disciple of Christ. Why is this such an important realization? Because only choices that are based on the reality of Christ – rather than on the illusions that spring from the consciousness of death – will bring you closer to the kingdom of

God. So the only way – the *absolutely* only way – for you to be saved is to learn how to make decisions based on the reality of Christ.

I know many people have an emotional reaction against this truth, but the main reason is that it makes them feel paralyzed. The reason for this sense of not knowing how to access the Christ mind is twofold:

- The ego can never access the Christ mind.
- You have been programmed by both secular and religious institutions to think you cannot access the Christ mind directly within yourself.

As I have now explained from different vantage points, the main purpose for my mission was to demonstrate that all people can access the Christ mind directly and thus they do not need to go through any external institution or authority, be it a religious, a political or a scientific establishment. In other words, the very fact that you were created in the image and likeness of God means that nothing can come between you and God—unless you allow it to do so. Your potential to experience Christ is your self-awareness. In fact, Christ consciousness can be seen as the ultimate self-awareness, the awareness of the Self as God.

Yet even if there is currently something that stands between you and God, the reality is that this something has attained that position as a result of choices you made in the past. Acknowledging this is extremely empowering, because you now see that your spiritual growth, your salvation, does not depend on any external institution who might deny it unless you make yourself a blind follower of its leaders. On the contrary, you can use your free will to undo the limiting choices from your past and thus free yourself from any tyranny on Earth. Truly, you have the option to know God's truth through the Christ mind, and that truth will make you free.

***

Ultimately, you must attain complete union with the Christ mind, which is the only way you can fulfill my promise to do the works that I did. Yet before you attain that union, you can still know the reality of Christ because your conscious self is an extension of the Being of the Creator. However, it might take some time for you to find the Christ mind within yourself, and therefore I offer you an intermediary. You can – right now – start making progress on the path to Christhood by taking advantage of the gift I gave to humankind:

> 16 And I will pray the Father, and he shall give you another Comforter, that he may abide with you for ever;
> 17 Even the Spirit of truth; whom the world cannot receive, because it seeth him not, neither knoweth him: but ye know him; for he dwelleth with you, and shall be in you. (John, Chapter 14)

This Comforter, this Spirit of Truth, can show you the reality of Christ, so that you have the best possible foundation for making right decisions. As I said:

> But the Comforter, which is the Holy Ghost, whom the Father will send in my name, he shall teach you all things, and bring all things to your remembrance, whatsoever I have said unto you. (John 14:26)

However, this does come at a price, for it requires you to allow the Spirit of Truth to "be in you" which means that it will expose the beam in your own eye—namely your human ego. You see, the ego always seeks to remain unseen, and it does so by hiding in the shadows. Yet when you let the Comforter into your consciousness, it will start shining a light. And as you allow it to grow brighter, it will remove the shadows and expose all that is hiding there. Thus, you must be willing to examine yourself and overcome all unreality in your being. This is no easy or comfortable task, which can be seen by the fact that millions of people think they are good Christians, yet they have not even fulfilled the very first requirement on the path to Christhood. They are still focusing their attention outside themselves instead of looking for the beam in their own eyes.

Now comes the essential realization. Only your conscious self has the ability to experience the Spirit of Truth, whereas your ego can *never* see beyond the illusions of death. Therefore, your ego will – with great force and with great subtlety – try to steer you away from the straight and narrow way that leads to eternal life and onto the broad way that leads to destruction. Only your conscious self is able to follow the Spirit of Truth, but the real question is whether the Conscious You is willing to follow the Spirit or whether it wants to continue to follow the blind leaders that promise it an external – and much easier – salvation? Is the Conscious You willing to make its own decisions, or will it refuse to accept full responsibility for your salvation—possibly by clinging to the graven image that Christ will somehow make the choices *for* you and change you into the kind of person that can enter heaven.

Do you see my point? The reality is that your salvation will be determined *exclusively* by the choices made by your conscious self. If you make choices based on the reality of Christ, you will find the kingdom of God within you. If you make choices based on the illusions of the consciousness of death, you will continue to look for the kingdom outside yourself, and this will keep you in outer darkness, where there is weeping and gnashing of teeth.

I earlier said that there is an interim period in which you have both elements of Christ and elements of anti-christ in your being. This is the period of "travail" that is referred to in many mythological stories, such as Odysseus' journey back to his home. The challenge during this period is to learn how to discern between the inner voices that are telling you what choices to make. There is a multitude of voices – represented by your ego and the prince of this world, even other people – who will tell you what to do based on the illusions of death. Yet there is also a still, small voice within, which will tell you what is the reality of Christ.

Your challenge – the challenge of the conscious self – is to learn to discern between the one true voice and the legion of false voices. This is not easy and you will inevitably make mistakes. Yet if you are willing to learn from every experience, you can learn to tell the difference between the One Spirit of Truth and the legion of false spirits. And *only* by developing this discernment will you attain your personal Christhood and find the inner kingdom. Only through Christ discernment can the Conscious You make fully conscious choices, choices where you *know* what is real and what is unreal.

We have now arrived at the very central question of the path. Will the Conscious You decide to enter the difficult path of learning how to discern between reality and unreality? Or will it continue to take the broad way that is so much easier to follow because it does not require you to discern? You see, by elevating the illusions of anti-christ to the status of infallible truth, it seems as if you already know truth from without, and thus you do not have to go through the subtle process of learning to distinguish the Spirit of Truth from the false spirits. Will the conscious self decide to finally start following the inner path, or will it continue to follow the external leaders who blindly lead you – and themselves – away from the inner kingdom?

There are many Christians who see themselves as disciples of Christ, yet they have not even taken the first step onto the true path. There are also many non-Christians who have been on the spiritual path for a while and who think they have made progress. Yet what I offer to all in this course is the real path of discipleship under the Living Christ. Ultimately, that path requires you to develop a personal relationship directly with me – the ascended Jesus Christ – and therefore this course is by no means a substitute for that direct, inner relationship. Yet it is the clearest description of the path so far released on this planet, and thus it can help you get started and build a solid momentum that can take you ever higher—until you meet me directly in your own heart. For as I promised:

> If a man love me, he will keep my words: and my Father will love him, and we will come unto him, and make our abode with him. (John 14:23)

In the following sections I will give you a series of keys that will help you anchor yourself on the path to Christhood. And we will begin with what for many is the most difficult step—deciding to start the real path as opposed to the broad way that leads to destruction.

***

Let me make it clear what *is* my purpose for the rest of this course. It is *not* my aim to give you knowledge, to teach you something, to give you an intellectual understanding of the path to Christhood. It is my goal to help you anchor yourself firmly on the path to Christhood by getting you to take the actual steps required to follow that path. In other words, this is not about learning—it is about doing, about becoming, about *being!*

It is not my goal to change your view of the spiritual path. It is my goal to empower you to go through the complete and fundamental transformation of consciousness that takes you from seeing yourself as a mortal, human being to knowing that you are the Living Christ on Earth.

Let me make it clear that this process of complete transformation – of spiritual rebirth – is not for the faint of heart. It is not for those who prefer to be comfortable or who prefer to always be in control. What I am offering you here is to partake of the oldest institution that was designed by the Ascended Host as the most effective means for raising up those who had fallen into the consciousness of death. That institution is the Master-disciple, or Guru-chela, relationship.

I am offering you an outer course that is an extension of the spiritual office I hold, namely as the primary teacher of the path to Christhood for planet Earth. If you are willing to participate fully in this outer course – knowing that the course *is not* and *must never become* an end in itself – you can qualify for the next step, namely to go beyond outer teachers and teachings and establish a direct, personal, inner relationship with me or with another ascended being who is your personal Master.

You see, the ascended teachers of humankind do not take on students until they have qualified themselves for working with us. What would be the point of a university professor taking on a student who is still in kindergarten? Let students follow outer teachers and teachings until they begin to understand and apply the central mechanism of the spiritual path, namely using their self-awareness to expose and pull the beam from their own eyes. Until a student has attained a high degree of willingness to go beyond his or her ego, we of the Ascended Host will not work personally with that student.

Let me briefly explain what it takes for a person to come to the point where he or she is ready to become a more direct student of the ascended teachers. I have briefly explained – and will later explain in more detail – that the consciousness of anti-christ is dualistic in nature, meaning that it always operates with two opposite polarities, such as good and evil, right and wrong. This duality will inevitably create internal contradictions and inconsistencies in any system – be it a religion or an entire civilization – that is based on the consciousness of anti-christ. These internal contradictions will actually cause the system to gradually self-destruct, which is the cause behind all of the problems you have seen throughout human history. In fact, it is precisely the internal contradictions that have led to the condition – described by the Buddha – where most people experience life as a struggle, as a state of constant suffering.

As a person experiences living in a society with such internal tension, he or she can eventually begin to realize that something is not working, and this can lead the person to finally cry out, "There must be a better way, there must be more to life!" At that point, the law of God mandates that the person is presented with a teacher and teaching that can lead the person to a higher state of consciousness. This law of God has been expressed as follows, "When the student is ready, the teacher appears!" If you consider your own life, you will see that you have – perhaps for your entire lifetime – had this inner sense that something was missing, that something wasn't right, that something was wrong.

What you need to do now is to realize that this sense can become a springboard to an entirely new approach to life. However, to do this, you must get your focus off the material world and the sense that something is wrong. Instead, you must adopt a positive outlook and realize that regardless of what is wrong on Earth or in your personal situation, you have the potential to follow the path to Christhood. And this will lead you to a state where you are *right* with God, no matter what you have experienced on Earth. In other words, stop focusing on the splinter in the eyes of other people, society or the world and start focusing on overcoming the blocks in your own consciousness.

You have no doubt already taken the steps necessary to bring you to the path to Christhood—or you would not be open to this course. What you need to do next is to take the steps that will anchor you firmly on the path and help you fully understand what the path entails and how you can make it work for you. This is a gradual process, and I will take you through the necessary steps based on my long experience with seeing how students respond to the path.

***

To facilitate the transformation of consciousness that will qualify you for a direct relationship with an ascended master, the rest of this course is designed as a work book. In the preceding chapters, I have given you a basic understanding of the essence of the path. The rest of this course is focused on helping you walk that path by beginning at the very first step. You may think you are beyond the beginning step – based on you having studied certain outer teachings and practiced certain techniques for a while – yet if you are not willing to follow the path I outline, then simply go elsewhere. When you eventually tire of following the false path of the ego, I will welcome you back with an open heart.

My point here is that no matter how advanced you think you are or are not, the following steps are designed to help you overcome the hurdles that *all* students must overcome on the path to Christhood. No matter who you think you are, you *do* have the potential to follow this course. The only thing required is an open mind and a willingness to TRY. There are two main obstacles to overcome, namely the inferiority complex or the superiority complex. Some people are affected by inferiority and think they are not worthy to follow the path to Christhood. Banish that thought, for if you have found this course, you ARE worthy and ready! Other people think they are so advanced that they do not need to follow any outer teaching or do not need to follow the beginning steps. Banish that thought, for if you have found this course, it proves you have something to learn. For that matter, the fact that you are still on Earth proves you have something to learn.

Again, official Christianity has created such an idolatry of my historical person that most people think I was born with full Christ consciousness. That is an illusion, and I can assure you that I had to go through every single step I outline in this course. There is no official record of me taking all of these steps, but there are records of me facing some of these initiations—when you read between the lines. My point being that if *I* followed these steps, then *you* should be content to follow them as well. God truly is no respecter of persons, a truth that the human ego will never fathom or accept.

Now, I have no problem with you reading the rest of this course from beginning to finish if you desire to have an overview of the steps and the path. There is much teaching on each step, and it can truly help you increase your understanding. However, neither do I have a problem with you beginning with Key 1 and only reading the next key when you have studied the teachings and performed the exercises outlined in the first key.

In other words, the absolute requirement that I make is that you do perform the exercises described in each key. You may read the rest of the course and then go back to Key 1 and start the exercises. Or you may start the exercise for Key 1 right away without reading beyond that key. Furthermore, it is an absolute requirement that you do not fall prey to the temptation to think that reading a key one time is enough. I am not seeking to give you intellectual understanding; I am seeking to help you truly internalize the lesson. Thus, you need to study a lesson for a time while performing the exercise for that lesson.

The exercise for each key is described at the end of the key. Obviously, the text of a key is so long that you probably will not read it all in one sitting. Thus, I recommend that you perform the exercises as you study the key. In other words, study a portion of the key each day and then perform the exercise after your study. It is better to study only a small portion of the key and then perform the exercise than to study more and exercise less. Study alone will *not* get you to Christhood.

Study and practice go hand in hand, and if you do not perform both, you will not make maximum progress. I will not put an absolute limit on how long you should perform an exercise, but as a recommendation, I set 33 days. Perform the exercise once a day for 33 days and spend some time every day studying the corresponding lesson. When I say study, I do not mean that you have to read the entire text in one sitting. I would rather have you read one paragraph and absorb it than having you read everything at a superficial – or an intellectual – level. If you feel a need to spend more than 33 days with a lesson, by all means do so. Sometimes a student can feel like things are moving so fast that there is a threat to his or her sense of continuity. It is then acceptable to back up and dwell on a certain lesson a bit longer.

However, I caution you against stopping the exercises or putting down the course completely. Keep the process of growth going by doing even a short exercise and studying a little bit in the course every day. And be aware that the ego is always seeking to prevent you from going beyond your current level, which means it will gladly keep you there indefinitely. Yet there is no stillstand, for the River of Life moves on, and those who do not keep up will inevitably fall behind.

The other requirement I make is that you do not skip a key or its exercise, not even to jump ahead and "come back later." The teachings and the exercises are designed to build upon each other and gradually – in a balanced manner – take you higher on the path to Christhood. As I said, this is a gradual process, and the wise students will not seek to rush it no matter what alluring arguments their egos serve up. As I said:

> In your patience possess ye your souls. (Luke 21:19)

I also said:

> The kingdom of heaven suffereth violence, and the violent take it by force. (Matthew 11:12)

If you want to be a true disciple of the Living Christ, then acknowledge that *you* are a disciple and that *I* am the Master. So allow me to fulfill *my* role and teach you, while you do not allow your ego to prevent you from fulfilling *your* role of being taught. For it is by allowing ourselves to go through the steps that we truly progress, as is explained in the story of my baptism by John:

> 13 Then cometh Jesus from Galilee to Jordan unto John, to be baptized of him.
> 14 But John forbad him, saying, I have need to be baptized of thee, and comest thou to me?
> 15 And Jesus answering said unto him, Suffer it to be so now: for thus it becometh us to fulfil all righteousness. Then he suffered him. (Matthew, Chapter 3)

Recognize that the essence of the path is that you come to see what you cannot currently see and that this is an ongoing process. Because I am ascended – and thus free of the human ego and the mind of anti-christ – *I* can see what *you* do not see. Thus, allow me to structure the program based on my higher vision, and do not let your ego make you believe that it knows better than the teacher. This is a subtle temptation, especially for experienced students—those who are closest to Christhood but still a world of – unrecognized – illusions away.

So let us get on with the cosmic dance between the willing teacher and the willing student, a dance whereby both are lifted up and magnified, becoming worthy to reach ever higher rungs on the infinite ladder of God's consciousness.

# PART TWO

## Key 1
## Decide to be teachable!

Let me summarize the essence of the path to personal Christhood. Right now, you have a self-image, a sense of identity, that is less than your actual potential. The Conscious You was created in the image and likeness of God and it has the potential to be – literally and with no qualifications – anything it can conceive of being. In the here and now of space and time, you are who you think you are. Thus, the essence of spiritual growth is to raise your vision, to increase your ability to think – to envision, to imagine, to know, to accept, to *be* – beyond the human identity that is defined based on the material universe.

Right now, your sense of identity is to a smaller or larger degree based on the conditions in the material universe and upon ideas that are unreal because they spring from a state of consciousness that is out of sync, out of oneness, with God's reality. I have called that state of consciousness "death," but we might also call it the consciousness of anti-christ or the consciousness of duality.

Why do I use the term anti-christ, which has – as virtually any other part of my teachings – been misused by overzealous Christians? I do so because the consciousness of Christ is – as explained earlier – designed to maintain oneness between the Creator and the created. Anti-christ is therefore that which is in opposition to oneness, namely separateness and division. The consciousness of anti-christ sees a difference, a distance, a chasm, a division between the Creator and its creation, between God and humans, between itself and the remote God. That is why this consciousness elevated me to being God on Earth and degraded all other people to being lesser creatures. The purpose was, of course, to prevent anyone else from following in my footsteps, declaring their oneness with God and doing the works that I did.

So the essential problem of human existence is that right now you have a sense of identity that is partly based on the consciousness of anti-christ. This causes you to identify yourself as a being who is different from – separated from – your source, your Creator.

What has given rise to this mortal sense of identity is that the Conscious You has come to accept certain illusions that have sprung from the mind of anti-christ. Thus, the essence of the path to Christhood is that you systematically uncover, challenge and let go of these illusions, replacing them with the corresponding truth of Christ.

Precisely because the concepts of anti-christ and the devil have been so misused by orthodox Christians – mainly as a scare tactic – most people have a very superficial understanding of what I am talking about. You have been conditioned to think that the devil always appears as an evil-looking creature, perhaps with hoofed feet, a tail and horns. This, of course, is a deliberately engineered lie, partly created to scare you and partly created to prevent you from realizing the profound truth that Paul encapsulated in this quote:

> 13 For such are false apostles, deceitful workers, transforming themselves into the apostles of Christ.
> 14 And no marvel; for Satan himself is transformed into an angel of light.
> 15 Therefore it is no great thing if his ministers also be transformed as the ministers of righteousness; whose end shall be according to their works. (2Corintians 11:14)

The stark reality is that it is not a straightforward matter to identify the representatives of anti-christ. They are good at camouflaging themselves as representatives of Christ, which you see in many Christian churches today. Yet my real point here is that it is likewise no straightforward matter to identify the illusions of anti-christ. For they are always presented in such a way as to appear to be the truth.

In other words, walking the path of Christhood is not a simple matter of identifying elements in your psyche that are clearly evil or dark. It is a much more complex matter of identifying the – sometimes very fine line – between the subtle lies of anti-christ – that might appear as perfectly benign and true – and the reality of Christ—which might at first appear to be so different from the norm that it seems to *not* be true.

Take note of what I am saying here. I realize that if you are open to this course, you have some willingness to change. Thus, if you came to the realization that you believed in an idea that came from the mind of anti-christ, you would be willing to let go of that idea. So the reason why you have not already let go of all ideas that spring from the mind of anti-christ is that you have not yet seen them for what they are. And the reason you have not seen them is not that you are stupid or deficient, but that these ideas are indeed very subtle and difficult to identify as what they truly are. They appear benign, beneficial and truthful. They are often confirmed by the traditions of your society and culture, and in some cases they can even seem to be confirmed by your experiences in life. Yet despite all appearances to the contrary, they are illusions, they are lies and they will – indefinitely – keep you from entering the kingdom within you.

***

The essence of the path to Christhood is that you become able to see – to identify – illusions that you do not currently see because they appear to be anything but illusions. The essence of my job as a spiritual teacher is to help you see what the Conscious You cannot currently see and what your ego will never be able to see—and thus does not want the conscious self to see either. Thus, we might say that my job is to get you – in whatever way necessary – to see what you cannot currently see by challenging your existing belief system, your mental box.

At this point you may think I am repeating myself, for surely I have said this before. But did you truly understand and internalize what I have been saying? You see, there is no question that you still hold on to illusions that spring from the mind of anti-christ. How can I say this? Because if you had let go of all such illusions, you probably would no longer be on Earth. You would either have ascended to the spiritual realm, or you would be able to communicate with me directly without needing this course!

This planet is currently a very dense environment in which all aspects of human endeavor are colored by the mind of anti-christ. Even matter itself is more dense than the way it was originally designed, and thus even matter seems to confirm the basic illusion that you are separated from God—even to the point that the density of matter makes some people believe there is nothing beyond matter.

My point is that it is wise to adopt the attitude that as long as you are on Earth, you need to be in a constant state of alertness, where you never allow yourself to think that you have nothing more to learn, that you have somehow reached some ultimate state of consciousness from which no further growth is needed or even possible. As the saying goes, "Constant vigilance – constant willingness to examine and transcend yourself – is the price of discipleship."

You are who you think you are, so if you think no more growth is needed, how could you be open to further growth? Yet Christhood is not a state of perfection that never changes. Christhood is being one with the process of life itself, the river that is always flowing.

When the Buddha was asked what kind of being he was, his extremely profound and powerful answer was, "I AM awake!" Being completely and totally awake is the ultimate goal of spiritual students, and it is a very difficult goal to attain in the density of the material universe. Thus, it is the role of a spiritual teacher to first take the student to a high state of "awakeness" and then make sure the student does not imperceptibly – as has happened to many people who thought they were advanced students, perhaps even masters – slip back into being less awake or even less *than* awake.

Do you see what I am saying? My job is to *always* challenge you to reach for a higher state of consciousness, to reach beyond your current beliefs and your current sense of identity. My job is to always challenge your sense of comfortability, your sense of equilibrium, your sense of status quo.

It is the ego that does not want to change, that does not want to be challenged—which is why it seeks to silence the Living Christ, even by killing him. The reason being that the ego needs security, which it – because it has no built-in divinity – seeks to attain through control. The ego is constantly seeking to maintain some sense of equilibrium, and thus the serious student must be willing to let the teacher challenge all sense of comfortability, even outer security. Again, look at this quote:

> 25 For whosoever will save his life shall lose it: and whosoever will lose his life for my sake shall find it.
> 26 For what is a man profited, if he shall gain the whole world, and lose his own soul? or what shall a man give in exchange for his soul? (Matthew, Chapter 16)

Being willing to lose your life means being willing to give up any sense of comfortability and security based on the things of this world in order to follow the Living Christ. Giving up security can be very difficult for new students, and, ironically, it can be even more difficult – but in a more subtle way – for older students who think they should be above being challenged. Yet – as I have attempted to explain – no one on Earth is beyond being challenged—that is, if they want to remain in the Master-disciple relationship with a true teacher. The mind has a tendency to form habits, and this makes a familiar illusion seem more attractive than an unfamiliar truth, causing people to cling to the lie simply because it is familiar and offers comfort or security.

It is extremely important for you to understand that although the ego will always resist being challenged, even the conscious self can build a resistance to growth, a resistance to learning. This resistance can be very subtle, and few students recognize it for what it is. Thus, let me explain it to you in clearer terms than has been done before.

***

Let us take a look at the ego's first line of defense. One of the great challenges for a spiritual teacher is the issue of complexity. Most people on this planet have been brought up with an extremely simplistic understanding of themselves and of life. If you grew up in a traditional Christian environment, you were taught to believe that God created your soul at conception and that you have had no prior existence anywhere. If you grew up in a materialistic environment, you were taught that your sense of self is a product of the brain, affected by inherited traits and environmental factors. Again, "you" simply appeared at birth with no prior existence.

In reality, the picture is much more complex, but the problem is that most students would feel completely overwhelmed upon hearing the full story of where they came from. One of the most common reactions encountered by spiritual teachers – a reaction I encountered often when I walked the Earth, as recorded in the scriptures – is that a student is presented with an idea that is so far beyond the student's existing beliefs that the student refuses to accept it and thus rejects the teacher and everything he or she stands for.

This reaction is actually described very well by the science of psychology, and it is commonly known as the "fight-or-flight response." When a person is confronted with a danger, the typical response is to avoid the danger by either fighting it or fleeing. For most people the default reaction will be to flee, but some have developed a default reaction of always fighting the danger instead.

So what happens when a student is presented with an idea that goes so far beyond the student's existing belief system that the idea is seen as a threat—because it threatens the belief system and thus the student's sense of status quo? Well, less mature students will experience a fight-or-flight response. They will typically seek to avoid having to think about the idea, often by rejecting it based on their existing world view. If they cannot justify ignoring it, they will often switch over to fighting it by arguing against the idea or perhaps even by attacking the person who presented it. If you read the scriptures, you will see that the scribes and the Pharisees –

sometimes even my own disciples – responded that way when I presented challenging ideas.

Why am I describing this reaction in a key that talks about your teachability? Well, is it not obvious that as long as you respond to challenging – or simply new – ideas with the fight-or-flight response, you are not teachable? This course is available for all people to read, meaning people from a wide variety of backgrounds. How can I say anything in this course that will not be new or challenging to some people? If you think about it, you will realize that the reason you are reading this course is that you hope it will help you improve your life. So if you already knew how to improve your life, you would have done so and have no need for the course. So how can I help you improve your life? I must tell you something you do not already know. Yet if your default reaction is to reject anything that goes beyond what you already know, you will severely limit my ability to teach you.

Thus, I have two options. I can say what I want to say and simply accept that a certain number of students will be filtered out because my ideas will be too challenging to them—too far away from their existing beliefs. Or I can seek to make the readers aware of the most common mechanism that prevents people from accepting new ideas. The former option has been chosen by many spiritual masters in the past, including myself when I walked the Earth. However, times have changed, and as humankind raises its consciousness, the law of God requires that the path to Christhood be explained in a more straightforward way than has ever been done before. Thus, I have chosen the latter option for this course.

The essence of the path to Christhood is – as I have attempted to explain from several perspectives – that you become able to see the beam in your own eye. That beam is the ego and the conglomerate of illusions behind which it is hiding. I have so far described two players in the drama of your path to Christhood, namely the Conscious You and the ego. The ego was created because the Conscious You came to accept certain illusions that spring from the mind of anti-christ. The essence of the path is that you become aware of these illusions and let them go, whereby you allow the ego to die as if it never existed—the conscious self, or rather the sense of identity built by the conscious self, being reborn in the process.

How can you become able to see through the illusions you currently hold? Only by allowing the truth of Christ to challenge those illusions! So is it not obvious that the ego – which has a strong survival instinct – does not want this to happen? Thus, the ego will do anything it can think of in order to prevent you from questioning your illusions and from accepting the truth of Christ. Its first line of defense is the fight-or-flight response that causes people to reject a new idea without actually giving it serious consideration. As the Buddha so eloquently put it: "Accept nothing that is unreasonable. Reject nothing as unreasonable without proper examination."

The hallmark of a true student of the Living Christ is that you are willing to perform a proper examination of any idea—meaning both your existing beliefs – that you might see as absolutely true – and any new idea presented to you. Only by adopting this attitude will you become teachable.

If you take an honest look at religious or spiritually interested people, you will see that most of them are simply not teachable. They spend a lifetime rejecting growth by allowing their egos to manipulate them into rejecting new ideas based on the fight-or-flight response. For example, a fundamentalist Christian would long ago have rejected this course because it threatens his so-called literal interpretation of the Bible, thereby making himself equal to the Pharisees who rejected me when I stood before them in the flesh.

Now, I am well aware that most of my readers will be more mature than the Pharisees. You have most likely already started to overcome the fight-or-flight response, being willing to consider challenging ideas and revise your world view accordingly. You have probably already gone beyond your childhood beliefs and accepted a more sophisticated view of life. Yet you still need to be aware of the fight-or-flight response as you read this course, for there will come a point when I will challenge one of your most deeply held beliefs.

Thus, in order to be fully teachable, you need to adopt a new approach and develop it into a habit. You must be willing to observe, to examine, yourself and your reactions to the ideas I present in this course. Whenever you feel the fight-or-flight response – however subtle – you should know that it is your ego trying to prevent you from letting go of an illusion. Self-examination – and I mean constant, no-nonsense, no-compromise self-examination – is the price you have to pay in order to qualify as a disciple of the Living Christ. The progress you make on the path to Christhood will be in direct proportion to your willingness to examine yourself, especially your reaction to ideas that challenge your ego's sense that it has everything under control.

I also need you to contemplate the necessity of challenging *any* and *all* ideas. As a disciple of the Living Christ, you must be willing to properly examine all ideas—both new ideas that come to you and the familiar ideas that have already gained entry into your mind. Why is this so essential? Let us move on to consider a more sophisticated picture of the ego's defense strategy.

***

As I have hinted, the reality of life is much more complex than what most people were brought up to believe. Even though this is a very long course, it is not my goal here to explain everything to you. This course is part of a series, and the preceding two books give you a fuller explanation of when, how and why you created the ego. The first of these books was released by the ascended being known as Mother Mary,[1] and she did indeed serve as my physical mother in my lifetime as Jesus. The second book was dictated by an ascended master who is not well known in the West. His name is Lord Maitreya,[2] and he was and is my spiritual master. When I talked about my "Father," I sometimes referred to my Creator, sometimes to my spiritual self and sometimes to Lord Maitreya, who as my Guru held the position of spiritual Father for me. My point being that in order to gain a fuller understanding of the origin of the ego, you need to study both of these books. What I will give you in this course is only what is necessary to explain the points I am making.

What you need to understand at this point is that the ego was created by the Conscious You and that this happened a long time ago. This is necessary in order for you to understand why the ego's defense strategy is so difficult for you to penetrate. It has been part of your being for so long that you either take it for granted, think it is necessary and beneficial, or even think it is an integral part of who you are—that you couldn't live – or be you – without it.

A traditional Christian will find it hard to explain the origin of the ego. If your soul was created shortly before you were born, then did God also create the ego? And if God did create it, how can you possibly overcome it? Can you see that the traditional Christian view of who you are and how you were created tends to pacify people and make them believe they can do little to qualify for their salvation? The reality is radically different, which is why most mainstream Christians will be unwilling to accept it.

Because you are open to this course, you have probably already realized that reality is more complex than your childhood beliefs. You have probably even begun to realize that the human psyche –

---

1 *Master Keys to the Abundant Life.*

2 *Master Keys to Spiritual Freedom.*

including your own – is more complex than most people think. As you go deeper into the psyche and encounter some of the very complex beliefs – beliefs that have literally taken on a life of their own – you will see even more complexity, and this will make it obvious to you that such complexity simply could not have arisen in one short lifetime. Thus, reincarnation will eventually become a self-evident reality to all spiritual students—as it was indeed a self-evident reality to me and my disciples. I did not teach it to the multitudes, but I surely expounded all things to my disciples, who knew full well that they had lived before and were therefore complex beings.

Why am I bringing up reincarnation at this point? Because it is the only way to explain why it is so difficult for people to see through the main defense strategy of the ego. As I said, the ego's illusions have been part of your being for so long that they have become very familiar. In fact, the Conscious You has come to believe that there are certain illusions that it should not, cannot or is not allowed to question.

When you realize that the path to Christhood requires you to question and discard *all* dualistic illusions, you will see that having certain illusions that you think are beyond questioning will inevitably put you in a bind, a spiritual catch-22, from which no progress is possible. You can think you are on the spiritual path – you can even think you have made great progress based on outer activities – but in reality you have come to a point from which you cannot progress any further—that is, until you question the illusions you think are beyond questioning.

The ego's strategy has two lines of defense. The first is to get you to accept certain illusions that keep you outside the kingdom by making you believe you are separated from God. The next line is to get you to accept other illusions that make you think the first illusions are beyond questioning, thus making it impossible for you to rise above those illusions—then building layer upon layer in order to produce a maze that keeps you trapped indefinitely.

If you look at people, you will see this mechanism at work in most of them. Most people have a set of basic beliefs that they never question. These beliefs form a barrier for their minds that their thoughts never venture beyond. The beliefs have become taboos, mental holy cows that are untouchable. How does the ego make people believe in these holy cows? Here are the most common methods and the reality of why they are fallacies:

- **Forbidden knowledge.** The claim is that there are certain ideas that no person is allowed to know or that only certain people – who form an elite – are allowed to know.

  The reality is that there is no knowledge that is truly forbidden for a sincere spiritual student. All true teachers know that it is the truth that will make you free and it is partial or erroneous knowledge that keeps you trapped. Thus, the true teachers want you to find the truth. The ego and the false teachers, on the other hand, are always trying to make you believe that questioning their illusions is forbidden.

- **Dangerous knowledge.** The claim is that questioning certain ideas or acquiring certain types of knowledge is dangerous and will send you to hell or have other negative effects.

  The reality is that the truth is not dangerous, so once you know the truth, you are beyond all danger. What *is* dangerous is having incomplete knowledge – a little knowledge is a dangerous thing – or incorrect knowledge—believing that illusions are true. Thus, a true teacher always wants you to increase your understanding, whereas the ego wants you to believe that going beyond certain boundaries is dangerous. Nothing is more dangerous than believing in an illusion and being afraid to question it, thus being unable to ever come to see that it is an illusion.

- **Impossible knowledge.** The claim is that there are certain things you simply can't know because you are just a human being.

  In reality, you are not a *human* being but a *spiritual* being who is an extension of your Creator. Thus, there is *nothing* that the Conscious You cannot know. The Conscious You is an extension of God's Being and thus has the ultimate potential to access the fullness of the mind of God. However, in order to know more sophisticated knowledge, you have to be willing to think beyond your existing beliefs—and that is precisely what the ego is trying to prevent you from doing. (It must be stated here that there are certain things you cannot know with the outer mind while in a physical body because the brain has a limited capacity, but the Conscious You is more than the brain.)

- **Your current beliefs are complete.** The claim is that you don't need to question your current beliefs, for they already give a complete view of reality and there simply is nothing more to know.

  In reality, no matter who you are, no matter how much you know, no matter what belief system you accept, no matter how much you have studied, I can assure you that your current beliefs are *not* complete. How can I say this? Because you are still in embodiment on Earth! The mind of God is so far beyond what human beings can imagine that there will always be more to discover. Even I as an ascended being have not explored all facets of the mind of God. Thus, you should expect that as long as you are in embodiment – and well beyond it, but that is not my primary concern in this course – there will be more to learn. A true teacher always wants you to question your existing beliefs, whereas the ego is desperately seeking to prevent you from questioning the illusions that keep it alive.

  When I say that the Conscious You has access to the fullness of the mind of God, I mean it, but the mind of God is so vast that no person in embodiment can hold all of the knowledge that is in the mind of God. In other words, for the conscious self to comprehend the fullness of the mind of God, it must ascend to the spiritual realm, so it is not hampered by the limitations of a physical body and brain. Yet it is still true that there are no boundaries to what you can – eventually – come to know.

- **Your current beliefs are infallible—they are absolutely true.** The claim is that because your beliefs have the highest authority – such as the Bible being the word of God, or science presenting objective facts – there could be nothing wrong or missing. Thus, any conflicting knowledge is simply false or of the devil.

  In reality, the material universe is a very dense environment. God is beyond the material universe, and the consequence is that no belief system in the material world can give you a complete or infallible image of God. God is simply too complex to fit into *any* of the mental boxes found on Earth. Thus, it is wise to always be open to learning more, to going beyond your existing knowledge. Again, the true teacher wants you to keep expanding your consciousness, whereas the ego wants you to stop at any level, perhaps by making you think you have reached the highest possible attainment.

Another concern is, as Maitreya explains in his book, that words are ambiguous, and thus it simply is not possible to express absolute truth in words. The consequence is that in order to truly know truth, you must understand the deeper meaning of my saying:

> God is a Spirit: and they that worship him must worship him in spirit and in truth. (John 4:24)

To fully know truth, you must go beyond any worded expression of truth, which is precisely why the Living Christ will challenge your beliefs, *no matter what those beliefs are*. The ego and the false teachers will vehemently deny what I have just said, and they will seek to make you cling to the belief that your belief system is the only absolute one and that it is all the others that are false.

Do you begin to see the pattern? The overall effect of this defense strategy is that the ego has created certain areas in your mind that it considers safe zones, because the ideas in them are safe from your questioning and thus cannot be exposed as illusions. These areas are off-limits to your conscious self, and thus you can never be free of the illusions that are hiding within them—that is, until you stop accepting the ego's division of your mind and adopt the willingness to question *any* idea. Do you see my point? Consider the following quote, which few Christians have truly understood:

> Every kingdom divided against itself is brought to desolation; and every city or house divided against itself shall not stand. (Matthew 12:25)

Do you now see the deeper meaning? The kingdom that is divided is your mind, and one of the factors that divides it is precisely that your ego has managed to create these forbidden zones in which reside ideas that the Conscious You will not question—for whatever reason. Therefore, your life is based partly on *true* ideas and partly on *false* ideas – for some people *entirely* on false ideas – and as long as you are not willing to penetrate the "Iron curtain" and shine Christ light into the "No-God's land," you will remain divided. The division will eventually cause your "desolation" or downfall. The reason for this is, as I have mentioned several times, that the River of Life is always moving on. Thus, it is a spiritual law that you cannot remain in the same place in consciousness, and if you are not growing, you will inevitably fall behind the river itself, eventually running out of opportunity since everything in time and space must have an end.

***

I earlier said that even the Conscious You can have built a certain resistance to change, and it is essential for you to contemplate this. You see, when the Conscious You has forgotten who it is, it is relatively easy for it to feel overwhelmed by complexity, to feel that it – being such an insignificant human being – could not possibly understand anything beyond its current belief system. Thus, it is easy for the conscious self to believe in the ego's lie – as I will examine later – that as long as you confine your mind to a particular thought system, you will be safe in some ultimate sense.

You must understand that this mentality has been hanging like a black cloud over this planet for a very long time. If you take an honest look at humankind, you will see that the vast majority of people have – without in any way understanding what is happening – accepted a set of very strict limitations for their potential. That is why I had to perform certain miracles to even get people's attention and demonstrate that there is indeed a higher potential to which all can aspire. The very fact that my example was so quickly turned into an exception only seeks to demonstrate how powerful is the planetary momentum of the denial of your spiritual potential—of the denial of self, meaning the spiritual self that you are.

My point being that for you to become teachable, you must be willing to recognize that this momentum of self-denial exists and has a very powerful magnetic force that seeks to pull the Conscious You into denying your true identity and potential. And precisely because you have come to accept some of the illusions that "justify" the self-denial, it will require a very determined effort by you to rise above the downward spiral of self-denial.

Your ego will always remain trapped in this spiral, but it is highly likely that even your conscious self has been affected by it. Thus, it is absolutely essential for you to realize that you must activate the conscious self's most important ability, namely the ability to be conscious of yourself, to look at yourself from outside your current sense of identity and mind. As I have said, the Conscious You is an extension of God's Being, meaning that it – you – has the ability to step outside of its current sense of identity and tune in to a higher part of your Being. This is what gives you the ability to be self-aware, to be aware that you have accepted certain illusions and to be aware of the truth that can set you free from them.

Yet the essential realization here is that this self-awareness is not something that comes automatically by praying, practicing meditation or by studying religious scriptures, not even this course. It can come *only* as a result of a conscious decision, the decision that you are willing to rise above your current sense of identity, your current sense of self, and BE MORE. Yet this decision must be a spontaneous decision that follows from an "Aha experience" in which you suddenly see, realize and experience who you truly are. It is my goal for this course to take you through successively deeper layers of this experience, until you can say with me, "I and my Father are one!"

You see, precisely because the Conscious You is an extension of God's Being, you have the same desire that propelled the Creator to create this universe, namely the desire to be more. The creator created the world of form – and self-aware extensions of itself – precisely because it wanted to be more. Thus, you exist because your Creator desires to be more *through* you, meaning that in the core of your being is the desire to be more.

Yet as I said, the Conscious You is – in time and space – who it thinks it is, meaning that it can come to identify itself *with* and *as* a mortal, human sense of identity. This can cause you to deny your potential to be more, to feel comfortable with your limited potential and to feel a sense of being overwhelmed at the thought of going beyond the limitations that seem comfortable. It is not uncommon for spiritual students to feel overwhelmed by the new knowledge they discover, but also to feel a sense of dread or resistance to the thought that you too can do the works that I did by unlocking your built-in ability to take dominion over the matter world. Or a sense that for you to reach this goal, there is an overwhelming amount of work to be done—as opposed to the outer path that promises instant salvation in some future kingdom.

Perhaps you already know exactly what I am talking about because you have recognized this resistance in yourself? Perhaps this concept is entirely new to you? In any case, it is essential for you to become more aware of the resistance, for as long as you are not aware of this, you will make your spiritual path much more difficult than it needs to be—because you will be a house divided against itself. Your built-in drive will propel you to rise on the spiritual path – as it propelled you to find and study this course – but another part of your being will pull you back toward the old momentums, the old comfortability. That part is the ego, but as long as your conscious self believes in some of the illusions of the ego, there will also be a resistance from yourself toward your progress. Thus, whenever you make progress, something will pull you back down and you often end up having to fight very hard for each step you climb higher on the path. It is my goal to help you rise above this unnecessary hardship.

There is an old joke about a man who has to walk home on a stormy night, when the streets are icy and slick as glass. When he finally makes it home, he says to his wife, "It was so slippery that for each step I took forward, I slid two steps backward!" She then asks the logical question, "Well if you kept sliding two steps backward for each step forward, how did you make it home?" His answer is, "Well, I finally figured it out, and I turned around and walked away from home!" My point is that for each step you take forward on the path, your ego will attempt to use any division in your mind to cause you to slide two steps backward. And eventually, this might make you give up on the path, which is the truth behind the old saying that discouragement is the sharpest tool in the devil's toolkit.

So you have to break the momentum by doing something you have never done before, something that will break the spell that the ego has over you. That something is to become aware of yourself and how you view the path. I am not saying this can or should be done in an instant. What I am saying is that at this point you need to become aware of the need to become more aware.

You do this by making the decision that you will begin to look for any resistance in your being toward the spiritual path—even toward the ideas I am presenting in this course. When you discover such a resistance, you will know that it either comes from the ego or from your conscious self's identification with illusions, with the mortal identity. You must then consciously decide to avoid the default reaction, which is to resist looking at the resistance. Instead, you must decide to force the resistance out in the open, so you can examine it in the light of Christ truth and thus see how and why it is unreal. By doing this, you can break down the wall that prevents you from seeing what is hiding in the deeper recesses of your mind. Thus, you must decide to start looking for the beam in your own eye, and you must be willing to expose it so you can consciously see through the illusion and let it go.

Here is the essential equation that I want you to fixate in your mind so that you will not forget it. It is quite possible to come to accept a dualistic illusion without understanding what is happening and how it will affect you. As I said, the illusions of anti-christ are carefully camouflaged as truth, and they are often presented as the *only* truth or as the easy way out. Thus, the Conscious You can come to accept a set of illusions without realizing what it is doing, because it is taking what seems like the path of least resistance. For example, it is easy for a child to accept the religion of its parents in order to avoid a confrontation. Yet you simply cannot overcome your illusions by remaining unaware or by taking the path of least resistance. You can overcome them only by deciding to become MORE aware, and this will require a deliberate effort on your part. It simply will not happen automatically!

It is possible to slide down the staircase of life with your eyes closed and without knowing what you are doing. Yet it simply is *not* possible to climb back up without opening your eyes and making conscious decisions. The planetary momentum of self-denial will easily take you down, but self-*denial* will never take you toward self-*realization*. You cannot become a self-realized being without awakening to your true identity, your true self. On Earth, most people are asleep; they are not awake. In heaven you find only beings who have been willing to make the effort to become fully awake. You cannot sleepwalk your way into heaven, so you must decide to become awake, to become aware of yourself.

The broad way that leads to destruction is indeed the path of least resistance, the path of mindlessly flowing with the planetary momentum, of blindly following the blind leaders. Though it may seem to promise a guaranteed salvation or an easy way out, it only leads you deeper into the jungle of duality, from which it will require effort to disentangle yourself. The straight and narrow path of Christhood is the path of making a conscious effort to examine every illusion that keeps you outside the kingdom within you. It is the path of recognizing that when you make an effort, you will indeed be rewarded accordingly, as I explained in the parable about multiplying your talents.

***

Why do I talk so much about the need to have an open mind, what in Zen Buddhism is called a beginner's mind, a mind that is flexible and is willing to look at things in new ways? Because it is a fact that those who have been on the spiritual path the longest are often the ones who have the least flexible minds. They think they know everything they need to know because they have studied an outer belief system. They have – in very subtle ways – started to become comfortable in the belief that they have the spiritual path and salvation all figured out.

Yet consider the popular Star Wars movie in which Luke Skywalker is being trained by Yoda to become a Jedi. Consider Yoda's remark that Luke must unlearn everything he has learned. It is often those who think they know the most who are the least flexible, and the effect of this is that they cannot take the last steps toward manifesting Christhood. This is unfortunate, for many of these students are only a few steps away from reaching a higher state of consciousness. Yet because of their inflexibility of mind, they might never take those last steps. This will then cause them to gradually solidify in the belief that they are "saved" based on outer criteria defined by their Earthly belief system. Thus, instead of becoming true followers of Christ, they end up as present-day scribes and Pharisees, whose righteousness is not sufficient to get them to the inner kingdom.

Consider the story of the Gordian knot, located in an ancient temple. The intricate knot was made in such a way that the knot itself hid all the ends of the ropes. An oracle had prophesied that he who could "undo" the Gordian knot would become ruler over all of Asia. Many tried, but they were not able to untie the knot. Finally, a man named Alexander cut the knot in two with his sword, thus undoing – as opposed to *untying* – the knot. The point of the story is that most of the people had looked at the problem with the same state of consciousness that created the problem. Thus, the only solution they could see was to untie the ropes, to reverse the process that created the problem. Yet this is impossible precisely because of what I earlier described as the ego's layered defense of creating illusions that prevent you from questioning deeper illusions, thus making it impossible for you to untangle the web of lies. Alexander stepped outside the consciousness that created the problem and was therefore able to see the situation from a fresh perspective, coming up with the only practical solution. The lesson from the story is that it is impossible to solve a problem with the same state of consciousness that created the problem. You cannot solve a problem created from the consciousness of death as long as you remain blinded by that state of consciousness.

The stark reality is that your ego has created a Gordian knot in your psyche by creating an intricate web of illusions that are all tied together in such a complicated knot that you cannot see the ends nor the beginnings of the lies. It simply will not be possible for you to undo this knot by using the dualistic state of consciousness, nor the human intellect. Thus, no matter how much you know, no matter how sophisticated is your intellectual understanding of spiritual teachings, you will be no closer to undoing the knot. In order to truly undo the knot, you need to use the conscious self's ability to step outside its current sense of identity, reconnect to your own Higher Being and then look at the knot from a higher perspective. Only when you see the knot from the non-dualistic perspective of the Christ mind, will you be able to see through the illusions and sort out the lies. Consider – once again – my saying:

> 14 ... Suffer the little children to come unto me, and forbid them not: for of such is the kingdom of God.
> 15 Verily I say unto you, Whosoever shall not receive the kingdom of God as a little child, he shall not enter therein. (Mark, Chapter 10)

As mentioned before, there are two approaches that are common among spiritual seekers. One is that people – especially those who are new to the path – fall into the trap of belittling themselves, what is often called the inferiority complex. They think they are too inferior to truly understand the path and do the works that I did. This is obviously a denial of the Christ in themselves, for the Christ is in everyone. Thus, every person has the potential to connect to the Christ mind, and through the Christ mind you can understand everything you need to understand in order to follow the spiritual path. Thus, if you are willing to reach beyond your present state of consciousness, you can indeed follow the spiritual path.

The other approach – common among people who have been following the spiritual path for a while, usually as members of an organization that promises its followers a guaranteed salvation – is that people fall into the trap of raising themselves up—the superiority complex. This causes people to think they are beyond learning certain basic things about the path, making them unwilling to reconsider their basic beliefs and preconceived ideas. And if those basic beliefs are partly or wholly based on illusions, the people cannot move on.

I might add that *any* belief that you are not willing to question is at least partly based on an illusion. For if you are flowing with the River of Life, you will be willing to question *any* belief in order to attain a higher understanding. And as I have said previously, it is *always* possible to attain a higher understanding of *anything*.

***

Being willing to question everything is a necessity for those who are serious about walking the path of Christhood. Yet as I will later explain in greater detail, the path of Christhood is not about jumping from one extreme to the other but about finding what I called the "strait and narrow way" and what the Buddha called the "Middle Way." This is a state of balance that is neither in one extreme, nor in the opposite extreme – nor in a compromise between them – but is above the dualistic game. Thus, even questioning everything can be taken too far, as it is by some seekers who continually question without ever finding any answers.

My point is that being willing to question everything does not mean that you think there is no truth or that you never accept any idea as valid. Instead, you realize that there are indeed valid ideas, but that these ideas are valid *only* for your present level of consciousness. Thus, you see them as tools that can be used to climb to a higher level of consciousness, and when you reach that level, you will need to question the ideas that got you there in order to climb even higher.

In other words, while you are willing to question everything, you still have certain ideas that you take as valid and use as a foundation for your upward climb. We might say that the real point of being teachable means that you recognize there is a higher truth that is beyond the dualistic mind and its relativistic reasoning. You recognize that it is possible for you to know at least fragments of that higher truth in your current state of consciousness. So you trust that there are certain ideas that are valid, while remaining open to the possibility that you do not yet see the full picture. Thus, when you eventually come to see the bigger picture, you might see these valid ideas in a broader context than what you can see now. This does not make them invalid, but it does change your perspective and understanding of these ideas.

Let me give you an example. As you start to learn about math, you first learn addition and subtraction. These are perfectly valid skills, but they do not give you the full picture of the potential of math. So if you were to insist that by learning addition and subtraction, you have learned everything there is to learn, or everything you need to learn, about math, you would severely limit yourself by clinging to a primitive view of math. As you learn more about math, you see that while addition and subtraction are valid and useful skills, there is so much more to math, and a college student may not consider addition and subtraction to be very significant. This illustrates that although you may currently have some knowledge of the spiritual path that is valid, there is likely to be much more to learn. And as you learn more, you might come to see that your current knowledge and beliefs are not nearly as significant as you think right now. Being open to this process is the hallmark of a true spiritual seeker, a true disciple of Christ.

***

How do you know what is true, what is a valid idea? You can know by making use of what I called the "Key of Knowledge," which basically is what people today call intuition. Yet even your intuition is not a faculty that is beyond being affected by your current state of consciousness, for your intuition is no better than the questions you are able – or willing – to ask. And your ability to formulate questions is highly dependent upon your current state of spiritual maturity.

Nevertheless, the fact is that no matter where you are at in consciousness, you have a way out, namely to make use of the gift I gave to all people:

> But the Comforter, which is the Holy Ghost, whom the Father will send in my name, he shall teach you all things, and bring all things to your remembrance, whatsoever I have said unto you. (John 14:26)

This Comforter is a portion of my Spirit – or the Spirit of another ascended master – that is "broken for you" in order to give you a guide who can "teach you all things" from within your own mind. This forms an inner teacher, which in some esoteric traditions has been called your "Christ self." Thus, we now have three players in the drama of your path to Christhood, namely your conscious self, your ego and your Christ self. The latter will help you know what is valid:

> 16 And I will pray the Father, and he shall give you another Comforter, that he may abide with you for ever;
> 17 Even the Spirit of truth; whom the world cannot receive, because it seeth him not, neither knoweth him: but ye know him; for he dwelleth with you, and shall be in you. (John, Chapter 14)

Your Christ self is your personal teacher – much more valuable than a personal trainer or Life coach – who will teach you through the inner voice of intuition. You have already received the guidance of your Christ self, or you would not have been reading this course. I will later give you more teachings on this as well as techniques for increasing your awareness of your Christ self. What I want to do at this point is to help you recognize that you *have* had the guidance of your Christ self, perhaps at important turning points in your life, perhaps on a more regular basis. Thus, you already have the foundation for learning everything you need to learn, and an essential part of being teachable is to work with your Christ self.

Your Christ self is the mediator between your outer mind, your conscious awareness, and your Higher Being and the spiritual realm. Thus, your Christ self is your guiding rod that can help you discern between the many relative "truths" that spring from the mind of duality and the one higher truth that is in the mind of Christ. Yet to fully hear and make use of the guidance of your Christ self, you need to recognize that there is a higher truth beyond what your ego and the forces of this world are telling you. This truth goes beyond what can be written down in this course or any religious scripture or interpretation thereof. You can know this higher truth only through a direct, inner experience, which means you must be open to input from a higher source, namely your Christ self.

Obviously, your ego and the forces of this world – including some people and institutions who might claim to be able to take you to salvation – will do anything to prevent you from following the direction from within, making you follow their outer direction instead. That is why I said:

> Woe unto you, lawyers! for ye have taken away the key of knowledge: ye entered not in yourselves, and them that were entering in ye hindered. (Luke 11:52)

Nevertheless, the fact that you are reading this proves that you already have some willingness to follow your inner guidance. Thus, you need to build on this by cleaning up all levels of your mind from the dualistic beliefs that have accumulated there. As you remove the debris, you will come to see more clearly, and thus your connection to your Christ self will become an unfailing inner guidance for you.

Do you see the basic mechanism I am describing here? Your ego and the false teachers of this world will seek to make you cling to an outer expression of truth as being complete and infallible. Your Christ self will seek to take you toward experiencing – eventually becoming one with – the Spirit of Truth, which is beyond all expressions in this world. Thus, if you cling to an outer expression – even if it is valid (a teaching can be valid without being absolute and infallible) – you shut off, overlook or explain away the voice of your Christ self. My point being that in order to make use of the Key of Knowledge, you must be willing to always look beyond your current beliefs and belief system in order to have a direct encounter with the Spirit of Truth, an encounter that goes beyond intellectual understanding and beyond the words and imagery of this world.

***

Let me reach back to my concept that you need to increase your self-awareness. As you are reading this course, your ego is not simply sitting passively by and waiting for you to discover a truth that will lessen the ego's control over you. On the contrary, the ego is working overtime on trying to prevent you from understanding or accepting the truth that will make you free. One way the ego will do this is by setting up an absolute frame of reference, made up of your existing ideas about the path to salvation, or whatever you might call it. Thus, as you read the ideas I present in this book, your ego will tempt you to compare them to your frame of reference.

You ego will seek to make you take the ideas I present and seek to fit them into your existing belief system. We might say that your existing beliefs can be compared to a number of boxes in your mind, each box with a label on it. Thus, your ego will want you to fit any idea I present into one of these predefined mental boxes. This, of course, is not something that is unique to you as a spiritual seeker, for indeed almost all people do this when presented with new knowledge. What I hope will be unique to you as a spiritual seeker is that you will become aware of this mechanism and the effects of it.

What is the main effect of this ego-controlled mechanism? I have said that the essence of the path to Christhood is that you are spiritually reborn. This is a radical change, not a matter of adjusting a few ideas here or there. So what happens if you fall prey to the ego's desire to fit every idea I present into a mental box as part of your existing belief system? Well, the effect of your existing belief system is that it allows the ego to hide so the Conscious You does not see it—which then allows the ego to remain in control. My aim is to free you from the ego's control, and in order to do this, I must challenge your present belief system, world view and self-image. Yet if you take an idea that I present and allow your ego to put it into a mental box that is part of your present belief system, then that idea will *not* challenge your present beliefs. Do you see the central mechanism here? That which has become part of the system has lost its potential to challenge the system. And only that which challenges the system can free you from the blindness imposed by the system.

In an attempt to help you overcome this tendency, I am asking you to enter into a new state of consciousness. In order to describe this "new mind" I will, in the following sections, repeat a teaching I have already given on my website.

***

## The hidden virtues of magnificent confusion

I am quite aware that most of the people who sincerely study my discourses on the ego will end up feeling somewhat confused. They will feel as if it seems almost impossible to distinguish between what is the dualistic "truth" of the ego and what is the real truth of the Christ mind. They will feel as if it seems very difficult to know when they are acting from the ego and when they are not. Some will even feel a sense of hopelessness, as if it seems impossible to ever overcome the ego and its subtleties.

I understand these feelings, but I hope I can help you see that this is simply a necessary phase on the spiritual path that all seekers must pass through before they can rise above the ego. Every person who has ever attained the Christ consciousness has passed through this phase, myself included. Thus, I hope I can help you realize that you are not alone and that it is indeed possible to pass through this phase, even though it can seem hopeless at times.

What I truly hope to help you see is that the state of honest confusion is actually a magnificent state of consciousness. Instead of feeling despair or discouragement, you should congratulate yourself for having won an important victory. By being willing to move into a state of confusion, you have taken a very important step on the path of freeing yourself from the ego. Why is that so?

What I have endeavored to explain in the ego discourses is that the ego has an insatiable desire to be in control of every situation. It is constantly seeking to set itself up as an authority figure that cannot be questioned or gainsaid. Yet being an authority figure comes with a subtle temptation that has caused many otherwise sincere people – especially in the field of politics – to fail their missions in life. And certainly, the ego has no way of resisting this temptation. The temptation is that if you are an authority figure, it seems as if you should always be right. If you are not right, your authority is brought into question, and this gives rise to the fear that you could lose your position and its privileges.

The ego lives in a constant state of fear that if it is proven wrong, it will lose its control over you and thus it will die. This is a well-founded fear in the sense that once the Conscious You begins to see the fallacy of the ego's dualistic, fear-based and control-seeking reasoning, the ego will lose its control over you and it will eventually die.

Now, here comes the subtle reasoning. The path that leads to freedom from the ego is that the Conscious You must stop identifying itself with the ego and the ego's dualistic beliefs. If a person is completely identified with his or her ego, the person will feel the ego's fear of losing control. Therefore, this person will feel compelled to defend the ego's beliefs as if it was a matter of life and death. In other words, the person will feel it is of utmost importance never to be proven wrong.

How does the ego attempt to avoid being proven wrong? The ego defines a world view, and as long as the person accepts this world view, the person can never be proven wrong. The person will always be able to twist any situation or argument so that it seems like he or she is never wrong.

Do you see the consequence of this approach to life? It truly gives a person a sense of certainty, which can make people feel very sure that they are right, that they are okay or even that they are superior to others. Yet, this is a false security that is in constant danger of being threatened or shattered by events over which neither the person nor the ego has any control. I referred to this false sense of certainty when I said:

> 26 And every one that heareth these sayings of mine, and doeth them not, shall be likened unto a foolish man, which built his house upon the sand:
> 27 And the rain descended, and the floods came, and the winds blew, and beat upon that house; and it fell: and great was the fall of it. (Matthew, Chapter 7)

When a person is completely identified with the ego, the person is using dualistic thinking to refute any idea or viewpoint that questions the ego's dualistic world view. Thus, such a person simply is not teachable, and a spiritual teacher has little opportunity to reach the person.

Do you now see my point? When you identify yourself with the ego, you have the ego's superficial certainty, and thus you can deny any confusion. In a sense, you are never feeling confused, because the ego always has ready-made answers to any question or situation. Therefore, the very fact that you now feel confused, and that you are willing to recognize that you feel confused, is a clear demonstration that the Conscious You is no longer completely identified with the ego.

***

I realize that in a certain way, the dissolution of the ego's superficial certainty will feel like a loss, but only when you look at it from a narrow perspective. Once you step back and look at the forest instead of the trees, you see that being confused is a major step forward because you have now become teachable for both your Christ self and your spiritual teachers. And as the old saying goes, "When the student is ready, the teacher appears." Thus, instead of looking back toward the "good old days" when you thought you knew everything and had life under control, you need to refocus your attention and look for the teacher who is here with you right now and is ready to help you take the next step.

I see many spiritual seekers who finally see through the ego's false certainty and who give up the security of the ego's old belief system or world view. However, they do so reluctantly and they immediately start looking for some other source of security. In so doing they are often attracted to a guru or organization who makes very strong – even absolutist – claims. This often gives them a sense that because they are now with the true guru or savior, they can feel secure again. Obviously, this approach simply gives the ego a new lease on life because it will now start using the new belief system to enslave you.

I also see some seekers who give up the security of an old belief system, yet they adopt a new one that makes them think they are on the path to enlightenment. They think that once they reach that state, they will once again feel secure and have the certainty of knowing everything. However, even an enlightened person does not know everything, as I will explain shortly.

What I desire to see happen is that seekers go beyond the need for outer certainty and security by making conscious contact with the ultimate teacher, namely the inner teacher of their Christ selves, and through that with their ascended teachers. The reason I said that the kingdom of God is within you is that you can enter the kingdom of God – the Christ consciousness – only through an inner process. It follows that in order to complete this process, you must make contact with your inner teacher.

I am not denouncing an outer teacher or teaching, as both can be very helpful. What I am saying here is that you will always attract to you both the true teacher that can help you take the next step and the false teacher that will make you feel like you shouldn't take the next step. If you look for certainty, you will inevitably be attracted to the false teacher. Only if you are willing to remain confused, will you find the true teacher. Why is that so?

The ego seeks to control you, and the last thing the ego wants is for you to become self-sufficient and spiritually independent. In return for letting it control you, the ego offers you the false sense of certainty—that you are always right, that you are guaranteed to be saved, that you are superior to others or whatever your particular need might be. In contrast, the true teacher wants you to become self-sufficient, and thus a true teacher will never seek to control you. Instead of offering you a superficial certainty, the true teacher offers you the true, inner path—and this is an ongoing process of expanding your consciousness.

The path never ends, meaning that there is no limit to how much you can grow in awareness and understanding. However, what exactly does that mean? If you are open to the possibility of never-ending growth in awareness, it means that there is no belief or viewpoint that can be considered absolute or infallible. In other words, the true inner path does not offer you the outer certainty of the ego, namely that this or that outer belief is absolute. On the contrary, on the inner path there are no absolute beliefs, for any belief can be expanded or replaced by a broader awareness. This leads to two essential considerations:

- It is not the essence of the inner path that you become codependent upon the inner teacher. It is the essence of the path that you become self-sufficient so that you no longer need your Christ self. This means that the true teacher will not tell you what to do, as the ego and false teachers will gladly do. The true teacher will give you a greater understanding, so that you have a better foundation for making choices. Yet it is *you* who must choose because only by choosing will you grow in self-sufficiency. Unless you are willing to make your own decisions, you might easily overlook the directions of the inner teacher, thus prolonging the state of confusion unnecessarily.

- On the inner path, there is no outer certainty or security. Therefore, it is essential that you develop an inner sense of certainty and security. The ego is trying to say that as long as you believe in its infallible doctrines, *you* are okay—which means that you are *only* okay when you believe in the right doctrines. Your self-worth depends on something outside your self. What you need to do is go beyond this need for an external security and find an internal source of security. This true inner security comes when you realize that the core of your being is the conscious self, and that you are an extension of the Creator. Your self-worth is now centered on your real self—which is *beyond* this world and thus cannot be threatened by anything *in* this world.

***

In reality, the ego has no inherent or self-sufficient sense of identity. The ego *is* its beliefs and viewpoints. That is why the ego must base its sense of identity and worth on its beliefs. And if one of those beliefs is threatened, the ego feels its worth, even its very existence, is threatened. That is why people who are identified with their egos are willing to kill other people in order to destroy a threat to their belief system.

The Conscious You does have an inherent sense of identity and worth that is independent of your outer beliefs, opinions and viewpoints. As you begin to focus on the fact that you *are* the conscious self, you can gradually reconnect to that pure sense of being. You can even experience a state of consciousness in which you are aware, but your mind is free of specific thoughts. You experience pure consciousness, and when you have such a transcendental or mystical experience, you know you are more than the contents of your mind.

All spiritual seekers have had at least brief glimpses of this pure consciousness or they would not be longing for something beyond what this world has to offer. Yet not all seekers are consciously aware of what they have experienced. Many even take these experiences for granted because they seem so natural or because they have never been taught what they mean. Yet as you begin to contemplate these concepts, you will realize that you *know* you are more than your beliefs.

And as you become more aware of the "you" that is behind the contents of your consciousness, you naturally become less attached to those contents. You begin to realize that any belief or viewpoint you hold on Earth is simply a particular expression of truth. Yet as *you* are more than the contents of your mind, *truth* is more than any particular expression. That is why I said:

> God is a Spirit: and they that worship him must worship him in spirit and in truth. (John 4:24)
>
> Even the Spirit of truth; whom the world cannot receive, because it seeth him not, neither knoweth him: but ye know him; for he dwelleth with you, and shall be in you. (John 14:17)

When you recognize that truth is more than *any* expression of truth found on Earth, how can you remain attached to one particular expression? And thus, you lose your fear of letting go of your present understanding of truth and letting it be replaced by a higher understanding.

As you stop holding on to the dualistic beliefs of the ego, you will become gradually more open to the non-dual directions of your Christ self and spiritual teachers. This will eventually give you a conscious connection to the universal Christ mind, and you will then begin to gain a foundation for avoiding the negative aspects of confusion, namely the sense that you don't know what is right and wrong, true or false. You will begin to experience the Spirit of Truth directly, and this will remove confusion although it will not give you an outer certainty as many people imagine.

***

The greatest advantage of this shift in consciousness is that you lose your fear of being wrong. Take a few seconds to step back and look at what a heavy burden has been put upon you by the ego and perhaps also by your upbringing. Take an honest look at how much the world revolves around the compulsive desire to always be right. See how it creates conflicts between people, often leading to wars. See how it creates conflicts in yourself, often putting you on a downward path, where all of your energy is fed into proving that you are right so you have no attention left over for enjoying life.

This obsessive-compulsive desire to be right springs from the ego's belief that if its viewpoints are proven wrong, then *it* is proven wrong. And this belief is perfectly true—for the ego. Yet it is not true for the Conscious You because you are *more* than your viewpoints. Thus, if one of your beliefs is proven wrong, it does not mean that *you* are wrong or that you are a bad person. And this means you can let go of the entire weight of having to always be right.

I can assure you that once you do this, you will literally feel as if the weight of the world has been lifted from your shoulders. You will feel reborn and feel that you have received a chance to start life anew. That is why I said:

> Verily I say unto you, Whosoever shall not receive the kingdom of God as a little child, he shall not enter therein. (Mark 10:15)

Look at a child who is learning how to walk. It does not carry the heavy burden that it has to be perfect every time or that it should feel guilty for falling down. It simply gets up and tries again, laughing at its own mistakes while still learning from them. When you separate yourself from the ego's need to be right, you too can become as joyful as a little child, and then the spiritual path becomes a joy-filled journey rather than the Via Dolorosa.

Take note that children are always eager to learn, meaning that they don't think they know everything or that they have to know everything. Thus, they have no resistance to learning something new. The ego will always resist having a belief proven wrong, but once you connect to who you are, you can actually see it as a great opportunity to have a belief proven wrong. Instead of continuing to live with a limited or incorrect belief, you can now rise to a higher understanding, which can only enrich your life. Thus, having a belief proven wrong becomes a stepping stone for growth rather than a loss.

***

The ego wants you to believe that if one of your beliefs is proven wrong, you will lose something and you will end up in a black hole. The reason is that the ego's sense of identity is based on its beliefs, so if one is taken, the ego loses part of its identity. Yet once you realize that the Conscious You is MORE than your beliefs, you can avoid this trap.

Instead, you can see that losing a limited belief never leaves you in a vacuum, for the limited belief is always replaced by a broader understanding. Your inner teacher will question your limited beliefs but will never leave you empty. Your inner teacher will always offer you a higher understanding to replace the limited one. And when you embrace this process, you will never feel a loss. Instead, your life will become a constant process of discovery that leads to a greater and greater understanding of life.

Yet for this to happen, you must become aware of the ego's fear of loss and you must consciously choose to dismiss it. Instead, you must embrace the true inner path as an ongoing journey that never stops. On the true path, you will never again have the outer security that is based on specific beliefs and viewpoints. Instead, you will develop an inner certainty that is based on knowing who you are and that who you are is perfectly worthy in the eyes of God.

The true spiritual path is the River of Life, and it is always flowing. Everything in the River of Life is constantly transcending itself and becoming MORE. The ego cannot be part of this process, but the Conscious You *can*—as long as you are willing to flow with the river instead of resisting it. People who identify with their egos are resisting the river, they are refusing to flow with it.

They are like people in a river who are desperately clinging to a branch on the river bank. They think flowing with the river is dangerous, and thus they cling to the sense of security and stability that the bank seems to offer. Once in a while, the current becomes so strong that they lose their grip and must let go. They feel a sense of panic and desperately grasp for anything they can hold on to. Thus, their entire lives are swallowed up by feeling threatened and by resisting their own growth.

The wise spiritual seekers realize that true growth means that you never stand still, and thus you never have the false sense of security that can only come from standing still. Instead, these seekers embrace the process and start enjoying the journey instead of either obsessing about or fearing the destination. They voluntarily let go of whatever they are holding on to on the river bank and lovingly embrace the river itself. They decide to flow *with* the current instead of resisting it. And they soon realize that flowing with the river is so much more enjoyable and peaceful than fighting the current that only seeks to carry them toward the ocean of self.

The really wise ones even realize that the ocean is not nearly as important as the journey. After all, the ocean is made of water, and so is the river. Thus, you will be no more wet in the ocean than you are in the river. In fact there is a distinct enjoyment in feeling the water moving and feeling yourself moving with the water. If you embrace the flow, you will not fear leaving the bank behind, nor will you feel that you will be incomplete until you reach the ocean. You will feel complete in being in the flow, and you will enjoy watching the journey unfold all around and within you. You will then BE ONE with the River of Life, and thus you will be one with the Creator's ongoing dance of self-transcendence.

There is no greater certainty than this oneness with the Spirit of Truth, yet it is not based on outer beliefs. In fact, in oneness with the process of self-transcendence there is no belief that cannot be expanded and replaced with a broader understanding. For if your present understanding could not be expanded, how could self-transcendence be possible? And if there is no self-transcendence, life itself will have stopped. Thus, stillstand is never a reality but only an illusion created by the ego.

Embrace the process of life and go with the flow. The sooner you let go of the need to always be right or the need for certainty, the sooner you can embrace the state of magnificent confusion. This means you have no outer certainty but that you have the inner certainty of knowing you are one with the River of Life itself. [End of quote.]

***

This concludes my quotes from the website, and I have only one additional thought for you to contemplate:

> **If your present beliefs are incorrect or incomplete—would you want to know?**

For a true disciple of the Living Christ, the answer to that question is always a "YES!"

## Exercise for Key 1

This is the practical exercise for Key 1. What I need you to do in the coming 33 days is to follow a regimen of two exercises. I want you to read or listen to[3] Archangel Michael's dictation and give his rosary once a day [See the Appendix for the text of both the dictation and the rosary]. In the beginning of the rosary, where you can make your personal calls, I want you to give the following call:

> **In the name of the I AM THAT I AM, Jesus Christ, I call to you, beloved Archangel Michael, to cut me free from any ties to the planetary momentum of the death consciousness. Cut me free from the downward pull of the collective consciousness, especially its resistance toward change and the tendency to reject new ideas without giving them proper consideration.**
>
> **Beloved Jesus, expose to me the beam in my own eye in the form of any resistance in my being toward expanding my awareness, considering new ideas and taking responsibility for my own path and salvation. Beloved Jesus, I am willing to be your disciple and to start by seeing the beam in my own eye—show me the way!**

The second exercise is that after you have given the rosary, I want you to take 5-15 minutes and contemplate the teachings in this key, perhaps by reading a few paragraphs. I want you to honestly consider where you might notice any of the elements of resistance in your own psyche. I want you to think back at your life and consider how you might have resisted learning something new or com-

---

3 A recording of the dictation and the rosary will be available as part of the Spiritual Crisis Toolkit. See *www.askrealjesus.com* in the Store section.

ing to a higher understanding. I want you to consider how you might still feel a subtle resistance in your being toward the teachings I give in this course, or even the entire idea of a spiritual path that requires you to question everything.

I strongly suggest that you buy a durable notebook in which you can write down your impressions. You will be doing a fair amount of writing in order to follow this course, so you might as well get used to the idea. Write down your impressions and describe how you have been reluctant to learn something new or see elements in yourself that need to change. Also write down how you have overcome such reluctance and eventually moved beyond and how this has made you freer than you were before. In other words, I want you to consider the process you have gone through in order to achieve the openness of mind that has made you willing to study this course. What opposed that progress, what aided it, what enabled you to overcome the opposition and how did it feel to do so.

By the end of the 33 days I expect you to have a clearer view – and a greater appreciation – for your willingness to go beyond limitations, so that you begin to see that you have already passed many hurdles and thus should be able to pass many more. Perhaps you might even begin to sense that if you are willing to surrender, you will be able to pass *any* hurdle that the forces of this world – including your ego – might come up with.

Obviously, we are at the beginning stages, but I want you to lock in to the fact that you have gone through a process in order to be ready for this course. This should spur you on to make greater progress, and by understanding the basic mechanism for how you got here, you should be able to avoid the trap of thinking you have already made it to the finish line. By understanding how you overcame limitations, you set a foundation for overcoming the more subtle challenges on the path, challenges that you do not yet have the awareness to even understand. By writing down your impressions, you also set the foundation for performing one of the tasks that is an integral part of the higher stages of the path to Christhood.

What I want to accomplish in this first key is to help you see that you have already been following the spiritual path for this – and likely many previous – lifetimes. You might not be consciously aware that you have been doing it, or you might not be fully aware of how you have been doing it. My point being that by coming to a more conscious awareness of the process of growth, you can take that growth to a much higher level and build an unstoppable momentum of self-transcendence. A momentum that neither the enemy within – your ego – or the enemy without – the forces of antichrist – can stop.

Take a look at how much humankind has progressed from the stone age to today. What is the central mechanism behind this growth? It is a growth in understanding, a growth in awareness. Humankind knows so much more today and modern people have a much more expanded awareness of themselves and their world. Thus, by *you* becoming more consciously aware of the spiritual growth you have already gone through, you can accelerate that growth immensely. Expanded awareness is the first step—and the second step, and the third step … and so on ad infinitum.

Yet now take this to a higher level. Where does expanded awareness begin? It begins by expanded *self*-awareness, the willingness to look at yourself and realize there is something you don't know, something you need to know—and then take action to expand your understanding.

This is a course in personal Christhood, and the one thing you should have learned by now is that the Living Christ will *never* accept status quo. Thus, you might as well realize that for the rest of your life – and beyond – you will be in the process or personal growth. As I said, you have already been engaged in this process, but I am now asking you to take this to a higher level by becoming more aware of the process. In other words, I am asking you to increase your *self*-awareness.

How can this be done? There is *only* one way—through objective, honest, penetrating self-observation. Why did I talk about those who look at the mote in their brother's eye and see not the beam in their own? Because the majority of human beings are looking outside themselves and refusing to observe themselves and recognize how *they* need to change. This is following the broad way that leads to destruction, and you simply cannot walk the path of personal Christhood if you are not willing to observe yourself.

Thus, I am asking you to have your notebook next to you as you study this book. Keep a certain amount of attention on your *reactions* to this book. An essential part of the path is to expose your ego, so the conscious self can separate itself from it. The separation will happen easily once you see the ego and see it for what it is, and your ego knows that its only chance of staying alive and keeping its control over you is to stay hidden. It is possible – not easy, but possible – to follow this course and have your ego stay hidden. So if you want to make it impossible for your ego to stay hidden, cultivate the habit of observing your ego's reactions to the ideas I present in this book. Be ready to write down any subtle or overt resistance to the ideas and the change I am calling you to make.

Do you see what I am saying? So far your ego has been able to fool you in many ways because you have not noticed its subtle manipulations. If you read this book without observing yourself, your ego will likely be able to continue to do this behind the scenes, because you will not be aware of how it manipulates you into not truly seeing or accepting what I will be telling you. You will not see the subtle ways in which it seeks to neutralize my teachings.

Yet if you cultivate the habit of observing yourself for the specific purpose of exposing your ego's resistance to change, you will put your ego in a dilemma—you will put *your ego* in a catch-22 instead of allowing your ego to keep *you* in a catch-22. How so? Because if the ego does nothing to manipulate you into resisting the change I will be calling for, you *will* change and then free yourself from its control. And if the ego *does* do something to get you to resist change, you will likely expose it and see it for what it is, whereby you will *also* free yourself from it.

Your ego and the prince of this world have – for a long time – attempted to manipulate you into situations where you are damned if you do and damned if you don't. It is time to reverse roles and put them in the same predicament.

# Key 2
# Confront your fears!

Why do I talk about *confronting* fear rather than *overcoming* fear? Because you cannot conquer fear through a passive measure! It is not a matter of performing some magical ritual that will automatically make your fear disappear. Fear is the most devastating of all feelings because it paralyzes you, it makes you afraid to move, afraid to change. Thus, there is no measure you can take that will *automatically* remove your fear. In the end, you will conquer fear *only* through an act of *will*, and *you* are the only person who can release that act of will. In order to do so, you must make a decision. In fact, we might say that your fears all spring from an unwillingness to make decisions.

Take note of the deeper reality here. I have said that the consciousness of anti-christ embodies a duality, a built-in, inescapable contradiction. The consciousness of anti-christ is based on separation from reality, yet what is reality? Reality is that everything is created from God's Being and energy. As the Gospel of John states, "Without him was not any thing made that was made" (John 1:3). Thus, the underlying reality is that all life is one through its common origin from the Being of God and the Christ mind, the WORD.

The consciousness of anti-christ is separated from reality, and since reality is one, the consciousness of anti-christ cannot be one (or it would be part of reality instead of being apart from it). Obviously, this separation exists only in the minds of self-aware beings who are blinded by the consciousness of anti-christ, and thus it is ultimately an illusion. Yet anything created by such beings will – by its very nature – be based on two opposing and mutually exclusive polarities, which means that it cannot have eternal life. Its internal contradictions will break it down, which is what turns life into a struggle, a constant struggle to maintain that which is in an inescapable process of self-destruction. In a sense one can say that anti-christ is in contradiction to Christ, but it would be more accurate to say that anti-christ is in contradiction to itself. It is in contradiction to the state of Christ in which there is no divisions and thus no contradictions. Much more on this later.

My point here is that for each quality you find in the mind of God – the mind of Christ – there is a perversion in the mind of anti-christ, a perversion with two opposing polarities. When the Creator created the world of form, it had to start with an act of will. In order to change any aspect of your life for the better, you have to start with an act of will. For each step you take on the path of Christhood, you have to start with an act of will. What is the perversion of will power? It is a duality in which one polarity is the tendency to make decisions without considering the whole (selfish decisions, prideful decisions) and the other polarity is fear, the fear of making a decision, the fear of setting in motion a cause. Thus, fear is dangerous precisely because it paralyzes you and prevents you from taking the very first step toward change—making a decision to change! Fear causes you to do nothing, to postpone making a decision, to avoid any decisive actions.

Why are you afraid to make a decision? You are afraid because at some point in the past you accepted an illusion. One example of such an illusion is the belief that if you do not follow the dictates of an external religious authority, you will burn forever in hell. Yet on top of that original illusion, your ego has built another illusion, namely that you must *never* look at the original illusion, you must accept it as absolutely and unconditionally true. You now have a cumulative effect, for the second fear prevents you from ever looking at the cause of the first fear. Yet what is the key to overcoming the original fear? It is to recognize that it springs from an illusion. And how can you recognize this as long as you are unwilling to make the decision to look at the belief?

This is the central mechanism that makes fear a catch-22 that traps most religious people, and even many spiritual people, in a blind alley where they can stay for a long time. Take note of the reality of the situation. *All* fear is based on an illusion, namely one of the illusions that spring from the consciousness of death, the mind of anti-christ. An illusion is something unreal, meaning that everything that you fear is ultimately unreal. Once you see that the cause of your fear is unreal, your fear will fade away, for you simply cannot fear something that you know is unreal. The fear springs from the belief that what you fear is real and thus has some kind of power over you. Yet how can something unreal have any power over you, and thus why fear it once you see it as unreal?

The problem is that in order to see the unreality behind fear, you must examine the illusion that started your fear. And you cannot do that unless you overcome the second fear, namely the fear of looking at the illusion. And you can overcome the second fear only by breaking the spell and making the decision – through an act of will – to look at your fear, no matter what reasons you have for not doing so.

This is the catch-22. Fear is anti-will, so it paralyzes you by making you unable – or rather unwilling – to use your will power. Yet any quality from the mind of anti-christ can be overcome only by bringing the corresponding reality from the mind of Christ. So fear can be overcome only through will. Yet how can you release the will power that will consume your fear, when your fear makes you afraid to use your will? You can do so in only one way, namely by understanding how fear works and seeing that it is unreal. Thus, it is the truth that will make you free.

The medieval Christian church literally had the minds of most Europeans in a straightjacket for almost a thousand years. How could this be done? Because the church had created layers of fear that effectively prevented people from taking a rational look at the church's doctrines. Thus, people were afraid to use their inner discernment to realize that some of the church's doctrines were out of alignment with the reality of Christ—even though the church claimed to be the only representative of Christ on Earth. Do you think it strange that I – the Living Jesus Christ – should have to challenge the very institution that claims to represent me on Earth? I do *not,* for I know that the role of the Living Christ is to *always* challenge the established powers of the time.

Do you truly understand what I am saying here? I have been spending a lot of time explaining that the essence of the path to Christhood is that you come to see what you cannot see right now—so that you can overcome your dualistic illusions. I have now explained that fear prevents you from taking a look at your beliefs and assumptions, so is it not obvious that as long as you have fear in your being, you cannot freely walk the path to Christhood?

As long as you are afraid to take a look at your illusions, how can you come to see them as illusions? Thus, one of the first steps on the path to Christhood is to become aware of fear and its paralyzing effects, so that you can build the understanding that empowers you to make the decision to confront – and then dismiss – all of your fears. Your ego hides behind your fears, so the only way to fully unmask the ego is to remove the fears so there is nothing left behind which the ego can hide. And doing this must start with an act of will.

***

The American president, Franklin Roosevelt, once said in a speech, "We have nothing to fear but fear itself!" That remark was inspired by the Ascended Host, and it is very important that you understand the reality behind this statement.

I have said that the two main players in the drama of your life are your conscious self and your ego. I have also said that all fear springs from an illusion, meaning that it is unreal. When you put these statements together, you get the following teaching.

Your conscious self is that part of you which is real in an ultimate sense, which means that it came out of God's Being and it was designed according to God's perfect vision. Only that which is created from God's Being has ultimate reality. In contrast, your ego was created by your conscious self after you started becoming blinded by duality. Thus, your ego is created based on the consciousness of duality and its illusions, meaning that your ego is ultimately unreal. It has only a temporary existence, it has no life in it. In fact, the ego can stay alive only as long as your conscious self feeds it life energy by believing it is real and identifying with it.

As I have explained, human beings on Earth have forgotten their true identity and have become blinded by the consciousness of death. The consciousness of death is based on the illusion of separation from your source, and because everything is created from God's Being and substance – what Mother Mary in her book calls the Ma-ter Light – separation is truly unreal. Yet because of free will, it is possible that self-aware beings can co-create from this state of illusion.

When you co-create based on the consciousness of death, the consciousness of duality, you will inevitably create something that has two opposites. You might recall that when the Serpent tempted Eve in the Garden of Eden, it said:

> 4 And the serpent said unto the woman, Ye shall not surely die:
> 5 For God doth know that in the day ye eat thereof, then your eyes shall be opened, and ye shall be as gods, knowing good and evil. (Genesis, Chapter 3)

The true meaning is that the "tree of the knowledge of good and evil" is a symbol for the duality consciousness, which is – as Maitreya explains in great detail in his book – an inevitable companion of free will. It is God's intent that you – and all other co-creators – should use your co-creative abilities within the overall vision and laws of God, whereby you will magnify all life, causing all of creation to become more. Yet because God gave you free will, God had to give you the option to go against God's law. And here comes a subtle mechanism that I need you to ponder.

God's vision is that all life should grow and become more. God's laws are set up to ensure that no self-aware co-creator ever needs to experience lack and suffering. Thus, when you co-create within God's law, you will never experience the conditions that many human beings consider a normal and inevitable part of life, namely limitations, loss and suffering. Why did I say that I am come that all might have life and that they might have it more abundantly? This does not mean that I will give all people the abundant life. The true meaning is that I am come to help people realign themselves with the vision and law of God – which he has written in their inward parts, meaning their higher selves – so they can co-create the kingdom of God instead of continuing to co-create the kingdom of lack.

When you use your co-creative abilities within God's law, you can only magnify all life, which means that you will not only enrich your own life but also the lives of all other people on Earth. The whole becomes more than the sum of its parts, which means that there is abundance for everyone. When you use your creative abilities *outside* of God's vision and laws, you will inevitably create lack, which means that the whole now is less than the sum of its parts. The logical consequence is that there is no longer abundance for everyone, which leads to competition for limited resources. This inevitably leads to a state where some people have – through deceit or violence – taken from others to the point where most people live a life of lack and suffering and a small elite live a privileged life of affluence.

I will later explain this point in greater detail, but I want to plant a seed in your mind. When you create *within* God's law, you affirm the oneness of all life, meaning that there is no conflict between you and other people. By raising yourself and becoming more, you are enriching the whole. You are creating from a state of oneness with all life and with your source, which is what I confirmed when I said, "I and my Father are one." When you step outside of God's law, you step into a realm that is based on separation from the source and separation from other parts of life. In this realm of separation, there cannot be oneness, meaning that instead of oneness, there is a state of division, separation and duality.

The logical consequence is that this realm of duality is characterized by opposites, which is what is truly meant by the expression "the knowledge of good and evil." When you are in oneness – innocence – you have no knowledge of duality, for you think only in terms of oneness. When you lose that innocence, you inevitably become blinded by the consciousness of death, in which everything is seen as being dominated by two opposite polarities, such as life and death, good and evil. And when everything must have an opposite, abundance must have an opposite, which means that lack and suffering suddenly become possible. This opens the possibility of a downward spiral that causes people to create more and more lack and suffering.

The inevitable conclusion is that humankind has collectively co-created all of the imperfect conditions you currently find on Earth, including all lack and suffering. These conditions were *not* – as many religions claim – created by God, thus they are neither God's will nor God's punishment. Although these conditions were created by using God's substance, they were not created in alignment with God's vision and God's laws. Thus, they have only a temporary existence, meaning that they are ultimately unreal.

***

Here comes a truth that I need you to fixate in your mind so you never forget it. I want you to contemplate this statement so that if I woke you up at four o-clock in the morning and asked you, "What is the basic truth of life?" you would be able to repeat it to me. Yet more than that, I want you to internalize this truth and keep contemplating it until it penetrates all aspects of your being. Here is the basic truth about life:

**That which is *unreal* cannot affect that which is *real!***

Now compare this statement to what I said above. There is a part of you which is real, namely your conscious self. Because this self is real, it cannot – in any way, shape or form – be affected by the imperfect conditions currently found on Earth! Although these conditions might seem very real, they actually have no power whatsoever over the conscious self. It is comparable to the sun, which is unaffected by anything that happens on Earth.

I need you to ponder this statement very carefully. You might fear many conditions on Earth, but these conditions are ultimately unreal. And since your conscious self is real, it does not make sense that the unreal conditions on Earth can affect that part of you which is real.

Do you see that this is why you have nothing to fear but fear itself? Fear is a feeling that paralyzes you by making you afraid to take a closer look at what you fear. Thus, you cannot come to see that what you fear is unreal and cannot affect that part of you which is real. Do you now see why it is so absolutely essential that a disciple of Christ comes to understand why fear itself is the only thing to be feared?

What is the consequence of fear? It is that it diverts your attention from cause to effect. You probably have certain conditions you fear, and thus your attention becomes focused on these conditions. Thereby, your attention is very effectively diverted from focusing on the fear itself. You are fooled into thinking that the cause of your fear is the outer condition that you – supposedly – fear. Thus, your focus is cleverly diverted from your psyche, away from the beam in your own eye. Instead, you focus attention on avoiding the outer condition, thinking that if you can eliminate the threat or protect yourself from it, your fear will go away. Yet in reality this is a lie, and let me explain why.

If you will contemplate fear, you will see that fear always has an element of uncertainty. For example, you might fear a certain condition, such as illness or losing a job. Yet most people find that when they actually face the condition they fear – when the uncertainly has been replaced by the certainty that the condition cannot be avoided – they shift from fear to a deep inner acceptance of the inevitability of the condition. And through that acceptance, their fear is dissolved, empowering them to deal with the condition in such a way that it leads to profound spiritual growth.

Do you see my point? Only as long as there is room for uncertainty is there room for fear. Once certainty has been achieved, the fear evaporates and thus people overcome their fear. It is a common realization that the best way to *overcome* your fear is to *face* your fear, meaning that when you experience the condition you fear, you realize it wasn't actually as bad as what you feared. In other words, the fear itself was worse than the actual condition, and this proves that it is not actually the condition that is the cause of the fear. The real cause of the fear has to be found somewhere else, for it is not located in outer conditions.

Now let us take the next logical step. Where is fear located? You might fear the loss of a job, and that condition is outside of you. Yet the fear is not *outside* of you; it is *inside* your mind, inside your psyche. Fear is a psychological condition, so is it not logical that the real cause of fear must be found inside the psyche itself?

I know that while this might seem logical, you have been programmed to accept that psychological conditions are caused by external conditions. Yet as we go through this course, you will gradually begin to understand that this is a lie perpetrated upon you – and upon humankind – by those who want to control you. Other people can control you only from the outside, so they must make you believe that outside conditions have power over you, including having power over your psyche. And while this belief is very persuasive on Earth, walking the spiritual path is a process of unmasking it for the lie that it is. However, let us not get too far ahead of ourselves; let us look at the inner mechanism that is the real cause of fear.

***

Before we look at the psychological cause of fear, let me clarify what I mean when I talk about the psyche. I mean a part of your being which is beyond the body and the physical brain, but there is more to it. Let me quickly summarize how Mother Mary and Maitreya have described the totality of your being in their books.

Your total being can be compared to a figure-eight with an upper and a lower part. The upper part represents your higher self or spiritual self, what we often call your I AM Presence. This is a part of your being which is permanently residing in the spiritual realm. The spiritual realm is made of energy of a much higher vibration than what you find in the material universe. Thus, your I AM Presence cannot in any way be affected negatively by anything you have done or experienced on Earth. No matter what mistakes you might have made, it has had no impact whatsoever on your I AM Presence. Your Presence is as pure and as perfect as when it was first created. Your Higher Being also contains your causal body, which is a storehouse for all of the positive, life-supporting experiences (meaning they were in alignment with God's laws) you have had on Earth. I referred to this in the following quote:

> 19 Lay not up for yourselves treasures upon Earth, where moth and rust doth corrupt, and where thieves break through and steal:
> 20 But lay up for yourselves treasures in heaven, where neither moth nor rust doth corrupt, and where thieves do not break through nor steal:
> 21 For where your treasure is, there will your heart be also.
> (Matthew, Chapter 6)

Your life-supporting experiences all become part of this causal body in which they can never be lost, meaning that you can never lose the ability to make use of them—as long as you are connected to your Higher Being.

The figure-eight also has a nexus, a meeting point between the upper and lower figure. This is where your conscious self resides, or at least where it is meant to reside. When your conscious self is centered in the nexus, it sees both the upper and the lower figure, which means that it can never forget that it is a spiritual being who is only temporarily expressing itself through the lower being and the body on Earth. Furthermore, by being connected to your I AM Presence, your conscious self will have dominion over your lower being and your outer circumstances. You will *be* the Living Christ on Earth, and thus God can work through you, as I described in the following quotes:

> I can of mine own self do nothing. (John 5:30)
>
> My Father worketh hitherto, and I work. (John 5:17)
>
> With men this is impossible; but with God all things are possible. (Matthew 19:26)

Take note that the nexus is one point, a singularity, meaning that you must be of one mind, you must have an undivided mind, in order to remain in the nexus. Once you allow your mind to be divided by the illusion of separation and the dualistic images, the conscious self will inevitably "fall" into the lower part of the figure-eight from which it can no longer see the upper part. There are two important things to understand about the conscious self:

- It is the seat of your imagination and your free will.
- Its primary task is to build your sense of identity as a co-creator with God in the material world. It creates the sense of identity that is the foundation for your creative expression in this world.

The practical implications of this are that your conscious self has the ability to imagine who and what it is, and it has the will to accept any given identity. In other words, at any given moment the conscious self literally is who it thinks it is. If it identifies itself as a spiritual being who is a co-creator, the conscious self will remain in the nexus even while expressing itself in this world. It is then *in* the world but not *of* the world.

Yet the conscious self also has the ability to imagine a lesser sense of identity and to identify itself fully with it. When the conscious self builds and accepts a sense of identity that is partly or fully based on duality, it cannot remain in the nexus. It inevitably descends into the lower part of the figure-eight, which means that it – partly or wholly – loses sight of your I AM Presence, even loses all memory of its origin in the spiritual realm. It may even deny that the spiritual realm exists.

This then brings us to the lower part of the figure-eight, which we might call your container of self, the psyche or even the soul (as is commonly done in spiritual teachings).

***

Here comes the essential realization that the forces of this world do not want you to understand or accept. I earlier used the analogy of the white light in a movie projector that takes on the colors and shapes that are on the filmstrip. When you build a sense of identity that is based on duality – a mortal self – it resides in the lower part of the figure-eight. Your conscious self can project itself into that lower part and experience the world through the filter of the mortal self. If it completely identifies itself with the mortal identity, it forgets its spiritual origin and inevitably comes to feel trapped in that mortal self. It might even believe that it *is* an evil or bad person because of the mistakes made through the mortal self.

Yet here is the essential reality. Your conscious self cannot be permanently affected by anything in this world or in the lower part of your being. Your conscious self is still as pure as the white light in the projector. You may temporarily identify yourself as a human being, but in reality you are more, which means that you can always return to your true identity. Even if you identify yourself as a human being, your conscious self has not *become* a human being. You are simply letting the white light of your being shine through a filmstrip that portrays you *as* a human being. If you look only at the movie screen – the appearances of the material world – you might believe there is nothing more to your identity than what you see on the screen. Yet you still have the ability to step out of that identity and experience that there is more to your total being.

We might say that there are two aspects to your identity. One is the spiritual identity that is anchored in your I AM Presence, the other is the temporary identity that you use to express yourself in this world. You were created with a certain spiritual identity, but you have added to it through your life-supporting experiences and decisions over many embodiments. Yet what is anchored in your I AM Presence – your treasure laid up in heaven – cannot be destroyed by anything in this world (because it resides in a realm of higher vibrations that makes it untouchable to any of the forces of this world). The temporary identity that you have created can be either *in* alignment with your spiritual identity or it can be *out of* alignment with it. One way to describe the path to personal Christhood is to say that it is a process of bringing your temporary identity into alignment with your spiritual identity, so you are no longer a house divided against itself.

How can you return to your true identity? It is a two-fold process of un-creating the mortal sense of identity while at the same time creating a spiritual sense of identity for how you express yourself in this world. Paul called it putting off the *old* man and putting on the *new* man (Ephesians 4:22-24). By doing this, you are not left in a vacuum with no identity (which the conscious self finds very difficult to handle). We might say that the light in the movie projector has forgotten that it is the pure light and has come to identify itself with the images that are projected onto the screen. In order to change what is projected onto the screen – meaning your outer, material circumstances – you must first become aware that the images are only projections of what is on the filmstrip—which is located in your psyche.

We might also say that your current sense of mortal or human identity forms a filmstrip that obscures another filmstrip, namely the spiritual identity that is anchored in your I AM Presence. This is a combination of the individuality that you were endowed with at your birth as a spiritual being and the individuality you have built – upon the rock of Christ – in past lifetimes. Thus, by removing the mortal filmstrip, you will not end up with an empty container. Instead, your spiritual identity will begin to shine through—as it is already doing in some situations.

You can now start the gradual process of erasing some of the images that are based on duality while replacing them with images that are based on the truth of Christ. This will cause you to project purer images onto the filmstrip – the Ma-ter Light – which means you will inevitably experience better material circumstances. When you change the filmstrip, you inevitably change the images on the screen. When you change the cause, you inevitably change the effect, when you change the action, you change the *re*action. We now see that the process of rising to the Christ consciousness is taking place largely in the lower part of your being, which we can also call your container of self.

The image of a container is fruitful because it illustrates that you have a container of your lower being, and your conscious self has chosen to allow certain elements from the material world to enter and accumulate. Thus, raising your consciousness is a matter of evaluating the contents of the container of self, purifying the container of imperfect images and beliefs while improving what can be improved. It is like spring cleaning. Some things need to be organized better, others need to be repaired and still others simply need to be thrown out.

What has all this got to do with fear? Well, if you are afraid to take a look at the contents in the container of self, how can you ever purify those contents? We now have the foundation for understanding where fear comes from, or rather which part of your lower being is the cause of fear.

***

I have said it several times, but have you fully grasped the essential truth:

- Your conscious self is real.
- That which is real cannot be affected by that which is unreal, meaning that your conscious self cannot be affected by any imperfect conditions on Earth.
- If your conscious self cannot be affected by any of these conditions, why would it – you – fear anything on Earth?

What I am actually saying here is that your conscious self truly cannot be afraid of anything. Yet then why do *you* have fear in your being?

Well, the answer is that there is a part of your being which is capable of being afraid of the things of this world, and that part is – of course – your ego. Yet do you understand why the ego fears the conditions of this world? It is because the ego is *not* created out of God's Being, and thus the ego has no ultimate reality. The ego is made from the vibrations, the energies, of the material world—and so are the outer conditions you see in this world. Therefore, your ego can indeed be affected by these conditions, which is why it fears them. The ego knows that external conditions have power over it.

Do you see the essential difference? Your conscious self is made from the higher, spiritual vibrations of God's being, and thus it cannot be affected by the lower, material vibrations of this world. Consequently, nothing from this world can touch your conscious self.

Do you understand why this is so? A sunbeam is made from light that vibrates at a higher frequency than mud. Mud – contrary to what your senses and everyday experience tells you – is also made from light – energy – only it has a much lower vibration than sunlight. Thus, you can throw mud at a sunbeam all day long without making it dirty. The mud – made of grosser vibrations – simply passes through the sunbeam without even touching it.

In contrast, the ego is made from the vibrations of the material world. Thus, it can indeed be affected by these vibrations, meaning that your ego can literally be hurt by some of the energies in the material world. Obviously, mud will not cling to your ego, but certain mental and emotional energies will, and we will later take a closer look at these energies.

Let us take another look at the concept that because the ego is made from the energies of the material world, it has reason to fear some of the imperfect conditions in this world. This means that it is understandable that the ego has fears. Yet no matter how understandable this is, a disciple of Christ needs to rise above these fears, and here is how this can be done.

The question is how the conscious self – who has no need to fear anything – can come to actually feel – or rather *believe* that it feels – fear? The reason is – as I explained earlier – that your conscious self has as its task to create a sense of identity for how you interact with this world. If the conscious self is centered in the nexus, it will retain its connection to the I AM Presence, and thus it will know it is above and beyond anything in this world, meaning it has nothing to fear. Yet when the conscious self begins to create a sense of identity that is based on duality, then it gradually forgets its spiritual nature.

Your ego – the mortal identity – forms the equivalent of a piece of colored glass, and when you shine a sunbeam through glass, it takes on the color of the glass. This illustrates that your conscious self can choose to look at the world through the colored glasses of the ego, and thus it can – temporarily – come to see the world as the ego sees it and thus take on – temporarily – the ego's fear. Yet while the ego can never escape its fear, the conscious self can escape this fear by reconnecting to who it is, whereby it will no longer be looking through the filter of the ego.

What actually happens is that a mortal, human, limited self is created, a self that lives in the lower part of the figure-eight, your container of self. We will later talk more about how this self is built, but for now the important point is that this mortal self is – by its very nature – afraid of the imperfections in this world. So when the conscious self begins to identify itself with – identify itself *as* – this mortal self, it will look upon the world through the filter of the mortal self—similar to a person wearing colored glasses. The conscious self will now look upon the world as a dangerous place with many imperfect conditions that can hurt it. One common effect of this is that you begin to fear that what can hurt your physical body can actually hurt YOU. That is one reason why I said:

> And fear not them which kill the body, but are not able to kill the soul: but rather fear him which is able to destroy both soul and body in hell. (Matthew 10:28)

This statement is – however – incomplete as quoted in present-day Bibles. Part of the meaning is that you should not fear those who can harm your body, for you are *more* than your body—meaning that the Conscious You should not fear anything in this world. The deeper meaning is that you *should* be concerned about him who can destroy the soul. Yet who can destroy the soul? Well, in reality only the conscious self can destroy your soul, and the reason is that the Conscious You has created the soul. I know that many people believe the devil or other dark forces have power over their souls, but this is a belief that must be understood from a higher perspective. If you know who you are, nothing in this world has any power over you. If your conscious self is in the nexus, it will be the gatekeeper of what enters your container of self. And since it will also have the discernment of Christ, it can keep out all elements of duality.

Yet if you have created a mortal self and if your conscious self identifies itself with that mortal self, then the ego becomes the gatekeeper to what enters your container of self. The ego does not have the discernment of Christ, because it is built from the consciousness of duality and thus cannot see through its illusions. Therefore, if you let the ego guard your mind, the forces of this world *do* have power over you. When you look at the world through the dualistic filter, you cannot see the unreality of the illusions of anti-christ, and thus the forces of this world can enter your container of self. Yet you can break that power by shifting your identification away from the *mortal* self and toward your *immortal* self, your I AM Presence.

Let me make it clear that the forces of this world do not have direct power over you. They have only an indirect power because you are the only one who can change your sense of identity. Yet if your conscious self identifies itself with the ego, it will think the ego's fears are real, and thus the forces of this world can manipulate you into changing your sense of identity. Yet the moment you see through the ego's illusions, the forces of this world can no longer influence you.

As an illustration, imagine you are at a tourist attraction and there are a number of telescopes for viewing the scenery. One of the telescopes has clear lenses while all of the others have lenses that are colored or distorted. Your conscious self has the choice of looking through the distorted lenses or the clear one. Is it not obvious that the way your conscious self sees the world will depend on which filter it is looking through?

***

The implications of this are many, but let me focus on one. If you take an honest look at humankind, you will see that many people – even some of the seemingly richest and most powerful people – spend their entire lives trying to protect themselves from what they fear. Their entire lives are literally controlled by their fears. What is truly happening to these people is that they have been fooled by the prince of this world into focusing their attention on the effects rather than on the cause.

Why did I earlier explain that humankind has created all of the imperfect conditions on Earth? I did so in order to help you realize that the conditions you might fear are ultimately the effects of an underlying, unseen cause. That cause is the fact that people have collectively used their co-creative abilities to create through the consciousness of duality. Thus, what you see on Earth – in the form of imperfect conditions – are the effects – the images projected upon the movie screen – of the underlying cause, namely the images on the filmstrip of the collective psyche.

We might say that human beings have collectively created the imperfect conditions on Earth, but because they are unaware of this, they think the conditions they face are real and are the result of external forces over which they have no control. Instead of being co-creators who have dominion over the Earth, they have allowed their own creation to take dominion over them—as Doctor Frankenstein's monster eventually killed him. My mission – including my miracles – was an attempt to demonstrate to people that their minds do have power over the material universe.

As a result of their blindness, people are trapped in a catch-22 of seeking to overcome the conditions they fear by controlling the external world. Yet because they focus on the external conditions, they cannot see that the conditions are the effects of their own state of consciousness. Thus, they seek to change the *external* world instead of seeking to change their own *internal* worlds. They focus on the world *outside* themselves instead of removing the beam in their own eyes. They do not see that the splinter in the eye of another is only a reflection of the beam in their own eye.

The effect is that people are trapped in an ego-game of seeking to attain some form of ultimate control over their environment, meaning other people, their society, even the physical planet. Consider how some of the most powerful people from history have been obsessed with controlling everything and everyone around them. Can you see that even though these people had great power on Earth, they were not truly powerful people? They were driven to seek power out of a need for control, and that need sprang from the fears centered in their egos. Thus, the greater the drive people have to seek Earthly power, the more they are controlled by their fear. In reality, some of the most powerful people in history have been the weakest. Real power is to control yourself so you are not driven by the ego's fears and tossed. As the old saying goes, it is greater to conquer yourself than to conquer a city. Or as I said, what shall it profit a man to gain the whole world if he has not gained control over his own soul and thus is still ruled by his own fears?

You now have a choice to make. You can spend the rest of your life – and many future lifetimes – engaging in this never-ending game of seeking to protect yourself from outer conditions, thinking that if you attain some perfect condition, your fears will go away. Or you can decide to become a disciple of Christ, which means that you no longer run away from your fears but face them head-on and walk right through them by seeing them as the illusions they are. I trust you will choose the latter possibility, so let us see what it will take to overcome your fear.

***

There is only one way for you to overcome fear and that is to see it as unreal, as the result of illusions. Yet the ego can never do this, for it is not capable of realizing that its very own existence springs from illusions. Thus, the ego will never see that what it fears is nothing but illusions. The consequence is that only the conscious self can overcome fear. Yet this cannot be done by working with the conditions in *this* world. No matter how ideal of an outer situation you might create, you still will not overcome fear. The ego will – by its very nature – fear the conditions – even the potential conditions – of this world. So the reality of the situation is that your conscious self must come to the point where it experiences that it is more than the ego, and thus it stops identifying itself with – seeing the world through – the filter created by the ego.

Let me sketch a concept that might help you see the point. I have talked about the mortal self, and this self can be seen as a conglomerate of different sub-personalities, each with its own role. It is almost like your container of self is a theater in which is being performed a play, the play of your life in the material world. Because the ego fears the conditions in the material world – and because it cannot see beyond this world – it seeks to deal with the fear by creating sub-personalities to protect itself from any potential contingency. In other words, the ego creates these roles in the drama of its life, and you might say that the theater of your container of self has all of these predefined roles. Your conscious self can shift from role to role, depending on the outer situation you face. Thus, in different situations, you might see the world slightly differently because you are looking through the filter of a different sub-personality.

My point here is that walking the path to Christhood is the process of disentangling yourself from these different roles and coming to see the world as it really is, meaning that you see through the non-filter of the Christ mind instead of the multiple filters of the mortal self. This is not something that can be done intellectually; it must be the result of a direct experience. However, there are two ways to have such a liberating experience:

- As mentioned earlier, many people have experienced fearing a certain condition for years, yet when they finally experience the condition, reality is not nearly as bad as what they feared. Or in some cases, reality *is* as bad as they feared, but the certainty of facing reality dissolves their fears. In any case, the experience of the actual condition dissolves the fear, which can either take people into a positive spiral of spiritual growth or a negative spiral of anger, a sense of injustice or feeling sorry for themselves.

  Yet the larger point here is that one way to overcome a particular fear is to actually experience the condition you fear. Once you confront the condition, you confront your fear and can thus overcome it. The problem with overcoming your fears this way is that it can be quite painful and time-consuming. There are numerous – in fact innumerable – conditions that the ego can fear, and one lifetime only lasts a finite amount of time, so there isn't time to confront all of your fears this way. Fortunately, there is a better way.

- Even when you experience the actual, physical condition you fear, the liberation from fear is actually the result of an inner experience, what is often called an "Aha-experience." You literally see or experience that your fear was unreal and you instantly, spontaneously, decide to let it go.

  As I have mentioned, an essential part of the path to Christhood is to realize that there is no inevitable link between outer conditions and what is going on in your psyche. Thus, you do not need to actually experience the

> condition you fear, for you can confront and overcome your fear entirely as the result of an internal process.
>
> You can confront your fears in the mind – which is where they originated and reside – instead of taking the intermediate step of confronting your fears by experiencing the condition you fear. In other words, you can realize that the fear is not caused by the external condition you fear but is created in the mind and must therefore be *uncreated* in the mind.

How do you start this internal process? It requires an act of willpower so that the conscious self overcomes the ego's built-in tendency to either flee or fight the conditions it fears. Do you see that some people spend their entire lives seeking to run away from the conditions they fear, while others spend their lives fighting those conditions, seeking to gain control over them? Both types of people are controlled by their egos and are not making progress toward Christhood (even if they use religion/spirituality in an attempt to escape or gain control). Why are they not making progress? Because they seek to avoid experiencing the conditions they fear and thus they cannot look at the fear itself.

We might say that you can overcome your fears in two ways, namely through the school of hard knocks – by experiencing the conditions you fear – or the internal way, by confronting your fears through a process of self-examination. Some people identify with their egos and thus have no other option than to run from or fight their fears. They can make spiritual progress only by actually experiencing the condition they fear, and since the universe is a mirror, they will often attract to them exactly what they fear. In fact, many spiritual people have – before coming into embodiment – vowed to overcome certain fears. And if they – after being blinded by their outer conditions – cannot do it the internal way, they will subconsciously want to do it the external way. Thus, many people will actually attract to them the conditions they fear most—out of a subconscious desire to be free of the fear and thus make significant spiritual progress.

My point here is that as a disciple of Christ, you simply do not have time to overcome your fears the external way. Thus, you must actively build a habit of confronting your fears through an internal process. And this begins by reaching for a higher will than the will of your ego or outer mind.

***

I will now describe a universal approach to dealing with limiting emotions. This is a technique you *can* – and *will* – use to deal with all types of limiting emotions, starting with fear and moving on to anger, hatred, non-forgiveness and so on. Here are the steps you need to take:

## Step 1

Recognize that you have fear (or whatever emotion). This is an important step, and it is often overlooked by spiritual seekers, especially those who have been on the path for a long time and feel they should be above certain emotions. The brutal fact is that if you are reading this course, you have – to some degree – fear and other limiting emotions. How can I say this? Because if you were above all such feelings, you would have attained mastery and thus you would not be reading this course.

I want you to understand that the ego is constantly trying to make you deny that you have a problem, and the reason is that this denial prevents you from dealing with the problem. As any psychologist will tell you, you cannot overcome a limitation until you acknowledge that you have a problem. Why is it that so many addicts have to "hit bottom" before they begin to recover? Because hitting bottom is actually the experience of finally acknowledging that they have a problem and that only *they* can do something about it. Before hitting bottom they were in a state of denial, either denying that they had a problem or denying that they could and should do something about it.

The simple fact is that in order to overcome a limiting feeling, you need to let it go, to surrender it. Yet it is a basic fact that you cannot give away what you do not own. As long as you have not taken ownership of a feeling – by acknowledging that it has gained entry into your container of self – you simply cannot give it away. And thus it will keep lurking in the shadows, from where it will drag you down. Many so-called spiritual people have simply compartmentalized their container of self and stuffed all unwanted feelings into a dark corner that they never look at and thus – at the surface level of their waking consciousness – have deluded themselves into thinking it doesn't exist. Yet I am expecting those who want to be disciples of the Living Christ to be willing to look for the beam in their own eyes—rather than seeking to define it out of existence.

There is no shame in admitting that you have fear, for it is virtually impossible to embody on this planet – in its current, highly imperfect state – and not be affected by fear (or other emotions). It sort of comes with the territory; it is part of being human. But now it is time to be MORE than human, and that begins by taking ownership of your human imperfections so you can give them away.

## Step 2

After you recognize that you *have* fear, you must acknowledge that you *are* not the fear—you are MORE than the fear. In other words, the fear is *not* your total being and thus it must *not* be allowed to control your attention or define your sense of identity. As I have said, your conscious self is a spiritual being, and you should know logically that there is no fear in the spiritual realm. Thus, fear cannot come from your I AM Presence, it can only come from the lower part of your being, namely your ego.

You already know that you are more than your physical body – or you would not be open to the path to Christhood – and so it is simple to take the next step and realize you are more than your fear, even more than the beliefs that give rise to the fear. However, to really take this step, you need to connect to a higher part of your being, namely your I AM Presence. You need to recognize – and actually experience – that you are so much more than your fear or the condition you fear. You have a greater purpose for being on Earth than to experience this fear. You did not come to this planet because you wanted to be crippled by fear, and thus you need to experience the infinite drive that caused you to come into embodiment. You need to truly experience that you have an important mission in this lifetime and that you simply will not let these unreal fears stand in the way of that mission. Your mission is real and you will not let unreality prevent you from fulfilling your reason for being. You will not let the shadows scare you into not shining your light—the light that is meant to consume all shadows on Earth.

How do you connect to this greater self? Partly through understanding and partly through the exercises I am giving you. The rosaries I am having you give are designed to help you re-connect to your Higher Being and then bring the insights and Light of your Higher Being into your container of self, where it can dispel the illusions and consume the imperfect energies that have accumulated there.

## Step 3

You must now consciously acknowledge that there is a fundamental difference between the condition you fear and the fear itself. You must understand that the fear is not a *material* condition but a *psychological* condition. The fear is not caused by the external condition, and thus you should not confuse cause and effect. You will never overcome a problem as long as you focus on the effect – the material condition – rather than the cause—the psychological origin of the fear. Thus, you can now take your attention off the external conditions and start looking for the real cause, namely the conditions in your psyche that hold the key to overcoming the fear.

You need to make the decision that you will take responsibility for your container of self. You do this by realizing that the conscious self is above material conditions, and thus no material conditions can truly affect you. You can then take command over your reactions to outer conditions, which means you can choose your reaction instead of allowing it to be determined by a preprogrammed response from one of the sub-personalities created by your ego. This is taking back dominion over your inner world of the self, and it is an essential step on the path to Christhood. How can you be the Christ, if you do not have dominion over your reactions to outer circumstances?

### Step 4

You now need to understand that fear – or any emotion – has two aspects. Everything is energy, and emotion is energy in motion. Thus, fear is a specific type of energy that has a specific vibration or frequency. There will come a point when science will be able to measure all emotions and even display a visual image of your energy field (your container of self), thereby making it easy to see what types of emotional energies have accumulated there. Yet for now, you simply need to recognize that a feeling has produced a certain amount of energy that has accumulated in your container of self, from where it exerts a magnetic pull on your emotions and your thoughts. Thus, this accumulated energy will intensify your feelings and – in the case of fear – make you more afraid to look at what you fear.

For many people their fear is so intense that they are afraid to acknowledge that they have fear or afraid to look at what they fear. Obviously, you are not in that category, or you would not be reading this course. Yet you can still make it easier for yourself to deal with fear by taking practical measures to reduce the magnetic pull of the fear energy in your energy field. You do this in a very simple way, namely by recognizing – as science has already discovered – that a wave of low-frequency energy can be changed by interacting with a wave of high-frequency energy. So the way to diminish the pull of accumulated fear is to invoke high-frequency spiritual energy and direct it into the fear energy in your energy field. This is precisely what Mother Mary's rosaries are designed to do, which is why I am having you give a rosary for each key.

### Step 5

You now need to recognize the other aspect of emotion. For as emotion is energy in motion, something needs to set that energy in motion, and that "something" is a belief. This belief resides in your thoughts, and it is a belief that is based on a dualistic illusion—which is why it sets energy in motion that has a low frequency and thus limits you.

Let me briefly refer back to my illustration of the figure-eight between your higher and lower being. What sustains your lower being is a stream of spiritual energy that flows from your I AM Presence into your container of self, where it becomes directed by your attention. It is your beliefs and attitudes about life that determine how that energy is directed. If you have beliefs that are based on the reality of Christ, you will use the energy to magnify yourself and all life, which means that it flows back up and becomes your treasure laid up in heaven. However, this returning energy – your multiplication of the talents – also forms the basis for your I AM Presence and spiritual teachers multiplying what you have used correctly, thus releasing more energy to you.

In contrast, when you have beliefs based on the duality of antichrist, you qualify the energy with a low vibration that cannot flow back up. Thus, this energy will accumulate in your container of self, and it will eventually gain more "mass" or strength to the point where it can affect – or even take over – your thoughts and feelings. For many people this has become a self-reinforcing spiral, where the accumulated energy pulls them into misqualifying more energy (you always receive a certain minimum amount to keep you alive), and they have lost control over their lives.

Obviously, part of breaking that self-reinforcing spiral is to invoke spiritual energy to consume the accumulated toxic energy. However, if you only invoke energy without dealing with the belief that causes you to misqualify energy, you will not break out of the spiral. You will simply misqualify energy as quickly as you purify it, and thus you are treading water or you are sliding two steps backward for each step you take forward. So to fully break the spiral, you need to look at the belief that is causing you to misqualify energy. You need to see that it is based on a dualistic illusion, and then you need to let go of that illusion, replacing it with the reality of Christ.

This requires you to do what I talked about earlier, namely to mentally confront your fear—without having to experience what you fear. You need to take a close look at the fear and what it is you actually fear. You need to discover the underlying belief, and then you need to understand why it springs from a dualistic illusion. You can do this by studying spiritual teachings, even by giving the rosaries, which contain affirmations that challenge your dualistic beliefs.

Yet you *must* understand that whereas purifying misqualified energy is a relatively mechanical process, overcoming an imperfect belief is *not* a mechanical process. I cannot give you a teaching that – by the mere fact that you read it – will automatically resolve your beliefs. You are the one who made a decision to accept that belief – which might have happened many lifetimes ago – and you are the one who must look at that original decision and replace it with a better decision. No one can do this *for* you, and this is why the path to Christhood is so demanding—it demands that you make an effort to uncover the beam in your own eye, to see what you cannot see.

What I *can* do for you is to challenge you to re-evaluate your beliefs, to question what you have not questioned. Yet if *I* could save you, you would – I can assure you – have been saved a very long time ago.

## Summary

Let me summarize what I am talking about. To use a simple example, let us look at the common childhood fear of the dark. What actually happens here is that a child builds an entire sub-personality – a role in the theater of your container of self – that is designed to deal with the fear of the dark. This personality is sustained by the energy that is misqualified by the fear, and the amount of accumulated energy will determine how much power the fear has over the child's conscious mind.

How did you overcome your childhood fear of the dark? Perhaps you went into a dark room, experienced that there were no monsters that came out to eat you and then decided that the fear was unreal and you would no longer allow it to have power over your mind? Perhaps you did this mentally by realizing that it simply didn't make sense that there were invisible monsters in a dark room or under your bed. So you did the same thing – dismiss the fear – without the actual, physical experience. In other words, the essence of overcoming a fear is to dismiss it as unreal, whereby you separate yourself from the sub-personality that was built to deal with the fear—whether deliberately dissolving it or allowing it to eventually atrophy for lack of energy. Here is a summary of the steps:

- Recognize that you have fear. Take ownership of your fear as a foundation for giving it away.
- Acknowledge that you *are* not the fear—you are MORE than the fear.
- Separate the condition you fear from the fear itself. See that the real cause is the psychological condition.
- Use a spiritual technique to transform the energy of fear that has accumulated in your energy field.
- Uncover the belief behind the fear, meaning the psychological condition that is the real cause of the fear (as opposed to the external condition you fear). See that this belief is based on a dualistic illusion and dismiss the illusion by replacing it with the non-dualistic truth of Christ.

***

Here is what I really want you to understand. One could say that there are only two basic emotions, namely love and fear. You are designed to be an open door for God's love and light to stream into this world. When your energy system is functioning according to its original design, the love of God flows unhindered from your I AM Presence into your lower being, where it is expressed through all of your activities. Yet when you go into the dualistic state of mind, you begin to believe that you cannot or should not express love in every situation. You begin to believe that you should only express love when specific conditions are met, and this causes you to start withholding love, to actually shut off the flow of God's love through your being.

There is a lot of anti-love in this world, and you will inevitably be exposed to it, which means some of that anti-love energy will enter your energy field. However, if your energy flow was in its natural state, the love from your I AM Presence would simply consume any anti-love before it could start accumulating. Yet the moment you start obstructing that flow, you disable that natural defense mechanism, and now lower energies will start accumulating—both as a result of what comes in from the outside and what you misqualify through your limiting emotions. That is why you need to use a spiritual technique to reestablish or reinforce that flow by deliberately invoking spiritual energy.

Do you understand what I am saying here? Fear is a specific type of low-frequency energy, and the natural way to overcome it is to consume it by allowing the opposite of fear to flow through your being. If you do this, you can live in this imperfect world without being touched by its imperfections—they simply will not be able to gain a foothold in your container of self. So your ego and the forces of this world trick you into shutting off the flow of love through your being, and they do so by making you believe in the dualistic lie that you should express love only when certain conditions are met—conditions that are rarely met in this unloving world.

The primary condition that causes you to shut off the flow of God's love is fear. The false teachers want you to believe that before you can express love, you must be free of fear, but since the ego will never be free of fear, you will never attain that condition. Which explains why many people are not letting God's love flow through them. It is the love that will consume their fears, but they think they cannot let love flow until they are free of fear—another catch-22.

Do you see that this is how you have been tricked into creating your own downward spiral? Do you see that it is time to break that spiral? And do you see that the *only* way to do so is to reestablish the natural flow of spiritual energy through your being? Do you also see that this can be done only by overcoming – one by one during a gradual process that is quite doable for anyone willing to make an effort – the blocks that stop or pervert this natural flow?

What is the opposite of fear or any other limiting emotion? It is love, but not human, conditional love. Look at this quote from the Bible:

> There is no fear in love; but perfect love casteth out fear: because fear hath torment. He that feareth is not made perfect in love. (1John 4:18)

Perfect love is God's unconditional love, which consumes all unlike itself and thus consumes all imperfect emotional energies. The expression that fear has torment means that you are in fear only because you have come to accept dualistic beliefs. These beliefs have built-in contradictions and opposing polarities, which pull you in different directions and thus make you a house – a psyche – divided against itself. Duality implies two opposing polarities, which means there is always an opposite to any quality—and thus there is always something to fear.

The way out is to "be made perfect in love" which means to overcome all of the dualistic conditions that cause you to shut off the flow of God's unconditional love through your being. What is the relationship between love and will power? When you have God's love flowing through you, you will effortlessly have the will to overcome any condition that limits you and prevents you from fulfilling your reason for being. Yet how do you get love to flow? You must start with an act of will, and that initial act of will must be based on the love you already have. How do I know you already have love? How else would you have been willing to study this course? So begin by recognizing that you have love and then turn it into a decision to confront your fears, gradually building a momentum that will take you beyond *all* of your fears.

I know that at this early point in your walk toward Christhood, this might seem like an abstract or unattainable goal. Yet I want to plant a seed in your mind that will gradually sprout and grow strong. And now I will turn to the more practical aspect of describing the exercise for this particular key.

***

## Exercise for Key 2.

What I want you to do for the next 33 days is to give Mother Mary's Rosary of God's Will[4] once a day. This rosary is designed to help you reconnect to your Higher Being and realize that *you* have a will for this lifetime, a will that is not external to you but is very much your own will, only the will of your total being—as opposed to the limited will of your outer mind and ego. You may already have done this rosary vigil after reading Mother Mary's book, but I am asking you to do it again and focus on opening the flow of will power that you need in order to confront the fears that keep you from moving forward on the path of Christhood.

After giving the rosary, I want you to spend some time meditating on your fears. Perhaps you already know your greatest fears, perhaps you will discover them as you go along. Yet allow yourself to look at one fear a day (perhaps spending several days on a big fear but not tackling more than one fear at a time). Write down what you fear and then seek to uncover the belief behind it, writing everything down as it comes to you. Simply meditate on a fear and

---

[4] See *www.askrealjesus.com* in the Personal Growth section.

write down whatever comes to you. The next day, make a call in the rosary based on your vision and also ask for a clearer vision.

I also want to make you a special offer. As you should know by now, I am not limited by time and space. Thus, no matter where and when you read this course, I am able to manifest my Presence with you if you allow me to enter your being and world. I will offer you that for the next 33 days I will manifest my Presence with you for the specific purpose of helping you confront your fears. So what I am asking you to do is to consider how *I* would look at a specific fear.

Visualize, imagine or experience my Presence with you and then seek to actually experience how I – as an ascended being who is beyond all fear – looks at your particular fear. Then visualize that – with my Presence over you – we go right into the heart of your fear, see it for the illusion it is, see the illusion behind it and see the reality of Christ that replaces that illusion. Finally, experience how we summon the unstoppable will of God and dismiss the fear as the absolute unreality that it is, thereby allowing the unconditional love of God to flow through your being, to flow into the darkest corners of your container of self and consume the misqualified energies as the darkness in a room is instantly consumed when you turn on the light.

As a help in confronting your fears, do the following. Once you have identified a particular fear, consider what would actually happen if what you fear came to pass. In other words, consider how you would deal with it if the worst happened. Yet I want you to consider this in two ways. First consider, and write down, how you would deal with it in your state of seeing yourself as a mortal, human being. Then consider how you would deal with the same situation in your state of knowing you are an immortal spiritual being who has the unlimited power of God to deal with any condition. If it helps you, envision my Presence over you and consider how *I* would deal with that condition if I was in your place.

Take note that I am not simply saying to imagine that you have all power and thus can make the condition go away. There are – as I will later explain in more detail – some conditions that you are meant to take on. So I am asking you to imagine how you would – as the spiritual being that you are – deal with the condition in a positive way, so that the condition would not prevent you from feeling at peace and from fulfilling your divine plan. In other words, my purpose is to help you see that no condition can prevent you from fulfilling your divine plan and being who you are, which is why you can dismiss your fear as unreal and unneeded.

I am not asking you to turn this into an elaborate ritual. In fact, I hope that after you get used to the process, you can feel my Presence over you whenever you encounter a fear. You then allow the process to take place, whereby we instantly go into the fear and consume it. If you will build this habit of inviting my Presence to help you consume your fear, you will soon overcome the very subtle fear that there might be a fear you cannot overcome. You will then experience the truth behind the statement that you have nothing to fear but fear itself.

And when you experience that truth, it will dismiss the very core of human fear, namely the fear that fears itself—the ego that fears its own shadow, for it is afraid to take a look at itself and see its own unreality. The ego fears to be no more, but when *you* know you are more than the fear, you will know that letting the fear die will not mean that *you* will die. On the contrary, it means that you will live in the eternal light of Christ Reality.

I am inviting you to share that reality with me!

# Key 3
# Loving yourself free from conditions

One of the important lessons from Mother Mary's book is that God has both a masculine and a feminine side. For disciples of the Living Christ, it is extremely important to contemplate and internalize this teaching, especially given the fact that mainstream Christianity has become part of the so-called monotheistic religions that largely ignore or deny the feminine aspect of God. Thus, you have likely been brought up with little understanding of the feminine aspect of God, possibly programmed to ignore or even degrade it. As Mother Mary explains, God the Creator started by dividing itself into two polarities, which I undeniably explained in the Book of Revelation:

> I am Alpha and Omega, the beginning and the ending, saith the Lord, which is, and which was, and which is to come, the Almighty. (Revelation 1:8)

Everything in the world of form is created from the interplay of these two complementary forces. Yet only when the two forces are in a harmonious balance, will their creation be sustainable. What is designed to balance the two is the Divine Son, namely the Christ mind. This Christ mind has a universal aspect, which unites all life and unites all that is created with the Creator. It also has an individual aspect that can be expressed through any co-creator, even those in embodiment on Earth. I came to demonstrate this potential and also demonstrate that when you become the individual expression of the Christ mind, you become one with both the Creator and with all life. This is embedded in the following quotes:

> I and my Father are one. (John 10:30)

> And the King shall answer and say unto them, Verily I say unto you, Inasmuch as ye have done it unto one of the least of these my brethren, ye have done it unto me. (Matthew 25:40)

Yet because self-aware beings have been given free will, it is possible that they can create by using the masculine and feminine – expansive and contracting, Alpha and Omega, yang and yin – forces in an unbalanced manner. By doing this, co-creators separate themselves from the oneness of all life, seeking to gain advantage for themselves as separate beings rather than seeking to raise up the All—often seeking to raise themselves in comparison to others.

This, of course, can be done only through the mind of anti-christ, which is a mind that is separated from the oneness of all life – the River of Life – and contains two polarities that do not complement and enhance each other but instead cancel out and diminish each other. This makes it possible that you can use one unbalanced polarity to raise yourself while using the other polarity to degrade others.

My purpose for giving you this teaching is to make you aware that in the realm of anti-christ, there are always two opposing polarities. In the previous key, I have had you invoke the higher will of your own being because overcoming fear must begin with an act of will. However, as I also explained in the last lesson, will power itself cannot banish fear, for only the perfect love will cast out fear. So to fully overcome fear, you must allow the unconditional love of God to flow through you, and thus we also need to address the factors that prevent this love from flowing through your being and expressing itself in the material world.

I have said that fear is dangerous because it paralyzes you, so you dare not move, dare not change. Instead, you cling to status quo, even a status quo that causes constant suffering. And since creation starts with an act of will – I will to create – fear is a perversion of will. Yet there are other paralyzing emotions, or one might say that fear has many expressions. Thus, we will next look at a variant of fear that can stop you from stepping onto the path of Christhood, even though you have recognized the path and started to overcome your fear.

***

If you look at mainstream, especially fundamentalist, Christians, you will see that most of these people would be afraid to contemplate the central idea behind this course, namely that all people have the potential to follow in my footsteps and attain the Christ consciousness. So this is a fear that would prevent them from even acknowledging the path to Christhood. They would deny that other people could follow me – thus denying my own words that those who believe on me shall do the works that I did – and they would say that I did not demonstrate a path to Christhood, for I was born in the fullness of that Christhood.

Obviously, *you* have overcome this level of fear. Now, I am not saying this to cause any pride or sense that you are better than others, for it is – as we will discuss in a future key – unnecessary to compare yourself to others based on a value judgment that makes you better or worse than others. However, the concept of a path does imply that you go from step to step, so it is valid to realize that you have risen above some of the lower aspects of the consciousness of death. This gives you a sense of momentum that makes it easier for you to overcome the next challenge.

So what *is* the next challenge? Well, when you have started to overcome the paralyzing aspects of fear and attained some will to experiment with the path to Christhood, you will face the challenge to overcome a set of obstacles that is designed to prevent you from exercising your will. In other words, the most paralyzing fear is meant to prevent you from even attaining the will power to change your life, and the next challenge is meant to prevent you from acting on your determination.

This challenge is the very subtle sense that although you now recognize the path to Christhood as a potential for all people, it doesn't *really* apply to *you*. You simply don't have what it takes to follow the path. You are not smart enough, spiritual enough or worthy. The path is too overwhelming or complicated for you. You have made this or that mistake in the past, and thus you are not worthy to walk the path. Or what if trying to remove the beam in your own eye exposes some incredibly bad flaw in your personality that makes you feel really guilty? You are simply too inferior—who do you think you are to even contemplate that you could follow in Jesus' footsteps?

One can characterize all of these feelings as guilt, but as you can see, there are many nuances. The overall theme being that although you now see the path, *you* are not able or worthy to follow it. In other words, this is an attempt to prevent you from stepping onto the path and accepting yourself as a worthy disciple of the Living Christ.

Where does this attempt come from? It comes from the ego and the consciousness of anti-christ. At this point, you might think of the ego as an active force in your container of self, a force that is always seeking to prevent you from taking the next step on the path of Christhood—because if you do, it will have lost some degree of control over the Conscious You.

In a sense one can say that each step on the path represents a particular illusion or aspect of the ego that the Conscious You needs to overcome. You do so by coming to see it for the illusion that it is, and thus separating yourself from it by realizing that you are MORE than this.

We have now seen that the first step on the path is to overcome the anti-will, and this anti-will is a perversion of the masculine principle. It is God the Father who has the will to create. Yet as I have explained, there are always two polarities, so the masculine perversion of anti-will must have an opposite, or feminine, polarity. And whereas the masculine is the *active* principle, the feminine is the *receiving* principle. So the perversion of anti-will is designed to prevent you from receiving that which you are entitled to receive when you have mustered the will to change—namely the help from above that empowers you to change.

As I explained in the last key, you can overcome fear only through the unconditional love of God. This love is beyond any form of love that can be produced in the material realm, so you simply cannot manufacture it on your own. You can only receive it from the spiritual realm, and the perversion of guilt/inferiority is designed to prevent you from accepting that you are capable of or worthy to receive God's love.

The first line of defense for the ego is to seek to prevent you from gathering the will power to confront your fears. The next line is to seek to prevent you from receiving the perfect love that will fully cast out your fears. In other words, the process of overcoming fear involves both the masculine and feminine aspects. You must gather the will power to confront your fears as a foundation for opening up the flow of love that will truly consume the fears.

Here is where I need you to contemplate something very seriously. If you have grown up in the Western world or in any religion that denies the feminine aspect of God, you have been programmed to approach religion as a passive measure. As I have said, I have been portrayed as the savior who is going to do all the work for you because you are not worthy in yourself. This has programmed you to – subconsciously – deny that you are worthy to receive God's love. As long as you have this programming in your subconscious mind, you will not be able to receive that love and you cannot fully escape your fears. Thus, we need to dispose of that programming, and how can this be done?

The essential key is to realize the full importance of the statement that everything is created from the interplay of the masculine and feminine forces but that a sustainable creation comes about only when the two forces are balanced by the Christ mind. The consequence of this is that any perversion of the two forces is attained through a perversion of the Christ mind, namely the consciousness of anti-christ. Thus, the key to overcoming any perversion of the two forces is to seek for the reality of Christ, which can expose the illusions of anti-christ and thus empower the Conscious You to separate itself from them. It is the truth – of Christ – that will make you free. With all thy getting, get the understanding of Christ.

***

Let us now look at the Christ reality concerning your ability to follow the path to Christhood and your worthiness to receive God's love. To fully understand this, you need to let go of several common illusions, and let us start by discussing the concept of original sin. This is the idea that you were born into a sinful state and thus not worthy of God's love.

Let me make it clear that I did not preach the concept of original sin, and it was indeed a later misinterpretation that gave rise to this idea. However, it is important for you to understand some of the ramifications of the idea because it has affected humankind's self-image in subtle ways.

One of the essential elements of Christ consciousness is the ability and willingness to ask penetrating questions, which empowers you to see the inconsistencies and lack of logic in ideas that most people take for granted and thus never question. In other words, an inescapable part of the path is your willingness to question ideas that you have been brought up – programmed – to accept without ever questioning them. So let us ask a few questions about original sin.

The concept implies that all people are born in an imperfect state, which makes them unworthy of salvation, and this is why they need an external savior, such as myself or an outer church. If we take the traditional Christian belief system, God created your soul shortly before your body was born, and thus your soul has never existed before. So if you are affected by original sin, it would mean that God either created you as a sinner or at least wanted you to start out life in a sinful state.

There are several problems with this line of reasoning. First of all, the traditional Christian view is that God is almighty – and thus perfect – and he is also loving. So it makes no sense that a perfect God would make a mistake and create you as an imperfect sinner. Yet if God didn't make a mistake, it must mean he wants you to be a sinner, and this doesn't sound like a loving God. So something is obviously inconsistent in the entire idea.

The concept of original sin says that since all human beings descended from Adam and Eve, they are affected by the original sin committed by those supposedly first people. Obviously, this is an erroneous concept, as Maitreya explains in great detail in his book. What I want to bring up here is that we have much the same problem as mentioned above. The Bible does not say that Adam and Eve were created as sinners, but unless God created them with a propensity to sin, how can we explain that they actually sinned? And why would a perfect and loving God create the first people with this propensity to sin?

Traditional and fundamentalist Christianity has no answers to this, but the obvious answer is that God did not create anyone with a propensity to sin. However, all self-aware beings are given free will, which gives them the *option* to go against God's laws. So we now see that Adam and Eve sinned because they used their free will to make a choice. We can also see that they did not actually make a *free* choice, for they were deceived by the Serpent and thus did not truly know what they were doing and did not understand the consequences. Again, Maitreya explains this in greater detail, but my point is that we now see that sin is not a condition created by God. It is the result of people using their free will while under the influence of the consciousness of anti-christ.

We can now see that if you were born into sin because of a choice made by two people thousands of years ago, this would actually be a violation of the principle of free will. You see, free will necessitates that you are created as a separate individual who is not inherently affected by the choices of other people. So if you were born into sin because of the choice made by Adam and Eve, you would not have been born with free will. *They* had the choice to stay away from sin, but *you* did not. Obviously, this would be a clear violation of the principle of free will.

Why is all this important? Because when we add reincarnation, we can now see that you might have been born with certain imperfections in this life, but they were not the result of some original sin. Instead, your particular karmic circumstances are the results of choices you made in past lifetimes. The essential implication of this is that you are not the helpless victim of some unjust God or of the choices of other people. You are the author and finisher of your own destiny, and thus no matter what mistakes you have made in the past, you have the potential to rise above them.

How can I say that? Because if your past mistakes were caused by anyone outside yourself – be it God, other people or the abominable snowman – there would be nothing you could do about it. You would be at the mercy of external forces. Yet if your mistakes were the results of choices *you* made, then *you* can undo those past choices. How do you undo the imperfect choices from the past?

Very simple! You realize that *all* imperfect choices were made under the influence of the consciousness of anti-christ and they *can* be replaced by making choices that are based on the consciousness of Christ.

It really *is* that simple, although there are numerous forces in the material world – including many secular and religious institutions – who will deny this basic truth. Yet contemplate what I am truly saying here.

God has given you free will, and the Creator respects its own laws. Thus, God will never take away your free will. This is proven by the fact that you have the ability to go against God's laws, whether you call this sinning, making karma or something else. Do you see the reality here? The very fact that you are in an imperfect state actually proves that God has given you truly free will. And this also proves that God will let you do whatever you want with that free will. Obviously, God will let you experience the consequences of your choices, but as Maitreya explains so profoundly, if your choices had no consequences or if you did not experience them, you would not actually have free will. You have the option to learn by following a loving teacher or learn by experiencing the consequences of your choices.

My point here is that God will *never* take away your freedom of choice, and this is actually the very mechanism that gives you the potential to walk the path of Christhood and enter God's kingdom. You see, what has caused you to "fall" into an imperfect state is that you started making choices while under the influence of the illusions of anti-christ, as depicted in how the Serpent deceived Eve in the Garden. Again, Maitreya explains this in greater detail, but my point here is that it is not *God* who takes away your free will but the consciousness of anti-christ and the beings who embody it. You see, Eve did make a choice to eat the forbidden fruit – meaning engage in the consciousness of duality – but it was not a truly *free* choice. There is an old saying that if people knew better, they would do better, and it is true. If people truly understand what they are doing, they will not deliberately hurt themselves.

The consequence is that you only made imperfect choices because you did not have the full understanding of what you were doing. Which means that you can seek a higher understanding – with all thy getting, get understanding – and this will give you a foundation for making better choices.

Why is this such an important idea? Because one of the most subtle tricks used by the ego and the prince of this world – even many Earthly institutions – is that once you have made a mistake, you can never escape it—at least not on your own. In other words, the fact that you have made mistakes in the past means that you cannot rise above them on your own. *You* made the mistakes, but you cannot "unmake" them. Which is why you need an external savior or church in order to be free from your sins. This idea is one of the most subtle and most effective lies in the devil's toolkit and most people have been affected by it.

So let me say this again. The consciousness of anti-christ is what takes away your free will. It does so by tricking you into making decisions based on limited or erroneous information. Once you have been blinded by this consciousness of duality, the prince of this world and your ego want to keep you blind, so that you continue to make unfree choices. In contrast, God never takes away your free will. God allows you to make the decision to partake of the consciousness of duality and make decisions based on it. But God leaves open your potential to – at any time – choose to reach beyond duality and seek for the truth of Christ, so that you can again get back to a state of consciousness in which you see reality and can thus make truly free choices.

Do you see the essential truth here? The forces of duality want to make you believe that once you have partaken of the consciousness of duality, you are caught forever and cannot escape on your own. Yet God's reality is that you can never lose the potential to reach beyond duality. Precisely because you have *free* will, none of your choices can be binding forever. *Any* choice you have ever made can be undone by making a better choice. *Any* choice based on the duality of anti-christ can be completely undone and erased by making a choice based on the reality of Christ. It is the truth that will make you free, but it does so by empowering you to make better choices!

God simply wants you to rise above the consciousness of duality, and you can never lose the potential to do so. The forces of anti-christ do not want you to rise, so they seek to prevent you from accepting your potential to come up higher by making you believe that – for whatever reason – you are stuck forever.

***

Having given you this teaching, we now need to deal with a very subtle point that is often misunderstood by spiritual seekers. What I have said above is that you are in an imperfect state as a result of choices *you* made. Thus, if you can get yourself *into* an imperfect situation through your own choices, you can also get yourself *out of* that situation through your own choices. In other words, your salvation depends *exclusively* on your choices.

However, here is where it gets subtle. You can be saved only based on the choices you make, but you cannot save yourself exclusively through your own power and faculties. In other words, you must act as if you *can* save yourself, but in reality you *cannot* save yourself. Let me explain.

I earlier said that you can't solve a problem with the same state of consciousness that created the problem. Thus, once you have become blinded by the duality consciousness, you cannot use the logic of the mind of anti-christ to overcome the duality consciousness. No matter how sophisticated an intellectual understanding of the material universe you might have – as materialistic science is striving to attain – you cannot use it to escape duality. In order to be free of suffering, you must reach for something beyond duality, namely the reality of the Christ mind.

I also said that what will truly consume negative emotions, such as fear and also guilt, is love. Yet the conditional love that is a result of the duality consciousness is not sufficient to consume fear. Thus, loving yourself in a human way will not help you rise above fear. What you truly need is the perfect, non-dualistic, unconditional love of God. You cannot produce this love from within yourself, but you *can* receive it from a higher source.

So what I am saying here is that you are currently trapped in an imperfect state, and you cannot save yourself from that state by using what is available to you in the state of duality. You can be saved only through the wisdom and the love of God. So in one sense you cannot save yourself, because you cannot produce what is needed for your salvation. Yet in another sense, you *can* save yourself by opening yourself up to the Divine energies that *will* produce your salvation.

Here is where we run into an even more subtle lie from the consciousness of anti-christ, a lie you have been programmed to believe over many lifetimes, a lie so subtle that over 99 percent of the people of this planet simply don't know enough to even question it. They take it for granted, because to them it appears that this is simply the way life is. Truly, this lie proves that once a planet sinks into duality, it becomes a self-fulfilling prophecy. What is this lie?

The lie is that in order to receive anything from God – be it grace, wisdom, forgiveness or love – you need to meet certain conditions, specifically conditions defined on Earth. In other words, this lie makes the claim that God's love is not unconditional but is given only to those who meet certain conditions. This is truly an example of how the consciousness of duality perverts everything. The Bible says that God created man in his image and likeness, but the reality is that after human beings fell into duality, they have created a god in the image and likeness of the dualistic self. This is a clear violation of the first two commandments, because it creates a graven – dualistic – image of God and elevates it to the status of a god, thus obscuring the real God. It is the ego's tendency to create mental images and project them onto the screen of life, thus worshipping the images instead of seeing reality.

At this point, you might be thinking that surely I cannot mean what I am saying, for clearly life in the material world confirms that God's love is conditional. You probably are not experiencing God's love at this moment, and does this not prove that God's love is conditional? Obviously, the reason you are not experiencing love must be that you are not meeting the conditions God has defined for receiving it. In other words, the logic is that *you* want God's love so the fact that you don't have it must mean that *God* is withholding if from you.

And while this is a logical line of reasoning, it is only logical based on your current state of consciousness. The reality is that God has defined NO conditions for you receiving God's love. *You* are the one who has defined – or at least accepted what is defined by others – the conditions that make you think you are not *worthy to receive God's love*. Thus, you are using your free will – the ultimate law for this universe – to close your being off and prevent God's love from flowing through you. Obviously, because God respects your free will, no Being in heaven will force you to receive love if you are not willing to open yourself to it. Let me give you a deeper understanding of the dynamic at work here.

***

The following is a brief summary of the process that has led to the creation of the material universe, based on what Mother Mary and Maitreya describe in their books. The material universe is only one part in a larger whole. The creation of this whole started when God the Creator created a void that had absolutely nothing in it. The Creator then projected itself into the void in the form of light, and this light formed a sphere that was set apart from the nothingness of the void. The Creator then used the light in this sphere to create structures that formed the basis for life. Finally, the Creator projected self-aware extensions of its own Being into the void.

These beings had the same creative abilities as the Creator, in the sense that they had the power of mind to use the Creator's light to form organized structures. They could not produce this light on their own, but they could be the open door for the light and give it form, thus serving as co-creators with the Creator. The co-creators in the first sphere were not created with the same awareness and mastery as the Creator, but through experimenting with their abilities, they gradually attained mastery. As part of this process, they served as conduits, through which the Creator could send more light into the first sphere, and they directed that light into forming structures that built upon the Creator's foundation.

When the first sphere had reached a certain stage of organization and light intensity, the creative process was taken to the next level. A new sphere was created, and the masters from the first sphere created structures within it. These masters then projected self-aware extensions of themselves into the next sphere, and these beings again served as co-creators who helped raise up their sphere from within. This process of creation has continued through several spheres, and the material universe is the most dense part of the latest sphere of God.

The point of this teaching is that the very fact that you are a self-aware being in the material universe proves that you are currently filling the position as a co-creator with God. The function of a co-creator is – as the name says – to help co-create the world in which it lives. A co-creator does this in the following ways:

- By connecting to the sphere right above it in vibration and receiving a stream of spiritual light from that realm.
- By connecting to the Christ mind and using that mind to direct the spiritual light into creating structures that are sustainable and that enrich both itself and all life in its sphere.

By fulfilling this role, a co-creator will grow in awareness until it can permanently ascend to a higher realm and continue its growth from there. It will also help raise its native sphere, until the sphere is so filled with light that it becomes the foundation for the next level in the creative process.

Why is this important? Well, it shows why you are here, namely to serve as a co-creator. The Bible actually describes this in veiled language by saying that God created humans in his image and likeness and gave them dominion over the Earth. Yet the real point is that you are *not* a material or human being, nor are you a miserable sinner. You were created as a co-creator with God, and you were designed to fulfill this position in the cosmic hierarchy.

Do you understand what I am saying? I have said that you have descended into an imperfect state from which you need to be saved. I have said that in order to be saved, you need the wisdom of the Christ mind and the unconditional love of God. I have also said that you have been programmed to believe that receiving this wisdom and love depends on you living up to certain conditions.

What you now see is that you do not need to live up to *any* conditions in order to receive wisdom and love. Why not? Because from the very beginning you were designed to have God's wisdom and love flowing through your being. You were designed to be a co-creator, and you co-create by directing the flow of love based on the wisdom of the Christ mind. Doing this is what you were designed to do. It is as natural for the Conscious You to receive wisdom and love as it is for your physical body to breathe, digest food or have your heart beat.

Do you see what I am saying? You do not need to fulfill *any* conditions in order to receive God's wisdom and love—you only ned to ACCEPT WHO YOU ALREADY ARE! The reason why you are not currently having God's wisdom and love flowing through you is *not* that you do not meet certain conditions on Earth. The reason is that you have forgotten who you are or that you have accepted certain lies that cause you to deny who you are. And it is *this denial* that shuts off the natural flow of love, light and truth through your being. Once you get out of this unnatural state of illusions, you will get back to your natural state of oneness with your source.

Imagine that you meet an eagle who is walking on the ground. You ask it – remember this is an imaginary example – "Why are you walking; why aren't you flying?" It answers, "I can't fly." You say, "What do you mean, there appears to be nothing wrong with your wings, surely you can fly, that's what eagles do!" It says, "No, I really can't fly. Other eagles might be able to, but I can't!"

My point being, of course, that eagles are designed to fly and thus they have an inherent ability to fly. Flying is a natural state, and the eagle in our example has simply been tricked into denying its inherent ability to fly. Likewise, most people on this planet have been tricked into denying their inherent ability to be the open doors for the wisdom of the Christ mind and the unconditional – meaning that it consumes all conditions and limitations – love of God.

***

As I have said, the consciousness of duality blinds you to reality. Thus, once you are blind, you can be controlled by the prince of this world and your ego. However, they can only control you as long as they can keep you blind, meaning that they will do *anything* to make sure that you will remain in a blind state. They would gladly have you believing that you are a material being or a mortal sinner with no potential whatsoever of escaping that state.

They want you to be imprisoned in a total way, meaning you think there is no alternative to the prison—you think it is normal to be imprisoned.

However, as I explained, most people will eventually come to see the internal contradictions in a dualistic world view, meaning that they become open to the concept that there is something beyond the prison and that escape might be possible. Yet all is not lost for the forces of duality, and their second line of defense is to portray God as a conditional being, meaning that you have to live up to certain conditions – conditions defined by duality – in order to qualify for entry into God's kingdom. Can you see that this is a blind alley that can never take you to your destination?

Do you see why this is an incredibly subtle and sinister strategy? I have explained many times now that you cannot solve a problem with the consciousness that created it. The problem is that you are trapped in duality, yet the prince of this world wants you to believe that the only way to escape duality is to live up to certain dualistic conditions. For people trapped in duality, this seems logical, but it is truly the broad way that leads to destruction. IT CAN NEVER WORK!

The *only* way to be saved is to rise above *all* dualistic conditions and *be* who you are. It is the conditions you have accepted that prevent God's wisdom and love from flowing through you, and thus only by overcoming all such conditions can you receive the truth and the love that will make you free. So it is not a matter of *meeting* certain conditions but of *abandoning* all conditions and the entire state of consciousness that defines conditions for everything.

My beloved, do you grasp what I have given you here? You may think this sounds abstract, theoretical or difficult to implement. Yet this teaching is very practical, realistic and it is actually easy to implement. In fact, it might be called the secret of life, the master key to salvation. Being saved is *not* a matter of becoming what you are not. It is a matter of overcoming the illusion that you are not saved and coming back to a state of consciousness in which you fully accept who you are and what you were created to be.

***

How can I say that this teaching is easy to implement? Because in reality, it requires NO effort!

You see, what I am telling you here is that having God's wisdom and love flowing through you is the natural state for a co-creator. Being in this state means that you are one with the forward movement of life itself, you are flowing with the River of Life.

What you are doing now is actually resisting the movement of life itself. You have stepped outside the River of Life, yet the river has not stopped flowing. Therefore, staying outside the river requires constant effort—and this is precisely what turns your life into an ongoing struggle.

Imagine being in a physical river and gently flowing with the stream. No resistance is necessary, no struggle is required, other than the willingness to flow with life. Now imagine that you decide to stem your feet against the river bottom and resist the forward movement. Obviously, this will not stop the river, so you need to exert a constant effort in order to stay in one place. You may feel as if the river is resisting your desire to stay in one place, but the river is simply doing what it was designed to do, and you are the one resisting the natural flow. You are refusing to transcend yourself by holding on to what you have now, whereas the river is constantly transcending itself—as God intended.

My point is that once you step into the duality consciousness, you are resisting the natural flow of the life force, and doing this requires a constant effort on your part. You have to continually resist the flow of life, and this is what turns your life into a struggle. Yet somehow the ego and the prince of this world have managed to make you believe in a set of illusions that gives you the impression that it is easier to stay in the duality consciousness and that it requires some superhuman effort in order to get back into the flow of life. In a sense, it *does* require a superhuman effort to walk the path to Christhood, the secret being that you were created as a superhuman being, and thus it is simply a matter of doing what you were designed to do.

Once you fully understand the path and stop resisting it, you will see that it is easier for you to return to oneness with the River of Life than it is to keep resisting the flow. This is what I expressed in veiled language in the situation of Paul's awakening:

> 1 And Saul, yet breathing out threatenings and slaughter against the disciples of the Lord, went unto the high priest,
> 2 And desired of him letters to Damascus to the synagogues, that if he found any of this way, whether they were men or women, he might bring them bound unto Jerusalem.
> 3 And as he journeyed, he came near Damascus: and suddenly there shined round about him a light from heaven:
> 4 And he fell to the Earth, and heard a voice saying unto him, Saul, Saul, why persecutest thou me?

> 5 And he said, Who art thou, Lord? And the Lord said, I am Jesus whom thou persecutest: it is hard for thee to kick against the pricks. (Acts, Chapter 9)

Kicking against the pricks means resisting the natural movement of life itself. Do you now see why I earlier said that the hallmark of the ego is resistance? The ego is created out of separation from the River of Life, and thus its very nature is resistance. Your ego will never stop resisting the River of Life, but when your conscious self separates itself from the ego's illusions, *you* can stop the resistance. You can then surrender yourself into the River of Life and be reborn of water and of Spirit.

***

On a more practical note, I fully realize that what I have given you in this key is a very advanced teaching, and you might not be fully ready for it. Yet what I wanted to do was to plant a seed in your mind, namely the idea that following the path to Christhood is not some superhuman activity but is a perfectly natural process. It is not a matter of becoming a saint but a matter of accepting who you were created to be and returning to that sense of identity. Thus, you have access to everything that is needed right within yourself, which is truly what I meant when I said that the kingdom of God is within you.

We now come to the conclusion of this key, which is the realization that what will fully consume your fear is that you receive the unconditional love that God has for you personally. And in order to receive that love, you simply need to allow it to follow its natural course and flow through you. Why do you think I said:

> That ye may be the children of your Father which is in heaven: for he maketh his sun to rise on the evil and on the good, and sendeth rain on the just and on the unjust. (Matthew 5:45)

You see, God's love is constantly being offered to every human being—without conditions, such as a dualistic evaluation of who is evil and good, just and unjust. *Your only choice regarding God's love is to accept it or reject it*. And it is precisely the illusions of anti-christ that have caused you to accept a set of conditions that makes you believe that – for whatever reason – you have to reject God's love until you have met these worldly conditions. What I am saying here is that perfect love will cast out fear, but in order to receive it, you must accept that you are worthy to receive it. Which means you must overcome the conditions that currently cause you to reject the perfect love that it is the Father's good pleasure to give you.

Yet I realize that giving you this teaching is not necessarily enough to help you stop rejecting God's love. For consider my sayings:

> And as ye would that men should do to you, do ye also to them likewise. (Luke 6:31)
>
> 1 Judge not, that ye be not judged.
> 2 For with what judgment ye judge, ye shall be judged: and with what measure ye mete, it shall be measured to you again. (Matthew, Chapter 7)

The deeper meaning here is that everything you do is a reflection of your state of consciousness. What you do to others, you have already done to yourself. So if you judge others according to certain conditions, you have already subconsciously judged yourself according to the same standard. My point being that if you are not currently able to accept that God loves you, it is because you are not currently able to love yourself. Which brings us to the exercise for this key.

## Exercise for Key 3

Even though I can tell you that God loves you because you are an extension of the Creator's own Being, you still may not be able to love yourself. And that is why I am asking you to do a very special rosary once a day for the next 33 days. This rosary is Mother Mary's Rosary for Loving Yourself,[5] and it is designed to challenge the many illusions that cause people to feel they are unworthy of love. And even though this is an advanced rosary at this early stage in the course, you can still benefit immensely from giving it.

So the exercise for this key is to give this rosary once a day for 33 days. After giving the rosary, take a few minutes to meditate on why you might not feel worthy of love, why you might reject love from other people or from God and why you feel a resistance toward truly accepting that God loves you and surrendering yourself into the flow of love. Then write down your impressions as they come to you without analyzing them. After you are done writing,

---

5 See *www.askrealjesus.com* in the Divine Feminine section.

reflect on what you wrote and then seek to uncover the belief behind your resistance to love.

On any day, read what you wrote the previous day before giving the rosary, and make a personal call in the beginning of the rosary based on your notes. Then repeat the meditation after the rosary and see if you can uncover deeper layers, deeper beliefs, of your resistance to love.

Of course, reread and contemplate my teachings in this key and we shall see whether we cannot change the way you look at yourself and help you accept that no matter what mistakes you might have made on this little Earth, in the greater scheme of things, you are as worthy of God's love as the day you were created in God's image and likeness.

# Key 4
# Seeking first the kingdom of God

We have now set a good foundation, and in this key, we will build upon it. I have had you go through the process of coming to a greater understanding of the path to Christhood and deciding to be teachable. I have had you tackle fear and work on loving yourself. Thus, you should now have reached a state of consciousness in which you are open to learning the deeper truths about life. This is a frame of mind in which you are not afraid to look beyond your existing beliefs and in which you are not paralyzed by guilt or a sense of being unworthy or incapable of following the path. Thus, you have the foundation for anchoring yourself on the path, and we now need to take a closer look at what exactly it will take for you to remove yourself from the path taken by most people – the broad way that leads to destruction – and place yourself permanently on the Way of Christ, the strait and narrow way that leads to eternal life.

As the next step, you need to realize that although I clearly want you to be open to receiving a higher understanding of the path, it is not my intention to turn you into a person who only *understands* the path to Christhood. I have no intention of turning you into a scribe who has the perfect intellectual understanding of how to follow that path but who has not internalized or applied that understanding.

I know I have not given a very flattering view of the scribes and Pharisees, and this might have given you the impression that they were stupid or malevolent people. In reality, most of them were highly intelligent people and they also had the best of intentions. They actually had a sincere desire to do the right thing, and in a sense we can say that they were actually doing the right thing—as they saw it. Yet how could they then fail to recognize the Living Christ and even want him condemned to death? The reason is that the human intellect cannot recognize Christ truth.

The human intellect is an analytical faculty, which means that it is designed to analyze by comparing any idea to what is known to be "true." In the spiritual field, the analytical mind works by comparing every new idea to a database of what it has defined as true and false ideas. Every new idea must be labeled, so it can fit within the categories defined in the database. Once labeled, it can easily be categorized as true or false, good or evil.

Do you understand the implication of this? The intellect has accepted a database which it believes is accurate, complete, infallible and thus beyond questioning. So if a new idea does not fit into any of the labeled boxes in the database, then it must per definition be false. The consequence is that the intellect can argue *for* or *against* any issue in a way that seems perfectly logical and rational to itself. Yet the outcome is predefined by the contents of the database that it uses as a frame of reference.

The problem is, of course, that because the collective consciousness of humankind has been dominated by the duality consciousness for so long, all of the man-made thought systems, all of the databases, are based on the duality consciousness. Thus, the Living Truth of Christ simply will not fit into any of the categories in such religious – or non-religious – databases. This means that people who cling to the security of the database – being unwilling to question it as the absolute frame of reference – will label the truth of Christ as evil or bad, thus being unable to recognize the Living Christ in any form. Consider how the scribes and Pharisees used their database – a particular interpretation of the Jewish belief system – to convince themselves that the truth I stated was of the devil. The only way they could *not* have reached that conclusion was if they had been willing to question their database, what in modern times is called their paradigms.

Do you see that the purpose of my mission was *not* to simply bring forth a few new ideas that could take the Jewish religion forward a notch? My purpose was to challenge people to fundamentally change their view of what it means to be human. I was challenging people to rethink the database that they saw as an infallible reference, the paradigm that defined what they thought was possible and impossible for human beings.

My point for bringing this up is to show you that the scribes and Pharisees were not stupid and they were not evil. They were very intelligent people and they were well-meaning. Yet you might have heard the saying that the road to hell is paved with good intentions. The real truth behind that saying is that the road to hell is paved with good intentions that are based on dualistic illusions. In other words, most of the scribes and Pharisees actually had the best of intentions. The problem was that they were so intelligent that they had used their intellects to convince themselves that they were already guaranteed to be saved, and thus they did not need the Living Truth that I brought. They had used their intellects – which could only refer to the database they had elevated to the status of infallibility – to convince themselves that the truth I expressed was not the truth but a lie. They were not willing to let me challenge their sense of equilibrium, in which they felt secure and comfortable because they had intellectually convinced themselves that they were sure to be saved. Thus, they were not willing to look for the beam in their own eyes when I pointed to such a beam.

This is the danger of the human intellect. It convinces people that they do not need to change because they are absolutely right. And this is what makes it possible that people can have a very sophisticated intellectual understanding of the spiritual path, but they nevertheless have not applied that understanding and actually changed their state of consciousness. They have taken certain outer steps, but they have not taken the all-important step of recognizing that there is a beam in their own eye and that they need to take active measures to remove it. Thus, they have used their sophisticated intellectual understanding of spiritual principles to convince themselves – as I explained earlier – that they can be saved without removing the beam, without looking in the mirror. They understand perfectly how others need to change or how "one" in general needs to change, but they have not looked in the mirror and acknowledged that *they too* need to change.

If you will take an honest look at history, you will see that every religion has had its scribes and Pharisees. If you take an honest look at the spiritual landscape of today, you will see that every spiritual movement has a group of people who think they understand the teaching and thus – because of the outer actions they have taken – they have actually applied the teaching to the fullest. They walk around like peacocks, strutting their superior knowledge and attainment, while in reality they have not even taken the first step onto the real path.

I need you to contemplate that it is perfectly possible for the intellect to use *any* spiritual teaching expressed in words to create a database and then use it as a justification for *not* looking for the beam in one's own eye. Yet I am determined to do everything possible to make sure that *you* will not be fooled by this subtle temptation, and thus I will give you certain teachings that might seem repetitive, but that nevertheless seek to shave off layers of illusions. You might consider your human identity as an onion that has many layers. If I were to remove all of them at once, you would lose all sense of continuity and experience an identity crisis. Thus, I take off one layer at a time, giving the Conscious You time to adjust to a new identity that is higher than the old one but not so much higher that you lose your bearings.

So what does it actually take to step onto the real path to Christhood? Well, you need to make decisions, but you need to make a special kind of decisions.

***

Take another look at the following passage:

> 16 And, behold, one came and said unto him, Good Master, what good thing shall I do, that I may have eternal life?
> 17 And he said unto him, Why callest thou me good? there is none good but one, that is, God: but if thou wilt enter into life, keep the commandments.
> 18 He saith unto him, Which? Jesus said, Thou shalt do no murder, Thou shalt not commit adultery, Thou shalt not steal, Thou shalt not bear false witness,
> 19 Honour thy father and thy mother: and, Thou shalt love thy neighbour as thyself.
> 20 The young man saith unto him, All these things have I kept from my youth up: what lack I yet?
> 21 Jesus said unto him, If thou wilt be perfect, go and sell that thou hast, and give to the poor, and thou shalt have treasure in heaven: and come and follow me.
> 22 But when the young man heard that saying, he went away sorrowful: for he had great possessions.
> 23 Then said Jesus unto his disciples, Verily I say unto you, That a rich man shall hardly enter into the kingdom of heaven.
> 24 And again I say unto you, It is easier for a camel to go through the eye of a needle, than for a rich man to enter into the kingdom of God.
> 25 When his disciples heard it, they were exceedingly amazed, saying, Who then can be saved?
> 26 But Jesus beheld them, and said unto them, With men this is impossible; but with God all things are possible. (Matthew, Chapter 19)

What is important here is the fact that the young man is telling me that he has followed the *outer* path all of his life, but now he wants more. I then offer him that more, namely that he can become one of my disciples and follow the path to Christhood. Obviously, I also tell him what is the first requirement he must meet in order to follow me, namely that he lets go of all attachments to anything on Earth.

Take note of a couple of things. One is that when I walked the Earth physically, I only had a short time, and thus I had to set some rather radical demands for those who were my direct disciples. Another is that it really isn't important that you let go of all your possessions. What *is* important is that you prioritize the path to Christhood higher than your Earthly possessions. Thus, I was giving this young man a test to see where his priorities were.

My point is that in today's world, I don't require my disciples to sell all their material possessions and withdraw from society. On the contrary, I generally prefer my disciples to be integrated in society, so they can demonstrate to others that there is an alternative to the typical materialistic lifestyle, even the typical religious lifestyle.

Yet it is still essential that you set your priorities straight. Why is this so? Because if you give your ego an inch, it will take a mile. If you prioritize anything in this world as being more important than the path to Christhood, your ego will trick you into stopping your progress at a certain point. And you will *not* progress beyond that point until you decide that you are willing to give up whatever is holding you back.

I am aware that we are at an early point in the course, and you may not yet be ready to give up everything on Earth. Yet I need to plant a seed in your mind so that you can begin to understand just how absolutely ruthless your ego and the prince of this world are in terms of using *any* opportunity to stop your progress. It is simply a basic fact of life that as long as your priorities and loyalties are divided, you cannot make maximum progress on the path. Here is why:

> No man can serve two masters: for either he will hate the one, and love the other; or else he will hold to the one, and despise the other. Ye cannot serve God and mammon. (Matthew 6:24)

Trying to serve the master of this world and the Master of the Living Christ will only make things harder for yourself, for you will be pulled in two opposite directions until something breaks—and that something is *you*. Incidentally, this is a point very few Christians have understood, for Christianity has been turned into an outer path based on the illusion of Peter, namely that you can be a disciple of Christ without removing the beam from your own eye. Why has Christianity perverted my teachings to the point of literally turning them upside down? Because the influence of the ego and the prince of this world is so subtle that it can use any spiritual teaching to justify the outer path. Yet look at how many attempts I made at explaining the essential, uncompromising nature of the path to Christhood:

> 19 Lay not up for yourselves treasures upon Earth, where moth and rust doth corrupt, and where thieves break through and steal:
> 20 But lay up for yourselves treasures in heaven, where neither moth nor rust doth corrupt, and where thieves do not break through nor steal:
> 21 For where your treasure is, there will your heart be also. (Matthew, Chapter 6)
>
> 44 Again, the kingdom of heaven is like unto treasure hid in a field; the which when a man hath found, he hideth, and for joy thereof goeth and selleth all that he hath, and buyeth that field.
> 45 Again, the kingdom of heaven is like unto a merchant man, seeking goodly pearls:
> 46 Who, when he had found one pearl of great price, went and sold all that he had, and bought it.
> 47 Again, the kingdom of heaven is like unto a net, that was cast into the sea, and gathered of every kind:
> 48 Which, when it was full, they drew to shore, and sat down, and gathered the good into vessels, but cast the bad away. (Matthew, Chapter 13)
>
> 16 And he spake a parable unto them, saying, The ground of a certain rich man brought forth plentifully:
> 17 And he thought within himself, saying, What shall I do, because I have no room where to bestow my fruits?
> 18 And he said, This will I do: I will pull down my barns, and build greater; and there will I bestow all my fruits and my goods.
> 19 And I will say to my soul, Soul, thou hast much goods laid up for many years; take thine ease, eat, drink, and be merry.
> 20 But God said unto him, Thou fool, this night thy soul shall be required of thee: then whose shall those things be, which thou hast provided?
> 21 So is he that layeth up treasure for himself, and is not rich toward God. (Luke, Chapter 12)
>
> 24 Then said Jesus unto his disciples, If any man will come after me, let him deny himself, and take up his cross, and follow me.

> 25 For whosoever will save his life shall lose it: and whosoever will lose his life for my sake shall find it.
> 26 For what is a man profited, if he shall gain the whole world, and lose his own soul? or what shall a man give in exchange for his soul?
> 27 For the Son of man shall come in the glory of his Father with his angels; and then he shall reward every man according to his works. (Matthew, Chapter 16)

Why is the path so uncompromising? Because for your ego, it is a matter of life or death to stop you from walking the path to Christhood! And you know very well that when people are in a survival situation, they will do almost anything to survive. Thus, you should never expect your ego to simply lay down and die. It will fight you every step of the way, and it will exploit any opening you give it. Meaning that as long as you have *any* attachment to *anything* on Earth, your ego will use it against you.

The simple fact is that your ego doesn't actually care about you at all—*it only cares about itself.* Take note of the following quote:

> 35 Then one of them, which was a lawyer, asked him a question, tempting him, and saying,
> 36 Master, which is the great commandment in the law?
> 37 Jesus said unto him, Thou shalt love the Lord thy God with all thy heart, and with all thy soul, and with all thy mind. (Matthew, Chapter 22)

The fact is that your ego loves itself with all its heart, soul and mind. Love is an attractive force, so the real factor that decides your progress on the path is the ratio between your ego's love for itself and the Conscious You's love for something beyond the ego. You have to decide that *you* love something more than your ego loves itself. Take note of my statement:

> If ye love me, keep my commandments. (John 14:15)

And my foremost commandment was to love God. Now, I am well aware that for many people in the modern world this is difficult because they have been brought up with such a distorted view of God. Yet if you cannot love God, then you must love something else, be it me, another person or your higher self.

> And the second is like unto it, Thou shalt love thy neighbour as thyself (Matthew 22:39)

How can you love your neighbor as yourself unless you also love yourself? Obviously, I am well aware that many spiritual seekers find it difficult to love themselves, yet you have started to overcome this condition, and I will give you further teachings and tools on this. For now I want you to contemplate what is your motivation for wanting to walk the path.

I especially want you to look for a motivation based on love, for if you look deeply enough, you will surely find it. You see, traditional religion has often sought to control people through fear, which has given many people a negative motivation. For example, many Christians seek to be saved because they are afraid of burning forever in hell. Such a negative motivation can be constructive for people in a low state of consciousness, because it can help them change their behavior and turn their lives around. However, a negative motivation will not get you very far on the path of Christhood.

As I explained in the last key, you were designed to have God's love flowing through you. And that is why I know that when you reconnect to your Higher Being, you will rediscover the positive motivation that made you decide to take embodiment on Earth. That motivation was based on love for something, and it is a stronger love than the ego's love for itself.

***

What I am saying here is that it is natural for you to be in the flow of love. And in order to get back into it, you have to make some decisions. But what kind of decisions? Consider the following quote from the Old Testament:

> I call heaven and Earth to record this day against you, that I have set before you life and death, blessing and cursing: therefore choose life, that both thou and thy seed may live: (Deuteronomy 30:19)

I have now also set before you life and death, meaning the life of Christ and the death of the consciousness of anti-christ. Thus, I also admonish you to choose life by making a LIFE decision. Let me ask you to read the following sections, taken from my website, in which I explain about these decisions:

## Making LIFE decisions or Death decisions[6]

Although I will describe the individual games used by the ego, I will start out by describing the master game. You may not be able to clearly see this game at this point, but I want to plant the seed in your mind so that it can germinate and eventually break through to your conscious awareness.

As I explained in my first discourses, the Conscious You created the ego by deciding that it would no longer make decisions. This is illustrated in the old fairy tale about the sleeping beauty. The princess is the Conscious You and one day she falls victim to a plot hatched by the evil Godmother, namely the prince of this world. Thus, the princess falls asleep and an impenetrable forest grows up around her castle. The forest, of course, is the ego and the individual trees are the illusions of the ego, the ego games. One day a prince comes by, penetrates the forest and kisses the princess, who awakens. The prince symbolizes the Living Christ who can take on many forms, both as an outer teacher and as the inner teacher of your Christ self. Regardless of the form, the Living Christ always serves to awaken the Conscious You to the need to come up higher.

In the fairy tale, the prince and the princess live happily ever after, and here is where the fairy tale departs from reality. In the real world, the Conscious You is not home free by being awakened. It/you must personally cut down all of the trees that surround the castle, and only *then* will you live happily ever after.

The master strategy of the ego involves two elements. The first one is that the ego will do anything it can to prevent the Conscious You from awakening to the realization that there must be more to your identity. For the majority of human beings, this strategy is still working and they still identify themselves completely with the identity that the ego has built in the material world. The fact that you are reading this means that you are a spiritual seeker, and thus your ego's first strategy has failed. You know there is more to your identity and you are actively looking for it.

Thus, you are now the target for the ego's second strategy, which is to prevent you from clearing the thorny trees around the castle. Each such tree represents a decision, a decision based on the mind of anti-christ, the mind of duality and separation. This is where I would like to leave the fairy-tale analogy behind and instead refer to the image of a spiral staircase. Each decision that was

---

6 This is one in a series of discourses on the ego and the games played by the ego found on www.askrealjesus.com.

based on the mind of anti-christ took you further down the spiral staircase, the staircase that leads into the darkness of separation from your Higher Being. This is what the Bible refers to as "the valley of the shadow of death" (Proverbs 23:4).

The separation from your I AM Presence and your true sense of identity truly is the consciousness of spiritual death. Thus, the decisions based on the illusions of the mind of anti-christ brought you further into the consciousness of death. We might say that each of these decisions was a Death decision. One kiss from the prince is not enough to raise you out of the shadow of death. You must consciously walk the staircase and undo each of the decisions that brought you down the staircase. And this is precisely what the ego will do everything in its power to prevent you from completing.

In order to take a step up the spiral staircase, you must come to see through the dualistic illusion that brought you down to your current step. You can do this only by seeing the Christ truth that counteracts the illusion, the truth that makes you free. And then you must choose the truth of Christ over the "truth" of anti-christ. You must choose life over death. I would like to call each of these decisions a "LIFE decision."

What I am hoping to help you see is that the ego will do anything to prevent you from making these LIFE decisions. And in order to accomplish this overall goal, the ego – and the forces of anti-christ – have invented a number of subtle games. The goal is to keep you entangled with a particular illusion, so that you cannot let go of it and rise to the next step on the path.

When I talk about LIFE decisions, I am not talking about minor decisions, such as whether to bring an umbrella or what to have for lunch. Nor am I talking about big decisions in your material life, such as what career to pursue or what person to marry. I am talking about the kind of decisions that affect how you see yourself, God, the world and the relationship between these three factors in your life. I am talking about decisions that affect your sense of identity.

As I explained in the previous discourses, when you descend one step on the spiral staircase, your old identity dies and a new one is born. Thus, in order to ascend one step, the old – human – identity must die and a new more spiritual one must be born. That is why I said:

> 5 Jesus answered, Verily, verily, I say unto thee, Except a man be born of water and of the Spirit, he cannot enter into the kingdom of God.
> 6 That which is born of the flesh is flesh; and that which is born of the Spirit is spirit. (John, Chapter 3)

This spiritual rebirth requires you to voluntarily and consciously – if it is not *conscious*, it cannot be *voluntary* – let the old human identity die and accept that you are reborn into a higher, more spiritual, sense of identity. To make this less abstract, let me give an example.

***

Many people struggle with alcoholism and use various programs to combat this condition. Some manage to stop drinking by using the force of conscious will to suppress the urge to drink. This is commendable, but it comes with a price, namely that you must struggle to uphold the decision, often for the rest of your life. A certain organization maintains that you are an alcoholic for life and that you must continue to suppress the urge to drink. I am not denouncing this approach for people at a certain level, but there is a higher approach.

You see, there is only one reason why you could become susceptible to alcoholism in the first place, namely that you have accepted a sense of identity as a human being who has no real purpose to life and who is powerless to overcome certain problems. Thus, if you can't overcome a problem (to stop the pain) and if you really are not worth anything, it is okay to dull the pain through alcohol.

You then gradually slide into a physical and emotional addiction, but one day the Conscious You wakes up and realizes this cannot go on or you will die. So you go into a treatment program and use the force of will to suppress what is seen as the cause of the problem, namely the urge to drink. However, the real cause is your sense of identity as a basically worthless human being whose life has no higher purpose.

The real solution is to transcend that state of consciousness, which you can do by internalizing the Christ truth that you are a unique, spiritual being who is infinitely loved by God and who came to Earth for a specific spiritual purpose. Once you accept this new sense of identity – once you let the old identity die and are spiritually reborn – you will see that you *are* worthy and that your life has a mission that is far too important to let alcohol stand in the way of its fulfillment.

Thus, you have not simply suppressed the urge to drink – which is only the effect and not the cause – but you have accepted a higher sense of identity. For the new person that you now are, drinking is simply unthinkable. It is not even an option and the ego and the prince of this world have no way to tempt you into drinking. You are so focused on your mission that you do not even notice their temptations. (This leads them to stop and attempt to come up with another kind of temptation that works at your new level of consciousness. Nevertheless, you have still made significant progress and it has become harder for them to tempt you.)

Do you now see the overall strategy of the ego? You have descended the staircase by accepting a lower sense of identity than your true identity, which is that you are a unique spiritual being. You have accepted that you are a human being with certain limitations. The ego is trying to prevent you from letting go of a limited sense of identity and accepting a higher one. It does this by either keeping you in spiritual blindness (so you don't see your limitations or the alternative) or making you so attached to your current sense of identity that you are not willing to let go of it.

Your current sense of identity is based on something in this world, it is a worldly or material sense of identity. Thus, the ego is trying to keep you so entangled with or attached to the "things of this world" that you either cannot see or cannot accept your true spiritual identity. The ego seeks to accomplish this through the individual ego games, each of which is designed to keep you so focused on something in the material world that you cannot or will not look beyond it. You are not willing to give up your limited sense of identity in order to rise to a broader sense of identity. You are not able or willing to let go of your belief that you *are* the lower identity and that there is nothing more to *you* than what that identity specifies.

***

Let us now consider how you descended the staircase that led you to your present level of consciousness. Here is where the fairy tale – and even the Bible – gives an incorrect description of the process. The Bible describes the Fall of man as one momentous event. In a sense it is true that losing contact with your spiritual teacher was a momentous event, but it happened as the result of a gradual process.

Many religions and many New Age teachings present the Fall of Man as one event and they present the solution – salvation or whatever it is called – the same way. This is one of the illusions created by the prince of this world. He wants you to believe that if only you belong to the right Christian church and believe all its doctrines, I – or rather the church's idolatrous image of Christ – will one day appear in the sky and save you. Or he wants you to believe that if only you are loving and kind to everyone, you will one day spontaneously wake up and be enlightened.

Both philosophies – and the many others that spring from the same consciousness – have the same goal, namely to pacify you so that you do not recognize the true key to salvation, spiritual growth, enlightenment or whatever you want to call it. That key is to understand the mechanics of how you *descend* and *ascend* the spiral staircase and the role of LIFE decisions. Let me explain.

The consciousness of anti-christ is subtle, which means that the Fall did not happen as the result of one decision on your part. You gradually started experimenting with the dualistic mind, and you gradually descended the spiral staircase. At some point the Conscious You did make the momentous decision that it would no longer be in command of your life, but most people did this without fully realizing what was at stake. They had already become so partially blinded by the duality of the mind of anti-christ that they did not fully understand what had happened. They did not understand that they had just made the quintessential Death decision.

Compare this to descending a staircase. If you walk down the steps, each step will send a jolt up your legs, and you know you have descended one step. You experience each step as a discrete and distinct event and you know you have gone one step down. Yet now imagine that you lie down on the staircase and allow gravity to pull your body down. You simply slide down the steps and because your body spans several steps, it becomes harder to realize that you have descended a step and that this is a discrete event. After all, which step did you just descend, the one under your head or the one under your feet? And when you do not clearly see that you have taken a step down, you can slide quite far down the spiral staircase before you even realize what has happened.

My point is that when you descended the staircase of consciousness, you did not clearly see what was happening. You did not realize that each step was a discrete event that caused your old sense of identity to die and a new – more limited one – to be born. The reason why you did not see this was that you were blinded by the dualistic logic of the mind of anti-christ, as Eve was blinded by the serpent in the Garden of Eden when he said, "Thou shalt not surely die" (Genesis 3:4).

Do you see that this is the very same lie that is behind each of the steps you have taken down the staircase? You think that you will not *surely* die by making a Death decision. After all, you have already gone part of the way suggested by the ego and you are still alive, so why not follow the ego a bit further? This is the logic that allowed you to slide down the spiral staircase until you could no longer see the exit door at the top and even forgot there is something at the top of the staircase. This is when the Conscious You accepted a sense of identity as a human being instead of a spiritual being.

Now, here is where we must once again correct the fairy tale. It is true that the Conscious You is asleep, but only metaphorically speaking. You are asleep in the sense that you do not see the reality of life, namely that you are more than a material, human being and that the world is more than the material universe. Yet you are not asleep in the sense that you are unconscious. Thus, you are painfully aware of the consequences of the ego-based decisions and you cannot escape experiencing those consequences. Here is where we need to take a closer look at what exactly it means that the Conscious You stopped making decisions.

***

In my previous discourses,[7] I said that at some point the Conscious You decided that it would no longer make decisions, and it allowed the ego to make decisions *for* you. This is true, but there is a deeper understanding that we now need to uncover.

The fact is that there are some decisions that *can* be made by the ego and there are some decisions that can *only* be made by the Conscious You. The Conscious You is an extension of your I AM Presence and a spark of God's Being. It is sent into the material world with the command to multiply and have dominion. This means that you must multiply your sense of identity as a co-creator, and only the Conscious You can make decisions about your sense of identity. Only the Conscious You can make a Death decision – a decision that leads you to a *lower* sense of identity – or a LIFE decision – a decision that leads you to a *higher* sense of identity. The ego cannot make such decisions, but it can influence how the Conscious You makes such decisions.

To illustrate this, consider a company that is owned by one person. The owner does not want to make all the day-to-day decisions and has hired a CEO to run the business while he spends time in his private office or in his country club. The CEO can make most of the decisions related to running the business, but some decisions must still be made by the owner. One year the CEO makes some bad decisions and the company loses money. Yet he does not admit this to the owner. Instead, he comes up with a plan that makes it seem like it was market conditions that led to the loss, and if only

[7] It is recommended that you study all of the ego discourses in the Spiritual Freedom section.

the owner will approve a loan from the bank, the company will regroup and be much stronger next year.

Because the owner really does not want to run the company himself, he believes the CEO and approves the loan. This obviously takes the company one step down the ladder of debt, but the owner thinks it will only be a temporary setback and he again retreats into his private world. The next year the company is still not showing a profit, but again the CEO comes up with a convincing plan and the owner – who really doesn't want to leave his private world – approves another loan.

Obviously, this process can continue for as long as the owner believes the CEO. As long as the CEO can avoid something that shakes the owner's trust, he can get away with quite a lot and the company can slide into hopeless debt before the owner realizes what is going on (as illustrated in my analogy of sliding down the staircase). Once the situation gets so bad that the owner can no longer ignore it, he will have to wake up and run the company himself (he experiences a discrete event that breaks the spell of blindness). However, what will it take to get to that point? That depends on the balance between the owner's desire to stay in his private world and his desire to avoid having the company go down. As long as there is no distinct event that shatters the owner's illusion, his sense of status quo, the slide can continue indefinitely.

Yet what is the real problem here? Although the owner has retreated from running the company, he is not completely isolated. He still feels the consequences of the company not making a profit and he still has to make the most important decisions. So although he might feel as if he is no longer making decisions, this is only an illusion. He is still making the Death decisions that take the company to a distinctly lower level, yet what he is *not* doing is taking charge of gathering the information UPON WHICH THESE DECISIONS ARE BASED. He allows the CEO to present to him a selective picture of the situation and then he bases his LIFE and Death decisions on the image presented by the CEO.

This is the exact dynamic between the Conscious You and the ego. The Conscious You decides that it no longer wants to be in command of your life, so it allows the ego to make the day-to-day decisions. Yet the ego cannot decide on your sense of identity, so the ego can only make decisions within the framework of how the Conscious You sees itself. The ego's decisions are based on the duality consciousness, which means they will inevitably lead to undesirable consequences.

The Conscious You will experience these consequences, but the ego will present you with a "company report" that makes it seem like this is just a temporary setback. You are the victim of circumstances beyond your control, but if only you will make the decision recommended by the ego, you will see that things will get better. The ego will present you with a view of the situation that is based on dualistic thinking. The ego really believes its solution will work, but in reality a solution based on the duality consciousness cannot solve problems created by the duality consciousness.

Yet if you still do not want to take back the responsibility for running the company, you might believe the ego. You will then make a Death decision that takes you down to a distinctly lower sense of identity. You might not realize what is happening, but the ego will now begin to make decisions based on this lower sense of identity. By accepting a lower sense of identity, you have given the ego more freedom to act, and this will lead to even more unpleasant consequences. Thus, you have already set the stage for the next crisis.

Do you see the mechanics? You make a Death decision that takes you to a lower level of identity. The ego now takes over and makes the minor decisions based on this new sense of identity. Each of these decisions leads to unpleasant consequences, and in order to escape those consequences, you will – as long as you refuse to take command of your life – make another Death decision that takes you further down the staircase.

When it comes time for the next company report, the ego will present a rosy picture that makes it seem like it is not the ego's fault, and certainly not *your* fault. Sure, things are tough right now, but they are sure to get better. And in the meantime, why don't you – the new *human* being – simply make yourself comfortable by taking advantage of the pleasures the material world has to offer. Stop worrying about the purpose of life and simply have a little fun. Live a little—until you have to die some more.

***

Once you have forgotten your higher identity, you cannot see any way out of your dilemma. You do not understand that the unpleasant consequences are the inevitable result of decisions based on the duality consciousness. You have forgotten that there is an alternative to this state of consciousness, so you think the only way to escape the unpleasant consequences is to make better dualistic decisions. You think you can solve your problems without transcending your current sense of identity—which is the source of your problems. And this is precisely what your ego and the prince of this world want you to keep believing. They want you to believe in the illusion that you can solve a problem with the same state of consciousness that created the problem (which is what *they* believe).

At some point, the Conscious You will experience such severe consequences that it will wake up and say, "I can't keep doing this anymore; I have to change something." Yet even after this awakening, the ego will do *anything* to prevent you from realizing the reality I have just described. That reality has the following components:

- Only the Conscious You can make LIFE and Death decisions, decisions that take you up or down the staircase of identity.
- You have descended that staircase because you made Death decisions.
- You made those decisions because you allowed the ego to gather the information upon which you based the decisions.
- Because the ego can see *only* the mind of anti-christ, all of its information was dualistic in nature and could only create more problems.
- The *only* way out is to start making LIFE decisions.
- Such decisions must be based on the reality of the Christ mind rather than on the illusions of the mind of anti-christ.
- Only the Conscious You can access the Christ mind. The ego can *never* do so.
- The Conscious You *always* has the option to reach for the mind of Christ. No matter how far you have descended down the staircase, you can still ask for guidance, and you will receive it. When the student is ready, the teacher will *always* appear, and the teacher will give the student exactly what is needed to take the very next step up the spiral staircase. The challenge for you is to recognize the teacher and be willing to follow his/her directions.

The problem is that before you can make use of this "open door that no man can shut," *you* – meaning the Conscious You – must decide to take back responsibility for your life. You must take back responsibility for making LIFE decisions and you must take back responsibility for gathering the information upon which you base those decisions. You must refuse to allow the ego to back you into a corner, where it seems like you have to make decisions based on two extremes that are both defined by the mind of anti-christ. You must refuse to be manipulated into a situation where it seems like your only option is to choose the lesser evil. You must take back your responsibility to discern between the truth of Christ and the illusions of anti-christ.

My overall point is this. Once you have made the decision not to take command, you allow the ego to provide the information upon which you make the big decisions, and you slide down the staircase without realizing what is happening. You experience it as a blur rather than as a string of discrete events, each one causing the death of the old you and the birth of the new you. However, you cannot ascend the staircase the same way. You cannot simply slide up the staircase—you must walk by your own efforts. You cannot expect a spiritual teacher to pull you up the staircase as the ego pulled you down. You must stand up and decide to walk by your own effort.

The real key is to realize that walking up the staircase requires you to take a number of discrete and distinct steps. In order to climb to the next step, you must remove both feet from the previous step, meaning that you must decide to leave that step behind forever. This requires you to willingly let the old sense of identity die and allow yourself to be reborn into a new sense of identity. This is what Paul described:

> 22 That ye put off concerning the former conversation the old man, which is corrupt according to the deceitful lusts;
> 23 And be renewed in the spirit of your mind;
> 24 And that ye put on the new man, which after God is created in righteousness and true holiness. (Ephesians, Chapter 4)

For each step you take up the spiral staircase, *you* must make a decision. This decision must be based on the following:

- You see that what brought you to your current step on the staircase was a decision that *you* made.
- You see that the decision was based on the illusions of the mind of anti-christ presented by the ego.
- You see why this illusion is wrong and why it could only lead to unpleasant consequences.

- You see this because you have recognized the truth of Christ that makes you free from the illusion.
- You now consciously and with no regrets or attachments choose to let go of the illusion and accept and internalize the truth of Christ.

By making this LIFE decision, you have allowed the old "you" to die and you have been spiritually reborn into a new sense of identity. This does not mean you are now saved and will live happily ever after. It means you have ascended one step on the spiral staircase, and you are now ready to face the next challenge. Only when you have faced every decision that brought you down the staircase, will you reach the top and live happily ever after.

***

Let me summarize what I have revealed in this discourse: You can sleepwalk your way *down* the spiral staircase of life, but you *cannot* sleepwalk your way *back up!* You can get down by making unconscious decisions, but you can get back up *only* by making conscious decisions.

Let me return to the analogy of the owner of a company. After several years of bad financial results, the owner finally wakes up and realizes his CEO has fed him a distorted view of the company's situation. Yet he now faces the crucial decision of whether to take back charge of the company or whether to simply fire the bad CEO and hire another one so he can continue to retreat into his private world. He decides to do the latter and hires a new CEO. Yet he is unaware that it is actually the old CEO who has taken on a disguise and has presented himself as a different person.

As a spiritual seeker, you have already made some LIFE decisions, and for each decision, you fired the ego which caused you to rise to a higher sense of identity. The problem is that the ego will immediately change its disguise and present itself as a capable CEO who can run your new company for you. My point is that many spiritual seekers have made significant progress, yet they have not yet come to the point of making the ultimate LIFE decision.

This decision is the firm commitment that you will take charge of your life and that you will remain in charge. You will make the important decisions and you will take responsibility for attaining the vision of Christ before you make such decisions. You will keep making one LIFE decision after another, and you will keep doing so until you reach the top of the spiral staircase. You will never again allow your ego to talk you into abandoning your responsibility to discern between the reality of Christ and the unreality of anti-christ.

Now, before you become discouraged and start feeling like it is an insurmountable task to overcome all of the ego's illusions, let me make it clear what you are up against. You might take an honest look at yourself and see that you still have a ways to go before you are free of the ego. And in your current state of confusion it might seem very difficult to see through the ego's illusions. Yet who ever said you have to see through the ego's illusions all at once or that you have to do so with your current level of consciousness?

Why do you think I keep talking about a spiral staircase? The key to climbing a staircase is to take one step at a time, and all you need to do is focus on two steps at a time—the step you are on right now and the one right above it. You don't need to look at the top step and you certainly don't need to climb the staircase by taking one giant leap. You simply keep putting one foot above the other, and as long as you keep taking one doable step at a time, you *will* make it to the top. The ego can stop you only by preventing you from rising above a certain step.

Let us say that the spiral staircase has 33 steps. You take stock of your life and realize you are on Step 10. At this stage you do not have the Christ discernment and insight to see through the ego illusion that prevents you from rising from Step 32 to Step 33. Yet you don't have to see through *that* illusion right now. You only have to see through the illusion that prevents you from rising from Step 10 to Step 11. And I can assure you that you *do* have what it takes to dismiss that illusion. You simply need to ask for the Christ vision you need, and if you ask with an open mind, you *will* receive an answer.

It is a spiritual law, that when the student is ready, the teacher *will* appear. The teacher may appear as the inner teacher of your Christ self or as an outer teacher that might have a variety of disguises. Yet the teacher will *always* find a way to present you with the insight you need in order to rise to the next step. If your mind is open, you will recognize the Divine direction and use it to rise to a higher level of identity. And once you have that higher sense of identity, you will have what it takes to dismiss the next ego-illusion and take another step.

I hope you now see what is the ego's master strategy. It is to prevent you from making the *ultimate* LIFE decision, but also to prevent you from making the *next* LIFE decision. It is precisely to accomplish this goal that the ego and the prince of this world have come up with a number of games that are designed to keep you stuck at a particular step. As you begin to study these games, you will see that you have already overcome some of them. And this should give you the inner knowing that you can overcome all of them by simply taking one step at a time.

I realize that it can still seem like climbing the staircase is an overwhelming task. Yet the fact that you are reading this teaching proves that you are not at the lowest step. So how did you rise to your current step? You did so because the Living Christ in some form reached out to you and you heeded the call. You accepted the teacher's directions and used them to make a LIFE decision that brought you one step higher. And you continued to do this until you reached your current step.

My point is that so far the teacher has been there for you every step of the way and you have followed the teacher's instructions. Based on this fact, is it rational to doubt that the teacher will be there for each of the following steps as well? Is it rational to doubt that you *can* and *will* follow the teacher as you have already done? Why not simply realize that you have already stepped on to the true path, and as long as you keep following it by reaching for the higher vision of Christ, you *will* make it all the way home. Thus, you should accept the message in the full quote that I gave in part earlier:

> Yea, though I walk through the valley of the shadow of death, I will fear no evil: for thou art with me; thy rod and thy staff they comfort me. (Proverbs 23:4)

Trust that the teacher will be with you each step of the way, and as long as you keep moving, you *will* make it to the goal. As the old saying goes, "A journey of a thousand miles begins with one step." However, the journey is completed only by those who keep taking the NEXT step. [End of quote]

***

This concludes my quotes from the website, and I will now use this teaching to summarize this key. We might say that life can be compared to a tug-of-war. There are two teams pulling on a rope. One team is made up of your ego and the prince of this world, the other team is made up of the Living Christ and the Ascended Host—and the rope is *you*.

The challenge of life is that there are two forces pulling on you. The prince of this world is seeking to pull you *down* the staircase of life and the Living Christ is pulling you *up*. Now, neither team can actually pull you up or down against your free will. The essential difference is that the worldly team will seek to deceive you into making Death decisions, even making the ultimate Death decision to give up your free will to the ego and the prince of this world. In contrast, the spiritual team will *not* deceive you and can pull you up *only* when you are willing to make conscious decisions, LIFE decisions.

We might say that the worldly team is pulling *with* the force of gravity and the spiritual team is pulling *against* gravity. So if you make yourself a dead weight, by refusing to make decisions, you make it easy for the worldly team to pull you down. The spiritual team can only pull you up when you are willing to put one foot in front of the other. You might recall the old saying that God helps those who help themselves. If you are not willing to help yourself, you give the advantage to the worldly team, and it will surely pull you *down*—for your spiritual identity will *surely* die when you refuse to take responsibility for your life.

***

What is it that makes it difficult for you to take a step up the spiral staircase of life? It is that you have become attached to something in the material world. If you look at the world, you will see that people are at many different levels of consciousness, and this is actually determined by their attachments. Some people are completely focused on sensual pleasure and act as if the highest purpose of life is to have more sex, more material possessions or more food. This is an attachment to the physical things of this world and the sensual pleasure it gives them. Other people cannot get enough power and are on a never-ending quest to control the world.

The fact that you are open to this course means that you have transcended such lower attachments. And the fact that you are still in embodiment on Earth means that you still have some attachments—they are simply more subtle. I will shortly talk about what such attachments might be, but my immediate point is that as long as you have *any* attachments to *anything* on Earth, you are making life harder for yourself. Take another look at this saying of mine:

> For the prince of this world cometh, and hath nothing in me. (John 14:30)

This is what will happen as you attain full Christhood; you will overcome *all* of your attachments and illusions so that the prince of this world and your ego cannot find anything in your being that they can use to pull you down the staircase. You have, so to speak, greased their side of the rope and they can no longer get a firm grip on you. It might still take you some time to reach this state of ultimate freedom, but you can take a very important step toward that state by making what I earlier called the ultimate LIFE decision, namely that you are willing to look at any aspect of your life and psychology and honestly make the following evaluation: Does this help me take the next step up the staircase or does it pull me down?

Again, take note that I am always talking about a gradual path. I am in no way requiring you to become perfect in one giant leap. What I am saying here is that by becoming aware of the tug-of-war, you can make it much easier for yourself to walk up the staircase and prevent the back-and-forth motion of sliding back down, thus having to take each step several times, perhaps even feeling like you are getting nowhere.

The key to doing this is to decide that you are willing to look at *anything* in your life and you are willing to seek a greater understanding of the aspects of your life that pull you down the staircase. You see, the first strategy of the ego and the prince of this world is to prevent you from even looking for the beam, so once you make a decision to do so, you take much of their power away from them.

Their goal is to keep you in a divided state – to keep you the house that is divided against itself and thus cannot stand against their downward pull – on an indefinite basis. This state of division is a lack of wholeness—if you were whole in knowing who you really are, you would know that the prince of this world has no power over you because … [Fill in the blank.] As a hint, think back to what I earlier said is the fundamental truth about life that you need to remember at all times. If you cannot immediately answer this question, go back and find my teaching on this and contemplate it again.

My point here is that I am leading you to reconsider your motivation for wanting to follow the path of Christhood.

***

Why are you here, why are you following this course, what is it that motivates you, what are you seeking to gain from the course?

If you take an honest look at spiritual and religious people, you will find a variety of motives that drive them to be involved with religious or spiritual pursuits. You will also see that some of those motives are clearly based on worldly desires and dualistic illusions. Some people turn to spirituality to overcome a health crisis or to gain financial abundance. Others seek some kind of status and come to a spiritual teaching with dreams of glory. This was even the case for some of my disciples, as mentioned before:

> 27 Then answered Peter and said unto him, Behold, we have forsaken all, and followed thee; what shall we have therefore?
> 28 And Jesus said unto them, Verily I say unto you, That ye which have followed me, in the regeneration when the Son of man shall sit in the throne of his glory, ye also shall sit upon twelve thrones, judging the twelve tribes of Israel.
> 29 And every one that hath forsaken houses, or brethren, or sisters, or father, or mother, or wife, or children, or lands, for my name's sake, shall receive an hundredfold, and shall inherit everlasting life.
> 30 But many that are first shall be last; and the last shall be first. (Matthew, Chapter 19)

Obviously, Peter feels that he has given up something in this world in order to follow me, and now he wants to know what he will get as a compensation. As said before, my answer here was not meant to give the full truth about this, for I was seeking to work with Peter's – relatively low – state of consciousness and turn his attention to a reward in the spiritual world rather than in the material world.

Do you now see the mechanics behind this situation? When you incorporate what I have said above, you will see that if your motivation for following the path of Christhood is based on a dream of attaining *anything* in this world, then the prince of this world will have an attachment in you that he can use to pull you away from the real path and onto the false path.

The path of Christhood is *not* about attaining anything in this world, which I demonstrated by allowing myself to be crucified like a common criminal instead of becoming the king of Israel, as many people at the time thought I was meant to become. I demonstrated that there was a higher goal than anything in this world, a goal that is *beyond* this world. That goal is the eternal life of the Christ consciousness that you attain by overcoming *all* attachments to the material world and ascending to the spiritual realm.

Perhaps this seems like an abstract and far-away goal for now. However, I still encourage you to consider your motivation. Seek to shift your motivation away from dreams of glory or other material results and onto something more intangible. My first suggestion is to make it your main motivation to seek wholeness, which will give you peace of mind, the peace that comes from no longer having divisions in your own psyche that pull you in opposite directions. Is that not an intermediate goal that is worth attaining and thus worth working for? If not, perhaps you should put this course aside for a while and go find yourself a guru who will promise you something that seems more appealing to your present level of consciousness. I will still be here when you have had enough of pursuing such goals, and I will receive you back with open arms.

***

I am sure you realize that I am saying the same thing in many different ways, but I am doing so in order to reach the greatest possible number of students, for this is truly a pivotal point in the course. If you do not fully understand what I am teaching in this key, you will *not* be able to lock yourself on the true path to Christhood. So let me say it another way by asking you to take another look at this statement:

> 13 Enter ye in at the strait gate: for wide is the gate, and broad is the way, that leadeth to destruction, and many there be which go in thereat:
> 14 Because strait is the gate, and narrow is the way, which leadeth unto life, and few there be that find it. (Matthew, Chapter 7)

What I am saying between the lines is that there are two distinct approaches to life. One is the approach taken by most people, and what you need to see here is that this approach is even taken by many religious and spiritual people. This is the outer approach of thinking that belonging to a certain teaching, following a certain guru or practicing certain exercises will save you without *you* having to look at the beam in your own eye. The narrow path that few people find is the true path to Christhood, which *does* require you to look at the beam in your own eye – psyche – and consciously heal the divisions in your being until you become whole.

Do you see what this means? The vast majority of the people on this planet are following a path that does *not* lead to Christhood, even though many of them are firmly convinced that they are among the elect who will surely be saved. Yet beyond that false path is a completely different approach to life, an approach that will give you real progress by removing the divisions that take away your inner peace. Yet in order to attain this inner peace, you *must* be willing to look at and overcome the divisions in your own psyche.

These divisions are created by your acceptance of certain illusions that spring from the mind of anti-christ, and many people are attached to these illusions, being unwilling to take a look at them or let them go. So you need to consider your priorities. Do you want to continue to follow the way of the world and ignore the need to do some spring cleaning in your psyche? Or are you willing to follow the true path of Christ, which requires you to deal with the elements of division in the psyche—a process that can only be completed *consciously*?

In order to follow the path of Christ, you *must* take command over your own psyche, so that the ego and the prince of this world cannot pull your attention away from your goal and trick you into focusing on lesser goals (that might be worthy goals in a worldly sense but will not lead you to the Christ consciousness).

This means that you must consciously clean out the elements of anti-christ in all levels, or layers, of your psyche, as I will shortly describe them. Doing this is actually completing the circle of Alpha and Omega.

***

You will recall that I earlier said that everything has an Alpha and an Omega aspect. Many people come to a spiritual teaching out of a valid desire to come closer to God and to understand God's truth. So they seek a higher understanding by studying spiritual teachings and they seek direct experiences – often called peak experiences – by practicing various techniques. There is nothing wrong with this, but many spiritual seekers fail to see that it is only one side of the coin and that they will never attain maximum progress – in fact they will never reach their goal – without also incorporating the other side of the coin.

Seeking understanding and direct experience of a higher reality is the Alpha aspect of the path. It is valid, but it cannot bring you to a higher state of consciousness on its own—regardless of the fact that many gurus claim that it *can* and that many students believe this claim.

I am Alpha *and* Omega, the beginning and the ending, sayeth the Lord. You will not attain Christ consciousness through the Alpha aspect alone. You *must* be willing to also fulfill the Omega aspect by doing the dirty work of cleaning up your psyche. As I have said, the ego dreams of creating the false path that makes it seem like you can be saved without pulling the beam from your own eye. The most obvious form of this dream is the claim that you are automatically saved by declaring me to be your Lord and Savior, and most people who are open to this course have overcome this illusion. Yet I need you to seriously consider whether you have fallen prey to a more subtle version of this illusion, namely the belief that by following this or that guru and practicing meditation or other techniques, you do not have to deal directly with your own psychological divisions.

This is simply a lie that is deliberately engineered to fool the more spiritually mature people into following the false path instead of doing what they are ready for, namely stepping onto the true path of Christhood. If you would rather follow this false path, I respect your free will. If not, then you need to recognize what it really takes to follow *my* path.

***

You have no doubt heard the saying that you can't have your cake and eat it too. Although this may seem like a trivial part of folklore, it actually contains an essential truth. I have said that God has given you free will and that he has given human beings dominion over the Earth. The deeper meaning is that you have a right to do anything you want in the material universe, yet the purpose of creating the material universe is to give you a platform for growing in consciousness. You grow by making choices and experiencing the consequences of those choices, meaning that everything you do – or don't do – has consequences. That is why you can't keep your cake – living a peaceful life with no adverse consequences – after eating the cake—doing whatever you want.

So you might approach life as a business that has a balance sheet with expenses and income. If your expenses exceed your income, you are not making progress on the path. Again, you have free will, so if you like the dualistic game of making money and spending/losing money, you can play it for as long as you like. Yet what I am offering you here is an alternative way, whereby you can eliminate the expenses altogether by overcoming the divisions in your psyche. Thereby, you can actually attain a state of consciousness in which you can keep the cake – of peace of mind – while making wise choices in the material universe and growing from those choices while raising up all of life. As I said:

> But seek ye first the kingdom of God, and his righteousness; and all these things shall be added unto you. (Matthew 6:33)

The kingdom of God is the Christ consciousness and "his righteousness" is the right use of your free will, so all of your choices are based on the wisdom of Christ and thus allow the love of God to flow through you. So in a sense, the path to Christhood can give you anything you want in the material universe, but it will not do so if you approach the path for the purpose of attaining anything in this world. That is why I am encouraging you to adopt the motivation of seeking first the kingdom of God, which is a state of wholeness, of having overcome the divisions in your psyche. For it is only when you attain this wholeness that the wisdom and love of God can flow through you and manifest anything you need in this world—that is, anything you need based on your divine plan and not the self-centered desires of the ego.

So my point is that you need to recognize that there are certain actions that will prevent you from making progress on the path. However, even more importantly, there are certain psychological conditions – the beam in your own eye – that will block your progress. The Alpha aspect of the path is receiving a higher understanding, as I have given you in this and preceding keys. Yet it is now time to get down to the Omega aspect, and in the following keys I will give you teachings and tools for overcoming the conditions in your psyche that create the most obvious blocks to your progress. However, there is an essential insight you need to have before we begin.

***

If you look at traditional Christianity, you will see that many Christians have – correctly I might add – recognized that certain types of behavior will block your salvation—and also your progress toward Christhood. Many Christians have even recognized that certain psychological conditions, such as anger, envy, greed or non-forgiveness, will block your progress. Yet the approach taken by most Christians is to either ignore such conditions, deny them or suppress them with the conscious will. Many people actually see themselves as "good Christians" because they have suppressed certain psychological elements to the point where they never express anger. Some people feel that because they have managed to suppress all these human, mortal or sinful elements, they are sure to be saved. Yet the stark reality is that these people have simply placed themselves in a state of consciousness that I addressed in the following quote:

> For I say unto you, That except your righteousness shall exceed the righteousness of the scribes and Pharisees, ye shall in no case enter into the kingdom of heaven. (Matthew 5:20)

This truth would be deeply shocking to such people, and many of them would refuse to believe it. Yet the fact is that by suppressing anger, you have *not* removed the division from your psyche. You have simply pushed it *to a deeper level,* like a forest fire that burns underground and may surface again at any moment. Who knows when you might encounter a situation in which you lose the outer control and are propelled into a fit of anger?

What I am calling you to embrace in this course is a higher approach, where you do not simply *suppress* that which you think is unacceptable according to some worldly standard. Instead, you seek first the kingdom of God, you seek first the inner wholeness whereby you are spiritually reborn by *resolving* your divisions and *healing* your wounds. You become a new person in Christ, and for this new person, the old behavior is simply no longer an option. You have healed the division in the psyche that caused you to respond with anger – or whatever the condition might be – so you no longer have a need to respond this way and can choose a response based on the mind of Christ.

This is not the via Dolorosa, even though it does require work. However, the via Dolorosa is a continued path of suffering. My path is a path where you temporarily deal with an imperfect condition in order to truly resolve it, and once you reach resolution, you are permanently free of the condition. In other words, it is not a quick-fix, but neither is it a state of ongoing suffering.

As you heal the most devastating divisions, you will overcome the suffering and begin to feel a new sense of freedom, peace and a bubbling sense of joy that is independent of any conditions on Earth. Thus, the prince of this world will have nothing in you whereby he can take away your peace and joy. This, my friend, is why I said that I am come that all might have life and that they might have it more abundantly. The abundant life is truly the freedom from the inner divisions that rob you of peace and joy.

I have earlier talked about giving up your life for Christ, but who – or what – is Christ? I said, "I am the way, the truth and the life," and the deeper meaning is that "Christ" is a symbol for a process that brings you from a state of *separation* from your source to *oneness* with your source. It leads you back to oneness with your higher self, your I AM Presence.

So the real question is whether you have had enough of following the ways of this world and have reached the point where you are willing to do what it takes to follow the Way of Christ. As I have attempted to explain in previous keys, you *do* have what it takes to follow my way. The only question is whether you are willing to do what it takes to follow the way? And I have now explained one of the basic requirements for following the way to wholeness.

## Exercise for Key 4

You are now at the point where you have all the elements you need in order to make a shift in consciousness, a shift that will take your focus away from the ways of the world and onto the inner path of Christ. In order to help you make that shift, I am asking you to give another 33-day vigil of studying this key while giving the Rosary for Clearing the Heart[8] once a day.

Repeat the technique of writing down your thoughts after the rosary and reading them the next day before you give the rosary. Focus especially on what motives and dreams you might have had about the spiritual path and what you should receive in return for giving up something in the world. Focus on your expectations about life and the path and consider whether they might prevent you from following the real-life path of self-transcendence leading to oneness.

Be willing to see and overcome anything that keeps you stuck in the state of separation. See it, surrender it and let it die:

> For whosoever will save his life shall lose it: and whosoever will lose his life for my sake shall find it. (Matthew 16:25)

Contemplate this truth: The ego is programmed to hold on to the things of this world. Yet you cannot take the things of this world with you to heaven, so any attachment to the things of this world will only pull you back. Meaning you have to reincarnate until you make the LIFE decision to give up your attachment. Thus, what will truly get you to heaven is not what you *hold on to* but what you *let go of*. What will a profit a person to gain the whole world yet lose the soul?

---

8 See *www.askrealjesus.com* in the Divine Feminine section.

# Key 5
# Freedom from cravings

In this and the following keys I will address some of the more obvious blocks that prevent you from being in the natural state of having God's wisdom and love flowing through your being. As you will see, these blocks are very much human in nature, and we might consider them kindergarten stuff for a sincere spiritual seeker. Yet there is great value in going over them with me, for these human conditions have inundated the collective consciousness. Unless you have a deeper understanding of them, it can be difficult for you to free yourself completely from all remnants of them. And I might say that unless you *do* free yourself completely from them, you will not attain ultimate freedom. Indeed, many sincere spiritual seekers have become stuck at a certain level precisely because they have not completely overcome one of these basic blocks. Thus, it is time to let them go, for you cannot pursue the path to Christhood while being burdened by these toxins.

In order to address the blocks, I need to give you some basic information. Some readers will already know this, but I need to make sure that all are on the same page. First of all, you need to have a clear understanding of your energy field. As you know from science, Einstein's theory of relativity states that the world is not made up of two separate substances, namely matter and energy. Einstein discovered that everything is energy, and by doing so he broke down the barrier between mind and matter. Energy is a more fundamental element than matter, which proves that thoughts are more fundamental than matter. This one realization is the foundation for all of my so-called miracles. Science has consistently proven that the more fundamental elements have power over the grosser elements. For example, all matter is made of subatomic particles, so the laws that work at the level of these particles have a fundamental influence on what form anything in the material universe can take.

Let me give a more visual example. You can carve a block of wood, and there are certain laws that guide how you work with wood, such as not cutting against the grain. Yet these laws function within a larger framework, namely the laws that guide how wood is formed at the molecular level. And these laws function within an even larger framework, namely the subatomic level, where pure energy is transformed into subatomic particles that can take on the form of any matter substance known on Earth. Do you see what I am saying? The same subatomic particles can form both wood, metal, water and air molecules. Thus, you see that all visible phenomena are created from a deeper underlying reality, which has a fundamental influence on everything in the material universe. Visible phenomena represent the level of effects, and the invisible reality represents the level of the real causes.

My point here is that in order to really change your life, you need to deal with causes and not effects, which means you need to look behind surface appearances. For example, as I said in the last key, many Christians traditionally seek to change certain types of behavior by suppressing them. Yet what I want is for you to go to the cause of these types of behavior and remove the cause – the beam in your own eye – so there is nothing left to suppress. And in order to do that, you need to know where the cause is located.

You need to understand that your total being – your mind – has more than one level. When you perform an action, it involves your physical body, your brain and your conscious mind. Yet you will never understand why you take certain actions by only looking at the brain and the conscious mind. You have no doubt heard the old saying, "Man, know thyself," and the deeper meaning is that you – man or woman – must know all levels of your mind. You must take command over your container of self.

The basic understanding you need is that your mind is an energy field, and as such it is made up of energies that vibrate at different levels. In fact, there are four main levels of your energy field, which in some esoteric traditions have been called your four lower bodies. However, I prefer to call them the four levels of the mind. They are:

- **The outer mind** that is closely linked to your physical body. This is the mind where you make conscious decisions and take many actions. This mind is very much affected by the physical brain and your environment, and for some people their conscious awareness is limited to this mind. Yet most spiritual seekers have expanded their conscious awareness to go beyond this mind, which is why they are open to the spiritual side of life. One of the main elements of spiritual growth is to expand one's conscious awareness beyond the physical mind, thus incorporating all levels of the mind and coming to know your full identity. Yet expansion is not enough, since it must be followed by purification of all levels of the mind.

- **The emotional mind.** This is obviously the level of your feelings, and as you know, feelings are very volatile and can easily be pointed in this or that direction. The emotional mind is above the outer mind, and thus feelings are a very powerful force for controlling your physical actions. You have experienced that when certain feelings build in intensity, the compulsion to take a certain action overpowers your conscious will. People who are completely controlled by their emotions have very little self-control, and thus they find it extremely difficult to make progress on the spiritual path. The reason being that since the emotional mind is more fundamental than the conscious mind, seeking to consciously suppress feelings is an uphill battle. As a sincere spiritual seeker, you need to attain control over your emotions, and one element of this is to remove the energies that pollute the emotional mind. Another is understanding where feelings originate.

- **The mental mind.** This is the seat of the intellect and your ability to understand the world. It is here that you analyze everything and can make more level-headed decisions. Ideally, your thoughts should lead to balanced emotions that lead to balanced actions. The problem is that the intellect is an analytical faculty, and I have already explained its inherent weakness. Thus, the intellect can find it difficult to know what is right, and this is what often plunges people into unbalanced emotions. They use the intellect to convince themselves that what they are thinking is right, which then gives them the belief that it is acceptable, necessary or unavoidable that they engage in certain limiting feelings. To overcome this pattern, you need to purify your mental mind from the energies and the dualistic illusions that prevent you from seeing that there is a deeper reality beyond the mental level—a reality that is *not* a matter of having the best intellectual analysis and argument.

- **The identity mind.** This is the highest level of your lower being, and it is the seat of your deepest sense of who you are in relation to the material universe (Your spiritual identity is anchored in your I AM Presence and can be accessed only by your conscious self, not by any of the lower minds.). As the most fundamental part of the lower being, the identity mind has a major impact on

> every aspect of your life, yet most people are unaware of its existence and thus have no control over it. They uncritically accept the sense of identity that is put upon them as they grow up, which then forms the foundation for all of their thoughts, feelings and actions. If people's identity is based on the consciousness of death, can their thoughts, feelings and actions do anything but follow? Thus, it is essential for a spiritual seeker to become aware of the identity mind and begin to purify it of all mortal elements.

We now need to add the fact that everything in the material universe is made from energy and that visible matter is actually a grosser manifestation of finer or more fundamental energies. Science has discovered how an energy wave can take on the form of a subatomic particle, even switching back and forth between a particle and a wave form. The implication is that beyond the material universe is a realm of finer energies – energies of a higher vibration – and this is, of course, what religious and spiritual teachings for thousands of years have referred to as heaven or the spiritual realm. My point being that the matter universe is created by lowering the vibration of spiritual energy, and thus this world is sustained only by a constant stream of energy from the spiritual into the material spectrum of vibrations. This flow of energy is replicated in the four levels of your mind.

You now see that the ideal state for a human being is that there is nothing to impede the natural flow of energy through the four levels of your mind. The spiritual energy flows from your Higher Being, your I AM Presence, and it first enters your identity mind. Here it is colored by your sense of identity, almost as if it passes through a filter. Yet if your sense of identity is based on your spiritual self, the energy flow will not be diminished but will simply be stepped down in vibration so it can enter the mental mind with full force. Again, the mental mind will color the energy, but if the images in this mind are based on the reality of Christ, the energy flow will not be diminished. It then enters the emotional mind, and if your emotions are pure, they will give the energy a positive direction that will be aimed at raising up all life. This will result in life-supporting actions that enrich both yourself and everyone else.

In the natural state, the energy that flows from your I AM Presence is stepped down and directed by your total being, and this happens in such a way that all life is enhanced. This is the form of life that I came to give all people by helping them reconnect to who they truly are. As I said:

> I am come that they might have life, and that they might have it more abundantly. (John 10:10)

When you express your spiritual identity through all of your thoughts, feelings and actions, you multiply the talents and thus God will give you even more creative energy. This is what gives you the truly abundant life.

So what happens when the four levels of your mind are polluted by imperfect beliefs and energies? Well, the natural flow is blocked and your creative power is limited. In reality, most of the energy that flows from your I AM Presence is blocked in your higher bodies and never reaches the level of the physical body, which means there is very little energy available for the person to be creative. In fact, many people have limited the energy flow to the point where there is barely enough to keep the physical body alive. Such people have very little energy left over to express their individuality, and thus they often mindlessly follow the mass consciousness.

How does this happen? Well, if you take God's energy and use it for selfish purposes, you are obviously not multiplying your talents and thus God has no return current that can be multiplied. You are limited to a certain amount of energy that enters your identity body. As you adopt selfish beliefs – meaning beliefs based on the mind of anti-christ that sees you as a separate being – you create certain blocks in the four levels of your mind.

To give you a visual illustration, compare the flow of energy to the flow of electricity coming into your house, the house being a symbol for the conscious mind. Now imagine that someone sneaks in and hooks up an electrical device to your power line before it enters your house—and that there is only a fixed amount of electricity coming to the house. One device might not make a noticeable difference, but as more and more devices are plugged in, there is not enough power to run everything in your house, so you are forced to shut something down. Furthermore, the devices that are plugged in before your house do not produce any useful output. All of the energy going into them is consumed by their own internal functions and there is nothing coming out that is useful to you or the world. The devices are simply spinning their wheels and producing heat that makes your house too hot for comfort.

My point being that the blocks in the higher levels of the mind are like devices that continually consume energy. As you become increasingly selfish, more and more of the fixed amount that enters your lower being is used up by your internal divisions, thus being blocked from flowing through you. As a result, you use up *internally* what should have been expressed *externally* to enrich yourself and all life. This is essentially the process behind what psychologists today call clinical depression. However, it can also lead to all other psychological imbalances, including a constant state of agitation, which is caused by the excess energy that makes your energy field an unpleasant place to be. The symptoms can be varied, and this can account for most psychological problems.

How do you break this self-reinforcing spiral? You do so by purifying the four levels of your mind from the energies that have accumulated there. And to do that, you must also overcome the dualistic beliefs that caused the downward spiral to start. This is the subject of this and the coming keys.

***

Now for another piece of basic information. As you might know, there is no record of my activities between the age of 12 and the age of 30. The last record of my early life is this:

> 41 Now his parents went to Jerusalem every year at the feast of the passover.
> 42 And when he was twelve years old, they went up to Jerusalem after the custom of the feast.
> 43 And when they had fulfilled the days, as they returned, the child Jesus tarried behind in Jerusalem; and Joseph and his mother knew not of it.
> 44 But they, supposing him to have been in the company, went a day's journey; and they sought him among their kinsfolk and acquaintance.
> 45 And when they found him not, they turned back again to Jerusalem, seeking him.
> 46 And it came to pass, that after three days they found him in the temple, sitting in the midst of the doctors, both hearing them, and asking them questions.
> 47 And all that heard him were astonished at his understanding and answers.
> 48 And when they saw him, they were amazed: and his mother said unto him, Son, why hast thou thus dealt with us? behold, thy father and I have sought thee sorrowing.
> 49 And he said unto them, How is it that ye sought me? wist ye not that I must be about my Father's business? (Luke, Chapter 2)

The next record of me is when I appear at the wedding in Cana, turning the water into wine (John 2:1). So what did I do in the meantime? Well, some assume I worked as a carpenter, others that I apparently did nothing, simply sitting around waiting for my mission to start. These assumptions are based on the mainstream Christian idol that says I was God incarnate and thus had to have been born already perfect. Yet is it not more logical to assume that in the 17 "missing" years I was not simply passively waiting for my mission to start but was doing what I said I was going to do, namely being about my Father's business? And what does that mean? Well, if I knew I had a mission for God, does it not seem logical that I was doing everything possible to prepare myself for that mission? In other words, I was walking the path of Christhood by studying and applying whatever spiritual teachings I could find?

The reality is that I did indeed engage in a pilgrimage of seeking out various spiritual teachings and teachers, and this journey brought me far and wide, from Egypt to India and Tibet. Many Christians vehemently deny this, but they do so because they fail to realize that I did not grow up in the Christian mental box in which they have grown up—there *was* no Christian mental box at the time. Thus, I was not a Christian, and if you want to put a label on me, you would have to say I was a mystic or a universal spiritual seeker who sought truth wherever it could be found. I knew – as all true mystics do – that God cannot be confined to any of the mental boxes – religious or otherwise – found on Earth. Thus, I knew that in order to prepare myself for my mission, I would have to find the universal spiritual path that runs like an unseen thread behind the world's outer religions. In fact, I knew that my immediate mission was to teach that path to the Jewish people—and beyond that to all.

During my spiritual journey, I studied – among others – the philosophy of Buddhism, which has many profound teachings and practical tools. In fact, some people have found parallels between my sayings and the sayings of the Buddha, which is not a coincidence. Partly because I did study the teachings of the Buddha and partly because we both drank from the same universal fount of truth. So what I want to do at this point is to introduce a teaching from esoteric Buddhism that relates to the topic of the blocks in your mind.

***

The concept I want to introduce is that of spiritual poisons. The traditional teaching from Buddhism is that in the beginning there was one, primordial Buddha, named Vajrasattva. This Being divided itself into five other Buddhas, in the West called Dhyani Buddhas. These are not Buddhas that embodied on Earth but they exist in a higher realm. Each Buddha embodies certain spiritual qualities, and the perversions of those qualities are the spiritual poisons. These poisons are what cause human suffering, and thus the way to overcome suffering is to free oneself from the poisons. This can be done partly by invoking the assistance and spiritual qualities of the Dhyani Buddhas and partly by overcoming the beliefs that open your mind to the poisons.

In the language we can use today, the Buddhas are actually members of the Ascended Host and their qualities correspond to certain spiritual energies that were used to create the material universe. The poisons are the perversions of the qualities of the Buddhas, in the form of energies with such a low vibration that they cannot flow back up to the spiritual realm. Thus, by engaging in the poisons, you diminish the natural figure-eight flow between your higher and lower being. To give you a feel for the poisons, let me list them:

- Ignorance and delusion.
- Anger and hatred.
- Spiritual and intellectual pride.
- Cravings and greed.
- Envy and jealousy.
- Non-will and non-being.

There are two ways for you to be affected by the poisons, namely by producing them internally and by taking them in from the outside. The two are connected, so let me explain.

You know that you live in an environment where you are, so to speak, surrounded by chemicals and microorganisms that can be dangerous to your health if they are allowed to enter your body. You do not live in constant fear of this, since you have learned to take certain precautions, such as cleaning and cooking your food, cleaning a cut and not breathing in dangerous fumes. Furthermore, you know your body has an immune system that repels or consumes dangerous substances.

You now need to realize that you also live in an environment where you are surrounded by unseen energies that can be equally dangerous if they are allowed to enter your energy field, meaning the four levels of your mind. The difference being that you were not taught this, so you have not built a habit of taking the necessary precautions to keep your energy field pure. Many spiritual seekers have actually learned to protect themselves from the poisons without being aware of it, yet there is great value in becoming consciously aware of the process so you can take even better precautions. The Earth is currently a very impure environment, where the collective consciousness of humankind is heavily affected by all of the spiritual poisons. So if you open your energy field to them, you can quickly be overwhelmed and lose control over your life.

As an example, let us take the poison of anger. It should be obvious that during the conflict-ridden history of humankind, enormous amounts of anger energy has been produced. Science tells you that energy cannot be created or destroyed, so once energy has been qualified with the distinct vibration of anger, it will remain in that state indefinitely—meaning until someone transforms the energy back to a higher vibration. If you engage in a fit of anger, you will often direct that anger at another person. This will – literally – blow or tear a hole in your energy field. And once the opening is there, anger energy from your environment can flow inwards through it and accumulate in your energy field.

Take note of what I am saying here. Your energy field has a certain structure that is designed to help you express life-supporting energies in the material realm. However, your field is *not* designed to facilitate the expression of anger or other emotions that do not enhance life. The consequence is that when you *do* express such emotions, you will damage the original structure of your energy field, often tearing rents in your garment. One instance of losing control in a fit of anger can literally tear a rent in your field that can open you up to an influx of energy from the outside. And as long as you stay in an agitated state, the energies will keep flowing in, which makes it difficult for your energy field to repair itself. The field can indeed heal itself as your physical body can, yet you know that if you cut your skin and keep scratching the cut or allowing dirt to accumulate, the healing process will take much longer.

Once energies have an inroad, they will pull on your thoughts and emotions, making you more prone to respond with anger in other situations. The next time you engage in anger, you reopen or reinforce the hole and more energy can come in. It should be easy to see that this can quickly create a downward, self-reinforcing spiral that can cause you to lose control of your life because your mental and emotional minds are simply overwhelmed with energy that turns your mind into a very chaotic environment.

As a parallel, consider how a chemical poison works in your body. A very small amount of a deadly poison will have no effect on your body. As more and more poison accumulates, you begin to see some long-term effects that still might not be deadly or even noticeable. Yet if you keep increasing the concentration, the chemical effect of the poison will eventually paralyze your major organs, and there comes a "point of no return" beyond which it becomes impossible to reverse the effect of the poison—leading to death.

Once a downward spiral of the accumulation of toxic energy has begun, it will take a very determined effort to reverse it and begin an upward spiral. Yet most people are not aware of how to even do this, and many of them don't care, for they have now become convinced that it is unavoidable or even justified for them to respond to certain situations – or life in general – with anger. This can even lead to the state of paranoia, where people feel the whole world is out to get them, and thus they are constantly in an agitated state, seeking to ward off attacks that often do not come or are largely imagined. This state is actually part of the explanation behind the concept of possession by evil Spirits, although there is also a deeper explanation. Can you see how easy it is for the ego and the forces of anti-christ to control people by keeping them in an agitated state, in which they have no attention left over to truly think about life but keep doing the same thing over and over, even for lifetimes?

Obviously, a person in such a state of inner conflict and division has no chance whatsoever of walking the path to Christhood. Thus, it is essential for all disciples of the Living Christ to learn how to break such a spiral by performing spiritual first aid.

***

Having set a foundation, I will now concentrate on the specific poison that is the focus of this key, namely cravings, lust and greed. I am starting with this poison because it is the lowest in vibration, being centered around the physical body. Thus, it is the most obvious, and it is also the poison that most spiritually interested people have already overcome to some degree. By showing you this, I hope to help you see that you already have some momentum on overcoming the poisons. And by becoming more aware of causes and effects, you can more easily free yourself from the downward pull of all the poisons.

As Maitreya explains in his book, there are many reasons why lifestreams find themselves embodying on Earth. Yet part of the motivation is that lifestreams want to experience the material universe and do the things that can only be done through a physical body. If you look at the world today, you will obviously see that people are at many different levels of consciousness. Some people are completely focused on experiencing the things of this world, including the pleasures of the body, be it drinking beer or having sex.

Now, take care to realize that I am not condemning this. God has defined the law of free will. It is not uncommon that a lifestream has to embody many times on Earth, sometimes spending several lifetimes focusing on a particular bodily pleasure or another Earthly pursuit, before it has had enough and begins to wonder if there isn't more to life. So within the framework set by the law of free will, there is nothing inherently wrong with people focusing on Earthly pleasure—if that is what they desire to experience.

However, the law of free will also states that while you are allowed to engage in Earthly pursuits, doing so is not the underlying purpose of your existence, meaning you cannot do this forever. The reason for this is that your lifestream was not created exclusively for the purpose of experiencing the material universe. It was created to be a co-creator with God and help raise the material universe to the point of becoming a permanent sphere in God's creation—again, as explained by Maitreya in greater detail. So there will come a point where your conscious self is beginning to awaken to its higher purpose.

Yet it is possible that your container of self has taken in so much of the poison of cravings that your conscious self cannot actually follow its innermost longing. The poison is pulling it into repeating the old patterns, meaning that you are no longer making a free choice to engage in the experiences of this world. Your free will has been overpowered by the poison, and you cannot free yourself from the downward pull. My point being that while there are some people who engage in worldly pursuits out of free will, there are many who have lost their free will to the prince of this world.

Let me give you a visual illustration. The poisons in the mass consciousness exert a gravitational pull on everything on Earth, including you. Yet you know that a physical magnet only attracts something made of iron. So if you walk through a strong magnetic field, it will have no noticeable effect on your body. Yet if you fill your pockets with pieces of iron, the magnet now has something to pull on, and this can prevent you from walking away from the magnetic field. Likewise, the gravitational pull of cravings will only have an attractive force on energies of the same vibration. Thus, if you have no such energies in your container of self, you can live on Earth without being affected by the mass consciousness, you can be *in* the world but not *of* the world.

Now imagine that you allow a small amount of the energies of cravings to enter your field. The effect is hardly noticeable, yet like attracts like, so the energies will gradually accumulate. As they do, they begin to exert more of a pull on your mental and emotional minds, which means you become susceptible to the belief that it is acceptable to engage in an activity that seemingly satisfies the cravings—you are now blinded by the energies. You also begin to feel an emotional craving to engage in such an activity, and the craving becomes gradually stronger. As the energies continue to accumulate, they can eventually become so strong that they can overpower your conscious will, and you have now become addicted to a particular activity. Yet no matter how much you engage in the activity, it never seems to be enough, and the reason is that the accumulated energy will continue to pull on you. You literally can never satisfy this craving, which is why people's lives can be consumed by an addiction that never leads to any ultimate satisfaction but becomes an end in itself.

The only way to break the vicious circle is to lessen the pull of the accumulated energy by invoking spiritual energy to consume it. Yet you also need to uncover the mental beliefs that made it seem acceptable or necessary to participate in a certain activity. By taking this two-fold approach, you can break any addiction—and let me assure you that there are many subtle addictions, even emotional and mental addictions. Even many spiritual people have addictions that they do not recognize. In fact, even the quest for peak spiritual experiences can become an addiction.

Obviously, if you had been completely blinded by the poison of cravings, you would not have been reading this book. Yet there are indeed many spiritual seekers who have only just begun to awaken, and thus – while not being entirely controlled by the poison of cravings – they are still very much affected by this poison. And this causes them to have to struggle very hard, often sliding backwards each time they think they have finally gained some ground. It is my goal in this key to empower you to avoid this see-saw pattern and instead turn your pursuit of spiritual growth into a steady, upward climb. And let me assure you that even more mature spiritual seekers can benefit from this lesson, for few are completely free from the poison of cravings.

***

As a spiritual seeker, you obviously know that you are more than your physical body. You are a spiritual being, who is only temporarily residing in this physical body, much like your body can get into a car in order to go somewhere. Yet have you really contemplated the relationship between the spiritual you and the physical body?

This relationship has two sides. One is, as already mentioned, that the body is not an end in itself but a means to an end, namely the spiritual purpose of helping to co-create the material universe. So obviously, you do not want the body to become a hindrance for that goal. Yet in order to make the best use of your body, you have to see the other side of the coin, which is that your body is not evil and it is not – inherently – an enemy of your spiritual growth and goals. This will require some contemplation.

Many spiritual traditions have depicted the body and the material universe as enemies of your spiritual growth. Some branches of Christianity have even portrayed the body and matter itself as creations of the devil, as being evil. Thus, there was a need to discipline the body, suppress bodily urges and starve the body of anything pleasurable. If you read Maitreya's book, you will see that the material universe is not evil and was not created by the devil. Matter was simply created at a relatively low vibration and people in embodiment were meant to raise it to a higher vibration. Because so many people have forgotten their original purpose, the vibration of matter has actually been lowered beyond its starting point, but that still doesn't make matter evil. It is simply dense, and while this does make it harder for people to contact the spiritual realm, it is not an insurmountable obstacle. You simply need to know what you are up against and how to overcome the downward pull of matter.

I hope you can see that in Christianity there was an obvious cause for this hatred of the body. It was the fact that the Catholic church made the wrongful decision that priests were not allowed to marry. Thus, priests had no outlet for sexual desire, and since it was seen as coming from the body, the body had to be evil and needed to be suppressed or even punished.

Beyond this there is, however, a deeper explanation. You are probably already aware that there are spiritual cycles in the life of this planet. I am the master for the 2,000-year cycle that started with my birth, normally called the Age of Pisces. We are now moving into the next cycle, called the Age of Aquarius. The fact is that during Pisces, the overall goal for people was to establish a connection to the spiritual realm and their higher selves. And because the collective consciousness of humankind was very dense during that age – as witnessed by the many atrocities in the history books – it was difficult to make that connection. Thus, for those who valued the spiritual connection highly, it was viable and necessary to eliminate any distractions. That is why you see a tendency for spiritual people to withdraw from worldly life into protected spheres, such as monasteries.

In the Aquarian age, the conditions are different. Despite many current world events, the consciousness of humankind has been raised significantly, especially over the past century. Thus, you now see many people who have a spiritual connection while living active lives in society. In fact, the focus for the Aquarian age is to bring spirituality into all aspects of life, including everyday activities. Thus, it is no longer necessary for spiritual people to withdraw from the world. Some can still benefit from doing so (perhaps only for a time) but most will make more progress by living active lives, where they demonstrate a spiritual approach to life through everyday activities.

***

As with everything else, there is an Alpha and an Omega aspect, and only when the two are balanced by the Christ mind, will you have sustainable growth. The Alpha aspect is that you are not here to simply experience the pleasures of Earth. In fact, you are not here to accept the current conditions on Earth. If you are a spiritual person, you have a divine plan, and part of that plan is to make your individual contribution – by expressing your spiritual individuality – to raising the vibration of Earth until God's kingdom – the abundant life – is manifest for all. So your physical body is meant to be a tool for this goal, and thus you need to see the body as a servant and the spiritual you as the master of your house.

This can only be done through the Christ mind. If you are unbalanced in the Alpha aspect, you will begin to see the body as a hindrance, even as an enemy, and you now engage in a struggle to suppress the body. Instead of working *with* the body, you are working *against* the body – feeling it is working against *you* – and this makes you a house divided against itself, turning your life into a struggle that eats up your creative energy so there is little left for expressing your divine plan.

On the other hand, if you become unbalanced in the Omega aspect, you fail to see your body as a servant, often coming to see it as an end in itself. Thus, what is meant to be your servant, will rule your life, and all of your creative energy will be swallowed up by pursuing bodily needs and pleasures. Again, the only way to balance the Omega aspect is the Christ mind, which helps you see that your body is not an enemy of your spiritual goals but the very foundation for fulfilling those goals.

I am an ascended master, and I have, as the Bible says, been given "all power in heaven and on Earth." This means that because

I have fully united with my Higher Being – heaven – I now have the all-power of mind over matter. I could – instantly – remove all disease from the Earth. Yet the law of God – the law of free will – states that I cannot use my power on Earth because I am not in a physical body. As Genesis explains, God has given dominion over the Earth to those people who are in a physical body on Earth. Thus, although I have the power to change the Earth, I do not have the authority to do so. Only people in embodiment have that authority, but they don't have the power. My purpose for coming into embodiment was to demonstrate that all people have the potential to attain the power of mind over matter, whereby they can use their authority to manifest the abundant life on Earth. I want to show *you* how to attain *my* power – or at least a measure of it – while you are still in embodiment and thus have the authority to produce real change.

So you now see that your physical body is the very platform for the fulfillment of your divine plan. Which means that instead of working *against* it, you need to learn how to work *with* it. You also see that in order to work *with* the body, you need to be in the driver's seat, for if you let the car drive itself, both of you will end up in the ditch. Whereby I mean that if you let the body and lower mind lead, they will blindly follow bodily cravings and you will then be a blind follower.

***

In order to put yourself in control of the body, I need you to begin a very deep shift in the way you look at the body, and even the material universe. I have told you that everything – even "solid" matter – is made from energy. Ultimately, even physical energy – such as electricity or sunlight – is made from spiritual energy that has been lowered in vibration into the material frequency spectrum. I have told you that there is a stream of spiritual energy that flows into the material universe and is gradually lowered in vibration through the four levels of the identity, mental, emotional and finally the physical spectrum. In the material level, energy first appears as energy waves, but then eventually is lowered to the spectrum that human beings call matter. This is still energy, but to the human senses, it appears as solid matter—even though you know that atoms have large amounts of empty space between the core and the electrons. How does this knowledge form the basis for a new view of the body?

Since you went to school, you have been programmed to view the world in a way that is very much based on the physical senses, which means it is centered around matter. Science is very much focused on matter, even to the point of many scientists believing that if a theory proposes a cause that is beyond matter, it is not a scientific theory. As one example of this, you have no doubt been shown a magnet and how there is a field around it in the form of concentric elliptical lines. You have been told since childhood that the magnet produces the field, and you have believed this statement, since you did not know better. Many spiritual people have come to believe that everything has an energy field around it, including their physical bodies. Yet most of them believe that this works the same way as a magnet, namely that the physical body produces the energy field. Can you see that this world view is a sensory-based world view? The physical senses can see the body but cannot see the energy field, so the senses automatically assume that what they see is the cause and anything unseen must be merely an effect.

In reality, science should have long ago set itself free from this – outdated – sensory-based world view. Thus, you should have been brought up with an expanded world view. Yet since that was not the case, it is now up to all spiritual people to free their minds from the sensory-based, materialistic world view in which every phenomenon must have a material cause.

So what is the consequence for the body? The consequence is that your body does *not* produce the energy field; it is the energy field that produces the body. Your energy field has four levels. The highest in vibration is the identity level. Even at this higher level, there is a blueprint for your physical body. If you have a correct sense of identity as a spiritual being with a higher purpose, the blueprint of your body will be one that supports your divine plan (which in some cases can involve dealing with a physical disease). There is another – more detailed – blueprint of your body in the mental mind and another in the emotional. Finally, there is a blueprint of the body in the material spectrum and this blueprint is – naturally – what spells out the physical characteristics of your body. In fact, the energy field in the material spectrum has a part of it that is so dense that it appears physical to your senses—which is what you call your body.

I need you to contemplate what I am saying here, although I realize that for most people it will take some time to integrate these ideas. You have no doubt seen the model of an atom that looks like a miniature solar system with a nucleus and some electrons orbiting it like planets. All so-called solid matter is made up of such atoms, but when you look at the model, you see that the atom is mostly empty space. You have no doubt heard that your body is made up of 70% water, so it is not nearly as solid as it seems. Yet now go one step further and realize that your body is made up of 100% atoms but that atoms are made up of over 99% empty space. The distances between the nucleus and the electrons in most atoms are relatively greater than the distance between the Earth and the sun. In other words, an atom is made up of a small fraction of so-called subatomic particles and the rest is empty space—and this is true for *all* matter.

What does this actually mean? Well, as one example, consider the question of whether people can walk through walls, as some spiritual teachers – myself included – are repudiated to have done. If your body is mostly empty space and the wall is mostly empty space, there is – theoretically – plenty of empty space in the wall for the very small percentage of subatomic particles in your body to pass through. So why can't your body pass through walls? Well, there is a technical explanation but science is not yet developed enough to actually have the vocabulary to explain it. So let us use every-day language and say that matter has two basic properties, an Alpha and an Omega aspect. The Alpha aspect is "emptiness" and the Omega aspect is "solidity." Of course, you can have various combinations of these two qualities, for example diamonds are very solid while air is more empty than solid.

So you have two options for viewing matter, and they are parallel to the old question of whether the glass is half full or half empty—it is all a matter of perspective. If you look at the world through the filter of the physical senses, you see the world in terms of solidity, and thus your body cannot pass through a wall. Yet if you could shift your perspective away from the senses, you would see the world in terms of emptiness, and then it would be easy for you to pass the body through a wall.

The point is that your mind can perceive the world through the senses or it can perceive the world beyond the senses—often called extra-sensory perception. The physical senses are designed to detect energy waves within a certain spectrum of frequencies, namely the material spectrum. Anything that vibrates within that spectrum will tend to appear solid to the senses. For example, you might have seen an airplane propeller that spins so quickly that it appears as a solid disc. Yet if you slow down the movements, you see that the disc it not solid at all. Likewise, matter only appears solid because it vibrates at a certain level that the senses perceive as solid. If you shift your perspective, you see that the appearance of solidity is only a matter of perspective. You cannot do this with the senses, but your mind can go beyond the senses—even though 99% of human beings have allowed their minds to be imprisoned by the senses.

Now consider the biblical account of me walking on water. Why did the weight of my body not sink into the water? Well, the senses view the body as solid and a wall as solid, but they view the water as softer – more empty – meaning that while a wall stops the body, the water allows it to pass through it. Yet when you shift your perspective, you see that when you focus on the body's emptiness and the wall's emptiness, the body can pass through the wall. So if you focus on the body's emptiness and the water's solidity, then the water can support the weight of the body—as can "thin" air, which explains the many reports of spiritual teachers levitating.

You will recall my statement that those who believe on me shall do the works that I did and even greater works. Does that mean I want my modern-day disciples to perform the miracles I performed 2,000 years ago? Not necessarily, since times have changed. My miracles were aimed at changing people's perception of what is possible, and this is always our aim for doing anything. Yet since humankind's consciousness has been expanded dramatically over the past 2,000 years, the situation is different today. So there will be different ways to demonstrate mastery in today's world. Nevertheless, I still want my modern-day disciples to develop the mastery of mind over matter, and that begins by understanding why it is possible for the mind to take command over "solid" matter.

***

The explanation is, as we have already touched upon, that everything in the world of form is made from one basic substance, namely the Ma-ter Light, which can take on any form. Yet the light takes on a specific form only when a self-aware being creates a mental image and uses the mind's ability to superimpose or project that image upon the Ma-ter light. My point is that everything in the material universe has no actual, or "objective" existence, as modern science calls it. Everything is a projection of mental images, which has actually been proven by the science of quantum physics. It might be helpful for you to read one of the many popular science books on the findings of quantum physics.

The consequence is that your physical body is a creation of the mind. Obviously, your conscious mind did not create your body, but your higher mind did. Yet your current body was not created "from scratch" as they say, since it is part of a creative process that has been occurring on this planet for millions of years. Therefore, your body was not created on a blank slate but is partly affected by the current state of affairs on Earth, including the density of the collective consciousness. This explains why most people think their minds have no power over their bodies—they are so overwhelmed by the "weight" of the collective consciousness that they cannot conceive of going beyond it.

Yet as a disciple of Christ, you need to realize that you cannot follow Christ and at the same time follow the mass consciousness. You cannot serve two masters, you cannot serve God and mammon—meaning the mass consciousness. So it is a natural and inescapable part of the path to Christhood that you raise your mind above the mass mind and begin to shift your sense of identity back to the spiritual being you are—reconnecting to the individuality that is anchored in your I AM Presence.

As a natural part of this process, you need to begin to see your body as a creation of the mind. Therefore, your body is subservient to your mind, meaning that it has the potential to be subservient *to* and supportive *of* your divine plan. For some people it is part of their divine plan to take on certain physical diseases or limitations, often to demonstrate how to overcome them, physically or mentally. Yet you need to move toward a point where your physical body is not in any way hindering or slowing down the fulfillment of your divine plan. This includes a greater awareness of cravings that center around the physical body and how they influence your mind.

I have said that your body is not your enemy but is the passport that gives your Higher Being entry into the material world. Yet because your body is in the material world and because your mind is intimately tied to it, the influence goes both ways. Because the body is truly a projection of a mental image in the mind, your conscious self has the potential to take command over your body. Yet unless you *do* take command, your body will overwhelm your conscious self, and your life will be controlled by the cravings of the body. That is why so many people identify themselves with – or even *as* – a physical body with nothing more to their identity, thinking they will cease to exist when the body dies—which truly is no way to live, for it is a state of spiritual death.

***

Let us now consider that your physical body is extremely complex, in fact far more complex and sophisticated than most technology. Your body has many functions that are so complex that if you were to direct them consciously, your conscious mind would quickly be overwhelmed. Thus, your body is designed in such a way that most of its functions can take place without your conscious mind telling the body what to do or how to do it. You do not have to tell your body to breathe in oxygen, to pump the blood around or to digest food. You might know that your body is made of individual cells, and inside each cell is a miniature "machinery" that is almost as complex as the organs and nervous system of the body. Yet, again, the cells function without you having to consciously direct them.

Your body is made of 50 trillion individual cells, yet all of these cells are tied together in a coherent whole. The 50 trillion cells can move as one body, and your conscious mind can tell the body where to go and it will – generally speaking – do so. Yet you also know that while your conscious mind can direct the body, the influence goes both ways. If your body has not had enough rest, it will influence your sense of well-being, and if your body is low on food, your mood is quickly affected. This can now give us a new perspective on cravings.

I generally do not like comparing everything to machines, but there is some value in likening the body to a very complex piece of machinery. In fact, the body "machine" is so complex that it is controlled by a very sophisticated computer. This computer has a number of individual programs that direct various functions of the body, such as breathing, metabolism and so on. These programs are generally speaking designed to ensure the survival of your individual body by meeting its physical needs, including food, shelter and rest.

Yet the computer that directs your individual body was not developed just to serve *your* body. In fact, it is part of a very long process of experimentation that goes back millions of years. The point being that your body computer has a very complex programming that is directed toward not only ensuring the survival of your individual body but also ensuring the survival of the human race as a whole. In fact, to continue in computer terminology, your individual computer is networked to a large mainframe computer, namely the collective consciousness of humankind. In some cases, an individual body computer can be taken over by the mainframe computer, which has programs that are designed to ensure the survival of the race. One example of such an overall program is the need for sex, which is not exclusively an individual need but is designed to propagate the race, even though bearing children is somewhat of a sacrifice for the individual. Likewise, an overall program can cause people to sacrifice the lives of their physical bodies to ensure the survival of a well-defined group, as for example to defend their family or by going to war to defend their country. The survival of the whole will sometimes override the survival of the individual.

I know this has been a long and round-about discussion, but you might remember that we started out talking about cravings. So it might be tempting at this point to reason that the subconscious computer programs that are designed to ensure the survival of the body and the race is what causes you to have cravings for food, sleep, sex and so on. This is both true and not true, but to understand this, we need to take a closer look at how I define cravings.

In the broadest sense, we might say that a craving is a longing or desire for something you don't have. It causes you to feel a need to act in order to get the object you crave, and you feel unsatisfied, hungry, unfulfilled, perhaps even unhappy or unwhole until you get it. Yet what I want to bring to your attention is that there are two layers of cravings. The lowest layer is a simple craving, such as a feeling of being hungry. This is the kind of craving that is born out of a program that ensures the survival of the body. You feel hungry, you eat, you feel full and the craving is forgotten. Yet beyond that is a craving that does *not* go away even when the physical need is fulfilled. It is a deeper craving, an emotional, even mental craving that cannot simply be fulfilled by acquiring the object of the craving. Let us consider a couple of examples.

Animals do not have a consciousness that is as sophisticated as that of humans. A cow, for example, is not aware that it is a cow and it does not consciously choose to behave as a cow—it instinctively behaves as a cow. Thus, we might say that the actions of animals are almost exclusively based on the need for the physical survival of the individual and the race. For example, all animals eat, but they eat only to survive, the consequence being that you rarely see an overweight animal. Compare this to humans, where an increasing number of people in Western countries are so overweight that it actually threatens the long-term survival of their bodies. In other words, animals eat to live and once the survival of the body is secured, they stop eating. Humans have the ability to go beyond the mere need for survival and eat because of a need that is not aimed at – and thus cannot spring from – the survival of the body. We now see that if people were functioning exclusively based on the programming of their body computers, they would eat only what was needed to ensure the survival of their physical bodies—and then they would stop eating.

As another example, consider that all animals breed, yet this is entirely directed by the need to propagate the race. At certain times of the year, the hormones kick in and both male and female representatives of a species develop a need for sexual activity. Yet once the optimal period is over, the need disappears and the individuals are now back to the behavior of eating and sleeping. Yet in humans, you see some individuals whose lives are consumed by a craving for sex. If you think about this logically, you realize that even in the animal kingdom, there is a limit to how many babies need to be born by one individual member of a higher species of mammals. Thus, there is no survival value in a human constantly feeling a craving for sex. Again, we see that humans have the ability to develop cravings that go far beyond the survival programs of the physical body.

My overall point here is that you are currently in physical embodiment, which means that you are expressing yourself through a physical body. In order to give you the capacities you have with a body, the body is a very complex biological machine, which means that it has certain built-in computer programs designed to ensure the survival of your individual body and the race.

Now let me return to the concept held by some spiritual people that your body is an enemy of spiritual growth or that it is evil. We can now see that this is simply a primitive form of reasoning. The reality is that your body is designed with survival in mind, meaning that the computer that runs the body is designed to ensure your individual survival and the long-term survival of the whole. As long as you are in the body, you will experience this as certain bodily needs, such as food, rest, sex and so on.

You obviously need your body to survive in order to have a platform for your expression in the material universe. Thus, there is nothing wrong with taking care of the physical needs of the body. It is a completely artificial construct that religious or spiritual people see the body as sinful and have a highly contrived view of the body's functions, including the need for sex. In reality, there is nothing wrong or sinful about spiritual people taking care of the needs of their bodies.

However, this is *not* the same as saying that spiritual people can eat as much as they want or have as much sex as they want. You need to realize that you only have a certain amount of time, attention and energy, so you need to decide how to spend it in a way that helps the fulfillment of your divine plan. Most people in the Western world have grown up without having any sense of spiritual purpose to their lives, so they have been programmed by society to be perfect consumers, meaning that people continue to consume. Many people do whatever feels good at the moment without considering long-term – let alone spiritual – consequences. This is obviously partly what I meant when I said you cannot serve both God and mammon. As a spiritual person you need to decide how you set your priorities.

Be careful to realize that I am not hereby saying you need to become an ascetic who deprives yourself of anything related to the body. In today's world, most spiritual people need to lead active lives, which involves taking care of their physical needs. However, what you need to strive for is a state of mind where taking care of your physical needs is driven by the natural drive for survival, whereby I mean that you do what is needed and then forget about the need. In other words, your life is not consumed by cravings for food or sex that are never satisfied and end up consuming your time, energy and attention, thereby preventing you from focusing on your divine plan.

In other words, there is nothing wrong with satisfying the natural cravings of the body, but you need to make an effort to raise yourself above any craving that is beyond the body's survival needs. And in order to do this, you need to understand where unnatural cravings come from.

***

The essential difference between a *natural* craving and an *unnatural* craving is that a natural craving can be filled, whereas an unnatural one can never be satisfied. You might have seen people who remain unsatisfied no matter how much they eat, how much sex they have, how much money they have or how much power they wield. An unnatural craving is like a bottomless pit that can never be filled, like a black hole that pulls everything into itself but never gives anything back.

Filling your natural cravings will not disturb your life or prevent you from fulfilling your divine plan. Taking care of your body's need for food – even sex – should be no more distracting than breathing. Yet trying to fulfill unnatural cravings is an impossible quest, and it can quickly take over people's lives to the point where their divine plans become secondary or forgotten.

You might have heard about the quest for the Holy Grail, which is actually a metaphor for the path to Christhood. Yet seeking to fulfill unnatural cravings is the quest for the *unholy* grail, the grail that can never be filled and thus is the cup that never runneth over.

Where do unnatural cravings come from? Well, since they cannot come from the survival programming of the body computer, they must come from the higher levels of the mind, namely the conscious mind and the emotional, mental and identity levels.

In order to understand the origin of cravings, you need to realize that your lifestream was designed to be a co-creator with God. Thus, you have two built-in desires that are very much God's desires seeking fulfillment in you. Take note that I have talked about unnatural cravings and not about desires. The word "desire" actually means "deity sires" and the Creator has a desire, which is the driving force behind the creation of the world of form.

One aspect of God's desire is the desire to become more through creating you and other self-aware beings. In your being, this is manifest as two separate but linked desires:

- The Alpha aspect is a desire for oneness with your source. This can ultimately be fulfilled only when you attain full God consciousness, but it is the driving force behind your spiritual quest and your sense that there is something more than the material world.
- The Omega aspect is a desire to become more in *this* world, namely by expressing your God-given creative powers in order to make the world more like the kingdom of God.

When you put these two desires together, you see that on one hand you have a desire that reaches *beyond* this world and on the other hand is a desire that seeks fulfillment *in* this world. This is designed to give you the desire to express yourself in this world without getting lost in this world. In other words, you naturally seek to experience more in the material world, but you always know that ultimate fulfillment can be found only in oneness with your source. As long as you are in a balanced state, there is no conflict between these two desires. By attaining the Christ consciousness, you will actually feel a great sense of oneness with your source – I and my Father are one – while expressing yourself in this world—my Father worketh hitherto and I work.

The problem comes in when a lifestream becomes blinded by the duality consciousness and builds an identity as a being who is separated from God. This causes the lifestream to believe in the image of the external God, and the consequence is that your longing for oneness with your source cannot be satisfied. How can you achieve oneness with a God that you see as being outside yourself, thus believing there will always be a distance between you and God? Instead, such lifestreams are tempted by the prince of this world to seek ultimate fulfillment in the material world by seeking to get more of what this world has to offer. Thus, they throw themselves into the quest of seeking some ultimate state in the material world, while not realizing it is an impossible quest. They seek more *of* this world instead of more *than* this world.

***

An unnatural craving starts in the identity body by you building the sense of identity that you are a being who is separated from your source, from God. Thus, you see yourself as being outside of God's kingdom and you see the material world as being separated from God's kingdom. You see yourself as unwhole, meaning that you are "condemned" to seeking wholeness in *this* world instead of seeking wholeness through oneness with your source.

On the mental level, this causes your mind to believe in the illusion of lack, namely that there is not enough resources in this world. The inevitable result is that you engage in the dualistic struggle of competing with other people for the scarce resources you think represent reality. You do this instead of following Mother Mary's teaching to bring more abundance into this world.

On the emotional level, you feel unwhole, and you think that in order to feel whole and fulfilled, you need to obtain something in this world. This gives rise to the fear of loss, which then opens your emotional mind to the many negative emotions that spring from the struggle against other people—whom you must perceive as trying to take from you the resources you need in order to obtain wholeness. Your emotional mind actually believes you can find wholeness in this world—if only you can get enough food, money, power, sex, possessions or whatever you have come to see as the means of fulfillment. Thus, on the conscious level, your attention is eaten up by the endless quest to acquire and accumulate what you see as the means to the ultimate end.

Once you have bought into this deception, you actually create several subconscious computer programs that will take the survival programs of the body and add a component. That is why the natural cravings of the body are now turned into *unnatural* cravings that can never be satisfied. And that is how the natural cravings become a treadmill that can keep you trapped for an indefinite period of time. Or at least until you begin to suspect that there must be more to life than this, which turns you into a spiritual seeker rather than a pleasure seeker.

***

Yet while this does explain cravings, I need you to go to an even higher level and realize what is really going on here. It all starts with the illusion that you are a separate being, living in a world dominated by lack. Once you believe in this illusion, the focus of your attention is to satisfy the desires of the separate self. Thus, you seek to possess something for the separate self, which means you must protect it from other people who are also seeking to possess for their separate selves. Yet now reach back to what I described as the design of your being. You are designed to be a co-creator with God. This does *not* mean that you seek to fulfill the desires of the separate self. It means you see yourself as one with your source – otherwise how can you co-create *with* God – and thus you see your *self* as an individual part of a larger whole, namely the Body of God.

When you have this correct sense of identity, you are *not* seeking to fulfill the desires of the separate self, for you have no separate self. Instead, you see the underlying oneness of all life, and thus you know that what is truly best for you as an individual being is what is best for the All. In fact, you know that the world of form is designed specifically to give the abundant life to *all* self-aware beings.

There are some spiritual seekers, even some spiritual teachers, who subscribe to the belief that the ultimate goal of the spiritual path is that your individuality disappears into union with God, or Nirvana, or whatever it is called. Yet your Creator did not create you for the purpose of having you go through a long process of building your individuality only to have it disappear. Instead, you are meant to win immortality for your spiritual identity through the process of the ascension. Once that goal is reached, you do not disappear, you start another phase in your self-expression. My point is that focusing on some distant end goal can be a subtle distraction on the path. You are designed to be a co-creator with God, so you do not find fulfillment in disappearing but in co-creating.

My point is that ultimate fulfillment does not necessarily come at the end of a long journey. It can be found on every step of the journey. However – and here is the crucial point – it can *never* be found when you approach the journey through the filter of the separate self. It can be found *only* by going beyond that self and realizing that you are co-creating *with* your God. And in doing so, you experience oneness with your source while still in the world of form. You are experiencing the ultimate fulfillment of being part of the outpicturing of God's desire to raise the entire material universe to the abundance of the kingdom of God.

Do you truly see the point here? The key to fulfillment is *not* the eradication of desire, as many spiritual people believe. Some have even misinterpreted the teachings of the Buddha and think he said the source of all suffering is desire, thus the goal of spiritual people is to destroy desire. However, doing so is seeking to destroy the very life force within you, which can never lead to spiritual progress. What the Buddha really said was that the cause of suffering is *wrong* desire, and we can now see that wrong desire is a desire centered around the needs of the separate self.

So what is the real key to overcoming cravings? It is *not* to destroy all desires. It is to elevate your desires and purify them of all selfishness by reconnecting to your spiritual identity and the reason why your lifestream originally chose to come into the material realm.

***

Obviously, reconnecting to your spiritual identity is the ultimate goal of the path to Christhood, and it might seem like it is far off at your present stage. However, I hope to help you see that you have already started this process. If you had not, you would not be studying this course but would be fully engaged in seeking fulfillment for some desire of the separate self.

So what you need to contemplate is that in a distant past, your lifestream was existing in the spiritual realm, and it made the decision to send an extension of itself down into the material world. You did this in order to express your spiritual individuality in this world and thus help raise the material world to the perfection that is the kingdom of God. In other words, you came here out of a true desire, and as you gradually reconnect to that desire, you will find it increasingly easier to let go of the desires of the separate self and rediscover the true desires of your spiritual self.

## Exercise for Key 5

In order to help you build a momentum on this process, I will give you some tools. I started out this key by talking about the spiritual poisons and the Dhyani Buddhas. The Buddha that is associated with desire or cravings is called Amitabha, and his particular God-quality is the perfect antidote to the spiritual poison of cravings, lust and greed. That God quality is wisdom, specifically discriminating wisdom, which gives you the ability to discern between the true desires of God and the false desires of the separate self.

So what you need to do in the coming 33 days is to contemplate the difference between true and false desires. You also need to become aware of when and how you are being tempted by your ego and the prince of this world to engage in a selfish desire. And when you feel the temptation coming on, you need to invoke the discriminating wisdom of the Buddha Amitabha. Each Dhyani Buddha has a mantra based on the Buddha's seed syllable. You may know that the oldest language known on Earth is Sanskrit, which is unique in the sense that there is a close connection between the sound and the form. Sound is a major creative force, as described in the Biblical statement: "And God said: Let there be light. And there *was* light." In other words, the Creator used sound to generate the energy impulse that created light. So there is great power in intoning the sound that invokes the Presence of a Dhyani Buddha, and the mantra for invoking the Presence of Amitabha is:

**OM AMITABHA HRIH**

Thus, during the next month, I want you to be very alert to the temptation to engage in selfish desires. As soon as you feel the temptation – and the sooner you notice it, the easier it will be to overcome it, as we will discuss in the next key – you start reciting the mantra – silently or aloud as the situation warrants – and you keep going until you begin to feel the peace of the Buddha Amitabha in your energy field. You can even visualize the Presence of this Buddha in your energy field as an image of complete serenity and peace. Why is the Buddha at peace? Because he has the perfect discriminating wisdom and thus can never be tempted by the false desires of the ego and the prince of this world. When you cannot be tempted, there is no need to fear temptation.

On top of this exercise, I also want you to give – once a day – Mother Mary's Rosary of Miracle Gratitude. However, I want you to substitute the standard Hail Mary with the one from another rosary, called the Nurturance Rosary.[9] Thus, instead of saying the standard Hail Mary for the Gratitude Rosary, you say this one:

**Hail Mary, I AM whole,**
**I AM complete within my soul.**
**I AM nurtured, I AM free,**
**one with God in eternity.**

**Holy Mary, by your Grace,**
**I AM transcending time and space.**
**I see God's perfect Light in me,**
**I AM the Sun, I love life free.**

I also want you to say the mantra of the Dhyani Buddha for this key one time after each verse and before the Hail Mother of Nurturance.

Why gratitude? Because gratitude is also an effective antidote against the cravings that spring from the fear of loss, the sense of being incomplete because you do not have something in this world.

---

[9] Both rosaries are found on *www.askrealjesus.com* in the Divine Feminine section.

Thus, as the writing exercise for this key, I want you to write down – after giving the rosary – instances from your life where you have felt that you did not have enough or where you have acted on a craving for more. Also, write down things for which you are grateful. Then look for a pattern to emerge that shows how your life has been affected by the sense of lack and how you have already taken some steps toward overcoming it.

Based on this understanding of the forces that have shaped your life, you can begin to evaluate which activities in the material world are aimed at fulfilling your true desires and which are based on false desires. Thus, you can begin to consider how to rise above activities that detract from your ability to fulfill your divine plan. You can then approach a point where all your activities either help fulfill your divine plan or do not detract from it.

In this way, you will be able to give up certain activities without forcing yourself to do so and thus experiencing it as a loss. Instead, you will give up an activity out of love, because you see that giving up something that limits you opens the way for greater freedom and fulfillment. No activity on Earth can give you the same fulfillment as seeing your divine plan come to fruition.

You may think this was a very long explanation to help you overcome cravings. However, we have also set a foundation for dealing with other spiritual poisons, and in the coming keys we will build upon it.

# Key 6
# Raising anger above fear

In this key we will deal with the spiritual poison of anger. The Dhyani Buddha who is the antidote to this poison is called Akshobya. His wisdom is the mirror-like wisdom and his mantra is:

**OM AKSHOBYA HUM**

As you study this key, tune in to the Buddha and repeat the mantra when you feel the poison of anger.

You should have learned something important from the last key. As a spiritual person, you obviously cannot allow your life to be controlled by cravings for the things of this world – you cannot serve God and mammon – and thus, from a certain viewpoint, one might say that you need to get rid of cravings. Yet as I showed you, it is not a matter of eradicating desires completely. For if you did so, what would be the point of you being in embodiment? You would actually be aborting the very purpose that brought you into this world, namely your higher self's desire to co-create with God, thus manifesting God's kingdom in the material world.

I also taught you about the four levels of your mind that correspond to the four levels of the material universe. I told you about the flow of spiritual energy through your four lower bodies. I told you about the higher purpose of raising up the material universe to the level of the kingdom of God, which can only be done by a critical mass of people becoming the open doors for God's light to stream through the four levels of their minds. So the last thing you want to do is to shut off this flow, and if you uncritically tried to extinguish all desires, you would be doing just that—stopping the flow of God's light through your energy field, the flow that springs from the deity's siring to be more through *you*.

As a spiritual person, you would probably say that anger is wrong, and it is something you need to get rid of. However, what I have been telling you is that human cravings are perversions of God's own desires. Thus, is it not likely that anger is also the perversion of a divine quality? And if you were to remove—not simply anger but the divine quality behind it, you would end up being completely passive?

Take note of what I am saying. Many spiritual seekers have an image that being truly spiritual means to be completely at peace, perhaps by sitting in a cave in the Himalayas and mediating on God 24 hours a day. I am not saying there is anything wrong with some people doing just that, but if you have been attracted to this course, it is most likely because part of your divine plan is to perform some active service to improve society. And you will not fulfill that purpose by making yourself completely passive.

Take a look at my life and see how I – in many instances – displayed something that could easily be interpreted as anger. See how I challenged the scribes and Pharisees and how I overturned the tables of the moneychangers in the temple. These were not the actions of a pacifist, in fact some have said they were not the actions of a spiritual master. However, here is where it is necessary to discern between various aspects of spiritual mastery.

To exemplify this, look at the difference between the Buddha and the Christ. What is your image of the Buddha? Is it not that of a spiritual master who sits in quiet contemplation and has withdrawn from the hustle and bustle of the world? And what is your image of Christ? Well, because Christianity has been so perverted, it is most likely the image of me hanging on the cross—the image that has been splashed in front of people's vision for almost 2,000 years. However, look behind that image. Why was I crucified? Was it not because I did *not* withdraw from the world but went out into the world to awaken the people and challenge the power elite who controlled them? I went out into the world to challenge the world's self-image by demonstrating that there is more to being human than the death consciousness.

I have talked about the Alpha and Omega aspect of God, and you now see that the Buddha represents the Alpha or father aspect, whereas the Christ represents the Omega or mother aspect. The Buddha withdraws from the hustle and bustle of everyday life, sits in complete peace and lets people come to him. However, who can come to the Buddha? Only those who are not completely trapped in the struggle of life. So how can those who are too overwhelmed by the struggle to even seek the Buddha be saved? Someone has to go where they are and show them that there is a way out of the struggle—and that is precisely the role of the Christ.

Do you see that both are expressions of spiritual mastery? It is not that one is right and one is wrong. It is not that one is better than the other. They are both equally valid and equally important—they are simply the two sides of the coin of spiritual mastery. God sends the Buddha to awaken those who *can* follow the path on their own and God sends the Christ to awaken those who *cannot* follow the path on their own. The Buddha is focused within, focused on the mind itself and on the spiritual world beyond this world. The Christ is focused without, focused on helping people improve this world. I am come that they might have life and that they might have it more abundantly—not tomorrow, not in the next world, but now, in this world. For the kingdom of God is at hand!

It is possible that you are meant to live the path of the Buddha, but if so I can assure you that this will become clear as you follow the path to Christhood. Yet because you have been attracted to this course, it is more likely that you are meant to exemplify the path of Christ, which is why this is a good working hypothesis for you. However, in the end, both paths lead to the same point of oneness with your source. In fact, only those who have walked the path of Christ will be able to truly become one with the Buddha—to *become* the Buddha.

Now, I am not trying to imply that the Buddha is a pacifist or is passive. What I *am* saying is that many spiritual people have adopted the mental image that in order to be truly spiritual, they have to sit passively in meditation and never rock the boat. And that is a viewpoint which for many people is detrimental to the fulfillment of their divine plans. As we will discuss in greater depth later, walking the path to Christhood will not pacify you, nor will it require you to withdraw from the world. As I said:

> For God sent not his Son into the world to condemn the world but that the world through him might be saved. (John 3:17)

The purpose of the Living Christ is to awaken the world from the consciousness of death, and that can be done *only* by going into the hustle and bustle of the marketplace in order to demonstrate to people that there is a higher way. What has that got to do with anger?

When you step back and look at humankind from an overall perspective, you see that the one word that characterizes life on Earth is the word "struggle." The Buddha said that one of the four noble truths is that life is a struggle. He also said that struggle is born from wrong desire. Well, wrong desire is a desire that springs from the duality consciousness, and as I have mentioned, this consciousness always has two opposites that are locked in a never-ending struggle. So we might say that the death consciousness has changed this planet from its original design – that was meant to give all people the abundant life – and has turned it into a giant struggle in which people are constantly battling each other, even battling the planet that gives them life.

Thus, we might say that there is a magnetic or gravitational force that is constantly pulling on your mind for the one purpose of somehow getting you to engage in this never-ending, pointless dualistic struggle. The cravings we talked about in the previous key is one way to pull you into the struggle by getting you to seek the fulfillment of desires that can never be satisfied. Yet there are many other ways, and one of the most effective ones is precisely anger. Thus, if you are to fulfill your Christ potential – by going into the marketplace to show people that there is a higher way – you absolutely have to overcome anger. For if you do not, you are sure to be pulled into the dualistic struggle by fighting for some cause or another, as has happened to many well-meaning people over the course of history. This is precisely one of the reasons why I said that until you pull the beam from your own eye, you cannot see clearly how to help others. So let us take a closer look at where anger comes from.

***

In order to illustrate the origin of anger, let me ask you to do something for me. Please go to your filing cabinet, or wherever you keep important legal papers, and pull out your Life Contract. This is the contract – signed by God – which specifies your rights as a human being on Earth, such as what you can expect from life, what you are entitled to have and what you are entitled *not* to experience. I would like to go over that contract with you, so please go get it.

What was that? You are saying you don't have any contract signed by God? Hmm? Well, then how come 99.9 percent of humanity respond to life as if they *did have* a contract from the highest authority, saying they are entitled to this and should never experience that? The result being, that when life does not meet their expectations, they get angry, often even blaming God for their problems!

Do you see what I am getting at? The origin of anger is your expectations about life. Now, the Buddha said that the cause of suffering is wrong desire, so one might think that the cause of anger is wrong expectations. But I will go one step further and state that the cause of anger is *any* expectation. Am I saying you should have *no* expectations about life? *Precisely!*

When you understand the reality of life on Earth, you know what kind of planet you live on, and thus you see the wisdom in not expecting *anything!* As the Living Christ you have no use for expectations, for you simply take life as it comes and respond to any situation in a way that will raise up all life.

I know this will require a major adjustment of your thinking, because from the cradle you have been programmed to have expectations about life. Some of these expectations may seem innocent, even reasonable or necessary, but I assure you that they are *not*. Don't be fooled by the fact that almost everyone has expectations about life, for have I not told you that almost everyone is trapped in the death consciousness? I know that many of your expectations have been taken over from parents or other people who had the best of intentions. I am not saying these are bad people. I am simply saying that today we have a situation on this planet where almost all people are blinded by the death consciousness, and thus they have accepted expectations that spring from that consciousness. And if you trace those seemingly innocent expectations back to their origin, you will see that they were deliberately crafted for the purpose of controlling people by manipulating them into a self-debilitating, disempowering response to life.

What is the nature of an expectation? An expectation is a mental image of how life should, or should not, unfold. Right there, you see that an expectation is separated from reality. There is a division, a space, between reality and the mental image that causes the expectation.

This should cause alarm bells to ring, because you are beginning to understand that the consciousness of death, the consciousness of anti-christ, is born from a separation from God's reality. As Maitreya explains in great detail in his book, the consciousness of Christ sees the reality of God, whereas the consciousness of anti-christ cannot see this reality. The consequence is that the consciousness of anti-christ sees *only* mental images that are created out of the separation from reality, meaning that they are *all* illusions. Once you are separated from reality, you see *only* illusions—mirages.

An expectation is *always* separated from reality. Why is this so? Because an expectation is about a future event that has not yet come to pass—it is about something that has not yet become reality. Thus, when the event actually happens, you are perceiving reality and have no need for an expectation. As an example, say you check the weather forecast at night and they promise sunny weather the next day. So you go to sleep expecting that you will wake up to a sunny day. Yet that expectation is only a mental image of what might happen at some future time. When you wake up and look out the window, you are perceiving the actual weather, so now you have no need for an expectation. You have direct perception of reality instead of a mental image.

I am sure you will agree that expecting sunny weather has little impact on the actual weather. So your expectation will have no influence on whether it will be sunny or cloudy in the morning. Yet your expectation *does* have an impact on whether it will be sunny or cloudy inside your own mind. If you expect sunshine but wake up to a cloudy day, you might have some kind of negative reaction, possibly even a reaction that puts you in a bad mood for the rest of the day. Do you see what I am saying? An expectation has no positive impact on what will actually happen in the world *outside* of you, but it has a potentially negative impact on what will happen *inside* of you.

***

Do you see why an expectation is such an effective tool for manipulating you? It causes you to create a mental image of what should or should not happen in the future. This has several effects:

- On an immediate level, the expectation ties up your mental energy and can give rise to both hope and fear. In fact, an expectation itself can have a profound impact on people's state of mind and their actions. Just consider how many people live in fear of some future calamity, such as disease, an economic crash or the end of the world.

- The expectation pulls your conscious awareness toward the future, which takes it away from the present moment. Thus, you are no longer living in the now but in a "no-man's land" that is somewhere between the now and the future. Yet when can you make LIFE decisions? Only in the *now,* for if you postpone your decisions to the future, that future will never arrive. When can you enjoy life? Only in the present moment, but how can you do so if you are not focused in the now?

- When the future arrives, you have the potential that reality can live up to your expectations or not live up to them. Yet either way, it is likely to create a reaction in you. For example, if reality does *not* live up to your expectations, many people get disappointed or angry. Yet even if reality lives up to people's expectations, many become prideful or overly optimistic, which can set them up for future disappointment.

You may have heard the saying that discouragement is the sharpest tool in the devil's toolkit. You can now see that the foundation for discouragement is expectations. You expect that life should be a certain way, and when you repeatedly experience that life is not that way, you eventually get discouraged and give up trying. Yet what would have happened if you had no expectations? Isn't it obvious? If you don't have any expectations of life, how can you possibly be disappointed and become discouraged? The prince of this world will come and have nothing in you.

The death consciousness is dualistic by nature, which means it has two opposites, such as happiness and unhappiness, hope and disappointment. Can you see that when you allow yourself to have an expectation, you set yourself up for a reaction that will be either positive or negative—yet *either* reaction is dualistic? Thus, expectation is a very subtle and thus very effective way to draw people into the dualistic struggle. Take a look at my saying:

> Take therefore no thought for the morrow: for the morrow shall take thoughts for the things of itself. Sufficient unto the day is the evil thereof. (Matthew 6:34)

Most Christians find it difficult to understand this statement, but do you now see that I was telling people to let go of their expectations? Why put yourself in a dualistic frame of mind by having expectations about tomorrow, when those expectations will not change what will actually happen but only set yourself up for a dualistic reaction? Tomorrow will be what it will be – what happens happens (at least in the short run) – so simply wait and deal with situations as they arise. Yes, I know there is a lot more to say about that point (as I will discuss later), but take a look at what I said before the above statement:

> But seek ye first the kingdom of God, and his righteousness: and all these things shall be added unto you. (Matthew 6:33)

Again, there is more than one meaning, but one is that you should focus your attention on seeking the Christ consciousness in the *now* rather than tying up your mental energies in inconsequential expectations about the future. Seek first the kingdom of God, seek it in the *now,* rather than thinking you can attain it only at some future time—the future that never arrives, because the only time you have is *now.*

Another meaning is that when you do strive for the Christ consciousness, God will give you what you truly need – not what your ego or outer mind might want – in order to survive and fulfill your divine plan. Thus, when you know that you will receive what you need, what use is there for expectations? You know that whatever happens represents the best possible opportunity for you to grow on the path and demonstrate Christhood—which is why you are here.

What I am saying is that there is a difference between expectations – based on a mental image – and an inner knowing, where you have no mental image but simply know that whatever happens is what is meant to happen, and you will spontaneously make the best of it.

***

If you will take an honest look at people you know, you will see that many people spend their entire lives chasing an impossible goal, yet at the core of this is an expectation about life that simply cannot be fulfilled—an impossible expectation. One common expectation is that right around the corner is a short-cut to riches, and you will see how many people live in the hope that one day they will win the lottery or in other ways strike it rich. Closely tied to this is the expectation that being rich or having specific possessions will automatically make you happy. In past times, this dream would often last a life-time because most people had no realistic possibility of ever becoming wealthy—so they would spend a lifetime dreaming about something that could not come to pass. Take a look at how many people have lived unhappy lives because of this unrealistic expectation. Take a look at how many others have taken all kind of shortcuts – even going into crime – in order to "get a break and get ahead," only to fall behind both materially and spiritually.

In these times, many people are actually acquiring greater material wealth and are thus experiencing firsthand that it does not automatically make you happy. On the contrary, when people actually get the material wealth they desire, they often discover that they feel even more empty than before. Instead of having the dream of becoming happy, they now have the experience that wealth does *not* make them happy. This gives rise to a sense of emptiness, because having been so focused on gaining something in this world – mammon – they have forgotten their spirituality and thus have no idea what will actually make them happy.

Perhaps you have already taken a look at yourself and seen that you have spent a considerable part of your life chasing one of the innumerable impossible expectations that have been designed by the mind of anti-christ in order to manipulate you into a catch-22 and prevent you from fulfilling your divine plan? If you are to successfully walk the path of Christhood, you obviously need to overcome such expectations, so you can be free to *be* who you truly are and fulfill the reason why you came into this world—both the long-term reason and the particular reason for this lifetime. So let us take a look at some of the impossible expectations that are designed specifically to trap the more mature spiritual seekers and prevent them from truly making progress toward Christhood. These, of course, are also the most common causes of anger in spiritual people.

***

There are a number of expectations that relate to Earth and what people should or should not experience on this little planet. Imagine someone going on a charitable mission in the heart of Calcutta with the expectation that it will be like a modern Western city. Well, many spiritual people come into embodiment on Earth expecting it to be somewhat of a paradise, and they are shocked and disappointed when they encounter the reality of life on this planet. The reactions can range from outright anger against God for "forcing" them to experience this planet to a more subtle sense of not wanting to be here, not wanting to engage in life and make the best of it—a reaction that also springs from – unrecognized – anger. As a disciple of the Living Christ, it is essential for you to examine your expectations and adjust them according to the spiritual reality of this planet.

So what *is* that reality? As Maitreya explains in his book, the Earth is currently very far below the level of purity and balance at which it was designed. The Earth is a mixed environment in which lifestreams from many different backgrounds have been allowed to incarnate as a cosmic experiment. Many of these are lifestreams that are very self-centered and have become firmly blinded by the illusions of duality. Many of them are lifestreams that could no longer remain in their previous environment because they refused to come up higher in consciousness as their environment – in this universe or in a higher sphere – ascended. If one wants to be direct, one could look upon Earth as a kind of cosmic refuse station, with a collection of lifestreams with a relatively low state of consciousness. The experiment is to see whether putting these lifestreams together will cause them to self-destruct or whether having to deal with their differences will help them transcend their closed mental boxes.

Naturally, we of the Ascended Host hold no negative image of any lifestream, so we do not consider Earth a refuse station. On the other hand we are keenly aware of the state of consciousness of every lifestream. Thus, we see that the basic choice on Earth is whether people will destroy themselves and each other or whether they will finally have enough of the dualistic struggle and realize that the *only* way out of it is for them to remove the beam from their own eyes. Obviously, there is a third option, namely that some lifestreams will misuse their opportunity – either by refusing to grow or by violating the free will of others – to the critical limit where they receive the judgment of the Living Christ and are no longer allowed to incarnate on Earth, being sent to an even lower realm.

My point is that you need to adjust your view of life on this planet, so you do not cling to some of the many unrealistic expectations that spiritual people have. Thus, let us examine where such expectations come from. Take note that I am not saying you should expect the worst or hold other negative expectations. I am not asking you to adopt a set of negative expectations. I am asking you to overcome *all* expectations and simply accept life on this planet for what it is right now, with no sense that it should be different or that you should not be exposed to this or that. As we will discuss later, this includes holding the vision that things will improve, but this must be done without human expectations.

Spiritual people obviously have a recognition that there is a spiritual world beyond the material universe, and they have some sense that things are better in the spiritual world. This gives them a clear sense that things are not right on Earth and that things need to improve. At the same time many spiritual people have volunteered to take embodiment on Earth precisely because they wanted to help bring about this improvement. It is therefore natural that spiritual lifestreams come into embodiment hoping to see some result of their efforts. The problem is that it is all too easy for the forces of anti-christ to turn this hope into a set of unrealistic expectations that sets a foundation for frustration and anger. These expectations fall into three categories:

- **Personal.** Many spiritual people have some variant of the expectation that there are certain things they should *not* experience, certain things that are below them. They often feel there are certain mistakes they should not make, yet they find themselves having made them and now they are angry at themselves for doing so and even angry at God for allowing them to be tempted. Yet the reality is that when you embody on this planet, you *will* be tempted, and you might ponder the fact that I was tempted after my stay in the wilderness. No one is exempt from this—not even *you*.

- **Other people.** Many spiritual people expect that other people should be as open to the spiritual side of life or to changing their lives as they are themselves. Yet this is a completely unrealistic expectation, given the kind of lifestreams that embody on Earth. Many spiritual people have spent a lifetime – even several lifetimes – seeking to convert others to a particular religion or belief system or seeking to bring about physical or political changes. Yet they continually experience frustration over the fact that most people do not respond and that a few respond with such outright negativity and hostility. Thus, they are easily tempted to engage in a dualistic struggle *against* other people or against institutions or belief systems. Again, this is fertile ground for frustration and anger against self, others and God.
- **The world.** Many spiritual people have come to expect that the world should be a better place and that it should be moving toward specific improvements that they believe are necessary or will bring about some ultimate breakthrough into an envisioned edenic state. And when the world does not respond as expected, we again have fertile ground for frustration and anger, even an anger against God for creating the world, for allowing people to have free will or for not forcing the desired changes upon humankind.

Here is one thing that is fundamentally wrong about these expectations. As Maitreya explains, there are many lifestreams on Earth who have long ago turned away from God and have become blinded by the illusion of separation. These lifestreams obviously cannot find any kind of fulfillment by co-creating with God as they were designed to do. So they have – often without understanding this whatsoever – condemned themselves to the impossible quest of seeking ultimate fulfillment in the material world.

Take note of my remark that "with men this is impossible, but not with God, for with God all things are possible." The deeper meaning is that you will *never* find ultimate fulfillment through the things and activities of the material world, for this can be found only by reuniting with your spiritual self and fulfilling your reason for being, which is to co-create the kingdom of God. The lifestreams who are blinded by separation are seeking ultimate fulfillment in the material universe, and as a result they have created a set of very subtle expectations. These expectations all say the same thing, namely that if only certain changes would come about – such as all people being converted to a particular belief system – paradise (as the state of ultimate fulfillment) would be manifest on Earth.

These expectations have permeated every aspect of life on Earth, and they have been used to fuel the dualistic struggle, with different groups of people pursuing mutually exclusive ways of bringing about the ultimate paradise—thus never being able to avoid the clash between them. Yet because these expectations are subtle, many spiritual and well-meaning people have been seduced by them and have thus engaged in the impossible quest of seeking paradise exclusively through something in the material universe. Take note that I am *not* saying that God's kingdom cannot be brought to Earth. I am saying that God's kingdom cannot be brought *without* God, meaning that it cannot be brought by lifestreams or through belief systems and institutions that are based on the illusion of separation, the duality consciousness.

What I am really saying here is that you cannot be a disciple of the Living Christ as long as you hold on to the expectations created through the mind of anti-christ or as long as you are are engaged – even with the best of intentions – in the dualistic struggle. So what is the way out?

It is to realize that the Living Christ does *not* come to Earth to bring about specific physical changes—such as making one religion the only religion on Earth, as many well-meaning Christians have believed for 2,000 years. So why *does* the Living Christ come to Earth? He or she comes to awaken people from the consciousness of death by GIVING THEM A CHOICE between the unreality of anti-christ and the reality of Christ. Take note of what I am saying here. The Living Christ does *not* come to force people in any way—not even to force them to do what is best for them. The Living Christ comes *only* to give people a real choice by presenting them with the reality of Christ, so they can see that there is something beyond the dualistic illusions of anti-christ.

The Living Christ has *no* expectations as to how people should respond or not respond. He or she leaves that to people's free will, even to the point where he is willing to let them crucify him if that is what they desire at the time. And no matter what people might do, the Living Christ does not judge them. Why not? Because the

Living Christ realizes that it is not his/her role to judge people, because there is another mechanism that will do so:

> He that rejecteth me, and receiveth not my words, hath one that judgeth him: the word that I have spoken, the same shall judge him in the last day. (John 12:48)

How does the Living Christ avoid judging people or becoming angry because they reject the truth they are offered, even to the point of killing the embodied messenger? Because the Living Christ understands that most people on this planet are blinded – to varying degrees – by the duality consciousness, and thus he or she can have no expectations about how people should respond. The living Christ understands what I expressed while hanging on the cross:

> Father, forgive them; for they know not what they do. (Luke 23:34)

This then leads us to the next level of expectations, namely those that revolve around yourself.

***

As it is with life on this planet, there is a host of expectations concerning yourself and what you are supposed to do and be. These expectations spring from – and some are deliberately designed by – the consciousness of anti-christ, and they very effectively put you in a catch-22 by causing you to pursue an impossible goal—thus condemning yourself to remaining unfulfilled for the indefinite future.

The essence of all these expectations is that they are based on the mechanism described above, namely that once you believe in the illusion that you are separated from your source, from God, you condemn yourself to seeking ultimate fulfillment in this world. The goal that has been created by these expectations is that there is some kind of ideal of the perfect human being and that you are supposed to live up to it.

To help you see beyond these very subtle expectations, I would like to ask you to quickly write down a description of the perfect human being, or go find such a description. Obviously, I realize that you have no such description. You might find various descriptions out there, but if you take a closer look at them, you will discover two things. One is that they are always based on a particular belief system or culture. For example, fundamentalist Christians have certain ideas of how the perfect human being should be while communists in China have quite different ideas. Obviously, an ideal that is so clearly based on a particular Earthly belief system or culture cannot be a universal ideal for the perfect human being. Thus, it cannot come from God—who is beyond all man-made ideas, for as the Bible says, "God is no respecter of persons."

The consequence is that these ideals are not a very clear or universal description of the perfect human being, yet let us go one step further. If you examine any Earthly ideals of perfection, you will discover that they are not very specific or detailed. While they might prescribe certain outer rules for behavior, they do not go into the psychological aspects. In other words, they describe the *outer* path that I have already explained can never lead to salvation, whereas they ignore the inner path, namely the transformation of consciousness.

This leads us to understand that the ideals for perfection are so vague or imprecise that you can never really pin down what a perfect human being is supposed to be like. This means that you can never actually live up to such an ideal, for how can you reach a goal that is not clearly defined? You are like a runner in a race who has started running, but the officials refuse to tell him what the final distance of the race is. Thus, he is condemned to running indefinitely – or until he gives up – without ever reaching the finish line. In fact, the false teachers and the ego are constantly moving the finish line, so no one can ever catch up.

What we have seen now is that there really is no clearly defined ideal for what the perfect human being is like, which means that it is practically impossible to ever *become* the perfect human being. Let us now consider whether – even if it *was* possible – becoming the perfect human being would actually lead to salvation? Obviously, I have already answered that question by saying that you will not be saved by following the outer path of the scribes and Pharisees and that you need to be spiritually reborn. However, let us take that to an even deeper level:

> And no man hath ascended up to heaven, but he that came down from heaven, even the Son of man which is in heaven. (John 3:13)

What was I really saying here? What I was saying is that the "man" that descended from heaven was your conscious self—a spiritual being that is an individualization of the Creator's own Being. After you fell into the duality consciousness, you created a separate self – the ego – that is based on the illusion of separation and thus can *never* see beyond or overcome that sense of separation from God.

The lie of the prince of this world is that it is possible for you to enter the kingdom of God *without* letting the ego die—that it is possible for the ego to do something in this world that will make it acceptable in the eyes of God. This is the outer path that causes spiritual and religious people to pursue the impossible quest of seeking to become perfect human beings or following an outer religion – the "only" true religion – in order to be saved. This is a decidedly non-constructive approach because it simply cannot *ever* end up in salvation. The ego – which has *not* descended from heaven – can *never* enter the kingdom. Only the conscious self – the person that *has* descended from heaven – can do so. However, the conscious self can do so *only* by letting its worldly sense of identity (the ego) die, which requires you to remove the beam from your own eye.

In other words, overcoming the ego is *not* an automatic process that will happen by following some religious ritual. *You* created the ego by making decisions. You can overcome the ego *only* by consciously looking at your past decisions, seeing that they were based on the illusions of the duality consciousness and then remaking those decisions by making decisions based on the reality of Christ. You must consciously remove the beam from your own eye and put on the wedding garment of the Christ consciousness:

> 11 And when the king came in to see the guests, he saw there a man which had not on a wedding garment:
> 12 And he saith unto him, Friend, how camest thou in hither not having a wedding garment? And he was speechless. (Matthew, Chapter 22)

This parable illustrates the fact that you cannot remain in the kingdom of heaven *without* putting on the Christ consciousness. The kingdom is open for *all* people, not just the chosen people as the Jews thought. Yet it is open *only* to those who let the ego die and thus are reborn into a new identity as the Living Christ. There simply is no cheating God, for God is not mocked and is no respecter of persons.

***

We now see that what has happened to most spiritual and religious people is that they have been seduced into adopting a set of unrealistic expectations about life on Earth and about their entry into the spiritual realm—however they define it according to their outer religion and culture. The most dangerous of these is the subtle belief that following an outer religion or a set of spiritual practices will automatically give you entry into the kingdom of God.

You may not realize this with your outer mind, but I can assure you that most people on this planet have gone through many lifetimes of believing in this lie—and then dying with the expectation that their salvation was guaranteed because they had faithfully followed the outer religion. They then experienced that their souls were not allowed into heaven but had to reincarnate on Earth, often facing the same temptation to believe in an outer religion.

After having gone through this for several lifetimes, many souls came to have a deep mistrust of all religion. There are many people in the world today who deny all religion and spirituality – often following the "religion" of materialism – precisely because they can no longer believe in the empty promises of the external road to salvation in any of its forms. The fact that you are a spiritual person proves that you have also come to doubt this outer path—or you would be happily – or at least blindly – following an outer religion.

My point here is that there are many people on Earth who have attained the spiritual maturity of seeing through the fallacy of the external path. Unfortunately many of them have become confused and no longer know which path to follow. And others have become angry, rejecting all religion and spirituality.

What I need you to do is to make the switch in consciousness, whereby you realize that the outer path is deliberately designed by the forces of anti-christ in order to do two things:

- First, it can cause you to spend many lifetimes pursuing the outer path without getting closer to salvation and most likely becoming embroiled in the ongoing struggle against people who belong to other religions.

- Secondly, as you begin to see through this illusion, it is almost inevitable that you develop a mistrust against not only religion but even God. This usually leads to a deep – and often unrecognized – anger against God. You come to believe that God is unjust, since you have faithfully followed an outer religion and God still won't let you into the kingdom.

I have earlier said that the concept of an outer path cannot lead to salvation. This demonstrates that this concept does not come from God, for God truly wants you to be saved and thus would never give you a path that cannot lead to the goal. As I said, it is God's good pleasure to give you the kingdom.

Do you understand what I just said? The subtle effect of these impossible expectations is that many spiritual people have actually come to doubt that God really wants to save them. As I have explained, many people in the world follow the outer path by believing that being a member of a particular church will guarantee their salvation. Most spiritual people have seen through this illusion, but instead they have come to doubt that it is actually possible to be saved, and the reason is that they have not critically examined the impossible expectation of perfection. In other words, some spiritual people have a subtle belief that being saved means becoming perfect, but because they also see the fallacy of seeking outer perfection, they think there is a gap that makes salvation unattainable. They think God requires them to be perfect and then makes it impossible for them to reach the goal.

The switch I need you to make is that all of these expectations spring from an unreal concept of God, namely the external God that is so often portrayed by religion as an angry being in the sky. In reality, it is *not* God who is refusing to let you into his kingdom. It is yourself – or rather your ego – that is preventing you from entering the kingdom. The actual situation is quite simple.

God has created a doorway to heaven that is two feet wide. Most people are carrying a beam – the ego – on their shoulders that is more than two feet wide. As long as you refuse to let go of the beam, you cannot fit through the door, for the beam hits the door frame and holds you back. God did not create the beam—*you* did. God cannot – because of the law of free will – take the beam away from you. *You* have to step back and come to see the beam that you have not seen thus far. You have to realize that it is the beam – and not something outside yourself – that is preventing you from entering the door. And then you have to consciously and willingly let the beam go. When you throw down the beam, the person that descended from heaven – the conscious self – will easily fit through the door to heaven and ascend back to where you came from. You have already gone through the door coming from above, so the same being can surely go through the same door from the opposite direction.

Do you see my point? All anger is – when it is stripped down to its naked origin – an anger against God. It all comes from an illusion about God and how God has designed the world, including the path to salvation. This illusion has created a set of expectations that can *never* be fulfilled, and this is what keeps you pursuing an impossible quest that can only add to your frustration and anger against God—thus making the beam in your eye longer and making it even harder to enter the doorway.

The *only* way out is to see through these illusions, whereby your expectations will be replaced by an experience – an inner knowing – of the reality of God. And when your expectations are gone, your anger will inevitably go with them—for both expectations and anger spring from a separation from God's reality. When you see the truth, you will be set free from both expectations and the anger they produce.

***

We now see something very profound about anger. Anger springs from the expectations that spring from the illusion of separation. Yet what is it about the illusion that you are separated *from* God that gives rise to anger *against* God?

The illusion that you are separated from God is what gives rise to the further illusion that you need to be saved, that you are outside of God's kingdom and that you need to fulfill certain requirements – defined by some thought system in this world – in order to gain entry into God's kingdom. And this entire mentality is what gives rise to the concept that you could fail to be saved, that you could become permanently lost, that you might be condemned by an angry god to spend an eternity in some kind of hell. And, of course, the entire concept of hell has been used very cleverly and persistently by the false teachers of anti-christ to generate fear in people—the fear of not being saved, the fear of eternal damnation and everlasting punishment.

In other words, the very simple psychological mechanism at play here is that anger springs from fear. The fear of not being saved is what gives rise to anger against God because people feel that they have no way to take control over their own salvation but must rely on a god who is seen as external to themselves. And precisely because there is a space between the external god and the self – or god would not be seen as external – there is room for an entire cornucopia of illusions that feed people's fears and thus their anger against this external god who is seen as unknowable, distant, uncaring, unjust, arbitrary and a whole host of other qualities. These are truly the qualities of the human ego that people project onto their graven images of god—worshipping them before the Living God who resides where…? Well, in the kingdom of God within you, of course.

In short, what I am saying here is that when you began to believe in the illusion of separation, a space was created between you – meaning your sense of self, your conscious self – and God. And in that space grew a host of illusions that make you feel trapped and at the mercy of a remote god who might or might not grant you salvation. It is precisely this sense of being stuck, of having no control over your own destiny, that has given rise to your anger against God.

Traditionally, many religious people have attempted to deal with their anger against God by suppressing it—and most mainstream Christians are examples of this. However, suppressing something never works, for the more forcefully you suppress your feelings, the more forcefully you imprison yourself in the catch-22. You will never see a way out until you become willing to look at the beam – in this case anger – in your own eye and deal with it consciously instead of suppressing it. So suppressing your anger against God will never set you free from it. The *only* way to overcome anger is to look at it consciously, realize that it springs from an illusion and thus set your anger free from the fear of not being saved.

And what happens when you raise anger above fear? You discover that your anger is not actually anger, but a special brand of fierce determination—the determination to bring change, the determination that things cannot be allowed to go on and cause so much suffering. And this was likely the very determination that caused you to volunteer to descend into the material universe in order to raise up planet Earth and set your brothers and sisters in spirit free from the treadmill of suffering on which they have been trapped for many lifetimes.

So you descended to Earth because of a positive desire, but when you became blinded by the illusion of separation, you saw no outlet for the positive desire, and thus the feeling behind it became lowered to what human beings call anger. Yet once you raise that sense of anger above fear, you will be left with the original determination, and then you will be free to fulfill the reason why you originally came to this planet.

***

Let me summarize the reality of why you find yourself in your current position—physically and in consciousness. You are here as a result of choices you made. You were not thrown into this world by an angry God and your salvation from this world does *not* depend upon God or anything or anyone outside yourself—unless you allow it to do so. Your situation *in* this world and your salvation *beyond* this world depend exclusively on choices you make—if you are willing to take full responsibility for yourself. And this, of course, is the problem.

The sad fact of life on this planet is that over 99 percent of the people refuse to take full responsibility for themselves. And as long as they do not take responsibility, they have no way of escaping the sense of being victimized by outer circumstances, other people or God. Thereby, they condemn themselves to remaining on the treadmill that will only increase their frustration and anger against the world, other people, God and themselves.

The equation is simple. If you do not accept that your present situation is the result of choices *you* made, then you make yourself a victim of forces outside yourself, forces over which you have little or no control, thus making it impossible for yourself to do anything to improve your situation. The *only* way you can improve your life is to accept the reality that *your* situation is the result of *your* choices. For by doing this, you take back the power to change your life through your own choices. How do you change your life? By looking at the beam in your own eye, admitting that your past choices were not the most constructive and then erasing your past choices BY MAKING BETTER CHOICES IN THE PRESENT!

As I have already explained, one of the most subtle lies perpetrated upon humankind by the false teachers of anti-christ is that once you have made a bad choice, you are bound by it forever. Yet consider the reality that God gave you free will, that God wants you to be saved and that God wants you to be saved through your own free choices. Based on what I said earlier – that God would not give you a path you could not walk – the logical conclusion is that God does not require you to be bound by your past choices—only the devil will attempt to make you think you are bound by the past.

God has given you the right to make any choice you want, which is what has given you the potential to descend into the illusion of separation. Yet God has also given you the power to rise above that illusion – the valley of the shadow of death – by instantly replacing dualistic choices with choices based on the reality of the Christ mind. God does not want you to stay in duality any longer than you desire to stay there. God wants you to rise above duality by choosing life over death, by choosing the eternal life of the Christ consciousness over the mortal life of the consciousness of anti-christ.

How do you overcome the ego? By finally accepting that you can walk away from it any minute and simply let it die! Of course, you can't walk away from the ego until you have consciously seen through and undone the choices that created the ego. For as long as those choices remain unchallenged, they will make you attached to the ego and make you think that if the ego dies, *you* will die.

God will not make choices for you, nor will any member of the Ascended Host. It is only your ego and the false teachers of anti-christ who will make choices for you, or rather seek to manipulate you into situations where you cannot make free choices because you have a limited understanding.

***

I have been building up to a point of helping you see that it is possible – in the blink of an eye – to fundamentally shift your attitude and approach to life away from feeling like a victim and then taking back your power to change your life. You can come to see that your expectations go so deep that they have distorted your sense of the purpose of life, making you believe that the purpose of life is to have something or to avoid something in this world.

In reality, the purpose of life is growth—the growth in your consciousness that leads to full Christ consciousness. When you accept this reality, you see that there is truly no point in having expectations. The law of free will reigns supreme on planet Earth, which means you cannot control what other people do to you. Not even God can control what people do. However, what you *can* control is how you *react* to what other people do to you. And taking control over your reactions to whatever happens to you on Earth is an essential part of attaining personal Christhood.

Do you see what I am saying here? For millennia there has been a false and a true path on Earth—the broad way and the straight and narrow way. The broad way is to seek to control your outer circumstances, including other people. Countless people have spent lifetimes on this pursuit, but they have never found inner fulfillment, for you can never truly control your outer circumstances—which inevitably leads people into anger. In contrast, the true path has always been the path of self-mastery, namely of taking command over your inner circumstances, whereby you become able to choose the highest possible response to *any* circumstance you encounter. And you cannot attain this self-mastery as long as you hold on to expectations, for they will inevitably pull you toward a dualistic reaction.

When you decide to follow the true path, you see that whatever happens is an opportunity to grow. For what is growth? True spiritual growth is *not* measured in your mastery over *outer* circumstances. True growth is measured in your mastery over *inner* circumstances, your *self*-mastery. Which means that a person committed to growth knows that in order to attain self-mastery, it is necessary to expose anything in one's psychology that causes a reaction that is less than peace. Thus, if something happens that takes away your peace, it is an opportunity for you to see the beam in your own eye and take active measures toward removing it.

In other words, those who follow the false path seek to control their outer circumstances so they never face situations that take away their peace—thus avoiding the exposure of the weaknesses in their own psyches. In contrast, those who walk the true path welcome the exposure of their own weaknesses, for it is only by looking at them that you can overcome them.

Most people go through life with a set of expectations about what should and should not happen. Thus, they meet every situation they encounter with the question of whether it will follow or go against their expectations, whether it will give them pain or pleasure. A disciple of the Living Christ has let go of such human expectations. Thus, he or she meets each situation with the attitude that it will provide an opportunity for growth, either by exposing something that needs to be overcome or by giving one the opportunity to demonstrate what one has already overcome. Pain or pleasure have become irrelevant, for every situation can only lead to a win by giving the opportunity to take another step closer to Christhood. For most people life is a question of win or lose, but for disciples of the Living Christ, life is a continuous string of victories, with each situation leading to growth toward the end goal of personal Christhood.

***

Having talked about the need to accept full responsibility for your actions, we need to deal with the fact that many spiritual people have already done so but that some have taken this too far by going into the blind alley of feeling guilty for their mistakes. In other words, by accepting full responsibility for yourself, you can overcome your anger against other people and God, but it can easily lead to anger against yourself. In fact, many spiritual people have expectations that cause anger against themselves when they are not fulfilled.

The first thing you need to understand here is that the mind of anti-christ always operates with two opposite polarities. The false teachers are always seeking to keep you on this scale, where there are two polarities and a gray area in the middle that is a mixture of the two opposites. The last thing they want is for you to see through the illusions of duality and raise yourself above the veil of dualistic lies—above the scale. So you need to smarten up and realize that in this case the two polarities are:

- You are in complete denial of your own responsibility, always projecting that other people, God, luck, fate or something else is responsible for your situation and there is nothing you can do to change that.

- You accept full responsibility for your situation but feel this makes everything your own fault. Thus, whatever happens to you is just one more straw of guilt and self-condemnation that will eventually break the camel's back.

My point is that one extreme is accepting no responsibility and the other is blaming yourself for everything. You obviously need to rise above both, but not by going into the gray area in the middle. You need to find the true Middle Way of the Buddha by becoming untouchable by dualistic thinking.

Let us begin by looking at a simple fact. You live on a planet with around six billion other people in embodiment. On top of that, there is a rather large number of disembodied beings who are attached to the Earth in the emotional, mental and identity levels. All of these beings combine their consciousness into what I call the collective consciousness, and this consciousness affects everything that happens on Earth, even nature, the weather and natural disasters. My point being that there are many occurrences that might affect you but which are not directly caused by you. Meaning that while you take responsibility for yourself, you do *not* take responsibility for everything that happens to you, for much of it is the result of the mass consciousness or other beings exercising their free will. Should I have felt guilty for my being crucified, or should I reason that I did exactly what I needed to do, namely expose the fact that many people are willing to kill the Living Christ instead of changing their consciousness?

The next step is to realize that God gave *you* free will, meaning that God gave you the right to experiment with your co-creative abilities. God attaches no guilt or blame to this process, for God has set up an entirely mechanical system that returns to you any energy impulse you send out, thus making you experience what you co-create. In other words, what I am saying here is that the entire consciousness of guilt and blame that is associated with so many religions on Earth did *not* come from God. It came entirely from the false teachers, who are seeking to trap humankind in the duality consciousness. The lie is that once you have made a mistake, you should feel guilty and blame yourself, which only drives you deeper into duality, making it harder for you to use even your mistakes as stepping stones for growth.

In God's reality there is no such thing as a mistake and thus no need to feel guilty. Any action is simply an experiment. It generates an energy impulse, and the impulse will inevitably be returned to you by the cosmic mirror. The returning impulse will have one of two effects. If the impulse you sent out was based on love, the returning impulse will *magnify* your life. If the impulse you sent was based on fear, the returning impulse will *diminish* your life. It is exactly what I described in my parable about the talents, where those who multiplied their talents had more given to them, whereas the servant who buried his talents in the ground – out of fear – had it taken away from him. So the real question is whether an action will multiply or diminish your own life. If you find that you receive a return from the universe that diminishes your life, you must reason that in the past you have sent out impulses based on fear. Thus, you can examine your consciousness and expose any elements of fear in your psyche. As you remove those elements by replacing them with the reality of the Christ mind, you will begin to send out impulses based on love, and in time they will inevitably be returned to you.

Let me use a crude analogy. Imagine you are playing one of these mechanical games where you use a spring to propel a metal ball into the machine and then use various dials and switches to control the ball's path and score points. This is a completely mechanical device, so there is no need to feel guilty for what happens to the ball. You are simply experimenting, and the ball's path is determined by mechanical factors. If you flip the right switch, you will score points, and if you don't, you will not score points. Well, while life is not entirely mechanical, my point is that God has given you the right to experiment with your free will, and he has given you a somewhat mechanical environment in which to do so. Thus, there is no need to feel guilty for your experiments. The real question is what the outcome of an experiment is, namely whether it multiplies your life or diminishes it. If you realize that the impulses you have sent out diminish your life, you don't need to feel guilty—*you simply need to change the impulses you are sending out by changing your consciousness!!!*

The problem is that most people have been seduced by the false teachers into believing that they don't need to change their consciousness—they don't need to remove the beam in their own eye or even look at that beam. They have been sold the lie of the outer path, which promises that they can escape the consequences of their actions – their sins – without changing the cause of those actions, namely the psychological condition that must precede any action.

Most people believe in this lie, whereas the disciples of the Living Christ are doing everything they can to remove all traces of that lie – however subtle – from their consciousness. This, of course, involves seeing every situation as an opportunity to expose some element of the duality consciousness and thus take another step closer to the total freedom that is the Christ consciousness.

My point is that life is an experiment. Your outer circumstances are to a large degree a reflection of what is going on in your consciousness. If you don't like what is coming back to you from the cosmic mirror, don't feel guilty about it and don't blame other people, God or yourself. Simply change what is in your consciousness, and the cosmic mirror will inevitably reflect back your new inner reality in your outer reality.

Do you see what I am really saying here? You are a co-creator and you grow in your ability to co-create *only* by experimenting. The false teachers are seeking to use your past mistakes to get you to shut down your co-creative abilities by losing your willingness to experiment. Yet the *only* true way out of the duality consciousness is to keep experimenting—only you seek to learn from every experiment and increase your Christ discernment so you can perform better experiments.

As I have said before, you cannot overcome a problem as long as you are trapped in the same state of consciousness that created the problem. The problem is *not* your experimentation. The problem is that for a long time you have exercised your co-creative abilities through the filter of the duality consciousness. The way out is *not* to stop experimenting but to keep experimenting while reaching for the discernment of Christ, so you can begin to base your experiments on reality rather than unreality.

When you accept that life is an experiment and embrace experimentation as the only way out of limitations, you can let go of all expectations, including the expectations about self that lead to anger against self. For you do not need to expect that you should have been perfect from the beginning. You are an experimenter, a researcher, and you are not required to be perfect. You are here to learn by continuing to experiment until you begin to see what multiplies and what diminishes your life. So keep experimenting and don't let anything – in your world or in your psyche – cause you to shut down your willingness to TRY. For as I have explained, the death consciousness becomes a closed circle, a self-reinforcing downward spiral. And the *only* way out of it is to TRY something new, to reach for something that is not colored by the illusions of the dualistic mind.

Consider the parable about the talents. The servants who multiplied their talents did so out of love, whereas the servant who buried them in the ground did so out of fear, the fear of loss. The false teachers are seeking to use your past mistakes to generate a fear of loss that causes you to stop experimenting. Yet it is not your failed experiments that keep you out of heaven, for even a failed experiment can be used to learn a lesson. It is only when you *stop* experimenting that you are keeping yourself out of heaven.

So far, your experimentation with free will might have taken you away from heaven. But the reason is that your experiments were based on the illusions of the mind of anti-christ. The way out is *not* to stop experimenting but to increase your discernment so you can begin to base your experiments on the reality of Christ. It is true that you have experimented yourself away from heaven. But it is equally true that the *only* way to overcome this condition is to experiment yourself back into heaven by making better experiments. Which means experimenting based on the reality that all life is one rather than the illusion of separation.

***

So let us now get to the core of the problem. You are – most likely – a spiritual being who volunteered to come into embodiment on Earth in order to help bring God's kingdom into manifestation on this planet. You did this out of love, but after you started embodying on this planet, your love – and the gift you came to bring – was rejected and most likely ridiculed and degraded by some of the more recalcitrant lifestreams on this planet. This has put you in a catch-22, and let me explain the nature of it.

On the one hand, you are not here for your own enjoyment. You are here because you know this planet is far below the level of the kingdom of God. Thus, you know things need to improve on this planet, and you also know that the only way to manifest such improvement is through the spiritual light and wisdom from a higher realm—which is precisely what you came to bring. Yet you have experienced over and over again that both the light and the truth is rejected by a majority of the people on this planet, and thus you cannot see how there can ever be an improvement. Because of this, you have built up a certain level of frustration that can easily cross the line to anger. You might not fear for your own salvation, but you fear for the salvation of other people or the planet.

My point for this entire discourse is to show you that this frustration is a product of the consciousness of separation, which has allowed fear to creep into your being. There are many variations of this fear, such as the sense of urgency that the world might come to an end or that there is a timeline that needs to be met.

Now, I am not saying that there is no timeline, for everything evolves according to cycles. However, let me make it very clear that THE WORLD WILL NOT COME TO AN END. Thus, I want to make it very clear that disciples of the Living Christ need to put behind them the fear of the world ending. When I was in embodiment, I was to some degree affected by this fear, for I did have a concept of the end of the world. However, the reality behind this is that for certain lifestreams, their opportunity to choose life over death will eventually come to an end on this planet, meaning that the world – or rather their opportunity to embody on Earth – will come to an end. However, this is *not* your responsibility, as it is all up to the law of free will.

My point is that you need to develop an uncompromising respect for free will. You respect the free will of other people to the point where, if they want to destroy themselves – or even if a majority want to destroy this planet – you allow them to have that experience. You also respect your own free will by refusing to allow other people's rejection of your light and truth to deter you from letting your light shine and from shouting your truth from the housetops.

What I am saying here is that there is *only* one way out of the catch-22 of frustration and discouragement. You need to decide that you are *not* here to change other people. You are here *only* to share your light and truth—for the purpose of giving other people the option to choose the light, which they do not have until they experience your light and truth. Yet you leave it up to their free will whether they will accept or reject your gift. For you are *not* here to make them accept your gift, you are only here to *offer* that gift.

I need you to make the switch in consciousness that you are here to be like the sun. The sun is constantly shining its light on planet Earth, and it is unconcerned about what people do with that light. Do they accept it or reject it? Well, either way the sun just keeps shining, and that is what you need to do as well. The role of the Living Christ is to be the open door through which the light and the truth of God can shine into this world. It is *not* the role of the Living Christ to get people to respond to that light in any specific way—for that is up to their free will. So the Living Christ is willing to allow other people to do whatever they want with the light, whereby the light becomes either their awakening or their judgment—according to their own choices.

You see, when you become the s-u-n that always shines, you become the S-o-n, the Son of God, the Living Christ (whether you are in a male or female body).

By going through this transformation, you will raise your anger above fear, whereby it will return to its natural God-quality, namely what we might call an unwavering determination, an uncompromising refusal to accept status quo. Which is precisely the driving force that caused the Creator to create the world of form and design it as a world that cannot stand still but is always transcending toward the ultimate goal of becoming the kingdom of God. The Living Christ *never* accepts any conditions on Earth as permanent or unchangeable. He or she holds the vision that things will improve, but in doing so, the Living Christ in non-attached – and I mean *completely* non-attached – to the choices of other people. That is why the Living Christ is absolutely determined *never* to shut off the light and truth but to *always* remain that open door.

Do you see the importance of this? Far too many spiritual people have gone through the stage of frustration and have then become seduced by the subtle lie that if the world does not want their light, they should simply hold it back. They should work on themselves, withdraw from the world and never rock the boat. It is *extremely* important for you to understand that this mentality is engineered by the forces of anti-christ specifically to prevent the most spiritual people from making a difference on this planet. It is engineered to make you stop shining your light, thereby effectively leaving this world in the control of the forces of anti-christ.

I need you to recognize that anger stems from a positive quality that is needed for Christhood, namely the unwillingness to accept stillstand, to accept status quo as unchangeable. Thus, you will do no good for God's cause if you allow yourself to withdraw from the world, to withhold your light and truth. Instead, I need you to awaken to your Christ potential and lock in to your original determination for coming to this planet, so you will not let *any* conditions in this world – including the conditions in your own psyche focused in your ego – prevent you from being that open door for the light and the truth that *will* – if it is allowed entry – change this world.

You see, when you believe in the illusion of separation, you believe that the world has to be saved by what is already *in* the world. And since a deeper part of your being recognizes that this is impossible, you feel – again – that you and the world are in a catch-22. Yet nothing is impossible for the light and the truth of God. They *can* and *will* change the world. However, the light and the truth of God can *only* work when they are allowed to enter this world. And this will happen only when a sufficient number of people decide to become the open doors by becoming the Living Christs in embodiment.

I came to Earth 2,000 years ago precisely to demonstrate the path to personal Christhood, so that others could follow in my footsteps and do the works that I did. So far only very few people have dared to do this, which is why there is still so much suffering on Earth. *You* have the potential to change the equation by becoming the open door. Will you join me, so that my example can bear fruit?

***

As the exercise for this key, I need you to work on forgiveness—forgiving all other people, forgiving God and forgiving yourself.

In order to do this, you need to understand an essential truth about forgiveness, a truth that even many religious and spiritual people have not understood. Many people think that when someone has harmed you, you should hold on to negative feelings toward them, and when you have harmed others, you should hold on to negative feelings toward yourself.

What I have told you here is that everything in this world is energy, meaning that your thoughts and feelings are energy impulses. When you have a thought or generate a feeling, you send out an energy impulse. In many cases it will last only seconds, but when you hold on to a negative feeling, you are constantly sending out an energy impulse. This will generate a continuos impulse, which is what scientists call an energy field. In other words, when you hold a grudge against a person who has harmed you, you create an energy field between your mind and the other person's mind. Take note that it does not matter what the other person has done to you. *You* are the one creating the energy connection, and I can assure you that energy can flow both ways over such a connection. I can also assure you that by allowing such an energy connection to persist, you open your energy field to influx from the collective consciousness.

When you consider how much non-forgiveness, anger and hatred has been generated on this planet, you should be able to see that you do not want to do anything to tie your personal energy field to that collective momentum. What I am saying here is that when *you* hold on to negative feelings toward any person, you open yourself up to an influx of energy, whereby the other person and the planetary force of anti-christ can exercise power over you. The more intense your feelings, the more likely that the force of anti-christ can agitate you into taking actions that will only continue the dualistic struggle and thus tie you to that struggle. There are many people who have been trapped in such a spiral or retaliation and revenge for many lifetimes. Obviously, you cannot be a disciple of the Living Christ as long as you are tied in to such momentums.

Likewise, there is a planetary momentum of anger against God and one of anger against oneself. When you hold a negative image of yourself, you make yourself vulnerable to the planetary momentum. In reality, you need to look for the beam in your own eye that caused you to hurt other people. When you have discovered and removed it, you need to accept that you are forgiven and thus there is no need to hold on to negative feelings about what you have done in the past. You need to accept that God has forgiven you and you need to forgive yourself.

How do you forgive? Well, most people find it hard to forgive because they think forgiveness – as everything else – should be tied to conditions on Earth. In other words, they think that if someone has harmed you, that person needs to change before he or she deserves forgiveness. Or they think there needs to be some kind of justice before there can be forgiveness. Yet this is a completely dualistic view of forgiveness, and it springs from the mind of anti-christ. Take a look at these sayings:

> But I say unto you, That ye resist not evil: but whosoever shall smite thee on thy right cheek, turn to him the other also. (Matthew 5:39)

> 21 Then came Peter to him, and said, Lord, how oft shall my brother sin against me, and I forgive him? till seven times?
> 22 Jesus saith unto him, I say not unto thee, Until seven times: but, Until seventy times seven. (Matthew, Chapter 18)

What I was really saying here is that you need to be in a state of *perpetual* forgiveness, a state of mind in which you never allow yourself to feel that you have been violated by others, and thus they are forgiven even before they do anything to you—which means you must overcome all expectations. Consider that forgiveness is normally seen as a selfless act that sets other people free. However, in reality it can be seen as an act of enlightened self-interest because it is actually setting *yourself* free.

What I told you above is that as long as you have *not* forgiven, you are maintaining an energy connection between yourself and the other person, a connection that also ties you to the collective consciousness. So by *not* forgiving, you are actually hurting yourself. Non-forgiveness is like climbing a mountain with a heavy boat anchor dragging behind you. My point being that you will only make it harder for yourself to walk the spiritual path if you hold on to non-forgiveness. When you let go and forgive, you will set yourself free to make much faster progress on the path.

The problem with non-forgiveness is that it can be characterized by the old concept that two wrongs don't make a right. Someone else is in an unbalanced state of mind and does something to hurt you. You – or rather your ego – then uses that unbalanced act as a "justification" for going into an unbalanced frame of mind. The ego thinks this is a natural reaction and that you are only doing what is just or necessary in order to pay back the other person and bring "justice." Yet in reality, you are harming yourself by putting yourself permanently in an unbalanced state of mind. And how can you hope to bring justice while you are in the same frame of mind as the person who harmed you?

So how do you forgive? There is *only* one way. You must let go of all the conditions created in this world and forgive UNCONDITIONALLY, which is precisely what I am telling my disciples to do—back then and today. There is only one form of forgiveness—unconditional forgiveness. You do not need to have another person change before you can forgive that person. You need to have *yourself* change so you can see that forgiving is enlightened self-interest, because it sets you free from any energy ties to people in an unbalanced state of mind.

You see, when someone hurts you, that person will make karma and what the person sent out will inevitably be returned to him or her by the cosmic mirror. That is why you have the saying:

> Dearly beloved, avenge not yourselves, but rather give place unto wrath: for it is written, Vengeance is mine; I will repay, saith the Lord. (Romans 12:19)

God has set up a mechanical law that returns to every person what that person is sending out. This is ultimate justice that no one can escape, so you have no need to worry about bringing other people to justice. You can leave that up to God's law, which is unfailing. So *your* concern should be your own growth, and in that respect let me make it clear that when you go into a negative frame of mind because another person hurt you, *you* will also make karma. For the cosmic mirror can only reflect back to you what you are sending out.

Do you now begin to see a deeper meaning behind my statement to turn the other cheek? If someone harms you, that person makes karma. If you take revenge or even hold a grudge, you too make karma. But if you turn the other cheek in unconditional forgiveness, *you* will make no karma from the situation. On top of that, your unconditional reaction will serve as the other person's judgment, whereby that person's opportunity to harm others will actually be shortened. On the other hand, when you go into a negative reaction, you engage in the dualistic struggle, and that cannot serve as the judgment of others—it only serves to perpetuate the struggle.

My point is that you have a decision to make over the next month. You need to decide whether you will forgive unconditionally, meaning that you forgive all people who have ever harmed you, forgive God and forgive yourself. If you will forgive unconditionally, then I welcome you to the next level of discipleship under the Living Christ. If you will not forgive unconditionally, then you are not yet ready to become a disciple of the Living Christ, and I ask you to withdraw from this course and return only when you have forgiven unconditionally.

## Exercise for Key 6

To help you forgive, I ask you to continue the pattern established of giving a rosary and then writing down what comes to you in terms of people you have not forgiven, things for which you hold anger against God and reasons for not forgiving yourself. Then examine those reasons and see how they are holding you back—creating an impenetrable wall between yourself and me. You simply cannot enter the wedding feast – and have your soul become the bride of Christ – until you have put on the wedding garment of unconditional forgiveness.

I also need you to monitor yourself for any elements of anger in your being. When you feel the vibration of anger, tune in to the Dhyani Buddha Akshobya, who is the Buddha that is the antidote to anger and hatred. His form of wisdom is the mirror-like wisdom, which you might envision as a completely calm mountain lake that is like a mirror undisturbed by anything in this world.

You may also think of it as a mirror that will – if you are open to seeing it – give you a mirror image of what is real and unreal, thus empowering you to discern and avoid being angered by anything unreal. If you ask the Buddha, he will reflect back to you what is unreal in your own consciousness. For I can assure you that nothing real will cause anger in the conscious self—only in your ego. And thus, when you see what is real and unreal, you have the opportunity to unmask the ego as it responds with anger to that which is real. Thus you need to build a habit of monitoring yourself for anger, and when you feel it, tune in to Akshobya and recite his mantra:

**OM AKSHOBYA HUM**

As the ongoing exercise for the coming 33 days, start by giving Mother Mary's Miracle Forgiveness Rosary once a day for two weeks. Use the same Hail Mary as mentioned in the last key. Then, give the Rosary of Unconditional Love for the remainder of the 33 days, again using the new Hail Mary:

**Hail Mary, I AM whole,**
**I AM complete within my soul.**
**I AM nurtured, I AM free,**
**one with God in eternity.**

**Holy Mary, by your Grace,**
**I AM transcending time and space.**
**I see God's perfect Light in me,**
**I AM the Sun, I love life free.**

I also want you to say the mantra of the Dhyani Buddha for this key one time after each verse and before the Hail Mother of Nurturance.

As my final word on anger, consider that anger is a perversion of determination. True determination is the will power to raise up the entire planet for the benefit of all. The perversion happens when fear enters the picture, which can only happen through the illusion of separation. Thus, the Divine determination to raise up the All now becomes centered around the determination to give the separate self a sense of security that enables it to live with its basic fear. Yet because the separate self has an inherent fear that it can never overcome, the determination to raise the All becomes perverted by the fear of loss. This causes it to be expressed as anger because the separate self can never feel fully secure and at peace, and thus disappointment and frustration is inevitable.

The very fear that causes you to seek an advantage for the separate self makes it impossible to ever feel at peace. In fact, the more you push to secure an advantage for the separate self, the more you reinforce the fear. This is a never-ending spiral that you can *only* escape by transcending the very consciousness that created it—namely the illusion of the separate self.

# Key 7
# Get off the treadmill of competition

In this key we will deal with the spiritual poison of envy and jealousy. The Dhyani Buddha who is the antidote to this poison is called Amogasiddhi. His wisdom is the all-accomplishing wisdom and his mantra is:

**OM AMOGASIDDHI AH**

As you study this key, tune in to the Buddha and repeat his mantra when you feel the energies we are dealing with.

As you will have learned by now, every human quality is the perversion of a divine quality, and the divine quality that corresponds to envy and jealousy is the desire to do well, the desire to achieve victory. There is a certain irony to the fact that the students who are most susceptible to envy and jealousy are the ones who have the greatest desire to do well. In other words, these are the most eager and dedicated students, the ones who truly want to follow their spiritual teacher and meet all requirements on the path. The problem comes in when these beings develop an attachment to doing well, an unbalanced desire to do well, an attachment to measuring "doing well" by the results achieved in this world.

Where does an imbalance come from? You will have realized by now that any imbalance comes from the illusion of separation. This illusion creates a "space" or distance between your conscious self and your Creator, which inevitably leads to fear—the fear that you could be lost. It is in this space, this no-God's land of fear, that the consciousness of anti-christ can exist and give rise to countless illusions that are designed to hide the basic fact that no part of God can be apart from God.

Since you are now beyond the beginning stages of this course, let me go right to the core of the issue. God is infinite, in fact a better word for God would be "The Infinite." Your conscious self is an individualization of the infinite Creator. As such, you are both infinite and an individual. As we have said, the conscious self *is* what it thinks it is. Your conscious self is created as an individual being, and as such it will look at the world from the perspective of an individual being. We might say that your conscious self is the Creator looking at creation from a particular vantage point—instead of the overall, omnipresent perspective of the Creator. God is looking at the world from the inside—through the prism of your identity. Because of that, the conscious self has the ability to instantly switch its perspective and see the overall perspective of the Creator.

Imagine that you are standing on a tall hill and have a commanding panoramic view. You now put a pair of strong binoculars in front of your eyes. Suddenly, you cannot see most of the view but see only a small slice of the whole. Furthermore, what you see is greatly magnified and thus seems more important. Yet you still have the potential to remove the binoculars and take in the entire view. The conscious self can always switch its perspective and see the world from God's perspective—it is often called a mystical experience but there is nothing mystical about it. It only seems mystical because most people have forgotten they are more than their separate selves, and thus they think they can see the world *only* through the "binoculars" of the separate self. Originally – meaning before you fell into duality – these binoculars showed simply a magnified view of reality. However, after you became influenced by duality, your personal binoculars showed a distorted or colored view of everything.

The conscious self can – so to speak – merge itself back into the Infinite from which it emerged—without losing its individuality. It can be both infinite and an individual at the same time—it can know that it IS the Infinite expressing itself through an individual identity. It is the Infinite expressing itself in the finite world. The importance of this is, of course, that when the conscious self knows that it is one with the Infinite, it can never be trapped in the illusion of separation. For the very nature of this illusion is that there is a finite world that is either set apart from God or is all that exists. When the conscious self believes in this illusion, it feels trapped in the finite world, and it then becomes vulnerable to all kinds of illusions for how to avoid this sense of being trapped—including the illusion that it needs to be better than other beings.

In reality, the only true antidote is the realization that although you live in a world that appears to be finite, even the finite world is created from the infinite energy and Being of the Creator. Thus, nothing is truly separated from the Infinite, which means there is no reason to feel trapped in the finite world. Simply go into the kingdom of the Infinite that is within you and reconnect to your true Being. When you realize you are an expression of the Infinite, how can you feel trapped in the finite world? For you will no longer believe in the illusion of separation, namely that the finite world is separated from God or that there is no God. Instead, you will do what you came for, namely to let the Infinite express its infinity through you, thereby bringing the finite world closer to infinity.

***

As Maitreya explains, a new lifestream is naturally focused on exploring its individuality, especially as it relates to expressing its creative abilities in the world where it is born. Yet a new lifestream always starts in a cosmic schoolroom under the tutelage of a spiritual teacher. Thus, a new lifestream has some awareness that it is part of something greater than the individual self and it has the loving guidance of an enlightened teacher. The goal of the teacher is to take the lifestream to the point where it becomes spiritually self-sufficient by becoming one with the Infinite—which is what some call enlightenment. Enlightenment means true self-knowledge, meaning that you fully know and accept that you *are* the Infinite expressing itself – through the prism of individuality – in the finite world.

The reason why you are not enlightened and why you are studying this course in Christhood is that you have come to believe in the illusion of separation. This illusion creates the sense that there is a gap between the conscious self and the Infinite, and this makes it seem like your individuality is what sets you apart from God, rather than making you a facet of the diamond of God's Being. In other words, when you believe in the illusion of separation, your individuality becomes a stumbling block that makes you think you are separated from God or that you will have to lose your individuality in order to become one with God (as some unenlightened teachers teach). In other words, you now begin to believe that individuality is synonymous with separation—that your individuality sets you apart from the Infinite and from other individualizations of the Infinite.

My point here is that in every spiritual school there are always some students who want to do well and some that are a bit more easy-going. When those who want to do well begin to believe in the illusion of separation, they become susceptible to three of the main illusions created by the consciousness of anti-christ:

- You are a separate being living in a world with other separate beings. You have your free will, but so do all other beings. And since *their* will is separate from *your* will, it is possible that they will do something that hurts you or makes you look bad in the eyes of the teacher/ God. In other words, free will means separate wills that can only create conflict.

- By becoming focused on your own separation from others, it becomes very easy to believe in the need to compare yourself to others. In other words, in order to do well and impress the teacher, you need to do better than others. This gives rise to the sense of competition and the need to rise above others—the desire to be a favorite son.

- When you believe in the illusion of separation, you inevitably come to focus attention on the material world. Thus, you become susceptible to the basic illusion of the outer path, namely that you gain entry into the kingdom of God by doing something in this world. In other words, the way to impress the teacher – the key to "doing well" or being saved – is to achieve certain results in this world. Of course, almost anything you can achieve in this world will depend on the choices of other beings, and this opens up another level of not simply competition but the need to control others. Some beings now become trapped in the further illusion that in order to make themselves look better than others, they not only have to raise up themselves, they also have to keep others down. Instead of focusing on bettering themselves, some beings now begin to focus on holding back others. And thus, the ongoing dualistic struggle is born.

***

When a being begins to believe in the illusion of separation and the dualistic illusions described above, that being now begins to believe that comparisons are not only possible but necessary. Do you truly understand what I just said?

Your outer mind has been programmed for your entire life – even for lifetimes – to believe in comparisons and to – automatically and without conscious thought – perform comparisons of many different kinds. You have grown up in a society that is based on and encourages the consciousness of comparisons, from grades in school to the social status or wealth of your parents to the importance of your nation or religion compared to others. In other words, your outer mind is so thoroughly programmed to engage in comparisons in the material world that it will require a major effort for your conscious self to disentangle itself from this consciousness – this energy vortex, this black hole – of comparisons.

As a student of the Living Christ, you are walking the path toward absolute spiritual freedom, and one aspect of this is that you rise above the consciousness of comparisons. Why is this important? Well, it should be fairly obvious that if you are to escape the spiritual poison of envy and jealousy, you have to rise above the illusion of comparison. For is it not obvious that envy springs from the illusion that it is possible or relevant to compare yourself to other people or to some standard defined in this world? If there is no comparison, how could there be a basis for envy?

Now consider the commonly known fact that although a snowstorm may produce billions of snowflakes, no two of them are alike. This has two implications that are relevant for our discussion. One is that a snowflake is a relatively simple structure. A co-creator with God is an almost infinitely more complex "structure" than a snowflake. In other words, the potential to create individual uniqueness is far higher in a complex than a simple structure. So if God can create individual uniqueness in as simple of a structure as snowflakes, do you see that it is far easier for God to create uniqueness in co-creators? My point being that you are created as an absolutely unique individual. There is no one like you in the entire world of form. You have the potential to bring a gift to planet Earth that no other being could bring. You are truly unique.

Now for the second point. Imagine you meet a scientist who has made it his life's work to study snowflakes. This isn't necessarily odd, but this scientist has taken his study in a peculiar direction. He has set up an entire system for comparing snowflakes and classifying them into "good" and "bad" flakes. He has created a scale upon which the value of snowflakes can be measured, and at the top of the scale is the perfect snowflake, which it is his life's goal to discover. Thus, he spends his entire life on a quest that is not aimed at helping humankind make better use of snow but is aimed entirely at finding the perfect snowflake and sorting snowflakes based on his self-created scale of value.

You would probably think this was an odd way to spend your life, and there are several reasons for this. One is that it is not a useful activity—it doesn't have any practical value that helps improve life on this planet. Another is that it is an impossible quest. When you think about it, you realize that snowflakes are unique, so what is the point of comparing them? How can you make comparisons between objects that are unique? And what is the point of assigning values to something like snowflakes? Can you really talk about good and bad snowflakes? And how could there be a perfect snowflake when they are all unique, since perfection implies a comparison to something imperfect?

Well, what is the point in making comparisons between people, when each person is a unique individual? What is the point in assigning values to people's uniqueness? And can you really talk about good and bad people according to some standard in this world? Is there any value judgment in the mind of God—who, after all, created all co-creators as unique individuals?

***

Do you begin to see the problem—the spiritual catch-22 of competition? You were created as a unique individualization of the Infinite. You chose to descend into the material world out of a pure desire to express your unique individuality in this world by allowing the light of the Infinite to shine through the prism of your individuality, thereby bringing light and your individual expression of truth to this world. In other words, you are here to BE the unique individual you were created to be. You are *not* here to live up to some standard defined in this world—by the mind of anti-christ. You are *not* here to make yourself look better than others in comparison to them, based on some criteria in this world. You are here to bring your light and truth, so that others may have a real choice to either accept what you bring – using it to raise themselves above duality – or reject it and thereby judge themselves. When you have shared your light and truth, you have fulfilled your mission—nothing more to be done.

Yet after you began to believe in the illusion of separation, you adopted a dualistic view of your reason for being here. You now began to believe that you were here not simply to let your light shine but to get other people to respond in a certain way or to produce certain outer results.

Do you see the subtle difference? In reality, you are *not* here to get other people to respond in any particular way. You are here to give them a choice and then leave it up to them what they choose. They will be judged by the law of God and that is truly not your concern. Thus, the success of your mission depends *only* on you sharing your light and truth, and thus it depends on nothing outside yourself.

Yet when the illusions of anti-christ started clouding your vision, you began to think your mission was about creating a particular result here on Earth, and this result involved getting other people to change. Suddenly, the perceived success of your mission became dependent upon the choices of other people. This made you believe in the possibility of failure—which had not been an option before. This fear of failure now – through the lies of the false teachers – became linked to your re-entry into the kingdom of God. In other words, the fear was possible only because you had come to believe in the illusion of separation, which then gives rise to the need to be saved. This creates the fear of not being saved, because your salvation depends on the results you achieve, and the results depend on the reactions of other people. In order to deal with this fear, you took one of two roads:

- You started believing that by following the outer path described in a religion in this world, your salvation – and your entry into the kingdom – would be guaranteed.
- You started believing that by achieving certain results in this world – and thereby making yourself look better than other people who did not achieve the same results – God would *have to* let you into his kingdom. This then gave you a desire to control others and keep them down in order to make yourself look better in comparison.

Yet either way led to the same result, namely to make you believe that by doing something in this world, you could buy or force your way into the kingdom of God. This plunged you into the consciousness of comparing yourself to others and to a standard in this world, making you vulnerable to the spiritual poison of envy and jealousy. And once this poison has entered your being, it will bind you to the treadmill of comparison and competition that will make it very difficult for you to see through the fallacy of what you are doing. There is always some goal, some carrot dangling in front of your nose: "If only I achieve such and such a result, if only I can make myself appear better than these other people, then I *will* be acceptable in the eyes of God."

Yet the reality is that you are already acceptable in the eyes of God—if only you let go of the separate self and return to the identity God created, namely as an individualization of your Creator. The kingdom of God is within you, meaning that it is a state of consciousness. Your entry into the kingdom is *not* dependent upon anything outside yourself, including anything in this world. Thus, the *only* way to enter the kingdom is for your conscious self to return to the original state of innocence that you had before you began to believe in the illusion of separation. In order to do that, you need to remove the beam in your own eye by seeing through the dualistic illusions that make up the beam and make up the smokescreen that prevents you from seeing the beam or the need to remove it.

So instead of comparing yourself to others, you need to switch into comparing yourself to yourself. You need to begin the process of rediscovering your true spiritual identity—as opposed to the human, worldly identity of your ego. You then need to evaluate how much of your spiritual individuality can shine through your outer mind and then make a sincere effort to remove all the layers of human identity, until the Sun of your I AM Presence can shine through unhindered, whereby you become the Son – the S-u-n – of God walking the Earth. Ask not what God can do *for* you—ask what God wants to do *through* you. Then contemplate how you can stop limiting what God can do through you, for Christed beings never resists having God work through them. My Father works hitherto, and I work.

***

Do you begin to see the reality I am describing? You are here to express your divine individuality, which is the gift that you wanted to bring to this world. We might even say it is the gift that God wants to bring to this world, and in order to deliver it, God created an extension of itself—*you*.

Yet the Creator is – of course – an undivided whole and the Creator has the overall perspective for the goal of the entire world of form (which Maitreya describes in his book as raising up each unascended sphere to become part of the spiritual realm). Thus, the Creator did *not* create individual extensions of itself in such a way that their individualities clash or work against the overall goal. There is no conflict between individual snowflakes—they all work perfectly together to create a snowfall. The Creator is fully capable of designing individual co-creators in such a way that their individualities supplement and complement each other—working together toward the same overall goal.

In other words, each individual co-creator is here to bring forth a unique facet of the overall goal. This means there is no competition between you and other co-creators. You were not created for the purpose of being the only or the best co-creator. You were created for the purpose of being a unique co-creator, doing something that is unique and thus cannot be compared to the unique efforts of other unique co-creators. Yet your unique contribution still fits perfectly into the larger whole, which means that your contribution magnifies the contributions of other co-creators and vice versa. The whole is more than the sum of the parts.

Do you see what I am saying? There is no *one* co-creator who can raise up the entire material universe to the perfection of the spiritual realm. Each co-creator has a unique role to play in this process, and your role will not conflict with or degrade the role of others. In fact, by working together, two co-creators can achieve more than simply twice as much as their individual efforts. Only when a critical mass of co-creators allow their light to shine through their lower beings, will the world be raised up. A diamond is beautiful because it has many facets, and each facet has a unique role to play. The diamond would not be complete if any one of the facets was missing, yet the whole of the diamond is more than simply a collection of facets. When all co-creators reconnect to their spiritual identities, they will form a whole – the Body of God on Earth – that is truly more than the sum of its parts. The goal of God is to see the formation of a community on Earth that is like the community we have in the spiritual realm, where people come into unity and thus manifest here below what is already manifest above.

My point being that when you reconnect to the infinite aspect of your own nature, all thoughts of conflicts, comparisons and competition simply fade away. Instead of comparing yourself to others, you focus on being who you are, focus on expressing your unique gift and enjoying your uniqueness. You no longer have a need for comparisons.

When you do this, your efforts will not threaten or diminish the efforts of others. On the contrary, you see that your efforts enhance the efforts of others, and the combined efforts form a whole that is more than the sum of the parts. Why do you think I said:

> For where two or three are gathered together in my name, there am I in the midst of them. (Matthew 18:20)

What am "I?" It is a symbol for the cosmic Christ, which is the consciousness designed to help everything become MORE and thus come closer to Infinity. The Christ is present *only* when people come together in the true spirit of oneness, where their individualities enhance each other. When people come together in my name, they will – if they truly understand the meaning of Christ – set aside the separate selves, their egos, in order to come into oneness with Christ and oneness with each other. By doing so, the whole becomes more than the sum of the parts, which means they have multiplied their talents. And thus the Living Christ will return to reward the servants who have been faithful over a few things by making them ruler over many things.

Do you begin to see the far-reaching implications of this? As an example, look at the fate of religious organizations. The true meaning of a spiritual movement is a coming together of people for the purpose of forming a greater union in the material world by seeking oneness with each other. This union then forms a chalice that will open up a doorway to the spiritual realm, whereby spiritual light and truth will be poured out from the Ascended Host. This can even lead to the opening of a direct connection to the spiritual realm that becomes a figure-eight flow of oneness as above, so below. In such a spiritual community, people might have different functions, but no person is more important or valuable than another.

Now look at the reality of how most spiritual and religious organizations function. They have a clear division into leaders and followers, with a small elite (perhaps just one person) as leaders and a large group of followers. The leaders are seen as having special abilities beyond the members—who on the other hand don't have to think or act for themselves but only have to do what the leaders tell them.

Can you see how such a system raises a few people up compared to the many and thus denies the Christ potential of *all* people? You see, even those who are raised above others deny the Christ potential in themselves. For the Christ is *not* above others, the Christ is ONE with all life and seeks to raise up all life. Thus, the Christ might be in a leadership position but is truly serving only to raise up the whole, as I expressed in this quote:

> And the King shall answer and say unto them, Verily I say unto you, Inasmuch as ye have done it unto one of the least of these my brethren, ye have done it unto me. (Matthew 25:40)

My point being that before you can do something to others, you must already have done it to yourself. Thus, before you seek to put others down and raise yourself up, you have already put yourself down. For if you had not put yourself down, why would you have the need to seem more important than others? Why would you need to compare unless you had already condemned yourself to the prison created by the illusion of separation?

***

Do you now understand that the goal for a disciple of Christ is to be completely free of the energy of envy and the illusion of comparison from which it springs? Your goal is to be free to *be* who you really are, to express your divine individuality—as opposed to the separate individuality defined by your ego. When you do this, everything you do will serve to further the overall goal that the Creator has for the material universe, including planet Earth. That goal is to raise up the entire universe to be so filled with light that it ascends to the spiritual realm.

When you are free of the illusion of competition, you see that you are here not to raise yourself up in comparison to others. You are here to help set them free from the illusions of duality—as *you* have become free from those illusions. You then understand the meaning of my statements:

> But he that is greatest among you shall be your servant. (Matthew 23:11)

> And he sat down, and called the twelve, and saith unto them, If any man desire to be first, the same shall be last of all, and servant of all. (Mark 9:35)

> And whosoever of you will be the chiefest, shall be servant of all. (Mark 10:44)

Do you see that the goal of the ego – the separate self – will always be to raise itself up in comparison to others? Thus, ego-driven people seek to make themselves appear more important than others, setting themselves up as leaders or as being somehow in a different class than the population.

The Living Christ has no need for being elevated above others, for he or she recognizes the oneness of all life. Thus, the only way to raise oneself is to raise the All—which is now seen as one's greater self. So how do you get to the point where you no longer feel threatened by others? Well, let us start by understanding the psychology of the separate self.

***

The psychology of the separate self – the ego for short – can be understood only by realizing that it is based on, springs from, the illusion of separation. When the conscious self sees reality, it knows it is an extension of the Infinite and thus it realizes the truth in the following statement:

> But Jesus beheld them, and said unto them, With men this is impossible; but with God all things are possible. (Matthew 19:26)

In other words, the conscious self knows that it is perfectly possible for it to fulfill its reason for coming into this world. In contrast, when the conscious self has accepted the illusion of separation, it now looks at the world and itself through the filter of the separate self. Thus, it believes separation is real, which means it now inevitably must doubt that it can fulfill its reason for coming into this world. It has inevitably become vulnerable to the fear that it might not achieve its goal and that it might not be able to get back to the spiritual realm.

Do you see the essential dynamic? The conscious self is an extension of the Creator's Being. When it realizes this, it knows that it can always ascend back to the spiritual realm, and it knows that by being the open door for the Infinite to express itself in the finite world, it can achieve its goals. This simply cannot fail, for when the conscious self sees itself as one with the Infinite, well then all things are possible to it as an extension of the Infinite.

Do you see that you are not necessarily here to accomplish specific results on Earth? An essential part of your mission is to bring more spiritual light into the material frequency spectrum, and by doing so, you *will* contribute to raising up this entire sphere, including planet Earth. Your main job is to be the open door and express the maximum amount of light in all situations. This is a task that does not depend on anything outside yourself, so if you make yourself open, your mission cannot fail.

The essential point here is that the *only* way for you to fulfill your goal and ascend back to the spiritual realm is for your conscious self to throw off the illusion of separation and return to a realistic self-knowledge—accepting who you really are as an individualization of the infinite Creator. This is the *only* road to salvation. It requires only one thing, namely that the conscious self separates itself from the separate self and allows the ego to die. When the conscious self is free from the separate self, it will not actually enter the kingdom of God, for it will realize that *it is already in* the kingdom and *has always been in* the kingdom. The kingdom of God is simply a metaphor for a state of consciousness, the state of being one with your source, with your Creator.

Yet when the conscious self sees itself as a separate being, it cannot see this as a viable path to salvation. It sees everything through the filter of the separate self, meaning that it thinks the separate self is real and that the goal is to preserve the separate self and make it acceptable in the eyes of God so it can enter the kingdom. Do you see the subtle shift here? The conscious self now believes that it is its task to save the separate self instead of letting it die. And since this cannot be done, the conscious self has bound itself on the treadmill of pursuing an impossible goal.

When you look through the filter of separation, the kingdom of God is seen as an actual place that is distant from the separate self.

The separate self has to enter this remote kingdom by qualifying itself through the means found in the material world—which is also seen as separate from the kingdom. Do you now begin to see the twisted logic of the separate self? It believes it is a separate being that is living in a world that is separated from the kingdom of God. Yet it also believes that it is possible for this separate being to enter the remote kingdom and that it can qualify for entry by doing something in this separate world.

When your conscious self sees the world through this filter, it becomes vulnerable to the illusion that by elevating the separate self to a superior status in this world, you can qualify for entry into God's kingdom. Yet can you now begin to see why this is a flawed logic? Anything you do to elevate the separate self in this world will only serve to reinforce the illusion that the separate self is real and that it is separate from other separate selves. The more special you seem compared to other people, the more separate you are from them. And this only reinforces the illusion that the separate self is real. So the more successful you are in setting yourself above others, the further you move into the jungle of duality. You are using your "superior" abilities to build a gilded cage for yourself.

The reality is that the kingdom of God is a state in which there is no separateness, for all life is seen as one—as an expression of the one Creator, for "without him was not any thing made that was made." So the *only* way to enter the kingdom is to overcome the illusion of the separate self. Thus, it is logical that the more you do to elevate the separate self, the more difficult you make it for the conscious self to overcome the illusion of separateness and let the ego die. The harder you try to qualify the separate self for salvation, the more you push salvation away from you. This is what I expressed in the following quote:

> 23 Then said Jesus unto his disciples, Verily I say unto you, That a rich man shall hardly enter into the kingdom of heaven.
> 24 And again I say unto you, It is easier for a camel to go through the eye of a needle, than for a rich man to enter into the kingdom of God.
> 25 When his disciples heard it, they were exceedingly amazed, saying, Who then can be saved?
> 26 But Jesus beheld them, and said unto them, With men this is impossible; but with God all things are possible. (Matthew, Chapter 19)

A "rich man" is a metaphor that can be interpreted as a person who thinks he has achieved a lot in this world—he is rich in thinking he has elevated the separate self to some superior status that qualifies it for salvation. The "eye of the needle" was actually a gate in the town wall around Jerusalem. My disciples knew that it was completely impossible for a camel to pass through that gate, which is why they suddenly feared that no one could be saved. And even beyond that, they had grown up in a culture that believed in the outer path, meaning that by faithfully following the outer religion, you were guaranteed to be saved. It was this belief they finally saw through and thus naturally began to wonder how salvation was possible without the outer religion. My answer was a coded message that only by letting go of the separate self and re-uniting with God can you be saved.

***

You now need to understand that the separate self will *never* see through the illusion of separation. Only your conscious self can see through this illusion, but even your conscious self will *never* do so as long as it looks at the world and itself through the filter of the separate self.

This means that the separate self will never overcome the fear that is the inevitable companion of the illusion of separation. This fear is born from the fact that the separate self is separated from the power of God and thus does not have the ability to fulfill your goal in this world nor the ability to take you beyond this world. In other words, the separate self cannot be saved because "with men this is impossible." And even though the separate self cannot see this, it knows that it cannot draw upon the power of God—since it feels separated from God. Thus, the separate self must of necessity seek to do everything by using the power that is available to it in the material world.

You now see the essential dynamic. Your conscious self can never quite forget that it has a purpose in this world, nor can it forget that it has a longing for something beyond this world—what many religions have explained as the need to be saved. The separate self can try to divert your attention from this longing, and for the majority of human beings, this is still working quite well—just consider how many schemes in this world are designed to simply keep people's attention focused on this world. Yet for the more mature beings, the tactic of diversion no longer works, and they will inevitably place importance on the goals that are beyond this world. To avoid losing control over the conscious self, the separate self has come up with the outer path, which says that you can fulfill your goals in this world and be saved by doing something *in* this world.

Of course, this is an impossible quest, but the separate self will never see this. Nor will it ever see why it is impossible—namely that you are meant to be the unique spiritual being God created and express that individuality. As a result, the separate self defines the path to salvation based on what it *can* see—namely this world. The reality is that you will fulfill your goals only by becoming one with your own Higher Being and thus one with God, whereby God can work *through* you. This is explained between the lines in the following statements:

> I can of mine own self do nothing: as I hear, I judge: and my judgment is just; because I seek not mine own will, but the will of the Father which hath sent me. (John 5:30)
>
> Believest thou not that I am in the Father, and the Father in me? the words that I speak unto you I speak not of myself: but the Father that dwelleth in me, he doeth the works. (John 14:10)

When you are *with* God, all things are possible to God *through* you. Likewise, the *only* path to salvation is to come into oneness with God, whereby you are in the kingdom of God no matter where you are. Yet because the separate self cannot see this, it defines the path based on this world.

This leads to the concept that the key is to elevate the separate self in comparison to other separate selves. For – in the mind of the separate self – it is logical that if *your* separate self is elevated far beyond the separate selves of other people, then God simply *has to* accept *your* separate self. The separate self believes it can be saved by qualifying itself in this world—in other words it believes it can enter the kingdom of oneness *without giving up its separateness but by elevating that separateness to some ultimate status*.

My point is that this comparative and competitive outlook inevitably has a built-in fear, namely that your separate self could fail to be good enough compared to others. And this inevitably leads to envy and jealousy, for you are constantly comparing yourself to others, fearing that if you do not meet some comparative criteria defined in this world, you can fail in this world and fail to reach the next world. In other words, you cannot separate the outer path from the fear of failure. This fear will be your inescapable companion for as long as you believe in the outer path and the illusion of separation from which it springs. And this fear of failure is precisely what perverts your constructive desire to do well in uniqueness and turns it into the non-constructive desire to do well in comparison.

The separate self is based on fear, so it seeks to do what is best for the separate self, namely what makes it seem better than other separate selves. This seduces the conscious self into focusing on doing what seems best in this world instead of focusing on expressing your uniqueness. Instead of simply *being* who you *are* – whereby you will inevitably raise up the All by sharing your light and truth – you now focus on making your separate self seem better than others—whereby you put down both yourself and all life. Yet at the same time, you believe this will actually lead to your own salvation. You might even believe that if you can get others to follow you in the only true religion, they too will be saved—the seduction is complete.

The separate self actually seeks to save itself by condemning those who are different from itself to everlasting damnation. In contrast, the Christ seeks to raise up all life, so that all can be saved.

***

The most subtle consequence of the energy of envy is that it prevents you from following the most essential requirement for the disciples of the living Christ. Let us look – again – at the quote in which I described this requirement:

> 1. Judge not, that ye be not judged.
> 2. For with what judgment ye judge, ye shall be judged: and with what measure ye mete, it shall be measured to you again.
> 3. And why beholdest thou the mote that is in thy brother's eye, but considerest not the beam that is in thine own eye?
> 4. Or how wilt thou say to thy brother, Let me pull out the mote out of thine eye; and, behold, a beam is in thine own eye?
> 5. Thou hypocrite, first cast out the beam out of thine own eye; and then shalt thou see clearly to cast out the mote out of thy brother's eye. (Matthew, Chapter 7)

What I am saying here is that you cannot even *begin* to walk the path toward Christhood as long as you are trapped in the consciousness of comparing yourself to others, thus focusing all of your attention on judging others instead of looking for the beam in your own eye.

Do you now see why this approach to life is so dysfunctional? As I have explained, everything in this world revolves around free will. You are responsible for your own choices, and you are not responsible for the choices of other people—*they are*. The consequence is that *your* salvation and *your* progress on the spiritual path does *not* depend on the choices made by other people. It depends EXCLUSIVELY on your own choices. The *only* way for *you* to be saved is to change *your* consciousness. Even if you managed to change the consciousness of every other person on the planet, it would have *no* impact on *your* salvation.

When your energy field is influenced by or filled with the poison of envy, you think you have the perfect excuse for focusing on the faults of other people and for ignoring the beam in your own eye. In other words, you think you have the perfect excuse for *not* doing the one thing that can lead to *your* salvation, namely changing your own consciousness.

Do you see the subtle seduction here? You came into this world out of a true desire to help raise this world into the light of the spiritual realm. In order to do this, many people have to be awakened, meaning that they have to change their consciousness by removing the beam in their own eyes. However, it is *not* your job to remove the mote in the eyes of other people. It is *your* job to give them an example of a person who is willing to remove the beam in his or her own eye.

Your job is *not* to force people through the separate self but to INSPIRE people by showing them how to unite with their higher selves. And when you are trapped in the consciousness of comparison and the poison of envy, you have effectively sabotaged your real mission on Earth—thus jeopardizing your return to the kingdom of God without doing anything to help others.

In fact, envy leads to the fear that you might fail. And this fear gives rise to the dualistic logic that if you seem to be better than others, then you cannot possibly fail. And since the separate self does not have access to the power of God, it can use only the powers in this world. Which means it is tempted to not simply raise up itself but to put others down. And when enough people are trapped in this frame of mind, you have a society and culture in which everyone is put down.

That is why you have grown up in a civilization that is – from a spiritual perspective – completely dysfunctional. A true civilization is focused on helping each child reconnect to its higher self and learn how to express its spiritual individuality—thereby bringing forth light and ideas that will benefit the whole of society. Instead, you have grown up in a society that denies the Christ potential of each person, instead trapping people into following a materialistic path of seeking pleasure and possessions in this world or the false spiritual path of seeking salvation through following a religion in this world. In other words, you have grown up in a culture in which everyone is put down to the lowest common denominator of seeking to be a good *human* being according to the dualistic standards defined by their society. It is high time for you to begin to consider how to escape this downward pull of the mass consciousness, and the place to begin is by overcoming the need to compare yourself to others or to the standard defined by your society. Personal Christhood is *not* a popularity contest.

***

## Exercise for Key 7

As the exercise for this key, I need you to do something that might be painful, but yet it is an absolutely necessary stage on the path to Christhood. I need you to look at your life and consider how you might have been involved with the entire consciousness of competition and comparison, causing you to, in various ways, compete with other people and to put others down. In order to assess this, I am asking you to continue the pattern of giving a rosary and then writing down whatever comes to you after the rosary.

I want you to spend as much time as you think is necessary on considering how you have been involved in competition in general. Of course, if you discover that your mental and emotional energies are still tied up in this pursuit of the impossible goal, I expect you to make the necessary changes, both in your mind but also in your outer situation. This may involve reconsidering or changing your involvement with work, business, sports or other pursuits.

When you have gone through this phase, I need you to take the next step, which is to consider whether your approach to the spiritual path has been influenced by the consciousness of competition and the poison of envy. I can assure you that there is a substantial portion of the people who think they are religious or spiritual who actually approach spirituality as a form of competition.

This has many overt and subtle expressions. Most obvious is the need to compare yourself to others in terms of how much you are doing in an outer way, be it by working in a spiritual organization, doing spiritual exercises or even contributing money. There are those for whom their spiritual involvement is simply another form of the old game of keeping up with the Joneses.

Yet beyond this is a more subtle game of using one's spiritual activities as a way to seek approval. This will often be in terms of seeking approval from others by being involved with a group or seeking approval from a spiritual leader or teacher. Yet in the end, it is all aimed at seeking approval from God, and it is based on the dualistic logic that if enough other people or a sufficiently elevated spiritual teacher approves of you, then God simply *has to* do the same. Yet you may fool every human being on this planet, but you will never fool God.

As the next phase, I need you to consider how you have been engaged in a mindset that is aimed at putting other people down by judging after the appearances of this world. I need you to see how you might have used a religion or a spiritual teaching to put others down by judging them according to some standard. Then, I need you to realize that what you do to others, you have already done to yourself. Meaning that you have put yourself down, which is truly a denial of your true identity, namely that you are a unique spiritual being, that you are an individualization of the Creator and thus inherently worthy of the Creator's love and approval—if you will only accept who you already are and stop trying to turn yourself into someone else.

As I have tried to explain in this key, only the separate self thinks it needs approval from God. When the conscious self raises itself above the dualistic illusions, it sees that it has no need for approval from God, for it *is* an individualization of God. Thus, stop seeking the approval of a god that can only be external and seek oneness with the true God—the internal God.

As the rosary for this key, use the Rosary of Miracle Nurturance and allow this very profound rosary to help you truly accept that when you seek first oneness with God, you *will* be wholly nurtured. And when you feel nurtured, you will know that with God you can attain all things, thus having no need for comparisons and envy.

Of course, do not forget the Buddha Amogasiddhi. Contemplate and invoke his wisdom, the all-accomplishing wisdom. For when you have the wisdom to accomplish all things, what is the need for envy? Also, use his mantra:

**OM AMOGASIDDHI AH**

I also want you to say the mantra of the Dhyani Buddha for this key one time after each verse and before the Hail Mother of Nurturance.

When you feel nurtured and know that with God all things can be accomplished, you can be free to *be* who you were created to be and to express that unique individuality with no fear or envy. This, my beloved, is true freedom, the freedom to BE your real self. Join me!

# Key 8
# Escaping the subtle trap of pride

In this key, we will deal with the spiritual poison of pride, specifically spiritual and intellectual pride. The Buddha who is the antidote to pride is called Ratnasambhava and his wisdom is the wisdom of equality. His mantra is:

**OM RATNASAMBHAVA TRAM**

Again, tune in to the Buddha as you study this lesson, and repeat his mantra as you deal with the energies and the illusions of pride.

What exactly *is* pride? It is the sense that you don't need to look at the beam in your own eye, or even the belief that there is not – and could not possibly be – anything to look for. In other words, it is the sense that you don't need to change, don't need to grow, don't need to self-transcend, for you have reached some kind of ultimate stage from which progress is neither possible nor necessary. It is the sense that you are already saved and thus have no need to transcend yourself in order to qualify for salvation. It is the sense that – because of some criteria in this world – you are superior to others—even in the eyes of God.

Yet if all beings are created out of God's Being, then would that not mean all are created with equal value in the eyes of God? For how could one extension of the Infinite be superior to another extension of the Infinite—how can there be comparisons in infinity? Thus, we see that pride springs from an illusion, from ignorance. The most prideful people are simply the most ignorant. This does not mean they know the least in this world—it means they do not know the reality of who they are and where they come from. Thus, contemplate the wisdom of equality, which says all beings came from the One God who is the All in all.

Pride is one of the most dangerous of all traps on the spiritual path because it primarily affects those who have started to mature. These are people who are ready to start the path to personal Christhood, but they are too often diverted into the blind alley of pride, in which they think they are very religious or spiritual. They think they are doing everything God wants them to do in this world and that they have already qualified for their entry into the next world. Thus, they refuse to grow any further, and – as I might have mentioned – continual growth, perpetual self-transcendence is the essence of Christhood. So pride has the effect of taking some of the more mature students and diverting them from the path of Christhood—just as they are getting ready to truly follow that path.

The net effect of pride is that it makes a person unreachable to a true spiritual teacher—the person is not teachable. People who are blinded by pride often take one of the following approaches:

- They reject a true spiritual teacher based on some criteria defined by their outer religion. This is why the scribes and Pharisees rejected me.

- They reject a true teacher based on a set of criteria defined in this world but outside religion. One example is materialistic science which denies the existence of the spiritual realm and thus denies the existence of spiritual teachers or the need for them.

- They reject a true teacher based on a set of personal criteria, which often makes them believe they are so sophisticated that they don't need a specific teacher because he or she doesn't live up to their standard for how the perfect teacher should be.

- They reject the need to follow any teacher and believe they don't need a teacher.

- They follow one of the many false teachers, elevating him or her to some ultimate status by idolizing the teacher.

- They reject a true spiritual teacher because they are not willing to look at the beam in their own eyes. A true spiritual teacher tells the students what they *need* to hear, what they cannot see because their vision is blocked by the ego.

- They follow a false teacher who tells them exactly what their egos *want* to hear—which makes them feel they are more special than other people.

Take note that people who are affected by pride are not completely ignorant or blind. Many of them have a sophisticated understanding of the spiritual path, and many of them can recognize the Living Christ in some form. Yet pride is the main reason why people fail the second challenge of Christ, namely whether you will allow the Living Christ to take you beyond the dualistic illusions of the ego or whether you will cling to those illusions and seek to force the living Christ into the mold. This is what Peter did, and based on that you might reason that Peter exemplifies a person who is affected by pride. Thus, the church based on Peter is likewise deeply affected by pride, which can be seen by its unwillingness to change and its failure to recognize its own shortcomings.

***

My esteemed colleague, Master MORE[10], has a saying, "If people knew better, they would do better." Thus, the essence of the spiritual path is to strive to get to know better. When you have an "Aha" experience and suddenly *know* better – thus having used the "Key of Knowledge" – you will effortlessly *do* better. You will have removed the beam from your own eye, and thus you will spontaneously do what you see as being in your own best interest.

The problem is that pride prevents people from getting to know better because it makes them think they already know better. They think they know all they *need* to know, even all there *is* to know. And if you are not willing to know better, how can you possibly do better? This becomes another catch-22 that closes people's minds and prevents them from having the openness that is the foundation for an "Aha experience." That is why I said:

> Verily I say unto you, Except ye be converted, and become as little children, ye shall not enter into the kingdom of heaven. (Matthew 18:3)

This is what Zen Buddhists call the "beginner's mind" and without it you have no opening for escaping the duality consciousness. Do you see that pride closes off the beginner's mind by making you think you are so sophisticated because you know the things of this world? Yet the things of this world are defined by the duality consciousness, and you cannot use the duality consciousness to escape the duality consciousness.

As I have been saying from the beginning, the essence of the path is that you come to see something that you do not currently see—and only *then* will you grow. So pride presents one of the greatest challenges for the true spiritual teachers of humankind. For how can you help students see what they cannot see, when the

---

10 Formerly known as the ascended master El Morya.

students believe there is nothing more to be seen or when they are unwilling to consider the need to look for even a splinter in their own eyes?

The unfortunate reality is that most students affected by pride leave off the true path of divine direction and thus join the school of hard knocks. Only when the knocks become so hard that their pride can no longer ignore or explain them away, do they wake up to the need to look in the mirror and change themselves. And even then, some do not truly get back on the true path. They only seek to make the minimal changes required to avoid the worst of the hard knocks. Thus, they seek to maintain their prideful, separate outlook on life instead of sincerely abandoning it and making themselves open to learning from the true teachers. I would like to see that anyone who studies this course escapes the trap of pride, but it is not *my* choice to make—it is *yours*.

Am I hereby hinting that all people are affected by pride? Well, here is a good working hypothesis: If you are on Earth studying this course, you are affected by pride. For if you were not affected by pride, you would be up here with me.

The brutal fact is that although you might not have personal pride, it is difficult to be in embodiment without being affected by the collective pride that hangs over this planet like a gray cloud—the gray fog of ignorance that makes it hard to distinguish between reality and unreality. So even if you have overcome personal pride, you have likely taken on a portion of the collective consciousness. In any event, pride will be a temptation for as long as you have not permanently ascended, so the wise disciple is always on the lookout for the subtle energies of pride.

***

You will have realized by now that the major – in a sense the *only* – challenge you face on the spiritual path is the illusion of separation. The ego is born from it, and the ego can never overcome it, which means the ego can never be saved. The ego cannot see this, and thus everything the ego does is an attempt to do the impossible. The ego does, however, know that it is cut off from the power of God, and this gives rise to a fear that the ego can never overcome. Thus, the ego is not only trying to do the impossible, everything it does is also aimed at dealing with the fear that it can never escape. Of course, the ego cannot see this, so it is always chasing the goal that if only it can achieve this or that, then the fear will be gone—like a donkey running after a carrot dangling in front of its nose on a stick attached to the cart. In other words, the ego is seeking to use the things of this world to compensate for the fear that can be overcome only by going beyond this world. Thus, another layer of the catch-22.

The problem is that the conscious self has stepped into the "reality distortion field" of the ego and thus sees everything – including itself – through the veil of dualistic illusions and lower vibrations. This is what we might call the energy veil, which is the origin of the more commonly used word "evil." The *only* possible solution is that the conscious self begins to see through the dualistic illusions of the mind of anti-christ, so that it can gradually separate itself from the veil of separation. The conscious self must come to see the unreality of duality, and thus it can step outside the reality distortion field and become one with the reality of God. This, of course, can only be done when the conscious self attains Christ consciousness, which truly means to attain oneness with the universal Christ mind, the mind that is the unifying element in the world of diversity. When this happens, the conscious self becomes an extension of the universal Christ mind, becomes the Living Christ in embodiment.

***

How do we begin to overcome pride? Well, as with everything else, the conscious self must come to see that pride is based on an illusion. The essence of pride is that you think you have it made, so the way to overcome it is to realize that this sense is an illusion, that it simply is not true. The problem is, of course, that the ego is most unwilling to have you come to this realization and will do anything to stop you. This includes playing on the fear that the pride is designed to push away. You see, pride is actually a way to push away the fear of not being saved, and thus prideful people will cling to the belief that they are guaranteed to be saved because of whatever condition in this world that is the object of their pride.

So you have the double problem of having to overcome pride but at the same time having to overcome the fear of not being saved. Yet the truth of Christ can set you free from both—through the wisdom of equality. For when you see that you are equal to all others because you are an extension of the Creator, you first see that the concept of being better than others is meaningless but you also see that the concept that you – the Conscious You – could be lost is equally meaningless.

In the previous key, we talked about envy. I explained that envy is an outcome of the ego's fear of not being saved, of failing to be acceptable to God. In order to deal with this fear, the ego creates the illusion that if only you are better than other people, then God simply *has to* accept you. When you believe in this, you can somewhat push aside the fear, although you can never fully escape it. The reason is that your way of dealing with the fear is to make yourself seem better than others, which binds you to the need to compare yourself to others. This leaves open the possibility that others can improve and thus upset the delicate balance that makes you seem superior. In other words, the ego's sense of equilibrium – which is what gives it a sense of relief from its primal fear – is very fragile and can easily be upset by other people. Is there a more effective way of dealing with the primal fear?

Well, there is, and it is to create other layers of the illusion that you are superior and to create them in such a way that you no longer need to be in competition with others. You have attained some kind of superior status that makes it impossible for others to catch up to you.

There are innumerable versions of this basic illusion, and let me mention just a few. There is the belief that a small tribe in the Middle East could be God's chosen people and the only ones who would be saved, a belief that many Jews and even some Christians accept to this day. There is the belief that only members of a particular religion will be saved and that all others will go to hell—a belief most Christians accept even today. There is the belief that members of a certain race are superior to all other races, or that citizens of a certain nation are superior to people in all other nations. There is the belief that being born into a certain class of royalty or nobility makes you superior to other people. There is the belief that those who have the most money are in a class of their own or that those who belong to a secret club of powerful people are superior. There are even many versions of the belief that certain people are intellectually superior and that they know better than God how the world came into existence—thus they have the right to define God out of existence through some philosophy on this Earth.

I am sure you can see many other versions, but they are all based on the idea that by belonging to a clearly defined group – defined by some criteria in this world – you are superior in a way that cannot be lost or threatened by others. Thus, you have no need to fear, and even your "salvation" is guaranteed. The more subtle message being, of course, that you do not have to look for the beam in your own eye, for since your salvation is already guaranteed, you have no need for self-examination. Once you step into this energy vortex of pride, you become completely blind. You can easily see the splinter in the eyes of other people, but you are completely unable and unwilling to look for a beam in your own eye. You have become unteachable.

So what is wrong with these illusions?

***

As Maitreya explains in great detail, nothing in the material universe is permanent. It is a fundamental law of God that everything must grow, and the evolutionary force will challenge anything that stands still. The majority of beings in the world of form are indeed growing, whereby they have formed the River of Life. This is a stream of consciousness that is constantly transcending itself and moving closer to oneness with the Creator's total consciousness. Those beings who refuse to grow cannot simply stand still. Since the River of Life is constantly moving forward, those who refuse to grow will inevitably fall behind. The consequence being that on Earth you can create a prideful sense of being in a superior class, but this state cannot be upheld forever. The forward movement of life itself will inevitably threaten your illusion of superiority, as for example happened to the royal and noble classes in feudal Europe—and many other societies throughout history.

One consequence of this is that pride does not actually set you free from the fear of not being saved; it can only give you a temporary relief. The price you pay is that pride binds you to the dualistic treadmill, for you must constantly defend your illusion of superiority—which consumes a substantial portion of your physical and mental resources. People who are blinded by pride spend so much attention on defending their sense of superiority that there is no attention left over for actually growing. Take for example people who feel pride because of their beauty. They have a standard for beauty, and they have to work very hard to live up to it. And although their sense of superiority might last for a decade or two, the harsh reality of aging will eventually shatter their pride.

However, to fully understand the futility of pride, we need to deal with an illusion that has been reinforced by every mainstream religion on this planet. The brutal fact – which you should now be able to see – is that the vast majority of the religions on this planet are dualistic religions that are either completely based on or strongly influenced by the consciousness of anti-christ. They are based on the primal fear of the ego, namely that you are separated from God, that you need to be saved and that you need to live up to certain conditions in this world in order to qualify for salvation. These religions therefore make the promise that if you are a faithful member of "the only true religion," you are guaranteed to be saved—even though you have not removed the beam of duality from your own eye. Thus, you can push aside the ego's fear of not being saved, but the inevitable consequence is that you enter into the energy vortex of spiritual pride by feeling superior to those who are not members of your religion. This also binds you to the need to defend your religion against any threat, real or perceived.

So a religion generally makes the promise that you can overcome the ego's primal fear without looking at the ego or its fear. You can solve a problem without rising above the consciousness that created the problem. This, as you will see by now, cannot be done. It is a complete fallacy.

Yet why does this false promise seem so appealing? It is because the ego has distorted everything, including the concept of what it means to be saved. In the ego's reality distortion field, it seems that being saved means gaining entry into some permanent state, call it paradise, heaven or the Garden of Eden. The underlying belief is that life on Earth might be fragile and ever-changing, but beyond it is this permanent state of peace, happiness and bliss.

As Maitreya explains in great detail, the reality is that the Garden of Eden – and any other concept of a paradise – is *not* a static state. Eden is a cosmic schoolroom, a mystery school, in which new co-creators are meant to grow toward Christhood, thereby becoming spiritually self-sufficient. When you attain Christhood, you attain oneness with all life, with the River of Life. Thus, Christhood is *not* a static state of consciousness. It is a state of consciousness in which you are now growing at the same pace as all life—as opposed to the state of separation in which you are growing slower than all life and thus essentially falling behind at a faster or slower rate. The difference is that when you attain Christhood, the oneness with all life will indeed give you complete peace. Yet it is a dynamic peace, where you are at peace and feel blissful about growing toward the ultimate goal of God consciousness. We might say that Christhood does not *stop* the journey—it empowers you to *enjoy* the journey.

As Maitreya explains, your conscious self is an individualization of the consciousness of the Creator. You descended into the world of form in order to give the Creator a way to experience this world from the inside and also give the Creator an open door for expressing itself in this world. What you gain from this is the opportunity to start out as an individual being and grow toward full God consciousness. This happens when you have transcended your initial sense of self to the point of attaining oneness with your Creator, whereby your individuality is not erased but becomes permanent—making you a Creator in your own right. In other words, you are a God in the making, which is what I expressed in the following passage:

> 34 Jesus answered them, Is it not written in your law, I said, Ye are gods?
> 35 If he called them gods, unto whom the word of God came, and the scripture cannot be broken;
> 36 Say ye of him, whom the Father hath sanctified, and sent into the world, Thou blasphemest; because I said, I am the Son of God? (John, Chapter 10)

Of course, you cannot attain ultimate God consciousness as long as you are in a physical body on Earth or anywhere else in the material universe. Thus, you need to realize that the nature of your life is – and will be for the foreseeable future – constant self-transcendence. *You* need to recognize that although there is an ultimate goal – oneness with God – even that goal is not static, for what is God but the Creator who transcends itself by creating out of itself?

My point here is that you need to seriously reconsider your concept of the spiritual path, your concept of Christhood, your concept of what it means to be saved. The vast majority of the people who begin studying this course will – as is virtually inevitable – have been affected by the mainstream religions and their distorted view of salvation. It is therefore likely that you have a subtle belief that what you are striving for is some kind of permanent state. Furthermore, this state is seen as desirable, which means it is better than – superior to – what you and most other people currently have.

Do you see the subtle deception here? Many sincere spiritual people are doing everything they can to attain some higher state of consciousness. Yet as long as their striving is colored by the two illusions I am talking about here, they simply cannot attain that state of consciousness. They cannot attain Christhood, for in Christhood nothing stands still. And when life is seen as a process of constant self-transcendence, comparisons – and the entire duality of superiority and inferiority – have no meaning.

The stark reality is that you need to reconsider your motivation for engaging in the spiritual path. Are you driven by a subtle belief that you will one day attain some superior state of consciousness from which no growth is necessary? Are you driven by a subtle belief that attaining this state of consciousness will make you superior to the people who have not attained this state?

What I am truly saying here is that permanency and superiority are illusions and that they are two sides of the same coin, the coin – the mammon – of duality. You cannot uphold the dream of attaining a permanent state without also binding yourself to the quest for superiority, which means you bind yourself to pride. And as I have said many times, you cannot serve two masters, you cannot serve God and mammon. So it is time to "choose ye this day whom ye will serve."

***

Let me make one more attempt to show you this from a different perspective. We have seen that the essence of pride is the illusion of separation. Yet why is separation an illusion—since it seems obvious to most people that God is not on Earth?

We have seen that in the very beginning of the world of form, there was nothing except the Creator. Thus, the Creator can only create out of its own Being, for there is nothing else. In other words, God cannot create something that is separated from itself.

We have seen that the Creator started by manifesting itself as the Ma-ter light that can take on any form. Thus, everything in the world of form was created out of the Creator's light, which is a manifestation of the Creator's Being—meaning that the Creator is present everywhere. And if the Creator is omnipresent, you cannot find a place where the Creator is *not* present, including planet Earth.

So the reality is that God IS present on Earth. The logical conclusion being that most people fail to see the reality of God's Presence. So why do people fail to see the obvious? Well, it is because they have entered a specific state of consciousness that blinds them to reality—they think the Earth is flat, whereas it has always been round. The reason is that they cannot see beyond the vibrations that make up physical matter, and thus they cannot see that matter is a manifestation of finer energies that can be traced to the Creator.

And what is the state of consciousness that blinds people? It is the dualistic mind, the mind of anti-christ, the consciousness of death, that springs from the illusion of separation. What I want to point out here is the basic fact that the illusion of separation gives rise to a primal fear.

You see, the Creator is all there is, the Creator is the very source of life. There is only one way to obtain eternal life, and that is through oneness with the Creator. The logical consequence is that ultimate peace can be found only through oneness with the Creator.

As we have seen, your conscious self is an extension of the Creator's own being. Your lifestream descended into the material universe for the purpose of starting out as an individualized being and then growing in self-awareness until you attain full God consciousness. The logical consequence is that your conscious self –

by its very nature and design – has the potential to attain a sense of oneness with God—and in attaining that oneness, you also find ultimate peace. You do not have to attain full God consciousness to obtain peace. It is sufficient to attain Christ consciousness, whereby you can see beyond the illusion of separation and the consciousness of duality. You then see that the real you is not and never could be separated from God, for you see the Creator's Presence within everything, including matter itself.

So we might say that the spiritual path is a process of overcoming the blindness that prevents you from seeing that you are an individualization of God and that God is within everything, even here on Earth. You overcome this illusion through the wisdom of equality—everything is God in disguise. Yet, what works against you overcoming spiritual blindness? Well, it is the fact that after you started believing in the illusion of separation, you created the separate self, the ego. Thus, you have now come to accept the "wisdom" of inequality—the spiritual poison of pride.

The ego can *never* overcome the illusion of separation—because it was born from this illusion. If the ego was capable of saying, "Hey, separation is an illusion," then it would have to make the only logical conclusion: "But if separation is an illusion, that means I – as a separate self – am not real, I do not actually exist!" If the ego made that admission, it would instantly cease to exist, and the cessation of existence is the primal fear of the ego. Thus, the stark reality is that the ego can never attain oneness with God – which is the *only* source of true peace – which means the ego can never overcome fear, can never attain peace. Meaning that *you* will never attain peace as long as you allow the illusions of duality to linger in your being. Do you now see why the ego will *never* be at peace?

***

In reality, the ego cannot see that it is not real because it has no sense of co-measurement from outside the illusion of separation. The ego cannot see the reality of God, so it cannot see that separation is unreal. However, the conscious self can indeed reach beyond separation and tune in to the reality of God out of which it was born. Thus, the conscious self can see that separation is unreal, which means that the conscious self can "uncreate" the ego. Thus, the ego will resist – driven by its survival instinct – the conscious self's awakening to the reality of the omnipresent God – the realization that the kingdom of God is within – and it will do so by seeking to create a catch-22 that makes it impossible for the conscious self to see through the illusions of duality. That catch-22 is the outer path that creates the impression that it is possible to make the separate self acceptable to God.

So the reality is that, for a long time, your separate self has been trying to get you to follow the outer path, and here is where pride comes in. Pride is the ultimate outcome of the separate self's attempts to become acceptable to God. Pride makes you feel that your separate self is – because it lives up to certain criteria defined in this world – finally acceptable to God. This allows you to live with the fear that springs from separation, the fear that the separate self will cease to exist.

Yet this sense of pride is based on the "things of this world," and in this world everything is presently colored by duality. The consequence is that everything has an opposite – every action has an opposite reaction – and thus the ego's pride will constantly be threatened by something. In other words, the ego can use pride to create a sense of equilibrium, but it is not true peace, for it is always under threat. Thus, you must spend a considerable amount of mental resources on defending the ego's source of pride from all threats—and for many people this literally eats up their lives.

I hope you can now begin to see where I am going with this. You are a spiritual seeker, and you are beyond the beginning stages of the spiritual path. So your striving on the path should be bringing you closer to Christhood, and you should be closer to this goal than before you started. However, the stark reality – a reality that many spiritual seekers and even many self-proclaimed spiritual teachers fail to acknowledge – is that those who are the most eager students are often the ones who are the furthest away from obtaining Christhood—even though they have seemingly done everything possible to follow the spiritual path. Yet consider my words:

> But many that are first shall be last; and the last first. (Mark 10:31)

The problem is that what such people have done is to follow the *outer* path, and everything they have done – all their studies, their practices of spiritual techniques and all their hard work – has only reinforced the belief that they are making progress toward making the separate self acceptable to God. For, after all, when that separate self has done so many spiritual things, surely God must be willing to accept it.

Can you begin to see the irony that those lifestreams who should be the most mature have been led astray into the blind alley of a spiritual pride that is so subtle that they do not see it or do not see it for what it is? Thus, those who should be the most advanced students have become blinded by their pride, and as a result they are like the scribes and Pharisees who fail to accept the Living Christ when he appears to them. They always recognize the Living Christ, but they fail the second challenge of Christ, for in their pride they are not willing to let the Living Christ take them beyond their mental boxes—the very mental boxes that are like towers of Babel that they think can allow the separate self to reach into the heavens.

Thus, it is a sad fact that I find it more difficult to reach many of the people who for decades and lifetimes have been very eager in following the spiritual path. They think they have already secured their salvation, so why would they need the Living Christ? And how could they possibly need to follow a teacher who says that they need to leave behind all of their striving and attainment – and let that sense of having elevated the separate self die – in order to be reborn and seemingly start all over again? Why on Earth would you have to suddenly give up everything you have attained on Earth? Well, the simple answer is that what you have attained on Earth cannot take you beyond the Earth. Only the being who descended from heaven can ascend back to heaven—the self created on Earth will *never* make it to the wedding feast of the Living Christ.

***

These considerations lead us to an inescapable conclusion. It is important – I should say, absolutely essential – for you to reconsider your approach to the spiritual path. The simple fact is that as you climb the path by following an outer teaching, you are educating your ego on how to use that outer teaching to maintain and even reinforce the illusions of the outer path. The brutal fact is that the more mature a lifestream becomes, the more subtle the ego becomes, making it better at defending the source of its pride, namely the outer path.

Do you see my point? This course is about attaining personal Christhood, and you cannot attain this state of consciousness as long as your approach to the path is influenced by pride—no matter how subtle. I am not interested in having you make great efforts to follow the spiritual path only to find out after you leave embodiment that you fell short of the mark—because you were following the outer path instead of the true inner path. I am interested in helping you lock yourself firmly on the true path and attain Christhood while you are still in embodiment. And in order to attain that goal, I have to give you the full truth, no matter how your ego might resist it.

Can you see that this also demonstrates why even the most advanced students need a teacher? The very fact that you are still on Earth shows that you have some form of a mental box. The more you climb the path, the more subtle that mental box will be, and thus it will be harder for you to see through the illusions that make up the box. Yet a true spiritual teacher is not inside your personal mental box, and thus he or she can see through the illusions that blind you. And that is precisely why even the most "advanced" students need an ascended teacher. Thus, the truly advanced students are those who recognize that they need a teacher—as opposed to those who think they are so advanced they no longer need a teacher.

We have now arrived at a point that is one of the crucial turning points in this course, a point that will determine whether you will actually enter the true path to Christhood or whether you will remain on the outer path—cleverly disguised as it may be.

The basic fact about the path to Christhood is that the true path puts your ego on the defensive—it presents the ego with a dilemma. Here are the two problems facing the ego:

- The ego can survive *only* by staying hidden from the conscious self. When the conscious self finally sees the ego, the ego will lose its power over the self. In order to see the ego, the conscious self simply has to use its built-in ability to tune in to the reality of God. In other words, in order to see the ego, the conscious self simply has to look, which means the ego must prevent the conscious self from looking. The ego *must* remain hidden from the conscious self.

- Once you discover the true path and begin to study a true spiritual teaching while practicing true techniques, the conscious self will inevitably make progress toward acquiring the insights, co-measurement, discernment and attunement that will expose the ego. So the ego can easily predict that if it does nothing, it will gradually be exposed. Yet if you truly understand the path, the ego will also be running a risk by actively doing something to resist your progress. The ego might be exposing itself because your conscious self can come to see the resistance to change as the hallmark of the ego.

So you see the dilemma. The ego cannot do nothing, but anything it does to resist your progress might expose it—if your conscious self is looking. My point being that you can now take a quantum leap forward by coming to the conscious realization of this dynamic. Your conscious self can then use this realization to actually expose the ego. What you need to do is to realize that the true path is all about giving up *anything* that takes you out of total inner peace. This state of inner peace is the natural state for your conscious self, for it is a natural consequence of the conscious self attaining true self-awareness.

When you realize that you are an extension of God's Being and that everything is created from God's being, you realize the oneness of all life. And when you see all life as one, you see that life truly cannot hurt itself. Thus, even if people trapped in duality nail you to a cross and kill your physical body, they cannot hurt the real you, which means you don't need to fear *anything*. And when you see this truth, the truth will set you free from all fear—even while you are still in a physical body that is subject to the free-will choices of people trapped in duality.

My point being that the true path to Christhood is actually about letting go of everything that keeps you trapped in the dualistic struggle, which means the path is all about surrendering – letting go of – all unreality. The ego will resist this surrender, and do you see why? The reason is that the ego is on the quest of seeking to use the things of this world to build a Tower of Babel that will reach into the heavens and thus take the ego to heaven. The ego will keep gathering and holding on to what it feels it has attained in this world – including knowledge of the spiritual path – in order to maintain its sense of superiority. Thus, for the ego, *you* letting go of what it sees as the foundation for its salvation will literally be seen as a matter of life and death. Meaning the ego will hold on to everything for dear life.

As a result, your conscious self can build a habit of looking for this inner resistance and use it to expose the ego. You can even deliberately practice letting go of anything in this world in order to provoke the ego to resist and thus expose itself. This can accelerate the process whereby your conscious self comes to see aspects of the ego and then surrenders them. Thus, you are now using the ego's dilemma – which it has so far used to manipulate you through the fear of loss – to put pressure on the ego. If the ego does nothing, it will be exposed and die. If it resists, its resistance will only hasten its exposure. This is the mark of a true disciple of the Living Christ—the willingness to pressure the ego and use its resistance to a true spiritual teacher as a tool for forcing the ego out into the open, where you can see it for what it is and then let it go as the illusion it is.

In contrast, the false disciples of anti-christ will seek to use a very subtle and sophisticated dualistic reasoning to reject or explain away the truth that the ego doesn't want the conscious self to accept. In other words, the false disciples will find some dualistic argument for rejecting the Living Christ and the truth of the message. They will reject the need to look for the beam in their own eyes, the need to change themselves. In doing so they will only bind themselves even more firmly to the treadmill of the false path, the path of pride that seeks to elevate the separate self to such superior status that God simply has to accept it—or so the reasoning goes.

You see, even with all their self-declared sophisticated reasoning, these disciples fail to see that they cannot fool God, for God is never affected by the dualistic mind. Thus, what seems logical to *them* has no effect on God. God truly is not mocked and is no respecter of even the most "sophisticated" persons—or their pride-intoxicated egos.

Do you see how this connects to pride? The essence of the path is to see the unreality of the ego and to see the reality of Christ. Yet pride causes you to resist having this shift in perception. You resist examining the illusions of the ego, resist looking for the beam in your own eye. And you resist acknowledging a true spiritual teacher and letting the Living Christ take you beyond your current mental box. Yet when you begin to understand how pride causes resistance to a new vision, you can actually use that resistance to expose the pride and thus see the pride for the unreality it is. And once the conscious self sees the pride as unreal, it will separate itself from it, and thus part of the ego will die. You, on the other hand, will be reborn into a higher degree of oneness with your source.

***

As I have said, every spiritual poison is a perversion of a God quality, and pride is the perversion of the God quality of peace, manifest in you as a desire for peace. As I said, you have a built-in desire for something more, which is what keeps pulling you to go beyond the material world and seek the spiritual path. Yet the drive for more is actually a drive for ultimate peace.

Do you see that what the ego is actually seeking through pride is a state of ultimate peace? Yet because it can use only the energies in the material universe, it is seeking to build this peace in a way that can never come to fruition. It is seeking to create permanent peace in this ever-changing, non-permanent world. It is seeking to create peace by elevating itself to some superior status. Yet its sense of superiority is defined based on the duality consciousness, in which everything must have an opposite. Thus, the ego can build a sense of peace, but it will always be threatened.

Your conscious self is susceptible to the ego's attempts to attain peace because it has an inherent desire for ultimate peace. That ultimate peace can be attained in only one way, namely by first becoming one with the River of Life – the forward movement of the totality of life – and then becoming one with your source, your Creator. Do you see the subtle difference? The ego thinks peace is a permanent state, meaning a state in which nothing changes. Yet real peace is the state of constant self-transcendence, of oneness with the River of Life.

In contrast to the ego, the conscious self can actually attain permanent peace, a peace that is *not* threatened by anything in this world. Yet it can do so only by giving up the illusions of separation, for as long as you hold on to this illusion, you will be compelled by the ego's fear to seek peace through the things of this world, the fragile peace of superiority based on inequality.

To attain true peace, contemplate the wisdom of equality. When you truly understand this wisdom, you realize that everything is equal because everything is God, everything is created from God's Being. Thus, you can overcome the drive for some ultimate state, for you realize there is no ultimate – in the form of non-changing – state. Peace cannot be found as long as you look for some ultimate state that is separated from what you have now. Peace can be found only by realizing that what you have, what you *are*, right now IS the ultimate state because it is part of God's ongoing process of self-transcendence, the dance of becoming MORE. Thus, the only ultimate state is the state of constant self-transcendence. Contemplate my two statements that the kingdom of God is within you and that the kingdom of God is at hand. You will never find the kingdom as long as you look for it outside yourself—even look for it in the future.

You will find the kingdom *only* when you let go of all illusions of inequality, for it is precisely the illusion of inequality that gives rise to the belief that the kingdom is not where you are. Consider how it is even possible for you to think you are outside God's kingdom? Is it not because you believe in inequality, which makes it possible that where you are right now is of a lower status than what you perceive as the remote kingdom of God? Yet without him was not any thing made that was made, meaning that everything is equal to God because everything IS God. You now realize that everything IS the kingdom because in reality God's kingdom is everywhere. Thus, you will find God's kingdom *only* when you recognize that it is HERE NOW! You recognize that you *are* in God's kingdom because you see that you *are* God expressing itself as you—and everything else.

Contemplate and acknowledge that your ultimate goal is a state of permanent and unassailable peace. And then realize that such peace – the peace that passeth understanding – can be obtained *only* by being who you are, by consciously recognizing and accepting that the real you is the conscious self, which is an individualization of your Creator. And precisely because you are out of the Creator's infinite Being, you cannot be threatened by anything in this finite world. You are *in* the world but not *of* the world, and in this realization lies the key to true – non-dualistic – peace.

***

Pride is the hallmark of the fallen angels, and they are the ones who created the original vortex of the energy of pride on this planet. However, it has since been reinforced by many people, even many who should have been following the path to Christhood. It should be obvious that you cannot be a true disciple of the Living Christ as long as you allow elements of the fallen consciousness to remain in your being. Thus, it must be exposed without "mercy," without compromise, so the conscious self can separate itself from it.

In that respect, it is essential for you to understand that the angels fell because they started believing that they knew better than God. They did so because they had started looking at everything through the filter of the dualistic mind. You see, in this mind there are always two opposite polarities, one which is good and one which is bad. So once you adopt this world view, it follows that if you belong in the one polarity, you must be right, whereas anyone – even God – who belongs in the other polarity must be wrong.

So this is what caused the Fall, and ever since the Fall, some of these angels have been engaged in a never-ending – because it can never succeed – struggle to prove that they are right and God is wrong. Many of the political, scientific and even religious theories and philosophies found on the Earth spring from this very desire to prove God wrong, even the desire to prove that there is no God.

You need to start unraveling these subtle dualistic illusions, and in order to help you, let me give you an example of what I am talking about. Pride obviously leads to a sense of being superior to others, a superiority complex. Yet have you ever considered that the opposite – the inferiority complex – also springs from pride?

Why is this so? Because the reality is that God created you as a unique extension of itself. As such, you are neither superior nor inferior compared to any other being. You are, as we saw in the last key, unique and in uniqueness there is no room for comparisons—thus no room for value judgments of inferiority and superiority. This is the wisdom of equality, for in your uniqueness you are equal to all other unique beings and have no need for the inferiority-superiority duality.

Yet when you step into the dualistic mind, you cannot see reality. You superimpose a dualistic image upon reality, and in this outlook there must be two opposites. Thus, to the dualistic mind uniqueness cannot exist without having a value judgment superimposed upon it. This is done by creating a standard for evaluating what – according to the standard defined in this world – is superior and what is inferior. Yet the real point is that this standard is in effect saying that you know better than God, because you now see God's creation "as it really is," namely where some beings are superior compared to others. As the Serpent said to Eve, you now have the knowledge of good and evil—meaning *relative* good and evil.

By imposing such a standard, you demonstrate that you believe you know better than God—and this is the pride of the fallen angels. So even if you think you are inferior, you still think you know better than God, meaning that inferiority – putting down what God created – is an outgrowth of pride.

Instead of seeing your unique individuality as equal to all other beings, you think your individuality is separated from them, meaning it is either better or worse than others. Instead of seeing yourself as one with all life, using your individual expression to raise up the All, you see yourself separated from life, using your individuality – seen through the filter of duality – to place the separate self in a unique position—as being worse or better than others. Yet when individuality is compared to others, it is not true, for true individuality is unique and thus comparison becomes irrelevant.

Naturally, in order to become a disciple of the Living Christ, you need to overcome the many subtle means whereby spiritual people feel they are better than others. But you also need to avoid the opposite extreme that causes many spiritual people to go into a false sense of humility. You now see that even if you put yourself down, you are still trapped in pride. God created you fully worthy, so if you judge yourself as being unworthy, you are saying you know better than God what God created.

There are many religious or spiritual people who have become aware of the dangers of pride, but they have gone into the opposite extreme of seeking to reduce themselves to nothing, to being completely "humble" in the sense that they seem unworthy. Yet even this is pride, for are you not saying that what God created is nothing?

In reality, the Creator did not create nothing when it created you. God created a unique extension of itself, and by the mere fact that God created you, you are inherently worthy.

My reason for going into this is that superiority cannot exist without inferiority. They are two sides of the same coin. In reality, the sense of superiority simply covers over the underlying sense of inferiority. The more prideful people are, the deeper their inferiority complex. They need the pride in order to cover over and deal with the sense of inferiority. Yet the more they rise into pride, the more they deepen – as a counterbalance – the sense of inferiority.

Where does inferiority come from? It comes from the illusion of separation. Obviously, that which is separated from God cannot enter the kingdom, meaning the ego will feel it is unworthy to enter. Therefore, the ego can never escape its primal inferiority just as it can never escape its primal fear. Meaning it is forever locked into the struggle of seeking to compensate for *inferiority* by creating the comparative sense of *superiority*.

This presents a catch-22, for in order to overcome pride, you obviously have to see it as the illusion it is, whereby your sense of superiority is often shattered. The problem is that this exposes the sense of inferiority – which had so far been unrecognized by the conscious mind – and this often shatters the person's self-esteem and plunges that person into a state of depression.

So I need you – as always – to strive for the Middle Way, whereby you can overcome your pride without destroying your self-esteem. I need you to overcome both of the unrealistic views of the separate self – that the separate self is both inferior and superior – and instead adopt a realistic view of self, namely that your real self, your conscious self, is a unique individualization of the Creator's Being. I need your conscious self to become conscious of and accept its true identity as a co-creator with God. In other words, instead of your present self-esteem that is based on the things of this world, you build a new self-esteem based on your true individuality as a spiritual being. And this self-esteem cannot be threatened by anything in this world, for since it is not dualistic, it has no opposite—it is based on the wisdom of equality.

How do you overcome the inferiority-superiority duality? By overcoming the belief that your ego knows better than God, by being willing to realize that it is only the ego who can feel inferior or superior, whereas the real you has no need for such feelings. The real you simply is who it is, and it is so focused on expressing its unique individuality in this world that it has no attention left over for any value judgments. The real you sees the wisdom of equality that consumes the illusions of superiority and inferiority. Thus, any concerns about comparing yourself to others are gone, and you are focused on being who you really are.

***

I now need you to go even deeper and realize that what gets lost in the inferiority-superiority duality is the real you. When your conscious self becomes trapped in the illusion of separation, you inevitably become trapped in the need to avoid feelings of inferiority by building and defending the sense of superiority. This will eat up your time and attention, but even beyond that, it will program you to deny your spiritual individuality and stop you from expressing it in this world.

You are an extension of a greater spiritual Being, who created you and sent you into this world for the purpose of bringing a unique gift to this world. As Maitreya explains in great detail, you are here to bring spiritual light into this world, thereby raising this sphere to be so filled with light that it can ascend and become part of the spiritual realm. So by expressing your unique spiritual identity, you bring light into this world and thus bring it closer to the kingdom of God.

Today, the Earth is a planet on which every aspect of life is deeply affected by the dualistic mind. So another purpose for your being here is to express your spiritual identity and thus demonstrate that there is more, that there is something beyond the dualistic mind. By daring to express your Christhood, you demonstrate that there is a way out of duality, which was the main purpose for my mission 2,000 years ago.

You now need to realize that there are many beings on Earth who are completely trapped in the dualistic mind. They think they own this planet, and they either think God gave them the Earth or that there is no God. Thus, the last thing these beings want is for someone to escape the illusion of duality and demonstrate that there is something beyond the dualistic mind. The last thing they want is a great number of people who are expressing their Christhood here on Earth. Consequently, these beings don't want your light and they don't want your truth—and they will do *anything* to discourage you from sharing it.

You see, they do not mind that you attain a high state of consciousness, as long as you sit in a cave in the Himalayas. What they don't want is for you to go out into the marketplace, as I did, and awaken the people. They will do *anything* to stop you from doing this, and in previous ages, they would kill people, as they did to me 2,000 years ago.

My point here is that in past lives you have experienced being brutally rejected when you attempted to share your spiritual light and Christ truth. And this has given rise to a sense of inferiority, the feeling that the world does not want your light and truth, that the world does not want *you*. So to compensate for this, many spiritual people have been pulled into the dualistic game of seeking to avoid the sense that their spiritual gifts are inferior by living up to an Earthly standard for what it means to be a spiritual and religious person. In other words, many truly spiritual people have spent lifetimes being diligent followers of one or several religions on Earth, always doing what is required according to the worldly standard. This has allowed them to push away the sense of inferiority and the pain of having your true self rejected by the world. However, the other side of the coin is that it has caused a subtle sense of pride, giving rise to the belief that the separate self – the self that is acceptable to the world – is superior.

So what I need you to do is to open up this old wound of being rejected and resolve these feelings. How can you do this? Only by coming to a full understanding of free will, which then leads to complete respect for free will.

You need to study – again – Maitreya's teachings on free will and realize that you are not – as we saw in the previous key – here to change other people. You are here *exclusively* to share your unique gift, to let the Sun of your higher self shine through your lower being. This means you must respect that other people have a right to reject your offering and that those blinded by duality will most likely reject it. Yet you also need to realize that their rejection is not a reflection on you or the worthiness of your gift. Their rejection is exclusively a consequence of their state of consciousness!

Do you see why this is so? When you shine your light, how does that light look to a person who is seeing the world through the spectacles of duality? Well, your spiritual light is undivided, meaning that it is different from anything in this world—that is why it offers people an opportunity to see beyond duality. However, a person trapped in duality cannot see the light as pure. What such a person sees is the light that has passed through his or her energy field, and thus it has been colored by the dualistic vibrations in the field. This means that what the person sees is *not* the pure light you are sharing but light that has been colored by duality and thus appears as one dualistic polarity. Yet even though it is seen as dualistic, your light will still be very intense, and as such it will disturb the person's sense of equilibrium. Instead of seeing this as an opportunity to transcend duality, the person sees it as a threat. And since the light is colored by duality, an image is projected onto it, whereby it is seen as opposing the very foundation for the person's sense of equilibrium, such as the person's sense of pride.

That is why the scribes and the Pharisees could not simply ignore me. The light I expressed was so intense that it stirred up their fear and challenged their pride, thus making it a matter of life and death for them to silence me. My point being that the more deeply people are blinded by pride, the more they will see Christ light as a threat. Meaning that when people reject your light, it has nothing to do with you but everything to do with their own, dualistic, state of consciousness. They are not rejecting *you*; they are rejecting an image of you that is generated in their own minds by their dualistic illusions.

When you recognize this, you can have complete respect for your own free will and determine that you will *not* let the world's rejection or acceptance have any influence on you. You will let your light shine and you will shout your truth from the housetops, regardless of whether the world accepts or rejects your gift. You will be the Sun who shines regardless of whether people accept or reject the sunshine. Only then will you be the Living Christ on Earth.

What I am seeking to help you accomplish here is to enter into a state of mind in which you have complete inner peace regardless of whether you are accepted or rejected by the world. You *know* who you are, you accept that you are a unique individualization of God's Being, and you fully accept that you have a right to be on Earth and to let your light shine. You see through the illusions of duality, and thus you know that even if every person on Earth rejects your gift – and, by the way, someone will always accept your gift – that does not mean you are wrong or that your gift is not worthy. You are infinitely worthy, for you are an extension of the Creator's infinite Being.

On the other hand, even if every person on Earth accepts your separate self, that will not make the separate self worthy in the eyes of God, and thus you can rise above the entire game of seeking to prove the superiority of the separate self. You can free up your attention to be who you were created to be and to express it in all aspects of your life. And when you are focused on being who you are – with no concern for how the world accepts or rejects you – you will have complete inner peace. You will also fulfill your reason for coming here, which was and is to be the open door that no man – including your separate self – can shut!

***

Do you see my point here? Pride can also be described as a perversion of the desire to do well, to be who you are, to express perfection in this world—and thus attain peace. In other words, it is possible to be perfect, but only by expressing your spiritual identity:

> Be ye therefore perfect, even as your Father which is in heaven is perfect. (Matthew 5:48)

Yet as always, the true desire is perverted by the fear of separation. Thus, the desire to express your spiritual perfection becomes colored by the fear of rejection—leading to a desire for acceptance in this world. So to avoid the fear of being rejected, you begin to adapt your behavior to the standard for "perfection" in this world. Of course, that standard is defined by the duality consciousness, and you are here to express your spiritual identity precisely to demonstrate that there is something beyond the duality consciousness. So when you seek to adapt your expression to the dualistic standard, you abort your purpose for coming here in the first place.

Thus, you need to leave behind the fear of rejection and raise your desire to express perfection above pride. You are not here to express perfection according to any standard defined on Earth. You are here to express the unique perfection of your spiritual identity, a perfection that fits no standard on Earth—for it is perfect precisely because it is beyond this world and its dualistic standards. You are here to be who you are already, to be who you were created to be—which is the riddle hidden in Hamlet's famous question, "To be, or not to be."

You are *not* here to become the perfect human being, for this is the lie behind the outer path, namely that by living up to a worldly standard of perfection, the separate self will become acceptable to God. You are here to be the perfect being that God created—to let God's perfection shine through your being, which has now become the open door.

> 1 Verily, verily, I say unto you, He that entereth not by the door into the sheepfold, but climbeth up some other way, the same is a thief and a robber.
> 2 But he that entereth in by the door is the shepherd of the sheep.
>
> 7 Then said Jesus unto them again, Verily, verily, I say unto you, I am the door of the sheep.

> 9 I am the door: by me if any man enter in, he shall be saved, and shall go in and out, and find pasture. (John, Chapter 10)

***

When you look at humankind, it is easy to see that people are at many different levels of consciousness, from extremely self-centered to more spiritual, whereby I mean God-centered—centered on the larger self. Why did I teach the multitudes in parables? Because I knew that at the time only very few people were ready to understand the path to Christhood. And even though many more people are ready in today's age, it remains a fact that only a small percentage of the total population can understand, let alone accept, the true path.

This then creates an interesting dilemma for the disciples of the Living Christ. The essence of the path is that you have to raise yourself above the average person—above the mass consciousness. Since most people cannot understand the path, they will tend to reject or ridicule the path and those who follow it. So in order to follow the path, you must be non-attached to the fact that you stand out from the general population. In fact, you have to work very hard to escape the pull of the mass consciousness that seeks to make you behave like everyone else, thereby rejecting the path.

This gives an inherent risk of elitism, because spiritual people can easily build a sense that, "We are better than others because we do something that most people don't want to do or can't do. We understand the true path and we are saving the world, whereas they simply eat, drink and be merry." In fact, there is a clear tendency that spiritual people are the "misfits" that cannot easily find friends and thus are not accepted by their peers. Which means some people actually follow the spiritual path precisely because it gives their egos ammunition for building a sense of superiority. In other words, these people use the path as a way to distance themselves from the average person, to compensate for the inferiority they built up by being rejected early in life. This is a constant and subtle challenge, and if you do not see the problem with it, it will undermine your path to Christhood and stop you at a certain point.

How can you overcome the temptation to use the path to reinforce the sense of being different, of standing out from the crowd, of being superior to those who are not on the path or not as far along as you are? You can do so *only* by recognizing who the Living Christ really is. The motto for the Living Christ might be, "It is not about me!"

The Living Christ realizes clearly that he or she is *not* in embodiment in order to secure his or her own salvation or in order to raise up the separate self in comparison to others. The Living Christ is here to demonstrate the oneness of all life, which means the Christ does not work for a personal goal—as this is normally defined. We might say that the Christ *does* work for a personal goal, but since the Christ sees him- or herself as one with all life, the Christ is working on the personal goal of raising up all people and manifesting God's kingdom on Earth. God's goal has now become your personal goal.

In other words, the only way to overcome the temptation of spiritual elitism, spiritual pride, is to develop the sense of oneness, whereby the separate self is allowed to die and thus concepts such as better or less have no meaning. Again, this is the wisdom of equality, leading to the vision of the underlying oneness of all life.

I fully understand that some of the students who come to this course will have a sense of elitism, will have a certain pride in being able to grasp the path and thus feeling they are above most people. I see this as a phase that many students go through, and thus I do not condemn anyone for feeling this. However, I see it as a *phase*—meaning that it is something that has a time limit rather than going on indefinitely. And it is now time to decide that the phase has come to an end, for you are ready to go into the next phase and work toward oneness with your own higher self, then oneness with God and then oneness with all life.

And if – perchance – you are *not* at that point, I suggest you put aside this course and go out there and find yourself a false teacher who will tell you what your ego wants to hear. I will not condemn you for this, I will simply wait for you to get tired of the school of hard knocks and decide to come back to the true path.

***

## Exercise for Key 8

The challenge for this key is to uncover your pride and see it for what it is, so you can let it go. Yet this involves exposing your pride without going into the opposite extreme of feeling guilty or worthless. In other words, I need you to stay on the Middle Way. The purpose of having you overcome pride is *not* to have you become like nothing and deny your Self, nor is it to have you feel guilty for having had pride. I want you to be neither proud nor humble but to rise above duality. My purpose is to give you a realistic sense of self-esteem that helps you accept that you are a unique co-creator with God and that you are here to share your light and truth.

To help you do this, I am asking you to do a 33-day vigil of reading or listening to[11] Mother Mary's dictation and then giving her rosary for Self-esteem [See the Appendix for the text of both dictation and rosary.]. Again, say the mantra of the Dhyani Buddha for this key one time after each verse and before the Hail Mary. After giving the rosary, write down in your notebook whatever comes to you on the following topics:

- Start by focusing on elements of pride or inferiority in your life, especially what you have been brought up with, such as pride over your nation, your religion, your family background, your accomplishments in school, your position in society, your wealth and so on. Expose them, and then write them down point for point. Use your inner attunement and my teachings to formulate a reason why they are unreal and pull you away from Christhood. Then let them go.

- Expose elements of pride or inferiority that have influenced or are influencing your approach to the spiritual path. Do you take pride in following a path that only few people can understand, of being able to understand complex teachings, of doing more spiritual exercises than others, et-cetera?

- Be willing to consider whether your approach to the path has been influenced by the inability to fit in or the desire to feel better than others. Is there an element of spiritual elitism in your approach to the path?

- Consider that as you follow the path and study spiritual teachings, you educate your ego on how to use the outer teachings to build a sense of superiority. Be willing to consider this openly and ask Mother Mary, myself and your Christ self to expose to you any elements of this spiritual pride. Again, write them down and then write down the reasons why they are unreal. Then, let them go.

- Finally, take an honest look at your reactions to this course. Have you been evaluating this course and my

---

11 A recording of the dictation and rosary will be available as part of the Spiritual Crisis Toolkit. See *www.askrealjesus.com* in the Store section.

teachings, sometimes feeling like I should have said things differently, that the course is not as sophisticated as you thought, that it is too basic for your advanced experience or other such feelings? Then be willing to admit that this sense can come only from the consciousness of the fallen angels who think they know better than God and thus think they know better than Christ. I am not hereby saying you *are* a fallen angel. I am only saying that the Conscious You has taken on the consciousness of the fallen angels and sees the world through this filter. Which you obviously need to shed before you can become a disciple of the Living Christ. On that note, also consider whether your reaction to this course has been the opposite, namely that the course is too difficult and that you are not worthy to follow it. Recognize that this is also the consciousness of the fallen angels, simply the opposite dualistic polarity of inferiority. It is also thinking you know better than Christ, for I know the reality that the Conscious You is out of God's Being and thus is fully capable of following the path to Christhood.

I expect that this exercise – if done with due diligence – will increase your sense of spiritual freedom. In fact, if you feel you need to take longer than the 33 days, by all means do so. This is a very important stage of this course, so please do not allow the subtle pride of the ego to rush you by making you believe you don't need to do this, or that you have already mastered it. Pride is dangerous precisely because it is subtle—it is unseen.

So when your ego tells you it is time to move on, your conscious self should know that it is time to step back and take another look in order to expose that which is ready to be exposed and which your ego does not want you to discover. It is time to begin to see through the tricks of the ego and to use its own resistance to your progress to unmask the ego and thus make unprecedented progress.

# Key 9
# Black-and-white ignorance

In this and the next keys we will tackle the spiritual poison of ignorance. The Buddha who is the antidote for this poison is named Vairochana and his wisdom is the All-pervading Wisdom. His mantra is:

**OM VAIROCHANA OM**

Use it as you study the following teachings.

Ignorance might seem to be the first hurdle you have to overcome before you can begin walking the spiritual path. After all, when you look at humanity, you see that most people are ignorant of the spiritual path. They either deny the existence of God or they follow – blindly – a mainstream religion that promises the outer path to salvation instead of the true inner path. So why didn't I start out by talking about the poison of ignorance? Well, the reason is that there are layers of ignorance. Those who are open to this course are not new to the spiritual path, so they have usually overcome the outer or innocent ignorance that affects most people on this planet. We can now define two layers of ignorance:

- Innocent ignorance is when you simply don't know. You are probably innocently ignorant of the latest discoveries of quantum physics, for example.

- Sophisticated ignorance is when you actually know something in the higher part of your being, but your conscious mind refuses to recognize it or to make the choices that follow from your knowledge. In a sense we can say that you do *know* better, but you refuse to *do* better. A practical example is that all people know smoking is dangerous to your health but some people continue to smoke anyway.

Why do I still call this ignorance? Because the conscious self really would *do* better if it truly *knew* better—if it consciously saw how it is refusing to acknowledge what it knows and how this is hurting itself. The problem is that the conscious self has come to believe in one or several of the dualistic illusions, and thus the conscious self cannot "see" that it actually knows better. So we might say that sophisticated ignorance is when you actually know better but you are not consciously acknowledging this. You have not actually seen the beam in your own eye, or you have not seen it for what it is.

You now see why I have started out by talking about the more obvious spiritual poisons, saving the more subtle poison of sophisticated ignorance until you had cleared away some of the energies that are covering over the deeper ignorance. Thus, we now have the foundation – provided you have actually done the exercises in the previous keys – for tackling sophisticated ignorance.

***

The problem with sophisticated ignorance is *not* that it causes people to know nothing. The problem is that it causes people to think that whatever they know – be it much or little – is all they need to know or all there is to know. Thus, they are not open to expanding or transcending their mental boxes, which means they have shut themselves off from the spiritual teachers of humankind. They think they know so much that they can safely reject the Living Christ, when he or she comes to free them from their mental prisons. This ignorance can, however, take two distinct forms, meaning that it leads to two distinct forms of thinking. We will tackle them in this and the next key, and I want you to begin by reading an excerpt from my website. You might have read this before, but I ask you to study it again with the deeper understanding you have as a result of following this course. You are bound to see deeper layers of understanding.

## Why the ego wants you to think the world is black and white

The most obvious example of the ego's relativistic, dualistic way of thinking is what I prefer to call black-and-white thinking. This plot by the ego makes blatant use of the basic duality built into the mind of anti-christ. It defines two opposites that are opposites in every way, meaning that there is no overlap or potential for compromise. There is no gray zone because the opposites cannot coexist but must cancel out each other—or so it seems. One opposite is defined as being absolutely good and the other is defined as being absolutely evil, thus setting up an inevitable, to-the-death struggle between them.

The ego makes people believe that the only way for them to please God and be saved is to take the side of good and to fight against evil. An extreme outcome of this scenario is the definition of two religions or ideologies that both claim to be the only true one, making their respective followers believe it is their duty to fight the other. The ultimate triumph of the prince of this world is to get two groups of religious people to kill each other in the name of the same God, as for example in the Crusades.

The result of this ego-manipulation is that people adopt a very simplistic view of the world. *Their* religion is completely true and all others are completely false. There is no room for any nuances in between, which means that people almost inevitably become extremists and fanatics. This is a very easy approach to life because it really does not require people to think for themselves. They simply accept the definitions created by the leaders of their society without making any personal attempts to discern whether their leaders are right according to the Christ standard. They believe these leaders are absolutely right and that God himself would agree with them.

The consequence of this approach to life is that once people have accepted that a particular belief system is absolutely good, they will never question it. Thus, they will blindly follow what the leaders of their religion have defined as absolutely right, and this has led to some of the worst atrocities in history. I described this scenario as follows:

> Let them alone: they be blind leaders of the blind. And if the blind lead the blind, both shall fall into the ditch. (Matthew 15:14)

Yet instead of leaving the blind leaders alone, people follow them uncritically. They never question that the black-and-white definition of life might not be in alignment with God's truth. As a result, many people have spent one or more lifetimes engaging all of their energy and attention in this dualistic struggle between two relative opposites. Such people have defined an enemy or scapegoat and they believe they must do God's work by destroying the enemy.

As long as people are trapped in this extreme form of black-and-white thinking, they are absolutely convinced that they are working *for* good and will be saved. Yet the stark reality is that everything they do to fight the self-defined enemy only serves to trap them more firmly in the dualistic state of consciousness. This obviously prevents them from putting on the wedding garment of the Christ consciousness, that is the *only* way to enter Heaven.

It can be extremely difficult for extremists to admit that they are wrong. They cannot admit that what they have seen as a work for God has not promoted God's cause but has only served to reinforce the dualistic struggle created by the forces of anti-christ. Such people tend to become very defensive and hostile toward anyone who questions the validity of their approach. This is why the scribes and the Pharisees wanted me dead and why some people in today's world become fanatical in defending their "truth."

The sad fact is that such people are unapproachable for a spiritual teacher. You see this illustrated in how the scribes and Pharisees rejected my attempts to show them the higher Way of Christ. They literally used their black-and-white viewpoints to justify rejecting the Living Christ, meaning that they had put their own graven image before the Living God. They used a relative image to justify not reaching for the direct experience of God's absolute reality—the experience I came to offer to all who were willing to lose their mortal sense of identity for my sake.

***

You will remember that I earlier said that the ego creates a false path to salvation. By using black-and-white logic, the ego creates the impression that being saved is a matter of belonging to the only true religion and meeting its outer requirements. The more people identify with their egos, the more prone they are to believe this illusion. It seems so easy that instead of doing the hard work of pulling the beam from your own eye, you simply have to believe a predefined doctrine and follow a set of outer rules.

At the beginning level of the spiritual path, people are prone to accept the black-and-white approach to salvation. Thus, they become very zealous – even fanatical – in following their particular belief system – be it religious, political or scientific in nature – and they absolutely refuse to question it. That is why some people can believe that by killing the enemies of God, they will instantly be saved.

Now comes one of the subtleties that the more mature spiritual seekers need to understand. The extreme outcome of being blinded by black-and-white thinking is that people become entirely self-centered and selfish. They often believe they have a supreme right to do what they want and that anyone who opposes them – including the rest of the human race – is wrong. They start acting like predatory animals who take whatever they want and are unwilling to consider how their actions affect other people, affect themselves in the long run or compare to higher principles. In the past, humankind was at a much lower level of consciousness than today, as illustrated by the cave man society in which the law of the jungle ruled. In today's world, you see this level of consciousness in many criminals, from leaders of organized crime to pedophiles or serial killers.

How do you take people who are completely selfish and raise them to a more spiritual level? Extreme selfishness is the ultimate outcome of the relative logic of the ego. In the Christ mind you see that all life is one, and thus when you hurt another, you are hurting yourself. When you are completely trapped in the mind of anti-christ, you think you can hurt others without hurting yourself, you even think you have the right to do whatever you want, regardless of how it affects others. You justify this by using the relative logic of the ego, which can truly make it seem like anything – including total selfishness – is justified.

How do people start rising above this level of consciousness? They do so by realizing that there is something beyond the ego's relative logic, that there is something that is right or wrong according to a higher standard. Do you see the point here? When you are completely selfish, you see nothing beyond the relative logic of your ego and thus you think you have the right to do anything you want. To begin the process of escaping total selfishness, you must realize that there is a higher standard for evaluating your behavior, so that you choose to limit certain types of selfish behavior.

For most people who are trapped in selfishness, this realization comes only when someone "puts the fear of God in them." In other words, these people begin to realize that there is such a thing as long-term consequences. Their souls can be affected in an afterlife by what they do in this life, and they will either be rewarded in heaven or burn forever in hell. Thus, from a purely selfish motive, these people begin to modify their short-term egotistical behavior according to a higher standard.

Because these people are still identified with their egos, they cannot yet see the limitations of the relative logic of the ego. So they need a very simplistic, black-and-white belief system with clearly defined rules for how to avoid hell and get into heaven. Here comes the subtle point. When people start modifying selfish behavior, they have reached a turning point from which genuine progress is possible. Yet there is a real danger that these people will be fooled by their egos to enter the blind alley of fanaticism, where they think they serve God by fighting what their belief system defines as the enemies of God. This will, of course, abort such people's progress.

However, if people avoid going into fanaticism, it is possible to make genuine spiritual progress by following a black-and-white belief system. The reason being that when you believe certain types of behavior will send you to hell, you gain a very strong motivation for modifying selfish behavior. This will cause a soul to make less karma, and thus the soul can gradually free itself from at least some of the downward pull of the dualistic struggle. When you are completely selfish, everything you do creates negative karma that only reinforces the sense that you are in a struggle against everyone else. When you relieve some of this pressure, you can begin to see through the more selfish beliefs, and thus you can free yourself from some of the illusions of the ego.

***

My point is that even though most fundamentalist Christians will reject this website as the work of the devil, there are actually people who have made progress by following a fundamentalist belief system. The problem is that this progress will only last for a time. A black-and-white approach simply cannot take you above a certain level of the spiritual path. And because this approach is still so heavily influenced by the relative logic of the ego, it can very easily become a blind alley that begins to take you into a downward spiral of judgment and pride, which is only marginally better than the downward spiral of selfishness.

The problem is that a black-and-white belief system automatically implies a value judgment. "The members of *our* church are automatically good and everyone else is bad." This inevitably causes people to judge others based on a relative standard, defined by their egos. As I said:

> 1 Judge not, that ye be not judged.
> 2 For with what judgment ye judge, ye shall be judged: and with what measure ye mete, it shall be measured to you again. (Matthew, Chapter 7)
>
> Judge not according to the appearance, but judge righteous judgment. (John 7:24)

Judging "according to the appearance" means that you judge based on a relative, dualistic standard created by the ego. Judging righteous judgment means that you discern absolute truth based on the vision of the Christ mind. When you judge based on the ego, you inevitably feel that you are better than other people, and this leads to spiritual pride, which binds you to the duality consciousness.

Do you see my point? The ego wants a relative standard because it allows it to build the appearance that it is better than others. It can then create the illusion that because you are better than certain other people, you are guaranteed to be saved. As I explained in a previous discourse, there is no such value judgment in the Christ mind. That which is in alignment with God's law is real, and that which is out of alignment with God is unreal. The Christ does not use the relative terms good and bad—it does not compare things on a relative scale that leads gradually from one extreme (good) to the opposite extreme (evil). The Christ mind does not judge based on appearances but is only concerned about whether something is real or not real.

One might say that the deepest level of ego-identification is to be completely selfish. You are completely identified with the dualistic struggle, thinking that life is a battle between you and the world. As you rise above this, you stop indulging in the most extreme selfish behaviors, but this makes you feel you are better than those who are still acting in "primitive" ways. At the lower level, you might engage in religion in order to destroy all threats to your religion, thinking God will reward you for doing so. At the next stage, your motivation for being involved with religion is to prove the superiority of your religion and thus create the appearance that you are so good that God simply has to save you.

***

The problem is that as long as you think the world is black and white, you cannot grow beyond a certain point. Black-and-white thinking sets up a scale with two extremes and then makes people think they have to choose one of the two polarities. In other words, if the world is engaged in an epic struggle between God and the devil, then you must obviously choose the side of God in order to be saved. Yet when this struggle is defined in black-and-white terms, it will seem as if choosing the side of God means choosing a particular religion in this world. And once you have chosen that religion, you must uncritically accept all of its doctrines—for if you don't, the devil will get you and take you to hell.

This line of thinking obviously leads to a fear-based approach to salvation, which gives rise to two problems. One is that you simply cannot enter the kingdom of God while there is *any* fear left in your being. That is why I said:

> 36 Master, which is the great commandment in the law?
> 37 Jesus said unto him, Thou shalt love the Lord thy God with all thy heart, and with all thy soul, and with all thy mind. (Matthew, Chapter 22)

Until you overcome fear, you cannot put on the Christ consciousness. Yet how do you overcome fear? Partly by using the rational mind to reason that your fear is based on a lack of knowledge and partly by reaching for a direct experience of God's transcendent reality, whereby you will experience the perfect love that casts out all fear. The problem here is that as long as you are trapped in a black-and-white belief system, you will be afraid of doing either.

Your belief system will strongly discourage you from thinking for yourself and questioning the beliefs that give rise to fear. And any black-and-white belief system on this planet states that you cannot experience God directly; you need the outer church and its priesthood as a mediator between you and God. That is why the black-and-white thinkers of the Jewish religion killed me after I stated that the kingdom of God is within you.

So fear itself makes a black-and-white belief system a closed circle, a trap for your mind. It creates a prison for your mind, and once the Conscious You is inside, your ego throws away the key. The Conscious You can step outside at any moment, but in order to do so, it must be willing to confront its fear and confront the fact that a black-and-white belief system is based on an illusion.

You see, the psychological effect of a black-and-white belief system is that it focuses your attention on a scale with two polarities, and then it makes it seem like truth has to be found somewhere on that scale. In other words, there is nothing beyond the relative scale. Yet any time – and I mean ANY TIME – you have a belief system with two opposites, you have a dualistic belief system. And in such a belief system BOTH OPPOSITES WILL BE DEFINED BY THE MIND OF ANTI-CHRIST.

I know this can be a startling statement considering the fact that most religions – including Christianity – define the world as an epic struggle between good and evil, between God and the devil. Yet as I have said, there is a stage on the spiritual path where people need to overcome the extreme selfish behavior by following a black-and-white belief system. However, there comes a point in your growth when you *must* move beyond that stage in order to make further progress. And you do this *only* by reaching for the Christ mind, which is beyond either of the two extremes defined by *any* black-and-white belief system!

Do you see my point? As I explained in previous discourses, the reality of God *cannot* be put on a relative scale and it has no opposite polarity. God's reality has no opposite because that which is outside of God's reality has no reality. And that which has no reality cannot be in opposition to that which has reality. Thus, in the Christ mind, there is only what is real and what appears to be unreal—because the law of free will has allowed it to take on a temporary appearance outside God's reality. Yet this unreality can exist only in the minds of co-creators who are trapped in duality.

It is only when you step into the mind of anti-christ that opposites become possible. In this frame of mind there seems to be two opposites, such as good and evil, true and false. These opposites cancel out each other, and because one can destroy the other, it seems like both of them have – the same – reality. This is what gives rise to fear of evil because people in a dualistic frame of mind think evil is real and has real power over them. When you attain the Christ mind and see that evil is not real and that its appearance has no power over you, you lose all fear. Yet as long as you believe evil has the same reality as good, you cannot overcome that fear. The trick is that evil *does* have the same reality as *relative* good. Thus, you need to use the Christ mind to see the absolute good of God.

My point here is that a black-and-white belief system makes you think that you have to move toward relative good and avoid its opposite, namely evil. It makes you think that a statement must be either true or false, meaning that you must side with what you – or your belief system – have defined as true and avoid anything that contradicts or goes beyond it.

People think that by moving toward relative good, they are moving closer to God. This is both true and untrue. If you move away from selfish behavior, you are moving away from the extreme forms of egotistical behavior. This gives you the potential – but only the *potential* – to rise above duality, which will bring you closer to God. The big question is whether you keep moving toward a relative extreme (good as defined by the ego) – and thus inevitably become trapped in pride – or make the leap and reach for something beyond the dualistic extremes.

Christ truth cannot be forced into a dualistic belief system, and thus Christ truth can *never* be found on a scale with two opposites! Christ truth is beyond duality and thus you can find it *only* by reaching beyond the black-and-white belief systems of this world. As I have said, only when a soul reaches a certain maturity, will it be ready to question its belief system and realize that the world is not black and white.

I could say much more about black-and-white thinking, but the most important fact you need to understand is that it becomes a trap for your mind. Once you accept any black-and-white belief system, the ego can always come up with a seemingly watertight argument for why you should not look beyond it. Many fundamentalist Christians believe Christianity is the only true religion, the Bible is the infallible word of God and their literal interpretation of the Bible is the only true one. Thus, anything beyond their present beliefs is of the devil and they should avoid thinking about it—which is why they reject this website as the fundamentalists of the Jewish religion rejected me when I walked the Earth in the flesh.

Likewise, many scientifically minded people believe there is nothing beyond the material universe. Thus, any belief system that proposes a "supernatural" cause is unscientific and the product of the subjectivity of the mind. The effect of a black-and-white approach is *always* that it closes your mind to growth. As I said in a previous discourse, you settle for a description of truth – a description created through the mind of anti-christ – and you use it to justify not reaching for a direct experience of the Spirit of Truth.

Billions of people are trapped in some version of a black-and-white belief system. Yet most of the people who are open to this website have already started seeing the fallacy of this approach to religion/life/salvation. They have started seeing through the illusion that there is only one true religion and that "our side is always right and the other side is always wrong." They have started realizing that life is not as simple as the black-and-white thinking implies and that a more sophisticated approach is needed. They have also started distancing themselves from the extremism and fanaticism – often even the value judgment and pride – that is so common for the black-and-white approach.

We might say that such people have started seeing through the black-and-white illusions of the ego. Yet although this clearly represents a higher level, it is extremely important for spiritual seekers to realize that they are still not above the relative logic of the ego. I have said that the ego has a built-in contradiction and seeks to create two opposite viewpoints in every situation. Obviously, black-and-white thinking defines such opposites, but this form of thinking also forms its own polarity. In other words, black-and-white thinking has its own opposite and when people start rising above black-and-white thinking, it is quite common that they jump into the opposite extreme. In the next discourse we will examine this extreme, and I hope I can prevent sincere seekers from being stuck in that extreme longer than necessary. [End of quote.]

***

Obviously, all who are open to this course have overcome the more obvious effects of black-and-white thinking. You are not likely to be a member of a Christian fundamentalist church or the communist party. Yet I need you to realize that black-and-white thinking has subtle effects that can take time and effort to overcome. I also need you to consider that most people on this planet have been affected by a black-and-white belief system—be it a religion, a political ideology or scientific materialism. Thus, as a disciple of the Living Christ, you need to understand black-and-white thinking so you can help others overcome it.

The most dangerous effect of black-and-white thinking is, of course, that it defines a clear distinction between ideas that are safe and ideas that are not safe. If you think about ideas that are not safe, you might end up in hell or you will become a religious nut case (a destiny worse than hell to materialists). And this clearly has the effect of confining people's minds to a mental box. We have already dealt with fear, but I need you to revisit it here and consider whether there are any ideas or beliefs that you are reluctant to think about?

As I have explained, there are clearly false teachers in this world, and they are constantly seeking to prevent people from attaining or expressing their Christhood by keeping them trapped in ignorance. So what I need you to begin to contemplate here is how these false teachers work. You first need to recognize that these beings – both embodied and disembodied beings – are trapped in and thus blinded by duality.

I ask you to step back from this and think more deeply about what I am implying here. You may have an image that there is some kind of ultimate evil being, such as the devil. We will later talk more about this, but what I want you to understand at this point is that there are many beings who are seeking to deceive humankind. In fact, there are various groups of such beings, and they are in a constant rivalry with each other, which is the main reason why they have not completely taken over this planet.

Why are they in a rivalry? Because they are divided against each other! Why are they divided against each other? Because they are trapped in the consciousness of duality, which always has two opposite polarities. Thus, they are divided within themselves – they are houses divided against themselves – and as a result they must inevitably be in conflict with each other. So you see that the very consciousness that causes them to go against God's purpose for the universe will also create the opposing forces that guarantee that they cannot ultimately be successful. They can have some temporary success, but in the end they can never win.

What I need you to understand here is that these false teachers cannot see what I have just explained. Why not? Because the very fact that they are working against God's purpose – by violating the free will of other beings – proves that they are trapped in duality. And precisely because they are blinded by the consciousness of duality, they are completely unable to see beyond it. They are completely unable to see the reality of Christ.

Take note of the subtlety here. The scribes and Pharisees were completely blinded by duality, yet they were still able to recognize me as being a threat to them. They did not recognize me as the Living Christ, but they felt sufficiently threatened by my truth that they knew they had to silence me. So while they could not see my reality, they *did* see me as a threat to their own beliefs, and thus they could not simply ignore me—they had to actively silence me.

My point is that the false teachers can recognize the Living Christ as a threat, but they cannot recognize the reality of the teachings of the Christ. Which means that they cannot see beyond the relative, dualistic thinking of the mind of anti-christ. Why is this important? Because I want you to understand that the traditional concept of the devil is quite primitive and is deliberately designed to scare people. The devil is sometimes portrayed as a being who is almost as powerful as God, in that – at least in this world – the devil has the power to take you to hell even against the best efforts of God and God's representatives.

So when you begin to understand that the devil seeks to deceive people, you might – perhaps subconsciously – accept this idea of an all-powerful devil and think the devil is as smart as God. In other words, the devil is far smarter than you, and thus you need to avoid even thinking about ideas that are spread by the devil so you don't end up in hell. This is how many Christians actually reason—perhaps without being consciously aware of it. And that is why they stay in the orthodox mental box, where even I – whom they claim as their master – cannot reach them.

I now need you to shatter this subtle fear by realizing what I have been saying here. The devil – and all false teachers – are truly very smart, but their abilities are limited to a certain level, namely the level of the dualistic mind. As I said, they cannot recognize the reality of Christ, which means they are completely blinded by duality. Their entire process of thinking takes place in the realm of duality, and they cannot see that duality is unreal. They are extremely skilled at using the dualistic mind to argue for their viewpoint, and thus they can often deceive people – who do not have the same sophistication of mind – into following them. People simply cannot see through their relative arguments, as Eve could not see through the lies of the Serpent.

Do you see the point? In the dualistic mind, there will always be two opposites—yet none of them have any ultimate reality. They exist *only* in relation to each other, meaning they are unreal because they are separated from the one reality of the Christ, the reality of God. Thus, what even the most sophisticated false teachers are doing is simply arguing that *their* dualistic, relativistic philosophy is better than any other dualistic philosophy—meaning that they are simply arguing *for* one unreal idea and *against* all other unreal ideas.

Now, I don't know about you, but I don't consider this to be very smart. I consider it to be a very immature form of "intelligence."

Don't get me wrong. I am not trying to make light of the false teachers, who represent a very subtle, and thus very dangerous, challenge to people on Earth. Yet what I am trying to help you see here is that these beings do not have some kind of magical power over you. And although they may have more sophisticated minds than you, this does not mean that they are automatically able to deceive you.

Do you begin to see my point? The false teachers can deceive you *only* as long as you allow your mind to stay in the realm of duality. Deception is possible *only* in the realm of duality, and thus those who are very good at using the relative logic of the dualistic mind can deceive those who are not as skilled in this – unreal – form of thinking.

Yet – as I attempted to explain even 2,000 years ago – all people have access to an antidote to dualistic thinking, namely the "Key of Knowledge" or the Comforter. If you are willing to reach for the reality of the Christ mind, you can find an undivided reality that immediately makes it obvious to you that the arguments used by the false teachers – no matter how clever they may appear – are out of touch with the reality of God. And once you see this, you cannot be deceived by them. Once you truly see the unreality of duality, you will never again be completely fooled by its logic. And you will see this when you experience a glimpse of the Spirit of Truth—as you have already done in order to find this course.

In other words, the devil is *not* deliberately using the consciousness of duality to ensnare people while he is above this consciousness. All false teachers are completely trapped in the consciousness of duality, and the more "sophisticated" they are at using its relative logic, the more trapped they are. Thus, the most "powerful" false teachers are in reality the most ignorant. Which means that if you are willing to make use of the Key of Knowledge, it is not difficult for you to be smarter than them, smart enough to see through their illusions so they no longer have any power over you.

So how do you begin to see through the illusions of the false teachers? By coming to understand how the dualistic mind works, so you can begin to see how they are using dualistic thinking to trap your mind in a particular mental box. Let me give you an example.

***

The main goal of the false teachers is to keep you in ignorance. Yet this does not mean that they want you to know nothing, for the more sophisticated of them realize that it is not possible to forever keep people in a state of knowing nothing. Because of the force of life itself, any society based on the people knowing nothing – such as the feudal societies of medieval Europe – will eventually collapse. And certainly, in the modern information age, keeping people in this form of ignorance is no longer seen as feasible by most false teachers.

So the next strategy of the false teachers is to satisfy people's quest for knowledge, but to do so by creating a predefined mental box and then – once people have stepped into it – manipulate them into never questioning the basic illusions that define the box. In other words, people are made to feel that the mental box can give them all the knowledge they need and that going outside the box is unnecessary, impossible or outright dangerous. They are ensnared by pride or fear, as we have discussed earlier. People are now trapped in the sophisticated ignorance of thinking they know all, but all their knowledge is based on dualistic illusions. Or it is at least so colored by duality that it will keep them outside the kingdom of God. One of the primary methods for creating such closed mental boxes is precisely black-and-white thinking.

Yet how does this make use of duality? As an example, consider fundamentalist Christianity, which is based on the fundamental assumptions that the Bible is the infallible word of God and that it should be interpreted literally. Once people accept these basic assumptions and refuse to question them, they are trapped in a mental box, and certain conclusions inevitably follow, such as the idea that they are sinners who can only be saved through me and do not have to take full responsibility for their salvation, meaning they can ignore the beam in their own eyes.

As I have said many times, the key feature of the dualistic consciousness is that it – by its dual nature – generates two opposing and mutually exclusive ideas. Thus, there is literally no idea, philosophy or belief system on Earth that does not have an opposite. Think about this! If you look at history, you will see that from time to time a new philosophical school of thought emerged, a school based on certain key ideas. Yet in most cases it did not take long before another school of thought emerged, and it was based on a rejection of the basic paradigms of the first school. This, of course, is a product of the false teachers, who are so good at using relative, dualistic logic that when one group comes up with a philosophy, there is always another group who can see how to use relative logic to disprove the other one.

My point being, of course, that the dualistic mind gives innumerable opportunities for defining a belief system that is clearly seen as being in opposition to another belief system. Yet this is only the first layer of deception. While the dualistic mind gives rise to innumerable thought systems that all have an opposite, it also gives rise to an even greater – more general – form of duality. This is the value judgment, which causes people to think that everything must be placed on a relative scale with good or right at one end and evil or wrong at the other end.

This now causes people to believe that their particular belief system is not just one among many possible belief systems, but is the one that represents absolute good or right, whereas the opposing belief system represents absolute evil or wrong. And thus it is their sacred duty to defend absolute good by seeking to destroy absolute evil—even to the point that it is justified to kill the people who represent evil. In this way people are fooled into promoting the endless dualistic struggle that can never – contrary to the claims made by the false teachers – produce an ultimate outcome. Why not? Because it is a *dualistic* struggle, meaning that any effort is opposed by an opposite impulse – any action has an opposite reaction – and thus no ultimate outcome is possible.

Do you now begin to see how subtle this deception is? As I have explained between the lines, humankind is engaged in a process that gradually raises people's consciousness. The entire planet is in an ascending spiral that will gradually set people free from the illusions of duality, which means the false teachers will lose their power on this planet. You can see this in history, for example how the feudal societies of Europe gave way to societies that gave greater freedom and rights to all people.

So what we see is that most people are entirely focused on themselves and their own immediate situation—which is clearly not Christhood (as Christhood seeks to raise all life). Yet as people begin to mature, they realize there is more to life, there is a higher purpose for life. They often begin to see the forward progression of humankind, and they begin to see themselves as being part of it with an active role to play. This is the very infant stage of Christhood, where you begin to see something bigger than your personal desires and situation—you begin to espouse a cause. Unfortunately, many people at this stage are deceived by black-and-white thinking into supporting a dualistic cause and engaging in the epic struggle between relative good and relative evil defined by the false teachers. Thus, instead of their efforts actually making a contribution to the forward movement of humankind, they only perpetuate the dualistic struggle that gives power to the false teachers. Instead of actually fighting *for* good, they are simply fighting *against* one relative idea that is in opposition to another relative idea—the sum total being no or very little progress.

As a historical example, consider the Crusades, where you had two groups of religious people killing each other in the name of the same God. Both sides were equally convinced that they were the ones who were right, since they had the only true religion. In hindsight, it is easy to see that they could not both be right, yet what I want you to do is to step back and look at the bigger picture. In reality, none of the two sides were right, for both of them had a dualistic approach to life. My original teachings were non-dualistic, but the official Christian church had turned them into dualistic doctrines. Likewise, Islam was from its very beginning based on divine revelation, but the consciousness of Mohammed was so influenced by dualistic thinking that the teachings of Islam were colored by duality at a very early stage.

My point is that as a disciple of the Living Christ, you cannot allow yourself to be pulled into such dualistic struggles. You need to free yourself from the dualistic illusions so you can help other people, even society, rise above the dualistic struggle and make real progress.

***

We now come to the more subtle effect of black-and-white thinking. As I said, this form of thinking puts your mind in a mental box with clearly defined boundaries, and then it makes you afraid or unwilling to think about ideas that are outside the box. This is what turns black-and-white thinking into an obvious example of a spiritual catch-22. You are trapped in a mental box defined by illusions, you are afraid to look at any ideas that are outside the mental box and could therefore help you see through the illusions. So how can you ever escape your illusions if you are afraid to see that they are illusions? In other words, as long as you are afraid to look at ideas outside your box, you can never escape the box. And this is precisely where the false teachers want people.

You see, because of the rivalry between different groups of false teachers, they have defined many mental boxes. From time to time, one group of false teachers gain power in a society, and they manage to draw people out of the old mental box – such as the

Catholic box of the middle ages – and into a new box, such as scientific materialism. Yet people are still in a box that sets boundaries for the ideas they are willing to consider, which prevents their ultimate freedom from dualistic thinking.

Let me now reach back to what I said earlier, namely that many people have come to fear that the devil is able to deceive them, and thus they dare not think about ideas that are outside their mental box. Do you now see how this works? The false teachers can influence you *only* as long as your mind is in the realm of duality, in which *every* idea is based on an illusion. This is why the false teachers *must* define a mental box and then make you afraid to look beyond it. It is the *only* way to prevent you from finding the truth of Christ that will set you free from the dualistic illusions!

My point being that the false teachers of humankind have cleverly manipulated most people into a frame of mind in which they are programmed to reject the truth of the Living Christ as actually being dangerous or even as being the work of the devil. This is precisely how the scribes and the Pharisees reasoned when they rejected my Living Truth.

The conclusion being that as a disciple of the Living Christ, you need to see through this deception and realize that it is *only* the false teachers who will try to prevent you from thinking about new ideas, ideas that do not fit in your current mental box.

Do you actually see the subtle deception here? Black-and-white thinking has been used for thousands of years to promote the subtle belief that the devil is the one who is trying to get you to think about ideas outside the safe box of your current belief system and that all such ideas are dangerous. In reality, the devil wants to herd you into a mental box that is defined by dualistic illusions and then keep you from ever questioning the box.

Do you see the plot? The false teachers have been working for a long time, and the result is that all of the world's belief systems are affected by duality. The main goal of the false teachers is to make people stay in a dualistic mental box—no matter which one. And as long as people do stay in a belief system affected by duality, their beliefs become self-fulfilling prophecies in the sense that no one can step back and see that duality is unreal, that the emperors of duality have nothing on. Do you now see why I need people in embodiment who will demonstrate that there is an alternative to dualistic thinking?

Certainly, it is true that there are ideas and belief systems in this world that are more destructive than certain other ideas. Thus, it is possible that a given person could be deceived by a new belief system that is more destructive than the system in which the person grew up. Likewise, there are competing groups of false teachers, so there are those who are seeking to pull you into a false teaching. Thus, I am *not* advocating that you uncritically open your mind to any and all ideas floating around in this world.

In fact, I do not advocate opening your mind to new ideas that are of this world, meaning that they are based on or colored by dualistic illusions. Instead, I advocate that you reach for the Key of Knowledge by coming to understand the concept of Christ discernment.

You see, in the realm of duality, every idea has an opposing idea. Thus, finding truth is *not* a matter of finding an idea in the realm of duality that is more true than other ideas. An inescapable part of the mind of duality is that it sets up a relative scale. So you might look at the ideas in this world and set them up on a scale, where one end represents ideas that are completely false, whereas the other represents ideas that have a higher degree of truth. Yet what I want you to see here is that as long as an idea fits on this scale, the idea is – at least to some degree – affected by duality. And your role as a disciple of the Living Christ is to raise yourself above dualistic thinking by reaching for the Key of Knowledge that empowers you to discern between the reality of the Christ mind and the unreality of the mind of anti-christ—no matter how cleverly the latter is disguised as being true within the confines of a dualistic system.

***

I have said that false teachers are trapped in and blinded by the consciousness of duality. Most of them are completely trapped in the struggle to assert one dualistic belief system as being superior to all other dualistic belief systems—as being the ultimate system. Yet some of the false teachers have actually come to see that this dualistic struggle cannot lead to an ultimate end—they see that all is vanity, that the struggle is pointless. So instead of believing in the struggle, they have learned to use it deliberately as part of the divide-and-conquer strategy. They use duality to divide people into factions that fight against each other, whereby the false teachers can control them and steal their life energy—using it to uphold their own separate existence. So even these beings are blinded by duality, only it is a deeper layer of the dualistic illusion. If they were not blinded by duality, they would see all life as one, and thus they would know that by hurting others, they are hurting themselves.

What I want you to do is to not only see the futility of the dualistic struggle but to rise above it, so you can see what even the most "sophisticated" false teachers will not see, namely the reality of Christ behind the veil of duality. I want you to see that the real goal of Christ is *not* – as has been portrayed by Christian churches – to elevate one particular belief system – not even Christianity – as the superior system on Earth, getting all people to become members and eradicating all competing systems. This very consciousness of turning Christianity into the dominant belief system is based on a dualistic misinterpretation of a couple of my statements:

> 15 And he said unto them, Go ye into all the world, and preach the gospel to every creature.
> 16 He that believeth and is baptized shall be saved; but he that believeth not shall be damned. (Mark, Chapter 16)

> Jesus saith unto him, I am the way, the truth, and the life: no man cometh unto the Father, but by me. (John, 14:6)

Can you see that when people are trapped in black-and-white thinking, these statements sound like I am saying that the outer religion of Christianity is the *only* way to salvation, and thus I want all people to become Christians? Yet can you now begin to grasp the non-dualistic truth in these statements?

The reality is that Christ represents a state of consciousness, a state that is above and beyond duality. The dualistic mind is born from a separation from God, from the Father, and thus no man can come to the Father as long as he or she is trapped in duality. How can you enter God's kingdom as long as you see yourself as separated from an external god? The absolutely *only* way to the Father is to let the dualistic self die and put on the mind of Christ, whereby you affirm that "I and my Father are one!"

Thus, the gospel I want preached to every creature is *not* that you need to be a member of an outer Christian religion in order to be saved. It is the non-dualistic gospel that you are saved *only* by rising above duality and putting on the mind of Christ. He who believes this and thus puts on the Christ mind – enters into oneness with me – is saved. Whereas those who do not accept this truth condemn themselves to remaining in the "outer darkness" of the dualistic mind, in which there will inevitably be "weeping and gnashing of teeth" because of the dualistic conflicts.

My overall point being that I need you to overcome all remnants of black-and-white thinking so you will be open to questioning *all* of your existing beliefs and considering any idea I present to you.

## Exercise for Key 9

As the exercise for this key, I want you to give a 33-day vigil of the Rosary of Oneness while using the Hail Mother of Nurturance from the Nurturance Rosary instead of the standard Hail Mary. I also want you to say the mantra of the Dhyani Buddha for this key one time after each verse and before the Hail Mother of Nurturance.

**OM VAIROCHANA OM**

After the rosary, contemplate and write down how your life has been affected by black-and-white thinking and how your society is affected by it. Then look for the dualistic belief that has been used to justify the black-and-white illusions you have encountered. Ask me to help you see how you can personally help set other people free from this unbalanced approach to life. Ask me to help you see you basic assumptions and how your current belief system actually supports or justifies those assumptions.

# Key 10
# Gray ignorance

In this key we will tackle another version of the poison of ignorance. Again, the Buddha is Vairochana. Use his mantra as you study this key:

**OM VAIROCHANA OM**

As I have described, there is a gradual process that leads from total spiritual blindness toward the complete awakening of the Christ consciousness. As they begin to awaken from being self-absorbed, people typically espouse a cause, but they often go through a phase of approaching that cause based on black-and-white thinking, causing them to participate in the dualistic struggle by battling an enemy who opposes their cause. After they have pursued a cause in this way – often for many lifetimes – they begin to see the limitations of black-and-white thinking, and they mature to the point where they can begin to question the idea that there is one absolute truth, or even that it is possible to find absolute truth in this world.

This leads to the next phase, where it is likely that people will have to go through what I call gray thinking, before they finally find the Middle Way of Christ discernment. So I ask you to study the teachings from my website on gray thinking, as it will set a foundation for a deeper understanding of how to find the Middle Way.

## Why the ego wants you to think the world is gray

As I have explained in previous discourses, the ego operates entirely in the realm of duality. When you go to the lowest aspect of dualistic thinking, you end up seeing the world as black and white, meaning that you are always right and anyone opposing you is always wrong. The reasoning is simple. People define a belief system as infallible and as the only true one, meaning that they think it is entirely true and not influenced by error at all. In the terminology I use in these discourses, people think *their* belief system springs entirely from the truth of Christ and is not influenced by the illusions of the mind of anti-christ.

In reality this line of thinking springs from the ego's desire to set itself up as an authority figure that cannot be questioned. It is an attempt to create the outer appearance that because you belong to the only true belief system, you are guaranteed to be saved. It also gives many people the sense that they are better than those who do not belong to their belief system. If you take an honest look at the world, you will see that even today many people are caught in this approach to life. They have a very obvious sense of righteousness, they judge others and they feel better than others. An obvious example is fundamentalists of any religion, including the religion of materialism.

If you have ever interacted with such people, you will know that it can be extremely difficult to carry on a normal conversation with them. And it is virtually impossible to discuss anything that goes beyond or seems to contradict their beliefs. If you try to make them see that their beliefs are limited or even incorrect, you are usually met with a very hostile reaction. In extreme cases, such people are willing to kill anyone who threatens their belief system, as for example a Muslim fundamentalist who carries out a suicide bombing to defend Islam. Or a Christian crusader defending a piece of real estate in the Holy Land—as if God – a spiritual being – ever wanted people to kill each other over anything in the material world. When people are less extreme, they will label you as being of the devil (or any number of other negative labels) and refuse to talk with you. This, of course, makes such people unreachable for a spiritual teacher.

***

What can bring people out of this state of having closed their minds completely? Well, the reality of the situation is that the conscious selves of such people have refused to make decisions. The conscious self has retreated into a self-made fortress and it has assigned the ego as a guard. The role of the ego is to build fortress walls that are impenetrable to anything that would require the conscious self to wake up and start making decisions again. Of course, as the medieval castles proved, any fortress built to keep the world *out*, will also keep its inhabitants *in*, thus becoming a prison.

The inevitable result is that the ego will act as a computer that mindlessly carries out its programming, taking the person further and further into the extreme of black-and-white thinking. This will cause the person to be in continuous conflict with other people, and when the conflict becomes extreme enough, the conscious self might finally wake up and realize, "I can't do this anymore. There must be a better way!"

If the conscious self is willing to take at least some responsibility for its situation, it can now reverse the downward trend, and it can then start the upward path that gradually leads it out of the prison built by the ego. Yet there are three main factors that can impede this growth:

- The mental prison was built as a fortress designed to "defend" the conscious self from having to make decisions. Thus, the conscious self might be emotionally attached to the security and comfortability of the prison. This might manifest as an unwillingness to run the risk of making decisions or as an attachment to the beliefs out of which the fortress is built. It might cling to this security in order to avoid feeling vulnerable.

- The ego wants the conscious self to believe in the lie that if you don't make any decisions, you can't make mistakes. Yet the reality is that because you have free will, not making decisions is still making a decision. If you don't make decisions, you are allowing the ego to make decisions *for* you. All of the ego's decisions are mistakes, in the sense that they will not bring you closer to oneness with God.

- The ego's survival instinct will seek to keep you inside the walls where it feels like it has you and the world under some form of control. So the ego will actively and aggressively seek to prevent you from rising to a new level of the spiritual path.

What do I mean when I talk about rising to a new level of the path? Well, there are many valid ways to divide the spiritual path into levels or stages. In this context, what I am talking about is that you come to the point where you begin to see the fallacy of dualistic thinking. You begin to see the forest itself rather than being blinded by the individual trees. This is when you can begin to consciously reach for the non-dual truth of Christ.

The ego and the forces of this world will mount a major offensive against any person who begins to rise above duality. They will do anything they can think of to keep you trapped in dualistic thinking. Yet their only way of doing this is to use the duality of the mind of anti-christ. However, this is a formidable weapon because it is much more subtle than most spiritual seekers realize.

***

As I explained in the previous discourse, many people have started rising out of extreme selfishness by being converted to a religion that talks about heaven and hell. These are what we normally call religious people, and they are still very much trapped in black-and-white thinking. They are largely unreachable to me, and most of them would reject this website outright.

In today's world, many people have started seeing the limitations of a black-and-white approach to religion. Some are still members of traditional religions while others seek a more universal spirituality or belong to a New Age organization. Common for all these people is that they have started to rise above the black-and-white, fear-based, judgmental approach to religion. Thus, they are what I call spiritual seekers. They realize there is more to know about the spiritual side of life than what can be found in black-and-white doctrines, and they are actively looking for a higher understanding. These are the kind of people who are open to the teachings that the Ascended Host are bringing forth in this age, whether through this website or other means.

My point is that spiritual seekers represent the greatest potential for turning around planet Earth and bringing humankind to a higher level. The problem is that at the present time this is only a potential. What keeps it from becoming a manifest reality is that too many spiritual seekers have become trapped in a form of dualistic thinking that is so different from black-and-white thinking that people believe it is above duality. Yet in reality, it is simply the opposite extreme of black-and-white thinking.

Here is one concept that I would like all sincere spiritual seekers to understand. You live on a planet that is like a twilight zone. Some spiritual light has started to penetrate the density of humankind's consciousness. Yet there is still so much darkness left that the light and the darkness can mix into shades of gray that make it very difficult to tell the difference between what is real and unreal. Therefore, the human ego and the prince of this world can still use the subtlety of the duality consciousness to blur the distinction between what is real and unreal.

The result is that there is currently no concept, truth or spiritual teaching on this planet that cannot be perverted by the human ego. The ego will try to turn any idea into a dualistic idea by putting it on a scale with other dualistic ideas—usually by setting up the idea in opposition to another idea. The consequence is that whenever you take a major step forward on the spiritual path, your ego will repeat its never-ending game of seeking to create two extremes and polarize you toward either one. When you come to the realization that you have had enough of one extreme, your ego will instantly try to make you jump into the opposite extreme. The purpose is to prevent you from leaving behind the dualistic way of thinking and rising to a higher plateau by finding the Middle Way.

As I have said, most spiritual seekers have had enough of the black-and-white approach to religion. They are done with the fanaticism and they see the fallacy of the value judgment that "Our religion is the only true one and thus we are always right and those who disagree with us are bad people and will go to hell." Most of them have distanced themselves from this approach, which is a step in the right direction. The problem is that the ego will try to make such people go into the opposite extreme, and in too many cases it is successful.

What is the opposite extreme of black-and-white thinking? It is a form of thinking in which nothing is black and white because everything is gray. This gives rise to a number of problems, but let me briefly outline the main ones:

- Religious people tend to think there is only one true religion—their own, which inevitably leads to religious intolerance. Spiritual seekers have distanced themselves from religious intolerance, but many have come to believe that religious tolerance means you must accept all religions as equally valid, meaning that you don't need to evaluate whether an idea is true or false. Just believe and let believe.

- Many religious people are judgmental and intolerant toward members of other religions. Most spiritual seekers make it a virtue to be non-judgmental, but the extreme outcome is that they see almost any type of belief or behavior as acceptable. Or at least they think you should never speak out against other people's beliefs or behavior.

- Many religious people feel threatened by those who disagree with them and often respond with hostility and anger. Obviously, this prevents them from following my command to love one-another as I love them—which leads to hypocrisy. They claim to be Christians, but they don't act lovingly. Most spiritual seekers see through such hypocrisy and are sincerely striving to be loving toward everyone. However, they also believe that being loving means you should be gentle and never challenge people's illusions.

The net outcome of this approach is that many spiritual seekers have come to believe that in order to do God's work and raise the consciousness of the planet, they simply have to avoid the obvious extremism of black-and-white thinking. They think it is enough to be tolerant and loving, but they do not see that this is simply another fortress built to prevent their conscious selves from making its own decisions. They do not realize that the ego that used to be judgmental when – in past lives – they were trapped in black-and-white thinking, has now morphed into an ego that is loving and kind toward everyone. Instead of truly overcoming their egos, they have allowed the chameleon of the ego to change color so that it blends in with their new world view, where being gray has become a virtue that is seen as being superior to being black-and-white. Let us take a closer look at the points raised above.

***

What caused the "Fall of Man" was the duality consciousness. The essence of the duality consciousness is that it is disconnected from God's reality. Thus, the duality consciousness sets up its own definition of what is good and evil—a definition that is out of alignment with the reality seen by the Christ mind. The ego is born out of this relative definition of "truth," and thus it cannot see any need to discern between what is God's reality and a dualistic unreality. It only sees a need to discern what is right and wrong according to the dualistic belief system that it currently accepts as infallible. The ego has replaced God's reality with a belief system created by the mind of anti-christ.

As I attempted to explain in previous discourses, anything you do in the duality consciousness – be it good or evil according to any man-made standard – will only take you further away from oneness with God. You cannot overcome the duality consciousness by using the duality consciousness. Thus, it simply is not possible to make true spiritual progress unless you are willing to discern between what is real – meaning that it is Christ truth – and what is unreal—meaning that it springs from the mind of anti-christ.

My point is that unless the Conscious You is willing to take up its responsibility and sharpen its ability to discern between God's truth and the unreality of a dualistic "truth," you will not make true spiritual progress. You will simply allow your ego to maneuver you into a form of self-righteousness that is different in appearance but essentially the same as what you see in many religious people. There are millions of people on this planet who claim to be truly religious or spiritual people, yet they have not truly begun to see the fallacy of dualistic thinking.

People who take a black-and-white approach are completely convinced that there is only one true belief system and that all others are false. The effect is that they do not have to discern between what is God's absolute truth and what is a dualistic illusion. Since their belief system defines what is the infallible truth, they have no need to think for themselves. Yet the people who think all belief systems are equally valid are also refusing to discern between Christ truth and a dualistic illusion. If there are no false ideas, you have no need to discern. Simply find a belief system you like – usually because it does not challenge your ego – and then allow your ego to make you feel that you are sure to be saved.

My point is that both black-and-white thinking and gray thinking give people a "perfect" excuse for not making an effort to discern between the non-dual reality and the dualistic illusions. This is a very easy approach to life, but it springs from the fact that the conscious self refuses to take responsibility for its situation. As I said in previous discourses, you are a co-creator with God, and you cannot turn off your creative abilities. You are either co-creating through the mind of Christ or de-creating through the mind of antichrist. Thus, it is your inherent responsibility to discern between reality and unreality to the best of your ability, while continuously sharpening your discernment.

Take note that in the current conditions found on Earth, discerning is not an easy task. Yet you are not required to be perfect; you are required to be willing to try. Those who run away from this responsibility are simply not making spiritual progress, no matter how convinced they are that because they belong to the only true church or because they never judge anyone, they are among the righteous ones who will surely be saved.

Take note of what I said earlier, namely that the ego is trying to create a false path and then convince people that by following it their salvation is guaranteed. Both the religious people who take a black-and-white approach and the spiritual seekers who take a gray approach are following this false path, namely the broad way that is taken by many people because it is easy. It does not require their conscious selves to take responsibility and make decisions. It gives the impression that you can be saved without discerning.

As I said 2,000 years ago, this approach will *never* get you into the kingdom of God, for it cannot take you to the Christ consciousness:

> For I say unto you, That except your righteousness shall exceed the righteousness of the scribes and Pharisees, ye

> shall in no case enter into the kingdom of heaven. (Matthew, 5:20)

The sense of righteousness of the scribes and Pharisees was based on their belief that they belonged to the only true religion. Yet behind that belief was an even deeper belief, namely that it is possible to define outer conditions in this world, and if you live up to these conditions, God has to let you into his kingdom. Defining such conditions is the basic programming of the ego, and it will *never* see that this is a fallacy. Yet the Conscious You has the potential to see the fallacy of this approach—but only when it decides that it is willing to take up its responsibility to discern.

When you step onto the path to Christhood – the true path to salvation – you realize that there *are* ideas that are false, because they spring from the mind of anti-christ. Thus, you are not showing tolerance by *not* challenging such ideas. However, this does not mean that you have to act like the people who take the black-and-white approach. They have a judgmental attitude, and they are condemning and judging anyone who disagrees with them.

As you begin to attain Christhood, you are no longer threatened by any ideas, so you have no need to judge or condemn other people. Instead, you can now look beyond the outer ideas and seek to genuinely help people rise above illusions. You never judge or condemn other people, but you freely challenge ideas and actions that are self-destructive and destructive toward other forms of life.

***

As I said, many people have started rising out of the tendency to be judgmental toward other people. You find them in liberal Christianity and in many New Age movements. Such people have made it a virtue to be kind toward everyone, and they often justify it by referring to my calls to turn the other cheek and do unto others what you want them to do to you. As I have said before, there are stages of the spiritual path, and there is a time when a person can benefit from following a black-and-white belief system.

Likewise, there is a phase where many people find it necessary to go into the opposite extreme and be non-judgmental. Yet this should only be a brief phase, and too many people get stuck in it because they allow their egos to convince them that it should be permanent.

Many such people allow the mind of anti-christ – focused in their egos – to convince them that the ideal behavior for a human being is to always be soft-spoken and kind. They will often justify this by referring to the behavior of spiritual leaders, such as the

Buddha and myself. Yet the reality is that neither the Buddha nor myself were always soft-spoken, and although we practiced kindness, it was not the human, dualistic form of kindness.

What is dualistic kindness—how can there be more than one form of kindness? When you are trapped in duality, you define kindness a certain way, usually by saying that it is soft-spoken and never challenges people. This causes many people to believe that if they are always gentle, they will always be kind. Such people often have made themselves believe that I or the Buddha always acted this way. Yet the reality is that both the Buddha and myself had come to set people free from the illusions of the ego. Thus, we often challenged the ego and its illusions.

If you take an objective look at the scriptures, you will see that I was not a soft-spoken person. I challenged the scribes and Pharisees and I overturned the tables of the money-changers. I even challenged my own disciples and in many situations acted in ways that could be considered unkind or even inconsistent. The reason was that I practiced Divine kindness, as do all other true spiritual leaders.

Divine kindness takes a fundamentally different approach than dualistic kindness. Divine kindness is based on Christ discernment – which the Buddha also practiced – and it clearly sees when people are trapped in a dualistic illusion. The ultimate form of kindness is to help people lift themselves out of their dualistic illusions so they are no longer trapped. Yet precisely because the ego has the effect of making people blind, it is often necessary to shake people awake so they can start thinking again instead of blindly following the ego or an outer leader.

My point is that when you begin to attain Christ discernment, you see that being soft-spoken and gentle is not necessarily true kindness. In fact, the Bible contains an important clue for those who are willing to read between the lines:

> There is no fear in love; but perfect love casteth out fear: because fear hath torment. He that feareth is not made perfect in love. (1John 4:18)

True love – Divine Love – is above duality, and that is why there is no fear in love. Instead, this perfect – undivided – love will cast out your fears. The problem is that as long as you identify with the ego, you will be afraid to accept perfect love because you think you are unworthy of it. Yet it is only the ego that is unworthy of perfect love; the Conscious You is always worthy. However, until you accept that you are worthy, you cannot accept the love that will cast out the fears that spring from the ego.

Why does fear have torment? Torment springs from the division between the Conscious You and God, a division that was not *caused* by but is *upheld* by the ego. So until the Conscious You overcomes this division, *you* will be in torment. And you cannot overcome the division between you and God until you decide to take up your ability to discern based on the one truth of Christ rather than the dualistic "truth" of the ego. Only when you are willing to let go of the sense of identity built by the ego and reach for your true identity in Christ can you be made perfect in love. As I said:

> For whosoever will save his life shall lose it: and whosoever will lose his life for my sake shall find it. (Matthew 16:25)

By letting go of the dualistic sense of identity, you can come back into alignment with your own Higher Being, your I AM Presence, and then you will always be able to practice Divine kindness. If you look at my actions in the scriptures, you will see that I was gentle with some people and challenged others. The dualistic mind will approach this by trying to analyze my actions and define patterns. It will then set up outer characteristics and say that in this type of situation one should be gentle and in that type of situation one should be challenging. The fact is, however, that my behavior was not based on outer characteristics or intellectual analysis. It was based entirely on the condition of the individual soul. I gave every person I met what that person needed to take the next step on the path. And what people needed is what could take them beyond a particular dualistic illusion.

Here comes a subtle, but all-important point. The ego and the dualistic mind cannot fathom its own illusions, so it can never turn Divine kindness into a system. You cannot use the duality consciousness to overcome the duality consciousness. Yet I hope the Conscious You can see the essential truth here. Divine love, Divine kindness, is above what the ego can fathom. It can be practiced *only* through the mind of Christ.

There are many people who have accepted that kindness and love should be the ultimate guide for their behavior. However, if they do not reach for the mind of Christ, they will inevitably begin to practice the type of kindness and love defined by the ego. And the ego will inevitably turn kindness and love into dualistic concepts. The ego will try to create an outer system which defines how to practice kindness and love. And for most people, this leads them to believe that if they are always gentle, they are always kind. Yet as I have now tried to explain from different perspectives, this is simply a refusal to exercise Christ discernment.

The conclusion is that there are many well-meaning spiritual seekers who have been maneuvered into a blind alley by their egos. These people are sincerely striving to rise above the judgment and anger of those who practice a black-and-white, fear-based approach to religion. Yet jumping into the opposite extreme will not enhance your spiritual growth beyond a certain point. It will simply trap you in another form of dualistic thinking.

***

Do you now see the central characteristic of dualistic thinking? It sets up a system in this world and then judges ideas and people based on that system. Remember my statement:

> God is a Spirit: and they that worship him must worship him in spirit and in truth. (John 4:24)

You cannot create a mental box in this world and then fit the unlimited Spirit of God into it. The ego cannot create a system that can contain and confine God—but the ego will never understand this because to the ego God is simply a concept. So as long as you allow your ego to try to fit God into a box, you cut yourself off from having a direct experience of the Spirit of Truth.

Fundamentalists judge everything based on their belief that there is only one true religion. And many non-fundamentalists judge everything based on their belief that there are no false ideas or that one does not need to discern. In other words, the ego always sets up a belief system by defining a certain concept or idea as infallible, meaning that it should not be questioned.

Black-and-white thinkers say there is only one true religion, and thus all others are false. Gray thinkers say we should always be kind toward everyone and it defines kindness as being gentle and soft-spoken. Yet both types of thinking spring from the ego and its need to create the appearance that as long as you stay within the confines of its infallible belief system, you are guaranteed to be saved. In reality – as I have attempted to explain in great detail – there are ABSOLUTELY NO CONDITIONS IN THIS WORLD THAT WILL GUARANTEE YOUR SALVATION.

The *only* thing that can guarantee your salvation is that you enter the kingdom of God, which is a symbol for the Christ consciousness. Yet the Christ consciousness cannot be fit into or be confined to any belief system created in this world. That is why the *only* way to attain the Christ consciousness is to reach beyond *all* of the outer belief systems. You can use a belief system as a foundation for reaching for the mind of Christ—which is the true function of all true belief systems. Yet you must *never* allow the ego to make you believe that because you belong to a certain belief system and follow its outer beliefs and practices, you are guaranteed to be saved.

In the beginning of this discourse, I said that people tend to define infallible belief systems and think they are not influenced by error or illusions. In reality, any belief system in this world *will* be influenced by the mind of anti-christ. The simple reason is that as long as people are not free from their egos, they will subconsciously impose the mental images of their egos upon any belief system. And if people claim their belief system is the only true one or is better than others, they demonstrate they have not risen above duality, thus giving proof that their belief system has most certainly been influenced by the mind of anti-christ.

In the following discourses, we will take a closer look at how the ego manages to convince people that they do not need to reach for the mind of Christ but can be saved by following a belief system in this world. I hope all true spiritual seekers will make a sincere effort to understand this point because it truly is the dividing line that separates those who attain true spiritual progress from those who believe they are spiritual but have used the illusions of the ego to build an appearance of spirituality—thus being hypocrites. [End of quote.]

***

We have now come to a crucial point, where I need you to understand how the ego and the duality consciousness work. To begin this discussion, let me refer to this quote:

> 36 Jesus answered, My kingdom is not of this world: if my kingdom were of this world, then would my servants fight, that I should not be delivered to the Jews: but now is my kingdom not from hence.
> 37 Pilate therefore said unto him, Art thou a king then? Jesus answered, Thou sayest that I am a king. To this end was I born, and for this cause came I into the world, that I should bear witness unto the truth. Every one that is of the truth heareth my voice.
> 38 Pilate saith unto him, What is truth? (John, Chapter 18)

There are many who have used this passage to reinforce a negative image of Pontius Pilate. In reality, Pilate is simply a symbol for the many people in this world – back then and today – who have begun to see through black-and-white thinking and who have realized how easy it is for the human ego to define "truth" in such a way that it seems to justify the ego's self-centered behavior. When you begin to see how everything in this world is influenced by selfish beliefs and desires, it is easy to feel almost hopeless, to feel as if there is no way to overcome the negativity and selfishness of this world. Such feelings are described in this quote:

> 2 Vanity of vanities, saith the Preacher, vanity of vanities; all is vanity.
> 3 What profit hath a man of all his labour which he taketh under the sun? (Ecclesiastes 1)

This sense of dread has caused many spiritual people to withdraw from the world, to give up on seeking to reform the world and to focus on getting out of this world by seeking to reach a higher state of consciousness. Yet while this approach is understandable, it is also in complete opposition to Christhood. Thus, it will not bring you closer to heaven but take you further away from it. Let me explain.

What is the Living Christ? It is a Being who comes into this world in order to awaken people from their state of spiritual death, so they can be reborn into a state of consciousness that is spiritual life. Thus, the disciples of Christ are *not* those who withdraw from the world and who refuse to engage in the world. Instead, they are the ones who are willing to raise themselves above both black-and-white and gray thinking, so they can help other people do the same. They have been willing to find truth, and thus they can help other people find truth. I am not hereby saying my disciples need to engage in the dualistic struggle. You need to find a higher way, so that you can engage in debate without doing so in a dualistic manner. And that requires you to find Christ truth, so let us look at what this means.

***

What have I said is the core of the consciousness of duality? It is that it is based on the illusion of separation from God. The ego is born from this illusion, which is why it will always see itself as separated from God, from all other egos and from the material world. In other words, the ego is separated from everyone and everything.

I earlier said that the only way to know God is to BE God, to be one with God. The ego can never experience this oneness, so what must the ego do? It turns God into a concept, a topic that can be studied from a distance. Yet what do you actually do when you study a topic from a distance? You have to build a mental image of it, because you cannot experience the real thing. Thus, the ego can never avoid violating the first two commandments:

> 1 And God spake all these words, saying,
> 2 I am the LORD thy God, which have brought thee out of the land of Egypt, out of the house of bondage.
> 3 Thou shalt have no other gods before me.
> 4 Thou shalt not make unto thee any graven image, or any likeness of any thing that is in heaven above, or that is in the Earth beneath, or that is in the water under the Earth: (Exodus, Chapter 20)

Can you now see the hidden spiritual meaning behind these commandments? The essence of the ego is that it creates mental images of *everything*. It then elevates its images to the status of infallibility, whereby it turns them into graven images, meaning images that you refuse to transcend and therefore will be trapped by indefinitely—keeping you from experiencing the true God who is beyond this world. Thus, if understood correctly, the first two commandments are actually telling people to transcend their egos—for that is the only way to avoid violating these commandments.

Consider the rampant superstition in medieval Europe, such as that the Earth was flat, even the religious superstition that caused people to believe the Earth was the center of the universe. What was such superstition based on? It was based on people creating a mental image and then elevating it to the status of infallibility, meaning that it never needed to be questioned or compared to anything outside their mental boxes.

What was the purpose behind the Ascended Host releasing the scientific method? It was to give people a tool for overcoming superstition by comparing their mental images – their theories – to something outside their minds by conducting experiments. Obviously, science can also be misused by the ego, but nevertheless the scientific method did lift humankind out of the medieval mental box and opened the way for further progress.

So what is my overall point? It is that the ego creates mental images of everything, and when the conscious self begins to accept – identify with – these images, it will be trapped in a mental box made of dualistic illusions. The ego will *never* see that its mental images are illusions, because it can never overcome the basic separation from which it was born. Thus, as long as the conscious self does not question the ego's mental images, it will be trapped by those images.

What does this really mean? The conscious self is an extension of God's Being, meaning that it can never actually be separated from God. Yet the conscious self *is* who it thinks it is, so as long as the conscious self thinks it is separated from God – based on the ego's illusions – the conscious self *is* – for all practical purposes – separated from God. Why is this so? Remember that the ego is separated from everything, so it creates mental images of everything, meaning that your ego has created a mental image of your conscious self. As long as your conscious self accepts this image – this mortal sense of identity – you will think and behave as if you really are that separate being.

So what is the path to Christhood? It is a process of gradually overcoming one dualistic illusion after another – thereby dismissing the ego's mental images – until you reach a critical mass and the conscious self sees beyond the dualistic mind and has an actual experience of the Spirit of Truth, namely its own Higher Being. Remember that the ego can never overcome separation and thus can never experience the Spirit of Truth. Yet because the conscious self is an extension of God's Being, it can indeed experience the Spirit directly. Thus, the ego will forever relate to God through its mental images, but the conscious self does not need a mental image in order to relate to God. Instead, it can build a relationship with God based on direct experience of God's Being. So the path to Christhood is a process of the conscious self disentangling itself from the ego's mental images of everything until it can finally stop identifying itself based on these images and instead accept who it really is as a spiritual Being. A being who is not bound by anything on this Earth or by the mental images created by the mind of anti-christ. Instead, you can be free to express your Divine individuality through the mind of Christ.

So what is the very foundation for this process? You can never complete it through intellectual reasoning. No matter how much you know about spiritual concepts – even if you have studied all of the spiritual teachings in this world – you will be no closer to enlightenment. You cannot solve a problem with the same consciousness that created the problem, so knowing everything is not the same as overcoming ignorance. Ignorance can ultimately be overcome in only one way, and that is through a direct experience of the Spirit of Truth. Such an experience demonstrates in an undeniable way that there is something outside the mental box of the ego.

And as you keep having such experiences, you will gradually begin to accept that YOU are outside the mental box of the ego and thus you no longer need the box. That is when you can give up the ghost and allow your mortal identity to die on the cross—whereby the Conscious You is reborn of fire into a Christed Being who will now serve to set others free.

***

Do you see what I am leading up to here? How do you begin to build Christ discernment? By being willing to question the mental images found in this world and see their inconsistencies, which then opens the way for a direct experience of the Spirit of Truth. Yet what does this means in practicality? Is questioning your mental images not simply another form of intellectual exercise?

Well, it can be—if you approach it with the intellect. Yet what I am suggesting is that you approach it by making use of the Key of Knowledge, which is your intuition. You learn to use the logical, rational mind as a way to set the foundation for an intuitive experience that gives you an Aha moment, in which you go beyond the mind and simply experience truth.

What does this mean? Well, it means you must realize a fundamental truth about truth—namely that in this world, there is no such thing as truth. Maitreya explains this in greater detail in his book, but the central concept is that even the words used in this world are relative and have different interpretations for different people. There are ascended master students who believe that in this age, we are using direct revelation to bring forth new spiritual teachings to replace all other spiritual teachings. The previous teachings all had flaws and were incomplete, but now we give direct revelation to bring forth the ultimate teaching, a teaching that will finally be complete and infallible.

This is a complete misunderstanding of our real purpose. We understand the truth expressed in the commandment not to have graven images. This does not simply refer to visual images but also to images based on words—such as holy scriptures. It is *not* possible to bring forth a teaching in words that is complete and infallible. Certainly, a teaching can be more or less influenced by dualistic illusions, but the simple fact is that no teaching in this world can give a complete and infallible description of God— for God is the Spirit of Truth who is *beyond* this world.

Why did I say the kingdom of God is within you? Because as long as you base your relationship with God on an outer teaching, you will never find God. You will find God only when you look beyond outer teachings and reach for a direct experience—and this experience can *only* take place inside your own mind.

Thus, the true purpose for giving a spiritual teaching is *not* to give people a complete description of God. It is to give them a foundation that can raise their consciousness to the point where they can reach for and actually have a direct experience of the reality that is *always* beyond the outer teaching. *No* teaching is God—God is *always* beyond – more than – anything in this world (although God is not separated from this world).

Do you begin to see the utter futility in arguing over which spiritual teaching is the ultimate one? So many sincere spiritual seekers have been trapped in this mindset, but in reality it only keeps them from attaining true progress. You will not even begin the path of Christhood until you stop engaging in the dualistic struggle to prove the superiority of one expression of truth and instead reach for a direct experience of the Spirit of Truth—who is beyond *all* expressions.

***

How does this relate to the topic of ignorance, including black-and-white and gray thinking? There are many people who think that overcoming ignorance is a matter of coming to know something you do not know. Thus, they seek for the complete and infallible teaching, thinking that when they find it and study it, they will automatically overcome ignorance. They see the mind as a container, and if you pour enough knowledge into it, you will fill it and overcome ignorance.

In reality, overcoming ignorance is not a mechanical but a creative process. Overcoming ignorance means making a fundamental shift in how you look at yourself and the world—and such a shift can *only* come from a direct experience of a reality beyond your current mental box. Some people have indeed had such an experience seemingly without any conscious preparation (in reality they prepared themselves in past lives). Yet you can do much to set the foundation for such an experience, and here are the main ingredients:

- You must acknowledge that your mind is currently in a mental box that colors how you look at everything. This box can never give you ultimate knowledge of reality. Even understanding this intellectually is a step in the right direction.

- You must develop a desire to go beyond the box, to know more.
- You must recognize that there is a reality outside the box and that you can know it. Yet this cannot happen through intellectual understanding but only through direct experience. You get this experience only by going beyond the intellect, which means neutralizing the intellectual mind that is always analyzing—like waves that obscure the stillness of the ocean.

Can you see that when people are trapped in black-and-white thinking, they are unable to see and admit that they are trapped in a mental box? They refuse to even consider that their mental box gives them a distorted and limited view of reality, clinging to the conviction that their belief system is infallible. Yet when people go into the opposite extreme of gray thinking, they refuse to acknowledge that there is an ultimate reality outside of all mental boxes. Such people can often see that people have created mental boxes, but they fail to see that there is an alternative. Black-and-white thinking causes people to cling to one box as the ultimate box, but gray thinking makes people believe there is no ultimate reality—everything is simply a matter of belief.

Can you now see that both approaches block your direct experience of the Spirit of Truth, meaning that you need to rise above both of them. And after you do so, you also need to help others rise above them—for this is the only way to help the world rise above the dualistic struggle.

***

Now for the real point I want to make in this discourse. I have said that the ego can never experience the Spirit of Truth and thus creates mental images as a substitute for direct experience. The conclusion is that people are living on a planet on which every aspect of life has been influenced by the myriad of illusions created by the duality consciousness. If you want to be a disciple of Christ, you need to free your mind from such mental images, and in order to complete this process, you must understand the real role of the Living Christ.

Did you understand the true meaning behind the concept that not even a teaching given by the Ascended Host through direct revelation can give an infallible description of God? The meaning is that once a teaching has been expressed in words, it has entered the realm where the duality consciousness can work. Meaning that the ego and the false teachers can pervert *any* spiritual teaching or concept.

Think about this. A spiritual teaching is *not* the same as God. In fact, a spiritual teaching is given *only* because people do not have a direct experience of God. If you were experiencing God directly right now, why would you need a spiritual teaching to describe God—including this course? Imagine that you are thinking about traveling to a specific location and you pick up a tourist brochure that gives a very vivid description of a natural wonder in that location, including describing what it looks like in great detail. Based on the vivid description, you develop a desire to experience the natural wonder for yourself, and you travel there. When you are standing in front of the wonder – and thus experiencing it directly – will you still be reading the brochure's description of what it looks like? Of course not—why do you need to read a description of what you can now experience directly?

Do you see my point? A spiritual teaching is meant to take you to the point where you can have a direct experience—it is *never* meant to be a substitute for that experience. Yet the ego cannot fathom this, and thus it seeks to turn any spiritual teaching you follow into an end in itself, rather than a means to an end. The ego and the false teachers can use *any* spiritual teaching – no matter how accurate or true it is – to reinforce the image of the outer path, where you just need to follow the outer teaching and your salvation will somehow happen at some time in the future. This is the mechanical path that does not require you to do anything creative—which truly means seeking a direct experience. For the true definition of creativity is that you experience the Spirit of Truth, the Spirit of your own Higher Being, and allow that Spirit to express its infinite creativity through your lower being.

So now what is the role of the Living Christ? The perverted view is that Christ comes into this world to give humankind the final and infallible teaching. The reality is that the Living Christ comes into this world to challenge people's mental boxes, the mental boxes that keep them from having a direct experience of the Spirit.

Do you see what this truly means? We of the Ascended Host have given several teachings through direct revelation over the past century. In every organization we have sponsored, a certain percentage of the students turned that teaching into the final and infallible revelation and thus turned it into a blind alley—another "infallible" mental box. The realization I am seeking to help you attain here is that the Living Christ does *not* come into this world to bring some infallible truth, for no such truth can be expressed in words. The *only* infallible truth is the Spirit of Truth, but this Spirit can *never* be reduced to words but can *only* be known through direct experience. The consequence is that for the Living Christ there is *no* absolute truth in this world. Meaning that the Living Christ does not have a consistent truth formulated in words. Instead, the Living Christ will challenge any and all mental boxes that people have created, even the boxes based on a spiritual teaching given by the Ascended Host.

Are you willing to grapple with this concept? Do you see that it challenges one of the basic illusions held by most spiritual seekers, namely the dream of finding the ultimate spiritual teaching? Do you see that it challenges another illusion, namely that a real spiritual teacher should have an entirely consistent message, meaning that he or she can never contradict any previous statement?

Do you see why it is entirely possible that the Living Christ will make contradictory statements? The Living Christ is here to challenge people's illusions so they will look beyond their current mental boxes and reach for the direct experience of truth. Thus, the statements made by the Living Christ are *not* based on some uniform expression of an infallible truth. They are based on an evaluation of what it will take to shake a particular person or group of people awake so they can begin to see beyond their current mental box. Thus, the statements of the Living Christ are aimed at producing a consistent result – transcendence – but the actual form of the statements is adapted to people's current mental boxes.

When I walked the Earth 2,000 years ago, I did not seek to bring forth a teaching that could stand for all time. I made many statements that were specifically formulated to challenge the mental box of the Jews, including their rigid adherence to a literal interpretation of the outer law. I attempted to show them that the Living Christ is above *any* teaching or law in this world—a truth that many of today's ascended master students have not even begun to understand. For example I said the following:

> 1 At that time Jesus went on the sabbath day through the corn; and his disciples were an hungered, and began to pluck the ears of corn, and to eat.
> 2 But when the Pharisees saw it, they said unto him, Behold, thy disciples do that which is not lawful to do upon the sabbath day.
> 3 But he said unto them, Have ye not read what David did, when he was an hungered, and they that were with him;

> 4 How he entered into the house of God, and did eat the showbread, which was not lawful for him to eat, neither for them which were with him, but only for the priests?
> 5 Or have ye not read in the law, how that on the sabbath days the priests in the temple profane the sabbath, and are blameless?
> 6 But I say unto you, That in this place is one greater than the temple.
> 7 But if ye had known what this meaneth, I will have mercy, and not sacrifice, ye would not have condemned the guiltless.
> 8 For the Son of man is Lord even of the sabbath day. (Matthew, Chapter 12)

People trapped in black-and-white thinking demand that a true spiritual teacher is entirely consistent, and when they see inconsistencies, they reject the teacher. People in gray thinking say there is no truth, so they refuse to consider that there can be true teachers and false teachers, thus being unable to recognize a true teacher. Those who go beyond this duality and begin to attain Christ discernment will see that a true teacher can very well make inconsistent statements but still be pursuing a consistent goal.

If a person is trapped in a particular mental box, the teacher must make statements that challenge the illusions that make up the box. Yet if the teacher then meets a person who is trapped in another mental box, the teacher must make other statements to challenge the second person's mental box. When the two statements are compared, they might seem contradictory to people who look at it with the linear, analytical mind. Yet behind the outer statements is the consistent goal of helping *any* person – no matter which mental box he or she is currently trapped in – by *always* challenging *any* mental box that is keeping people from a direct experience of the Spirit of Truth. For that matter, it is entirely possible that a true teacher will say one thing to you at the beginning stages of the path and then say the seemingly opposite at a later stage. Again, the purpose is to shake you out of whatever mental box you are in at the moment, so you always keep transcending your current level and never get stuck in thinking you now know it all.

If you can internalize and accept this truth, you have taken an essential step toward building the discernment that is the very foundation for Christhood, the discernment that takes you beyond the judgment after appearances and allows you to see the undivided truth that is behind all of the dualistic appearances in this world. And this will then help you overcome the really sophisticated ignorance that we will talk about in the next key.

## Exercise for Key 10

I ask you to give a 33-day vigil of the Rosary of All-pervading Wisdom. Say the mantra of the Dhyani Buddha for this key one time after each verse and before the Hail Mary.

**OM VAIROCHANA OM**

After giving the rosary, consider your current mental box and then ask me to expose to you any aspect of the box that is keeping you from a direct experience of the Spirit of Truth. After formulating this question, write down whatever comes to you without analyzing it in any way.

I also want you to ask me and the Buddha Vairochana to help you have discernment in your daily life, so you can begin to see reality and unreality in every situation.

# Key 11
# Truly sophisticated ignorance

In this key we will tackle the most subtle form of sophisticated ignorance. Again, the Buddha who is the antidote for this poison is Vairochana and his wisdom is the All-pervading Wisdom. As you study the following teachings, use his mantra:

**OM VAIROCHANA OM**

In a sense, one might say that I have been talking about sophisticated ignorance since the beginning of this course:

- I have said that the essence of the path to personal Christhood is that you come to see what you cannot see, that you come to see the beam in your own eye.
- I have said that the second challenge of Christ is whether you will allow the Living Christ to take you beyond your current mental box, which means you must be willing to see and acknowledge the limitations of that box.
- I have talked about the outer path versus the inner path and said you need to leave behind all of the illusions of the outer path.

Yet what exactly does that mean for *you* at your current level on the path? The most dangerous aspect of sophisticated ignorance is that it makes you absolutely convinced that you are right, while in reality you are wrong. You are out of alignment with God's reality because – in your mind – you have elevated an illusion to the status of "reality." And when you have this belief, you obviously will not be willing to heed the Living Christ, when he or she comes to take you beyond your current mental box. You see no need to go beyond that box, since you are convinced it is complete and infallible—which means you have to reject the teacher. In effect, sophisticated ignorance makes you think that you know better than the teacher how to walk the path to Christhood. You think you have found the ultimate knowledge, belief or understanding and that you have no need to question it. This reaction is typical for people who are trapped in both black-and-white and gray thinking, as both forms of thinking offer the ego plenty of justification for staying where it is comfortable and rejecting the teacher.

So what is wrong with your current mental box? Isn't it possible that you really have found the ultimate understanding of life and the spiritual path? Well, as we saw in the previous key, there is no such thing as the ultimate spiritual teaching. However, just to make sure you understand this point, let me propose a simple way to determine whether you need to question your current mental box. You need to consider the fact that you are sitting on Earth reading this book, while I am dictating it from the spiritual realm. This means that *you* have not ascended, while *I* have made my ascension. So the essential question here is why you have not ascended and I have?

The logical answer is that I must have figured out something that you have not – yet – figured out. Why is that so—could it not be that you have all the knowledge you need for your ascension but it simply isn't your time to leave the Earth behind (the ego can *always* reason with any argument raised by the teacher, which is a good way to expose the ego)? Well, consider a simple test. Can you – this instant – raise yourself into the spiritual realm? If you *can,* then come up here and join me, so we can continue this conversation "face to face."

If you are still reading this, it can mean only one thing. No matter how sophisticated you think your knowledge is, it is still not sophisticated enough to propel you to the spiritual realm at will. You still have a ways to go before you get here—for if you did not have a ways to go, you would already be here!

If your conscious self is willing to acknowledge that I have ascended and you have not, then you should be able to accept a couple of conclusions. One is that since I have ascended, I really do know something you don't know. Thus, you should listen to *me* rather than one of the many false teachers found in the material world or in the emotional, mental and etheric realms—including your own ego.

Another conclusion is that since I have ascended, I must have figured out something your conscious self has not yet figured out and which your ego will *never* figure out. So what might that be? Well, let me expose to you the ultimate secret about the spiritual path.

Now, I want you to take a few seconds to consider what kind of reaction you notice inside yourself to the statement that I will give you the ultimate secret. Do you notice any particular thoughts or sensations? If so, explore them to find out what they are.

No matter what sensations you might have noticed, they came from the ego. How can I say that? Because – as I have attempted to explain in previous keys – the ego is always on the impossible quest of finding the ultimate secret that will make it acceptable to God. So what *is* the ultimate secret?

**It is that there is NO ultimate secret!**

There is no magical formula that will suddenly take you to a higher state of consciousness. There is no outer path that will automatically make you qualify for salvation, ascension, enlightenment or whatever you want to call it.

The essential key to reaching the spiritual realm is the process of ongoing growth that I have called the River of Life. And the essence of this growth is that you are constantly expanding your mental box, your sense of identity. You are constantly questioning your beliefs and even the way you look at yourself. You are willing to let your old identity die, so that you can be born again – of water and of fire – into a higher sense of identity. Yet this does not happen in one dramatic moment – where the heavens open and you see flashes of light and hear angels singing, or whatever people imagine – it happens as the result of daily choices to put off the old man and put on the new man—as Paul put it. He also said, "I die daily!"

So you should now be willing to question one of the most dearly held illusions of the ego, namely that you are working toward some ultimate peak experience that will suddenly turn you into an entirely different person. I can assure you that every person who discovers the spiritual path – even the *inner* path – must face the temptation to deal with this illusion. And although you might have overcome it at the layers of your mind that are close to your conscious awareness, it is time to dig deeper and make sure you have overcome it at deeper levels as well.

You see, this dream of an ultimate breakthrough is the carrot that the ego is dangling in front of the nose of the conscious self. And as long as the conscious self believes in the illusion, you will keep running after the carrot—and in doing so, you will be running away from the true key to growth. What is that key? It is that you stop looking for an experience from outside yourself and start looking for the kingdom of God inside yourself—realizing you will reach it only by taking small, daily steps toward expanding your sense of identity—until you fully accept yourself as a co-creator with God and thus find yourself in the state of oneness that IS the kingdom of God.

We might say that the ego is on a quest to perfect your mental box and reach some ultimate state where your salvation is guaranteed. The real key to the path is that you continue to expand your mental box—which means you *never* hold on to your current box. You gladly let it go, knowing you will only gain greater freedom. There is an ultimate expansion, which is God consciousness, but the more important intermediate stage for you is to reach the Christ consciousness, which opens you to a perception of the spiritual realm—whereby you will be *in* the kingdom of God even while still in a physical body.

Do you see that Christhood is not a mechanical process, but a creative process in which you expand the self *consciously? You* are charged with defining the self through which you co-create in the material world, so *you* must define your identity as a Christed Being. This will not happen as a result of you doing outer things, not even following this course.

***

If you will take a look at spiritual people, you will see that many of them are chasing what they call "peak experiences." Some are traveling to what they see as the spiritual places on the planet in order to be there at just the right time to get a peak experience. Others seek it in meditation, retreats or other spiritual courses. Others chase for the ultimate spiritual teacher who can give them the experience and still others look for the ultimate chemical high. Yet can you see that they are all looking for an experience coming as the result of something outside themselves?

Now, I know very well that if your conscious self truly is beginning to awaken from the ego's ultimate illusion, you will be feeling something that is akin to the withdrawal symptoms that addicts experience when they give up their addictive substance. It is quite possible that you have actually been addicted to this chase for some kind of spiritual fix, and it is inevitable that you will have to go through a period of recovery to overcome the addiction.

What I have done here – that is, if you have understood and acknowledged what I have been saying – is that I have taken all the mystery – some will say all the fun – out of the spiritual path. Look at how many people think there needs to be some kind of mystery involved with religion and spirituality. Many spiritual seekers talk about mystery schools and a mystical path—and they love the sense that they know something most people don't know or receive secret initiations. They love the concept of a path of initiation, where there is still something unknown ahead of you, but on the other hand *you* are ahead of those who are below you.

What I am saying here is that there truly is no mystery. The path is a very pragmatic process of taking one small step at a time. It is a matter of always looking for the next illusion you need to overcome, seeing why it is an illusion and then consciously dismissing it. This is how you make progress on the path—by letting the old sense of identity die and being reborn into a new identity that is only a degree beyond the old one.

But what about the mystery? Am I saying that there are no breakthrough experiences that suddenly expand your vision? Well, there are certainly breakthroughs, but the further along you move on the path, the less dramatic they become. And the final shift between being unascended and ascended is not nearly as dramatic as some people – especially ascended master students – tend to think. It is extremely important that you understand why this is so.

You may look back at your own path and realize that you have had some dramatic breakthrough experiences. Many spiritual seekers had such dramatic experiences when they first found the path, feeling that an entirely new world, an entirely new world view, opened up to them. You may even have felt that after that initial phase, you have had few or no dramatic experiences. You may even feel like something must have gone wrong and that you must have lost something you had in the beginning. In fact, this sense of a let-down, of an anti-climax, of feeling the path has become routine or dull might have been part of what motivated you to begin this course—hoping I could provide the drama you perceive to be missing. So let me explain to you what has happened.

What is the mechanical aspect of a dramatic experience of any kind? It is contrast! For there to be drama, there must be contrast, meaning that there must be two opposites. And this mention of opposites should make alarm bells start ringing, for what is the very nature of the ego? It is that it is based on duality—the duality that always has two opposite polarities.

So why was it such a dramatic experience to find the spiritual path? It was because you were brought up in a culture that has no knowledge of the spiritual path. Thus, you were brought up in very deep ignorance, which means finding the spiritual path provided a dramatic contrast. Yet can you see that the intensity of the contrast was determined by the depth of your ignorance? The deeper the darkness, the starker the contrast when the light starts shining!

You may have heard that heroin addicts have a dramatic experience on their first fix and spend the rest of their lives chasing that ultimate fix. Well, the reason is that it is only the first time that there can be the ultimate contrast between people's normal state of consciousness and whatever experience they have on drugs—

which I can assure you is never a true spiritual experience. My point here is that there are spiritual people who likewise had a very dramatic experience upon finding the path and who have become addicted to chasing that ultimate experience.

Obviously, I don't want you to be among them, for this chase can never take you to Christhood. Why not? Well, the essence of Christhood is that you rise above the ego, meaning that you rise above the consciousness of death, the consciousness of anti-christ. And what is the nature of this consciousness? It is that it is dualistic, meaning that it will always have two opposite polarities. And precisely because it always has two opposites, it will always provide plenty of contrast. Meaning that the consciousness of anti-christ can offer you dramatic experiences—which the consciousness of Christ simply cannot offer.

Why not? Because the consciousness of Christ is above duality. It has no opposite polarities, only the oneness with God, the oneness with all life. This is a state of peace that is very joyful. In fact, Buddhism calls it bliss or Nirvana and I called it the kingdom of God. Yet this bliss is *not* the kind of happiness that most people long for on Earth. For on Earth, happiness is currently seen as a dualistic concept. Happiness is opposed to unhappiness, whereas bliss has no opposite. Bliss has no contrast, meaning that there cannot be the dramatic shift from darkness to light.

Do you see what I am saying here? When you first found the spiritual path, you had a lot of false beliefs and imperfect energies in your mind and energy field. You had a lot of darkness, which means that when you first saw the light, you experienced a dramatic contrast between the light and the darkness. And this contrast is what gave you what seemed like a peak experience. Yet do you see that the intensity of this experience was in direct proportion to the amount of darkness in your being? The more darkness, the more intense the experience, for the greater the contrast?

Yet what is the path to Christhood all about? It is about overcoming your false beliefs and purifying your energy field from all lower vibrations. So if you successfully walk the path, you will decrease the intensity of the darkness in your being. Meaning that when you have breakthrough experiences, there will no longer be the dramatic contrast between light and darkness—and thus the experiences will inevitably seem less intense. In fact, they will gradually begin to seem perfectly natural.

Can you see that this is actually a sign that you have made real progress? Yet the ego and the false teachers are always looking for a way to nullify your progress, so they have created the very clever concept of seeking for the ultimate breakthrough experience. And since you are not experiencing anything dramatic, they can make you believe that you are no longer making progress. So you must be doing something wrong, which means you can easily be diverted into the following extremes or one of the blind alleys in between the extremes:

- You become discouraged, feeling like what you are doing is not working, perhaps giving up on the path or resigning yourself to the fact that you will never break through.
- You begin the quest for finding the ultimate way to force a breakthrough experience, thus seeking to take heaven by force. This actually "works" for some people in the sense that they open themselves up to dark forces that enter their beings, whereby there is once again enough darkness to provide contrast. Yet the drama does not equate with true spiritual progress. Thus, these people are not moving closer to Christhood, for they are tied up in a see-saw that takes them up, then down, then up, then down—ad infinitum.

What I want you to see here is the fact that as you move higher on the real path to Christhood, you remove darkness from your being, and thus there will be less contrast to provide you with dramatic experiences. Thus, you need to let go of the dream of having dramatic experiences and instead begin to look for the "ultimate" experience, namely that of constant, unwavering peace of mind—which is truly a state of bliss, only it is not a state that has an opposite.

This points to a new definition of "ultimate." The dualistic definition is that an ultimate experience is one that provides maximum drama, which can come only from maximum contrast. A non-dualistic definition is that ultimate means that opposites have been eliminated or transcended, so that there is no longer any contrast.

***

It is helpful to consider how your physical senses have an influence on this desire for contrast. The senses are designed to detect phenomena in the material world, and this world is characterized by differences that provide plenty of contrast, such as night and day. You might know, or even have experienced, that your eyes are easily fooled by a very slow, gradual movement, such as the hands of a clock. If something moves slowly enough, there is not enough contrast for your eyes to detect the movement, which demonstrates that your physical senses are designed to detect contrast. It also explains why people who identify with the physical body can become addicted to experiences that provide contrast. This is why some spiritual teachers have stressed the need to overcome the pull of the physical body and the senses, so you free the mind to have experiences beyond the senses. Yet I have no intention of taking you through some ascetic discipline, for what you truly need to do is to see how the ego and the false teachers seek to magnify the mindset built on the sensory experience into a never-ending quest for dramatic experiences.

Many spiritual seekers are obsessed with the concept of expanding their consciousness, thinking that there is some ultimate state of consciousness, whether they call it God consciousness, enlightenment or whatever. They seem to think that this is a very dramatic state of consciousness, so the closer they get, the more dramatic must be their experiences. If God is the ultimate, then the closer you get to God, the more dramatic must be your experience. Yet again, the dramatic experience is possible only when there is contrast, and contrast implies distance. So you can have a dramatic experience of God only if your normal state of consciousness is far away from God.

Yet Christhood is a state of oneness with God. In oneness there is no contrast, for there is no separation to provide the contrast. You might think there will be a contrast between separation and oneness, but oneness cannot be attained in one dramatic leap. It can be attained only by taking one small step at a time. In the beginning of this process, there will be contrast for each step you take, but the further you move along, the less contrast there will be. The closer you are to seeing God *inside* yourself, the more natural God consciousness will feel and the less dramatic the experience. Oneness comes so naturally that you almost don't notice the difference—until you one day realize that you are no longer feeling the contrast and thus know that you have arrived. As I said:

> Every valley shall be filled, and every mountain and hill shall be brought low; and the crooked shall be made straight, and the rough ways shall be made smooth. (Luke 3:5)

So contemplate Christhood as the great equalizer rather than as the dramatic peak experiences. This is the wisdom of equality, the wisdom that pervades all appearances of contrast.

***

Ignorance means you cannot tell the difference between what is real and what is unreal, and thus you are imprisoned by illusions. When you come to know the truth, the truth will set you free, but what *is* truth? Let us revisit the discussion from the previous key and go into a bit more detail. Take another look at this passage:

> 37 Pilate therefore said unto him, Art thou a king then? Jesus answered, Thou sayest that I am a king. To this end was I born, and for this cause came I into the world, that I should bear witness unto the truth. Every one that is of the truth heareth my voice.
> 38 Pilate saith unto him, What is truth? (John, Chapter 18)

Pilate represents a person who is in ignorance because he does not know what truth is. Yet at least he was willing to recognize that he did not know—instead of doing as the scribes and Pharisees who had elevated their own erroneous beliefs to the status of an absolute truth. Thus, they thought they knew truth, while in reality they had no recognition of truth whatsoever. So the next question we will consider is precisely, "What is truth?" Again, look at the following quote:

> 22 Ye worship ye know not what: we know what we worship: for salvation is of the Jews.
> 23 But the hour cometh, and now is, when the true worshippers shall worship the Father in spirit and in truth: for the Father seeketh such to worship him.
> 24 God is a Spirit: and they that worship him must worship him in spirit and in truth. (John, Chapter 4)

Here is a concept that can be very difficult for spiritual seekers to understand. Truth is *not* the same as knowledge, not even the same as wisdom or understanding. Why not?

You have grown up in a society that is heavily influenced by a scientific mindset, which is based on the – genuine – desire to know how the material world works. This has led to the subtle paradigm that understanding the world is a matter of accumulating knowledge. If only we gather enough knowledge, we will eventually uncover the secrets of life. You see many spiritual seekers who have the same attitude, thinking that if only they study enough spiritual teachings – especially the ones that seem very complex and difficult to understand – they will eventually have a breakthrough experience and discover the ultimate truth, the secret formula that will give them whatever they want. Why is this an impossible dream?

Well, let us revisit our analogy about the movie theater. What you can see with your physical senses and even with current scientific instruments is equivalent to what you see on the movie screen. Yet no matter how often you watch the movie and no matter how carefully you study the screen itself, you will not fully understand what is going on. Where do the images on the screen actually come from—what is their cause? Why do the people on the screen act the way they do? To understand this, you need to look beyond the screen – the material realm – and look for deeper causes.

If you think the cause of what is happening on the screen can be found at the level of the screen, you will never know the cause. You need to recognize that the images on the screen are projected from the projection room, but you even need to go beyond and understand that somewhere a group of actors recorded the movie, which was based on a script written by the screen writer. Meaning that when you see people on a movie screen, you can understand their actions only by going into the mind of the writer—not by studying the visible phenomena.

My point here is that the spiritual teachings found in this world are all expressed in the words, concepts and images found in this world. And when the "truth" is expressed in words and images, it is drawn *into* this world, meaning that it becomes a visible phenomenon, just like the images on the movie screen. Yet God is a Spirit, meaning that God is *beyond* this world. As we have discussed before, you cannot describe God accurately or fully through words and images in this world, which is why the only way to know God is to *be* God—to be one with God. And that is precisely what is hidden behind the admonishment to worship God in Spirit and in truth. You realize that God is a Spirit, so you cannot fully worship God through teachings or rituals found in this world. You must go beyond anything and everything in this world and seek a direct experience of God's Spirit. Which means that ultimate truth cannot be expressed in a spiritual teaching—not even in the "infallible word of God." Thus, the purpose of a spiritual teaching is *not* to bring forth an ultimate truth but to be a stepping stone for reaching beyond the teaching to a direct experience of the Spirit of Truth. I wish all who call themselves Christians would understand this, but for now I would settle for *you* fully understanding it.

Most spiritual seekers have had glimpses of mystical experiences, which is why they are on the spiritual path. The challenge for all seekers is to come to understand the true meaning of the second challenge of Christ and then apply it to their experiences.

The second challenge of Christ is – as you will recall – whether you will allow the Living Christ to take you beyond your current mental box or whether you will seek to force your encounter with the Living Christ to fit inside your box—thus reinforcing the box and its hold over your conscious self (its ability to make the conscious self accept its current sense of identity and that it cannot or should not go beyond it).

So here is a pattern that I see in many sincere seekers. Some people had no prior religious or spiritual beliefs and suddenly have a spiritual experience that awakens them to the path. Others had religious or spiritual beliefs but then had an experience that made them see that there is more. In any case, the mechanics are the same. When you have a spiritual, mystical, intuitive or breakthrough experience, your conscious mind touches the Infinite, touches the Spirit of Truth. Yet your conscious mind is limited by its present beliefs, its present sense of identity—what I call your current mental box. Thus, the conscious self cannot fully fathom or integrate the experience of God's infinite Spirit. It simply doesn't know what to do with it because it is so different from, so far beyond, its daily experience in the material world.

We might say that an experience of the Infinite threatens your sense of identity. However, it is very important for you to understand that your conscious self can be described as an individualized sense of identity. Thus, the only fear that truly has any hold over the conscious self is the loss of its sense of identity.

Now what is your ego? It is also an individualized sense of identity. Thus, the only real fear of the ego is the loss of identity, which in the ego's case means the loss of existence. The difference between the ego and the conscious self is that the ego is born from separation, meaning that it is ultimately unreal. The ego's sense of identity is based entirely on the illusion of separation, so if the ego truly lost its sense of identity, it would cease to exist.

The conscious self is an extension of God's Being, meaning that it is ultimately real—it can never be lost. The conscious self – in this moment – sees itself through the filter of a particular sense of identity that is influenced by the "things of this world," including the illusions of the ego. Yet if it lost that sense of "mortal" identity, it would not cease to exist—it would be reborn into a higher sense of identity that is closer to its infinite or spiritual identity as a co-creator with God.

The problem is that if the conscious self has come to identify itself based on the illusions of the ego – the sense of identity based on separation from God – then it obviously cannot fathom that letting the mortal sense of identity die will cause it to be reborn into a more eternal sense of identity, leading it – eventually – to its true identity as an immortal spiritual being. In other words, the conscious self will believe the ego's illusion that the loss of its current sense of identity means that it will cease to exist—and since it resists non-existence, it will hold on to its current sense of identity.

What has that got to do with having a spiritual experience? Well, your conscious self is an infinite spiritual being who is currently trapped in a finite sense of identity. When you experience a glimpse of the Infinite Spirit of Truth, this experience, and the sense of reality associated with it, threatens your sense that you are a finite being and that there is nothing more to your existence. We might say that when you have a mystical experience, it is a signal that you are ready to let go of the old and adopt an expanded sense of identity. Yet if you have not understood what I have just explained, you will not be able to let go of your current sense of identity—you will cling to it as the ego clings to it, thinking it is a matter of life and death. But since you cannot deny that you had an experience of something beyond your current mental box, you have to find a way to explain the experience by using the beliefs in your current mental box—perhaps by expanding the box somewhat but in a way that does not threaten your basic sense of identity as a separate being.

That is why people who have a mystical experience often seek for an expanded belief system that can explain their experience. But without realizing it, they adopt a belief system that explains their experience in such a way that they can keep their current sense of identity as beings who are separated from God. You even see some people who have a mystical experience but use it to reinforce their outer belief system and its supposed infallibility.

Do you begin to see what is truly happening here? A spiritual experience is a gift that is meant to give you a boost on the path that leads from a finite to an infinite sense of identity. Yet if you do not understand the basic dynamic of the path, you cannot separate the conscious self from the mortal identity of the ego. Thus, you cannot let the mortal identity die, and you must now find a way to explain the mystical experience within the context of an Earthly belief system.

Now, here comes the subtle point. At a certain stage of the path, this is perfectly natural and unavoidable. As I have explained, the true path is a gradual process. There are some spiritual seekers who think it is possible to have an experience that instantly – in one giant leap – propels you from a mortal to an immortal sense of identity. This simply is *not* possible, for it would shatter your sense of identity and you would end up having no sense of identity—as has indeed happened to people who attempted to take heaven by force and ended up in a mental institution.

So in the beginning stages of the path, it is natural that you have a mystical experience and use it to expand your mental box a bit but do not challenge your basic sense of identity (which you are not yet ready to confront). Yet when you reach the higher levels of the path – when you desire to become a disciple of the Living Christ – you can no longer proceed this way. You will hit a glass ceiling, and you will not rise higher on the path until you are willing to question what you have so far seen as unquestionable.

You now have to consciously come to see how you have used your current mental box to force your mystical experiences into an Earthly framework. You have to understand why and how this aborts your progress beyond a certain point. And then you have to consciously decide to let this ego-based, fear-based sense of self die. You must master the second challenge of Christ and stop trying to force the Living Christ to fit into your mental box, instead allowing the Living Christ to take you beyond your current box—and eventually beyond *all* mental boxes found on Earth.

***

There are many sincere spiritual seekers who have walked the path diligently for many years, even decades. They have studied various spiritual teachings and have built a good intellectual understanding of spiritual concepts. They have practiced spiritual techniques and have built a momentum in meditation, yoga or the like. They have practiced a spiritual lifestyle and have built habits of living according to spiritual precepts. Such people often feel that they have made great progress and are headed toward enlightenment. They often feel like an ultimate breakthrough must be right around the corner, and if only they keep doing what they are doing, the breakthrough will happen—soon.

Again, we face a subtle point. These people often *have* made great progress. When they look back at the point when they consciously found the spiritual path, they can see that tremendous changes have taken place. I am not hereby questioning that you have made progress up until this point. However, the big question is whether what you have achieved so far, and the way you have achieved it, will take you to the next level? Or whether it will keep you trapped at your current level of the path, a level where the ultimate breakthrough seems close—and can seem close for an indefinite period of time! You see, I am not interested in having you be close to breaking through—and having you remain close forever. I am interested in you actually breaking through and rising to an entirely different level of the path.

How can you do this? By overcoming ignorance. How do you overcome ignorance? By finding truth, so we are back to where we started: What is truth?

My point is to help you see that at a certain stage of the path, it is acceptable to accumulate knowledge of spiritual topics. However, you now need to step back and realize that no matter how long you keep accumulating knowledge, it will bring you *no* closer to finding truth. In fact, accumulating knowledge beyond a certain point will make it more difficult for you to find truth! There are many spiritual people who have studied for many years and think they have God and spirituality all figured out, yet they fail to see that the more they know about God, the further they are from actually finding – *experiencing* – God.

I have already said that a spiritual teaching that is expressed in the words, concepts and images of this world is not the same as the Spirit of Truth, but have you understood what this really means? God is the Infinite. A spiritual teaching in this finite world must – by its very nature – be finite. NO FINITE TEACHING CAN EVER PORTRAY THE INFINITE! Thus, you can study all of the finite teachings in the world without finding the infinite God. In fact, doing this will make it more difficult to experience the infinite God.

One reason for this is that the ego is always looking for the automatic, outer path, and it will seek to superimpose its basic belief upon everything you do. So when you start studying spiritual teachings, the ego will seek to steer you into the belief that if only you find the ultimate teaching or accumulate some ultimate knowledge, you are guaranteed to be saved. God simply *has* to save you because you know so much. Or perhaps you will discover some ultimate secret that will give you salvation without God. There are as many versions of these beliefs as there are false teachers, and they are legion.

You have heard the old saying that, "The more I know, the more I realize I don't know." That is the statement of a true seeker, who realizes that – at least in this world – there will always be more to know about God. Yet many people are tricked into a state of consciousness where the more they know, the more they feel they don't *need* to know—the more they feel they don't need a teacher or don't need to look at the beam in their own eyes. Thus, we find a considerable number of spiritual seekers who have become trapped in a subtle form of intellectual and spiritual pride, which is very comparable to the scribes and Pharisees who rejected me—and felt fully justified in doing so by their "superior" knowledge. This is one form of sophisticated ignorance, because these people think they have a sophisticated knowledge and thus they don't need the Living Christ.

Yet beyond this more obvious form of ignorance is a more subtle, and thus far more deceptive and dangerous, form of ignorance. Let me attempt to explain.

***

Look at any spiritual teaching expressed in words. What does it do to God? As mentioned before, it *objectifies* God! It turns God into an object that can be studied, analyzed and categorized by the intellect.

A teaching presents knowledge about God, and in so doing, it turns God into an object for study. Yet the teaching itself is in the finite world and the human intellect is a finite faculty. The intellect not only has a finite capacity for understanding, it can *only* understand that which is finite. For the intellect is an analytical faculty, meaning that it analyzes by comparing one thing to another. And since God is the one, indivisible infinite, there is nothing that compares to God.

Meaning that the intellect truly cannot deal with God. So what does the intellect do? It turns God into a finite object by analyzing an IMAGE of God. However, this image must of necessity be finite, for how could you possibly create an infinite image in the finite world? Take a look at this saying:

> 24 This is the disciple which testifieth of these things, and wrote these things: and we know that his testimony is true.
> 25 And there are also many other things which Jesus did, the which, if they should be written every one, I suppose that even the world itself could not contain the books that should be written. Amen. (John, Chapter 21)

The coded message here is that I too was and am an infinite being. Obviously, I had a finite number of years on Earth, so one could only write a finite number of books, meaning that the world could actually contain the books. Yet the deeper meaning is that the world and the expressions in this world could not "contain" my infinite teachings. Likewise, if you want to know God, you must look beyond finite expressions, which the intellect cannot do. However, by turning God into a finite image, the intellect can compare one finite image of God to another finite image of God, even to the finite paradigm of materialism which says there is no God.

Yet do you see that *any* spiritual and religious teaching is *not* God but can only present an image of God? And can you see that the more you study such a finite image – the more you feel you know about God, the more finite knowledge you feel you have accumulated – the more you turn this image into a graven image? For you begin to believe in the subtle illusion of anti-christ, namely that God truly *is* a finite object that can be quantified and analyzed by the intellect. And the more you believe in this fundamentally flawed illusion, the more you begin to worship your graven image of God instead of the Living God who is beyond *all* images in this world. That is why there can be no absolute and infallible spiritual teaching.

So we now have people who worship a graven image, a finite image of the infinite God, but they are absolutely convinced that they are worshipping the only true God. And this is the most subtle form of sophisticated ignorance and the one from which it is most difficult for a spiritual teacher to awaken people—as demonstrated by how the scribes and Pharisees rejected me when I stood before them in the flesh. The point being, of course, that you have to look beyond *any* and *all* spiritual teachings and reach for a direct experience of the infinite God.

I am not saying there is anything wrong with spiritual teachings. You need to study them in order to expand your mental box. Yet you also need to recognize the mechanism I have just described, whereby you realize that if you refuse to look beyond a specific teaching and reach for a direct experience of the Spirit of Truth, then that teaching is no longer *expanding* your mental box; it is *reinforcing* the box. And *any* box in this finite world will be less than the infinite God!

Now take a look at this book. What have I been doing throughout this book? I have talked about the Living Christ, but in doing so, I have objectified the Living Christ. I have turned the Living Christ into an object that can be studied and analyzed by the intellect, and if you will look honestly at your reaction to this book, you will see that your intellect has indeed analyzed and quantified what I have said. Yet it is now time to go beyond this and ask the question: "Studying this book has increased your knowledge of the Living Christ, but has this brought you closer to *experiencing* the Living Christ or has it brought you further away from a direct experience by causing you to worship a graven image of the Living Christ?"

You see, I have no desire to have you become very knowledgeable about the Living Christ, so you can go out and flaunt your knowledge and feel superior to those "unfortunate" people who have not studied this course. I desire to have you go beyond knowledge and actually *experience* the Living Christ. More than that, I desire you to *become one* with me, and then go on to *become the Living Christ in embodiment*. And for this to be accomplished, I need to take you beyond even the most subtle forms of sophisticated ignorance.

***

So what *is* the most subtle form of sophisticated ignorance? It is the one that reinforces the illusion of the separate self.

I have told you that the core of your being is the conscious self. I have told you that your conscious self is an extension of God's own Being—it is the Creator individualizing itself as *you*. The meaning is that your conscious self is not, never has been and never could be separated from God in reality. Separation is an illusion that seems real only when the conscious self is looking at itself through the filter of the ego—the separate self.

This will seem like a paradox or a mystery to the intellect, for how can your conscious self be an expression, an individualization, of God and not be separate? And no matter how much you study this topic, your intellect will never resolve the paradox. However, your conscious self can resolve it by having a mystical experience of its own oneness with the Infinite, thereby opening up for the inner knowing that you are not a separate puddle of water but a wave on the infinite ocean of God's Being. In the beginning you will have these experiences of oneness in short glimpses, but if you are willing, they will increase in frequency and duration, until they become a constant backdrop to your every-day life and you spontaneously exclaim, "I and my Father are one!"

So can you see that the more you study spiritual teachings, the more you might reinforce the illusion of the separate self? By objectifying God, a spiritual teaching will inevitably create the basic impression that you are separated from God. You – the subject – are studying God – the object – and subject and object are separate. If you were not separated from the object, how could you study it? And why would you need to study it?

Do you see the subtle mindset here? You need to use a teaching to study God only because you are separated from God. If you were not separated, you would be *experiencing* God's Presence, and then what would be the need to study God as a remote object? In a sense, we can also say that in order to objectify God, you must first objectify – or should we say *subjectify* – yourself. Before you can turn God into a remote object for study, you must have turned yourself into a separate being who can study a remote God.

Thus, you see that the more you study – the more you think you know – the more you reinforce the basic illusion from which the ego was born, the illusion that it is possible for a wave to be separated from the ocean. This often leads spiritual and religious people to build another layer of illusion by comparing themselves to others, feeling they are better than others because they understand this sophisticated knowledge or belong to a particular church or teaching. And you will not be able to overcome this illusion of comparison unless you overcome the underlying illusion of the separation between subject and object. This is what I talked about earlier as *Gnosis,* and you now have a deeper understanding of why this is essential. Which should help you take the next step of consciously giving up the quest for knowledge and redirecting your approach to the spiritual path into seeking gnosis, into seeking oneness with the object, oneness with the Infinite from which you emerged in the fiery sunrise of life's beginning.

***

What I am calling you to face here is the necessity to question *everything* that brought you to this point on the path. I am even calling you to realize that the self – the sense of identity – that brought you to this point must be allowed to die. For if you are not willing to lose your life for my sake – and *I AM* eternal progress – you will lose your life. Let me give you an analogy.

You probably know that a triathlon is a sporting event where the participants first swim a distance, then ride bicycles and then run to the finish line. Imagine a participant who finishes first in the swimming leg and then goes on to ride the bike. He really loves riding a bike and is so good at it that he arrives at the end of the bike leg far ahead of the other competitors. Yet he is so proud of his abilities on the bike that he simply cannot toss the bike aside and leave it behind. So he straps it on his back and starts running. Is it likely that he will finish the race in first place, or will he be taken over by those who saw the bike simply as a tool that brought them to a certain point, thereby making itself obsolete and needing to be left behind?

Likewise, the spiritual path has distinct phases. The outer tools that brought you to the top of one phase simply will not serve you on the next leg—which is why you need the innocent mind of a child that easily moves to a higher level without holding on to the past. In fact, the sense of self that brought you to the top of one phase will not serve you on the next leg. For what is *real* spiritual progress? It is *not* that you acquire knowledge or skills. It is that you overcome a limited sense of identity and that your sense of self is reborn into an expanded sense of self. And that is why you cannot truly begin the next phase until you have allowed that self to die and have left behind the outer tools that have now served their purpose and have made themselves obsolete.

So this is the essence of the second challenge of Christ—can you leave behind what brought you to the feet of the Living Christ, or will you insist on carrying it with you—thinking you can find a way to make it acceptable to the Living Christ? Or even falling prey to the illusion of the fallen beings that you can fool the Living Christ by hiding or camouflaging the old self, thinking that you can serve two masters. These fallen beings – in their pride – refuse to let go of the separate self, and that is why – no matter how much they know intellectually about spirituality – they will never reach the finish line first. They think their separate selves are so sophisticated that they could not possibly let them die and do not *have to* let them die, for they are so sophisticated – according to their self-created dualistic standard – that they *must* be acceptable to God. Consider the deeper meaning behind this saying:

> 23 Then said one unto him, Lord, are there few that be saved? And he said unto them,
> 24 Strive to enter in at the strait gate: for many, I say unto you, will seek to enter in, and shall not be able.
> 25 When once the master of the house is risen up, and hath shut to the door, and ye begin to stand without, and to knock at the door, saying, Lord, Lord, open unto us; and he shall answer and say unto you, I know you not whence ye are:
> 26 Then shall ye begin to say, We have eaten and drunk in thy presence, and thou hast taught in our streets.
> 27 But he shall say, I tell you, I know you not whence ye are; depart from me, all ye workers of iniquity.
> 28 There shall be weeping and gnashing of teeth, when ye shall see Abraham, and Isaac, and Jacob, and all the prophets, in the kingdom of God, and you yourselves thrust out.
> 29 And they shall come from the east, and from the west, and from the north, and from the south, and shall sit down in the kingdom of God.
> 30 And, behold, there are last which shall be first, and there are first which shall be last. (Luke, Chapter 13)

My point is, of course, to help you do a critical re-examination of what brought you to this point of the path. When you do so, you will discover that part of your motivation for walking the spiritual path was the ego's drive for a guaranteed salvation. This caused you to engage in certain games aimed at making the separate self seem superior.

Take note that I am in no way saying this to make you feel guilty or to destroy your true self-esteem. I *am,* however, saying it to shatter your false self-esteem, your ego-esteem. Yet you are far enough along on the path that you should be able to see these games and simply rise above them, simply leave them behind without feeling guilt or lowering your self-esteem. So let us look at some of the ego games that are relevant to this key.

***

The most obvious game is, as we have already talked about, the game of comparison. Yet let us apply it to how people approach spirituality and religion. The ego is always looking for the guaranteed path to salvation, and at the same time it is thinking in dualistic terms. Duality means there are two opposing polarities and we can apply a value judgment, making one polarity good and the other evil. The consequence is that the ego will look at the religious landscape with the basic paradigm that the one polarity is the "one true religion" and the other is a religion that is absolutely false. All other religions must fall somewhere in between, depending on how close they are to congruency with the one true religion. Yet, of course, unless they are in total congruency, they cannot lead to salvation and their unfortunate followers must go to hell.

I realize that most spiritual seekers are beyond this black-and-white approach to religion, but there are many spiritual people who are trapped in a more subtle form of this game. They are still looking for the ultimate guru or teaching. In fact, in previous teachings released by the Ascended Host we have deliberately tested the spiritual pride of our students by making remarks that played upon this subtle pride. For example, some ascended master students to this day believe they have the highest teachings on the planet, which implies that they – since they can accept and follow this teaching – must be the highest or most advanced spiritual students on the planet. In other words, by the mere acceptance of this teaching and membership of an organization, you suddenly move from being a "nobody" to being one of the most important people on the planet.

As I have hopefully made clear, we of the Ascended Host have risen above duality, so we do not make value judgments. Thus, we do not think in terms of the highest or lowest teaching—it is a concept we use exclusively to test people who are still trapped in duality. Thus, we might say that the idea that a particular teaching is the highest on the planet does not come from us, it comes from the dualistic mind.

Yet what I really want to point out here is what this concept does to your quest for Christhood. As I have attempted to explain, the path to Christhood is the path of overcoming the illusion that you are a separate self who is set apart from your source – God – and other people. When you become the Christ, you acknowledge your oneness with God and you acknowledge that all other lifestreams came from that source, meaning you are one with the All. Thus, you now see that the only realistic way to raise up yourself is to raise up your *whole* self, meaning all life. What this does for you is give you the ultimate form of self-esteem, a self-worth that is not tied to any conditions in this world and is *not* based on the sands of a value judgment. You are worthy because you are a unique expression of God's Being, meaning your self-esteem is based on the rock of Christ.

So what gives people the need for self-worth that makes them seek out a religion that claims to be the only true one or the highest teaching on the planet? It is that they have a lack of self-worth, but where does this lack come from? It can only come from the ego, the separate self, for when you see yourself as separate from God, you can never attain ultimate self-esteem. My point being that when you are in a teaching – in a culture and environment – that operates with the concept of one true religion or the highest teaching on the planet, you are only reinforcing the illusion of the separate self, seeking to raise the separate self in contrast to other people. Meaning that your involvement with such a teaching or organization is *not* bringing you closer to Christhood, but is taking you further away from it!

Now, you are, of course, free to pursue your own path, but please do not remain in this mindset and at the same time entertain the notion that you are a disciple of the Living Christ. For you simply cannot be a disciple of Christ if you are playing the dualistic game of making the separate self seem better – for any reason – than other people. You cannot serve God and mammon. For *my* way is the path of oneness with me and oneness with all life. Anything that reinforces the "reality" of the separate self is *not* my way.

***

Here comes a more subtle point. What are you actually saying when you believe that you belong to the highest teaching on the planet? You are saying that you have the ultimate teaching, which makes you better than all other people who are not in that teaching. But you are also saying that you don't need anything beyond that teaching, meaning that you don't need a Living Spiritual Teacher.

It is a stark reality that there are millions of people who claim to be Christians, but in reality they will have nothing to do with the Living Christ. They cling to the teaching that was written down almost 2,000 years ago, and they completely refuse to consider that I might be speaking to humankind today or that I could speak to them in their own hearts through the Comforter, their Christ selves. Yet even more ironic is the fact that in this age, the ascended masters have sponsored several organizations that published a more modern spiritual teaching. So there are now thousands of students who believe they are following a teaching that came directly from the ascended masters, and thus must be the most advanced on the planet. Yet in this worshipping of an outer teaching, they often shut out the Living Masters. For they will not acknowledge that when we no longer speak through a particular organization, progressive revelation has not stopped. In fact, progressive revelation will *never* stop as long as there is one person on Earth who has not attained Christ consciousness.

My point here is that when you are trapped in a dualistic approach to spirituality, you allow your ego to set up outer criteria that give you a superior status compared to other people. But the subtle effect of this mindset is that you inevitably come to believe in the ego's claim to superiority, meaning that you don't actually need a Living Teacher to come and tell you what is wrong with your current mental box. Thus, you inadvertently shut out the Living Teacher, the Living Christ. You believe your salvation is secured, for if only you keep studying the outer teaching and practicing the outer rituals, then surely one day – perhaps after the end of this lifetime – you will qualify for your ascension. Thus, you are no longer open to letting the teacher expose the beam in your own eye. You have forced the teacher – or rather your image of the teacher – into your mental box.

But if you have a superior teaching, why do you need a teacher? There are actually many of the more mature spiritual seekers on this planet who have come to believe in one of the many subtle lies that deny the need for a teacher. Some even deny the need for ascended masters because they think they can contact God directly with no intermediary.

You should now be able to see why you need a teacher and why you will need a teacher as long as you have not ascended. The reason is that as long as you are in embodiment, you will be in some kind of mental box. And in order to grow beyond that mental box – ultimately making that final leap that takes you into the ascended consciousness – you need a connection to something outside your current mental box—no matter how expanded that box might be.

What I am saying here is that as long as your conscious self is expressing itself through a physical body, you will have some mental box—for if you did not, you simply could not remain in embodiment. Thus, you need to be humble enough to recognize that in order to continue to grow, you need a teacher who is *not* inside your mental box and who can thus serve as the connection, as the bridge, as the open door to the reality that cannot fit in your mental box. For if you have no such connection, you will inevitably fall prey to the oh-so-subtle temptation to think that you have now found the ultimate mental box, and thus God's reality can finally fit inside your superior box.

Can you finally grasp the reality that God is the Infinite and will *never* fit into any of the mental boxes that can be created in the material universe? Therefore, growth means that you *never* seek to hold on to any mental box, but that you continually let your current (separate) self die and allow yourself to be reborn into a more expansive sense of self. And you continue this process as long as you are on Earth, and only *then* will you one day cross the line that brings you into the ascended realm (from which you will still continue to expand your sense of self until you reach full God consciousness and start a different cycle).

As we have seen, knowing truth does not mean knowing a teaching expressed in the words and images of this world. Truth is a state of being, it is oneness with the Spirit of Truth. You have access to that Spirit right inside yourself, which means that you do not need anything on Earth, anything outside yourself, to contact that Spirit. Yet how do you contact the Spirit of Truth? You do so through the spiritual hierarchy that is above you, namely the Ascended Host.

There are those who in their spiritual pride think they can contact God directly, even think they are God in embodiment or manifestation. Some of them deny the reality of the Ascended Host, some say we are impostors trying to make people think they need us so we can take their energy. Yet thinking that you – while in embodiment on Earth – can contact the Spirit of Truth or God directly is like talking on the telephone with a person on another continent and denying that you make the connection through the telephone lines and thus you have no need for the phone company.

You see, the Creator has indeed manifested itself *as* and *in* everything that has form. Yet that manifestation has happened in a hierarchical structure, as Maitreya explains in great detail in his book. You live in the latest sphere of God's creation, but your sphere is created out of the energies of the sphere that came right before yours. And it is created by the Beings in that sphere, meaning that they have embedded their own beings in your sphere—as you and all other co-creators. Your conscious self is an extension of the Creator's Being in the sense that there truly is only ONE Being out of which everything is created. But you were not created directly by the Creator. Your conscious self came out of the Being of a spiritual master in a higher sphere who had attained oneness with the Creator. You can have a spiritual or mystical experience of oneness with God, oneness with the Spirit of Truth, but in order to reach God, you must go through the "telephone" line of all ascended beings who are between you and the Creator. You might not realize that you are doing this, but you are still doing it.

And that is precisely why you need contact with a Living Teacher who is at the level above yours and thus knows exactly what you need in order to escape your current mental box and stay in the process of perpetual self-transcendence. The job of this teacher is to keep you on the true path, which – as you should have realized by now – is the path of perpetual self-transcendence. This is in contrast to the path of the ego and the false teachers, which is based on the belief in some ultimate state from which self-transcendence is no longer necessary.

If you actually were able to contact the Creator directly, the Creator's light would be so intense that it would instantly burn away all of your mental boxes and consume your separate self. This would be such a shock to your being that you would be thrown into an identity crisis and likely go insane. This has happened to many people who invoked more spiritual light than they could handle in a balanced way—something that is possible by using some of the techniques offered by false teachers.

So the reason why you need the Ascended Host is that we are at the level right above you, and thus we know how much light you can handle at any given moment. We will multiply what you bring to the altar, and thus we never give you back more than you can handle. We will facilitate your experience of the Spirit of Truth, but we will step down the Creator's light to a level and an intensity that will accelerate your growth in a balanced and thus sustainable way. In contrast, the false teachers will trick you into invoking more light than you can handle because it gives them an opportunity to steal the excess—something we have no need for doing because we are spiritually self-sufficient and need no light from human beings.

***

Here is another subtle point. I have said that the essence of the path is self-transcendence, but how does this happen? Take note that I am saying *self*-transcendence, meaning that it is a conscious process—not something that happens automatically. Again, the ego will have you believe that if only you follow an outer teaching, progress will happen automatically. Yet as I have explained over and over again – because I know how difficult it is for people to integrate this truth – progress happens *only* as a result of you looking at the beam in your own eye, understanding how it limits yourself and then making the conscious decision to leave behind an element of the duality consciousness.

So what I am saying here is that in order for you to walk the path, you need to be constantly looking for some element of unreality. When people are new to the spiritual path – and especially if they come from a fear-based religion – they will often approach this process as something unpleasant, even something to be feared. They will do this because they see it as a process whereby they have to acknowledge and admit that they have been wrong, that they have believed in the lies of the devil, or however they phrase it. In other words, there is a certain trauma involved because you see that you were "wrong" or stupid for believing in a lie, and it can even give rise to a certain fear that since you have believed in so many subtle lies, you will never be able to see the truth.

Most spiritual seekers gradually overcome this and adopt a love-based approach to spirituality. But some get stuck in a subtle blind alley that is born from the ego's default reaction. You see, the ego is born of separation from God. Separation from God is *not* the same as denial of God's existence. There are clearly some thought systems on Earth that deny the existence of God, but these are actually not the most dangerous blind alleys for a spiritual seeker. The most dangerous illusion is the original illusion that caused the fall of the first beings who fell in higher spheres, and that illusion – again as explained by Maitreya in greater detail – was that they knew better than God. So the underlying mindset of the ego is that it is born from separation from God, and it can never become one with God. The ego will forever see God as the remote being in the sky, for it is only in separation that it can continue to exist.

As I have explained, separation is truly an illusion, which means the ego's existence is based on a lie. Yet the ego can never admit that it is born from a lie, for if it did, it would cease to exist. Thus, in order to maintain its existence – a result of its survival instinct – the ego must at all costs uphold the illusion of separation. Yet here is the subtle mechanism. God's reality is that everything is one, thus separation is not real. The ego says it is separated from God, and in so doing the ego is actually saying that it knows better than God. It feels it is absolutely right in saying that God is not here, that God is in a remote heaven. And this is the definition of spiritual pride—that you think you are right and that you know even better than God what is real and what is unreal.

Can you begin to sense that this is the fundamental illusion of the ego? Can you begin to see that it is the most subtle illusion of the ego and thus the most dangerous form of sophisticated ignorance, in fact the "mother of all ignorance?" So can you now see the dilemma faced by spiritual seekers?

You have come to believe in some of the illusions of the ego. There might be a number of such illusions, but we now see that underneath them all is the illusion of separation from God, which inevitably leads to the belief that one knows better than God. So you need to be saved because you have come to believe in the illusion that you are separated from God. Yet this illusion is so subtle and persuasive that once you are inside of it, you cannot see the illusion or cannot see that it is an illusion. You think that what you experience on Earth is real and that you truly *are* separated from God. And as both Mother Mary and Maitreya explain, this belief becomes a self-fulfilling prophecy, because the Ma-ter light will take on any image projected upon it by self-conscious beings. Meaning that human beings have actually made matter more dense, which makes it seem even more real that matter is separated from Spirit and thus they are separated from God.

So what do you have to do to escape this illusion? Let us compare the path to a spiral staircase. You were born at a certain level, and you were meant to ascend the staircase toward higher and higher states of consciousness. Instead, you were deceived by the duality consciousness – as Maitreya explains – and started descending the staircase. For each step you took down, you came to believe in another dualistic lie. So what does it take to reverse the process? You have to walk back up the staircase, and for each step you take up, you have to unmask and consciously dismiss the lie that took you that step down.

Now, here comes the point. The ego has a life-and-death need to maintain the illusion that it knows best, that it is always right—

or it fears it will lose control over your conscious self. So it will vehemently resist that the conscious self comes to the recognition that takes you a step up through a LIFE decision. The ego will feel that for you to admit that you have believed in a lie is the same as admitting that you were wrong. However, the real issue is that it will be admitting that *the ego* is wrong, for how did you come to believe in the dualistic illusions? You did so because they were presented to you by the ego, who presented them as infallible truths.

As long as the conscious self is still partly identifying itself with the ego, it too can easily come to see this with a negative overlay. In other words, admitting that you have been wrong is seen as a negative to be avoided, which of course aborts your potential to make progress on the path—for the essence of the path is to consciously leave your illusions behind by admitting that they are illusions and accepting the truth of Christ in their stead.

Obviously, I have no desire whatsoever to see my disciples fall into this trap of trying to uphold the subtle illusion that you are always right. Many sincere spiritual seekers have fallen prey to one of the subtle traps set by the false teachers. These teachers prefer that no lifestream ever enters the upward path. Yet when a person refuses to be distracted and actually starts the path, the false teachers work overtime on taking the person into a blind alley. There are numerous versions, but one of the more subtle ones is the idea that because you have found this advanced teaching and belong to this ultimate organization, you have been redeemed. Thus, you no longer need to look for faults in your beliefs, for you have now adopted an infallible belief system that will take you to heaven.

As I said, the ascended masters have given several teachings aimed at setting people free from the duality consciousness. Yet in every case a certain percentage among the students have turned the living teaching into a dead outer doctrine. They now believe that because they have this advanced teaching, they no longer need to look for the beam in their own eyes, to look for more dualistic illusions. Essentially they have become deceived by the ego's ongoing, never-ending attempt to prove that it is right. Thus, they have allowed their egos to take a teaching given by the ascended masters for their liberation and turn it into a gilded cage that entraps them in the mindset that they know better than anyone else. And this implies that they know better than the Living Teachers or the ascended masters, even better than God.

Do you see what I am saying here? The ego and the false teachers will have you believe that you can rise to such a sophisticated stage of the path that you can no longer be fooled by the dualistic illusions, that you can no longer be wrong, that you can no longer be tempted by pride. You are not prideful in thinking you have superior knowledge, for you really *do have* superior knowledge—or so they whisper in your ear. Yet what I am saying here is that as long as you are in embodiment, you face the test of pride, the test of thinking you have reached some superior stage from which self-transcendence is no longer necessary or even possible.

It is a sad fact that those who are actually the more mature students often are trapped into this very subtle form of sophisticated ignorance and thus stop their growth just before they would have manifested Christhood. And precisely because such people have so much outer, analytical knowledge of the path, they are very good at arguing their case and defending their decision to stop at their present level. They are very good at using the intellect to actually reject the Living Teacher when he or she comes, often disguised in a humble form that they can easily reject based on their "superior" knowledge.

One obvious form of this game is the desire to argue that your religion or outer teaching, guru or organization is better than all others. This is another outcome of the ego's fear of not being acceptable to God. The ego thinks that if it is always right among men, it must be acceptable to God. Thus, it has an extreme fear of being proven wrong, and this can cause spiritual seekers to endlessly argue with others—instead of going beyond outer teachings and seeking the direct experience of the Spirit of Truth that can settle all arguments. But beyond that is the very subtle game of arguing that you are always right, that you could never be wrong.

***

I know this is a long discourse, but the reason is that we have reached a stage of this course where every lesson counts. If you get the lesson, you move on toward Christhood. If you don't get it, you will stand still at your present level until you *do* get it. So if you are to move on, you *must* see the subtleties of sophisticated ignorance.

The real danger of sophisticated ignorance is that it causes you to think you know everything, whereas in reality you don't see the full picture. You may actually be very knowledgeable, only you have not seen that the essence of the path is to overcome the separate self—which means that although you have a lot of outer knowledge of the spiritual path, you are still ignorant of the essential aspect of the path. The problem is that the more you think you know, the more difficult it becomes for you to admit your ignorance. And if you do not see and acknowledge your ignorance, how can you possibly overcome it? In other words, you have attained a sophisticated knowledge of the spiritual teachings that are in this world, and you are using that knowledge to defend your ignorance of the real truth, your failure to become one with the Spirit of Truth.

We might also say that sophisticated ignorance causes you to defend ideas that are wrong simply because you have declared them to be right. Yet that declaration was based on the ignorance of duality, which is the consciousness of anti-christ. Thus, you are defending anti-christ. It should be obvious that you cannot be a disciple of Christ and continue to do this.

What is another word for sophisticated ignorance? It is a word I often used, especially when I addressed the scribes and Pharisees, who in their sophisticated ignorance thought they did not need the Living Truth that I brought. Here is one example:

> 1 Then came to Jesus scribes and Pharisees, which were of Jerusalem, saying,
> 2 Why do thy disciples transgress the tradition of the elders? for they wash not their hands when they eat bread.
> 3 But he answered and said unto them, Why do ye also transgress the commandment of God by your tradition?
> 4 For God commanded, saying, Honour thy father and mother: and, He that curseth father or mother, let him die the death.
> 5 But ye say, Whosoever shall say to his father or his mother, It is a gift, by whatsoever thou mightest be profited by me;
> 6 And honour not his father or his mother, he shall be free. Thus have ye made the commandment of God of none effect by your tradition.
> 7 Ye hypocrites, well did Esaias prophesy of you, saying,
> 8 This people draweth nigh unto me with their mouth, and honoureth me with their lips; but their heart is far from me.
> 9 But in vain they do worship me, teaching for doctrines the commandments of men. (Matthew, Chapter 15)

So a valid word for sophisticated ignorance is hypocrisy, because it makes you think that since you know so much, you are better than others. Take an honest look at spiritual seekers you know and see how many are seeking to make themselves look like they are special because of their astrology, their knowledge, their diligent practice of this or that technique, their following some superior guru, their self-professed righteousness in following outer rules, their not eating this and eating plenty of that, the way they dress, or their ability to win any argument. Can you see that all this has only one aim, namely to reinforce the illusion of the separate self that if it seems to be superior to others based on a standard in this world, it *must* be acceptable to God?

Can you also see that God is not mocked, for the illusions of men do not change reality. The Earth was still round when most people thought it was flat. The fact that everyone in medieval Europe thought the Earth was the center of the universe did not make it a fact.

So what is the essence of hypocrisy? It is that you refuse to compare your beliefs to reality, and thus how could your beliefs ever be proven wrong? You refuse to compare your mental image to the reality that is outside your mental box—which can only be done through the Living Teacher, who is your link to that reality (no one comes to the Father, but by me). A hypocrite is a person who has used his knowledge in this world to argue why his beliefs do not need to be compared to the reality that is beyond this world. A hypocrite is a person who rejects the Living Truth and the Living Christ, but who has managed to convince him- or herself that this is actually a virtue that makes one superior to other people. Because the universe really *can* fit into the hypocrite's mental box. Obviously, you should now see the essential requirement for becoming a true disciple of the Living Christ: *Hypocrites need not apply!*

## Exercise for Key 11

In the coming 33 days – or more if you feel like it – repeat the pattern from the previous exercises of giving a rosary and writing down your thoughts. This time, I need you to give Jesus' Invocation for Victory Over Death.[12] Say the mantra of the Dhyani Buddha for this key one time after each verse and before the Hail Christ Within.

I need you to apply the technique from all previous keys in order to discover where you have any remnants of sophisticated ignorance that cause you to resist the Living teacher, cause you to resist having your present knowledge and beliefs compared to the undeniable reality of Christ Truth.

I ask that after giving the invocation, you meditate on sophisticated ignorance and ask your Christ self and me to expose to you the elements of this ignorance – even any hypocrisy – in your being. And then write down whatever comes to you without analyz-

---

12 Found on www.askrealjesus.com.

ing with the outer mind. Later, go over what you have written, examine the beliefs behind it and look for the dualistic illusion that caused those beliefs. Then let them go.

To help you let go of sophisticated ignorance, invoke the Buddha Vairochana and his wisdom of the All-pervading Wisdom. Use his mantra:

**OM VAIROCHANA OM**

This will invoke the wisdom that will pervade all of the subtle illusions of the mind of anti-christ. If you feel you need more than 33 days to complete this cleansing, by all means take the time you feel is needed. You can't rush the quest for eternal life.

# Key 12
# Rediscovering your will to BE

The spiritual poison for this key is called non-will and non-being. This may mean little to you at first, but I will explain it as we go along. The Buddha who is the antidote to this poison is named Vajrasattva, and his wisdom is the Wisdom of God's Diamond Will. You might notice that a diamond is the hardest substance and thus not affected by anything on Earth. You may also notice that a diamond has many facets that shine individually but together form the beautiful whole. As you study the following teaching, focus on the Buddha and use his mantra:

**OM VAJRASATTVA HUM**

If you read Maitreya's 600-page book and then step back in order to look at the big picture, you will see that the entire purpose of the book is to help people understand and overcome the psychological mechanism that caused them to be separated from their spiritual teachers—thereby condemning themselves to the learning environment of the "school of hard knocks" rather than the Divine Direction found in the Garden of Eden. Maitreya does everything possible to explain how a spiritual teacher is always and exclusively seeking to help the students grow. The concept that the teacher is seeking to point out the students' mistakes is a projection upon the teacher, born from the fact that the students have been blinded by the ego and are thus projecting a dualistic image upon the teacher. The central feature of the ego, of course, being that it projects its dualistic images upon everything.

So let me briefly summarize the essence of the master-disciple relationship. A lifestream is created as an individualization of the Creator, but it starts out with a very limited sense of self that is naturally focused on itself and its immediate environment. As an example, go back several centuries and you will see that most people lived in a small village and had little awareness of what was going on outside a 20-mile radius around their birthplace—which would often also be the place where they died. Today, most people have an awareness that the Earth is very large and they know about, or have even traveled to, countries far away, countries that have a culture very different from their own. So we can see that humankind has moved from a localized toward a more global form of awareness. Yet how did this shift in consciousness happen? It happened because people were forced to acknowledge that there was a reality outside their mental box—there was a world outside their immediate environment. So the function of a spiritual teacher is to help a new lifestream expand its mental box by demonstrating that there is a larger reality outside the box—and thus growth is both possible and desirable. Now look at my statement:

> Verily I say unto you, Except ye be converted, and become as little children, ye shall not enter into the kingdom of heaven. (Matthew 18:3)

What is the characteristic of children that gives them entry into the kingdom? As I have attempted to explain over and over again, the kingdom of God is *not* a static state of "perfection." It is an ongoing process of self-transcendence, the River of Life. And because children are open to learning, are always seeking to grow, they have access to that kingdom. Look at a small child who is learning to walk. The child often falls down, and sometimes it hurts itself. But what you do not see in the child is an overlay of guilt or blame, causing the child to blame itself for falling down. In other words, the child learns from every experience. If it falls down, it does not waste time blaming itself for not being perfect. It simply gets up and keeps experimenting. Sometimes the child makes the same mistake over and over again, but because it keeps experimenting, it will eventually get it right and learn to walk. Every single child, who is not physically impaired, eventually learns to walk. Yet the reason for this is that the child keeps experimenting without having the interference of guilt or blame.

As Maitreya explains, this was precisely the learning environment that he attempted to create in the Garden of Eden. I say attempted to create because, as he also explains, the garden was a mixed environment with lifestreams who had fallen into the duality consciousness in higher spheres. And these lifestreams found it very difficult to enter into the childlike mind, which means they projected their own dualistic state of consciousness upon the garden and the teacher. They also attempted to pull other students into their mindset, as demonstrated by the story of the Serpent. So what *is* that mindset?

Well, as I have explained, when a lifestream accepts the illusion of separation, it creates a separate self – the ego – which is born from duality. The ego is on an impossible quest of seeking to make itself acceptable to God, of seeking to force its way into the kingdom. It attempts to do this through the outer path, which essentially divides human actions according to a dualistic standard. Some actions are right and some are wrong. Thus, if you train yourself to avoid *wrong* actions and only perform *right* actions, the ego reasons that you are guaranteed to be saved. However, this dualistic path is based on an inescapable fear. For in dividing actions into right and wrong, there inevitably comes the fear that if you cannot avoid wrong actions, you could fail to be saved. It also introduces guilt, for if you commit a wrong action, you should feel guilty as a way to "force" yourself to avoid such actions in the future.

What is the psychological effect of this? It is that it kills the innocence of the childlike mind, and this aborts experimentation. What drives the child to learn to walk is that it has a desire to walk, but underneath it is a desire to "get it right." The love for getting it right is what drives the child to keep experimenting. However, the dualistic mind is not driven by a love for what is right; it is driven by a fear of what is wrong. The childlike mind is seeking to get closer to what it loves, whereas the dualistic mind is seeking to get away from what it fears.

We can also say that the childlike mind is innocent because there is no fear or guilt associated with learning, there is no risk involved in learning. Everything the child does is part of the process of experimentation, and the process goes in only one direction, namely toward a positive goal of self-transcendence. There are no mistakes, for the child can learn from every experience. If it falls down, it learns that this was *not* how to walk, and when it does not fall down, it learns that this *is* how to walk. Thus, there is never a failed experiment, only experiments that did not produce the desired outcome, but since you can learn from those experiments, they still bring you closer to the goal. And when you have learned from an action, what is the point of calling it a failure and feeling guilty for it? The real purpose of life is growth, and anything that helps you grow is a success, regardless of the physical outcome.

Do you see the subtle difference? The material world is a schoolroom, a laboratory, created for the sole purpose of your growth in self-awareness. The material world is not ultimately real, so it really doesn't matter what happens in this world. The Christ mind is exclusively focused on your growth and puts no ultimate importance or permanence on what happens in this world. The Christ is not concerned about you making a few mistakes, the Christ is exclusively concerned about bringing you closer to the ultimate goal of oneness with your Creator. In contrast, the mind of anti-christ is based on separation, so it cannot conceive of the real goal for this universe. It sees the material universe not as a means to an end but as an end in itself. Thus, it places undue importance on what happens in this world, meaning that certain actions are seen as mistakes or sins and are now given some ultimate and permanent importance.

Do you understand what I am saying here? When your conscious self is unimpaired by the filter of duality, you are in the childlike mind. Life is a continuous process of experimentation, and there are no failed experiments, for every action becomes a learning experience that expands your mental box and increases your sense of self. This is precisely what you were created to do—you were created in order to grow toward an expanded sense of self, leading to God consciousness. And you can do this in only one way, namely by experimenting and learning from your experiments. Some experiments teach you what works and some teach you what doesn't work, but they all teach you something that brings you higher in awareness. Thus, as long as you are in this childlike mind, you are *always* right because you are in alignment with God's purpose of growth! You were not created to be perfect in doing everything that can be done in this or any other world. For the only way to know how to do *everything* is to be in God consciousness. You were not created in God consciousness; you were created to grow *toward* God consciousness. And as long as you are transcending your sense of self, you are *right* with God.

Yet what is the *one* condition that *must* be fulfilled in order for you to grow? It is that you are willing to experiment, you are willing to act and to learn from every action. In order to do this, you must be willing to observe yourself and evaluate your actions based on the consideration, "Did it work or didn't it work—did it take me closer to oneness with God or did it take me further into separation?"

Do you see that this is a fundamentally different equation than what you have in the duality consciousness? The ego does not ask, "Did it work or didn't it work?" The ego asks, "Was it right or was it wrong?" The first evaluation encourages experimentation, whereas the second one kills experimentation. When you are in the childlike mind, you want to experiment, for every experiment helps you grow and this is rewarding. When you are in the dualistic mind, you do not want to experiment, for every experiment carries the risk that it could be wrong, increasing your fear and guilt. Thus, you want to only do what you know to be right according to a worldly standard, and this – of course – stops you from expressing your built-in creativity. Instead of acting like the creative spiritual being you truly are, you begin to act like a mechanized being, a kind of robot that mindlessly repeats patterns that have been programmed into it—you become a blind follower of the blind leaders. And such mechanized beings have no place in the perpetually creative world that is God's kingdom. For they violate one of the basic creative principles, a principle I expressed this way:

> Judge not according to the appearance, but judge righteous judgment. (John 7:24)

Do you see the point? The dualistic mind is a relative mind in that it always relates everything to a worldly standard—to the appearances of this world, which it sees as real. It is also a judgmental mind in that it always judges whether something is right (causing it to feel pride) or wrong (causing it to feel guilt). The net effect is that it kills experimentation, kills creativity. In contrast, the childlike mind – the mind of Christ – is not relative, for it has no standard and thus cannot judge based on any appearance in this world. The Christ mind does know God's reality, but as I have said, God's reality is the River of Life, which is constantly transcending itself—so the Christ mind does not have a fixed standard. The Christ mind does not ask whether something is right or wrong, but whether something helps you grow or impedes your growth. And what is growth? You grow when you express your God-given creativity and thus become more than you thought you were—you transcend your sense of self.

The Christ mind is not even comparing to some divine standard, for God is infinite and you are created as an extension of the Infinite. You are meant to express the infinite creativity of God in a localized place, and when you do, the finite world is raised up toward the Infinite. Thus, there is no standard for how you should behave when you are expressing your unique, spiritual individuality. Creativity cannot be related to any standard, nor can it be judged in terms of right or wrong. It simply is what it is. Which is why God said to Moses, "I am that I am," which is more correctly translated as, "I will be who I will be!"

***

We now need to take this one step further by considering what it really means that something works or doesn't work. As you should be beginning to realize by now, the dualistic mind can pervert anything, so it can play the game of asking whether it works rather than whether it is right or wrong. Yet what the dualistic mind cannot do is to step outside its inherent duality. Thus, the dualistic mind will define what works and doesn't work based on a dualistic view, which means it invariably defines it as what works for the separate self in terms of elevating it toward the superior status that it invariably sees as the end goal.

So what is the real definition? Well, the Creator has created innumerable extensions of itself. God loves all of its offspring with an infinite love, which means it has no meaning to consider that God loves some beings more than others. There can be no comparisons in infinity (obviously, the dualistic mind cannot fathom infinity, other than as a theoretical, mathematical concept). As the Bible says, "God is no respecter of persons."

So the Creator did not create the world of form for the purpose of elevating some extensions of itself to a superior status and setting them up as overlords over other extensions of itself. As Maitreya explains, there is a natural hierarchy in that some beings have transcended themselves and thus hold certain positions in hierarchy, but this does not make them better than others. It simply makes them better qualified to fill that position, as a teacher is better qualified to teach than those who have not yet learned to read. Yet by applying themselves, the students can obviously qualify to become teachers.

What the Creator wants is for *all* extensions of itself to engage in the River of Life, whereby they continuously transcend their sense of self until they reach full God consciousness. When you are trapped in duality, you see yourself as a separate being, and thus you believe in the illusion that you can raise yourself in comparison to others. When you see the reality of the Christ mind, you see all beings as part of the Body of God, and thus you see that the only way to truly raise yourself is to raise the All. This is what I expressed when I said, "Inasmuch as ye have done it unto the least of these my brethren, ye have done it unto me." In other words, the real definition is that what "works" is what raises up all life and what "doesn't work" is what seeks to raise up the separate self but in reality limits all life—including the separate self.

One example is what Mother Mary explains in her book, where she says that those blinded by the ego seek to hoard the abundance that is already in the material world, whereas those who are not blinded use their God-given ability to draw spiritual energy into the material world and thereby expand the total amount of abundance available in this world. The first action seems to raise the separate self, whereas the second action truly raises the All. And this is what works for God. So what is the second action based on? It is based on creativity, the creative potential that is built into every lifestream. God is obviously the ultimate creative being, but since you are an extension of the Creator, you have the potential to express infinite creativity in a finite situation. Doing so is what works for God, for it raises all life.

When you compare this to my parable about the talents, you will see that if everyone is multiplying their talents, God will multiply their offering and the total multiplication will be exponential. In other words, if everyone is selflessly seeking to increase the abundance on Earth, God will give such a huge increase that poverty could be eradicated very quickly. The present poverty is a function of the fact that some people have sought to monopolize and hoard abundance by taking from others—and that those others have allowed the elite to get away with it. The net effect is that there is not as much for God to multiply, which is why there is not enough abundance in the material world to raise all above poverty.

So what is the function of the spiritual teacher? The teacher has escaped the illusions of duality and is no longer seeking to raise the separate self. The teacher has seen through the illusions of duality and can see that what truly raises up the individual being is actions that serve to raise up all life. Thus, the function of the teacher is to give the student a standard, a measuring rod, whereby the student can see which actions work for the greater good and which actions don't. The function of the teacher is to give the student a glimpse of what his or her actions look like when they are not seen through the filter of duality, when they are not seen from inside the student's own mental box.

You can now see the essential problem between student and teacher. When students have become blinded by duality, they are seeking to raise the separate self to a standard of perfection defined by some system in this world. They think they are well on their way toward or have already achieved this goal, yet it is all an illusion. Seeing this, the teacher can help these students only by helping them see that they are living a lie and that they will *not* go to the real heaven—and not even to the imagined heaven they have created. Yet the students – blinded by the duality of their egos – will see this as a threat and will see the teacher as an unwelcome intruder. The ego might even conjure up the belief that the teacher is a threat to their religion, and since that religion is the only true one, the teacher is a threat to God's plan for salvation—and thus must be an agent of the devil. Which is precisely why the scribes and Pharisees rejected me and called me a tool of the devil.

As I said, "I have come that all might have life," and the reality is that "life" means that you are in the River of Life, in the childlike mind where you are experimenting and transcending your sense of self. You are *being*, which means that you are living a spontaneously joyful life—as the child who expresses spontaneous joy. Going around putting yourself down through fear or guilt or raising yourself up through pride (to cover over the fear) is no way to live—it is not life. When you have stopped experimenting, or when you are experimenting only to raise the separate self, you are in a state of consciousness that is spiritual death. Yet since you think you are guaranteed to be saved, this could also be called an extreme form of ignorance or a state of non-being. You are not being who you were created to be, you are being less than you were created to be.

What will it take for people to escape this state of non-being? Well, somehow their sense that they know everything, or know everything they need to know, must be shattered. This can happen the hard way—for example by people pounding their heads against a concrete wall until they finally realize they cannot break down the wall. Or it can happen through the divine direction of the teacher, which the student uses to trigger an "Aha-experience." When people are completely blinded by duality, they can only awaken the hard way. As a side note, this awakening happens because duality always has or creates two opposing forces. Thus, people can never attain complete peace in the consciousness of death, since the contradicting dualistic forces will always threaten their peace. And this conflict is precisely what gives people opportunities to awaken from the illusion, thereby sensing that there must be something outside duality, there must be a better way to live.

When a person begins to awaken from duality, that person becomes open to direction from a spiritual teacher. This often starts with openness to an outer teaching, but will eventually lead to an openness to inner direction, both from the student's Christ self and from the Ascended Host. Obviously, you have already come to this point, so why this long discourse? Because I need you to see that the illusions of the ego are subtle. And although you have so far been willing to grow, it is virtually inevitable – having incarnated on Earth a number of times – that there are still remnants of the ego's resistance toward the teacher left in your subconscious mind.

As long as these elements of willful, or sophisticated, ignorance remain in your being, you will resist the teacher when he comes to point out that you are still repeating patterns of beliefs or actions that "don't work" because they do not raise the All but seek to raise the separate self. Obviously, this resistance will slow down your progress, but more importantly, it will actually prevent you from going beyond a certain level of the path to Christhood.

Specifically, it will prevent you from going beyond the level demonstrated by Peter, who recognized the Living Christ but would not let the Living Christ take him beyond his mental box, thus seeking to force the Christ into his box. As I have said, this is what mainstream Christianity – building on the foundation of the Catholic Church – has been doing for 2,000 years. But – as I trust is obvious to you – you cannot become a disciple of the Living Christ by repeating this pattern. Thus, it is an absolute, inescapable requirement that you free yourself from the last elements of resistance toward the teacher. You cannot BE my disciple as long as you are trapped in non-being.

***

A very subtle and dangerous result of the pride that springs from sophisticated ignorance is wanting to always be right, to never be wrong. This prevents you from admitting what the ego sees as mistakes, but which God sees as simply experiments that did not work. Yet when you will not admit that an experiment did not work, how can you learn from it and avoid repeating the same pattern?

Of course, you do not think you have to rise above the pattern, for the ego defines it as being right in this world. Thus, you are seeking to be right among men rather than seeking to be right with God. Which is a deeper interpretation of my statement that you cannot serve two masters, that you cannot serve God and mammon. You cannot simultaneously be right with God and right with the world—the reason being that the world (the collective consciousness) is so infused with the duality of the ego that it has defined a standard for what is right that is out of alignment with God's reality.

As I have said in previous keys, every spiritual poison is a perversion of a true God quality. Thus, ignorance is a perversion of the desire to know. The desire to know is truly a desire to expand your sense of self to the ultimate, which is God consciousness, oneness with your Creator. Yet this expansion of self is a vertical growth, whereby you become *more* than your present sense of self. The ego's perversion of this drive is the desire to be more of what you already are. This is a desire to perfect the separate self, which can never come closer to God. It is a desire to become the perfect human being who knows everything in this world, but never goes beyond the level of a human being. This is similar to the citizens of Babylon who got the idea that they wanted to build a tower that could reach into the heavens, so they could reach God. With your modern knowledge of cosmology, you can see just how naive this quest was, yet the ego's quest is equally naive.

If you want another illustration of this, consider a person who is overeating and becoming fatter and fatter. We cannot say that this person is standing still, for he is clearly expanding and even transcending his former state. Yet this is a horizontal expansion that takes place in the material universe, rather than a vertical expansion whereby you rediscover your true identity as a spiritual being who is not limited by the material world. Thus, we see that God does *not* want you to become the perfect human being. This is a drive motivated solely by the ego's illusion that it can force God to let it into his kingdom by living up to a standard in this world. God wants you to be a spiritual being who is expressing your God-given individuality in the material world and thus raising the material world and co-creating the kingdom of God on Earth.

Do you see the point? Many people on Earth – even many religious people and spiritual seekers – are engaged in the horizontal quest of seeking to expand, to inflate, their egos. The subtle, underlying illusion is that if the ego is inflated to some ultimate extent, to "perfection," then God simply *has* to accept it. This can never work, but the ego will never see that it cannot work. Thus, people will be trapped in this fruitless quest until the conscious self sees through the illusions of the ego and separates itself from those illusions—penetrates the veil of illusions, the veil of Maya. It is the function of a spiritual teacher to help the student begin and complete this process from non-being back to being. Yet the work of the teacher is made more difficult as long as the student is still so blinded by sophisticated ignorance that he or she – often without seeing it – resists the teacher, resists self-transcendence.

***

We now need to go even further with this. We have seen that the ego wants to be right in this world and that it thinks being right in this world will guarantee it entry into heaven. Yet what is really happening here is that underneath the surface is an even deeper layer of deception.

The ego wants to be right in this world because in this world, it can always argue that it is right. Why is this so? Because the ego is based on the illusion of separation. And the illusion of separation gives rise to two opposite polarities, namely a dualistic thought system. Do you understand why this is so? In God, there is no division, there is only oneness. So how can you separate yourself from oneness? Only by creating a state of division. Yet how can division be created? Only when you create two polarities that oppose each other.

The essence of a dualistic thought system is that it has opposing ideas—which makes it very easy to define one idea as being right and the opposite as being wrong. And since the ego is born of duality, it can always use the dualistic thought system to argue that it is right—compared to an opposite which is wrong. And the ego can always convince itself that it is right. Yet where does this consciousness come from?

As Maitreya explains, creation has occurred as a gradual expansion of concentric or interpenetrating spheres. The concept is that a sphere is set apart from the void, and self-conscious beings are sent into that sphere. As they grow in self-awareness, they learn to use their co-creative abilities to bring more spiritual light into their sphere, until the entire sphere ascends and thus becomes what I called the kingdom of God. In the beginning, all beings in the new spheres ascended, but there came a point when the next sphere reached such density that some beings became blinded by duality and could not ascend when their sphere ascended. These beings had "fallen" into the duality consciousness, and when their sphere ascended, they fell into the newly created sphere in order to receive another opportunity to join the River of Life.

What caused these beings to fall? It was ignorance, but it was a very sophisticated form of ignorance, expressed as an unwillingness to grow, an unwillingness to be more—a form of non-being. These beings were actually wisdom angels, meaning that they had the highest knowledge of how the world of form works. However, despite their high knowledge of the world, they still became entrapped in the consciousness of separation and began to believe they knew better than God how the universe should be run. Specifically, they thought God made a mistake by giving free will to unascended beings, because they could misuse their co-creative abilities to destroy themselves and others, even an entire planet. They also thought the true teachers of unascended beings were wrong in giving so much room for free will and that the angels could do a better job by controlling unascended beings, thus forcing them to grow. However, what these angels did not understand is that true growth is a creative process that cannot be forced—a self-aware being can grow only from within, by raising its self-awareness.

My point here is to get you to consider how you could possibly come to feel that you know better than God? Well, is it not obvious that you can do this only if you have separated yourself from God? For unless you see yourself as a separate being, how could you feel you know better than this other separate being—which you have now turned God into (in your mind, not in reality, of course).

So what caused the original wisdom angels to fall? It was their wisdom, their ability to project what was likely to happen as a result of giving unascended beings free will and sending them into a sphere of such density that some of them would become "lost" in duality. And the angels were – in a sense – right. Some beings have become trapped in duality, and they have descended very far below the level at which they were created (a level from which they were meant to go only up). As a result, these beings have a very long and arduous road back to even the point where they were created—and then from there on to God consciousness. And some beings have indeed become so lost in duality that they have run out of time and opportunity, and have then been dissolved as individual lifestreams, being reabsorbed into the Creator's Being.

Yet how can wisdom cause beings to fall? Because the wisdom angels were not yet one with God, and thus for all their wisdom they looked at the world from a specific, individualized, localized point of view. Yet they gradually began to feel that they knew everything, and this gave rise to the subtle belief that their point of view was the ultimate, the absolute point of view. They had now confused their individual world view with the universal world view—that only the Creator can have.

So here is what the angels – for all of their wisdom – did not understand. You see, the angels failed to see that they had become focused on the self, their own selves. They felt that their selves were the center of the universe, and thus their world view should be the only true one. Because of this, they failed to see the real purpose behind having co-creators with free will descend into an unascended sphere, meaning they came to see themselves as separated from the co-creators. In essence, the angels were meant to serve as the guardians of the beings descending, which means that the angels would be committed to this task for as long as it took for the co-creators to ascend. Some of the angels did not like the prospects of being tied to unascended beings for so long. Others did not like the prospect that once these beings had ascended, they would assume higher positions in hierarchy than the angels themselves. The reason being that the ascended beings have more experience with the world of form and thus know what it is like to rise to a position rather than being created into that position.

What the angels failed to see was that they were not willing to serve the co-creators because they had failed to attain oneness with the co-creators. Yet the Creator was willing to serve – as Maitreya says, the Creator is the ultimate servant – in the sense that the Creator was willing to let a part of its own Being be embedded in the co-creators, even giving them free will to do with it as they saw fit. In other words, the Creator was willing to do whatever was necessary to give co-creators an opportunity to grow and to do so for a very long time. The Creator has a sense of oneness with the co-creators—and with the angels. The angels were not wiling to do what the Creator was willing to do, and in this non-will they separated themselves from the Circle of Oneness that is the Creator's Being. They were not willing to be one with the co-creators but since the co-creators are out of the Creator's Being, the angels were no longer willing to be one with the Creator. This unwillingness to be one with those above and below you in the Chain of Being is the essence of non-will and non-being.

What I desire you to understand here is that what happened to these wisdom angels was a very subtle shift in consciousness, in fact so subtle that they did not notice what was happening. Why – with all of their wisdom – did the angels fail to see this? Because they had never experienced what it was like to be outside the Circle of Oneness—they had no contrast, no perspective. There were beings – masters – who had experienced what it was like to descend into a newly created sphere and then ascend back to oneness, so they could see what the angels could not see. Yet because the angels thought they had superior wisdom, they would not listen to anyone else. They thought that, *surely,* they could not need a spiritual teacher to realign them to the reality of God.

***

Let us take another look at the very subtle ignorance that caused the angels to fall. You see, the angels were created to reside in the ascended spheres, never to take embodiment in an unascended sphere. So their entire mindset was to help spheres – and the beings in them – ascend into the oneness and perfection of God's kingdom. Yet because they had never experienced what it is like to be inside an unascended sphere, they came to view an unascended sphere as being in an imperfect state, as being less desirable, as being of lesser value than the perfection in the ascended realm. This gave rise to a subtle sense of judgment, yet what is the reality here?

You are obviously living in an unascended sphere, and you might not have had any mystical experiences to give you a sense of the perfection found in the spiritual realm. Yet you have an inner sense that the many imperfections you see on Earth clearly could not exist in the spiritual realm, and thus there is a higher state in Spirit. The angels were even more keenly aware of the contrast between the latest unascended sphere and the spiritual realm. Yet what they failed to see was that even though an unascended sphere has not reached the perfection of the spiritual realm, it is not "bad" or even imperfect. For why was the unascended sphere created as less than the spiritual realm?

It was to give God's co-creators the opportunity to start out with a localized, individual sense of self and then rise to the ascended realm, entering it with a deeper appreciation because they had experienced the contrast and had experienced the climb toward the ascended state. This gave them the joy and sense of accomplishment of having attained this state of consciousness and the joy of helping to co-create their sphere and raising it to the ascended state. And this has value in the eyes of God, a value that the angels failed to appreciate.

Yet beyond this is an even deeper layer. You see, when you compare an unascended sphere to the ascended realm – such as comparing Earth to heaven – you see an enormous contrast, a contrast that has only grown bigger after unascended beings fell into duality and thus took parts of their sphere lower than the level at which it was created. Thus, the Earth is today far less than what it was created to be.

So when you focus on this contrast, you clearly see that the unascended sphere has a long way to go, but you also see that it *must* and will eventually ascend. It is thus easy to fall into a value judgment and say that the unascended sphere is not as good as the spiritual realm. You might even think there is something wrong with the unascended sphere and that the beings in it have made mistakes or have sinned by taking a planet below the level at which it was created, thus going against the ascending process rather than flowing with it.

Yet there are several illusions involved in this. The reality is that it is the will of the Creator that co-creators have free will. The Creator was fully aware that by giving co-creators free will, they could take their environment below the original level, potentially even destroying a planet and becoming lost. Yet the Creator also saw that free will is the only way for a being to ascend with a full appreciation for oneness by consciously choosing that oneness over a separate existence. Thus, even though the current imperfections seen on Earth are not what the Creator wants to see for human beings, they are still within the sphere of God's will. For it is God's will that human beings have free will—and thus are given an opportunity to learn by experiencing the consequences of their own actions and state of mind.

Another illusion is based on a failure to see that – as Mother Mary explains – the material universe is created out of a substance called the Ma-ter light or the Mother Light. This is a substance that has no form but can take on *any* form. A planet is created out of the Ma-ter light by spiritual beings who use the creative powers of their minds to envision a blueprint for the planet and then superimpose it upon the Ma-ter light, causing it to coalesce into the envisioned form. The co-creators who embody on that planet are then given free will to do what they want with their environment. It is the vow of the Ma-ter light to take on any form that the co-creators impose upon it, thus allowing them to see the outpicturing in matter of their own state of consciousness, giving them maximum opportunity to learn. The Ma-ter light has consciousness and is aware when an imposed form is not the highest possible, but it has no judgment. It will take on any form, for it knows that any form is temporary. And thus, even if human beings superimpose an imperfect form on the light, this will give them an opportunity to learn. And thus, in the long run even an imperfect form will serve the overall goal of the Creator—namely the growth in consciousness.

When beings focus on current imperfections, they think that an unascended sphere, especially one that has been taken below its original level, is somehow imperfect or bad and thus must be separated from God—who is associated with the perfection in heaven. Yet everything in an unascended sphere – no matter how imperfect – is created from the Ma-ter light and where does the Ma-ter light come from? It too is an extension of the Creator's Being, meaning that an unascended sphere is *not* separated from God. God is all there is—without him was not any thing made that was made. God is omnipresent, so how can you find a place where God is not? Meaning that behind all of the appearances on Earth – even the worst imperfections – is the smiling face of God.

Why is this important? Because the essential element of attaining Christ consciousness is that you overcome the illusion of separation, the illusion of duality. And that means you must overcome the illusion that anything – no matter how imperfect of an appearance it might have taken on temporarily – is separated from God, is *not* God. You attain Christ consciousness when you see God everywhere, when you see *only* God.

***

The wisdom angels failed to see these illusions, and this lack of vision caused them to separate themselves from the Circle of Oneness. They did not see that this was caused by choices they made, the choice to refuse to enter into oneness with the co-creators they were meant to serve, the choice to resist serving those they considered below them. Which was really a choice to refuse to be one with the one above them—the Creator, who is serving all life. Yet as Maitreya explains, a being in the ascended realm cannot enter into duality and remain in that realm, meaning that the angels fell into the highest level of the unascended sphere. And although the angels did not see that they entered into the consciousness of separation, they clearly saw when they had fallen below their previous level.

They saw this as a clear degradation of their status, yet because they did not acknowledge that this happened as the result of their own choosing, they felt that God – whom they now saw as the external God – had done this to them, and furthermore that he had done this unjustly. They became even more convinced that they were right and that God was wrong. And they now used their understanding of the law of free will to demand that they be given an opportunity to prove it. Their thought behind this was that if they could prove that they were right and God was wrong, they would have redeemed themselves. And thus, God would not only have to reinstate them to their rank of Archangels, but would have to make them rulers over the entire world of form—which meant they could then impose their vision upon everyone and everything. They could become as powerful as God, they could become *as* God or *become* God.

The real problem was that the angels failed to see that all extensions of God have the opportunity to become God—only this must be done through the Path of Oneness. The reason being that in order to attain the ultimate power, you must have demonstrated that you are the ultimate servant and therefore will not abuse your power. Thus, ever since the Fall, the angels have been on the impossible quest of trying to become God through the path of separation. This, as I have attempted to explain, cannot be done, but when you are blinded by duality, you cannot see this. Yet why is duality so persuasive, why is the illusion of duality so difficult to penetrate once you have entered into it?

God is one, the indivisible whole. Thus, when you are in oneness with God, there is no room for separation. The beings in the spiritual realm are all in oneness with God, which means they are in oneness with each other while remaining individual beings. In this oneness there is no competition or conflict between individual beings, for they all share a common vision that unites them in fulfilling the Creator's overall purpose for creation.

The consequence of this is that there is only one way to separate yourself from oneness and that is to enter into duality. Oneness is one, meaning there is no room for divisions. So to leave oneness, you have to enter into a divided state with (at least) two divisions. Thus, separation leads to duality, meaning that in the separated state of consciousness there will inevitably be two opposing forces, two mutually exclusive possibilities. Take note that when the Creator began the process of creating the world of form, it first expressed itself as two polarities, namely the expanding and the contracting force. Yet these are not opposites in the sense that they do not cancel out each other. They complement each other, and thus their union gives rise to more. Yet in duality, the two basic forces become opposites that cancel out each other, which results in there being less than before the interaction.

So we now see that in duality there will always be two opposing viewpoints that are mutually exclusive. And once the wisdom angels had become blinded by separation, they entered into this dualistic state of mind. Their knowledge of the world of form did not disappear, but it became colored by an overlay of duality, meaning that they now started to see the world as the product of two opposites, which they judged as right and wrong.

Do you see what happened here? In oneness, right and wrong cannot exist, for there is no division and thus there cannot be two opposing and mutually exclusive polarities. Yet the consciousness of duality sees everything in terms of a conflict between two opposing polarities, which gives rise to the judgment that one polarity is wrong and the other is right.

So do you see what the angels did? They thought they had demanded an opportunity to prove God wrong and that this was a possible goal. But all they had really done was to enter into the state of duality. Because this state is based upon two opposites, it now becomes possible to prove that one polarity is right and the other is wrong—yet both polarities are separated from the one reality of God. This is why the angels thought they had the opportunity to prove themselves right and to prove God wrong.

Can you see the flaw in their argument? It is that God had not entered into duality. In reality, God is still the indivisible One. Thus, God sees no division between itself and the angels and God sees no conflict with the angels. God is not seeking to prove the angels wrong. God is simply allowing them to outplay free will until they hopefully tire of the dualistic game and decide to – consciously and voluntarily – come back to oneness.

God was not in any way, shape or form changed by the angels' decision to separate from oneness. What *was* changed was the angels' perception of God—and that change took place entirely within their own minds.

The mind of anti-christ must turn God into an opposite of itself—which is how it seems to have power as being in opposition to God. However, this cannot be done with the real God who is infinite, thus is indivisible and thus can have no opposite. So the mind of anti-christ can do this only by creating a graven image of God and then setting itself up as the opposite of this graven image. Yet the mind of anti-christ has defined both the false god and itself as the opposite of that god. Both are unreal, and if people believe in either the false god or the devil, they will never find the infinite God. Do you see what this means?

The fallen angels are to this day trying to prove themselves right by proving God wrong, and they clearly believe God is engaged in this struggle. In reality, the "god" that they oppose is not the Living God, the Creator. The god they are opposing is a graven image of god that they have created by projecting their own duality outside themselves. They have created their own dualistic god, and they have then set themselves up against this god in an epic struggle. They think the outcome of this struggle is control of the world of form, but in reality the outcome is control of the minds of the angels themselves. The angels are not fighting God, they are fighting themselves. They have created two false selves that are fighting each other, and the only real question is when the conscious selves of the angels are going to realize this and decide to give up the dualistic struggle, to let the separate selves die and be reborn into their original state of non-duality.

So do you begin to grasp that the fallen angels are engaged in an impossible quest? They think they are working toward the goal of proving God wrong. And they think they can attain this by turning all co-creators in the material universe into their followers and then "forcing" them to be saved through the outer path, the path of separation. And they think that if they can attain the goal of making everyone follow them, then God will simply *have to* change and make the outer path lead to salvation—because if God doesn't do this, everyone will be lost.

However, it is only when seen through the filter of duality that this can seem like a possible (or desirable) goal. For in reality, there is only ONE road to salvation, and that is ONEness.

***

Do you begin to see what the angels have done and how the law of free will allows this to outplay itself? The angels had used their free will to enter into separation. They had used the dualistic mind to create the belief that they were right and God was wrong. God respects free will and thus had no intention of *forcing* the angels to see the error of their ways. They had to come to see this voluntarily. Yet how could this be accomplished?

Well, angels were not created to descend into an unascended sphere and take embodiment. They were meant to remain in the spiritual realm. So when an angel began to accept the illusion of separation, it had aborted its own reason for being. Thus, one possibility would have been that the angel would have destroyed itself and ceased to exist—it would have been reabsorbed into God's Being. Yet because God is merciful, the angels were allowed to descend and embody in an unascended sphere, thereby essentially becoming like co-creators in the sense that they had to work their way back up.

Yet the angels, of course, did not see the reality of what had happened. They thought they had forced God's hand and had forced God into giving them the unascended sphere as their domain. They thought God had given them the right to use that sphere in their attempt to prove God wrong, meaning that they had the right to subvert and control all of the other beings in that sphere—using them to prove their scheme for "salvation." So they took advantage of their opportunity with the firm conviction that they were right and that they had a God-given right to do whatever is necessary to subdue all other beings in their sphere—getting them to worship the fallen angles instead of God, or rather, worship the angels *as* gods.

Why am I telling you all this? Because in order to become a true disciple of the Living Christ, you need to understand that you have to free yourself entirely from the consciousness of duality, the consciousness of the fallen angels. You need to understand that everything on Earth is currently influenced – at least to some degree, but in most cases to a large degree – by this consciousness and the graven images it has projected onto the Ma-ter light. The reason being that the fallen angels have set themselves up as the false teachers who are seeking to lead humankind into becoming the blind followers of the blind leaders. They are seeking to make humankind believe in the false path to salvation, the outer path, the path of inflating the ego to some ultimate status rather than simply surrendering the separate self and returning to oneness.

And how can you free yourself from these false teachers? Only by understanding how they are attempting to seduce humankind and why their dualistic illusions seem so persuasive, seem like reality. And we can now see the essence of this seduction. As I have said, in the duality consciousness there must of necessity be two divisions that will seem like opposites. This invariably causes beings trapped in duality to judge one division as being wrong and the other as being right. The reality, of course, is that both divisions are separated from the oneness of God, which is the underlying reality, meaning that both dualistic divisions are "wrong" in the sense that no matter which side you are on, it will keep you from oneness. Even fighting *for* what you think is a good cause will keep you engaged in the dualistic struggle and thus keep you from oneness.

Do you see the point? The dualistic divisions have no actual existence—they simply do not exist in the reality of God. They do have a temporary existence in the minds of the beings trapped in duality, but this is a relative existence. One division has existence only because it is defined in relation to the other division. None of the divisions have existence in relation to God's reality—they *only* have existence relative to each other. They have a relative – meaning temporary – existence and no absolute existence.

This, of course, is incomprehensible to the dualistic mind, which sees one division as right and the other wrong, meaning that the dualistic mind thinks the "right" division does have absolute existence because it is the same as God's reality. Once a being is convinced of this, it has great persuasive power and can thus convince those who are not as sure of themselves or not as skilled in reasoning.

Yet why does the dualistic "reality" seem real to some people? Because it is based on a dualistic, relative belief system. What does this mean? It means that it gives beings the opportunity to define "reality" in such a way that they are always right, that they cannot be challenged or gainsaid. Let me give you a concrete example.

I have explained that God is the Infinite and is beyond any finite expression, meaning that no religion can give a complete description of God. In order to know God you have to go beyond the outer religion and experience the Spirit of Truth. The consequence being that there can be many true religions, for any religion that helps you go beyond its outer teaching serves the true purpose of religion.

Yet the ego cannot fathom this, and thus it thinks everything must be evaluated in terms of right and wrong. The ego thinks there can be only one truth, and thus the existence of other religions than its own must be seen as a threat. It *is* truly a threat to the ego's sense of superiority, its belief that by belonging to the only true religion, it is guaranteed to be saved. Yet the ego projects a different image onto the situation and defines other religions as a threat to God's plan for the salvation of humankind, meaning it is now justifiable to kill the followers of those religions for the greater good of saving the entire universe.

Yet can you see that this absurd belief is a product of the fact that the separate self has defined its own image of reality? It has used the relative, dualistic logic to argue that reality is obviously divided into two opposing factions, of which one is right and the opposite is wrong. It then defines that its own relative polarity is not actually relative, but is absolutely right, meaning that the opposing polarity is absolutely wrong.

Can you see that this is what some people have called the "privilege of formulating the problem" or the "privilege of setting the tone for the debate?" In other words, if you can define the terms for how the world should be viewed, you can define them in such a way that you always seem to be right. Let me give you an example.

In ancient Greece, there was a group of philosophers who used a special definition of logic. For example, they might go through the following scenario:

A philosopher asks a person: "Is that dog yours?" The answer is "Yes," and the philosopher then asks: "Is that dog a father?" The answer is "Yes," and the philosopher then concludes: "Ergo, that dog is *your* father."

This is, of course, an absurd example, but to the ancient philosophers, this was simply the inevitable – and thus logical – outcome of *their* definition of logic. What I hope you can see is that the fallen angels have set themselves up as the false teachers of humankind, and they have done so by using logic that is equally absurd although far more subtle and harder to expose. Logic is based on a certain assumption or paradigm. Yet once you accept this paradigm as infallible or beyond questioning, your mind is locked on a track. And the track can lead to only one destination, namely the one defined by the basic assumption.

The essence of the logic of the fallen angels is the firm belief that they truly *are* separated from God. This separation gives rise to a fundamental and – as long as you are trapped in separation – inescapable duality, a division into two opposing factions. The angels have imposed the value judgment that one faction is right and the other wrong. They have then defined their own reality in such a way that *their* faction is always right and any opposing faction is always wrong.

This has created an epic struggle between what is defined as good and what is defined as evil. Yet both sides in this dualistic struggle are separated from God's reality, meaning that as long as you are engaged in the dualistic struggle between relative good and evil – thinking you are fighting for the ultimate good – you cannot question the underlying illusion of separation. In other words, the dualistic struggle is the second layer of illusion that is built on the first layer, namely separation itself. And the second layer obscures the underlying illusion, keeping your mind trapped in the struggle while never being able to question the original illusion.

Do you now see that the struggle is not actually real? It is simply a function of the fact that the fallen angels have defined their world view based on their own localized perspective. They have defined themselves as the center of the universe, and thus they are always right for everything is defined based on the one inescapable axiom, namely that the angels – the ego – could *never* be wrong. For if the separate self was proven wrong, it would be forced to admit that separation is an illusion, and thus the separate self could no longer exist (as separate but would have to die, whereby the conscious self would be reborn into oneness). Thus, the fallen angels would cease to exist, for they would be reborn into a new identity that is no longer a fallen being. Yet for this to happen, a fallen angel would have to voluntarily let its separate identity die, so as long as a being is not willing to do that, it must resist reality.

***

Step back and take another look at this. Any being is born with a localized sense of self, which gives that being a particular view of the world. The being looks at the universe from a localized vantage point. This is not wrong, as long as the being is aware that it is part of something bigger and that it can grow toward that something by expanding, or rather transcending, its localized view of the world. Yet when a being falls into duality, it now elevates its localized perspective to the status of universality and infallibility. Obviously, any localized view *can* and *will* be opposed by another localized view. You might have heard the ancient parable of the blind men who encountered an elephant and touched different parts of the elephants' body, causing them to identify the elephant as various other life forms.

So the problem here is that when you fall into duality, you define your *localized* view as the *universal* view, and it follows that any opposing or diverging view is defined as being wrong. Yet in order to maintain the ego's sense that – because it holds the universal view – it is guaranteed to be saved, you must seek to convert other people to accept your view and suppress all opposing views. Thus, you engage in a struggle to elevate your localized view by suppressing or destroying all other localized views. And this struggle will go on until you tire of it and decide to transcend your localized view instead of defending it.

So do you now begin to see the essential problem of the separate self? It is that the *individual* world view is thought to be the *universal* world view, meaning that it is the *only* right view. Thus, the world view of the separate self forms a closed lop, a closed mental box, a spiritual catch-22, from which there seemingly is no escape.

Yet the Creator is not unintelligent, and thus the Creator foresaw what could happen as a result of giving self-aware beings free will. And thus, there is a built-in safety mechanism, which is the very nature of duality. You see, originally, there was one group of fallen angels who fell together, and they fell because they were in agreement that God was wrong. Yet after they fell into duality, they started using the relative dualistic logic, and thus each angel defined its own world view with itself as the center, meaning that the angels now began to oppose each other. Since then, other angels have fallen and co-creators have fallen. So the result is that on Earth you now have a large number of opposing philosophies, religions, political ideologies and so forth.

This diversity is the inevitable result of the fact that duality is relative and thus makes it possible to raise a logical, rational argument for – literally – any possible idea. There is not one idea that cannot be supported by rational, logical arguments. To some, these arguments will seem absurd, but to others they will seem convincing. What is the difference?

Each idea is based on one particular localized view of the world, one particular assumption. In other words, it is based on selecting a particular point and then DEFINING it as the "center" of the universe. Once you accept that this particular point really *is* the center of the universe, all else must revolve around it, meaning that you now see the world from this particular vantage point. And thus, the world will truly look like this vantage point *is* the center, meaning that your idea or belief system will seem to be the only true one—as long as your conscious self sees the world from that particular "center."

This is why human beings during the Middle Ages believed the Earth was the center of the physical universe with the sun and all of the stars revolving around it. They had created a very narrow world view and had then placed themselves at the center. They looked at the universe only through the physical senses, and when you look up into the sky, it seems perfectly logical that the sun is moving in the sky and that the stars are revolving around the Earth—around you.

Likewise, many other people have defined similar world views. For example, mainstream Christians have defined an ego-centric world view that projects a false image upon Christ, namely that I was the *only* Son of God—which then confirms that all other people are separated from God. Modern scientists have defined a world view based on the "infallible" paradigm that there is nothing beyond the material universe. Communists have defined another world view based on infallible assumptions, and so on in an almost infinite variety over the same basic theme.

Why did people rise above the medieval world view? Because they were willing to question their basic world view, to mentally project themselves outside the senses and realize there was a more expanded perspective. Modern society will change only if a critical mass of people are willing to question their "infallible" paradigms, and that is why I need my modern-day disciples to be the forerunners for this process by questioning the beam – the unquestionable assumptions – in your own eyes.

I hope you can now see where I am leading with all this. What is the essence of Christhood? It is that you expand your mental box, which truly means that you overcome the illusion that your localized world view is the same as the universal world view. You let the sense of self based on your former localized world view die, so you can be reborn into a greater sense of self. And you keep doing this until your personal world view is expanded to where you can see that the only truly universal world view is that of the Creator. This helps you see that God is the true center of the universe, for God is everywhere—*including in you*. Thus, even while you are still in a physical body on Earth – and thus inevitably must see the world (outwardly) from a localized viewpoint – you can have a direct experience of the Spirit of Truth (inwardly). And thus, you can never be trapped in the localized world view—you see it as simply a practical way for the infinite self to express itself in the finite world.

You see, Christhood does *not* mean that your individual self is dissolved. It means that your individual self now comes to see itself as an expression of the Infinite Self. It sees itself as the Infinite Self expressing itself in a particular point of the world of form *without* being separated from the ocean of the Infinite Self. Thus, you can never see the individual self as the center of the world, for you know the Infinite Self is your center. The world does not revolve around you, you revolve around the Infinite Self that you are. I and my Father are one.

By attaining Christ consciousness, your individual self is not dissolved. What is dissolved is the illusion that the individual self is a separate self. What *is* dissolved is the separate self that was never real to begin with. What is left is the part of you that is real.

***

What has all this got to do with non-being? Well, non-being is a refusal to enter into oneness, oneness with the Creator and the spiritual hierarchy above you and oneness with all beings below you in the cosmic hierarchy. And this inevitably leads you into a form of denial. You deny not only God and other beings, but you also deny yourself, you deny your true identity. This inevitably leads you to stop your growth, for instead of entering the River of Life that leads to a continual expansion of your localized sense of self, you now cling to that localized sense of self. You set yourself outside the River of Life, which automatically makes your life a struggle. Yet instead of realizing you have made a mistake – as witnessed by the fact that you have to struggle – you go into a defensive mode. You seek to defend the separate self, and this, of course, only intensifies the struggle, causing you to be caught in a downward spiral from which there seems to be no escape—and there *is* no escape as long as the conscious self sees the world from inside the infallible paradigm of the separate self.

Modern psychologists have identified the ego's tendency to go into denial, which is really a selective form of self-awareness. Obviously, the core of your being is the conscious self, and it is named the conscious self precisely because it is *conscious*, it is self-aware. Yet the effect of non-being is that you define certain areas where self-awareness is shut off, areas where your self-awareness is denied entry, areas that you simply cannot look at. As I have described, the ego cannot look at the unreality of duality, for if it acknowledged that separation is unreal, it could not continue to exist. So to the ego there are certain basic beliefs that *cannot* be wrong and thus should never be examined. There are certain actions or events from the past that are defined as being so painful that they cannot or should not be examined. There are certain repetitive patterns in the psyche that are defined as being off limits, and so on.

The net effect of this is that the ego has managed to define a safe zone for itself. The ego knows it is safe – and has you under its control – as long as you do not examine certain beliefs, actions or patterns. What I am hoping to help you see here is that this leads to a completely warped way of life, for you are forced to adjust everything around avoiding the forbidden zones. It is like having a thorn under your foot. Every move you make must be adjusted to avoid the pain. This causes you to walk in an abnormal way that puts strain on other parts of your body, and soon your muscles start feeling sore or stiff. Yet you keep trying to compensate for this instead of doing the sensible thing of removing the thorn.

My point being that you can never turn off self-awareness. Therefore, when you enter into the state of non-being, you do not become unaware. You simply create a new sense of self, and that self will be constantly under attack. Why is this so? Because it is a dualistic sense of self, and thus no matter what viewpoint this self has, there will *always* be a dualistic opposite that threatens its sense of equilibrium. In other words, the dualistic self is out of balance, is not centered, which means it must constantly strive for some sense of equilibrium, some sense of being safe. Obviously, the only true form of equilibrium is oneness with your source, which is why the separate self can never find peace. Furthermore, the River of Life itself is a force that is constantly pulling on the separate self to expand and grow. So we might say that the separate self is being "threatened" both *internally* – by the dualistic forces in the realm of separation – and *externally* by the life force itself seeking to pull your conscious self out of illusion. This is what I described in my parable about the unwise man who built his house on sand – the relativity of the duality consciousness – and the wise man who built on rock, the rock of the Christ consciousness, centered in reality.

Do you see that you will never find peace as long as you allow this struggle to go on, for you will be a house divided against itself? As Maitreya explains in his book, the conscious self often falls because it refuses to make decisions, and thus it creates the ego to make decisions for it. In a sense, the conscious self is hoping that it can avoid being conscious by letting the ego take over. Yet this can never work, for although you can numb your awareness, you can never switch it off completely. Thus, the ego forces you into what we might call a negative self-awareness in which you always feel threatened by forces that seem to be beyond your control. You go into what psychologists call the fight-or-flight response, where you are constantly seeking to escape external threats and having to fight what you cannot run away from.

This leads to the development of what psychologists call unnecessary defense mechanisms, leading to all kinds of psychological imbalances, even the outright paranoia of thinking the entire world is against you. Obviously, spiritual seekers have overcome the most common and obvious forms of such defense mechanisms, but I need you to take a serious look at the possibility that you still have some subtle defense mechanisms that are set up to defend the basic illusions of your ego.

Am I saying you definitely have such mechanisms? Well, let me suggest a test. If you have no unnecessary defense mechanisms, then you will – naturally and with no hesitation or resistance – be willing to look into any area of your psychology and see if there is any tendency to defend anything, any tendency to resist the teacher. In other words, if you are free of all defense mechanisms, then you have no resistance toward looking at any aspect of your psychology, your past, your life and considering what needs to change. So if you feel any resistance toward such completely open self-examination, if you have any tense feelings about this, you obviously have some defense mechanisms left. And I can assure you that your ego is hiding behind the barrier created by these defenses.

Some people might feel like I am sticking a knife in an open wound and deliberately twisting it. Others might be wondering if I am going to keep exposing anything in their psychology until everything is laid bare. To the first response, let me say that only the ego can feel this way and to the second the answer is simple: I do intend to expose absolutely everything in your psychology that springs from duality and keeps you from the infinite freedom and abundant life that can only come from oneness with your source. If I leave any stone unturned, the ego will hide under it, and that will keep you from entering into the Circle of Oneness and attaining complete peace. Why would I want anything for you that is less than your highest potential—and why would *you* want anything less for yourself? Only the ego will cling to what is less instead of accepting the abundant life that it is the Creator's good pleasure to give you.

***

We now see that non-being has a price, namely constant self-consciousness, the constant need to defend something that is under perpetual attack. This causes you to go into a frame of mind based on avoiding pain—which has the effect of also avoiding growth.

Am I saying you cannot grow without pain, that there is no gain without pain? Well, at a certain point that is true, for you cannot escape the illusions of the ego without consciously looking at them, and that will bring you in touch with the memories and emotional pain that came from the actions that sprang from a certain illusion. However, who is feeling that pain? Only the ego! Thus, *you* will feel that pain only as long as the conscious self is identifying itself with the ego and is looking at life through the filter – the localized perspective – of the ego. My point being that the conscious self has the potential to – instantly – shift its sense of focus, its sense of self, away from the ego and toward the infinite world view of your Creator. Doing this is true spiritual freedom.

How do you make that switch? It might help you to consider that there is a fundamental difference between being self-conscious and being self-aware. Self-consciousness is a dualistic state of mind, which means it is constantly torn between two opposites, such as right and wrong. It is also based on an unavoidable value judgment that forces you into constantly defending why you are right in order to avoid the pain of being wrong. Self-consciousness stops growth by making you compare yourself to an external standard—in this world. This shuts off creativity by turning you into a predictable person who never goes beyond the mold—in order to uphold the sense of equilibrium that is the basis for the ego's sense of superiority and safety. The price you pay for this fleeting sense of superiority is that you are constantly judging yourself, and since the world has a nasty habit of not living up to your dualistic expectations, safety will not last forever. Pride truly does go before the fall because pride creates the fall.

In contrast, self-awareness is non-dual, meaning that it is a neutral state of observing yourself and the world without needing to judge it based on a dualistic standard. This is the natural state for the conscious self. You need to be self-aware in order to consciously raise up your self and flow with the River of Life. The River of Life is the process of becoming more, the process of vertical self-transcendence, and this is a creative process. You can *only* become more through creativity, and creativity is inherently unpredictable. So self-awareness will not hold you back but will neutrally evaluate any event based on whether it is a full expression of who you are. Thus, self-awareness constantly spurs you on toward becoming more—which is true creativity.

We can say that self-consciousness causes you to base your sense of self on something *outside* yourself, something in this world. Self-awareness causes you to base your sense of self on something *inside* yourself, namely your own Higher Being and the spiritual hierarchy out of which you came. *You* decide which way gives you access to the kingdom of God, which is, as I might have mentioned a few times, *within* you.

We now see that the ego feels threatened by creativity precisely because it is unpredictable and thus cannot be controlled. Which means the ego thinks it cannot avoid pain and stay hidden as long as you are creative. Thus, the ego wants you to enter the state of non-being that shuts off the creative flow through your being. Yet since the conscious self was designed to be in this flow, shutting it off carries the steep price of making you feel like life has no meaning, like you are not getting anywhere, like you have no worth. In other words, it truly takes all the joy out of life, which is why the only way to be fulfilled and at peace is for you to re-enter the River of Life. The ego seeks to compensate for this by engaging you in the dualistic struggle to raise the separate self, thereby giving you a false sense of accomplishment by being better than other people. Yet even though this can divert your attention for a time, it can never be ultimately satisfying, meaning that you will eventually have to go back and remove the beam from your own eye—so you can find the kingdom of God that is within you and not in this world.

In order to do this, you must raise your self-consciousness above the fear of separation and reconnect to the divine quality of seeking perfection—you must let self-consciousness transcend into self-awareness. Perfection is ultimately God consciousness. Yet the intermediate stage on the way to this perfection, the Christic stage of perfection, is complete willingness to self-transcend and to keep doing so. This requires a willingness to look at anything in your psyche and simply transcend it by allowing the separate self to die. You give up any aspect of the separate self as soon as it comes to your conscious awareness, whereby you take another step toward complete freedom. Once you lock into this process, it does not cause pain, for instead of being trapped in the sense of loss of the ego, you are focused on the sense of gain that the conscious self experiences every time it takes another step closer to the freedom to be who you are.

In other words, by making a switch in the way you look at life, you can overcome the resistance to change and thereby also overcome the stage where giving up something old leads to pain. You can have gain without pain because it no longer causes you pain to give up that which prevents your gain. In fact, the more of the separate self you give up, the more free you feel, which means you welcome the exposure of the dualistic illusions. And this is the point where you can truly follow a spiritual teacher and allow the teacher to help you make maximum progress.

***

As we have already talked about, many spiritual people have a subtle fear of having something exposed, something that will threaten their sense of equilibrium. This is truly what the ego is always seeking—a sense of equilibrium. The ego is constantly seeking to set itself up in a position where two conditions are fulfilled:

- The ego feels it is in control.
- The ego feels its control cannot be threatened.

In order to accomplish this, the ego wants you to accept certain dualistic beliefs and then elevate them to the status of infallibility, so you never question them, and so you always defend them against any attacks—if necessary by going into complete denial, where you simply refuse to think about anything that threatens your basic paradigms. This can give rise to a certain sense of pride or superiority, where people actually use the spiritual path to build the pride of the separate self. Yet many spiritual people cannot maintain the pride and often get stuck in a subtle and unrecognized passivity, where they feel they simply have to stay within certain boundaries and wait for their future salvation. The ego would like for you to expand your sense of superiority indefinitely, but if that cannot be achieved, the ego wants you to go into the passive state of thinking you will be saved if only you keep doing and believing the same thing.

You can see this in fundamentalist Christians, who think they simply have to believe in a literal interpretation of the Bible without questioning it, and then they are guaranteed to be saved. Yet what you need to consider is that even many spiritual seekers have accepted that their egos have defined barriers for their self-examination. They have allowed their egos to make them self-conscious, which means they have set aside certain areas from the penetrating light of self-awareness. You need to expose and overcome this dysfunctional self-consciousness, and here is why.

Self-consciousness always judges whether something is right or wrong. And since the ego cannot be wrong, you are tricked into defending any aspect of the ego that is threatened by your current situation—and there is always some aspect of the ego that feels threatened. In contrast, self-awareness simply evaluates whether something sets you free or imprisons you. Thus, when you objectively see that something is taking away your freedom, you can effortlessly let go of that something and be reborn into a new, freer sense of self. You can effortlessly let the old unfree self die.

What I am leading up to here is the recognition that the state of non-being has the effect of pacifying you in a spiritual sense. As I have said, you were designed to be a co-creator with God, and you originally descended into an unascended sphere with the intention of helping to co-create the kingdom of God in that sphere. Yet the state of non-being has completely aborted that goal by causing you to defend everything that prevents you from achieving that goal, namely the separate self and the illusions behind which it is hiding.

You need to get to the point where you are free to *be* your spiritual self and do what you came here for. Your divine plan cannot be fulfilled through the ego and cannot be fulfilled by being passive. You are here to help change the world, not watch the world continue doing the same thing—because *you* are doing the same thing in order to uphold the ego's sense of equilibrium.

This leads to the conclusion that the state of non-being is a prison in which you are condemned to defend that which cannot be defended, namely the ego's sense of equilibrium that is threatened both by the River of Life and by its own internal duality. You may be very active in terms of defending the separate self (by fighting *against* other people or fighting *for* causes), but you are passive in terms of fulfilling your reason for being. This then gives the conscious self a sense of being unfulfilled, which the ego interprets as a threat to its sense of equilibrium, causing it to redouble its efforts to keep you on the defensive, possibly by making you think you are working for some ultimate cause. And this little game can go on for lifetimes before people have finally had enough and start looking for a true spiritual teacher.

A true spiritual teacher will help you enter into a state of *being,* where you are self-aware without judging yourself or anything else. You are flowing *with* the River of Life and allowing your Infinite Self to express itself through you. This is truly a state of *life,* whereas non-being is a state of *death*.

***

Have you fully grasped why non-being kills creativity? As we have seen, the ego is trying to achieve through control what the River of Life offers you freely—if you will only flow with it. What does it take to control something? Well, you have to be able to predict what is going to happen next. Predictability is the foundation for effective control. The more predictable a person is, the easier it is to control that person. The fewer variables that are present in a situation, the easier it is to control that situation. So the ego wants to eliminate unpredictability, and that is why it *has* to eliminate creativity—*for creativity is inherently unpredictable!*

Think about this. Creativity is a spontaneous activity that cannot be planned in advance. Creativity is the spontaneous emergence of better solutions than anyone had consciously thought of before. An activity that is planned ahead of time is not a creative activity—it is a *controlled* activity. There is no such thing as planned creativity. There is no such thing as controlled creativity. Creativity is the spontaneous expression of that which is new, that which is alive. Control leads to death, whereas life is always spontaneous.

The Conscious You is designed to be a wholly creative being. You are designed to be in the creative flow that *is* life itself, to be the open door for that flow to express itself in the material world, thereby bringing forth new solutions to old problems. And that is why your ego must kill the creative flow through you. How can it control you if you are open to this flow? And how can the ego build and maintain any type of security and safety if it never knows what you might do next?

What is the effect of killing your inherent creativity? It is that it turns you into a mechanized being, a kind of self-conscious robot. The Earth is currently populated by almost six billion of such robots, and that is why humankind is so amazingly predictable. That is why there are so many unspoken beliefs that are never questioned. That is why people act as sheep that always stay within the fold, where they are controlled by a power elite—the blind leaders.

Besides your personal ego, there is another force that wants to control you. This force is made up of embodied and disembodied beings that form the planetary force of darkness, sometimes called the false hierarchy. The core of this force is the fallen angels and the disembodied beings – or beasts – that Maitreya describes in his book. How can this force control you? By making you predictable, and they can do this only by getting you to shut off your creativity, which is why there are so many aspects of human society that are aimed at either killing your creativity or channeling it into activities that do not threaten the status quo.

On a grand scale, the purpose is to control humankind, so those who have aligned themselves with the false hierarchy can form a power elite that can attain and maintain positions of privilege and power in human society. Who was it that had me killed 2,000 years ago? It was the power elite of the time, those who felt they were in control of society and did not want the Living Christ to threaten their control over the people. Of course, the most effective way to control the population is to go to the individual level and shut off the flow of creativity through each person.

The blind leaders do this by luring you into denying your God-given individuality and reducing yourself to the separate self, which is not a *creative* being but a *mechanical* being. Thus, as long as you identify yourself with and as the separate self, you are easy to control. Your ego is predisposed – programmed – to always stay within boundaries and never enter the unpredictability of creativity. Why? Because, as we have seen, the ego looks for the outer path which promises that if only you follow the outer rules of a belief system – if only you blindly follow the blind leaders – you are guaranteed to be saved. This is what has created the entire myth of the outer path, which is a mechanical path. However, on an even deeper level, your ego is actually created out of certain dualistic beliefs, and that is why the ego cannot question the very illusions that brought it into existence.

In contrast, I hope you are now beginning to see that the true path is a creative path. The Living Christ is not a *mechanical* being but a *creative* being. Not even God can predict what a Christed being will do, for the Creator did indeed create extensions of itself and gave them a Christ potential because the Creator wants to be surprised by the individual creativity of its offspring. This, of course, contradicts the doctrines of traditional religion, but the reason is that for thousands of years religion has been one of the primary means for shutting off people's creativity and turning them into blind followers of the blind leaders—the fallen angels.

***

This leads us to an entirely new perspective on what the true path is all about. Let me summarize what we have discussed. We have seen that the conscious self starts out with a limited sense of identity, a localized world view. The path is a process of expanding your sense of identity until you attain full God consciousness. And here is the essential point. The localized sense of identity with which your lifestream originally came into being is *not* the same as the separate identity of the ego!

Your original sense of identity was *localized,* but it was based on oneness. You saw yourself as an individual being who was part of something larger than your self, as a wave on the ocean. Yet in reality, you were an *extension* of the ocean, which means you could transcend your sense of self until you saw yourself as one with the ocean—as one with both the Creator and all other waves on the ocean. This is *not* the same as expanding your separate self—it is transcending all sense that the self is separate.

The essential illusion of the ego is that the separate self is real. Thus, the logic of the ego says that the spiritual path is about expanding the separate self. The separate self is like a puddle of water disconnected from the ocean. The ego is trying to expand the puddle until it becomes as big as the ocean. This is an impossible quest. The real quest is to expand the individual sense of self to oneness with the ocean rather than to expand the separate self to be the size of the ocean but still separated from it.

So those blinded by the ego are seeking to inflate the ego, thinking if it only becomes big enough, it will – like the tower of Babel – reach into the heavens and God simply *has* to accept it, since it is so much better than the separate selves of other people blinded by duality. This is *not* the path of the true disciples of Christ, but the false path of the anti-disciples.

Which leads us to consider what is the true purpose of this course. This course is *not* an automatic, mechanized path, as are many schools on Earth. Consider for example the education of many priests. They go through a course in a theological seminary, and if they fulfill all of the requirements of the course – the main requirement being that they don't question the basic doctrines of the religion offering the course – they automatically become ordained as priests. The requirement is outer learning and adherence to a predefined system. There is little room for considering the student's state of consciousness, nor the degree to which the student dares to be creative and look for an understanding that is beyond doctrines.

In this course, everything is different. There is no exam and you will not get a diploma. It is entirely possible that a person can take this course without understanding the reality I am seeking to explain, without understanding the nature of the path. Out of ten people who study this course, some will understand and some will not. The reason is that this is a creative course, and the outcome is entirely a matter of how much of your God-given creativity you are willing to apply to the process of following this course. You cannot be mechanical about this course, for if you are, you will emerge as a person who has great intellectual knowledge of Christhood but who has never touched the Spirit of Truth and thus is unworthy to touch the hem of the garment of the Living Christ.

What have I actually done with the description of the path that I have given you up until this point? Well, if you have understood what I have been saying, I have taken all the mystery out of the path. Instead of some mysterious process of seeking for the hidden secret, the ultimate teaching or the enlightened guru hiding in a cave in the Himalayas, I have described the path as a very pragmatic process of questioning, exposing and surrendering the illusions of the separate self—until you can finally see the separate self itself and surrender it.

This path leaves no room for the sense of security that you will automatically be saved, nor does it feed the ego's desire to feel better than others. For such a false path only reinforces the illusion of separation from God—and this is *not* Christhood.

So the question at this point is whether you are still interested in following a path that offers no security and no superiority. If you are, I need you to consider making a decision—the decision to BE.

You see, what caused the fall of the original angels was their decision *not* to be. They did not want to choose the state of being one with their Creator and they were not willing to serve those below them in hierarchy, they were not willing to be one as above, so below. This non-will and non-being is – as everything else – a specific form of energy, a spiritual poison. Since the first fall, this energy has accumulated, and it has formed a formidable force that exerts a very strong gravitational pull on the beings of all people on Earth.

You have been exposed to this force for many lifetimes, and it has likely overwhelmed you. And the sheer magnetism of this force has given rise to a new form of non-being and non-will, namely the sense that it is too difficult, too overwhelming, to rise above the downward pull of the world. When you begin to understand what the spiritual path is really all about, you might look at where you are today and you might look forward to the goal of personal Christhood. And you might have a "moment of truth" that makes you realize just how far you are from attaining the goal—now that you are awakened from the ignorance that is not bliss but does give you the blissful sense that your salvation is in the bag. So you might look at the long road ahead and feel a sense of dread, a sense that it is overwhelming to walk the path. You might feel that it seems easier to just give up and merge into the mass consciousness, flowing along with everyone else—flowing along with the river of death that has been created by the fallen angels and all of their followers.

They have attempted to create the antithesis to the River of Life, a force that overwhelms people and pulls them into mechanically repeating certain patterns of thought and behavior. These false teachers and your ego will do anything they can – depending on your personal history and psychology – to discourage you from following the true path. Thus, I need you to make the decision that you will *not* follow the false path, even though it seems like the path of least resistance—but it is truly the path of maximum resistance, the resistance created by the inherent conflict in a dualistic world view. I need you to decide that you will allow me to show you the true path, which is the path of *no* resistance.

How do you make this decision? By reconnecting to the diamond will within your spiritual self—the very power of unassailable will that brought you here in the first place. You see, you did not descend to the material universe for the purpose of becoming trapped in the duality consciousness and clawing your way back up the spiral staircase. You descended with a positive purpose of expressing your God-given creativity and thus making a contribution to manifesting the kingdom of God on Earth. This desire is based on an immovable will to be part of God's creation, to be part of the River of Life, to BE who you are, to BE here below all that you are above.

And when you rediscover that diamond will, the decision to leave behind the false path and join the true path will come spontaneously. However, to help you rediscover your inner drive to BE, I will give you the exercise for this key.

## Exercise for Key 12

In the coming 33 days, repeat the pattern of giving a rosary and writing down your thoughts. This time, I need you to give the Invocation for Creative Freedom of Will.[13]

After giving the invocation, write down how you have been programmed to deny your creativity, how you have been conditioned to *not* express that creativity.

Yet I also want you to set aside some time where you simply write whatever comes to you without placing any restrictions on it whatsoever. Center yourself in your heart, and then write whatever comes. If nothing comes, then simply stay centered for as long as you feel like it and wait for the writing to flow spontaneously. If you need help in getting things to flow, consider this question: "If I had absolutely no restrictions for my creativity, what would my higher self desire to express through me?"

---

[13] Found on *www.askrealjesus.com* in the Golden Age section.

# Key 13
# The non-violence of the Living Christ

It is time to step back and take a look at what we have achieved so far. If you have performed the exercises, you have gone through a period of purification. This is always the first stage when a student comes to a spiritual teacher. The teacher must require new students to cut the ties to the energies, beings and beliefs that will prevent the students from following the teacher's instructions. Thus, the students must learn to protect themselves from influences from the world, and they must learn how to expose and let go of the impulses that have already entered their beings. The students must move toward the point where the prince of this world will come and have nothing in them that can pull them away from the teacher.

Each teacher has a right to define his or her own process for allowing students to enter the teacher's Circle of Oneness. Each teacher has a right to set his or her own barrier of entry for those who want to be students of that teacher. Students who are not willing to go through the process of purification defined by the teacher, are simply not a match for that teacher and should thus seek out a different one. You see, a true spiritual teacher has no judgments. True teachers do not say that those students who will not follow their instructions are bad or will go to hell. They simply say that such students are not a fit for the teacher, because their consciousness does not resonate with the consciousness of the teacher—as that consciousness is expressed through a specific vessel. Thus, the teacher cannot help that student.

I am the Ascended Jesus Christ, and I cannot be restricted by any expression on Earth, whether the Bible, this course or anything else. I can and do express myself in many different ways. This course is a true expression of my Being, but it is not the only one. Thus, if you do not resonate with this course, you should seek out another expression of the one true teacher.

Why am I telling you this at this late stage in the course? Well, perhaps you haven't noticed, but I have been telling you this indirectly in every key. Why have I done this? Because as a spiritual teacher I have learned that it is impossible to bring forth any manifestation that will help everyone. Thus, my overall goal is to show you that behind this and any other true expression is an inner path. Your primary concern should be to lock yourself on that inner path and to seek out a teacher that can help you take the next step on your personal path—continuing to seek out the teacher who can take you to the next level.

However, I also have a more subtle reason, which is to test my students—as it is my right and my commitment to do. What am I doing by telling you to abandon this course if you do not resonate with it? I am offering your ego an easy way out! You see, the ego is constantly looking for a way to pull you away from the true path and back onto the outer path. And by offering you a way out I am – now that you have purified your being from the more obvious spiritual poisons – giving you an opportunity to unmask the ego. If you will look honestly at your reactions to this course, you might indeed spot the ego's attempts to pull you back into the fold. And this can then assist you in separating the real you even more from the ego. Certainly, I hope you can avoid the trap of "guru-hopping," where people jump from guru to guru – thinking the next one will be the right one who will do all the work for them – instead of looking at the beam in their own eyes. Or they find a guru who tells them exactly what their egos want to hear.

I do, however, have another reason for talking about whether you should continue with this course. The reason is that we have reached a turning point. Beginning with this key, the course will take a different direction. It is possible you are not yet ready to go in this direction and that you need more time to integrate the lessons learned so far. There is not necessarily anything wrong with this, as each person has an individual path to walk and should not try to take growth by force. Some people will have such deep psychological wounds that they need time to heal and are not yet ready to engage in the next stage of this course. In fact, many people could benefit immensely from seeking the help of a professional in the field of psychological healing before they continue with the course or as they continue with the course. I hope you will be sensitive to your personal situation and follow your inner direction in seeking out the healing that can help you heal your personal wounds and see through the blocks in your psyche. A professional can be the personal extension of the teacher in the sense that such a practitioner will not be *inside* your personal mental box.

I have no illusions of creating a course that fits everyone. It simply is not possible to take people through a 10-11 month period and have them all be at the same level at the end. So if you feel you are not yet ready, then do not seek to force yourself. On the other hand, recognize that your ego can also use this to get you to procrastinate making the decision to be ready—and to do so indefinitely. For in the end, "being ready" is all about making the decision to be ready—it is *not* something that happens as a result of external conditions.

Take note of how you respond to these statements. Do you sense a frustration or anger over me saying that the course cannot guarantee results? If so, recognize that it comes from the ego, which is still desperately seeking to use this course to build a sense of outer security—to reinforce its sense of equilibrium, its sense of having control over you and the world. "Surely, if this course is a real course, following it diligently for so many months should entitle me to some kind of status! And if I am not getting it, then there must be something wrong with the course or the teacher."

But what did I show you in the last key? I showed you that the path to Christhood is *not* a mechanical process. It is a *creative* process! Thus, there is no way to guarantee results—for how do you even define what the results of a creative process should be? Everything is a matter of how well you integrate the lessons I offer and how willing you are to express what you have internalized. I can only offer the lessons, I can only lead you to water—I cannot make you drink.

Furthermore, there is no standard outcome, as you see in many schools on Earth. Contrary to popular belief – even among ascended master students – there is no standard for what it means to be the Christ. Thus, a true course in Christhood cannot take you to a final exam in which every student gives the same answers to a set of standardized questions. As I said, Christhood is a creative process, and how can you standardize creativity? It is *not* my goal to make you a clone of me. It is my goal to help you be the unique individual that you were created to be and to express your unique gift to this world—for *this* is Christhood.

What is the new direction we will take in this and coming keys? Well, we will finally get started on giving you the keys to walking the path to Christhood. What is that? You thought I have been giving you the keys to the path to Christhood all along? Not exactly! So far I have been giving you the keys to the path of personal growth, the path of raising your consciousness. For a time, the path of raising your consciousness overlaps the path to Christhood in the sense that you *do* need to raise your consciousness to a certain level before you can even begin the path to Christhood. Yet it is now time for you to acknowledge that the path to Christhood is *not* the same as the path to personal growth. There will come a point on the path of personal growth where you must make a choice. You can continue on the path of personal growth or you can enter the path to Christhood. In this key, we will explore the differences, so you can make an informed choice.

If you want the difference in a nutshell, here it is: The path of personal growth is the path of raising *your* consciousness. The path of Christhood is the path of raising consciousness.

***

So far we have talked about the first two challenges of Christ. The first one is that you recognize the Living Christ and recognize that it is possible for you to attain a higher state of consciousness, a higher form of life. The second challenge is that you allow the Living Christ to help you attain that higher state of consciousness by taking you beyond your mental boxes, your mortal sense of identity. Can you see that until you are willing to let the Living Christ take you beyond your mental box, you cannot actually start the path of Christhood? Instead, you will be seeking to use the Living Christ to elevate the separate self, which is the path of personal growth.

It is now time to talk about the third challenge of Christ, which is that you recognize that you can go beyond simply following an external teacher. You can actually become one with the teacher, whereby *you* become the Living Christ.

Do you see the progression here? We can also describe it in terms of the separate self. Most people are trapped in a state of consciousness that is spiritual death, meaning that they are entirely blinded by the dualistic illusions of the separate self. They are completely convinced that they *are* the separate self, that they are mortal, human beings—however they define that based on their religious or materialistic world view. The first challenge of Christ is to recognize that there is a reality beyond the world created by the separate self, that it is possible to escape the mortal identity of the separate self and attain a higher sense of identity.

The second challenge of Christ is to go through the process of systematically exposing, consciously recognizing and then letting go of the illusions that make up your personal separate self. As you do this, you will gradually attain a higher understanding, a higher sense of freedom and a higher sense of self—yet you still have not necessarily challenged the basic illusion of the separate self, namely that it is real and separate. In other words, it is possible to go through the process of raising your consciousness – making genuine progress – but still maintaining the sense that you are raising *your* consciousness. You can come to see through many of the illusions created by the dualistic mind while still not seeing the basic illusion of separateness—and this truly is the hardest illusion to overcome. Which is why death is called the last enemy:

> 20 But now is Christ risen from the dead, and become the firstfruits of them that slept.
> 21 For since by man came death, by man came also the resurrection of the dead.
> 22 For as in Adam all die, even so in Christ shall all be made alive.
> 23 But every man in his own order: Christ the firstfruits; afterward they that are Christ's at his coming.
> 24 Then cometh the end, when he shall have delivered up the kingdom to God, even the Father; when he shall have put down all rule and all authority and power.
> 25 For he must reign, till he hath put all enemies under his feet.
> 26 The last enemy that shall be destroyed is death. (1Corinthians, Chapter 15)

My point is that if you take an honest look at spiritual seekers, you will see that one of the primary motivations that drives people is the desire to attain a higher state of consciousness, but to do so in a way that is still focused on the self—the separate self. This is not necessarily done in a prideful or comparative way, as we have talked about in the last few keys. It is done in a very subtle way that gives people the impression that raising your consciousness is a personal goal. You are seeking to attain a state of enlightenment in which you understand everything, you are seeking to attain a state of bliss, you are seeking to attain mastery over matter, you are seeking to attain oneness with God—or however the ultimate goal might be defined.

Now, here comes the subtle distinction. There is not necessarily anything wrong with seeking enlightenment, bliss or union with God, but the crucial question is *why* you are seeking this? Are you seeking this with a sense that *you* – meaning the separate self – can attain this and that this is desirable for the separate self? Or are you able and willing to raise your motivation to a higher level?

Do you see the subtlety? As you start the path, you need to have a motivation. Yet what motivates you at the level where you start the path must of necessity be a reflection of your state of consciousness at that point. And what is that state of consciousness? It is that you are still very much identified *with* and *as* a separate self. So to get started on the path, you need a motivation that makes it seem like the path offers something that is valuable to the separate self—otherwise why go through the trouble of seeking spiritual growth, why not simply eat, drink and be merry? So people formulate their own individual motives in order to start the path. As they climb the path, they attain a greater understanding, which forces them to face a choice.

The question is whether people can raise their motives based on their new understanding? You see, as you acquire a higher understanding, you will come to a "moment of truth" that makes you see that the path will not actually give you what you were seeking when you started. In other words, you started with a motivation centered around the separate self, but as you grow in understanding, you begin to see that this motivation was a house built on sand. Some people go through a period of experiencing a sense of disappointment or even anger, perhaps by feeling they were lied to by an outer teacher or religion. That is why you see many people in the modern age who become disgruntled with religion in general or with a specific religion or teacher. Some go into a blind alley of blaming a religion or teacher, whereas others raise their motivation and formulate a new goal. This new motivation will be higher than the previous one, but it will still be a reflection of your state of consciousness at the time. So the process of refining your motives will be ongoing.

For some people this becomes a source of stress, where they feel each cycle like a traumatic event that causes them a sense of grief or loss. What I am hoping to help you see here is that you can shift your perspective and overcome this pain.

You simply need to realize that as your understanding grows, it is only natural that your motivation will shift. On top of that, you can now begin to realize that you must of necessity start out with a motivation centered around the separate self. The separate self thinks it can gain something from walking the spiritual path. Yet when you walk the true path, the separate self actually will not gain anything, as the path is all about the real you overcoming identification with the separate self, whereby the separate self dies. So what you realize is that every motive that is influenced by the separate self is bound to lead to disappointment (unless you switch to the false path that does offer the separate self the illusion that it is superior to others).

So when you realize the mechanics of this, your conscious self can now step back and look at the process from an overall perspective. Thus, you can decide not to identify with the disappointment of the separate self, whereby you will avoid feeling its pain and loss. You can then begin to look for a higher motivation by contemplating the third challenge of Christ. Let us take a closer look.

***

What is the motivation you can build by understanding the third challenge of Christ? Well, again, that will depend on your current state of consciousness, but let us begin with a broad motivation. What have we achieved by taking you through the process of purification outlined in the previous keys? We have reduced the magnetic, gravitational pull that draws you toward the dualistic struggle. The net effect of this is to give your conscious self the opportunity to free itself from this struggle. We have set your attention free to contemplate who you really are. Thus, we might say that the process has been one of taking you toward spiritual independence, spiritual freedom.

Is that a goal that resonates with you? Do you have a desire to be free, to be truly independent of anything on Earth? If so, you are on the way to developing a higher motivation based on the third challenge of Christ. For what does it mean to become the Christ? It means to become completely and utterly independent of *anything* in the material world. You have become spiritually self-sufficient, meaning that you no longer believe – as most people do – that you need anyone or anything from the material world in order to be whole. Thus, you can truly say that the prince of this world comes and has nothing in you because you and your Father are one. My point being, of course, that I suggest you make it your main goal to attain this state of spiritual independence, which will then allow us to begin considering what it will take for you to be spiritually free.

Obviously, one goal of this course is to make you a true disciple of the Living Christ, which means you cannot at the same time be on the false path. Thus, in order for you to be free to follow the path of Christhood, you cannot have any hooks in your being whereby the false teachers can pull you away from the true path and toward the false path. So let us take a look at one of the more subtle of these hooks, namely the concept that someone else has the power to do something to you. Certainly, you cannot be free as long as you entertain the belief that someone – or some exterior force – actually has power to do something to you against your will.

One of the greatest lies foisted upon humankind by the forces of anti-christ is the concept that someone or some force from outside yourself has power to do something to you against your will. This lie springs directly from the illusion we talked about in the last key, namely that a group of fallen beings believe they have the power to create an alternative to God's creation, that they have been given the material universe as an opportunity to prove God wrong and that they consequently have the right to force or fool others to follow them. Thus, they have perpetuated the lie that they actually have the power to force you to follow them—meaning that they have actual power over you.

At this point, you might be wondering what I am talking about, since your every-day experience is that there are people who have physical power to hurt you. For example, someone might strike you on one cheek—to use my own saying. And even though I was supposedly the only son of God, the leaders of the time still had the power to condemn me to death and nail me to a cross—or so it would seem. Yet who was it they nailed to that cross? Was it me or was it just a physical body that I was temporarily using as an instrument to express my real self on Earth? Was it the real me, or was it a material expression, a mere mirage that I, the Living Christ, used to make their own evil more visible—thus giving them an opportunity to rise above it, if they so chose?

What I have been taking you toward in previous keys is the recognition that you are *not* the physical body, that you are a spiritual being who is only using the body as a temporary vehicle for expressing yourself in the material world. So if you are more than the body, how can anything done to the body hurt the real you? Unless, of course, you identify with the body and thus believe in the illusion that what is done to the body is also done to you. If you look at my crucifixion, you will see that I did not identify with my body. That is why I could forgive those who crucified me and why I could give up the ghost as a final act of separating the real self from the physical envelope. I thereby demonstrated that although the powers of this world had the power to kill my body, they could not even begin to touch the real Being that I AM. You, of course, must do the same. You must come to the point where you know that you are more than anything in this world, and thus no power in this world can hurt or even affect the real you.

As Mother Mary and Maitreya explain, everything is made from energy and there are different levels of vibration. As an illustration, consider the hardness of physical matter. A block of wood may seem hard if it hits you over the head, but try scratching a diamond with it and you will get nowhere. Wood is simply not hard enough to have any effect on a diamond. A sound wave is pure energy, and you can create a sound wave powerful enough to shatter buildings. Yet try using sound to affect sunlight and you will get nowhere. The reason being that material sound has a lower vibration than light and thus can have no effect on light whatsoever. My point being, of course, that you are a spiritual being, meaning that the real you is made from energy of a vibration that is much higher than any vibration found in the material universe. Thus, it follows logically that nothing in the material universe can have any direct power over the real you. It is like trying to scratch a diamond with a toothpick.

The fallen angels and the beasts they have created have been condemned to the material universe. This universe has four levels, and each level is made of energies that vibrate within a certain spectrum of frequencies. You have four lower bodies, four levels of the mind, and each body exists within the corresponding frequency spectrum. Your physical body obviously exists within the physical frequency spectrum or octave, and it can be affected by other energies within that spectrum. So other people in a physical body can hurt your body. However, beings who are *not* in a physical body cannot harm your body. Thus, the age-old concept that there are demons or other dark beings who can affect you physically is simply out of touch with reality. It was a concept perpetrated by the false teachers for the purpose of perpetuating the lie that others have power over you—and the fear that springs from it.

There are dark beings in the emotional realm, and they do have the power to affect your emotional body. However, in order to do this, they have to go through your mind, and thus you can protect yourself by having your emotional body be controlled by your mental body, which can easily see through the manipulations of beings in the emotional realm. Of course, your mental body can be affected by dark beings in the mental realm, so you also need to have your mental body controlled by your identity body, which can easily see through the mental lies. And finally, you need to have your identity body controlled by your conscious self in oneness with your Higher Being, your Christ self and I AM Presence, so you will know you are more than anything in this world. And thus, no power in this world can influence you against your will.

***

Let us look at this from another angle. Say someone slaps you on one cheek. Most people would feel that *they* have been hurt, but you are a spiritual person, so you know you are more than the body. You are the conscious self, which is an extension of the Creator's own Being. Obviously, the Creator is above and beyond *any* vibration in the material universe, even the entire world of form. Thus, the core of your being cannot be affected by anything in this world.

Yet the conscious self is who it thinks it is—at least in the moment. Thus, if you are not consciously aware of who you are, you might identify yourself with and as the physical body, as most people do. It now follows that you will believe that if someone hurts your body, they have hurt *you*. What is the net effect? The effect is that those who hurt your body do have power over you—but only because you give them that power.

Take another look at my crucifixion. What was it that the religious authorities were trying to do to me? From an outer perspective, they were trying to silence me because I was a threat to their control over the people. Yet what was really going on was that the fallen angels were trying to stop me from expressing my Christhood in this world. Remember that the fallen angels believe they own the material universe (all four levels). Thus, when the Living Christ appears in any form, they feel threatened to the ultimate degree. So what they were really trying to do to me was to stop me from being the Christ in this world. They were essentially saying, "You have no right to be the Christ in *our* world!"

How could they stop me from being the Christ? Well, they have no physical power to stop me, because my conscious self is an extension of the Creator's being. This is what gives me the potential to be the Christ and thus be the open door for the Creator to express itself in this world. Yet my conscious self is who it thinks it is, meaning that if I believe I am not the Christ or believe I should not express my Christhood on Earth, then they *can* stop me.

Yet can you see the essential mechanism here? They cannot actually stop anyone from being the Christ, so they have to work through deception. They have to get you to *believe* that you do not have the ability or the right to be the Christ. Yet this also demonstrates that they have no actual power, for they can exercise power *only* through the medium of your free will. *They* cannot stop you, so they have to get *you* to stop yourself, for *you* are the only one who can turn on or off your Christhood. How can you avoid falling into this trap? By knowing the secret of life I gave you earlier, the secret you are not supposed to forget and which is...

Do you begin to see how this ties in with the third challenge of Christ, which is to recognize and accept that *you* can be the Christ on Earth? In order to meet this challenge, you have to demonstrate that you will not be affected by the forces of anti-christ—who will do anything they can think of to prevent you from turning on your Christhood. This includes making you believe that it is fine for you to be the Christ *after* you leave this world—anything to prevent you from being the Christ *in* this world.

Yet who is the Living Christ? He or she is the open door for setting free those who are trapped in the consciousness of death! And in the spiritual realm, everyone has risen above the consciousness of death or they would not be here. So there is no need for the Living Christ in the spiritual realm, meaning it is meaningless for you to become the Christ *after* you leave this world. The need is for you to be the Christ while you are *in* this world. I came to Earth to demonstrate this and to set the foundation for other people doing greater works than I did. So the third challenge of Christ means that you must stand up to the forces of anti-christ until you are absolutely undivided in your inner knowing that they have no power over you whatsoever. You don't actually have to demonstrate this outwardly as much as you have to do it inwardly. The third challenge of Christ is still focused primarily on bringing about change within yourself.

***

Who *are* you? You are the conscious self! Who is the conscious self? You are who you think you are, and you will act on Earth according to who you think you are, according to your sense of identity. If you think you are a human being who is limited by the conditions in this world, you will act like a human being. And thus, you will not challenge the status quo in which most people are blinded by the dualistic illusions created by the forces of anti-christ. These forces will do anything they can to maintain status quo by preventing you from letting the human identity die and being reborn into a new identity, where you recognize who you really are. Yet – again – they can do this *only* by making you think you are less than who you really are, by making you think you cannot be the Christ in this world.

So what is the path to Christhood all about? It is about shifting your sense of identity, so you do not identify yourself with and as anything in this world. The most obvious example is, of course, the physical body. The body is made from energies in the physical octave, and thus the forces of this octave have power over it. If you identify yourself as the body, you will believe these forces have power over *you*—and you either will not think you can go beyond them or you will be afraid to try. You will therefore, for all practical purposes, *be* a human being—as it is currently defined by the mass consciousness.

Can you begin to gain a deeper perspective on my statement that the path of personal growth must, at some point, deviate from the path to Christhood? It is possible to expand your consciousness and gain a greater understanding of the spiritual side of life without actually seeing the basic illusion of the forces of anti-christ. Many religious and spiritual people have achieved a higher understanding, but their entire focus is on what happens to them *after* they leave the material world. In fact, most Christians have been deceived into thinking that they could not and should not ever attempt to become the Christ. They claim to be my followers, but they do not follow my example. My point is that it is possible to continue to focus on your personal growth and on attaining some higher consciousness either by withdrawing from the world or after you leave this world—and you can do so for the rest of this lifetime. Yet that is *not* the path to Christhood.

Thus, there comes a point where a person has reached a sufficient understanding, and the person is now ready to consciously acknowledge the potential to become the Christ. If a person is *not* willing to do this, then that person will continue on the path of personal growth. This can still lead to some progress, but it will *not* qualify lifestreams for their final ascension into the spiritual realm—for reasons I will explain later.

Yet *if* a person recognizes his or her potential to actually become the Christ *in* this world, then that person starts on the real path to Christhood—which at this point takes a dramatic turn and forever transcends the path of personal growth.

What does it take for a person to make the shift and start the path to Christhood? It begins with a momentous decision. You must do what I talked about earlier, namely accept full and complete responsibility for yourself and your own growth. What exactly does this mean? It means that you recognize and accept the logical consequence of what I have taught you in this key. You must say, "No one ever did anything to me!"

What is the basis for this saying? It is the recognition that the core of your being is the conscious self, which *is* who it thinks it is. Thus, the only way someone can do something to you is by affecting what you see as your identity. If you identify with the body, then someone else can do something to you by doing something to your body. Yet the reality is that the only being who can change your sense of identity is *you*. Thus, *you* are ultimately responsible for your sense of identity. You can neglect that responsibility by identifying yourself as less than a spiritual being, which then gives forces outside yourself (the ego is also outside your real self) power to change how you see yourself. Yet such forces can *only* exercise power over you to the extent that *you* give them that power by projecting the power outside yourself.

In other words, when you take full and complete responsibility for yourself, you acknowledge that no outside force has actual power over you, and thus no one ever did anything to you. Take another look at my saying:

> And fear not them which kill the body, but are not able to kill the soul: but rather fear him which is able to destroy both soul and body in hell. (Matthew 10:28)

Traditionally, Christians have interpreted this to mean that they should fear the devil, who seemingly has power to destroy the soul. Yet what I am showing you here is that the *only* being who has power over you is *you*. Thus, "him which is able to destroy both soul and body in hell" refers to the conscious self, for only the conscious self has power to change your identity to that of a mortal being. And only a mortal being could end up in hell by refusing to reunite with its Higher Being. Thus, the devil cannot condemn you to hell—only *you* can do that.

***

To make that point even clearer, let me give you an excerpt of a dictation given by Gautama Buddha at the New Years conference 2007-8.[14] These are the Buddha's words:

## Understanding the false hierarchy

Thus, my beloved, we have sometimes talked about the fact that there is a certain percentage of lifestreams who have been allowed to embody on this planet, and that they form – together with lifestreams in the mental and emotional realms – a hierarchy which we have called the false hierarchy. Now my beloved, this is the force that I earlier said has destroyed many previous Golden Age civilizations.

And so you who are spiritual people have gone through a phase, many of you, where you saw the necessity to make calls or decrees or call forth the judgment of the false hierarchy. And this was a necessary step, not only in the planetary unfoldment but also in your own personal growth. But many of you, my beloved, have reached a point where you are, as again was discussed earlier, ready to truly free yourself from the last very subtle remnants of the duality consciousness. And thus, I, as the Lord of the World – who truly holds the spiritual balance for all lifestreams who em-

---

[14] The entire dictation can be found on *www.askrealjesus.com* in the Golden Age section.

body on Earth – I have determined to give you a teaching that is beyond what we have released earlier.

Thus my beloved, let me take you through a little bit of a thought experiment, an exercise of your imagination. You might, my beloved, start out with the image that was given in the books and movies that were popular in the recent time about the little hobbit Frodo who received the ring and had to bring it back to its creation point [*Lord of the Rings*]. And in so doing had to fight against this dark force that seemed to be permeating the universe and seemed to be emanating from a central point, where supposedly there was an evil emperor or sorcerer who was directing not only the force, but who was directing millions upon millions of orcs or other beings who were doing his bidding and were under his control.

Yet my beloved, I desire to give you a twist on this story. Now imagine, my beloved, that you look at the world and see that there are certain people who are seemingly committed to destroying peace and prosperity in the world. And you see deeper and realize that they are committed to this because they are in a certain state of consciousness. And you see, my beloved, that they are in this state of consciousness primarily because they are afraid. They are afraid that if they do not pursue a certain course of action, well, some calamity will befall them, such as burning forever in the hell that is the worst thing they can imagine.

So out of that fear of going to hell, they are afraid of going against those who command them to kill others in the name of God. And thus, you see that on Earth there is a certain hierarchy, as you have seen for example in past ages, where the leaders of a particular religion – even the supreme leader, such as the pope of the Christian religion – would command those below him to make war with the members of another religion. Thus killing other human beings in the name of their god, which they at the same time claimed was a god of love who had given the commandment, "Thou shallt not kill." And who had sent his only begotten son into the Earth, who gave the commandment to turn the other cheek and to love your neighbor as yourself.

Yet somehow, the logic was that if you killed in the name of this god, you would avoid a fiery hell that would otherwise come upon the Earth—if those of the other religion were allowed to spread their religion unhindered. And so my beloved, you have an Earthly hierarchy but when you are a spiritual person and see deeper, you see that there is a non-material hierarchy that is actually pulling the strings, so to speak, of the marionettes that dance around on the Earth. But even those who seem to have great power, such as popes and emperors, are truly robots who are doing the bidding of some greater force behind them.

***

And so you might, as some of you have done, open your awareness to the fact that there is a force beyond the material. And in the beginning, you might feel some fear about this force. And you might think, my beloved, that as there is a hierarchy of darkness on Earth, well there is an even greater and more powerful hierarchy in the higher realms – in the non-material world – so that that false hierarchy has unlimited power, or almost unlimited power, over those who have been pulled into their sphere of influence.

And this, of course, has given many people on Earth – from various religions including ascended master students – a great fear of being influenced by this false hierarchy, my beloved. So that in that fear of being influenced by the false hierarchy, you become so concerned about keeping your consciousness pure that you actually – without realizing it – shut off the flow of the River of Life through your own being, shut off your own creativity by thinking that you need to be so afraid of experimenting with your own creative ability for fear of opening yourself to the false hierarchy.

So my beloved, many spiritual people who have gone beyond the "ignorance is bliss" of "seeing no evil, hearing no evil" have come to believe that there are these dark forces. And indeed, there *are* dark forces—I am not in any way denying that. But the image I want to give you here is that there truly is a false or dark hierarchy, a dark force that is organized into a hierarchy, my beloved. And so you can look at Earth and you can see that there are individual people who are driven by this evil force, who are blinded by it and some of them, for example, become serial killers.

But there is also a more organized form, where at certain points an entire society can come under the spell of the false hierarchy, so that they now unite their forces in seeking to kill the members of another society. And of course, if you want an obvious example of this, you can see the Nazi force in Germany as one modern example. But if you dare to look a little more closely, you can see that many societies have elements of this. Even modern-day America has certain people who are in high positions of power, who have come under the spell of this false hierarchy and thus become instruments for precipitating war and conflict on a planetary scale.

And yet, my beloved, when you look beyond these people on Earth – who have been blinded or taken over by the false hierarchy – you see that beyond them is a non-material hierarchy. And you might think of it in terms of evil spirits, demons, discarnates, entities, whatever you want to call them. But the main image here is that there are beings who are completely blinded by the consciousness of duality and thus are completely focused on and committed to expressing some form of darkness—even though they often believe it is for some greater good.

And so my beloved, if you conceive of this false or dark hierarchy as a pyramid, where the physical manifestations you see are the lowest level of the pyramid and beyond it is another level, and beyond that is another level—and all of it leads up toward the top of the pyramid. And you know, my beloved, of course, that the pyramid ends in one single point. And thus, you have the popular image that at the top of the pyramid of the dark hierarchy is the devil or Satan or Lucifer or whatever that being has been called in various cultures and religions.

***

Yet my beloved, now imagine that we put on the full armor of Archangel Michael, so that we are invulnerable to the dark forces, and we set out on a journey like Frodo who traveled to the depths of Mordor, the depths of darkness. We are traveling now through the different layers of the false hierarchy, the forces of darkness. We are traveling higher and higher toward the apex, the very top point of the pyramid.

And as we come closer and closer, we encounter various manifestations of darkness, as Frodo encountered on his journey toward Mordor. And we expect, of course, that as we come to the very top, we will find the ultimate temple of darkness, the ultimate building that houses the dark lord himself, who is at the very top of this dark hierarchy. And indeed, my beloved, as we penetrate through the deeper levels of darkness, we do see such a temple, a structure constructed with all kinds of evil or ugly manifestations of figures, of dragons, of gargoyles of whatever you can imagine on Earth.

And yet my beloved, as we get to this very temple itself, we see something peculiar. We see that surrounding the temple are beings who worship the temple, but those beings are so afraid to enter the temple that they never, ever enter the temple. They always reside outside. But we see that these beings form, so to speak, the top level of the dark hierarchy that we can see from our position outside the dark temple. And we see that they are so hypnotized, so focused on promoting or perpetuating a particular idea that they believe has been given to them by the dark lord himself. But we realize that none of these beings has ever seen the dark lord, has never actually received that philosophy or matrix from the dark lord.

They believe it was given in the distant past, my beloved, to their forefathers, and they are simply continuing to carry out the instructions that they think were given in the past. And they pass those instructions on to the next level of the pyramid, to those below them. And so those below them blindly carry out the instructions of their overlords, which they believe came directly from the dark lord himself, and so on down through the levels of the pyramid. And now my beloved, we look at these that are – so to speak – the most advanced dark beings we have encountered on our journey, and we see that although they have great power over those below them, we see that they are actually driven by fear themselves—rather than being the powerful beings that their followers see them to be.

We see through them and see that they are hollow shells because they are driven by fear. And in their fear, they are actually mechanically carrying out what they believe to be the instructions of their dark lord. And although they believe that the dark lord is the counterpoint to God – and thus as powerful as God – they really have no proof of this, for they have never seen the dark lord himself, my beloved. So when we realize this fear – and again, of course, being protected by the full armor of Archangel Michael – we say, "Well, perhaps we should do what they are afraid to do. Perhaps we should walk into that temple and take a look at this dark lord, who is supposedly as powerful as God himself."

And now my beloved, we gather our courage, and we walk through the temple gates and we encounter a great hall, and at the end of that hall is a great throne. But to our surprise we discover that there is no one sitting on the throne, save a little mouse, my beloved, who has snuck into the dark temple looking for food, but has found none and thus quickly runs away as it hears us coming. And thus, we stand there in front of that dark throne—and suddenly it dawns upon us, my beloved, that *there is no dark lord!*

***

There never *was* a dark lord! There never *was* an evil being who was the counterpoint of God and who was thus as powerful as God. You see, my beloved, what we realize in an instant is that all of the different levels of the hierarchy of darkness are worshipping a complete illusion, my beloved. They are worshipping something that is not there, something that has no reality, my beloved. And thus, we see something very profound.

The beings at the lower levels of the pyramid are afraid to disobey those above them because they believe those above them have power over them. And to some degree this is true, for when you are at the lower levels, well those above you have certain powers of black magic that they can use against you.

But we also see that the entire hierarchy leads toward the very highest level of the beings who are outside the temple, and we see that those beings are worshipping the dark lord that they think resides in the temple. But they do so because they believe that the dark lord is there and that he has real, actual powers over them, and thus will destroy them if they do not do his bidding. But we see that those beings – even though they have power over all of the beings below them in hierarchy – they are actually the most to be pitied—because they think that the dark lord above them has power over them. But since the dark lord is not there and the temple is empty, there is no power over them and thus there is no one who can destroy them if they do not do the bidding of the dark lord that is nonexistent.

And thus, we suddenly see, my beloved, that this false hierarchy – which might appear to have power on Earth, or in the mental or emotional realms – actually has no real power. It is all an illusion, and that which is unreal cannot have power over that which is real—unless that which is real has fallen into the illusion of believing that the darkness is real, thereby – by affirming the reality of the darkness – giving the darkness power.

So do you see, my beloved, that we suddenly realize that those on the lower levels of the hierarchy of darkness are using their own energies to feed the illusion. And in so doing, they are sending their energies into a false matrix, and thereby they give their own energies to create a force which those at the next highest level of the pyramid can then use to control them.

In other words, those who are being controlled are themselves giving their own energies to those who control them. And thus, if those who are being controlled would stop feeding the energy to their overlords, well then they would take away the power that the overlords have over them. And when you see that this is repeated at each level of the pyramid, you see that it is not actually true – as you see portrayed in many myths around the world – that those who are immediately below the dark lord are receiving power from the dark lord himself.

For you see that there is no dark lord, so how could those who are at the top level of the pyramid receive power when there is nothing above them but emptiness? And so you see now that the entire superstructure of the false hierarchy is not fed by the dark lord. They are fed by those below them, going all the way back to the human beings in embodiment who are not completely empty of light but still have some reality, some light in them. But who have been tricked into misqualifying this light through illusions and thereby feeding the entire superstructure of dark beings and the false hierarchy.

And so we suddenly realize that evil is not real and its appearance has no actual power over human beings—except what human beings give to darkness by misqualifying their own light with the illusions created by darkness—the illusions that people believe are real.

***

Now my beloved, you who are the spiritual people, many of you are right at that point where you are ready to fully integrate this truth that I have given you. Where you are ready to take that step, which finally and fully brings you out of the reach of the forces of duality. Which brings you to the point, my beloved, where the prince of this world will come but have nothing in you, whereby he can force you to go into a negative reaction that feeds your light to the darkness.

You are right at the point where one more step will set you free, so that you can sit as the Buddha under the tree and be confronted with the demons of Mara, the forces of this world. But no matter how they attempt to attack or tempt you, there is no attachment in you, whereby they can cause you to give power to their illusions. For you see through the illusions, and thus you are unmoved through your own perpetual surrender of all that is unreal.

And do you see, my beloved, that many of you are at the point, where a slight turn of the dial of consciousness will suddenly open up your vision to see the complete unreality of all that is dark and evil? This my beloved, would not instantly remove that darkness from the Earth, for the law of free will allows that there are still many people who believe in the illusions of darkness. But there are two important aspects of you overcoming that illusion.

First of all that you, of course, are free of the pull of duality, free of the fear of the false hierarchy. You are anchored in the infinite peace of the Buddha, the infinite peace of Christ, the infinite peace of the Divine Mother, the infinite peace of the Divine Father, the infinite peace of the Holy Spirit. And by being anchored in that peace, well then you can step up to an entirely new level of holding the balance for the Earth, so that you can serve as a counterbalance to the people who are still blinded by duality and still think they have to do the bidding of the evil lord and those above them in the dark hierarchy. Which they often do not see as a dark hierarchy but see as the hierarchy of their own religion or the hierarchy of their political party. Or whatever illusion you have on Earth that is designed to trick people into giving their obedience and energies to the dark forces while thinking they are working for God or some ultimate cause.

And this, truly, is how you hold the counterbalance, my beloved, against the forces of darkness—when you realize that there is no dark lord. There is no reality to the forces of darkness, but you also realize that too many of your brothers and sisters are still blinded by that illusion—that darkness is real and that it has actual power over them. And so you recognize that there are many people who are not yet ready to let go of that illusion.

And why are they not ready my beloved? Because they are not ready to take a look at darkness. They are not ready to acknowledge that if they are engaged in the dualistic struggle – even though they believe they are fighting for a good cause – they are actually working *for* the hierarchy of darkness. They are afraid to acknowledge that—because they would feel such remorse and self-condemnation that it would take them lifetimes to heal from that wound. And even those who are willing to acknowledge that fighting can never come from the hierarchy of light, they still are afraid to take a close look at the hierarchy of darkness, following it all the way to the top and then finally seeing that there is nothing at the top and therefore it can have no power.

And so you see that it is necessary that there is a certain percentage of people who will hold the balance that gives the rest of humanity more time to build up the maturity and the courage, where they are then able to look at the darkness, to see it for what it is and thus use their free will to abandon it. And you see that it is necessary that some will hold the balance, so that the people who are blinded by the darkness will not plunge this Earth into a negative spiral of violence that will prevent the manifestation of the Golden Age. [End of quote.]

***

My first purpose for inserting these teachings is to help you finally accept that there is no external force that has any power over the real you—except the power that you give to it through your free will. You can only give up your power by making a decision to do so. An external force might influence your decision, but only *you* can make it. Which means that you can never lose the ability to take back your power. How do you take back your power? By reversing the process through which you gave it away—by making a new decision that neutralizes the old decision.

The problem is, of course, that the decision that gives away your power is always made without a full understanding of what is happening—it is based on ignorance. Thus, the only way to make a new decision that neutralizes the old decision is to overcome the ignorance. You can make an *unconscious* decision to give away power, but you cannot take it back without making a *conscious* decision. Yet it obviously becomes easier to make that decision when you realize that you have the full power and authority to do so and that no force in this world can stop you.

You might contemplate the fact that the forces of darkness are always seeking to incite fear in people. Yet why do you need to control people through fear if you can control them through physical force? In other words, the tactic to control people through fear proves the absence of physical power.

Another purpose is to help you see that although there is a temporary force of darkness in this world, it has no reality in God. This is why it has no power over the conscious self—which *does* have reality as an extension of the Creator's Being. So the forces of anti-christ have a temporary existence in the material world, but they can exist *only* because people keep feeding them their life energies. If humankind would stop misqualifying energy tomorrow, the forces of darkness would quickly wither away, for they have no ability to receive light from the spiritual realm.

This leads to the inescapable conclusion that as a disciple of Christ you cannot allow yourself to feed your life energies to these dark forces. Which means you have to make it an absolute priority in your life to attain complete spiritual freedom from these forces. And how do you do this? By overcoming all tendency to respond to life – and particular situations – in a dualistic manner—in a violent manner. This requires you to attain what the Buddha called non-attachment, and let me give you some teachings that will help you achieve this goal, which is an inescapable goal for any disciple of Christ.

***

We have already talked about the fact that when you understand the importance of free will, you can set yourself free from feeling responsible for other people's salvation. We have talked about the cosmic mirror and that the material universe basically is a device that is designed to give self-aware beings any experience they want. But let us revisit the most important aspect of this.

The universe will outpicture in physical circumstances what is in your consciousness, and the effect of this is that most people reason that their beliefs have been confirmed by the universe and thus must be true. For example, there are many people on Earth who have a division in their psyches which causes them to see life as a struggle. They are sending out the subconscious message that they want to experience a struggle, and the cosmic mirror must obediently give them circumstances that do make their lives a struggle. People then see this as a confirmation that life really *is* a struggle, which means that the universe has a potential to become a closed loop, a catch-22.

When people do not understand that the universe simply reflects back what they send out, they cannot see that there is an alternative to their present form of life. They cannot see that although life is a struggle, this is a self-created condition and the universe would gladly reflect back a more pleasant image. They think they have no other option than to continue the struggle indefinitely—they feel trapped in the struggle and see no way out. This self-reinforcing spiral must then continue and the struggle must intensify until people become so burdened that they finally give up the need to fight and start looking for a better way by being willing to change themselves. This is truly the school of hard knocks, for the knocks must become harder and harder until people have finally had enough.

What is the function of the Living Christ? It is to embody on Earth – in a particular culture – and demonstrate that there is indeed an alternative to present conditions, that there is a way out of the human condition—*any* human condition. The Living Christ does this by first being born into a set of limiting conditions, thus demonstrating that he or she is just like any other person in that culture—which is why I called myself the "Son of Man" instead of the "Son of God." Then, the Living Christ demonstrates that he or she can rise above those conditions, thereby hopefully setting forth an example that others will follow.

So we now see that there are lifestreams who had attained a certain degree of Christhood in previous lives and who volunteered to embody in limiting conditions in order to demonstrate how you rise above them. This includes embodying in particular cultures, but also being born with various handicaps, being born in a poor family, having physical diseases or any other type of limiting condition. In other words, for any limiting circumstance there is one or more persons who volunteered to embody with that limitation in order to demonstrate how to rise above it. Since you are interested in this course, it is highly likely that you are one of these lifestreams.

So what will it take for you to fulfill your mission? Well, you must demonstrate how to rise above the limitations into which you were born, and that must begin by you freeing yourself from these limitations—in your mind. Take note that this can be interpreted in various ways. For example, some people might have a physical handicap and are not necessarily meant to jump out of a wheelchair. They might be meant to demonstrate how to have such a handicap and *not* let it prevent you from pursuing and expressing personal Christhood. In other words, the mission of the Living Christ is to challenge people's mental boxes—which is often done by *not* doing what most people would want to do in a given circumstance. The mission of the Living Christ is to demonstrate that you can be the Christ regardless of *any* conditions on Earth. For example, you will notice from the scriptures that I did have the opportunity to walk away from the crucifixion but did not do so.

Beyond such individual demonstrations of overcoming, there is one overall goal that is the same for all Christed beings. That goal is to demonstrate in every circumstance that it is possible to rise above the dualistic struggle, that there is an alternative to the dualistic state of consciousness. This, of course, makes it absolutely necessary that you free yourself from the duality consciousness, and this can be done *only* through total non-attachment, complete non-violence.

***

We now come to a point that has confused many sincere spiritual seekers throughout the ages. In fact, this one point has prevented many people from expressing their Christhood and instead tricked them into perpetuating the dualistic struggle.

As a Christed being, you have an inner sense that you are here to improve conditions, to rise above them. Yet this means it is easy to reason that current conditions are not what God wanted for the Earth. In a sense this is correct in that God never wanted people on Earth to experience the current suffering. Yet in another sense, it is God's supreme will that co-creators are given free will and thus allowed to create for themselves any experience they desire to have—continuing that experience until they have had enough of it. Therefore, God and the Ascended Host are *not* looking down upon Earth with disdain, judgment or anger. Contrary to the widespread image of an angry and judgmental God, God simply wants people to rise above their current limitations—God wants people to be free to be God.

Yet if you do not understand this, it is easy to look at current conditions on Earth and enter into a judgmental frame of mind that causes feelings of frustration, fear and anger. And this very easily causes you to act on your genuine desire to improve the Earth in a way that is colored by such limiting emotions and thus perpetuates the struggle.

How can you avoid this trap? By changing your perspective! What is behind the feelings of frustration, anger or even a sense of injustice? It is a form of non-acceptance. You will not accept current conditions, and thus you struggle against them.

At this point you might be thinking, "But I thought I was here to improve current conditions, so doesn't that imply that I do not accept those conditions? I mean, if I accepted current conditions, why would I have a drive to improve them?" This is an understandable reaction, but it is now time to rise above it by seeing beyond the dualistic logic and increasing your discernment. You need to come to understand that you will never *change* current conditions until you fully *accept* those conditions.

What have I said is the underlying cause of all human limitations? It is the duality consciousness, which has a fundamental division between two opposite polarities. So when it comes to acceptance, there are two dualistic opposites. One is that people accept current conditions as being caused by the laws of nature or the will of God, and thus they reason they can do nothing to go beyond them. The other reaction is to reason that since current conditions cause suffering, this is wrong. Thus, someone must have caused this, and we need to destroy those people in order to make things right. The dualistic mind always judges everything based on a dualistic scale with right and wrong as opposites.

Can you see that both of these reactions only perpetuate the dualistic struggle—which is the cause of current conditions? In other words, whether people accept current conditions as unchangeable or fight some external cause of those conditions, they only perpetuate the dualistic struggle. As always, those trapped in the dualistic mind will see no alternative to these two reactions. Yet what is the Middle Way of the Christ? It is to fully accept current conditions for what they truly are.

Current conditions *are* the will of God *in the sense* that it is God's will that human beings have free will and thus have the right to create any experience they choose. Current conditions *are* a result of the laws of nature *in the sense* that the universe is designed to reflect back to you what you send out. Current conditions *are* the result of someone causing them, but destroying those people or forces will *not* correct current conditions. The reason being that those forces and people created current conditions by struggling against the River of Life. If you struggle against *them,* you also struggle against the River of Life, and this can never correct the initial problem of separation from the river.

My point here is that when people have not gone through the first two challenges of Christ, they mindlessly accept current conditions as absolute limitations. Those who have passed these first two initiations no longer do so. However, they can easily be mislead into fighting the perceived cause of current conditions, and this will cause them to fail the third challenge of Christ. To master this challenge, you must accept that current conditions are indeed allowed by God because people have free will to create any experience they want. Thus, current conditions are the result of people exercising their God-given free will.

The conclusion is that the Living Christ is *not* here to judge people as being wrong for creating current conditions. Take note of my words:

> For God sent not his Son into the world to condemn the world; but that the world through him might be saved. (John 3:17)

The Christ does not judge based on appearances, which means the Christ does not judge current conditions as being ultimately real. The Christ sees that current conditions are simply temporary projections upon the Ma-ter light, and the light can instantly outpicture better conditions—as I demonstrated when I healed the sick by instantly overriding the projection of illness with a projection of health.

Yet this means that the Christ is *not* here to force people or to change conditions *for* them. This is the lie perpetrated by orthodox Christianity—that I came to save people by paying for their sins with my blood on the cross. I did not come to change the world *for* people. I came to help people escape the closed loop that caused them to think current conditions were unchangeable. In other words, the Living Christ sees that current conditions on Earth are the outpicturing in matter of people's current state of consciousness—they are projections upon the Ma-ter light that are no more real or permanent than the images on a movie screen. Thus, the way to change current conditions is to demonstrate to people that there is an alternative to the closed loop of their current state of consciousness—that there is an alternative to the dualistic state of consciousness. And when a critical mass of people *do* expand their mental boxes, then they will project a different image upon the Ma-ter light—and outer conditions will automatically change. In other words, the Living Christ is not blinded by effects and thus focuses on the underlying cause, namely the duality consciousness. This is in stark contrast to those trapped in duality, who focus on the effects and thus think they have to fight other people.

We might say that the Living Christ realizes that planet Earth is a schoolroom in which people must learn by seeing the Ma-ter light outpicture their consciousness. Thus, the Living Christ is focused on helping people learn their lessons, so they can voluntarily and consciously change their consciousness and thereby change outer conditions. If the Living Christ did all the work *for* them, how would people learn and then how would the purpose of planet Earth be fulfilled?

In other words, if the Living Christ changed conditions on Earth, he or she would actually sabotage the learning process that is the purpose for Earth. When you understand this, you see that it is only the representatives of anti-christ who seek to force people—even if doing so seemingly is for their own good or to further some greater cause. The ultimate cause is the growth in consciousness, and it cannot be forced, for it is a creative process that must come from within. The Living Christ seeks to facilitate this process by being the example and *only* the example.

When you see this, you overcome all frustration, all impatience, all sense of injustice. You accept things for what they are—temporary and unreal projections upon the Ma-ter light that can be changed in the blink of an eye. Thus, you do not feel trapped in or afraid of current conditions, for you know that that which in unreal cannot affect that which is real. Instead, you seek to help people remove the beam from their eyes, so they are free to "see" a higher vision and project *that* upon the Ma-ter light. For when the eye is single, the entire Earth body will be full of light—for it is made from light.

So the Living Christ sees that the ultimate purpose for life is the growth in self-awareness. Thus, the Living Christ accepts that current conditions are the perfect tool for helping people expand their self-awareness. This is done by helping people see that their current conditions are the outpicturing in matter of their current state of consciousness. Thus, if people do not like their current conditions, they must begin by changing their consciousness, and the material universe will inevitably respond in kind. Do you see the key here? Instead of struggling *against* current conditions, you can now begin to *use them as the perfect teaching tool*. When you seek first the kingdom of God and his righteousness, all these things will be added onto you. And when you help others do the same, you will gradually build a critical mass that adds onto humankind the kingdom of God on Earth.

***

What causes frustration, what causes you to struggle against outer conditions? It is that you feel trapped, and why do you feel trapped? Because you think you are up against conditions that you have no power to change. In order to be the Living Christ, you have to completely overcome this sense of being trapped and powerless. How can you do this?

It begins with total respect for free will. This allows you to see that you are not here to change conditions—you are here to help other people change their consciousness—which will then change conditions. And when you respect their free will, you will not feel powerless to change current conditions—for you will *not* see it as *your* job to change those conditions. Thus, you can let go of the sense of being up against conditions you have no power to change. You should not *want* power to change current conditions, for as a representative of Christ you have no desire to have power over people's free will.

When you have realized and integrated this truth, you can begin to challenge one of the most persistent illusions created by the duality consciousness, namely that the past has power over the present and the future. Why do people feel trapped? Because they think that mistakes they have made in the past can still influence them now and thus will have an influence on their future. Since they cannot change what was done in the past, people think they are powerless to avoid the pain they feel in the present and avoid further pain in the indefinite future—thus the concept of an everlasting hell.

Yet what is the psychological mechanism at work here? When you feel trapped, you *resent* current conditions. You are struggling against those conditions and against what you see as the unchangeable cause from the past. Thus, you project a struggle into the cosmic mirror, and guess what the mirror must reflect back to you? In other words, when you struggle against something, you give it reality in your mind. And this means that you reinforce it by giving it your vital energy. As the saying goes, *what you resist persists*.

The reality here is that there is no such thing as past, present or future. The sense of time is an illusion that springs from the illusion of separation. Only the separate self can believe in time. The conscious self is an extension of the Creator's Being, and you do not seriously believe that the Creator is limited by time, do you? The Creator exists in the eternal NOW, which is *not* the same as what people call the present moment.

Look at this from a different angle. Sure, you did something in the past that you now see was limiting to yourself and others. Yet when did you actually do this? You did not do it in the past, you did it in what was then the present. Why is this important? Well, let us go back to the movie theater analogy. What you are seeing on a movie screen is an image that is projected from the filmstrip. That image has no permanency, as it is made of individual pictures that change many times each second. My point being that what is seen on the screen at any given time is simply an image that is projected at that specific moment. The image is not permanent. Sure, you can have a filmstrip on which each image is the same, meaning that for a long time the image on the screen will not change. But nevertheless, the screen would instantly display a different image if the image on the filmstrip was changed.

What is the real-life equivalent of the filmstrip? *It is your mind!* Meaning that if you change the images in your mind, the images on the movie screen – the screen of life – will also change. Can you see what I am saying here? The separate self believes in the reality of separation, and separation gives rise to a separation between past, present and future. Thus, it seems to the separate mind that mistakes made in the past will have an impact on the present and thus will continue to have an impact into the future. It seems that present conditions were created in the past and that they have a lasting existence. And since it seems like you cannot change the past, it seems like you cannot change outer conditions. In reality, conditions are created in the now, and thus they can also be changed in the now.

The conditions you experience at any given moment are the results of the image you hold in the four levels of your mind at that moment and thus project upon the Ma-ter light. If you changed that image, the Ma-ter light would reflect back a different image—instantly.

How does the past influence the present? Only when you allow a mistake you made in the past to remain in your consciousness and affect your self-image, so you continue to project that image upon the Ma-ter light. The moment you truly change the image in your mind, the Ma-ter light will instantly reflect back the new image. The trick being, of course, that you cannot simply change your self-image at the level of the conscious mind. You must go all the way back up through the emotional, mental and identity levels. Only when the new self-image is the reality in all of the four levels of your mind, will you see the outer manifestation of that image.

I realize that time is a very difficult illusion to overcome. Yet can you at least begin to see that the conscious self is an extension of the Creator's Being and thus must be beyond time? You are who you think you are, but when do you think what you are? You can do so only in the present moment. What you are thinking right now is something that exists only right now. You may be repeating a self-image created in the past, but the past is gone, and thus that image has already disappeared. It has no reality and thus can have no effect on the present—unless your mind actually recreates the past image in the present.

Do you see that your mind is like a filmstrip? Many times a second an image is projected onto the screen of life. Your mind has the power to change that image at any moment. Yet if you do not, then you will keep projecting the same image—you will draw images from the past into the present. And then the cosmic mirror must reflect the same conditions back to you. As they say in the computer world, "What you see [in your mind's eye] is what you get!"

Can you see the inescapable conclusion? One of the most persistent illusions is that the world has some kind of permanence, some kind of continuous existence. This is an illusion that is fed by your senses because they are designed to work in the material frequency spectrum. They are designed to detect contrast and change, which means they easily overlook gradual movement. This is why your eyes are fooled by a movie into seeing a continuous motion, when in reality the movie is a series of still images. You will notice that in old movies there were fewer images per second, which made people's movements appear jerky. In modern movies, this is no longer the case because there are so many images displayed that your eyes cannot detect the breaks between individual images and thus sees a continuous motion. This is also how your conscious mind is tricked into thinking that the material universe has a continuous existence.

The stark reality is that the material universe is *not* permanent and has *no* continuous existence. The entire material universe is a projection upon the screen of the Ma-ter light, and that projection is repeated many times a second by conscious minds projecting images upon the light, as a filmstrip is projecting images upon a movie screen. There are spiritual beings who are projecting the basic image of the Earth, but on top of that image, people in embodiment are projecting their own images, which is what creates the current conditions of limitations, struggle and suffering. Yet these images could change instantly—if only people would change the images in their minds.

As a representative of the Living Christ, you must work to overcome the illusion that the past has any influence on the present and the future. You must overcome the illusion of time and realize that everything is created in the *now*—through the images people hold in their minds *right now*. Thus, you can change *anything* by changing the images in your mind, and here comes the all-important realization. When can you actually change the images in your mind? You can do so *only* in the present moment, in the NOW.

As you very well know, you cannot change your past, for the past is gone irretrievably. Likewise, you cannot change the future, for it has not yet arrived and is thus beyond your grasp. All you have to work with is the now. Yet you can actually change your past by changing the way you look at the past in the now. When you change the self-image you created in the past, you change the image you project into the cosmic mirror—and this will also change what is reflected back in the future. You have then transcended the past so it no longer has any power over you.

My point being, of course, that in order for you to master the third challenge of Christ and actually *be* the Living Christ on Earth, you must first escape the illusion that any condition on Earth has any power over you. And this includes the condition of past, present and future. Which begins by internalizing the reality that your past need not have *any* power over your present—unless you give it that power by holding on to a self-image that is no longer real. Yet even if a self-image was created a long time ago and has been reinforced over many lifetimes, you still have the potential to change that image instantly. Yet you must decide that the image is to change—right NOW!

***

We now come to an essential point that will either take you on the path of Christhood or take you on the path of personal growth. As Maitreya explains in great detail, the essential problem on Earth is the illusion of separation, which has caused most people to separate themselves from their spiritual teachers. Yet what causes this separation? It starts when a student has a moment of truth and realizes it has disobeyed the teacher's instructions. The question now becomes whether to go back to the teacher and confess the mistake or whether to withdraw from the teacher.

The more a student is blinded by separation and duality, the more it will tend to respond by withdrawing from the teacher. Only when there is a space between yourself and the teacher, can you believe the illusion that you can hide your mistake from the teacher. Paradoxically, this reaction often comes from those who are the most diligent students, those who are most eager to please the teacher. They cannot bear to admit a mistake because they think it will disappoint the teacher. So they withdraw, and in their withdrawal they fall prey to the illusion of a separation between past, present and future. This gives rise to the illusion that by withdrawing from the teacher, they gain time to correct their mistakes. You can use the present to compensate for a mistake made in the past, and then at some future time you can go back to the teacher and present yourself in your original state as if you had never made the mistake—or so the reasoning goes.

This is the path of personal growth, meaning that you want to walk the path on your own—without working with the teacher. Can it work? Yes and no! You were the one who made the decisions to descend down the staircase of life into the depths of the duality consciousness. You have made every decision that took you down, and you can thus "unmake" every decision and climb back up—theoretically. The problem is – as I have now explained from almost every possible angle – that the duality consciousness becomes a closed loop, a self-fulfilling prophecy. The Ma-ter light reflects back what you send out, thus seemingly confirming that you are right in believing life is a struggle. Thus preventing most people from seeing that it is the *sense of struggle* that generates the struggle.

So how do you break the closed loop? You can do so *only* by making contact with something above and beyond your mental box. That "something" is the spiritual teacher, and the teacher is always trying to reach you with an impulse that will help you rise above your illusions. It is quite possible that you can receive such an impulse and use it to take a step back up the staircase. Yet those blinded by duality will often fail to acknowledge that the impulse actually came from the teacher, and some will believe they came up with it on their own. This is what causes people to enter the path of personal growth, where they think they are making progress based on their own efforts. This can work, but it can *only* take you to a certain level. There will come a dividing point, the line in the sand.

You see, the true path is the path of oneness. This path ultimately leads your individual, localized self back to oneness with the universal self, your Creator. Yet no person on Earth can make that leap in one giant step. Thus, the path of oneness begins with you attaining oneness with the spiritual beings who are at the next level of the spiritual hierarchy, namely the members of the Ascended Host who serve as spiritual teachers for humankind. This is the time-honored method, and it is – quite frankly – the *only* way to grow on the path of oneness. You see, in the spiritual realm, all beings are one, so whether you attain oneness with me or oneness with God—it is the same thing, for I and my Father are one. Furthermore, you are actually an extension of the Ascended Host, for your Higher Being came out of a member of the Ascended Host. The illusion of separation caused you to forget this, so the only way above separation is to once again accept your true origin and come into oneness with your own Chain of Being.

The false teachers have come up with many descriptions of the path which claim you do not have to attain oneness with the teacher, that you can elevate the separate self until it is worthy to attain direct entry into God's kingdom. Thus, they have created the outer path, the path of personal growth. There is a stage on the path where people are still so blinded by the duality consciousness that they cannot see that they are receiving impulses from the true teachers. This is the stage where the path of personal growth is still leading you toward Christhood. Yet there comes a point when a student has recognized the Living Christ and has been willing to let the Christ take the student beyond some of the most primitive dualistic illusions. The student is now ready to fully embrace the teacher—and see that the path is a process of coming into oneness with the teacher and thus *becoming* the teacher in embodiment. So the question becomes whether the student will do this or whether the student will still want to maintain a space between itself and the teacher?

This course has now reached the point where you have to decide whether you are ready to fully and finally overcome the space between you and the teacher—me! I can take you no further unless you are willing to come into oneness with me. Thus, you need to decide whether you will continue to hide your past mistakes from me or whether you will allow me to help you leave behind the self-image based on those mistakes?

Do you see what this means? Any mistake you could have made in the past was a result of the duality consciousness, which springs from the illusion of separation. As I have tried to explain, you cannot overcome a problem with the same state of consciousness that created the problem. You may overcome one problem created by the duality consciousness, but you will instantly create another one that is more cleverly disguised. So the *only* way to overcome the illusion of separation is the path of oneness, the path of coming into oneness with the teacher who is above you in the cosmic hierarchy that leads from your current level to the Creator. There is NO way to get to God without going through the hierarchy of beings that have come into oneness with God. The reason being that your lifestream was created out of the Beings who are above you in hierarchy.

***

The space between you and the teacher is actually a space between you and reality. For the teacher is one with God and one with all life, which is the ultimate reality—all life is ONE. When you are one with all life above you, and when you seek to raise up all life at your level, then you are the open door for God to act through you, which means that God can instantly manifest what to most people seems like a miracle. When you are one with all life, how can the Ma-ter light fail to instantly outpicture in matter what you project upon it through your undivided mind—that only seeks to raise the All? We now gain a deeper perspective on my statement that those who believe on me shall do the works that I did and even greater works because I go to the Father.

"Believing on me" is a metaphor for coming into oneness with me. When you come into oneness with me, you are not acting alone. *You* are one with *me* and with my momentum of co-creative ability. Thus, your own momentum combines with my momentum—which is greater than yours because I have already ascended. Thus, our combined momentums can manifest greater works than you – or I when I was in embodiment – could do alone. Yet the inescapable requirement is your oneness with me. As long as you do not have this oneness, you can still co-create, but it will be subject to a time delay as the creative impulse cycles through the four levels of the material universe and is subject to interference from the mass consciousness and your own subconscious mind at each level. Yet when you come into oneness with me, there is no such delay and the manifestation is instantaneous.

The Christ consciousness is one with reality, which opens up for instant manifestation. This is not really a miracle, even though for most people it seems to defy the laws of nature. Yet remember that the ultimate law of nature is that you create your own limitations by projecting dualistic images into the cosmic mirror. So when you rise above the dualistic consciousness, you are no longer bound by the "laws of nature" created by that consciousness.

How can you come into oneness with me? Only by overcoming the distance between yourself and reality! And that means you must be willing to stop believing that you can hide or can gain benefit from hiding your mistakes from me. I have no intention of condemning you for any mistake you could possibly have made. I am only interested in helping you overcome the one mistake from which all others spring, namely the illusion that any part of God can be apart from God.

So be willing to compare your world view to reality—the reality that I AM. Acknowledge that your present world view is localized and thus limited. Then let that world view go, for as long as you hold on to it, you keep superimposing it upon the Ma-ter light—and the universe must reflect it back to you. This is truly why you carry the past with you and cannot seem to escape it. You need to contemplate these statements:

> 21. And another of his disciples said unto him, Lord, suffer me first to go and bury my father.
> 22. But Jesus said unto him, Follow me; and let the dead bury their dead. (Matthew, Chapter 8)

> 21. Peter seeing him saith to Jesus, Lord, and what shall this man do?
> 22. Jesus saith unto him, If I will that he tarry till I come, what is that to thee? follow thou me. (John, Chapter 21)

***

Let me summarize this key in order to make sure you understand the non-violence of the Living Christ. Take a look at the following statement:

> Fear not, little flock; for it is your Father's good pleasure to give you the kingdom. (Luke 12:32)

This simple statement contains the key to understanding life. It truly is God's good pleasure to give you the kingdom of the abundant life. Yet in order to receive it, you have to be in oneness with God. If you separate yourself from oneness, if you step outside the River of Life, how can you possibly receive the kingdom? You cannot be outside the river and still get wet.

So the reason why life on Earth is a struggle is that people have stepped outside the River of Life, and that is why God's kingdom of the abundant life is not currently manifest on Earth. People have instead become blinded by the duality consciousness, which causes them to reject God's kingdom. Why do people reject what God offers them freely? Because they have entered into duality, in which there are two opposite polarities. Thus, people cannot simply accept that God will freely give them the abundant life, because they think the only way to get something is to take it by force. They think they have to struggle for what God offers them freely—or resign themselves to the belief that it is forever beyond their reach. And because they have separated themselves from the River of Life, they do have to struggle for everything, as expressed in this quote:

> 13. And the LORD God said unto the woman, What is this that thou hast done? And the woman said, The serpent beguiled me, and I did eat.
>
> 16. Unto the woman he said, I will greatly multiply thy sorrow and thy conception; in sorrow thou shalt bring forth children; and thy desire shall be to thy husband, and he shall rule over thee.
> 17. And unto Adam he said, Because thou hast hearkened unto the voice of thy wife, and hast eaten of the tree, of which I commanded thee, saying, Thou shalt not eat of it: cursed is the ground for thy sake; in sorrow shalt thou eat of it all the days of thy life;
> 18. Thorns also and thistles shall it bring forth to thee; and thou shalt eat the herb of the field;
> 19. In the sweat of thy face shalt thou eat bread, till thou return unto the ground; for out of it wast thou taken: for dust thou art, and unto dust shalt thou return. (Genesis, Chapter 3)

Can you see that this is a metaphorical way of describing the process of people falling into the duality consciousness, thus separating themselves from the River of Life and having to struggle to obtain everything? They now have to take by force what God would have given them freely—if they had stayed in the Circle of Oneness. Take a look at this quote:

> And from the days of John the Baptist until now the kingdom of heaven suffereth violence, and the violent take it by force. (Matthew 11:12)

There are some who in their pride have thought this means that you can actually enter the kingdom of heaven by force. The real meaning is that the kingdom of heaven suffers because it is not manifest on Earth as it wants to be. And why isn't it manifest? Because so many people are trapped in duality and thus seek to take by force what God offers them freely.

The deeper understanding being that what God offers freely is the abundant life for *all* people. Yet on Earth you currently have certain lifestreams who do not want abundance for all. They want to have more than most people, and this can be obtained only in an unbalanced system where some take from others through force. Obviously, such a privileged elite cannot exist in the kingdom of God, which is why the elite does not want people on Earth to inherit their Father's kingdom. This is why the false teachers seek to keep people trapped in the duality that causes them to reject abundance—because they believe in the lie that they are cursed to struggle because of the mistakes made in the past by Adam and Eve.

The Living Christ sees that the only problem on Earth is the duality consciousness, perpetuated by the false teachers. Yet the Living Christ also sees that he or she is *not* here to destroy the forces of duality. The Living Christ is *not* here to win the epic battle between good and evil, for this is a dualistic battle, and as such it can never remove duality. The Living Christ sees that this battle is based on the use of force and knows that it cannot be overcome through force. Thus, the Living Christ never uses force but simply claims his or her right to BE in the oneness of Christ and to express that oneness in the face of all divisions.

The Living Christ sees that only the ego uses force, for only the self that is separate from the River of Life needs to use force. The Living Christ may seem to be in opposition to the false teachers – as the scribes and the Pharisees saw me as opposing them – but in reality you are not opposing anyone. You are simply *being* who you are and expressing who you are—and who *is* the Living Christ? *I AM the way, the truth and the life*.

It is inevitable that this will be a threat to those who want to preserve their dualistic system, and thus they will do anything possible to draw you into a dualistic struggle with them. If that does not work, they will do anything in their power to silence you. Yet you must see through this and stay clear of all their snares.

As the Living Christ, you know that only when there is separation from the River of Life is there a need to obtain anything through force. You also know that force can exist *only* in a dualistic environment. For only when there are two opposing polarities is there a need for one polarity to use force against the other polarity. You also see that any use of force is guided by the law of action and reaction—for every force there is an opposite force of equal strength. Thus, you see that the dualistic struggle can never lead to any ultimate victory—as many well-meaning people on Earth have claimed (thinking they need to use force to win an ultimate battle and establish their religion as the superior one, which will bring God's kingdom to Earth).

So the Living Christ is *not* here to win the dualistic struggle, which is why I refused to become a warrior king and lead Israel in an uprising against the Romans—as some people wanted me to do. The Living Christ is here to awaken people from the futility of the dualistic struggle by demonstrating that there is an alternative to the dualistic consciousness. Thereby, you give people a real choice between continuing the struggle and receiving God's kingdom, a choice they do not have while they are blinded by duality and think there is no alternative to the struggle.

As an illustration of this, imagine that you have an entire civilization whose members for centuries have lived in a dark cavern beneath the Earth's surface. They have never seen the light and think there is nothing outside of darkness. You are now sent to that civilization to help them awaken from this illusion and show them there is something outside their dark cave—a world of light. Yet how can you do this? You cannot fight the darkness, for it has no actual substance. You can seek to persuade people that their basic world view is wrong and then seek to convert them to *your* world view. Yet this will be very difficult because they have never seen light, and thus you easily end up in a dualistic fight to destroy their present belief system.

So what is the only possible solution? You must help people experience that there is an alternative to darkness, and how can you do this? By pulling out a flashlight and turning on the light! The moment a light shines in the darkness, it is impossible for people to reject that there is an alternative to darkness, it is impossible to continue to believe that there is only darkness.

People can still refuse to walk into the light by using many different means, such as elevating you to the only person who has light. Yet at least you have given them a choice, and that is the only reason you are here. So as the Living Christ, you are here to turn on the light that is inside of you and to let that light shine so that others have an opportunity to first see that there is an alternative to the darkness of duality and then perhaps discover that they too have light inside themselves.

So the non-violence of the Living Christ is to be a light shining in the darkness, even if the darkness comprehends it not. Your job is to stay free of the dualistic struggle and let your light shine. As I said:

> Then spake Jesus again unto them, saying, I am the light of the world: he that followeth me shall not walk in darkness, but shall have the light of life. (John 8:12)

> As long as I am in the world, I am the light of the world. (John 9:5)

> Ye are the light of the world. A city that is set on an hill cannot be hid. (Matthew 5:14)

> Let your light so shine before men, that they may see your good works, and glorify your Father which is in heaven. (Matthew 5:16)

## Exercise for Key 13

As the exercise for this key, I want you to do a 33-day vigil of the Invocation for Rising above the Past. After the invocation, center in your heart and contemplate the following koan. As you probably know, a koan is a teaching device used by teachers of Zen Buddhism. It is a seemingly contradictory or nonsensical statement that is designed to neutralize the analytical mind and help you attain an "Aha experience." This is the koan for this key:

> Who is the "you" that is conscious of itself at the present moment?

# Key 14
# Find your Self by losing your self

Let us begin this key by talking about what I call the guru paradox. As I have explained, once you are trapped in the duality consciousness, your conscious self is effectively inside a mental box of its own making, and it has forgotten that it has an existence outside the box. We might say the conscious self cannot actually see the box, for since it has no contact with anything outside the box, it has no comeasurement to help it see that it is in a box. If you go back a thousand years, you will see that there were several cultures that lived in isolation from each other. Each culture thought theirs was the only possible culture, and since they had no contact with other cultures, they had no comeasurement to see that it was possible to live in a very different culture.

As I have said, the problem is that the conscious self has become fixated on a localized perspective of the world and has forgotten that it is out of the universal mind. It has forgotten that it has the ability to connect to the overall perspective while being focused in a particular point—thus it has become trapped in the localized view. In order to help lifestreams escape this trap, we of the Ascended Host send teachers to Earth to show people that there is something outside the mental box created by individuals or an entire culture. So the very foundation for spiritual growth is that you have contact with a teacher, or guru, who is outside your personal mental box. The teacher can give you a sense of comeasurement that empowers you to see that there is indeed something outside the box—and thus your conscious self does not have to remain trapped in the box.

Yet as everything else, your interaction with a guru will very much be influenced by your current state of consciousness. Your separate self will indeed project graven images upon the guru and will then demand that the guru lives up to them. If he or she does not, then the ego will declare that it must be a false guru or deny that the person is qualified to be *your* guru (making you seem superior). This brings us to a trap that many spiritual seekers have been led into because they could not see the dynamics of their egos.

The ego is based on duality, which means it has a built-in contradiction that the ego cannot escape because it will refuse to see the inconsistency of its approach to life. The conscious self is capable of seeing this contradiction, and it is indeed one of the primary ways in which people grow—they see an inconsistency in their viewpoints and start looking for a higher understanding. Take the story of how I confronted a group of people who were ready to stone a woman caught in adultery. They were blinded by their egos, but when I asked that the person who was without sin should cast the first stone, they saw the inconsistencies in their approach and walked away (John 8:7).

So here is the paradox created by the way in which the ego approaches any guru. The ego is looking for a way to build its sense of superiority, so it wants to find a guru who appears to have some kind of status according to the norms of its society. The ego is seeing only the outer path, so it feels that if it follows a guru who has superior abilities or status, then the guru can do something for it. This is exactly why orthodox Christianity has built me up to be an absolutely unique individual – the *only* son of God, as if an almighty God could have only one son – who has the power to absolve all sins committed by humankind, past, present and future. The paradox is, of course, that this pacifies you and causes you to look outside yourself for your salvation. In other words, the ego puts you in a situation where you cannot be saved, and thus the ego's expectations must be shattered before the real you has an opportunity to find the true path to salvation.

Another aspect of this quest for the ultimate guru is that many otherwise sincere spiritual students think they cannot learn from other people. This is especially true of those who have been on the path for a long time and have attained some kind of position in a spiritual organization or in society. Such people often fall into the subtle trap of spiritual pride and think they cannot learn from those who are beneath them in their self-created hierarchy. Yet as I have explained, the only true teacher is the Christ and he/she can appear in many disguises. And this is the reason for Master MORE's saying that you must heed the guru even when he appears in the form of an ant. In many cases, we test our students by sending them someone who appears in a humble form, so we can see if the student is willing to listen for the truth regardless of the disguise in which it is presented. As I said, inasmuch as you have done it to the least of these my little ones, you have done it unto me. My point being – again – that your concept of the guru can block you from heeding the guru, and thus your graven images of the "ultimate guru" must be shattered before you can truly step onto the path to Christhood. The problem is how the conscious self reacts when the ego's expectations are shattered.

Do you see the paradox? A false guru will use the ego's expectations to bind you more firmly to the guru, meaning that a false guru will not threaten but confirm your ego's expectations and sense of superiority. Yet a true guru has the goal of setting the conscious self free, so a true guru must of necessity shatter your ego's expectations and sense of superiority. And in so doing, the true guru must run the risk that if the conscious self cannot free itself from identification with the ego, it will believe the ego's reasoning that the true guru must be a false or incompetent guru because he or she does not live up to the ego's dualistic expectations. Once again, a catch-22 that can be broken only by the conscious self overcoming its ignorance.

What is the real problem with building up the guru as an idol? An idol is a mental image that the ego creates and then elevates to the status of infallibility, which means it becomes a graven image because you never question it. One problem with this is that no human being can possibly live up to the ego's desire for perfection, so any guru on Earth will eventually fail to live up to your ego-based expectations. This often causes people to become either angry with the guru or discouraged about the spiritual path, which is exactly what the false teachers want. Yet how can you become angry because a guru did not live up to your expectations? Only because you refuse to take responsibility for yourself! Thus, you feel you cannot secure your salvation on your own power, and you then project the image that the guru will do it for you. When that illusion is shattered, you feel you have been cheated, which only blocks you from taking responsibility. It is much the same with discouragement—you have given away your power over your own growth and believe in the illusion that the guru will do it for you. When this expectation is shattered, you feel discouraged and give up on the path.

***

Another problem is that no true guru can possibly live up to the ego-based dualistic illusions, so such expectations often block people from following a true guru and steer them onto the outer path offered by the false gurus—of which there are many. My point being that idolatry is very much a spiritual poison that must be overcome. An idol actually has the effect of standing between you and the true God, between you and the freedom that can be found only in oneness. Thus, when you have allowed your ego to set up an idol, the idol must be broken down before the conscious self can be free. In many cases, people's egos actually break down their idols, for the ego is dualistic, so it is easy for it to switch from seeing *nothing* wrong with a person to seeing *everything* wrong with that person. This is the basis for the love-hate relationship that is readily observed by any student of psychology.

The fact is that only when you stop idolizing the guru, can you develop a true relationship with the guru. Which means you do not expect the guru to elevate the separate self but to help the real you transcend the separate self. The ego will always see the guru as superior as long as its expectations are intact. When they are shattered, the ego will dethrone the guru and see it as a false guru, projecting all kinds of negative images upon the guru—images that reflect the ego's internal division rather than an external reality. So the ego will always have a superiority-inferiority interaction with the guru. A "true" guru will always be seen as *superior*, whereas a "fallen" guru will always be seen as *inferior*.

The highest relationship with a true guru is one of equals, or rather a relationship where value judgments – that create the superiority-inferiority dynamic – have fallen away. The core of *my* Being is the conscious self, which is an extension of the Creator's Being. The core of *your* Being is the conscious self, which is also an extension of the Creator. The Creator is Infinite, thus it is meaningless to compare the value or status of one extension of the infinite to another extension of the Infinite. You and I are both extensions of the same God, which means it has no meaning for one to be superior to the other.

I have no desire to be seen as superior by you, for as long as you see me as superior, you will always see a distance, a space, between yourself and me. Can you see why this is so? Superiority can exist only when there is separation, for only then can there be a comparison between two separated entities. When there is oneness, no comparison is possible and thus inferiority and superiority are irrelevant.

I am a true spiritual teacher, which means I teach the path of oneness. You can follow my teaching only by coming into oneness with me, and you cannot do that as long as your view of me is filtered through the inferiority-superiority glasses of the ego. As I said when I won my Christhood, "I and my Father are one." Yet as a teacher I long to say, "I and my student – *you* – are one." Which requires you to come to the point where *you* can say, "I and my Father – my guru – are one!"

Take note of a subtle point. The ego can twist anything through the duality consciousness. Thus, when I say we are equals, that too can be misused by people's egos by making them think that if we are equals, they don't need to listen to me. The reality is that you and I are equals in terms of our intrinsic value. Yet you have not fully realized and accepted your potential, whereas I have. Thus, I serve as the teacher, meaning that you need to respect that I have insights that are beyond your mental box, and thus you need me in order to see beyond the ego. You need to see me as having higher authority than your ego and the false teachers of this world—so that you will listen to me even when they tell you the opposite.

We might also say that your ego is *not* an equal with me—although it very much thinks it is, even that it is superior to me. Thus, your conscious self needs to see that I do indeed have a greater insight than the ego and the false teachers, which is why you need to pay attention when I tell you something that is beyond what your ego wants you to hear. We might also say that the reason why there is an advantage to you in coming into oneness with me is that I have a less localized perspective, and this is the only way for you to transcend your current perspective. Do you see the point? Separation is based on division, so the only way to overcome it is to come into oneness with a Being who is beyond duality. You cannot overcome duality while retaining a sense of identity as a separate being.

Obviously, coming into oneness with the teacher means you have to stop seeing me as a teacher, for the student-teacher relationship implies distance between student and teacher.

***

How can you come to a real sense of oneness with me? Well, you can do so by questioning another illusion that is implicit in the dualistic world view. You might begin to see that I am taking you through a process of questioning your illusions about the spiritual path. For unless you question the ego-centered view of the spiritual path, you cannot move from the path of personal growth to the path of Christhood.

I have said that those who are completely blinded by the duality consciousness cannot see that there is anything beyond the material world, and thus they cannot grasp anything beyond the mental box of the dualistic mind. The only way to go beyond that stage is to attune to beings who are outside duality, meaning the spiritual hierarchy. We have been called by many names in the world's religions and spiritual traditions, but the important point is that we have risen above duality and thus can lead people beyond duality.

Yet when people first come into contact with us, they will again project their dualistic images upon us. And once again, anything – even the reality of a spiritual hierarchy – can be used by the ego to reinforce the illusion of separation.

What does the image of a spiritual hierarchy imply? Well, when you look at it through the separate self, you can only see it in a linear way. In pre-scientific times, people conceived of this in terms of heaven and God being above the physical Earth. So if you traveled up into space, you would quickly enter heaven. In today's age, spiritual seekers have a more sophisticated view, but they still tend to look at this with the linear mind. For example, you might see yourself as being at a low level and God is far above you in a level with much higher and purer vibrations than what you see on Earth. This gives rise to the illusion that God is at the top of the spiritual hierarchy and is *only* found by going to the very top level. Which can reinforce the dualistic illusion that you are separated from God—meaning that God is *not* found where you are.

As I attempted to explain 2,000 years ago, and as I have attempted to explain in this book, you will enter God's kingdom *only* when you stop looking for God outside yourself and start looking for God the only place you can possibly find God, namely inside yourself. So you need to overcome the illusion that you can find God only by going up the linear staircase and that you will experience God only at some future time when you are in a different place. God exists in the eternal NOW, and you will experience God *only* in that NOW—meaning whenever you decide that the time to experience God is NOW.

However, as with everything that involves the ego, there are always two polarities. One is that you deny God where you are and one is that you think you can contact God without going through the spiritual hierarchy. In other words, you think there is nothing between you and God, that you can contact God directly. This has led several people to develop an extreme form of the ego's superiority, where they think they are chosen by the highest God for a special mission, that they are the only ones who can contact God directly, that they need no spiritual teacher above them or even that they are the incarnations of the superior God—in whatever form they perceive it.

Do you see the subtlety here? On the one hand, you should not deny God where you are (which is inferiority), but on the other hand you should not fall prey to the ego's illusion that God is exclusively where you are, meaning you use God to build the ego's sense of superiority. You must – as always – find the Middle Way. What *is* the Middle Way here? It is to recognize that you *can* indeed find God within yourself, but what you find within yourself is still a localized view of God. In other words, your conscious self is an individualization of the Creator's Being, but it is focused in a localized sense of self. Because your conscious self is an extension of God's Being, you can go within and experience what feels like the fullness of the Creator's Being right inside yourself. This is a very important experience, and once you have had it, you can never again be fully blinded by the ego's illusions, for you can never believe that the separate self is all there is.

However, what can confuse people is that when you experience God within yourself, the experience can – especially at the lower levels of the path where the contrast is greater – be so overwhelming that you think you have experienced the fullness of God. Yet what you have experienced is the Creator's Being seen from the localized perspective of your conscious self—for that is the *only* perspective from which you can see anything!

This might require some contemplation, but it is important for you to think about this. What you have right now is a localized perspective. How localized it is depends on your current sense of identity, but the very fact that you are still in embodiment on Earth proves that you have *not* transcended the separate self completely. This is simply a matter of realism.

Because the conscious self is an extension of the Creator's Being, it has the potential to grow toward the fullness of God consciousness. How can it do so? It can do so *only* by expanding its localized perspective to become more encompassing. Yet how does it do this? By becoming one with the Beings who are above it in the spiritual hierarchy. In other words, it simply is not possible for you to expand your sense of self while remaining separate from the beings who have attained oneness with the All, with the River of Life, with their source. If you try to expand the self without coming into oneness with the Ascended Host – perhaps even, as some people do, while denying our existence or reality – you will only be expanding the separate self.

One example of this is how various people have had mystical or spiritual experiences, yet have used them to confirm their existing beliefs or their existing religion. For example, some people talk about *Christian* mystics as people who have had a deeper experience than the average person, yet all of their experiences confirmed or conformed to the Christian belief system, perhaps even a specific church within that system. As I have said throughout this book, the role of the Living Christ is to take you beyond all man-made mental boxes. Yet when you are new to the mystical path, it is very easy to allow the ego to – in subtle ways – impose an overlay upon your mystical experiences. This is tempting because a true mystical experience can be quite paradigm shattering, so immature students will often seek to fit it into their existing belief system in order to regain some sense of security. Obviously, the mature student will go beyond this and will thus rise above all man-made belief systems, while potentially still expressing itself within a system in order to help other people.

***

Because this is subtle, let me give you another perspective. I have said that the Creator is the Infinite. The Infinite cannot be divided, and thus the Infinite God cannot express itself in or as form. In order to create anything, the Infinite Creator must express itself as something that can be divided and thus can take on form. We might conceive of this by referring to the traditional view of seeing God as two polarities, such as yin and yang or masculine and feminine. Again, this is a linear view, but there is value in considering it for the purpose of this discussion.

So we can say that the Infinite Creator is God the Father, who then expresses itself as God the Mother, thereby creating the Mater light that can take on any possible form. Your conscious self is an extension of the Creator's Being, but since you are created to go into the world of form, you are actually created out of the Mother aspect of God. You have the potential to unite with God the Father, but this will happen only as you go through the ultimate self-transcendence—and this cannot happen while you are on Earth.

So when you go within and have a mystical experience of God's Presence, what you experience is actually God the Mother; it is an *expression* of the Infinite God—not the *totality* of the Infinite God. The reason is that as long as you are seeing the world from a localized perspective, you cannot see the Infinite God. You can see *only* an expression of that God, and any *expression* is in the realm of God the Mother. To paraphrase the Tao Te Ching, the God who can be perceived is not the real God.

My aim with this discussion is, of course, to help you overcome the one extreme of denying God where you are without jumping into the opposite extreme of thinking you are the highest God where you are. You need to find the Middle Way of knowing you are a localized expression of God, moving toward oneness with the universal perspective of the omnipresent God. This leads you on to the path of Christhood, which is the path of transcending your current localized perspective—and continuing to do so indefinitely without actually seeking some superior status.

Do you see the point? Denying God where you are is affirming your sense of identity as a separate being. But thinking that you are an incarnation of the highest God, that you alone are God in embodiment, is also affirming your identity as a separate being. One illusion simply says that no one is God, whereas the others says that no one is God besides *you*. In contrast, the Christ mind sees that all beings are extensions of the Creator, and thus the Living Christ works to raise up all life—instead of degrading all life or raising up only itself.

***

The ego is always looking for a way to elevate you to some superior status. If you look honestly at spiritual seekers you know, you will see that many of them are still trapped in this game of seeking to be someone special. People have numerous ways of seeking this, such as their astrology, their past lives, their interaction with a special guru, what a psychic told them, an experience with spiritual beings and so on ad infinitum.

On the one hand, everything the ego does is a perversion of a true God quality, and in this case the source is your genuine desire to expand and express your true God-given individuality. This is your reason for being here, namely to multiply your individuality and have dominion over the self and through that over the Earth. Yet when this is colored by the ego's fear, it becomes expressed as a desire to set yourself apart from others, or rather to elevate yourself above others. The ego's fear leads to a lack of self-esteem, and the way to compensate is to raise yourself in comparison to others. This then leads to idolatry or self-idolatry, where one person is seen as being so special that no one else can follow.

In contrast, the Living Christ knows it is an extension of the Creator's Being and is a unique, individual expression. Thus, there is no fear and no need for comparison or value judgments. This sets you free to express your Christhood, which means you have no desire to be better than others. You desire to express your individuality and you desire to show people that there is something beyond their current mental box and world view. Yet you do this in such a way that you become an example to follow by demonstrating that what one has done, all can do.

This is spiritual freedom, and it comes from a sense of equality with all, which springs from the true knowledge that all are extensions of God and thus part of the Body of God. When people see this about themselves, they can come together to form a true community, namely the community of Christ that I sought to build 2,000 years ago and which some of my early followers did indeed build, at least for a time. It is our hope that it can be recreated in this age.

Yet in order to attain this state of oneness with life, you have to leave behind the false individuality that the ego has built. Again, this individuality is based on your God-given individuality, but it has been colored by the illusion of separation and the fear that it generates. The ego expresses this individuality out of fear instead of out of love, which perverts everything. Thus, you need to rise above fear and embrace your spiritual individuality, which does not compete with others but seeks oneness with all life in order to raise up all life.

The false individuality wants you to believe that you are so special, and thus there is something you need to do on Earth that no one else can do—and that something is somehow essential for God's plan, the salvation of Earth or whatever tickles the fancy of your personal ego. In reality, there *is* something no one else can do, but it is *not* to glorify your ego—it is to be the unique spiritual Being you are.

In order to uncover that Being, you need to look at your expectations and realize they are all unreal and spring from ignorance—the ignorance based on separation. As I have said, all expectations spring from separation, which is the ultimate form of ignorance. Ignorance leads to fear, which leads to a desire to control. Thus, the ego thinks it has to take through control what God offers you freely—if you give up the ego. It is the Father's good pleasure to give you the kingdom, but in order to receive it, you must overcome ignorance so you can accept what God gives you and thereby be in the flow of the River of Life. You can receive God's kingdom *only* by *being* in that kingdom, which requires you to overcome the illusion that you could ever be separated from God's kingdom.

Do you see the mechanism? Ignorance leads to fear, which leads to the need for control, which causes you to overcompensate by seeking control. You seek control by creating mental images of everything and then seeking to force reality to fit the mental image. The more you overcompensate, the more you move away from the River of Life and actually reject what God is offering you. Thus, you must overcome the ignorance so you can see the futility of the ego and surrender it, thereby plunging yourself into the River of Life. You must acknowledge that your expectations spring from a desire to control the teacher and the path—which is ultimately the desire to control God that came from the original fallen angels. THIS MUST GO!!! You simply cannot even begin the path to Christhood as long as you are still seeking to elevate the separate self in comparison to others. Nor can you begin the path while you are still holding on to your mental images and trying to make the entire universe, other people and God fit into the mental box formed by the images.

The River of Life is God's power, love and wisdom. It wants to flow, but it flows only for the good of all life. Thus, if you seek to get power, wisdom or love in order to raise the separate self, you block the flow. The more you seek to take it by force, the more you create a counter-force – your action creates a reaction – and this will get you nowhere nearer to oneness with all life.

There truly is no way to "beat the system," even though the ego and the false teachers claim they have discovered all kinds of ways to take heaven by force. The simple fact is that you can receive unconditional love only when you have no conditions that stop you from directing it for the growth of all life—your greater self as opposed to the separate self. Do you see that the ego sets up conditions that seek to direct the flow of life into raising up itself? The River of Life sees through all such attempts, no matter how subtle, and thus you will get nowhere. I have seen people who for many lifetimes have been looking for a shortcut, for a way to force their way into having special powers that can set them apart from others. Some have even developed a certain ability to manipulate matter with their minds, which can impress those who do not have the spiritual discernment to read people's hearts. Yet such people are nowhere nearer to actually entering heaven, for they have not even started the path to Christhood.

It is an enormous sense of liberation when you finally realize that nothing – absolutely nothing – can fool God or the Ascended Host. Thus, there is nothing hidden from God or from your true teachers. It is amazing to me how many people continue to believe in the lie that what they can hide from other people is also hidden from God. It is such a liberation to realize the folly of this illusion. For when you do, you see that there truly is no point in seeking to hide your past mistakes from the teacher. For in seeking to hide, you maintain a space between yourself and the teacher, and this space will prevent you from entering the true path of Christhood, which is the path of oneness. There can be no space in oneness, for as long as there is a distance, there cannot be oneness.

***

Let us now look to the world of science, specifically classical physics. Isaac Newton formulated three laws of motion, and the third of them is the law of action and reaction. This law is commonly understood to mean that for each force (the action) there is an opposite force of equal strength (the reaction). However, these forces do not necessarily work on the same "body," and it is important to understand why.

When you move your body, your body is generating a force, an action. There must be an opposite force (a reaction) that is of equal strength. Yet if these two forces were working on your body, you would not be able to move—the *re*action would cancel out your action and you would stand still. So the very reason why you can do anything in the physical universe is that this universe is designed to allow you to perform actions on a local scale. You can act on your immediate environment and you can generate what seems like a decisive force that produces a particular result. Yet according to Newton's law, this is possible *only* because the universe compensates for your action by allowing the reaction to work on another part of the universe.

What I am saying here is that the spiritual understanding of Newton's law is that the total amount of force generated in the universe is a constant. Every action has an opposite reaction, meaning that there is balance on the macrocosmic scale. The universe as a whole is in balance. Yet on the microcosmic scale, you can perform an action that seems to have no opposite reaction, meaning that it produces what seems like a decisive outcome. You can move your body from point A to point B.

Yet these localized actions are bought at a price, in the sense that the universe compensates by allowing the opposite reaction to work somewhere else (the large mass of the universe – or the Earth – absorbs the force generated by your actions). Thus, your action – performed in one location – creates an imbalance in another location. This is what Eastern religions call karma, yet we can now gain a deeper understanding.

Karma is *not* a form of punishment. Karma is simply the reaction from the universe to a localized and unbalanced action. When you perform an action that is aimed at benefitting the separate self – instead of seeking to raise up the All – the universe allows you to do so by moving the reaction somewhere else, so that it does not immediately cancel out your action. This is the only way you can actually take an action that is *not* aimed at raising up the All but only seeks to raise the localized self. However, this karma is created by you and thus it is *your* responsibility. Before you can permanently ascend from the material universe, you must restore the balance in the localized area where you created the imbalance. If you made karma on Earth, you must balance it by reincarnating on Earth until you have restored the balance caused by your actions.

So what you see here is that after people become blinded by the illusion of separation, all of their actions are motivated by the ego, by the separate self. And thus, they are aimed at raising the separate self in comparison to other separate selves. Such self-centered actions will inevitably create an imbalance in the universe, and thus they create karma for you. Now, there are some ascended master students who believe that by balancing this karma, you will be free of the Earth and can ascend. However, this is a slightly incomplete understanding of karma.

It is correct that one of the requirements for making your ascension from Earth is that you must balance the karma you have made here. However, you were not sent here to make karma, balance that karma and then leave. You were sent here to be a co-creator with God and help bring the Earth closer to manifesting the kingdom of God. In other words, you were sent here to create a decisive action that lifts the Earth, and until you make that contribution, you will not be free to ascend.

This might seem to contradict what I just said, but not when you understand it correctly. You see, the material universe was not created to be a static place, as some materialistic scientists and many religious people have envisioned. The universe was created as a platform for the spiritual growth of self-aware beings. Thus, it is meant to rise higher in sophistication and intensity of light – as Maitreya explains – until the entire universe ascends and becomes part of the spiritual realm. You make an individual contribution to this process by letting your light shine, by letting the light of your I AM Presence shine through your lower being and by directing that light – with the conscious self – in such a way that it raises the All.

Consider my saying that "with men this is impossible, but not with God, for with God all things are possible." Consider how I produced the so-called miracles that seemed beyond the powers of ordinary humans. The reality here is that when you are trapped in duality, you are confined to acting within the sphere of action-reaction. You can perform selfish actions, but they will always be opposed by a reaction, meaning that your creative power is limited because you are actually pushing against the River of Life. Thus, "with men," with the consciousness of separation, many things are impossible.

Yet when you rise above the illusion of separation, you see the oneness of all life. Thus, you see that what truly raises your self – your sense of self based on oneness – is what raises the All. As I said, "Inasmuch as ye have done it to the least of these my brethren, ye have done it unto me." Thus, when you do not seek to raise yourself but seek to raise the All, you are in alignment with God's purpose for the universe—which is precisely to raise the All. You are now acting "with God," you are flowing with the River of Life and thus all things are possible to you because you are working with the deeper forces of the universe, the forces that are beyond the action-reaction duality. This allows you to perform actions that do not simply have local consequences – which are opposed by reactions elsewhere – but have universal consequences that raise all life.

So what I am saying here is that most people on this planet are caught in the dualistic struggle of performing self-centered actions that are opposed by the entire universe and thus have limited power. Yet they still create karma that must be balanced before people can be free. You have free will, so you are free to continue playing this game for as long as you like. Indeed, many people who see themselves as spiritual are still playing the dualistic game—they have simply disguised it in a clever appearance of being spiritual. Yet they are still seeking to raise the separate self in comparison to others. This raising of the separate self can give the illusion that you are making progress on a localized scale, but in reality it has nothing to do with Christhood. As I said, the path of personal growth must be abandoned before you can truly step onto the path of Christhood.

You now see – once again – that Christhood is not about *you*—when "you" is defined as a separate self, no matter how cleverly disguised with spiritual imagery. Christhood is about one thing only, namely raising the All. As long as you see yourself as separated from the All, you have not actually started the path of Christhood, no matter how good you are at putting on an appearance of being spiritual.

There is an ancient Greek myth about a man named Sisyphus. As a punishment for thinking he was equal to the gods, he was condemned to rolling a boulder up a hill only to see it roll back down and having to roll it up again—ad infinitum. So he was trapped in a never-ending game that produced no decisive action, but only gave the appearance of such an action. This is the game of the ego. It makes you repeat the same actions over and over again, but regardless of localized appearances, they never produce any decisive action in terms of raising the All.

If you still want to play this game, you are not ready for the path to Christhood, and thus I cannot help you. Simply leave this book and then come back to me when you are ready to learn how to perform truly decisive actions, actions that are in harmony with the overall purpose of creation. Actions that do not produce a *re-*action but a *de-*action, a *deified* action.

***

Let me take this one step further. I have talked about the pattern of action and reaction, but we can also say that most people on Earth are not actually performing decisive actions, what I have called *de*-actions. Instead, they are completely trapped in a pattern of *re*acting to the current conditions on Earth. They have been trapped in this pattern because they have become blinded by the consciousness of duality, which has the effect of making people believe that the current chaos and suffering is real. This makes people feel trapped in their limited situation, and thus they – in most cases without being consciously aware of it – react *against* these limitations based on the state of duality. This is what happens when someone strikes you on one cheek and you *do not* turn the other cheek. Instead, you strike back *or* resign yourself to the fact that you can do nothing to escape the abuse.

The effect of such a reaction is that you are now pulled even further into the pattern of reacting to current conditions in a dualistic way, which of course only perpetuates those conditions. Can you see what I am saying? The fallen beings brought their dualistic consciousness to Earth, and they quickly caused an imbalance on this planet. They performed selfish actions aimed at controlling, manipulating and abusing other people, and this caused many of those people to react in a dualistic way by either seeking to fight back or by submitting to the control of those they thought were superior to themselves. This quickly created a situation in which just about everyone is reacting against conditions that spring from the dualistic mind, and they are doing so in such a way that it only reinforces the dualistic illusions, including the overall illusion that this planet is separated from the kingdom of God and that God's perfection can never be manifest here.

Do you see what this means? Humankind is now locked in this dualistic struggle, and the net effect is that this has created a self-reinforcing downward spiral in which the original violence of the fallen beings has generated so much violence and counter-violence that very few people have any attention or awareness left over for looking at the big picture and saying, "Why are we continuing to struggle against everything and everyone—isn't there a better way?"

How can this downward spiral be broken? Only by some people – on an individual basis – refusing to engage in the struggle. These people must demonstrate that it is possible to avoid a dualistic reaction and instead respond to life in a non-dualistic manner—by refusing to resist evil and instead turning the other cheek, no matter how hard you are stricken! And when enough people do this, a critical mass can be reached that gradually awakens more and more people, until the dualistic consciousness is exposed for what it is and thus people have a real choice to rise above it. Right now the vast majority of people on this planet simply do not have this choice, for they have never seen a person who did not respond in a dualistic manner. They have only seen people trapped in duality who are responding to other people trapped in duality, and they have been given no understanding of the duality consciousness and how it affects every aspect of life.

Obviously, I count on my true disciples to be the forerunners for this non-dualistic movement, yet how can you accomplish this? Well, it cannot be done the way traditional Christians do it, namely by using the outer mind to force themselves to act in a way they think is in alignment with my commandments. It can *only* be done by truly changing your consciousness, so you pull the beam of duality from your eye, whereby your eye is no longer divided but is single. What exactly does this mean?

Look back at the history of this planet and consider how much violence and abuse there has been. Now allow yourself to recognize that you have embodied on this planet for many lifetimes, meaning that it is virtually impossible for you to have avoided all of the atrocities in history. Thus, you have most likely gone through some of these atrocities and have been exposed to extreme forms of abuse. Perhaps you have been a slave, perhaps you have been killed for taking a stand for truth or perhaps you have been in many wars and have been killed in the prime of life? And because you were somewhat blinded by the duality consciousness, it is likely that you have responded to some of these dysfunctional situations in a dualistic manner. And what is the effect of this?

Well, as I have said, the ego is born from separation and all of its reactions are based on duality. Thus, the ego can only respond to an abusive situation in a dualistic manner. It is only the conscious self who has the potential to respond to situations in a non-dualistic manner, but it can do so only when it takes full responsibility for making decisions and bases its decisions on the recognition that it is a spiritual being who is more than the body and thus is not ultimately affected by the abuse of the body. So when the conscious self is not able to do this, it will respond to a limiting situation by *not* wanting to make decisions. In a sense, the Conscious You responds to abuse by deciding that it does not want to even experience it, it does not want to be conscious of it. So it seeks to withdraw into a cave, in which it thinks it can avoid making decisions as to how to respond—and thus it hopes it can avoid being conscious of the situation.

Obviously, the conscious self cannot avoid being conscious, but it can give the ego the authority to make decisions about how to respond. Yet because the ego can respond only in a dualistic manner, the ego's responses will only serve to get you even deeper into the dualistic struggle. This happens because what the ego will do is to create a sub-ego, a new separate self, that is designed to deal with the particular abusive situation you are experiencing.

This separate self is similar to a computer program in that it unconsciously carries out its programming. Thus, whenever you experience a situation that resembles the abuse that created the separate self, that self is activated and now takes over your reaction to the situation. Which means you mindlessly repeat the patterns from the past and get yourself even deeper into the dualistic struggle. Which is why so many people on this planet are not growing spiritually but are simply repeating the same patterns lifetime after lifetime—until they finally have had enough and decide to take back their responsibility to change their reactions to life.

***

Obviously, you have already broken the downward spiral of repeating old patterns and have taken back a large degree of responsibility for yourself. Yet it is highly likely that you still have some of these old separate selves residing in your subconscious mind. These are the skeletons in the closet, the ghosts that haunt the mansion of your mind.

What I am saying here is that these dualistic selves, these ghosts from the past, simply cannot follow you into the kingdom of God, which means you must "give up the ghost." You must come to consciously see these old separate selves, see that they were created out of the duality consciousness and therefore do not serve any constructive purpose on your path to Christhood. Thus, they must be allowed to die, they must be given up—and this must be done consciously.

Does the expression to "give up the ghost" ring a bell? If you have read the scriptures, it should remind you of my last moments on the cross:

> 33 And when the sixth hour was come, there was darkness over the whole land until the ninth hour.
> 34 And at the ninth hour Jesus cried with a loud voice, saying, Eloi, Eloi, lama sabachthani? which is, being interpreted, My God, my God, why hast thou forsaken me?

> 37 And Jesus cried with a loud voice, and gave up the ghost.
> 38 And the veil of the temple was rent in twain from the top to the bottom. (Mark, Chapter 15)

Do you begin to see the deeper symbolism here, a symbolism you should have been taught in Sunday school but were not? My crucifixion is *not* something that was exclusive to me. It was a physical outpicturing of what every human being is going through in a spiritual manner—it is an illustration of a spiritual initiation. What is the cross? It is a device that keeps you fixated in a certain position from which you seemingly cannot extricate yourself. And this is precisely what your ego and the forces of anti-christ are doing to you—and to every human being who is trapped in duality. Almost all people on this planet are crucified in a spiritual sense because they have been nailed to a cross by their own egos, a cross that they were sentenced to by the false leaders, the fallen beings, who condemned them to spiritual death in order to prevent them from expressing their spiritual potential to be co-creators with God.

Do you begin to see that what I intended to do by allowing myself to be physically crucified was to illustrate the fact that all people – namely their conscious selves – are more than the body? And thus, even if they seek to crucify – paralyze – you in a physical sense, you are more than this and can rise above it. Thus, even though the false leaders on this planet have sought to box you in by trapping you in a mental box based on duality, you do not have to accept this state of paralysis.

Instead, you can rise above their illusions by realizing that they are unreal and therefore that which is unreal cannot affect that which is real—namely the Conscious You who is an extension of the Creator's own Being. How do you free the conscious self from the dualistic identity? By giving up the ghost, as a symbol for the separate selves that you have created to deal with the abuses you have encountered on Earth. Yet instead of seeking revenge for such abuses or even seeking to set them right, you simply decide to give up all attachment to anything on Earth. Whereby your mortal self dies – as symbolized by my physical body dying on the cross – and the conscious self can now be resurrected – can be born of fire – into a new identity as the S-u-n of God you were created to be.

And when that happens, the veil in the temple will be rent, the veil that symbolizes the separation between matter and spirit, between the material realm and the spiritual realm. When that veil is rent, the separation is shattered and you have now become the open door that no man can shut, the open door for your Higher Being to express itself in this world, whereby you can finally fulfill your role of helping to co-create God's kingdom on Earth.

So do you now see that my crucifixion is a symbol for the very process that can free all people from the ghosts of the past? Which should give a new meaning to the expression to "take up your cross and follow me." And which should then give you a firm motivation for exposing the ghosts – the separate selves – from your past and coming to the point where you can consciously, unconditionally and lovingly give them up and let your mortal self die. Knowing full well that the real you will not die but will be resurrected into a new identity in which you see yourself as one with all life above you and one with all life below you.

***

Let me try to make sure that you truly understand why these separate selves and the ego are unreal. Do you truly understand that all of your separate selves are based on graven images? The reason being that they are created by the ego, which cannot experience God's reality. This might be difficult to understand for a spiritual seeker, especially if you are aware that you have had spiritual experiences that confirmed God's reality. You then tend to think that your ego can fathom these experiences and has changed as a result. However, this simply is *not* the case. Your ego cannot fathom or recognize a true mystical experience. What the ego *can* do is to change its behavior when it sees that *you* are changed by such an experience. The ego will once again morph itself into a different entity, so it can use your new world view to stay hidden in the shadows.

I have been explaining the central feature of the ego from many different angles, but have you actually understood the modus operandi of the ego? The ego will forever be separated from reality, which means that it cannot experience reality directly. Thus, the ego creates mental images of what it thinks reality is like, and it then elevates them to the status of infallibility, which makes them graven images. The ego cannot compare its mental images to reality, but your conscious self *can*. Thus, by trying to make you believe its mental images are infallible or above questioning, the ego is trying to prevent the conscious self from exercising its ability to use the Key of Knowledge and compare your beliefs to reality, to perform a reality check. For if you *do* see that one of your beliefs is unreal, then you will immediately abandon it, which then causes the ego and the false teachers to lose some degree of control over you.

Do you now see what is actually driving most people on this planet and what is fueling the dualistic struggle? Most people are blinded by their egos, and the egos have created dualistic images that they have projected onto reality. Thus, people are trying to make reality fit into their mental boxes, their belief systems, and in order to do that, they must convert or eliminate all people who do not accept their belief system. The ego simply cannot accept any threat to its belief system and will seek to eliminate it with all means possible. Which explains why there have been and why there still are so many struggles between different belief systems.

Do you see that the vast majority of people on this planet are locked into the struggle of seeking to make the entire universe, other people and God fit into their specific mental boxes? Do you see that this can never be done, which means it is a futile endeavor that can only lead to struggle and suffering? Can you see that I need people who will go out and expose the mechanism behind this struggle by demonstrating that it is possible to rise above the veil of illusions created by the dualistic mind? And can you see that in order to do this, you *must* begin by removing the beam from your own eye, for that is the only way you can see clearly how to help other people do the same?

You must give up the ghosts created by your ego so that your conscious self can be resurrected into a new sense of self, an identity *based on* reality because it is *one with* reality. And how can you qualify for this resurrection? By coming into oneness with a true spiritual teacher, by coming into oneness with the spiritual hierarchy above you, the Beings who have already attained oneness with the Beings above them, and thus have oneness with the Creator. In other words, you must come to the point where you no longer see yourself as a separate being but as one link in the Chain of Being, as one member of the Body of God—above and below.

***

What I am taking you toward is a point where you have overcome all divisions in your psyche, where you are no longer a house divided against itself, where you are of one mind, where your eye is single. When your vision is no longer divided by the ghosts of the separate self, you can make an informed, conscious decision about leaving behind the path of personal growth and stepping on to the path to Christhood—leaving behind for good the desire to elevate the separate self or the desire to make the universe fit into your mental box. As I have attempted to explain, the path to Christhood takes you into oneness with the All, but this must begin in seeking oneness with the spiritual hierarchy above you.

Thus, the path to Christhood is the path of oneness with me—or with another ascended master who is close to your heart. You can follow the path by seeking oneness with any ascended Being—for we are all one. Yet I do hold the office of planetary Christ, and no man cometh to the Father except by going through that office. And going through my office means coming into oneness with me. So you will, sooner or later, have to make your peace with me, which ironically is easier for people who did not grow up in a Christian culture. For mainstream Christianity has provided such a distorted image of me that most people from a Christian background find it very difficult to even contemplate coming into oneness with me. Nevertheless, an inescapable part of the path to Christhood is that you rise above your background, whatever it might be. Which is why I said:

> 32 Whosoever therefore shall confess me before men, him will I confess also before my Father which is in heaven.
> 33 But whosoever shall deny me before men, him will I also deny before my Father which is in heaven.
> 34 Think not that I am come to send peace on Earth: I came not to send peace, but a sword.
> 35 For I am come to set a man at variance against his father, and the daughter against her mother, and the daughter in law against her mother in law.
> 36 And a man's foes shall be they of his own household.
> 37 He that loveth father or mother more than me is not worthy of me: and he that loveth son or daughter more than me is not worthy of me. (Matthew, Chapter 10)

The real meaning here is that the path to Christhood is uncompromising. In order to follow it, you cannot stay within the mold defined by the mass consciousness of your culture and family. You must be willing to go beyond convention, for if you seek to adapt to *anything* on Earth, you cannot come into oneness with me. For I do not conform to any graven images, and I am in no way taking part in the dualistic struggle. I have given up my personal ghost and I am one with reality, thus having given up the attempt to fit the universe into a box. My overall point here being to help you realize that we have now reached another dividing line in this course.

In order to progress beyond your current level, you need to realize that the next level of the path requires you to come into oneness with me as a spiritual Being. And precisely because I am a *spiritual* Being, I am beyond any of the limitations – beyond the ghosts – found on Earth. If you seek to hold on to your worldly identity, how could you possibly come into oneness with me? For as I said:

> 24 Then said Jesus unto his disciples, If any man will come after me, let him deny himself, and take up his cross, and follow me.
> 25 For whosoever will save his life shall lose it: and whosoever will lose his life for my sake shall find it. (Matthew, Chapter 16)

Denying yourself means denying the pressure to conform to the worldly identity—the pressure that comes both from without – from false teachers, society, family and the mass consciousness – and from within, namely from your ego. Taking up your cross means taking on the challenge to unravel your dualistic beliefs, which is precisely what keeps you nailed to the cross and prevents you from moving beyond it. So if you seek to save that worldly life, the ghostly identity, you cannot possibly come into oneness with me. And here is the real point you need to understand.

As I have tried to explain, the ego and the false teachers have come up with a false path that has many clever and subtle disguises. Yet the essence of them all is that they are based on a failure to understand the second challenge of Christ. Thus, they create the subtle impression that it is somehow possible to keep your worldly identity – your ghosts – and still be saved, or even come into oneness with Christ. In other words, the underlying belief is that instead of you leaving behind your mental box, it is possible to somehow get Christ to enter and conform to your box. You do not *surely* have to lose your life in order to follow Christ, for it is possible to make Christ accept your separate self, to make the separate self worthy in the eyes of Christ.

I hope you can now begin to see that this is a complete and utter illusion. I will *never* compromise my office, which is dedicated to setting you free from the prison made from the illusions of antichrist. Thus, I will *never* conform to the expectations and the graven images of the separate self.

There are many sincere spiritual seekers who have made some progress on the path, but who have then entered a gray zone, a twilight zone, in which they are making progress so much harder for themselves by holding on to certain subtle beliefs that are based on the very illusion I just explained—namely that you do not really have to make an all-out choice, that you can keep holding on to the separate self – or certain dualistic images – while still making progress beyond a certain point. I have seen so many people over the centuries who have sincerely striven for decades to make spiritual progress, but who have stopped at a certain point precisely because they did not understand the uncompromising need to give up all ghosts and let the separate self die on the cross.

Do you understand what this truly means? Study the accounts of my crucifixion again and see what actually happened. At first, I thought God would save me from the cross, but I finally realized this was not going to happen. I then gave up the ghost that made me believe in a mental image and finally accepted reality, namely that I had to let my physical body die on the cross—without actually knowing what would happen afterward. This is a symbol for the fact that you have to give up a ghost without knowing what will happen as a result. It is almost as if you have to take a leap of faith into the unknown. However, the more you have truly understood that you are a conscious self which is out of God's Being, the less of a leap and the less faith is required—for faith will be replaced by knowing that you are an immortal, spiritual Being who will not die because you let the mortal self die. Thus, the *real* you cannot die on the cross, only the *unreal* you. Yet only when you come to see the difference, will you be able to let the unreal you die without fearing you will lose your existence.

You would make life so much easier for yourself if your conscious self would come to the realization of the basic illusion of the ego, and that the ego will never let go of it, but that *you* can still let go of it. Thus, you can stop trying to force reality into your mental box and instead focus your attention on becoming one with reality. How do you get to know truth? By becoming one with the Spirit of Truth, by *becoming* truth. That is why I said:

> I am the way, the truth, and the life: no man cometh unto the Father, but by me. (John, 14:6)

Do you see how this connects with what I said above? As long as you hold on to the ego's basic illusion, you are keeping yourself in the twilight zone of action and reaction. You may take two steps forward, but your internal division pulls you one step backward, making your progress much harder and slower.

What I am hoping to help you see here is that I have now taken you as far as I can take you while you are still in this divided state. You can still make some progress, and perhaps you still have wounds that need psychological healing, which might entail seeking professional help. So I am not saying there is anything wrong with not being ready to make the all-out decision I am describing here. Yet you also need to be aware that your ego will use *anything* as an excuse for postponing that decision forever. Thus, there *must* come a point where the conscious self recognizes that *it* needs to make that decision and that it can *only* be made in the NOW.

So I need you to seriously contemplate whether you are ready to make the decision that you are willing – not out of fear or a sense of obligation but out of a sense of love – to come into oneness with me, or whether you still want to keep me at some distance and maintain a space between you and me, a space in which your ego can hide?

If you are not ready, I am not condemning you. Yet I do recommend that you do not continue with this course until you are ready. You might do the preceding keys over again or go back to Mother Mary's book and let her help you heal your psychological divisions. Or you might seek some professional help with exposing and dismissing the ghosts from the past. If you need more time before making the decision, perform the exercise for this key for as long as you feel necessary.

What I am saying here is that I expect that when you read beyond this point, you have come to a clear decision that you are willing to pursue a path of oneness with me. Obviously, I do not expect you to have attained that oneness, and I am certainly going to take you through a process of working toward that oneness. But I am expecting you to have made a decision that you are willing to move toward oneness—with whatever that entails.

## Exercise for Key 14

Again, I want you to give a 33-day vigil of Jesus' Invocation for Victory over Death. After giving the invocation, sit with your notebook ready and contemplate the following koan. Then freely write down whatever comes to you. This is the koan:

> I am a full-grown, young eagle and my wings are ready to carry me soaring into the sky for the first time. I am sitting on the edge of the nest, my wings eager to cleave the air, yet my claws holding on to the nest. What forces within me cause my claws to grasp the nest so firmly that I cannot trust my wings and let go?

Obviously, what is holding you back is the separate selves you have created in the past, as explained earlier. Ask me to help you see these selves, so that you can recognize them consciously. As you become aware of those past selves, I want you to connect to the fact that you *are* the conscious self and that you are more than any self created to deal with the appearances of this world.

I want you to contemplate that even though your past situations seemed very real at the time, they only seemed real to the separate self. The conscious self can see that these situations were only appearances in a world that is ultimately unreal. These unreal appearances have no power over the real you, and thus they should not be allowed to continue to affect your sense of self.

Thus, you can now imagine that you are hanging on a cross created by a specific self from your past. As you take ownership and acknowledge that you created the past self, you can sense that you are paralyzed on the cross. Then you can raise your vision and see that the real you is above and beyond the material cross. Thus, you can give up the ghost of your past identities and allow them to be consumed by the Flame of God that you are. For our God is indeed a consuming fire that can consume all unlike itself—and will do so if you let go of it and allow it to pass into the flame instead of using your free will to give it continued existence.

Since I am the Being who represents the crucifixion for humankind, I am both capable of and willing to go through this experience with you. Thus, envision that I am hanging with you on the cross and that I am offering you my momentum of total and unconditional surrender. By tapping in to this momentum, you can indeed overcome any burden that is holding you back from the total spiritual freedom that is the master key to the abundant life. For what are the separate selves doing but rejecting the abundant life by confirming that life is a struggle and that God is an angry and conditional God who is not willing to give you his kingdom? By using this technique diligently, you can literally rise above *any* and *all* limiting conditions. For the only thing that can limit you is an unreal sense of self. So be willing to give up every ghost in order to be resurrected as a new Being in Christ, as the Sun of God.

My beloved, do you see the underlying point? You may have grown up to fear the crucifixion and see it as something to be avoided. You may be willing to do just about anything to avoid being nailed to a cross from which you cannot move. Yet do you see that you are already crucified in a spiritual sense and that you have been hanging on your personal cross for many lifetimes? What I offer you is to help you come to the point where you can transcend the cross by finally giving up the ghosts that cause you to remain nailed to the cross. This release is not something to be feared—it is something to be accepted with great joy, for it will finally set the captives free and take you across the sea – by parting the sea of duality – to the promised land. So will you not accept your freedom instead of continuing to resist it by holding on to the ghosts from the past?

> 27 All things are delivered unto me of my Father: and no man knoweth the Son, but the Father; neither knoweth any man the Father, save the Son, and he to whomsoever the Son will reveal him.
> 28 Come unto me, all ye that labour and are heavy laden, and I will give you rest.
> 29 Take my yoke upon you, and learn of me; for I am meek and lowly in heart: and ye shall find rest unto your souls.
> 30 For my yoke is easy, and my burden is light. (Matthew, Chapter 11)

# Key 15
# Understanding who Christ really is

Before you can begin to understand what it takes to come into oneness with me, you need to have a clearer understanding of who I really am. This will require you to consider what images of Christ you were brought up with—as it is virtually impossible to grow up on this planet without having been affected by one of the many false images of Christ floating around in the turbulent sea of the mass consciousness.

Obviously, you have already started to challenge and leave behind your childhood images of Christ—or you would not have been able to follow the course up until this point. In fact, I have systematically challenged many of these images in previous keys. Yet I still want you to take some time during the next 33 days to consider your images of me as Jesus and your more general images of Christ. What does it mean for you to be the Christ—what images and what limitations are associated with the concept of Christ? Do you see it as something exclusive to me, or do you see that "Christ" is more than Jesus? And thus, there is a potential that other people could attain Christhood and that other people have.

As I am sure you are aware, language has certain limitations. For example, I have said that you *are* God in the sense that you are an extension of the Creator, an individualization of the Creator's Being. Yet I have also said that you *are not* God, meaning that you are not all that God is, you are not the fullness of God. You are an expression of the whole but not the whole.

Now, it would be inaccurate to say that the Creator has no individuality, but the individuality of the Creator is far beyond that of any human being, in fact so far beyond that no human being can fathom the individuality of the Creator. So I propose we say that the Creator has a universal sense of identity and that you have an individual or localized sense of identity.

The important point here is that every being in the world of form has such an individual sense of identity. As I have said, there is a spiritual hierarchy stretching from human beings to the highest spiritual Beings. Yet even these Beings are still individualizations of the Creator. So what happens as you move up into the layers of this hierarchy? You encounter beings who have moved away from a very localized sense of identity and toward the universal identity of the Creator. Yet even the highest Beings in the spiritual hierarchy have not lost their individuality—in fact they have strengthened it, but not in the sense you see on Earth. So we might say that rising in the spiritual hierarchy means moving toward a universal form of identity, and this is actually a strengthening of a being's identity as an individual. However, this strengthening happens by the Being growing toward a more universal sense of identity—which to a human being sounds contradictory, again, the limitations of human language. So to make this clearer, take another look at my saying:

> For whosoever will save his life shall lose it: and whosoever will lose his life for my sake shall find it. (Matthew 16:25)

What I am saying between the lines is that in order to move up to the next level of the spiritual hierarchy and become a Christed being, you must be willing to lose your life for my sake. If you seek to save "it," you will lose "it." Yet if you are willing to lose "it," you will find "it." The key is to realize that it is not the same "it" I am talking about.

My point here is to show you that even the highest Beings in the spiritual hierarchy have *not* lost their individuality. They have actually found a more expanded, more universal individuality. Yet what is it you have to lose in order to find this new individuality? You have to lose your present sense of individuality—whatever that is.

The highest Beings in the spiritual hierarchy are Beings known on Earth only as Alpha and Omega. Yet "Alpha and Omega" is actually a spiritual office, much like the president of a country. At any given time, the office is held by an individual, but the office is more than that particular individual. This is also the case with the office of Alpha and Omega. It is currently held by two individual Beings, but there have been other individual beings in that office before and there will be others after.

So in one sense, the image I am painting here is that even spiritual beings have to be willing to let go of their old identity in order to move to a higher level in the spiritual hierarchy. It is possible that even a spiritual being can become attached to a particular sense of identity and refuse to let it die, which explains why spiritual beings – such as angels – can fall. This is all explained in greater detail by Maitreya, so I will not go further into it here. However, I *will* point out that the way a spiritual being moves to a higher level in the spiritual world is that it makes itself a servant of those below it in hierarchy. For the Creator is the ultimate servant and only those who serve unconditionally can approach the Creator's level of consciousness.

The big difference between human beings and spiritual beings is that you are living in a sphere that has not yet ascended, meaning there is room for duality. Thus, you have built a sense of identity based on the duality consciousness, which means you see yourself as a separate being. And it is this separate sense of identity that must die, for only when you lose the "it" of the separate identity can you find the "it" of your true, spiritual identity. And only then will you be a whole being instead of a house divided against itself. Only then have you been reborn of fire.

My purpose for bringing this up is to address the only type of fear that has any hold over the conscious self, namely that it could lose its individuality, lose its existence. The conscious self is born as an individual being, and it is charged with the desire to expand and strengthen its individuality, until it reaches the level of the universal where it then becomes a God in its own right—a being who can create its own world of form, if it so desires. Yet because the conscious self has come to identify itself fully or partially based on the separate, dualistic identity, it can come to believe that if the separate self dies, *it* will die. And this will obviously be a belief that will stop you from going beyond a specific point of the spiritual path. Thus, it is essential – absolutely essential – for your conscious self – for *you* – to overcome this illusion and realize that the separate self is *not* you. *You* are MORE than the separate self.

If you want a metaphor for this, consider the concept of an office, as I just spoke about. The separate self you currently have is like an office on Earth, for example like the headmaster of a school. You may choose to take on that job and even hold it for many years, which means you come to see yourself as "the headmaster." Yet you know you are more than the job, and even though it will require some adjustment to let go of the office, you know there is life beyond the job—or at least there should be. In other words, you have simply chosen to step into a separate sense of identity, but you are more than that identity and can step outside of it any time. Stepping outside this separate self does not mean that your life comes to an end—it means you find a new life, a new sense of identity, that offers you greater freedom. For, of course, in stepping into the "office" of your separate self, you also have to take on all of the duties of that office, which eats up most of your attention. For while you are "the headmaster" you cannot be someone else.

So do you see my point? It is to help you overcome the fear that "coming into oneness with me" means that you lose your individuality, your identity. You only lose the separate identity but find a new one that is much more than the old one. What I am saying here is that the ego will actually see Christhood as a loss, so it is up to the conscious self to step outside that self-centered viewpoint and gain a less localized perspective. Whereby you will see Christhood as a gain of spiritual freedom that is far more attractive than anything offered by the limited identity of the ego.

***

So let us go over – again – the characteristics of the separate self. The first characteristic we notice about the ego is, of course, that it is focused on itself. We might say that the ego is a localized sense of awareness that has become so localized that it sees itself as the center of the universe with all other beings – from other humans to God – there only to serve itself and fulfill its needs. As people become more egotistical, they become less sensitive to other forms of life and more willing to control others in order to fulfill their own desires—regardless of what consequences that has for others.

Obviously, spiritual seekers have moved beyond these forms of ego-centeredness and would not knowingly hurt other people. Yet there can still be remnants of ego-centeredness left in how people pursue the spiritual path. As I have tried to explain, this can still propel you forward on the path of personal growth, but it will get you nowhere on the path of personal Christhood.

What are some of the more obvious signs of self-centeredness on the path? Here are a few:

- The desire to raise one's own consciousness purely for one's own sake. It may be a desire to escape negative self-esteem, fear or other hurtful feelings. It may be to build one's pride and sense of being better than others.

- The desire to acquire special powers to either impress other people and establish superiority, or to control other people, the world and even God. Some people actually come to spiritual teachers hoping to learn magical powers that will allow them to control their environment—the ego's ultimate dream.

- The desire to feel like an important person who is doing work to save humanity or the planet or who is doing something for God that will be recognized in heaven. This can also be a desire for fame or celebrity status in human society.
- The desire to acquire special powers in order to – supposedly – awaken other people to the spiritual path. Nevertheless, the desire is to be the only one who does this, even on a planetary scale.
- A savior complex, where the person's ego wants to be seen as the ultimate savior. I have had many people approach me as an ascended master wanting to learn my "secret" so they could set themselves up as being as important as they think I was when I walked the Earth. It might help to consider that in my lifetime I had very few followers and a very localized "fame."
- Many variations of the desire to receive something in return for one's efforts to grow spiritually or to help other people by converting them to one's beliefs. This can even be an expression of the ego's desire for ultimate security, which it thinks will come if everyone else is converted to its religion or political belief system.

Behind all of these approaches is the essential mechanism of the ego, based on its self-centered way of thinking: "What's in it for me?" The ego cannot stop thinking this way, so again it is up to the conscious self to step outside the reality distortion field of the ego. Take a look at this passage:

> 27 Then answered Peter and said unto him, Behold, we have forsaken all, and followed thee; what shall we have therefore?
> 28 And Jesus said unto them, Verily I say unto you, That ye which have followed me, in the regeneration when the Son of man shall sit in the throne of his glory, ye also shall sit upon twelve thrones, judging the twelve tribes of Israel.
> 29 And every one that hath forsaken houses, or brethren, or sisters, or father, or mother, or wife, or children, or lands, for my name's sake, shall receive an hundredfold, and shall inherit everlasting life.
> 30 But many that are first shall be last; and the last shall be first. (Matthew, Chapter 19)

For 2,000 years this has been a guiding rod for many Christians who have sincerely pursued the path of growth—as they saw it based on the distorted doctrines available to them. They have reasoned that I came to Earth to offer them something that they could not have in this world but only in the next world. In other words, they have thought that if they did the right outer things in this life, they would reap the reward in the future—thus seeing a gap between themselves and the reward. This is not necessarily wrong in that many people have had such karma that they could not manifest their Christhood in the current lifetime. Thus, they had to be willing to work in the *now* in order to gain an advantage in a distant *future,* for this was the only way they could make progress. Thus, my teaching was adapted to the state of consciousness that humankind had 2,000 years ago and which many people still have.

Yet we are now moving into the final stages of the spiritual cycle I came to inaugurate, which means there are many people in embodiment who do have the potential to manifest full Christhood in this lifetime, and many more who can manifest a degree of Christhood. And this, of course, relates to the third challenge of Christ, which is that you begin to see yourself as the Christ. In the above quote, you can see that Peter was the archetypical example of a person who has mastered the first challenge of Christ but has become stuck in the second one. Thus, while he is willing to follow me – even give up much to do so – he is still doing this from a self-centered motive of wanting a reward. He is still feeling he has to give up something to follow Christ and that he should be entitled to a compensation for doing so.

But now look even deeper. What is Peter actually doing? He is feeling that he has to discipline his separate self and give up part of his separate self in order to follow me, and he is willing to do so. Yet in following me, he is seeking a reward *for* the separate self. So even in his willingness to follow me, he is affirming the reality of his separate self—which, of course, means he cannot follow me beyond a certain point as the separate self cannot enter the kingdom. So we now see that you can master the first challenge of Christ – and think you are a real disciple of Christ or in other ways define yourself as a very spiritual person – while still being stuck in the consciousness of seeking to elevate the separate self. This is the consciousness that you need to overcome in order to master the second challenge of Christ and move on to the third challenge.

I know I have said this before, but it is consistently the one thing that trips up sincere spiritual seekers and takes them into a blind alley for lifetimes. It is essential that you uncover, examine and leave behind all desire to walk the path in order to get something in return, even – or especially – the tendency to do good on Earth in order to receive a reward in heaven. You must overcome all tendency to pursue the path for self-gratification, for this can *only* come from the ego. And as long as you seek to gain *anything* for the separate self, you will not be able to follow Christ into oneness. Look at this quote:

> 36 Simon Peter said unto him, Lord, whither goest thou? Jesus answered him, Whither I go, thou canst not follow me now; but thou shalt follow me afterwards.
> 37 Peter said unto him, Lord, why cannot I follow thee now? I will lay down my life for thy sake.
> 38 Jesus answered him, Wilt thou lay down thy life for my sake? Verily, verily, I say unto thee, The cock shall not crow, till thou hast denied me thrice. (John, Chapter 13)

Again, Peter represents the consciousness of a person stuck in the second challenge, thus thinking he is ready to follow me even though he has not given up the separate self. The lesson here is that Peter did indeed deny me three times, thus denying his oneness with me. This denial came from his identification with the separate self, which is also why he wanted to follow me—thinking he would gain something for the separate self by following me. This, of course, shows that he had not understood what it means to follow Christ because he had not understood the consciousness of Christ. So let us do what we *can* to make sure *you* will not get stuck at the level of Peter. For whereas the Catholic church might be content to follow Peter, I desire my true disciples to go beyond that level of consciousness entirely. I desire them to follow me—*not Peter.*

***

So what will it take to follow Christ, what was it Peter was unable to see? Look at this quote from Paul:

> 1 If there be therefore any consolation in Christ, if any comfort of love, if any fellowship of the Spirit, if any bowels and mercies,
> 2 Fulfil ye my joy, that ye be likeminded, having the same love, being of one accord, of one mind.
> 3 Let nothing be done through strife or vainglory; but in lowliness of mind let each esteem other better than themselves.
> 4 Look not every man on his own things, but every man also on the things of others.

> 5 Let this mind be in you, which was also in Christ Jesus:
> 6 Who, being in the form of God, thought it not robbery to be equal with God:
> 7 But made himself of no reputation, and took upon him the form of a servant, and was made in the likeness of men:
> 8 And being found in fashion as a man, he humbled himself, and became obedient unto death, even the death of the cross. (Philippians, Chapter 2)

The essence of this quote is, of course, to "let this mind be in you, which was also in Christ Jesus." And what mind is that? Well, it is, of course, the Christ mind. As we have talked about before, this is a universal mind that is meant to maintain oneness between the Creator and its creation and between all levels of that creation by empowering all individual beings to be "of one accord, of one mind."

I have earlier talked about an office, and again, the Christ mind can be seen as an office that is beyond any individual. Yet anyone can aspire to that office, meaning anyone can put on the mind of Christ. In other words, the Christ mind can take upon itself any form, even being "made in the likeness of men" and "being found in fashion of a man." This signifies that all have the potential to take on the Christ mind, whereby they become the Living Christ in embodiment.

Yet what is this mind? It is a mind that is completely beyond the separate mind of the ego. The Christ mind knows it is "in the form of God" and thus it thinks "it not robbery to be equal with God," meaning being one with God and God's purpose for creation, being a co-creator with God. Yet what is the purpose of the Creator? It is to raise up the All, which is why the Christ mind takes "upon him the form of a servant," seeking to awaken all people on Earth from the consciousness of death. This includes being willing to demonstrate that one can rise above death, even by becoming "obedient unto death, even the death of the cross" in order to show people what is possible. So you now see that the Christ mind is the ultimate servant, which is why it is greater than the separate mind:

> 33 And he came to Capernaum: and being in the house he asked them, What was it that ye disputed among yourselves by the way?
> 34 But they held their peace: for by the way they had disputed among themselves, who should be the greatest.

> 35 And he sat down, and called the twelve, and saith unto them, If any man desire to be first, the same shall be last of all, and servant of all. (Mark, Chapter 9)

So you see – I hope – that when you let the Christ mind *be in you,* you overcome all desire for gain for the separate self. Instead, you attain the total spiritual freedom of never having your attention and energy swallowed up by the gain-loss duality of the separate self. Instead, you enter into a state of mind in which there is no loss but only the non-dualistic gain of knowing you are *being* in the River of Life and thus doing exactly what you originally came here to do—to bear witness to your truth and let your light shine. Once you begin to experience the incomparable flow of the River of Life – the Holy Spirit, through you – you will know that this state of mind is infinitely more joyful and fulfilling than anything the ego can offer. You will know the truth in the words:

> For what shall it profit a man, if he shall gain the whole world, and lose his own soul? (Mark 8:36)

So I trust you are beginning to see that the turning point you have reached is the dividing line between the path of personal growth and the true path of Christhood. In order to rise from the path of personal growth to the path of Christhood, you have to be willing to come into oneness with me. Yet who am "I?" I AM an individual being who has come into oneness with the universal Christ mind, and as such I am the servant of all. Which means I am focused exclusively on raising up the All by seeking to awaken all from the consciousness of death and constantly seeking to help them take the next step on the path to oneness.

So do you now see the inescapable conclusion? You will *not* make any progress on the path of Christhood as long as you are focused on yourself—even if you think you are seeking to raise your consciousness or doing something for others. As long as your motives are self-centered, you cannot even take the first step on the path of Christhood. In order to walk that path, you must do something for others, and you must do so selflessly and unconditionally. Why is this so? Because the only way to fully overcome the separate self is to do something for others—and to keep refining your motives until you can do it unconditionally, meaning without expecting anything in return.

The reaction of the ego to this statement will be, "Well, then why do something for others if you don't get anything in return!" And that is precisely how you can unmask the ego. For while the conscious self will not receive something in return for doing something for others, it will not go unrewarded—only it will not be the kind of reward the ego can fathom.

***

Let us consider that – as everything else – Christhood has an Alpha and an Omega aspect. The Alpha aspect is that you do seek to raise your consciousness so that you establish a greater sense of oneness with your own Higher Being and with the Chain of Being above you in the cosmic hierarchy. From a superficial viewpoint, this might seem to be what I have called the path of personal growth, and indeed many students – even some self-declared spiritual teachers – have seen no difference. Yet there is an *essential* difference! The simple fact is that if you pursue this growth out of a self-centered motive, you will never actually attain oneness with your higher self or the spiritual hierarchy. Why not? Because we are beyond the dualistic self, so how could you possibly make progress toward oneness with us unless you too move beyond the separate self?

In other words, the Alpha aspect of Christhood requires you to let go of the separate self and gradually become selfless—which is not the same as having no individuality (although it seems that way from the dualistic perspective of the ego, since you becoming selfless means becoming ego-less). So what happens as you begin to attain oneness with the Beings above you? Well, you naturally begin to see what the separate self cannot see, namely the true purpose of creation. You begin to see the purpose of raising your sphere to the level of the spiritual realm and that you can become an open door for this process. Yet you also see that beyond this purpose is the goal of raising up individual beings toward God consciousness. You begin to see this first for yourself, meaning that you see that *you* came out of the Creator's Being and that you can grow toward oneness with your source.

Yet as this happens, you also begin to see that all other self-aware beings came from the same source, which means all beings are one because they are connected through their common source. You then begin to see yourself as part of the Body of God, and then you begin to see all other people as part of that body too. You begin to see that the only way to raise your physical body is to raise all parts of it—you do not raise your body by raising one finger. And then it dawns on you that the *only* way to truly raise yourself is to raise the entire body, which means raising up all beings. You even begin to see that your expanded self *is* the entire Body of God.

And this will naturally bring you in tune with the Omega aspect of Christhood, which is that you leave behind all desire to raise up the separate self and instead focus all of your attention on raising up the All. In other words, seeking oneness with what is above you no longer has the purpose of raising your own consciousness. Instead, your striving is entirely focused on raising your consciousness for the purpose of being able to better help others. And this, of course, is when you truly make progress because now you are in alignment with God's purpose. And as you multiply your talents, God can truly multiply your own efforts. Which is why those who adopt the consciousness of being willing to serve all are truly raised up. As we say, "The reward for service is more service." The more you are willing to do for others, the more God is willing to act through you, and God acting through you is, of course, the true source of power and the ultimate reward. It is also the only way for you to feel one with the Creator.

***

Do you now see that being the Living Christ, the Christ in embodiment, is more about fulfilling the Omega aspect of serving others than the Alpha of raising your consciousness? In fact, most spiritual seekers have this reversed and think they somehow have to reach a superior state of consciousness *before* they can begin to serve others. This, of course, is the illusion of the ego, which is always striving for some ultimate state and often has formulated seemingly altruistic motives for wanting it. As I have said, the ego is quite capable of using your striving on the path in order to hide itself. Thus, it creates the concept that you are really here to serve God or serve others or serve some cause, but you just have to attain these spiritual powers before you can fulfill that mission. Of course, the ego can never attain the state of oneness that is the key to spiritual power, so as long as you believe in this illusion, you will never reach your goal and the ego is safe.

Do you see the point? It is a fallacy to think that you *first* have to reach some superior state of consciousness, and *then* you can serve God, other people or a cause. In reality, you will *never* reach a higher state of consciousness *until* you begin to serve others with whatever powers and abilities you have. Why is this so? Because there truly is no superior state of consciousness that suddenly appears out of nowhere. The path is a gradual process of you multiplying your talents and God giving you more in proportion to your effort. You then multiply the more you have and God again gives you more. This is the path of Christhood, and it does not actually begin until you decide to do something that selflessly serves others—using whatever "talents" you have right now. And with serving others, I do not mean simply performing outer actions, but actually doing so from a genuine motivation of wanting to raise up the All—rather than scoring points in some game conjured up by the ego or the false teachers.

Only when you serve selflessly will you perform what I earlier called de-actions, namely the de-ified actions that come when you know you are *not* the doer because you know it is God acting through you. Thus, you do not take pride in producing certain results, for you know that with men this is impossible and only with God is it possible to produce truly decisive actions. Which means actions that raise up the All rather than raising up a localized part of the universe only to create an imbalance elsewhere.

De-actions spring from genuine oneness with the All and an unconditional desire to raise up the All. And this can come only from putting on the mind of Christ, from being one with Christ—because you realize that the true role of Christ is to awaken all people. Thus, you dedicate your life to raising up humankind rather than pursuing some self-centered goals or desires.

In order to attain this state of mind, you must overcome all tendency to want something in return for your service. As an image of the Christ, consider the sun, which simply gives its light unconditionally to the Earth without needing, wanting or expecting anything in return. You see, the Christ is content to be the open door and knows that the only real reward is to feel the light and truth of God flowing through you and to direct that light into raising up all life—thus fulfilling your reason for being, namely to be a co-creator with God.

The Christ knows that when you give selflessly and unconditionally, you have no need for any reward or return from any source on Earth. Why would you, when every action you take – regardless of its outer results and the response from other people – produces the reward of releasing more light from God and thus increasing your sense of joy and fulfillment.

Deified action is when you act with no expectation of a return from Earth, thus without creating a reaction to a self-centered – and thus unbalanced – action. Do you see that karma is not a form of punishment but a teacher? When you act to raise up the localized self, you create an imbalance, and it will pull on you to set things right. This pull will continue until you realize that by raising your awareness and acting selflessly, you will receive a much greater reward than could ever be obtained from ego-centered actions. Thus, you truly change your consciousness and can now act on Earth without creating a reaction, without creating the kind of karma that pulls you back toward Earth. Instead, you create the kind of karma that pulls you toward the spiritual realm.

***

Another way to look at this is to say that your mind is like a radio receiver, and the question is which station you choose to tune in to. Do you tune in to the mass consciousness or to the Ascended Host? If you are still motivated by a self-centered desire – no matter how cleverly disguised in religious or altruistic garments – you will inevitably tune your consciousness to the mass consciousness, in which you find billions of other people who are still focused on the separate self. *Only* when you overcome self-centeredness will your mind start tuning in to the Ascended Host.

Take note that I am not hereby talking about spiritual experiences. There are actually people who have so-called spiritual experiences even though they are still in a self-centered state of mind. Yet this phenomenon is caused by the fact that for most people, anything above the material level of consciousness is considered spiritual. Yet as I have mentioned, there are three levels of the material universe between the physical level and the spiritual realm. It is possible to establish a connection to beings in those realms while still being self-centered, and this makes it possible that people can have all kinds of unusual experiences – even receive messages from so-called "spiritual" beings – while still on the path of personal growth. This is what I described when I talked about those who take heaven by force, only it is not heaven but an imitation of it that they take.

My point is that it is necessary to distinguish between experiencing the higher levels of the material universe and the actual spiritual realm. There are beings in the emotional, mental and lower etheric realms who mimic ascended masters to the point that they must be called impostors. There are people on Earth who have established some contact with such beings, even to the point of channeling them and bringing forth messages that can sound impressive to the immature seeker. Yet such messages will always seek to boost the egos of the students rather than speaking about the need to overcome the ego.

Which leads to the understanding that we of the Ascended Host *never* go below a certain frequency in vibration. Meaning that if you want to contact us, you need to raise your consciousness so you can tune the radio of the mind to *our* frequency. This can be viewed as a mechanical process in the sense that you know very well that if you do not tune the radio the right way, you simply cannot receive a certain radio station. Thus, as long as you try to reach us with the radio tuned to the selfish band of frequencies, you will never have success. You might still reach the impostors in lower levels, and they might make you feel like a very important person, but you still have not reached the true teachers of humankind, for we do not take on students who want to use us to boost their egos. Which leads us to a conclusion that might seem shocking to some, but it is time you understood the reality of how you can relate to us. For how else can you come into oneness with me?

***

You see, the brutal fact is that I have absolutely no interest in, concern for or love for *you*—meaning your separate self. This is a misunderstanding found in both Christian and New Age circles. It is a false understanding based on an illusion created by the false teachers. For example, many Christians believe that if only they meet certain outer requirements, such as being baptized or confessing me as their Lord and Savior, I simply *have* to save anyone. Likewise, many New Age people believe that I was so loving and kind that I included and accepted anyone. In both cases, these people are actually believing that they can somehow get me to afford them salvation without them having to remove the beam from their own eyes. They think they can receive the reward without meeting the requirements. You should now be able to see that this is a complete fallacy, and you should be able to name several reasons why this is so. Take another look at my statement:

> 32 Whosoever therefore shall confess me before men, him will I confess also before my Father which is in heaven.
> 33 But whosoever shall deny me before men, him will I also deny before my Father which is in heaven.
> 34 Think not that I am come to send peace on Earth: I came not to send peace, but a sword. (Matthew, Chapter 10)

The sword I represent is the one that divides the real from the unreal. I am *not* come to save you by doing all the work *for* you. I am come to give you the ingredient that will empower you to raise your consciousness to the level of the Christ mind—which is the *only* possible salvation. That ingredient is the Key of Knowledge which allows you to divide the real from the unreal in your own mind, whereby *you* can pull the beam from your own eye. And *then* you shall see clearly how to help others do the same.

So when *you* have multiplied the talents I give you and have pulled the beam from your eye, *then* I will confess you before the

Father, which gives you entry into the Father's kingdom. Yet what will it take for me to confess you before the Father? *You* will have to confess *me* before men—which means you must put on the mind of Christ and then express it before other people.

Do you see my point here? I am *not* here to save your separate self, your ego. I am here to save the *real* you, the conscious self that is an extension of the Creator's Being and has temporarily accepted a lesser sense of identity. And I can save the real you *only* by helping that real you separate itself from everything that is unreal—meaning everything based on the illusion of separation.

Both of the above categories of people believe I have some kind of love, compassion or concern for them as they are right now. Because they are still so identified with their separate selves, they actually think I care for their separate selves. This is a complete fallacy, as I have ABSOLUTELY NO CONCERN WHATSOEVER for people's egos.

What *is* true is that I have infinite and unconditional love for people's real selves. Obviously, in the here and now, the conscious self is who it thinks it is, which means I do have concern, compassion and love for you in whatever state of consciousness you are in right now. However, you must understand the crucial distinction. You may think that who you see yourself as being right now is all there is to your identity, but I can never fall prey to that illusion. I *never* see you as a limited, self-centered human being. I *only* see you as the spiritual being that you truly are. Thus, my concern, love and compassion is *not* for the separate self but for the real self. I do not love you for what you are right now; I love you for what you have the potential to become—when you rise above unreality. Or one might say that I *do* love you for who you really are—regardless of how you see yourself.

***

We now come to an absolutely essential point which very few people have understood. Take a look at the following quotes:

> 16 For God so loved the world, that he gave his only begotten Son, that whosoever believeth in him should not perish, but have everlasting life.
> 17 For God sent not his Son into the world to condemn the world; but that the world through him might be saved. (John, Chapter 3)
>
> 30 I can of mine own self do nothing: as I hear, I judge: and my judgment is just; because I seek not mine own will,

> but the will of the Father which hath sent me. (John, Chapter 5)

God did not "send" the Christ into this world in order to condemn the world but so that the world might be saved. How can the world be saved? By people rising to the Christ consciousness! And how can they do that? By separating the real from the unreal, by rightly dividing the word of truth, by learning how to make the just judgments of the Christ mind. And what is a just judgment? It is one based on the only distinction that counts: Is it real or is it unreal? Now read these quotes:

> Judge not according to the appearance, but judge righteous judgment. (John 7:24)

> 15 Ye judge after the flesh; I judge no man.
> 16 And yet if I judge, my judgment is true: for I am not alone, but I and the Father that sent me. (John, Chapter 8)

The vast majority of human beings are still trapped in the consciousness of judging after appearances by using some standard created in this world – and thus created based on the value judgments of the dualistic mind – to judge everything in their personal lives, in society and even in their relationship with God. As we have discussed before, this is a judgment based on the mental images created by the ego—the mind that can never experience oneness with God's reality and thus *must* create mental images and judge everything by them.

Do you begin to see that as a Christed being you rise above *all* such dualistic judgments? The Christ has no personal likes and dislikes, no judgments about what is right and wrong, good or bad. The Christ *only* evaluates whether something is one with God's reality or still – wholly or partially – separated from that reality. The Christ does not evaluate people based on personal likes and dislikes. The Christ only evaluates whether a person is teachable or not.

The Christ has unconditional acceptance for any person in whatever physical or mental state that person is in right now. The reason is that the Christ has unconditional respect for God's law of free will. Thus, the Christ recognizes that a person's present state is the result of that person exercising its God-given free will. And since the Christ has complete acceptance of God giving all beings free will, the Christ also accepts each being's right to create whatever experience it desires for itself.

Of course, the Christ also sees that most people on Earth have created an experience for themselves that is outside the River of Life and thus keeps them from the abundant life that it is the Father's good pleasure to give them. And while the Christ accepts people's right to experience separation, the Christ is ever ready to help people overcome their unreal situation and their unreal identity and find their way back into God's kingdom of oneness with all life.

Thus, when the Christ meets a specific person, the Christ does not judge that person based on *any* standard—as most Christians do. Neither does the Christ start preaching the highest spiritual truth to any person. The Christ looks at the person's current state and sees the path that the person has to take from that point to oneness. The Christ does not expect or demand that the person covers the entire distance in one giant leap. Instead, the Christ plots a very practical, realistic path and then focuses on helping the person take the first step.

The Christ does this by giving the person a morsel of truth and light. Yet the Christ does not judge how the person uses that initial offering. It leaves this up to the person's free will and simply stands ready to work with those who multiply their talents rather than burying them in the ground.

Do you see that this is completely free of judgment? The Christ looks at a person and sees the very first step that the person must take to journey from its present state to the Christ consciousness. It then gives the person what he or she needs in order to take that step. If the person multiplies what is given, the Christ will give more. If the person chooses not to multiply the offering, then the Christ moves on and finds other people to help.

The Christ has no judgment of any person and thus has no attachment to any person, has no desire for the person to respond in a certain way. The Christ is completely free of such judgments and thus the Christ sets itself and all other people free. Which is why the Christ is one with the reality of God, namely that free will reigns supreme in this world.

Do you understand the underlying meaning? The false teachers and fallen beings are the ones who disagreed with God's decision to give co-creators free will. Thus, they are the ones trying to control people into making certain choices—they are trying to force people to be saved. These false teachers have influenced virtually every religion on Earth and have spread the subtle mindset that it is acceptable to herd people into the fold of religion so they can be saved and avoid eternal damnation. Yet this is a complete misunderstanding of God's intent, which is that people enter the kingdom of God as a result of a free-will choice to leave the separate identity behind. Only by freeing yourself *completely* from this subtle consciousness can you *be* the Living Christ and avoid being pulled into one of the many subtle dualistic games that are supposedly aimed at saving people but have no chance of ever doing so. For that which is unreal is forever separated from that which is real and thus cannot bring you into oneness with that which is real.

***

As the Living Christ, you accept what *is,* you accept any condition as what it is without in any way being concerned about it having to be different. Thus, you avoid the trap, that is so common, of going into a negative frame of mind, such as guilt or regret, in which you want the present to be different and thus focus on the past—before things were the way they are. You also avoid the opposite extreme of hoping for a better future, always waiting for things to get better. As a result of avoiding these extremes, you stay in the NOW, which is the *only* time when you can bring about change.

As the Christ, you accept what *is,* but you do not accept it for *what it is*—you do not accept it as real or permanent. Instead, you see current conditions as the springboard for growth, which means that people learn their lessons and move from duality toward oneness. You meet people where they are, but you have no sympathy, not even compassion as it is understood by most people. Instead, you have an unconditional love for a person's real self and a desire to help the person transcend its current limitations.

You *never* accept limitations as real or permanent. You always see beyond outer appearances and see the conscious self within, the conscious self that is an extension of God's Being and has the potential – no matter how far it has descended into duality and separation – to return to oneness with its source. You have acceptance of the self in its present state, but also of its potential to transcend that state. You accept people as they are, but you also accept that they have the potential to transcend any condition they are currently facing.

Why do you have this acceptance? Because you see that no matter what the current condition might be, it was created by the conscious self by projecting dualistic images upon the Ma-ter light. And you know the Ma-ter light can instantly shake off such conditions and instead outpicture images projected through the Christ mind. Thus, you see that the conscious self can indeed overcome any *outer* condition by transcending its *inner* condition—and *that* is your focus.

Your focus is on helping people transcend, and if they won't, the Christ leaves them and moves on to those who *can* be helped—because they are willing to help themselves. The Christ is a practical realist and is quite aware of the limitations of time and space, which means it uses its opportunity to the maximum effect by focusing on people who are willing to multiply their talents. The Christ is aware of the overall goal, namely to raise up all of humankind, which can be done by the top ten percent raising their consciousness. Thus, the Christ seeks what has the greatest possible effect on the overall goal and does not become lost in details, such as trying to "save" one person who is not willing to multiply the talents. The Christ sees the big picture that most people don't see, which is why I said to my Earthly father at the age of 12:

> 42 And when he was twelve years old, they went up to Jerusalem after the custom of the feast.
> 43 And when they had fulfilled the days, as they returned, the child Jesus tarried behind in Jerusalem; and Joseph and his mother knew not of it.
> 44 But they, supposing him to have been in the company, went a day's journey; and they sought him among their kinsfolk and acquaintance.
> 45 And when they found him not, they turned back again to Jerusalem, seeking him.
> 46 And it came to pass, that after three days they found him in the temple, sitting in the midst of the doctors, both hearing them, and asking them questions.
> 47 And all that heard him were astonished at his understanding and answers.
> 48 And when they saw him, they were amazed: and his mother said unto him, Son, why hast thou thus dealt with us? behold, thy father and I have sought thee sorrowing.
> 49 And he said unto them, How is it that ye sought me? wist ye not that I must be about my Father's business?
> 50 And they understood not the saying which he spake unto them. (Luke, Chapter 2)

***

We have now arrived at the point where you should be able to grasp and fully internalize the essential point about Christhood. *Christhood is not a passive frame of mind!!!*

It is a frame of mind in which you are focused on one thing and one thing only, namely how you can *serve*. How can you serve the overall purpose of the Creator – to raise up the material universe to be the kingdom of God – which can be achieved by raising up each individual to the Christ consciousness? In order to find your place in this grand adventure, you must be willing to actively go out to awaken people and shine your light of truth on the issues and the situations in your localized environment and/or on the planet.

My point being to bring you to the very simple realization that the *only* way to become the Christ is to dedicate your life to *serving* a greater purpose than any defined by your separate self. Thus, if you are not active, you are stuck in the no-man's land of the ego, a dead end, a catch-22.

If that is the case for you, I have only one thing to say to you: GET OUT OF IT—RIGHT NOW!!!

Take a look at the world you live in. There is an infinite variety of needs for raising up life in some way. There is so much suffering, so much lack, and there is a crying need for those who will not simply try to alleviate the suffering but who will seek to help people transcend the suffering by rising to a higher state of consciousness. There are so many people to help, so many causes to promote, so many new ideas and inventions to bring forth that no one who truly understands Christhood can possibly remain passive—unless they are trapped in one of these ego-traps:

- Some people have become so focused on their own growth that they think they will actually serve God and humankind by raising their own consciousness indefinitely. I have now explained that you are here to fulfill your divine plan, and while that requires you to raise your consciousness, it does not require you to raise it indefinitely—only enough to do what you came to do. Thus, continued personal growth simply becomes a black hole that swallows up your attention and keeps you from doing what you came here to do. Get out of this trap and start focusing on the real self, rather than the ego and its insatiable desire for self-elevation.

- You have become trapped in a – perhaps unrecognized – fear of expressing your Christhood. This is a state created by the false teachers who – as Maitreya explains – think they own planet Earth. Thus, the last thing they want is for anyone to express their Christhood on this planet. It is fine with them if you sit in a cave and raise your consciousness, but the moment you go out into the marketplace and overturn their tables in the temples of the world, they will come after you—or so they want you to think. Yet realize that this is all an illusion, for that which

> is unreal cannot threaten that which is real. Thus, realize that you are here for a higher purpose and that God has given you the right to express your Christhood on this planet—which is one of the main things I came to demonstrate. I also demonstrated that even if they kill your body, God will raise you up and thus you have no need to fear him who can kill the body.

So what you need to decide is whether you will follow Christ and express your Christhood or whether you will follow anti-christ and hide your light under a bushel. Here are some excerpts to clarify the situation you face:

> 10 Blessed are they which are persecuted for righteousness' sake: for theirs is the kingdom of heaven.
> 11 Blessed are ye, when men shall revile you, and persecute you, and shall say all manner of evil against you falsely, for my sake.
> 12 Rejoice, and be exceeding glad: for great is your reward in heaven: for so persecuted they the prophets which were before you.
> 13 Ye are the salt of the Earth: but if the salt have lost his savour, wherewith shall it be salted? it is thenceforth good for nothing, but to be cast out, and to be trodden under foot of men.
> 14 Ye are the light of the world. A city that is set on an hill cannot be hid.
> 15 Neither do men light a candle, and put it under a bushel, but on a candlestick; and it giveth light unto all that are in the house.
> 16 Let your light so shine before men, that they may see your good works, and glorify your Father which is in heaven. (Matthew, Chapter 5)
> 16 Behold, I send you forth as sheep in the midst of wolves: be ye therefore wise as serpents, and harmless as doves.
> 17 But beware of men: for they will deliver you up to the councils, and they will scourge you in their synagogues;
> 18 And ye shall be brought before governors and kings for my sake, for a testimony against them and the Gentiles.
> 19 But when they deliver you up, take no thought how or what ye shall speak: for it shall be given you in that same hour what ye shall speak.
> 20 For it is not ye that speak, but the Spirit of your Father which speaketh in you.

21 And the brother shall deliver up the brother to death,
and the father the child: and the children shall rise up
against their parents, and cause them to be put to death.
22 And ye shall be hated of all men for my name's sake:
but he that endureth to the end shall be saved.
23 But when they persecute you in this city, flee ye into
another: for verily I say unto you, Ye shall not have gone
over the cities of Israel, till the Son of man be come.
24 The disciple is not above his master, nor the servant
above his lord.
25 It is enough for the disciple that he be as his master,
and the servant as his lord. If they have called the master
of the house Beelzebub, how much more shall they call
them of his household?
26 Fear them not therefore: for there is nothing covered,
that shall not be revealed; and hid, that shall not be known.
27 What I tell you in darkness, that speak ye in light: and
what ye hear in the ear, that preach ye upon the housetops.
28 And fear not them which kill the body, but are not able
to kill the soul: but rather fear him which is able to destroy
both soul and body in hell. (Matthew, Chapter 10)

32 Whosoever therefore shall confess me before men, him
will I confess also before my Father which is in heaven.
33 But whosoever shall deny me before men, him will I
also deny before my Father which is in heaven.
34 Think not that I am come to send peace on Earth: I
came not to send peace, but a sword.
35 For I am come to set a man at variance against his father, and the daughter against her mother, and the daughter in law against her mother in law.
36 And a man's foes shall be they of his own household.
37 He that loveth father or mother more than me is not
worthy of me: and he that loveth son or daughter more
than me is not worthy of me.
38 And he that taketh not his cross, and followeth after me,
is not worthy of me.
39 He that findeth his life shall lose it: and he that loseth
his life for my sake shall find it.
40 He that receiveth you receiveth me, and he that receiveth me receiveth him that sent me.
41 He that receiveth a prophet in the name of a prophet
shall receive a prophet's reward; and he that receiveth a
righteous man in the name of a righteous man shall receive a righteous man's reward.

> 42 And whosoever shall give to drink unto one of these little ones a cup of cold water only in the name of a disciple, verily I say unto you, he shall in no wise lose his reward. (Matthew, Chapter 10)

## Exercise for Key 15

Do you understand what you are going through at this stage of the course? You are moving from the third challenge of Christ – which is to stop seeing Christ outside yourself and accept that you can become the Christ – to the fourth challenge of Christ. The fourth challenge is to realize that Christhood is *not* about you – as the separate self – but about YOU as the greater self that is one with the All and thus naturally serves to raise the All—thereby also raising its localized self. In other words, you become the Christ *only* by expressing your Christhood in service to others. If you do not, you cannot move on from the second challenge of Christ, which means you get stuck in a no-man's land that some mystics have called the "dark night of the soul." Which is really a state of being stuck between the path of personal growth and the path of personal Christhood. I will not talk much about this here, for the only way to overcome it is to get out of your self-created dark cave and start serving others.

So what you need to do as the exercise for this key is to consider and write down any hang-ups in your being that are preventing you from expressing your Christhood in service to life. To help you, I am asking you to do a 33-day vigil of a rosary or invocation of your choice. After the rosary/invocation, go through the attunement exercise below. When you have entered the garden and are sitting across from me – or the ascended master of your choice – ask me to show you what is keeping you from being the Living Christ in action. I *will* show you, for if ye ask, ye shall receive. It is *only* your willingness to receive an answer that will limit the answer.

### Inner attunement exercise:

1. Go into a quiet room where you can remain undisturbed for some time (at least 10-15 minutes). Seat yourself in a comfortable chair so that you are not disturbed by discomfort in your physical body.

2. Give the rosary or invocation of your choice.

3. Visualize that the angels of Archangel Michael are surrounding your personal energy field. There are four angels, one on each side. These angels are 12 ft. tall and they carry swords that burn with a bright blue flame. They are fierce and able to protect you from the forces of this world.

4. Turn your attention to your higher self which is located right above your head. Silently give the following affirmation:

**In the name of Jesus Christ, I invoke a wall of brilliant white light around my body, mind and energy field. I accept that this energy seals me from the things of this world. I now invoke a violet flame to burn inside the wall of light and to consume all imperfect energies in my own being.**

Allow yourself a few moments to feel that you are completely sealed from the energies of this world.

5. When you feel at peace, focus your attention at the center of your chest at the height of your physical heart. Visualize that a spiritual flame burns inside your chest. This spiritual flame does not require fuel to burn. It is the unfed flame.

6. Focus your attention on this flame and allow your attention to enter the flame itself. Behind the flame, you see a doorway. Enter that doorway. As you go through the doorway, you move into a tunnel. As you move forward, you see the proverbial light at the end of the tunnel.

7. Keep moving forward until you emerge from the tunnel and walk into the light.

8. You now see that you have entered an exquisitely beautiful garden. The garden is surrounded by tall hedges. It has beautiful flower beds and walkways. In the center of the garden is a fountain that gently whispers. All over the garden, birds are singing cheerfully.

9. As you walk into this garden, you feel that the cares of the world are simply falling away from you. The further

you move into the garden, the more light and peaceful you feel.

10. Simply keep walking and allow yourself to feel how the peace and tranquility of the garden absorbs all of your worries and cares. When you feel uplifted and at peace, take a moment to look around.

11. As you look around, you see two seats carved from stone. Allow yourself to sit down in one seat and make yourself comfortable. Then, focus your attention on your heart and close your eyes. Allow yourself to feel that you are completely at peace in this beautiful garden. In fact, you somehow feel that this is home.

12. Now imagine that you open your eyes and look at the seat in front of you. To your surprise, you notice that someone is now sitting in that seat. When you look closer, you realize that it is indeed I, your Jesus, who is sitting before you.

13. Allow yourself to get comfortable in my Presence.

14. Now focus your attention on my heart and allow yourself to feel that my heart radiates an unconditional love for you. Give yourself a few moments to accept that I love you unconditionally.

15. Then, allow yourself to absorb my unconditional love for you and feel how it consumes everything that is imperfect and unreal. This is indeed the perfect love which casts out all fear and all other imperfect emotions.

16. While you are seated in front of me and fully absorbed in my love, allow yourself to think back to your situation on Earth. Do not allow yourself to be disturbed by any aspect of that situation. Simply bring your situation to your conscious awareness for a moment. Then, look at me again, and in your mind formulate a silent question, covering what is keeping you from being the Christ in action.

17. After you formulate the question, send it to me.

18. Then close your eyes and focus your attention on my love. Allow yourself to be so absorbed in that love that you forget all the cares of the world.

19. After some time of being absorbed in my love, your attention might naturally drift back to the question. Simply focus your attention on my heart and listen for an answer. If you do not receive an immediate answer, be not disturbed. Simply focus on my unconditional love and allow yourself to be absorbed in that love for as long as you like.

20. When you feel you have absorbed what you can, when you feel that your heart has become the cup that runneth over with my love, then visualize that you quietly leave the beautiful garden and walk back through the tunnel.

21. You are now seated in the chair in your room. Give yourself a few moments to return back to your normal state of consciousness.

22. Now write down whatever comes to you without analyzing or judging it with the outer mind.

# Key 16
# The Alpha and the Omega of Christhood

As I have said, Christhood has an Alpha and an Omega side. To give you a deeper understanding, study this excerpt from a dictation I gave at the Easter conference in 2008:

## The kingdom of God is at hand—through the union of the Divine Father and the Divine Mother

Greetings, my beloved, on this Easter Morning—meant to symbolize my resurrection from the grave, from the tomb. But yet I, Jesus, did not come to this Earth to symbolize this for myself, I came to symbolize the potential – for all human beings – to let the human self, the mortal self, die. And thereby be resurrected – not into a new physical life or spiritual life in some higher realm – but to be resurrected, my beloved, into a new sense of identity, where you no longer deny the reality that you are a co-creator with God.

Thus, you acknowledge that the kingdom of God is within you, that you are one with your Father, that your Father has worked hitherto, and that you are willing to work by being the co-creator that you were sent here to be. So that you can play a part in bringing the kingdom of God to Earth. This is the purpose for which I came, this is the purpose for which I went through the physical events of the crucifixion, my death on the cross—in order to symbolize what is possible for all human beings spiritually, my beloved.

***

For you see, 2,000 years ago, it was indeed necessary to give people physical, visible, outer manifestations, or they would not have been able to lock in to the potential for overcoming death, the consciousness of death. But of course, in giving those outer manifestations, it was foreseeable and inevitable that many people would focus on the outer manifestations, failing to see the hidden symbolism behind them, and thereby failing to see the universal aspects of my mission and message. Thinking that it only applied to the Jews, thinking that certain things only applied to me, or that certain things only applied to Christians.

For truly, my beloved, the Christ consciousness is universal. The entire idea of the Christ Consciousness, my beloved, is that it unifies the material and the spiritual. It unifies what you might call the Divine Father, and the Divine Mother, so that there is no separation between the Creator and its creation. For of course, as it is stated in the Gospel of John, without him was not anything made that was made.

And that is precisely why the kingdom of God is within you, because God – God's Being, and God's Presence – is embedded within everything, my beloved. And it is only a religion that is based on separation that could have turned Christianity into a monotheistic religion, thereby raising up the graven image of the external God. The angry, remote being in the sky, looking down upon you, ready to judge you for any transgression and send you to hell for all eternity.

My beloved, it is time that the Christian people, those who call themselves Christians today, wake up to the reality of my true message—that I did not come to create another religion that denies their Christ potential, as the Jewish religion did at the time (and still does, for that matter). I came to awaken all people to the potential to find the kingdom of God within you, and thereby become an extension of that kingdom on Earth, the co-creator who cocreates that kingdom and brings it into manifestation. Thereby giving the abundant life to all people, both the abundant material life and the abundant spiritual life.

***

For you see, my beloved, in God's mind, in God's vision, there is no difference between the material and the spiritual. This is an illusion created from the duality consciousness, the consciousness of separation that was brought to this planet by the fallen beings from higher spheres, but that has also been espoused by many people on this Earth. And you see, my beloved, only the duality consciousness makes it possible for the ego to exist. And the duality consciousness also gives the ego the potential for creating the illusion that the ego has attained what it craves the most, namely some kind of superior status, compared to other people on Earth.

And *that,* my beloved, is precisely why so many people in so many different areas of the world – and in so many cultures and religions – will not let go of the duality consciousness. This even applies to those who call themselves Christians. They will not let go of the duality consciousness, for if they were to let go of it, they would have to realize and recognize that the salvation I brought to this Earth is not exclusive to themselves, to the members of their own particular little church—that they have defined for themselves, thinking that they can thereby exclude all others from being saved.

So my beloved, what does it then take to overcome that duality consciousness? Well my beloved, it takes a recognition, a realization, that God the Father was never separated from God the Mother. For you see, what has happened in the duality consciousness is that you have created these gender roles, and you have created these images – dualistic images – that makes it almost impossible for us to communicate the reality, the spiritual reality. For when we say a word, you immediately start – you meaning the people on Earth – to impose your dualistic images upon them.

So when I say "God the Father," immediately people project an image based on the gender roles that have been defined in human society. And when I say "God the Mother," they project another image based on their image of women. But those images are both dualistic, are both unbalanced, and thus they cannot lead you to the correct understanding of what it actually takes to be saved, as the Christians call it. Which truly means that you enter the kingdom of God—which as I said is within you, as the symbol for the fact that the kingdom of God is not a physical state, is not a spiritual state; it is a state of consciousness.

It is not that you have to travel somewhere physically in order to enter the kingdom of Heaven. It is not even that you have to shed the body and ascend to some spiritual realm in order to enter the kingdom of Heaven. The message I came to bring to Earth was embodied in the saying I preached in my early days, where I said, "The Kingdom of God is at hand." Meaning you can experience it right now by entering the state of consciousness that *is* the Kingdom of God.

And what *is* that state of consciousness? It is the state where you have overcome the illusion of this world, the illusion created by the prince of this world, so that you overcome the illusion that God in the Father aspect, in the Alpha aspect, could ever be separated from God in the Mother, Omega aspect. For you see, my beloved, it is true that there are two aspects of God. There is the one Creator which is the Infinite, which is undivided, indivisible. Yet that infinite Creator has expressed itself in the world of form, but in so doing has expressed itself *as* form, has embedded its own Being in form, has created everything out of its own Being. And therefore, even though there is still an aspect of God that is the undivided Creator, nevertheless God has also divided itself into the world of form, the Ma-ter light that has taken on form.

***

So you see that God the Father is not separated or distinct from God the Mother in the way you think of it, based on gender roles on Earth. God the Mother is another expression of God the Father, and your role as self-aware beings in the matter realm is to awaken to the reality that you are extensions of God the Creator. And thus, you can be the open doors for God the Creator to bring its kingdom into manifestation on Earth. But you can be those open doors *only* when you overcome the sense of separation from your source, from your Creator, so that you finally say, "I and my Creator are One." And you recognize that you were never separated in reality.

For my beloved, if God is infinite, it must mean that the Creator is everywhere, so how could you ever be separated from the Creator, separated from your source? It cannot happen, except as an illusion created in the mind that is based on separation.

So you see how this relates to the topic for this conference, of restoring the Divine Mother, the Divine Feminine. For do you see, my beloved, that in order to walk the path of Christhood, you have to overcome the illusion that the Divine Mother – that the feminine aspect of God, that the matter realm – could ever be separated from the Father, the Creator?

You then become the open door for spreading that truth to others, for giving that life-giving truth to others, that they too might be awakened, and realize that they are extensions of God the Father. But when they attain union with that God the Father, then they *become* God the Mother, they become the representatives of God in the matter realm. And thus, you become the Father-Mother God in embodiment. You become the union of the Father-Mother God right here in this realm.

This is the role of the Christed being. This, my beloved, is the true path to Christhood. There are levels of the path, but as you go toward the higher levels of the path to Christhood, you need to integrate the Father and Mother aspects of your being. Where you realize that your lower being – the identity you have built in order to express yourself in this world – needs to come into oneness with God the Father, whereby you actually become God the Mother in the pure sense of God the Mother.

***

For you see, my beloved, be not confused by appearances—do not judge after appearances. Make the subtle distinction here. Everything you see around you in the material realm is created out of the Ma-ter light that has taken on form. The Ma-ter light is an expression of God the Mother—in a sense we can say that the Ma-ter light in its pure form *is* God the Mother.

Yet God the Mother has vowed to allow the self-aware beings, the co-creators, to experiment with their free will, meaning the Ma-ter light will take on any form that they impose upon it through the power of their minds. And thus, what you see on planet Earth is manifestations of God the Mother, but not in a pure form, not in a form that is in accordance with the vision of God the Father, or the immaculate concept of God the Mother.

So you cannot look at the imperfections on Earth and say that this is God the Mother. God the Mother can never be in any impure form, even though God the Mother allows her energies, her light, to take on an impure form in order to give God's co-creators the opportunity to reap what they have sown.

Yet God the Mother forever remains pure, remains undefiled by any imperfect manifestation in this world. God the Mother has always been pure—and will always remain pure. And when you obtain the Christ consciousness and see that there is no separation between God the Father and God the Mother, well then you become the purity of God the Mother in embodiment. You become an expression of the purity of God the Mother.

And so you see, whether you are in a male body or a female body has no impact on this whatsoever. You still – when you attain the Christ consciousness, my beloved – you become God the Mother in embodiment. For do you see that the Creator in its pure, infinite, undivided form does not express itself in this world? It is the Creator expressing itself *as* God the Mother that has created the world of form. And thus, you need to even go beyond the expressions of God the Father and God the Mother, and perhaps find a more universal expression, such as the infinite God and the expressed God, the manifest God.

***

And my beloved, you as self-conscious beings are evolving toward God consciousness. And when you obtain that God consciousness, you can experience the Creator in its pure form. But as long as you are in embodiment in the world of form, you do not experience the Creator in its pure form, you experience the Creator in its expressed form, as God the Mother. And that truly is the God that you become one with while you are still in embodiment.

Now you see, my beloved, you will know that I said, "I and my Father are One." The reality behind that statement is that when you are in embodiment, you hold a female polarity with the beings in the spiritual realm, namely we who are the Ascended Host. So when I said "I and my Father are One," I acknowledged my oneness with my teacher and guru Lord Maitreya, my oneness with my I AM Presence, my oneness with my spiritual lineage that leads all the way to the Creator. And thus, in acknowledging that oneness, I acknowledged the oneness of Spirit and matter, the spiritual realm and the matter realm.

But what I am talking about here is an even deeper awareness of God as the infinite, unexpressed Creator and God as the expressed Creator—that has expressed itself in the finite world. And thus forms a different polarity than the polarity between the spiritual realm and the matter realm.

So you see, again, there are layers, there are wheels within wheels, but you need to contemplate here that your goal as Christed beings is to work toward the state of consciousness where you have unified the two aspects of God—that have traditionally been seen as masculine and feminine, Alpha and Omega, Father and Mother. Where you no longer see any separation, even any difference, between them because you realize that they have become one in your being. For it is the Christ consciousness that unifies the two aspects of God, so that you overcome the separation – that is possible only in the world of form – that any form could be separated from its source.

***

And thus, my beloved, what I am telling you here is that the path to salvation that I came to bring to this planet was indeed the path to personal Christhood, but the path to personal Christhood is not a path that can be walked without the Divine Feminine.

Do you see, my beloved, what has happened to Christianity is that instead of becoming the religion it was meant to be, it became an extension of the Jewish religion. Which was a religion focused on the Father aspect of God, and the denial of the Divine Feminine, that sprang from the falsified version of the Garden of Eden story, which blames women and the Feminine for the Fall of Man.

And thus, Christianity became another religion that denies the Divine Feminine. This was not my original intent, and that is why it is true – as some people are beginning to realize – that I had an entirely different view of women and women's role in spirituality and religion than what has been portrayed by the later establishment of the Catholic and later Christian Churches. Almost all of which are based on blaming women for the Fall, and therefore raising man and the male aspect to some superior status, using it as an excuse for suppressing women physically and spiritually.

So you see, when you obtain Christhood, my beloved, you rise above the gender roles on Earth. It no longer matters whether you are in a male or female body, for you rise beyond human sexuality, and you do not see yourself as one or the other. It is simply of no consequence what your body is, or what your sexuality is, as is so commonly discussed today. For it no longer has importance when you obtain that state of oneness, when you obtain that union of the Father-Mother, the Feminine-Masculine, the Outer and the Inner. And you realize that there was never a separation, for how could God be separated from itself, when God is infinite and thus is everywhere and thus must be in everything—and not the remote being in the sky.

So you see, my beloved, that is why I said that the Kingdom of God is within you. For as long as you picture God as the remote being in the sky, you will never obtain union with that God. You will only obtain that union when you find the God that has expressed itself as you – as form – and you acknowledge your union with that God. Then you overcome the sense of separation.

Then the masculine and feminine come together in perfect union, in perfect harmony. Then the inner has become the outer, and the outer has become the inner, as is quoted in the book of Thomas:

> 22. Jesus saw some babies nursing. He said to his disciples, "These nursing babies are like those who enter the (Father's) kingdom."
> They said to him, "Then shall we enter the (Father's) kingdom as babies?"
> Jesus said to them, "When you make the two into one, and when you make the inner like the outer and the outer like the inner, and the upper like the lower, and when you make male and female into a single one, so that the male will not be male nor the female be female, when you make eyes in place of an eye, a hand in place of a hand, a foot in place of a foot, an image in place of an image, then you will enter [the kingdom]."

And *then* you overcome that separation. Now you know who you are, now you know why you are here. And at that moment, you are reborn, my beloved, as I attempted to explain to Nicodemus—who could not understand it because he could not separate himself from the linear, analytical mind based on duality and separation.

But what did I say, my beloved? "No man can ascend back to heaven save he that descended from heaven." Only the conscious self can ascend back to heaven. And it can only "ascend back" to heaven when it realizes that it was never separated from heaven, it was never separated from its source, for it is an extension of the Creator's own Being.

That is when you are reborn into the realization of who you always were, who you always have been. But this does not mean that you then disappear, for it now means that you can take the individuality you have created in the world of form and raise it up and resurrect it so that it becomes one with the divine individuality anchored in your I AM Presence. But in order for that to happen, you must let the unreal individuality – the individuality that is based on separation and duality, the mortal human self, the ego – you must let that identity die on the cross by giving up the ghost—the ghost that is some sense that you are separated from God.

And when you finally give up that ghost, then the human self will die. Then you can be reborn into knowing who you are, and then the Divine Mother and the Divine Father will come into perfect union in your being, and you will be as above so below. You will be here below all that you are above.

***

So my beloved, what I am saying here is that the Christianity that you have today has deliberately been perverted in denying the importance of the Divine Feminine, in denying the teachings I have just given you. And which I did give in a veiled form 2,000 years ago, and which some of my disciples did indeed grasp and did indeed teach to others—although, again, few people understood it at the time.

So you see the consequence here: the Christianity you have today, the male-dominated form of Christianity, can never lead people to salvation! Do you understand, my beloved? It can never fulfill its promise of leading people to salvation. It is impossible, it is a false promise—and every Christian church that promises salvation to its members is making a false promise. Christianity can only fulfill its potential when the role of the Divine Feminine is restored in Christianity.

This does not necessarily mean that we need to have a role-reversal, where suddenly women take over all positions formerly held by men. But it does mean that we need to create a new Christianity, where it is of no consequence whether you are in a male or female body, for you can hold any position, fulfill any role in that religion, in that movement. As you indeed see in your own movement that you have started here.

***

My beloved, the Christian churches of today are so stuck in this male-dominated mindset that the only way that they could possibly transcend is that women are acknowledged as being completely equal to men, and are allowed then to hold any position in Christian churches. *That* has the potential that they can balance the male element and eventually bring balance to the churches. But it is a rather low probability that the mainstream Christian churches will be willing to make that transition.

Thus, it is far more realistic to expect that new Christian churches need to spring up, new movements need to spring up, so that people come out of the old churches and join new churches, new movements. This does not mean that I envision most mainstream Christians joining a movement such as this one that recognizes direct revelation from the Ascended Host. For many Christians are not ready for this, but I tell you clearly, as also emphasized by Mother Mary and Kuan Yin, that women hold the key to the potential for transforming Christianity.

And thus, I ask you, who are the more spiritually aware people, to envision that women are raised up in all Christian churches, and that they either are allowed to transform the churches, or that women stand up and say, "We must then come apart from these inflexible rigid churches, and start and find a new way to approach the mysteries of Christ, so that we can unify the Divine Feminine and the Divine Masculine."

Thus, my beloved, this is the vision I desire you to hold on this Easter Sunday and beyond—that the Divine Mother is restored in the Christian religion. Especially that the value of the Divine Mother is finally recognized and understood, recognizing also that it is not only women who can be in contact with or be extensions of the Divine Mother. But that both men and women must become extensions of the Divine Mother, as I have explained it in this discourse, my beloved.

For only when both men and women are balanced in the Divine Feminine and the Divine Masculine, will you reach your full potential, individually and as a spiritual movement that can pull up the collective consciousness. So that you can be the top ten percent who pull up the eighty percent of the people and bring forth the judgment of the lowest ten percent—so that if they will not change, they will be removed from this planet and have opportunities elsewhere.

***

Thus my beloved, hold that vision. Hold the vision that Christianity will be resurrected, that there will be an awakening so that a critical mass of people in all Christian churches, or at least in as many as possible, will be willing to give up the ghost of the old male-dominated unbalanced Christianity. Will be willing to let that identity, that mass identity, die so that the movement that I came to start can be resurrected and we can have a truly balanced spiritual movement. Where the Father and Mother, the Masculine and Feminine, work in perfect harmony and union, so that people can overcome separation between matter and spirit, between the Creator and its creation, between the unexpressed God and the expressed God in all of its expressions. So that all of its expressions are indeed aware of themselves as expressions of the One indivisible God.

This is the vision I hold. This is the vision Mother Mary holds. I ask you to also hold that vision, and see that this movement will start, especially with the women in Christian churches who will wake up and say, "The old ways are no longer working! This cannot go on. We must take on a more active role, not in setting up ourselves against the men, but in helping the men see that they too are trapped in their traditional roles. And that they too would experience greater freedom by rising above them, by going beyond them, by simply letting that ghost die, that is holding them nailed to the cross of an unbalanced religion, an unbalanced world view." This is my call, this is my vision.

And I also wish to extend my great gratitude to all of you who are participating in this conference, whether you are here physically, whether you are on the broadcast, whether you are out there giving rosaries at the same time, so that you are adding to the momentum that has been created. For I can assure you that you have already precipitated a major breakthrough in the collective consciousness. You have achieved the goal that we envisioned for this conference.

And thus, I congratulate you for this, and I wish you to feel the gratitude that all of us have for your willingness to be the spearhead, so to speak, to break through this old encrusted male-dominated consciousness, and carve a pathway for the resurrection of the Divine Feminine in all areas of spirituality. And even in the area of religion, so that religion can become spiritualized instead of the current condition, where most mainstream religions no longer have any spiritual element, any spiritual fire, any spiritual teaching. And thus, of course, cannot satisfy the spiritual needs of today's spiritual people, who will not settle for doctrines and dogmas, but want answers that make sense and take them into an intuitive recognition, an intuitive experience, of what I called the Spirit of Truth.

Thus, my beloved, I seal you in my Flame of Infinite Joy, for, truly, I came to bring joy to the world, as this is my keynote, my beloved. Thus, I bid you catch my Joy and bring it to the people. For if you truly understand what I have told you in this discourse – that the Kingdom of God is at hand – then how could you not feel Joy? [End of quote]

***

There is much to study in this message, and I encourage you to read it several times. However, the point I want to make here is that one of the most important tasks of the Alpha aspect of Christhood is to overcome the illusion that the world of form is separated from God, that God is not found here, that God is somewhere else, perhaps even *anywhere* else but here. This, of course, is the illusion that the false teachers of humankind, the fallen beings, do not want you to overcome and – especially – do not want you to shout from the housetops. Thus, it is precisely the illusion *I* need you to overcome and then share it with others.

The overall fact is that the entire material realm is in an upward spiral and is rising toward its ascension into becoming a permanent part of the spiritual realm. The driving force behind this process is the free-will decisions made by billions upon billions of lifestreams in all four levels of the material frequency spectrum, lifestreams who form the River of Life. There are small pockets of the material realm that are pulling in the opposite direction or are moving slower than the general speed of the universe. Earth is in one such pocket, but even the Earth is in an upward spiral. As a Christed being, you need to be very clear and firm in holding the vision of this reality—a reality that cannot be altered by human beings on Earth because they simply do not have the power of mind – being divided by duality and thus having their powers reduced – to pull against the upward force of the rest of the universe.

It really is not a question of *if* the Earth will rise to a higher stage; it is only a matter of *when* and *how* this will occur. If a majority of human beings continue to learn only from the school of hard knocks, how hard do the knocks have to become before people awaken to the reality that there is a better way?

As you will know, I was the spiritual hierarch for a cycle called the Age of Pisces, and the Earth is now moving into the next cycle, called the Age of Aquarius. The hierarch for this new cycle is my brother Saint Germain, who has a vision of the Earth rising into a Golden Age. However, this vision was created even before Saint Germain became an ascended master. I came into embodiment at the start of the Piscean age precisely to set the foundation for the Golden Age of Aquarius. And what *is* that foundation? It is that a critical mass of people attain personal Christhood *and* express that Christhood.

As I have explained in the book *The Christ Is Born in You,* there are currently 10,000 people who have attained Christhood at inner levels but who have not yet realized and accepted this with their outer minds. There are also millions more who have attained a high degree of Christhood and who can climb even higher in this lifetime. When a critical mass of these people decide to consciously claim *and* express their Christhood, they will create a force that will pull the rest of the population up, and this is the foundation for the Golden Age. For as we have explained, the current conditions on Earth are created by the collective consciousness of humankind projecting unbalanced, dualistic mental images upon the Ma-ter light. Thus, the only way to change current conditions is to raise the collective consciousness, purify it of imperfect images – by people no longer accepting the dualistic lies – and filling it with more positive images—by people coming to see and accept the reality of Christ.

Yet someone must be the forerunner for this shift in the collective consciousness, and most people open to this course came into embodiment at this special time precisely to be part of this movement. Thus, as the Alpha aspect of your divine plan, you need to stop "judging after appearances" and judge the righteous judgment of Christ by seeing that everything is an expression of God. And therefore, there is a very real potential for instantly changing any imperfect appearance into the reality of God's perfect vision.

In fact, as I have explained, the universal Christ mind is precisely created to uphold oneness between the Creator and the creation. Thus, as you become one with that mind, you too must uphold the vision of oneness by never allowing yourself to see any imperfect manifestations as real or permanent. Take note that I am not hereby telling you to stick your head in the sand and ignore the many imperfections currently outpictured on Earth. This is precisely what the false teachers want you to do. It is – once again – the image of a spiritual person withdrawing from the world and meditating on God in a cave. As I have said, the false teachers know the potential for Christed beings changing the equation on Earth, and they are desperately trying to stem the tide by making as many people as possible deny their Christ potential. And this includes getting such beings to withdraw from society and thereby denying the Omega aspect of Christhood—which also denies the Alpha aspect and instead traps you on the path of personal growth.

You see, when you truly fathom that everything is God in disguise, how could you withdraw? How could you avoid being so on fire with a desire to free the imprisoned God that you simply have to shout this from the housetops? How could you acquire spiritual light and then hide it under a bushel, instead of letting it shine so it can light the path of other people who are following behind you? You see, all human beings are connected through the web of life. Those who are in the top ten percent have vowed to be the forerunners, meaning that you have a number of people who are meant to follow in your footsteps as you carve a path from a particular state of consciousness through the jungle of duality to the summit of the Christ mind. Thus, if you withhold your light and truth, they have nothing to follow and many of them will be stuck, for they are not yet ready to walk the path on their own. And why do you think *you* are ready? It is because others before you – such as myself, Mother Mary, Saint Germain, the Buddha, Kuthumi, Master MORE and many other masters have been willing to come into embodiment in order to carve a trail that *you* have followed. Look at this quote:

> 19 What? know ye not that your body is the temple of the Holy Ghost which is in you, which ye have of God, and ye are not your own?
> 20 For ye are bought with a price: therefore glorify God in your body, and in your spirit, which are God's. (1Corinthians, Chapter 6)

Those who have gone before you have paid a price in order to give you the infusion of the Holy Spirit that has lifted you to your current level. It is up to *you* to multiply the talents you have been given by helping others, so that the momentum can be carried forward instead of being stopped in its tracks. I have talked about a chain of being above you, but it also extends below you, to lifestreams who have not yet reached your level of consciousness but are meant to follow in your tracks and thus cannot rise until you carve a trail for them.

So the Alpha aspect of Christhood is to hold the vision that God is behind all appearances and that the Golden Age is already the only possible reality. The Omega aspect is to act on that vision by going out into society and freeing other people to see the reality you see. For if one person could manifest the kingdom of God on

Earth, I would surely have done so 2,000 years ago. Yet the law of free will mandates that a critical mass of people must be awakened and must choose to accept a new vision—which then becomes the next manifest reality.

Thus, it is necessary that many Christed beings – from all possible backgrounds – preach a new message, namely that there is so much more to life than what most people are experiencing right now. And therefore, you see that the Omega aspect of Christhood can take on many different forms. For it is not our intent to preach one particular doctrine or spiritual philosophy. It is our intent to challenge any and all mental boxes on Earth by showing people that there is more to life than what is defined by their current box. Thus, we need Christed beings to embody in all kinds of situations, and then to demonstrate how to shatter your mental box and claim something more from life, manifesting it on Earth as an undeniable reality. For in order for the law of free will to be fulfilled, people must choose to accept the vision of MORE before it can be manifest. Yet if all they have ever seen is the lies of duality, how can they choose the MORE of the reality of Christ? Thus, demonstrating this MORE is indeed the task of the Living Christ, and it can be done in numerous ways, some of which are not even what most people will see as spiritual. For the Living Christ meets people wherever they are in consciousness, and then seeks to raise them from there, taking them one step at a time until they are anchored on the upward path and can start moving on their own momentum.

***

You see, Christhood is all about closing the gap between the present moment and a better future, between God's reality and the "reality" that people can accept on Earth. For what good does it do to give people a vision of some future salvation – as Christian and other religions have done for millennia – when there will always be a gap between people's present reality and the salvation they envision? Do you see that if your perceived salvation is in the future, then it will always be in the future, for the future never comes. The only time you have in which to make decisions is the now, and thus until you decide that you will claim your Christhood now, there will always be a gap between you and Christhood. And you will *never* cross that gap until you decide that the gap no longer exists and that you will accept the MORE as a manifest reality—NOW!

So the *Alpha* of Christhood is to see the vision of a higher reality, and the *Omega* is to act as if that vision is already a reality. Do you see that when I healed the sick, raised the dead, walked on water and turned the water into wine, I was not making a prayer? I saw beyond the present imperfect conditions and accepted the MORE of the reality of God as the *only* possible reality to be manifest in the situation. And it was in this complete, undivided acceptance of God's reality as the *only* reality that I had the mastery of mind over matter.

In today's more scientific language, we could say that I accepted that matter is a creation of mind, and thus whatever is now taking on a certain imperfect appearance was created by the mind. Which means that it can be *changed* by the mind – instantly – when that mind is undivided by a dualistic illusion. The dualistic illusion, of course, being what creates a division, whereby it seems like matter can exist independently of mind and thus the mind does not have the power to change matter.

Does that mean I want my disciples to go around and change matter to provide people with visible phenomena? Well, yes and no. You see, this is where many spiritual seekers have completely unrealistic dreams of creating some kind of phenomenon that will convert people to the spiritual path or their particular guru or teaching. Many seekers have had ego-centered dreams of performing such feats in order to raise themselves up—often disguised as the "altruistic" desire to convert millions of people. There are a few things you need to be aware of.

The temptation for a spiritual master to demonstrate some visible phenomenon has always been there—as demonstrated by the devil tempting me after my stay in the wilderness. I also said:

> 38 Then certain of the scribes and of the Pharisees answered, saying, Master, we would see a sign from thee.
> 39 But he answered and said unto them, An evil and adulterous generation seeketh after a sign; and there shall no sign be given to it... (Matthew, Chapter 12)

Those who want to see a sign will not see it and those who want to show it will not be able to show it. Why? Because, as I just said, you must *accept* the vision as reality before it can *become* reality—for that is how you co-create!

As I also said, I can of my own self do nothing. It is indeed the Father within, the power of God that changes water into wine, but it does so only when needed, and not when determined by the outer minds of people still colored by duality. So what I want my disciples to do is to be open to the power of God working through them—and then to be completely non-attached concerning what that power does or does not do.

Yet you also need to be aware that the Age of Aquarius is the age of community, in which individual demonstrations of special powers is not what we are looking for—only the false teachers will encourage this. What we desire to see happen is that people come together and realize that when they unite their collective minds, they can indeed co-create a new and higher reality on this planet, in anything from individual affairs, such as healing disease, to collective matters that affect the entire planet.

Yet the overall mission of the Christed beings of this age is to realize that you have volunteered to embody in many different, and often very difficult, situations in order to demonstrate the potential for overcoming all limitations and circumstances. You do this by acquiring the Alpha vision that God is behind all appearances and then applying the Omega vision that you can overcome whatever limitation you face and manifest a more abundant form of life—meaning first of all a more abundant spiritual form of life.

***

Let me say this another way. The Alpha aspect of Christhood is that you hold the vision that everything is God and is created out of God's Being and light. The Omega aspect is to overcome the very longing that brought you to this point on your personal path, namely the longing for something beyond the material world. Do you see that what has driven you to this point is your inner knowing that there is more to life than what the material world has to offer, and your longing to find that more?

Yet what I am telling you here is that the path of Christhood has phases, and what helped you complete one phase will not help you move forward on the next phase. So the first phase of the path is that you must come apart from the current downward pull of the mass consciousness. You must dare to go against the norm and pursue spiritual growth over material comfort and experiences, and this *does* require you to set yourself apart from other people.

Yet in order to rise to the next level of Christhood, you absolutely need to leave behind you the longing for something beyond the material world. Instead, you need to see God *behind* the appearances of the material world. You need to see that the kingdom of God is not only within *you* but is within *everything!* You now need to find God within the material world and be fulfilled in being in the material world with whatever experiences it offers you. You need to see any experience as an opportunity to transcend and thus demonstrate the reality that there is more to life than any present appearance in this world. You need to demonstrate that regardless of what imperfect manifestations are currently appearing in this world, they are not ultimately real and it is possible to transcend them. Thus, transcend any experiences and circumstances you have encountered and are encountering. See the cosmic dance of God behind all appearances – judge not after appearances – but see the kingdom of God as the *only* reality regardless of material appearances.

See that everything that is not manifesting Christ perfection is a – temporary and ultimately unreal – appearance. And then see beyond it and affirm that *only* Christ perfection is real!

***

I earlier said that it was not my intention for this course to give you some ultimate secret, some magical formula that will instantly turn you into a Christed being or give you supernatural powers. Obviously, I said that in order to shatter your ego-created mental box of desiring special powers to raise the separate self. So let me now move on to giving you the secret formula for manifesting Christhood, the ultimate secret that has been overlooked by the vast majority of religious people and spiritual seekers on this planet. A secret so mysterious that it will turn you into a unique being with special powers—if you truly grasp and apply it.

The formula is simple. How will you become one with me? *By seeing me in everyone and everything,* and then seeking to raise everyone so that they too can see Christ, first within themselves and then within each other.

Do you see the point? For almost 2,000 years official Christianity has portrayed me as a remote being up in heaven. Yet in reality I am the servant of all, so only if you too serve the All can you be one with me in that service. *You cannot be one with Christ by being apart from life, only by serving all life!*

Take note of one of the most important passages in the New Testament, a passage that the false teachers of Christianity did not have the wherewithal to remove or distort because they could not grasp its significance:

> 31 When the Son of man shall come in his glory, and all the holy angels with him, then shall he sit upon the throne of his glory:
> 32 And before him shall be gathered all nations: and he shall separate them one from another, as a shepherd divideth his sheep from the goats:
> 33 And he shall set the sheep on his right hand, but the goats on the left.

34 Then shall the King say unto them on his right hand,
Come, ye blessed of my Father, inherit the kingdom prepared for you from the foundation of the world:
35 For I was an hungered, and ye gave me meat: I was
thirsty, and ye gave me drink: I was a stranger, and ye took
me in:
36 Naked, and ye clothed me: I was sick, and ye visited
me: I was in prison, and ye came unto me.
37 Then shall the righteous answer him, saying, Lord,
when saw we thee an hungered, and fed thee? or thirsty,
and gave thee drink?
38 When saw we thee a stranger, and took thee in? or naked, and clothed thee?
39 Or when saw we thee sick, or in prison, and came unto
thee?
40 And the King shall answer and say unto them, Verily I
say unto you, Inasmuch as ye have done it unto one of the
least of these my brethren, ye have done it unto me.
41 Then shall he say also unto them on the left hand, Depart from me, ye cursed, into everlasting fire, prepared for
the devil and his angels:
42 For I was an hungered, and ye gave me no meat: I was
thirsty, and ye gave me no drink:
43 I was a stranger, and ye took me not in: naked, and ye
clothed me not: sick, and in prison, and ye visited me not.
44 Then shall they also answer him, saying, Lord, when
saw we thee an hungered, or athirst, or a stranger, or naked, or sick, or in prison, and did not minister unto thee?
45 Then shall he answer them, saying, Verily I say unto
you, Inasmuch as ye did it not to one of the least of these,
ye did it not to me.
46 And these shall go away into everlasting punishment:
but the righteous into life eternal. (Matthew, Chapter 25)

Do you now see the deeper meaning? Many Christians have interpreted this to mean that only Christians will be saved, but what is the deeper meaning of "Christian" in this context? It is not simply a person who is a member of an outer church. It is a person who sees Christ in every situation and in every person, always seeking to raise up everything to the perfection of Christ reality. Now, I am well aware that many – Christians and non-christians – will say that they have indeed done all these outer things, and thus they surely must have earned entry into the kingdom. Yet I have now explained that if you do these outer things out of a desire to raise the separate self – no matter how cleverly it is disguised (from you, for nothing is hidden from Christ) – then you have *not* done what I asked. You are still on my left hand.

I am *not* asking you to serve all life in order to get a reward. I am asking you to serve all life because you have come to see yourself as one with your source, you have come to see all other people and all material appearances as originating from that same source. And thus, you have naturally felt the desire to raise up all toward also knowing their oneness with their source and thus outpicturing the vision of that source, namely the manifestation of God's kingdom on Earth. As I said:

> 34 But when the Pharisees had heard that he had put the Sadducees to silence, they were gathered together.
> 35 Then one of them, which was a lawyer, asked him a question, tempting him, and saying,
> 36 Master, which is the great commandment in the law?
> 37 Jesus said unto him, Thou shalt love the Lord thy God with all thy heart, and with all thy soul, and with all thy mind.
> 38 This is the first and great commandment.
> 39 And the second is like unto it, Thou shalt love thy neighbour as thyself.
> 40 On these two commandments hang all the law and the prophets. (Matthew, Chapter 22)

Do you see the greater secret veiled in the expression "love thy neighbour as thyself?" It is that you love your neighbor *as* yourself because you see that your neighbor *is* yourself, is part of your greater self, which is the Body of God on Earth.

Do you now see that you cannot attain oneness with me by sitting in a cave? You may need to withdraw from the world in order to rise above the mass consciousness. Yet it is a fallacy to think that if only you stay long enough in your cave, you will eventually find Christ, that I will some day appear to you in clouds of glory. Once you have risen above the downward pull of the mass consciousness, you will attain no further progress by withdrawing from the world. You will find Christ *only* by going back into the world and seeking oneness with me by seeing me in other people and then seeking to raise them up to see Christ in themselves and each other. You can find oneness with me only in service to others, for I am not on the path of personal growth, I am only on the path of Christhood—which is the path of raising all life. Thus, I will appear to you *only* as you serve all life and suddenly realize that I am the one looking at you through the eyes of a person you have served unconditionally.

***

The need to go out and minister onto others can even be seen as the most powerful tool for exposing and out-maneuvering your personal ego. As I have attempted to explain, the ego is subtle and as you grow on the path, it will morph into different disguises in order to stay hidden. The ego and the false teachers will use anything to get you to stop at a certain level of the path and thus prevent you from reaching full Christhood.

As I said, in order to walk the path, you need to withdraw from the world and go beyond the mass consciousness. Yet what I have explained throughout this course it that the ego can use this in order to disguise itself. Thus, many spiritual people have created an inner world view and an outer situation for themselves in which they feel very comfortable and feel as if they have life, the path and even the world under some form of control.

Thus, they are quite comfortable in that mental "cave," and their egos are very comfortable too since they know they can stay hidden. The sign that you are in such a cave is very clear. If you are reluctant to leave it in order to serve others, then you have clearly created a mental box for yourself, and you can be sure your ego is using it to hold you back.

Thus, what I am saying here is that if you truly want the ultimate progress toward Christhood, you need to see this mechanism and then take active measures to flush your ego out of hiding, so the conscious self can see it and then separate itself even more from it. And the best – in fact the *only* – way to truly do this is to engage in some form of service to others. And then watch for anything in your psyche that prevents you from serving others unconditionally and with complete inner peace and non-attachment. *Any* condition that takes away your inner peace, hides the ego. So when you recognize this, you can look behind the inner reactions that disturb your peace and unmask your ego.

Why is this important? Because your ego has certain universal aspects that are the same as for all other people. These are the aspects of the ego that I have exposed in this book. Obviously, I cannot write this book specifically for *you*. Which means that for *you* to get the full effect from this course, you need to use the universal teachings in the book to gain specific insights into your personal ego. You will get this by asking me and your Christ self, but your conscious mind can receive those insights *only* if you are open to seeing what you have not seen so far.

Thus, you need to recognize that your personal ego has all of the universal aspects I have exposed in this course, but that it has applied them in ways that are individual to your situation in this and past lives. Thus, it has managed to use your specific situation to camouflage itself in ways that make it harder for you to see it, because you take certain things for granted and don't see the need to question them. You look at the ego from inside the mental box created by the ego, and thus you cannot see the box.

Therefore, it is up to you to go beyond this course and ask for the inner direction to expose your personal ego and the disguises that you have not thus far seen. Only by doing this actively will you make maximum progress, and in order to expose your ego, you need to serve others. There is no other way, for until you begin to serve others, your ego will stay within its comfort zone in which you will be unable to see it. This is another secret formula that most spiritual seekers have not understood.

***

We have now reached the final point, where you should be able to see what this course *can* and *cannot* do for you. Obviously, this is a general course that is aimed at reaching any sincere spiritual seeker. Yet this course is *not* conceived of as being an end in itself. It is only a *means to an end,* namely that you establish a direct, personal contact with your Christ self and with me – or another ascended master who is close to your heart – and then continue the process of getting personal directions directly from us inside yourself. The entire goal of this course is to take you to the point where you have that inner direction and thus no longer need the course.

There are now two possibilities. One is that you feel you do not have such a connection and one is that you feel you do:

- If you do not feel you have a connection or if you are not sure that it is accurate, then study this course again. Or use Mother Mary's book to gain deeper insights into and healing of your psychology. Or use Maitreya's book to increase your overall understanding of how the universe works. Then come back and continue to work with the course until you begin to feel the inner connection. As I have said, if you are taking this course, it proves you are self-aware. If you are self-aware, it proves you have a conscious self that is out of the Creator's own Being. And this conscious self *will* be able to connect to its source—as long as your outer mind stops blocking that connection. So it is truly a matter of removing the blocks in your psyche until the light can shine through. As I said:

7 Ask, and it shall be given you; seek, and ye shall find; knock, and it shall be opened unto you:
8 For every one that asketh receiveth; and he that seeketh findeth; and to him that knocketh it shall be opened. (Matthew, Chapter 7)

- If you feel you do have a connection, then do what I have said. Go out of your cave and find a way to serve others. Then continue to refine your ability to receive inner direction by realizing and never forgetting that your ego will try to interfere with and color your direction or your interpretation of it. Thus, it is an ongoing process of refining your connection by sharpening your ability to discern what comes from the ascended realm or what comes from or is colored by lower minds. It is always spiritual pride to think you have risen above the need for self-examination leading to self-transcendence.

There are many spiritual seekers who are aware that they were born at this time for a purpose, that they have a divine plan for this lifetime, and they are eagerly trying to find out what it is. Yet some have the illusion that if only they sit in a cave long enough, then one day their divine plan will be revealed to them in all its glory. Again, this is a trap of the ego and the false teachers.

How do you truly get to know your divine plan? By multiplying the talents you have been given and serving others with the insight and vision you have *right now*. Then – AS YOU ARE SERVING – and *only* then, will you be given further insights. It is *only* when you start moving that we will direct your course. What is the point of giving directions to one who is standing still, refusing to move? So if you don't know how to get to your destination, there is only one way to find out: START WALKING!

***

How do you start walking? Simply look at the world and consider that there are infinite needs for improvement, an infinite number of causes to work for, an infinite variety of services to be rendered. Then pick a cause that appeals to your heart and pursue it until you get further visions and directions.

Consider that the overall cause is to raise people's awareness of every aspect of life but also of the overall purpose of life. And there have never been better opportunities for raising people's awareness by using the internet to contact people you could never contact by meeting them physically.

At this point, there are two possibilities:

- You are on fire for serving life.
- You are not on fire.

If the latter is the case, recognize that there can be only one reason. You are still stuck in the self-centered focus that comes from the ego. If you are not willing to go beyond this, there is nothing I or any other true spiritual teacher can do for you. The false teachers will make you feel great about your current situation, but I obviously will not do that. My only suggestion at this point is that you go through the course again and seriously look for the psychological mechanism that is putting you in this catch-22, this state of spiritual paralysis. If you will honestly look, then I have incorporated many subtle keys that you obviously missed the first time you went through the course. I also recommend that you seek a professional therapist who can help you see what is holding you back.

If you *are* indeed on fire, then recognize that there are no rules for how to express your Christhood. Indeed, there are two ways to deny your Christhood, one is to deny that you can be the Christ and the other is to think that in order to be the Christ, you have to behave a certain way. As I have tried to explain, the Christ comes to challenge any and all of your mental boxes, so if you think the expression of your Christhood needs to fit into any mental box on Earth, then you will not be able to express your Christhood. And this can be another reason why people feel stuck and cannot seem to express the Christhood that they have actually earned—which puts them in the dark night. So consider the fact that being the Christ is being creative in an ultimate way that goes beyond all preconceived opinions.

You are here precisely to help people go beyond their mental boxes, and how can you do that if you think you have to conform to any man-made boxes, including your own? Surely, there is a balance to be found, and the Christ is never provocative for the sake of being provocative. The Christ realizes that in order to help people, they might have to accept you as one of their own, which means you have to conform to some degree to their mental box. Yet you never allow any mental box to define you or to hold you back from doing what is necessary to help people go beyond the box. You are not here to be popular—you are here to change the world by changing the way people look at the world. Changing the world is a creative endeavor, and creativity cannot be predicted. So allow yourself to be creative and allow the Spirit of God to express its creativity through you without seeking to force it into any mental box.

It is one of the great fallacies of the ego and false teachers that they think the Christ must behave a certain way, that he must follow the rules and fit into their mental box. And if the Christ doesn't fit into their box, they have the perfect justification for rejecting him, as the scribes and Pharisees rejected me. Yet learn from me and realize that even if people reject you, they have still been given a choice, and giving people this choice is your real job. Always remember that if you conform to people's boxes, how will life ever change? You will simply be engaging in the common form of insanity, which – as Einstein said – comes from doing the same thing and expecting different results.

Another mental box is that once you have done something in one situation, you should always do the same in similar situations. Yet remember that the goal is to shake people out of whatever mental boxes they are in, so in some cases this may require one type of action and in other cases it might require a seemingly opposite type of action. Consistency is good only when it is consistency in following the inspiration of the Spirit. Once you allow the need for physical consistency to shut off the inspiration from above, your consistency has become a prison. Thus, be consistent in seeking first the kingdom of God and his righteousness, and allow all other things to flow from that oneness.

Recognize that creativity doesn't come out of nowhere. Creativity is the pearl of great price, but God will not cast his pearls before swine. Thus, the only way to be an instrument for God's creativity is that you turn your mind into a chalice that can receive the creative impulse but also has the psychological wholeness and the practical knowledge to make use of it to serve others. Look at how some people have minds that are open to all kinds of creative ideas, but they do not have the psychological wholeness or practical knowledge to turn them into something that actually helps humankind. Look at how others are concerned about bringing forth new ideas only to enrich themselves.

Consider that many spiritual people have established a connection to their higher selves, but they do not have the practical knowledge to make use of any creative impulse they receive. So seek the balance of psychological wholeness and practical knowledge. Educate yourself in whatever practical aspects of life appeal to you. You need a good knowledge of spiritual topics and of human psychology. But besides that, there should be one area of society where you are an expert and know far more than the average person. Only when you have both wholeness and practical knowledge, will your mind truly be a chalice for God pouring his creative Spirit into it. As the Bible says:

> Bring ye all the tithes into the storehouse, that there may be meat in mine house, and prove me now herewith, saith the LORD of hosts, if I will not open you the windows of heaven, and pour you out a blessing, that there shall not be room enough to receive it. (Malachi, 3:10)

***

As I have said, find the cause for which your heart is on fire, and then pursue it according to your inner direction. Be not afraid to follow your personal vision, but if you desire some direction, here is a list of causes that are certainly within the framework of the overall mission of the Ascended Host yet offer you infinite room for personal creativity:

- The awakening of people to the fact that there is more to life. The expanding of people's understanding of the spiritual side to life—a cause that goes beyond both science and religion.

- Changing the tone and purpose of the religious debate, as described by Maitreya in his book. Opening people to understanding the influence of the human ego on religion—and every other aspect of society. This includes helping people understand the difference between dualistic and non-dualistic thinking, as explained in neutral terms in the book *The Art of Non-war.*

- The empowering of people to heal their psychology and manifest the abundant life, as described by Mother Mary in her book.

- The awakening of people to an understanding of the true purpose of my mission and my inner teachings, as described in this and my other books.

- The restoration of the Divine Feminine and the restoration of balance in religion.

- The unification of science and religion as two complementary ways for humankind to fulfill its quest for answers to the questions of life.
- The manifestation of Saint Germain's Golden Age, which included bringing forth new ideas in every area of society as well as new inventions and technology.

If one of these causes does not speak to your heart, then find another one that does and pursue it with a desire to become an open door for the Spirit to express itself through you in advancing the cause of making life on this planet MORE. And as you multiply your talents, allow yourself to receive the reward as an increase in creative power that allows you to give even more service. The reward for service is more service, a growth process that never ends but becomes the source of perpetual joy. I *am* that flame of joy, and I came to give my joy to the world. *Catch it by giving it to others!*

***

Christhood is a choice—but not just one choice. Christhood is a string of many choices, made constantly as long as you are in embodiment—and beyond. Christhood is to choose the oneness of LIFE over the separation of death—and to do so in every situation you encounter, regardless of outer appearances that compel you to accept death as a reality.

Stop seeking oneness with Christ as a being who is above you in a remote spiritual realm. See me in other people and then seek oneness with me in seeking oneness with others, thus forming the community of Christ, the community of the Holy Spirit on Earth.

The Aquarian age is an age of community—of coming into unity with God above – God the Father – and God below—God the Mother.

When Father Mother are as One,
we know the victory is won.

Christhood is not about heaven. Christhood is about improving conditions on Earth by bringing the Mother realm into oneness with the Father, by making matter a reflection of Spirit, so that God can again be the One, the undivided Spirit even while expressed in form. The Christ is a being who knows it is God even while expressing itself in form.

Find me by allowing me to express myself through you in service to all. For I am indeed the servant of all, which is why I have earned the title and hold the office as Lord of all, as the planetary Christ.

This book is my mind, my Being, which is broken for you. Take, eat and in remembrance of me, *serve all life*.

## Exercise for Key 16

As the exercise for this key, I want you to give a 33-day vigil of the Invocation of the Eternal Now. After the invocation, use the attunement exercise given earlier and ask me to help you discover your personal cause and all elements of your divine plan that you are ready to receive at this point. Yet remember that I will only be able to give you according to your multiplication of your talents, meaning how you use what you have right now in service to life.

# Key 17
# Transcending the path to Christhood

My goal for this course has been based on practical realism. What can be done in a book, where you cannot interact with an outer teacher? Thus, my goal has been to help you establish contact with the inner teacher and thus anchor yourself firmly on the path to personal Christhood. If you make use of what is given in this book and what you will be given from within, you have everything needed to get yourself on the right path. And you can then continue to make progress according to your willingness to multiply what you have received. However, making progress on the path to personal Christhood cannot go on forever. For there must come a point where you transcend even the path. Why is that so? Because as long as you see yourself moving forward on a path, you obviously envision yourself as a being who has not yet arrived. And how will you ever arrive, unless you transcend the very concept that you are moving toward a goal but you are not there yet?

As I have said over and over again, it is the role of the Living Christ to help you transcend *any* mental box. Thus, I must do my work and seek to shatter the mental box based on the concept of a path toward a goal that is seen as remote—and will thus remain remote until you change your vision and accept that you have arrived.

Do not misunderstand me. There are phases in Christhood, and it is necessary and unavoidable that you go through a phase, where you see yourself as a being walking a gradual path toward the remote goal of the Christ consciousness. And in order to traverse this part of the path, you need to go out and render service to other forms of life until you find oneness with me within yourself by seeing me in all life. The goal of this course has been to give you the understanding and the vision to help you navigate this phase. Yet as the last act of this course, I will point you beyond this phase to the logical conclusion.

For the concept of a path implies that there is an end goal. Yet how will you reach that goal as long as you think you are still separated from it? The path of Christhood is the path of oneness, and the logical conclusion is that you arrive at a point where you accept that you are not separated from the end goal—you now accept that you have arrived—you are one with Christ.

This is where things get subtle. There is a phase on the path where you are simply not ready to accept that you have arrived—because you still have too many divisions in your being, too much untransmuted energy and too many dualistic beliefs and images. Yet there will come a point where you have attained enough inner wholeness that you are ready to stop seeing a gap between yourself and Christhood. Yet because of the intense and subtle programming in this world, it is quite possible that you can be ready at inner levels, but your outer mind simply cannot accept this. One of the most unfortunate effects of official Christianity is that it has prevented a considerable number of people from claiming their Christhood, thinking it was something reserved for me or something they could attain only after they leave this world. So it is my hope that this course can help people – who are ready for it – overcome this last hurdle and consciously accept that they have arrived, thus claiming their Christhood and proclaiming it *as directed from above*.

If you think of me as a teacher, you might realize that I came to this planet 2,000 years ago to teach people how to attain Christhood. Yet after 2,000 years, how many of my students have actually graduated? And what kind of a teacher can engage his students in pursuing a course yet not have any of them make it through the final exam? So it is my hope that this course can help correct the obvious deficiency, so that my teaching efforts can finally – and not a moment too soon – bear fruit and produce students who are no longer students but who are ready to be teachers and do the same works that I did, and even greater works by building on the momentum created by my ascension to the Father.

***

The danger of giving you the image of a path is that you will see Christhood as always being in the future, as being away from where you are right now. Thus, you are always seeing a gap between yourself and Christhood, and the fact is that as long as you accept that there is a gap, you will never cross the gap. This is illustrated by the ancient Greek philosophers in what is called Zeno's paradox. The concept is that a person is trying to get to another location by first crossing half the distance, then half of the remaining distance, then half of that distance and so on. Yet because you can always keep dividing the remaining distance in half, you can never make it—there will always always a gap between you and the destination.

The ego can never cross that gap and move from separation to oneness. So the only way for you to cross the gap is that your conscious self keeps moving closer to the goal until the distance is so short that you can cross it in one leap. The ego cannot make that leap, but the conscious self *can*. Yet you will not make it until you make what is traditionally called a "leap of faith" but which I hope you can see is truly a leap of inner knowing. When you know you are more than the ego, you can give up the ego and let the mortal identity die, knowing that the real you will not disappear but will be reborn into your true spiritual identity.

If you take an honest look at spiritual seekers and religious people, you will see that many of them have – some for decades, some for lifetimes – been chasing some goal that always seems to elude them. So many religious people are seeking a paradise that they think is far way and far into the future. Others are chasing some big breakthrough on Earth, but they also seem to always be one step away from it. Or they realize they have been chasing an impossible dream—only to turn right around and start chasing the pot of gold at the end of another rainbow. I hope you can see that in the realm of duality there will always be another rainbow, for the ego and the false teachers can come up with an infinite variety of them. Yet none of them have a pot of gold at the end, for the pot of gold is the Christ consciousness, which is found only by looking for it inside yourself.

If you have diligently followed this course and gone through all of the exercises – especially the writing exercises – you should have gone through a dramatic transformation of consciousness. Yet in case you have not experienced this transformation, I submit to you that the reason is that you are still looking at this course through the filter of the ego and its never-ending dream that someone will do it all for you. Thus, it would be wise to take an honest look at your unfulfilled expectations about this course, for behind them you will find how your personal ego is trying to prevent you from making the decision to take full responsibility for your path by acknowledging that if the equation of your life is to change, you must begin by changing yourself. As I have said, I cannot do it *for* you—I can only set before you life and death and then leave it up to you whether you choose oneness or separation.

My point being that you won't find Christhood until you stop seeing it as "out there" or in the future. You won't find it until you accept that ultimately, *you* must make the decision to *be* the Christ. And you must do so by accepting that Christhood is HERE NOW.

However, only *you* can determine when that point in time and space has arrived. In some cases it has not yet arrived and in some cases all that is missing is your decision that the acceptable time is NOW.

***

I have earlier said that the ego and the false teachers are very subtle and that they will do anything to stop you at any level below full Christhood. So how do you avoid that they find a clever way to make you think that you have arrived before you are actually ready to claim your Christhood? If you look at the mental institutions of the world, you will see quite a number of people who have made the claim to some ultimate status yet obviously did not have the psychological wholeness needed to back up the claim. Obviously, I have no desire to see any student of this course fall into this category. And I know there will be people who have gone through this course diligently but who are still far from the point where they are ready to claim their Christhood—still needing psychological and spiritual healing in order to find the Middle Way and attain balance. Please be realistic in assessing whether you are among them.

I have said that the path is an ongoing process, meaning that you walk the path by *always* taking the next step. So the way to avoid that the ego and the false teachers stop you in your tracks is to *always* take the next step and to *never* let them make you think you have arrived. Yet how can you transcend the path if you are to always take the next step? How can you overcome the gap between you and the end goal if you are to never think you have arrived?

The key is to understand what I have said several times earlier, namely that Christhood is not a state of stillstand, but a state of dynamic creativity, where you are moving with the River of Life. So the key to transcending the path is to never leave the path, to always take the next step but to do so with the attitude that you are not seeking to gain something or to reach some ultimate state. You are taking the next step in order to be in the River of Life and in order to raise up others. In other words, you are no longer seeking something for your separate self, you are no longer seeking to raise your ego to some ultimate state. Instead, you are seeking to raise yourself in order to render better service in helping raise others and thus carry on the momentum of the River of Life.

Do you see how the duality consciousness colors everything and thus makes you think having arrived at the end of the path to Christhood means that you no longer need to move? In fact, having arrived at the end of the path to Christhood means you are now one with the River of Life and thus flowing with it as it is constantly transcending its current state and becoming MORE. Thus, you are constantly taking the next step, but you are taking it with unconditional love, never letting any condition stop your growth or stop you from enjoying the moment. You are taking the next step but you see no distance between yourself and some final destination, for you see that the final destination is the river itself.

Your path is no longer a process of feeling inadequate because you have not yet arrived at some predefined goal. Your path is an ongoing joy of finding total fulfillment and peace in every instance of transcendence. You no longer take the next step in order to get to some final destination. You take it for the sheer joy of taking that step, of seeing the cosmic dance unfold, of seeing the currents of the River of Life swerve and twist as they glide their way toward the ocean—that is no longer an ocean, for the river is now seen as all that IS.

You no longer feel that you cannot appreciate life until you have arrived. Instead, you appreciate what IS in the present moment—and then let that moment pass and now appreciate what IS in the present moment—and then let that moment pass to appreciate the next present moment—thus turning your life into a constant process of ever-growing appreciation for what IS. And when you fully appreciate what IS, you have arrived, for "I see now with the single eye, that I am God and God IS I."

***

It is likely that you will follow this course and make significant progress in many areas, but that you will still have one area of your life where it seems like there is no change, like you cannot break through. The reason is that in this particular area, you are still fighting *against* life instead of flowing *with* it.

Many spiritual students have not yet found the very delicate balance that I call the Middle Way in one area of their lives. Thus, they have a vision and understanding of what they want to have happen, but they cannot make it happen—no matter how hard they try. My advice is – as always – to step back and look at the bigger picture, instead of continuing to do the same thing and expecting different results. Why isn't change happening? There can be only one reason. You still have an attachment that is preventing change from manifesting.

It is easy for the conscious mind to lock onto the idea that a certain change should happen—often because it seems mandated by a religious teaching. Yet you need to recognize that the underlying purpose for your life in the material universe is to learn certain lessons. Before you came into embodiment, you decided that you wanted to learn a certain lesson, and you chose to embody in circumstances where you would be confronted with physical conditions that "force" yourself to face the lesson. Thus, you will – subconsciously – prevent the outer circumstances from changing until you have learned your lesson. Which means that although your outer mind thinks the change should have happened, your subconscious mind – and in this case your higher mind – is blocking the change.

What I recommend in such situations is that you recognize there is a lesson you have not yet seen. Thus, instead of trying harder and harder to make change happen, you let go of all desire to see change happen. You accept what is, and you accept that you can be perfectly at peace with what is—even if it does not change in this lifetime. And then you go about fulfilling your divine plan to the best of your current vision. In other words, you do not allow the circumstance that will not change to block you from moving forward in your service to life.

What I am saying here is that the underlying lesson is not the material circumstances. The underlying lesson is always that the Christ does not let any conditions on Earth prevent him or her from being the Christ in action. The real reason why change is not happening is that you have built a false identity which says you cannot be the Christ until such and such changes have occurred. This is a fallacy, as nothing on Earth can stop your Christhood—unless you think it can. Thus, you need to let that false identity die so that the real you can be reborn—which often will open up for the change to happen. Yet the change will not happen until you no longer think you need it.

You see, the Living Christ is completely self-sufficient. You look to God for everything and never think you need anything in this world in order to express Christhood. Thus, you realize that God will – and already has – given you everything you need to express Christhood right now. Which means that if you don't have it, you don't need it—you just need to realize that you don't need it and then be the Christ anyway.

As always, there is a balance. As the Christ, you are not passive, so you sometimes take active measures to make things happen. Yet when you cannot "make" things happen, it is time to step back, look at yourself, surrender all expectations and mental images and simply flow with the River of Life—letting things happen. If you can't *make* it happen—*let* it happen.

***

Speaking of mental images, your ego loves the concept that you are here to make a difference, to help change the world, even to help save the world. In fact, your ego would single-handedly save the world if it could—and for some people their egos really think they *can* save the world (and take all the credit). Thus, your ego and the false teachers will try to make you believe in an array of dualistic images about what it means to save the world and how the world needs to change.

I have earlier said that you need to let go of all expectations, but be careful to realize that I am not saying you need to let go of all mental images. You have to let go of all *dualistic* mental images, but if you let go of *all* images, how could you fulfill your role as a co-creator with God? You see, you co-create by creating mental images and using the power of the mind to superimpose them upon the Ma-ter light, which then takes on the envisioned form.

The Earth currently has suffering and imbalances because, for a long time, humankind has created mental images based on the duality consciousness. The way out of this is *not* to free people's minds from all mental images. The way out is to help people formulate new images based on the reality of the Christ mind, for this is the only way God's kingdom can be manifest on Earth—and it is God's good pleasure to have the abundant life manifest on this planet.

Yet how can you free your mind from dualistic images, how can you discern what is dualistic and what is not? Why not simply let your ego show you. By now you should have learned that the Christ never resists life and never holds on to anything. Thus, when you feel resistance, when you feel that something in your mind is holding on to a particular image or belief, you know this is the ego. And thus, you know that what the ego is holding on to is a dualistic image, for the ego can see nothing else.

Dualistic images are graven images because they are formulated on Earth and then elevated to the status of being absolute and infallible. The Christ – as I have tried to explain – sees no absolute truth or image because the Christ is always flowing with the River of Life in which everything is constantly transcending itself. Thus, while the Christ mind contains mental images, these images are always open to transcendence.

When you become aware that there is a resistance within you to letting go of a particular image – such as how to save the world – you know this is the ego at work. You can then choose to consciously let go of the image and instead surrender yourself to letting God – or your Higher Being – give you a new vision. Make it a habit that when you sense resistance, you will deliberately let go and let God. You will stop trying to hold on to an image and instead decide to let God be the doer and manifest a change through you.

You see, the ego uses mental images as a way to control "reality," although reality can never be controlled by the ego. Thus, the ego seeks for some ultimate thought system on Earth and then formulates images based on it—seeking to force reality to comply with the system. In contrast, the Christ has no system and is not pursuing mechanical changes but creative changes. Which sometimes means that you become the instrument for a change that you did not envision beforehand with your conscious mind. In such cases, it might seem as if you did not have mental images that you superimposed upon the Ma-ter light, but in reality the mental image simply wasn't known by your conscious mind. The image was still there in the higher parts of your mind, and what you did was to give up the images in the conscious mind so that the higher image could manifest. When you do this, you will often find that what actually happens is far better than what you had envisioned with your conscious mind. It is the Father's good pleasure to give you the kingdom, and in many cases you simply have to get your outer mind out of the way.

As you see the unexpected unfold, you gradually build the trust that your Higher Being knows best. And this can then lead to a point where you are no longer seeking to formulate images with your conscious mind. Instead, you allow those images to descend to your conscious mind from the higher parts of your mind. This does not mean that you are not creative at the level of the conscious mind. But it does mean that you allow your higher mind to give you the overall image, and then you use the conscious mind to fill in the details. Thus, your Father – your own Higher Being – works hitherto and you – your conscious mind – work.

When you find this balance between above and below, you will find that instead of struggling to make things happen, you simply have to allow a greater plan to unfold. This is what is called effortless manifestation and it is a sign of the higher stages of Christhood. For as with everything else, Christhood is not a static state of perfection but has its own stages. For even the Christ – or rather, *especially* the Christ – is participating in the cosmic dance of the Creator becoming less in order to rise toward becoming MORE. All self-aware beings are part of this dance, but the Christed ones are consciously aware of the dance and can thus appreciate it to the fullest.

***

Some students like to have a measuring rod for how they are making progress. Although I have said that there are no rules for Christhood, no standard for how to be the Christ, I will give you one way to gauge your progress. Thus, consider that the ultimate goal for a Christed Being is to have complete inner peace in every situation. The Christ has transcended all Earthly identity and thus inner peace is the natural consequence.

You can now see that as long as you are not completely at peace, you still have some kind of attachment based on a dualistic belief. For only such attachments can take away your inner peace. As I have said, the conscious self is ultimately *real* because it is out of the Creator's own Being. Anything in the material realm is ultimately *unreal,* and – as you should know by know – that which is unreal has no power over that which is real. So if anything in this world can take away your peace, it is because you think it is real. And this is a denial of who you are and the fact that "with men this is impossible, but not with God, for with God all things are possible." When you know and accept that you are an extension of God's Being, then nothing in this world can threaten you—and thus how could you not feel inner peace? Things in this world are not perfect, but what is that to thee—follow thou me into the peace of God.

So when you see something that takes away your peace, be willing to look at your own reaction—rather than focusing on the outer conditions. What is your belief that causes you to lose your peace? Do you have a desire to have other people agree with the truth you see? Do you seek approval, recognition or attention from other people or even from the whole world? Do you want to produce certain changes in the world, and are you frustrated that the world does not want to go along?

Again, do not focus on changing other people but allow them to be who they are at any given moment. Instead, focus all your attention on being who *you* are—sharing your light and truth regardless of the reactions from other people.

How can you come to this point of inner peace? Again, there is an Alpha and an Omega aspect. The Omega aspect is that you focus on cleaning out the dualistic beliefs that make you think anything in this world is real and has power over you. The Alpha aspect is that you focus on uniting with your own Higher Being, whereby you become spiritually self-sufficient, you become a spiritual sun that shines its light without needing anything from Earth.

As you begin to tune in to your Higher Being, you will begin to discover that this Being is a spiritual Being, which means it is made of very high-vibration energy. You might picture this as a fire, as a God Flame with certain qualities that you will learn to know. Thus, your major purpose for coming to Earth is to let the light of your God Flame shine in the darkness that covers the land. You are here to be the open door through which the light can shine. And even if people reject your light, the light will still enter the material realm, and it will contribute to dispelling the darkness and raising the vibration of the entire material universe. As more and more people do this, it is only a matter of time before the Earth throws off the darkness and ascends into the light of a higher vibration. Thus, you can feel fulfilled and at peace in shining your light, for you know this is your primary job, a job that no force on Earth can stop you from performing—if you do not let that which is unreal have power over that which is real.

What are the qualities of your God Flame? You will discover them as you gain greater attunement, but begin by considering what gives you great love and what has given you great opposition. You have a love for your God Flame, and you have volunteered to take on the consciousness that is a perversion of your God Flame, thus often encountering these qualities as challenges and opposition. For example, if your God Flame is one of the many shades of freedom, you will feel a great love for freedom but will likely have encountered people or conditions that oppose freedom. If your God Flame is one of the shades of truth, you have a love for finding and expressing truth, but you might have been challenged to lie in order to keep peace, or you have encountered situations in which people or institutions sought to prevent you from expressing truth.

I am deliberately being vague because at this point I do not want to give the analytical mind ammunition for turning the concept of God Flames into another mental box. God Flames cannot be confined to Earthly words or even qualities. You can use any positive quality as a way to describe a God Flame, but the God Flame is always more than any Earthly words, so be careful not to limit your concept of the Flame, for thereby you will limit yourself by limiting the Flame's expression through you. Our God is a consuming fire that consumes all unlike itself, so allow your personal God Flame to consume everything in your Being that is unlike your higher self.

In a sense, your God Flame is the ultimate tool for spiritual growth because it can consume all opposition to your growth and the manifestation of your divine plan. I have not talked about it earlier because until you have cleared your consciousness of dualistic images, you will not be able to fully tune in to the Flame and allow it to flow through you. You see, your God Flame will not burn away more of the lower self than what the Conscious You can handle at any given moment. The Flame will burn anything unlike itself, but it knows that at this moment you have a limited sense of self, and if it was instantly burned away, you would be in an identity crisis. Thus, the Flame will wait until you have been reborn of water by raising your sense of self. And *then* you will be reborn of Fire and become a SUN of God on Earth.

Consider how many times I talked about light and hinted between the lines of how important it is for you to let your spiritual light shine:

> 14 Ye are the light of the world. A city that is set on an hill cannot be hid.
> 15 Neither do men light a candle, and put it under a bushel, but on a candlestick; and it giveth light unto all that are in the house.
> 16 Let your light so shine before men, that they may see your good works, and glorify your Father which is in heaven. (Matthew, Chapter 5)

> 22 The light of the body is the eye: if therefore thine eye be single, thy whole body shall be full of light.
> 23 But if thine eye be evil, thy whole body shall be full of darkness. If therefore the light that is in thee be darkness, how great is that darkness, Chapter 6)

> What I tell you in darkness, that speak ye in light: and what ye hear in the ear, that preach ye upon the housetops. (Matthew 10:27)

> 28 Come unto me, all ye that labour and are heavy laden, and I will give you rest.
> 29 Take my yoke upon you, and learn of me; for I am meek and lowly in heart: and ye shall find rest unto your souls.
> 30 For my yoke is easy, and my burden is light. (Matthew, Chapter 11)

> 18 He that believeth on him is not condemned: but he that believeth not is condemned already, because he hath not believed in the name of the only begotten Son of God.
> 19 And this is the condemnation, that light is come into the world, and men loved darkness rather than light, because their deeds were evil. 20For every one that doeth evil

hateth the light, neither cometh to the light, lest his deeds should be reproved.
21 But he that doeth truth cometh to the light, that his deeds may be made manifest, that they are wrought in God. (John, Chapter 3)

I am the light of the world: he that followeth me shall not walk in darkness, but shall have the light of life. (John 8:12)

As long as I am in the world, I am the light of the world. (John 9:5)

9 Jesus answered, Are there not twelve hours in the day? If any man walk in the day, he stumbleth not, because he seeth the light of this world.
10 But if a man walk in the night, he stumbleth, because there is no light in him. (John, Chapter 11)

35 Then Jesus said unto them, Yet a little while is the light with you. Walk while ye have the light, lest darkness come upon you: for he that walketh in darkness knoweth not whither he goeth.
36 While ye have light, believe in the light, that ye may be the children of light. (John, Chapter 12)

44 Jesus cried and said, He that believeth on me, believeth not on me, but on him that sent me.
45 And he that seeth me seeth him that sent me.
46 I am come a light into the world, that whosoever believeth on me should not abide in darkness. (John, Chapter 12)

Take note of the saying: "As long as I am in the world, I am the light of the world." The meaning is that as long as the universal Christ mind is in the world, it is the light of the world, yet if there was no Christ light in the world, the world would self-destruct in a scenario akin to a fiery cataclysm. While I was in physical embodiment, I was the light of the world and held the spiritual balance for the planet. Since then a few people in every age have held that light, but it was my hope and vision that millions of people would understand my true teachings, so they could follow in my footsteps and do the works that I did by being the light of the world. And when enough people do this, you can do even greater works than I did and lift the world out of the darkness of ignorance and into the light of true self-knowledge—the knowledge of the

Self as God. Thus, for as long as *you* are in the world, *be* the light of the world!!!

***

Why is death called the last enemy? Well, how do you defeat an enemy? From the perspective of the dualistic mind, you defeat an enemy by destroying the enemy—of course, no one in the dualistic frame of mind has yet figured out how to destroy death. From the perspective of the Christ mind, you defeat an enemy by turning the enemy into a friend.

Am I telling you to see death as a friend? Well, what is death? Death is the final cessation of something. For example, you know that when you die physically, you leave the body and all of your material possessions behind. You have the popular saying, "You can't take it with you."

Normally, people would say that death means the cessation of life. However, as a spiritual student, you know this is not true. First of all, you are more than the body, so you do not die when the body dies. Furthermore, you can receive other bodies, so even on the physical level, death is not the total cessation of life. Now consider that while you cannot take anything material with you, you do actually take something with you as you lay down one body. You take the spiritual self, but you also take the separate self. Your ego and the separate selves created by the ego will follow you from lifetime to lifetime.

How do you finally overcome the ego? By letting it die, meaning that you allow the ego to go through a final and total cessation of being. In other words, the only aspect of your being that is subject to death is the ego. Meaning that your fear of death does not come from the conscious self but from the ego, which will indefinitely resist its own death and thus seek to get *you* to resist its death. Meaning that the ego will resist your growth toward Christhood until the very end. My death on the cross was meant to symbolize the death of the ego, as I finally gave up the ghost of my resistance to letting the ego die. And it was in this act of total, final and unconditional surrender that I opened up for my resurrection into the total freedom of an ego-less existence.

Do you see that when you fully integrate this truth, you know that nothing real *can* die and you know the conscious self is real. You also know that anything unreal *must* die, and the ego is unreal. Thus, you see that any resistance to death in your being can only come from the ego, which fears the cessation of existence. Yet the real you, the conscious self, has no reason to fear the cessation of existence, for it is out of the Creator's own Being and can never die. Thus, you have no actual reason to fear death. In fact, to the conscious self death will – when you are awakened to reality – be your ultimate friend, for death means the total and final cessation of something unreal. And when you allow the ego to go through that total and final cessation of being, the conscious self will finally be free to be here below all that you are Above. So why resist losing your "life" for my sake?

## The final assignment

It is now time to give you the final assignment of this course. It is to write down your story of how you found the spiritual path and how you walked it to your present level. How did you begin to question your childhood belief system? How did you learn to see through the dualistic lies? How did you learn to unmask your ego and rise above it? What challenges have you faced, and how did you overcome them? What experiences have you had with spiritual organizations and teachers and how did they help or hinder your growth?

As you write, consider what takes away your peace about writing and then seek to find your center, your peace.

Be honest, be straightforward, but first of all *be yourself.*

Allow yourself to be creative and let the story flow!

Write this as if you are writing for a person who has not yet discovered the path but who senses that there is more to life. Then take that person from the beginning stages of spiritual awareness to your present level by allowing the person to share your personal journey.

As always, there is an Alpha and an Omega aspect to this. The Alpha is that by writing down your story, you will achieve greater clarity and this will help you process elements of your being that are not yet resolved—it is a therapeutic process. The Omega is that you will help others and bear witness to the fact that there is an alternative to the duality of traditional religion and atheism. Consider how many people today become dissatisfied with traditional religion but think there is no alternative other than atheism based on scientific materialism. Thus, I need millions of people to demonstrate that there is indeed a Middle Way between these to dualistic extremes.

Then publish your story as you see appropriate, but at the very least make it available on the internet.

# Appendix

# I give you the tools to overcome a spiritual crisis

A message from Archangel Michael.

Archangel Michael I AM, and I AM the Presence of the LORD who can withstand the onslaught of any force on Earth. Thus, I come with a special dispensation for those people on Earth who are burdened by negative energy by the mass consciousness, by their own momentums of the past, or by those dark forces that have manifested themselves on this planet for eons.

You are those who know that you are facing a spiritual crisis, for you have come to the point of being willing to admit that you are being attacked by forces outside yourself, forces that seem to be beyond your control. Thus, you have taken a step that most among humankind have not been willing to take, for they are not willing to acknowledge that there are such forces in the world.

Thus, my beloved, my concern for this particular release is to help those who can be helped—because they are willing to acknowledge that they have a problem, that they are attacked by forces beyond their immediate control. And so, I come to give you my assistance by giving you a part of the momentum that I AM, the momentum of God's Will, the momentum of God's protection.

But, my beloved, I need you to understand the reality of an archangel, for I must tell you that regardless of how angels and archangels have been portrayed by various religions, I must assure you that I, Archangel Michael, am not locked in a dualistic battle with the devil and the demons and the forces of darkness. For I am not in duality, I AM above and beyond all dualistic consciousness and that is precisely why the power of an archangel is beyond any force on Earth. And therefore, no force on Earth can prevail against us when we manifest our Presence in the full power that we are.

So you see, my beloved, why are we not simply manifesting our Presence and wiping all darkness from the Earth? Well, it is because the Law of Free Will mandates that the people who are in physical embodiment on Earth are the ones who determine what is allowed to remain on the Earth and what is allowed to manifest on the Earth in the form of Light.

You, my beloved, are facing a spiritual crisis. You feel like you are powerless, you feel like you are paralyzed, you feel like you are being attacked or weighted down by burdens and forces that you cannot prevail against with the strength that you have with your outer mind and being. And while this may be so right now, I must tell you that it is all an illusion. And the bottom of this illusion is that *you* are the one who must be in control of your forcefield.

My beloved, the essential difference between an archangel and the forces of darkness is this: I will not violate your free will, whereas the forces of darkness *will* violate your free will. But you see, my beloved, they can violate your free will only to the extent that you use your free will to allow them to do so. And that is why, my beloved, I cannot step into your forcefield and banish the darkness from your Being—I must be invited. But I must be invited in a profound way, where you understand that you are the one who has to choose to let go of the darkness before it can be consumed by my Presence.

Do you see, my beloved, the equation here? There are many ways that you can invite the forces of darkness into your being, and many of those ways are even unbeknownst to you, for this world truly is so saturated with the subtle serpentine lies that many people invite the forces of darkness into their beings without knowing what they are doing. Yet I must tell you that there is always a choice made somewhere, and ultimately you cannot be free of darkness until you undo the choice that allowed them to enter and allows them to remain.

So you see, my beloved, you must be willing to awaken – to come up higher – and ultimately to move towards the point where you can take full and final responsibility for yourself, your own being, your own path in life, even your own salvation. For you see, my beloved, the forces of darkness do not simply enter through activities that you see as clearly dark, such as drug and alcohol abuse or other forms that are clearly dark. They often enter through seemingly innocent means, even religious activities that portray the eternal lie that you need an external savior in order to be saved because you cannot save yourself.

Thus, my beloved, you must awaken, you must take responsibility before my power and my Presence can enter your being. For if you do not, then my Presence in your being will only increase the tension—for you will be fighting not only against the dark forces, but a part of your own being will be fighting against my Light because it will want to hold on to the darkness.

Do you see, my beloved, the essential equation here? If you could let go of the darkness – if you could consciously let go of the illusions that allow the darkness to remain in your being – then my Presence could enter and the darkness would be banished. Yet until you let go, there will be a part of your being, a part of your ego, that holds on to the darkness because, in reality, your ego is comfortable with the dark forces because they do give it some sense of power or control over you.

And thus, my beloved, I cannot – as has been portrayed by so many traditional religions – simply walk into your forcefield and banish all your darkness, even based on a simple prayer to do so. There must be the equivalence from you of the willingness to take a look at why you invited the forces of darkness in in the first place.

And I know, my beloved, that when you are truly burdened and feel paralyzed, it is almost impossible for you to contemplate that you could ever have allowed this darkness into your being voluntarily. And in many cases, as I said, it was not a conscious, voluntary decision. It was a seemingly innocent decision that was made, but nevertheless I am telling you that unless you are willing to look at the decision and consciously undo it, you cannot be ultimately free.

What I can do for you, what I *will* do for you, is that through your listening to this dictation, over and over again while giving my special rosary for this purpose, I will manifest as much of my Presence in your being as you can withstand without being thrown into a conflict that is worse than what you are experiencing right now.

So what I offer you is a gradual path, my beloved. And on that path I require you to do several things. I require you right now to open your heart and give from within or aloud, a simple prayer to invite me into your being and to banish the darkness that is burdening you so you feel like you cannot take another step higher.

Thus, my beloved, when you make this simple request, I can manifest a certain amount of my Presence that will allow you some relief from your current burdens. But, my beloved, this offering from my heart will not work if you use that relief to say, "Ah, now I don't need to worry about my burdens, now I don't need to look at my illusions, I can, after all, suddenly survive so I will simply go on."

My beloved, this cannot work, for there will come a point where you will again be burdened by the darkness, and you will again feel paralyzed and overwhelmed. And thus, I need you to be the wise workman who will do what Jesus said and multiply the talents you have been given. My beloved, only by multiplying it will I be able – according to the Law of Free Will – to give you further and further protection and relief—as you warrant it by your own willingness to keep doing my rosary, to keep listening to this dictation, and to keep studying the teachings that you need to study in order to take command over your own psychology.

And my beloved, the teachings that you first and foremost need to study in order to overcome any spiritual crisis, is the wonderful book by Mother Mary, *Master Keys to the Abundant Life* and also the book *Master Keys to Personal Wholeness*. Thus, I recommend these two books for everyone who faces a spiritual crisis and is willing to do some work, is willing to look for the beam in their own eye to overcome that crisis.

My beloved, why am I stressing the need for you to do something? Well there are two reasons for this. My beloved, traditional religion portrays you as the passive recipient of the Grace from Heaven. And thus, you have been conditioned to think that if I really am an archangel and have all power in Heaven and on Earth, then you should be able to ask me to relieve your burden, and I should immediately step in and do it for you. This, my beloved, is false religion, promoted by the forces of darkness in order to give them an inroad into your being.

And that brings us to the second reason. You see, my beloved, it is the very belief that you are passive, and that you have no power on your own, that makes you vulnerable to the dark forces in the first place. So do you see, that if I did something to confirm that belief, I would actually prevent your ultimate freedom from those dark forces? Surely, I could – on a temporary basis – relieve your burdens. But it would not permanently relieve those burdens until you take charge and say, "No, I must be responsible for my own household, I must be responsible for my own path in life. And thus I must be willing to look at the illusions that I have come to believe, the conditions I have set up, the expectations of life that I have. And therefore, I must be willing to see what is unreal, let go of what is unreal, and instead accept the truth of Christ that will make me free from the unreality."

This my beloved, is the difference between the true representatives of God in the Ascended Host and the myriad of false teachers who exist in the physical plane, in the emotional plane, in the mental plane, and even in the lowest levels of the etheric plane. You see, my beloved, they all want to tell you that you cannot save yourself, that you cannot rise up on your own power, and that you need them to do something for you.

Well my beloved, you need nothing outside the power in your own Being, and why is this so? It is so because the Kingdom of God is within you, meaning that you are created out of the Being of your Creator. My beloved, the difference between you and I is that I have ascended to the rank of an archangel because I have been willing to acknowledge the power of God within me—that I AM an extension of God's Being, I AM an individualization of the Creator. And thus I have been able to let go of the illusion of separation that once upon a time caused me to believe also that I was separated from my God and separated from the rest of creation.

And this is the essential illusion of the serpentine consciousness and those in the fallen consciousness who want to enslave all people on Earth, so they can milk them of their light and their energy. For these dark beings have no longer the ability to receive light from God, for they would not be able to withstand that light, they would not be able to use it at all. And thus, they must have you – who still receive that light from above – misqualify that light so they can absorb it—once you have qualified it with a negative emotion.

Do you see, my beloved, that this is why they are pounding on you day and night to get you into an inharmonious and unbalanced state of mind? This is why they have set up so many lies and illusions, so many activities on this Earth, that have no other purpose than to very gradually fool people into getting into a state of consciousness, where they can be spiritually raped because they have no longer the protection of the auric field that is natural to all human beings.

That field has been broken down—so many openings have been created that there is an inroad for the dark forces to walk in at any time of the day or night and take over your being. And suddenly, you realize that you are no longer in control of the situation, you are no longer in control of your actions, your emotions, your thoughts. Even your sense of who you are has now been taken over, and you do not recognize yourself—compared to the moments where you feel uplifted and at peace.

Thus, my beloved, you must recognize that there are certain outer activities in this world that are designed for one purpose only, and that is to open you up to the forces of darkness. And I must tell you that if you think that you can give my rosary and listen to this dictation and study the books while still indulging in these activities, then you are indeed mistaken because this simply cannot be done. For as I have said, my multiplication of your efforts will be only a multiplication of *your* efforts, my beloved.

And thus, if you are not willing to put forth the effort of freeing yourself from certain outer activities, well then I cannot continue to help you. I can help you get a clarity and a peace that will allow you to free yourself from these activities, but I must tell you that it will never happen automatically because you got into your present state of consciousness through choices you made, and you will get out of it only through choices you make.

Do you understand this? I know very well that your ego does not understand this, but I am not talking to your ego—I am talking to your conscious self. And if you do not yet know what the conscious self is, then study the book by Mother Mary, so you will know and understand that there is a part of your being that is real, there is a part of your being that is an extension of God, the Creator himself. And that part of your being has the ability to make the choice to come up higher, to make the choice and say, "This outer manifestation of imperfection and unreality, this outer manifestation of inharmony and imbalance, is not the true being that I AM. And therefore, I will no longer indulge in this, I will no longer indulge in the illusion that it has any power over me."

For my beloved I must tell you that there is no condition in this world that has any ultimate reality to it whatsoever. And with ultimate reality I mean that there is no condition in this world that has any power over the real You, the conscious self, your higher being. And thus, my beloved, the ultimate way to be free from the forces of this world is to realize that they are unreal—and when they are unreal, they have no power over you.

Nothing that is unreal can possibly threaten that which is real. And so what is the key to overcoming unreality? Well it is, my beloved, as we have said over and over again, Christ discernment. And I realize full well that while you are burdened by this or that energy and force, you cannot have full Christ discernment. But I tell you that there is a reality in your being that can know right now what is real and unreal in your immediate situation. You can know right now what is the next step you need to take to overcome your present burden, to come out of your present crisis.

And my beloved, I am talking to that reality in you right now, and I say, "Wake up and realize that you are God—you are an individualization of God! And then make the choice that God would make in your present situation so that you can overcome the burden that seems insurmountable with your human consciousness. And it *is* insurmountable with your outer consciousness because did not Jesus say that with men this is impossible but with God all things are possible?

Thus my beloved, there is a spark of God in your being. You may not yet have the full internalization of that reality, and therefore you cannot unleash the power of God from within yourself. And that is why I am giving you this release, because I offer to be the vicarious power of God for a time. But, my beloved, do not mistake this for the vicarious atonement, where they think that Jesus will come and save them.

For I, Archangel Michael, will not come and save anyone permanently. I will only come on a temporary basis to uplift you, so that you can have freedom and peace to connect to the power of God within yourself. And so that, after a time, you no longer need my Presence as the external power of God, for you have now discovered the internal power of God that you truly are.

And therefore, do you see, my beloved, when you come to that point, you no longer need the power of God to stream through me as an external being that you must see as external. Because you realize that in the inner parts of your being, you are one with the entire Ascended Host, with the entire Body of God. So you realize that Archangel Michael is not truly outside of you.

For I have a universal Presence that cannot be confined to time and space, and thus I am also inside of you. And when you realize that, you realize that I simply represent the power of God, and that power of God can stream through you from the inside. And that is when you become spiritually self-sufficient, and that is when the demons of darkness will run from you, because they will know that they have lost their power over you as you saw them lose their power over Christ.

But my beloved, to attain that ultimate freedom, you must be willing to look at every illusion, every serpentine lie that has crept into your consciousness, sneaking along the ground, sneaking through the bushes and the grass, and suddenly entering your being when you least expect it. And my beloved, this can be done, for again, you have a Christ Self that is internal to you. And when you connect to that Christ Self, you can get the inner recognition – often when you read an outer teaching – you can get an inner recognition that says, "This is how this outer teaching applies to me in my immediate situation."

And when you are alert and when you are true to that inner prompting, then you can take the step that goes beyond the outer teaching. You can take the step that is specific for your immediate situation that will help you rise one step higher on your path and attain a greater degree of freedom from the darkness. And therefore, you can gradually overcome that darkness.

For I tell you – even though you might feel burdened right now – I can tell you that if you were suddenly free from all darkness, you would experience an identity crisis. For you have become so used to the illusions—even the presence of dark forces can become almost an addiction, where your outer mind is so addicted to these dark forces and what they do through you and to you, that even though it is unpleasant, you cannot let it go.

And if you want a visible example of this, then look at the people who are smoking cigarettes. And even though they have already experienced lung cancer, they cannot stop. Look at the people who have had throat cancer and had a voice box implanted, yet they smoke a cigarette through that voice box. Look at those who have had one lung removed but continue to smoke. This, my beloved, is the addiction where you feel, your outer mind feels, that it cannot do without the darkness. It has so internalized the darkness and made it part of its own being that it literally could not maintain a sense of continuity and identity without it.

And my beloved, if you are that deep into identification with the darkness, then I say to you: "You have a long road ahead of you, but I am willing to walk with you every step of the way—as you are willing to keep taking one small step at a time. I do not expect that you can come up to the full freedom in an instant, in the blink of an eye. It may take days, it may take months, it may take years, it may take decades and for some people it may even take lifetimes, but I tell you, the forces of darkness will keep you trapped in the illusion that this is too much, that this is too overwhelming."

"But I tell you, a journey of a thousand miles begins with one step, but a journey of a thousand miles is completed only when you keep taking one small step at a time. And if you will decide right now that you want to be free of this darkness, and if you will decide that you will keep taking one small step at a time, then I can assure you that eventually the forces of darkness will lose their grip over your outer mind. And you will realize that you can indeed be free, that you *will* indeed be free—if you keep taking one step at a time. And I must tell you that no matter how burdened you are, you can always take some small step—if you are willing to do so."

And thus, I must tell you again, I cannot help those who are not willing to help themselves. It is impossible because the law of free will mandates that I cannot help those who are not willing to make decisions.

My beloved, it may be difficult for your outer mind to understand, but when you look at the Earth, and look at the darkness that is rampant on this planet, you have only two options. You must say that either God created this darkness or allowed it to be on Earth, or that it is created through the Law of Free Will, whereby the people on Earth have allowed this darkness to enter this planet and have continued to allow it to maintain a presence here.

My beloved, there is no other logical option. And I can assure you that it was not God who wanted the darkness. For the many serpentine beliefs that God and the devil are two polarities in the dualistic whole is simply a lie. The ego will never understand this, but the Conscious You can understand this because the Conscious You has the ability to connect to the reality of God, and experience that it is beyond duality. And thus, my beloved, if you are willing to keep taking one small step at a time, you *will* rise in consciousness until you come to the point where the clouds part and you suddenly see a glimpse of the non-dualistic reality of God. And thus, my beloved, at that point you will know that what I say is true, even though you cannot know it with the outer mind right now.

Thus, my beloved, my program is simple: this dictation, this release, has given you the impetus you need to take the next step. So after listening to this, give my rosary. Then listen to the dictation again, give the rosary again. I am not saying to do this in a 24 hour vigil, I am saying do it as often as you feel you need it until you sense a definite release, a definite relief, from the forces and the energies that are burdening you right now.

If you are truly burdened, if you are truly at the end of your rope, as they say, then continue doing this until you feel you have some control over your being. For after all, my beloved, what else will you do with your time? Continue the same old momentums of letting your emotional body and your thoughts run wild because they are taken over by the darkness?

So is it not better, then, to remain in my Presence for as long as you need, until you feel that the darkness has receded enough to allow you to make some kind of clear decision. Then go on with your daily life enough to keep you going but enter a program of listening to this dictation and giving my rosary once a day while at the same time studying the books I have recommended.

My beloved, God helps those who help themselves. If you will be honest, you will see in the world that there are those who have gone down in a downward spiral, a black hole of self destruction. And they have done so because they were not willing to make their own decisions, to help themselves to come up higher—and to keep taking that one small step at a time.

Sometimes they expected some immediate relief, other times they just got discouraged or bored, or started doubting that this would work in the end. I tell you, my beloved, discouragement has been called the greatest tool in the devil's toolkit, and it is so for a reason. For the dark forces will try to discourage you, and I must tell you that there are millions of people who have come within an inch of breaking through to a higher level of consciousness, yet have allowed some doubt to creep into their minds and have become discouraged at the last minute before they would have experienced an entirely new phase in their lives.

This, my beloved, *can* happen to you or it *cannot* happen to you. I cannot make it happen or not make it happen, for you must make the choice. What I *can* do is give you the tool, and I have done so. And my beloved, I must tell you one thing—if you have been willing to listen to this dictation, then it is because you have the potential to come up higher and turn your life around into a positive spiral. For had you not been at that point, had you been so far gone that you had no ability to take control over yourself, you would have been unwilling to listen to these words—because the dark forces would long ago have prompted you to accept some kind of excuse for why you should turn off this very unpleasant release of light that makes them so uncomfortable that they can barely stand to be in your auric field while your outer mind is listening to my words.

For indeed, there is much more than words released through this dictation. My beloved, my Presence is indeed with you, for it has entered your being inasmuch as you have allowed it, and as much as it can be done without throwing you into an unbalanced situation. Thus, my beloved, listen to my words but listen beyond the words to the vibration that I bring. Listen to the reality that even though the forces of darkness that have burdened you and controlled you may seem to have power, I Archangel Michael do not accept that they have any power over *me*. Neither do I accept that they have any power over *you*.

Although I do accept that you have free will. But what I want you to understand is that right now you are not making fully free choices. Because the forces of darkness and your own ego, have controlled your ability to make choices to the point where you cannot see the reality that allows you to make free choices.

Thus, you can continue to allow the forces of darkness to influence your choosing, or you can take up my offer to listen to my determination, and my reality and thereby gain strength from that to make your own choices—by taking back your power to make choices, by finding some element of peace, comfort, some sense that there is hope ahead, that there is still a sun shining above the storm clouds that have gathered over and in your forcefield.

Thus, will you continue to listen to the demons and the ego that howl their songs incessantly, trying to overwhelm you? Or will you listen to the voice of an archangel, who is here to say: "There is a God, that God is real, and that God is everywhere, including in you. Find the God within, and accept the reality of that God and that it is the only reality and that all manifestations on this Earth are ultimately illusions that have no power over the real spiritual being that you are. Thus, reach for that reality, and accept the Presence of an archangel until you can accept the Presence of your own Higher Being."

Thus, be sealed in the God Power of the first ray of the Will of God—the infinite faith that is beyond doubt because it is not faith, it is not belief, it is Oneness with reality, the reality that I AM.

# Archangel Michael's Rosary for Overcoming a Spiritual Crisis

In the name of the unconditional love of the Father, the Son, the Holy Spirit and the Miracle Mother, Amen.

Beloved Archangel Michael, I dedicate this rosary to the manifestation of God's will and God's kingdom in . . .

(Describe the situations and conditions that you want Archangel Michael and his angels to resolve.)

## Lord's Prayer

My Father-Mother God who is within all life, I honor your Presence, the I AM, within me. I accept your kingdom manifest on Earth through me. I accept my responsibility to manifest your will on Earth, as it is manifest in Heaven.

I accept that you are giving me my daily opportunity to be all that you are. I acknowledge that you forgive me my imperfections, as I forgive others and surrender my will to the higher will within me. I therefore accept the truth that the universe returns to me what I send out.

I take responsibility for my mind and my life. I vow to rise above the temptations of the lower self, so that you can deliver me from all imperfect energies. I affirm that your kingdom, power and glory is manifest in my being, now and forever. Amen.

## Archangel Michael, I am willing to take an active approach

1. Archangel Michael, I acknowledge you as the Presence of the LORD who can withstand the onslaught of any force on Earth. I want to be part of your special dispensation and rise above all negative energy, the mass consciousness, my own momentums of the past and all dark forces.

Hail Michael

**Hail Archangel Michael, Lord of Angels,**
**Your Presence is always with me.**
**Protect me from all forces of darkness,**
**and bind the enemy within me.**
**I take dominion over my mind,**
**and manifest God's kingdom in my life.**

**Holy Michael, Defender of Faith.**
**I invoke your Blue-flame Sword.**
**Cut me free from the lies of anti-christ,**
**so I can pierce the veil of separation.**
**I affirm my oneness with God,**
**and join the Body of God on Earth.**

2. Archangel Michael, I know that I am facing a spiritual crisis, and I am willing to admit that I am being attacked by forces outside myself, forces that seem to be beyond my control. I now consciously place myself in the group of those who can be helped—because I am willing to acknowledge that I have a problem. Archangel Michael, I ask for your assistance and I am willing to receive part of the momentum that you are, the momentum of God's Will, the momentum of God's protection.

**Hail Michael**

3. Archangel Michael, I acknowledge that you are not locked in a dualistic battle with the devil and the demons and the forces of darkness—that you are not in duality. I understand that this is why no force on Earth can prevail against you, when you manifest your Presence in the full power that you are. I acknowledge the Law of Free Will, which mandates that I must determine what darkness I allow to remain and what Light is allowed to manifest in my forcefield. Thus, I say, "I want to rise above the darkness and rise into the Light of your Presence, the Light of God!"

**Hail Michael**

4. Archangel Michael, I know that my ego and the forces of darkness do not want me to give this rosary, for the Light I invoke will make them uncomfortable. Yet I will not fall prey to their subtle temptations to give up. Instead, I will use their resistance to expose them by monitoring my reactions and using my God-given will power – assisted by the infinite will power of Archangel Michael –

to walk right through the opposition and establish a personal relationship with Michael, the Archangel of God's Will.

**Hail Archangel Michael, Lord of Angels,**
**Your Presence is always with me.**
**Protect me from all forces of darkness,**
**and bind the enemy within me.**
**I take dominion over my mind,**
**and manifest God's kingdom in my life.**

**Holy Michael, Defender of Faith.**
**I invoke your Blue-flame Sword.**
**Cut me free from the lies of anti-christ,**
**so I can pierce the veil of separation.**
**I affirm my oneness with God,**
**and join the Body of God on Earth.**

5. Archangel Michael, I acknowledge that when I feel like I am powerless, paralyzed, under attack or weighted down by burdens and forces that I cannot prevail against with the strength of my outer mind and being, this is all an illusion. And the core of this illusion is that I am the one who must be in control of my forcefield.

**Hail Michael**

6. Archangel Michael, I acknowledge that you will not violate my free will, whereas the forces of darkness WILL violate my free will. I understand that they can violate my free will only to the extent that I allow them to do so. Archangel Michael, I hereby invite you into my forcefield to banish the darkness from my Being. I understand that I am the one who must choose to let go of the darkness before it can be consumed by your Presence.

**Hail Michael**

7. Archangel Michael, I understand the equation of free will. I am willing to see how I have invited the forces of darkness into my being, even the ways that are unknown to me. I see that the world is so saturated with the subtle serpentine lies that I have invited the forces of darkness into my being without knowing what I was doing. I am willing to see the choices that I made, and I am willing to undo the choices that allowed the darkness to enter and allow it to remain.

**Hail Michael**

8. Archangel Michael, I am willing to awaken, to come up higher, and ultimately to take full and final responsibility for myself, my own being, my own path in life, even my own salvation. I know that the forces of darkness do not simply enter through activities that I see as clearly dark, but also through seemingly innocent means, even religious activities that portray the eternal lie that I need an external savior because I can do nothing to save myself.

**Hail Michael**

9. Archangel Michael, I am willing to awaken, to take responsibility, so that your power and Presence can enter my being. I will not fight against your Light, and I will not hold on to the darkness. I see that my ego holds on to the darkness because my ego is comfortable with the dark forces that give it some sense of power and control over me. Yet I know my conscious self is more than the ego, and thus I am willing to take a look at why I invited the forces of darkness in. I am willing to look at every decision that opened my being to the darkness and consciously undo it, so that I can be ultimately free.

**Hail Michael**

## I Choose Life!

**Beloved Archangel Michael, save me or I perish!** (3X)

Archangel Michael, save me from the consciousness of death that causes me to identify myself as a mortal human being who is separated from my God.

Beloved Archangel Michael, thou Defender of my Faith, if people knew better, they would do better, and by the authority of my God-given free will I hereby declare that I am willing to know better. I am willing to be cut free from the lies of anti-christ that have enveloped my soul, so that I am caught in a spider web of lies from which there seems to be no way out.

Archangel Michael, I am willing to rise above the consciousness of death and be free to see the truth of Christ and the shining reality of God. I am willing to see my God and no longer live as a human being but live as the spiritual being that I truly am.

Archangel Michael, I am willing to change my life. I am willing to lose my mortal sense of life, my mortal sense of identity, that is based on the limitations of this world and the duality of the carnal mind. I am willing to let mine eye be single, so that I can see beyond the subtle lies of the serpentine mind and be filled with the Light of Christ. I am willing to surrender my emotional attachments to the things of this world and the limitations that seem so real. I am willing to lose this sense of life to win the immortal life of the Christ consciousness and accept my true identity as a co-creator with God.

Therefore I now say, with the full authority of my free will and the power of the Christ Flame within me:

**I CHOOSE LIFE!** (4X)

I choose the consciousness of life, the Christ consciousness, and I accept that am alive forevermore in the light of Christ. I accept that behind all appearances of this world is the reality of my God, and therefore I vow to nevermore give permanency to any worldly appearances. I affirm that God is everywhere and therefore also in me.

I choose to be one with my God, and therefore I am the Presence of Archangel Michael in this world.

## Archangel Michael, I acknowledge the power of God within me

1. Archangel Michael, I call to you to manifest as much of your Presence in my being as I can withstand. I vow to follow the gradual path that you offer. I hereby invite you into my being to banish the darkness. I will use the relief from my burdens to look at my illusions and undo the choices that make me vulnerable to dark forces and energies. I want to come up higher in consciousness and attain oneness with my own Higher Being, my I AM Presence. I am the wise workman who will multiply the talents so I will not again be burdened by the darkness.

**Hail Michael**

2. Archangel Michael, I want to enter an ongoing relationship with you, so that when I multiply what I have received, you can give me further protection and relief—as I warrant it by my willingness to keep doing your rosary, to keep listening to your dictation, and to keep studying the teachings that I need to study in order to take command over my own psychology.

**Hail Michael**

3. Archangel Michael, I realize that for me to enter into a personal relationship with you, I must take an active approach. I hereby let go of the illusions of traditional religion that portray me as the passive recipient of the Grace from Heaven. And thus, I do not expect

that I should be able to ask you to relieve my burden, and you should immediately step in and do it for me. I see that this is false religion, promoted by the forces of darkness in order to give them an inroad into my being.

**Hail Archangel Michael, Lord of Angels,**
**Your Presence is always with me.**
**Protect me from all forces of darkness,**
**and bind the enemy within me.**
**I take dominion over my mind,**
**and manifest God's kingdom in my life.**

**Holy Michael, Defender of Faith.**
**I invoke your Blue-flame Sword.**
**Cut me free from the lies of anti-christ,**
**so I can pierce the veil of separation.**
**I affirm my oneness with God,**
**and join the Body of God on Earth.**

4. Archangel Michael, I recognize that it is the very belief that I am passive, and that I have no power on my own, that makes me vulnerable to the dark forces in the first place. I see that if you did something to confirm that belief, you would prevent my ultimate freedom. I now take charge and I say, "I AM responsible for my own household, I AM responsible for my own path in life. And thus I AM willing to look at the illusions that I have come to believe, the conditions I have set up, the expectations of life that I have. And therefore, I AM willing to see what is unreal, let go of what is unreal, and instead accept the truth of Christ that will make me free from the unreality."

**Hail Michael**

5. Archangel Michael, I see the difference between the true representatives of God in the Ascended Host and the myriad of false teachers who exist in the physical plane, the emotional plane, the mental plane, and the lowest levels of the etheric plane. I know they all want to tell me that I cannot save myself, that I cannot rise up on my own power, and that I need them to do something for me. I recognize the truth that I need nothing outside the power in my own Being, because the Kingdom of God is within me, meaning that I am created out of the Being of my Creator.

**Hail Michael**

6. Archangel Michael, I am willing to acknowledge the power of God within me—that I AM an extension of God's Being, I AM an individualization of the Creator. I hereby let go of the illusion of separation that causes me to believe that I am separated from my God and separated from the rest of creation. I see that this is the essential illusion of the serpentine consciousness and those in the fallen consciousness who want to enslave all people on Earth so they can milk them of their light and their energy. I understand that these dark beings can no longer receive light from God, and thus they must get me to misqualify light so they can absorb it.

**Hail Archangel Michael, Lord of Angels,**
**Your Presence is always with me.**
**Protect me from all forces of darkness,**
**and bind the enemy within me.**
**I take dominion over my mind,**
**and manifest God's kingdom in my life.**

**Holy Michael, Defender of Faith.**
**I invoke your Blue-flame Sword.**
**Cut me free from the lies of anti-christ,**
**so I can pierce the veil of separation.**
**I affirm my oneness with God,**
**and join the Body of God on Earth.**

7. Archangel Michael, I now understand why the dark forces are pounding on me day and night to get me into an inharmonious and unbalanced state of mind. I know why they have set up so many lies and illusions, so many activities, that have no other purpose than to manipulate me into a state of consciousness, where I can be spiritually raped because I no longer have the protection of my auric field. I am determined to close up all openings in my energy field that give an inroad for the dark forces to walk in at any time of the day or night and take over my being. With your help, I will be in control of every situation, I will be in control of my actions, emotions, thoughts and my sense of who I am, so I can always feel uplifted and at peace.

**Hail Michael**

8. Archangel Michael, I recognize that there are certain outer activities in this world that are designed to open me up to the forces of darkness. I recognize that I cannot overcome a spiritual crisis

and attain peace of mind while indulging in these activities. Thus, I am willing to put forth the effort of freeing myself from any and all outer activities that steal my peace. I seek the clarity and the peace that will empower me to free myself from these activities by taking responsibility for my past choices and making better choices in the present and the future.

**Hail Michael**

9. Archangel Michael, I recognize that my ego will not understand the advantage of letting go of these activities, but I know I am more than my ego, and my conscious self will recognize the truth. I recognize that this part of my being is an extension of God, the Creator himself. Thus, I have the ability to make the choice to come up higher and I say, "This outer manifestation of imperfection and unreality, this outer manifestation of inharmony and imbalance, is not the true being that I AM. And therefore, I will no longer indulge in this, I will no longer indulge in the illusion that it has any power over me."

**Hail Michael**

## I Choose Life!

**Beloved Archangel Michael, save me or I perish!** (3X)

Archangel Michael, save me from the consciousness of death that causes me to identify myself as a mortal human being who is separated from my God.

Beloved Archangel Michael, thou Defender of my Faith, if people knew better, they would do better, and by the authority of my God-given free will I hereby declare that I am willing to know better. I am willing to be cut free from the lies of anti-christ that have enveloped my soul, so that I am caught in a spider web of lies from which there seems to be no way out.

Archangel Michael, I am willing to rise above the consciousness of death and be free to see the truth of Christ and the shining reality of God. I am willing to see my God and no longer live as a human being but live as the spiritual being that I truly am.

Archangel Michael, I am willing to change my life. I am willing to lose my mortal sense of life, my mortal sense of identity, that is based on the limitations of this world and the duality of the carnal mind. I am willing to let mine eye be single, so that I can see beyond the subtle lies of the serpentine mind and be filled with the Light of Christ. I am willing to surrender my emotional attachments to the things of this world and the limitations that seem so real. I am willing to lose this sense of life to win the immortal life of the Christ consciousness and accept my true identity as a co-creator with God.

Therefore I now say, with the full authority of my free will and the power of the Christ Flame within me:

**I CHOOSE LIFE!** (4X)

I choose the consciousness of life, the Christ consciousness, and I accept that am alive forevermore in the light of Christ. I accept that behind all appearances of this world is the reality of my God, and therefore I vow to nevermore give permanency to any worldly appearances. I affirm that God is everywhere and therefore also in me.

I choose to be one with my God, and therefore I am the Presence of Archangel Michael in this world.

## Archangel Michael, I am willing to be spiritually self-sufficient

1. Archangel Michael, I recognize that there is no condition in this world that has any ultimate reality to it whatsoever. There is no condition in this world that has any power over the real me, the conscious self, my Higher Being. I see that the ultimate way to be free from the forces of this world is to realize that they are unreal—and because they are unreal, they have no power over me.

**Hail Michael**

2. Archangel Michael, I realize that nothing that is unreal can possibly threaten that which is real. Thus, I call to my Christ self to help me attain Christ discernment to separate the real from the unreal in my being and world. I realize that while I am burdened by this or that energy and force, I cannot have full Christ discernment. Yet I know there is a reality in my being that can know what is real and unreal in my immediate situation. I can know what is the next step I need to take in order to overcome my present burden, to come out of my present crisis.

**Hail Michael**

3. Archangel Michael, I recognize the inner reality of my Being and I am awakening to the realization that I am God—I am an individualization of God! Thus, I am making the choice that God

would make in my present situation, so that I can overcome the burden that seems insurmountable with my human consciousness. I acknowledge the truth in the words of Jesus, "With men this is impossible but with God all things are possible."

**Hail Archangel Michael, Lord of Angels,**
**Your Presence is always with me.**
**Protect me from all forces of darkness,**
**and bind the enemy within me.**
**I take dominion over my mind,**
**and manifest God's kingdom in my life.**

**Holy Michael, Defender of Faith.**
**I invoke your Blue-flame Sword.**
**Cut me free from the lies of anti-christ,**
**so I can pierce the veil of separation.**
**I affirm my oneness with God,**
**and join the Body of God on Earth.**

4. Archangel Michael, I acknowledge the spark of God in my being. I also see that I cannot yet unleash the power of God from within myself. Therefore, I ask you to be the vicarious power of God for a time, until I am fully connected to the power of God within myself, and thus I am spiritually self-sufficient.

**Hail Michael**

5. Archangel Michael, I am not expecting you to save me permanently. I ask you to come on a temporary basis to uplift me so that I can have freedom and peace to connect to the power of God within myself. And so that, after a time, I no longer need your Presence as the external power of God, for I have now discovered the internal power of God that I truly am. And thus I realize that in the inner parts of my being, I am one with the entire Ascended Host, with the entire Body of God.

**Hail Michael**

6. Archangel Michael, I realize that you are not truly outside of me. I recognize that you have a universal Presence that cannot be confined to time and space, and thus you are also inside of me. I know you represent the Power of God, and the Power of God can stream through me from the inside, making me spiritually self-sufficient. And that is when the demons of darkness will run from me because

they will know that they have lost their power over me, as they lost their power over Christ.

**Hail Archangel Michael, Lord of Angels,**
**Your Presence is always with me.**
**Protect me from all forces of darkness,**
**and bind the enemy within me.**
**I take dominion over my mind,**
**and manifest God's kingdom in my life.**

**Holy Michael, Defender of Faith.**
**I invoke your Blue-flame Sword.**
**Cut me free from the lies of anti-christ,**
**so I can pierce the veil of separation.**
**I affirm my oneness with God,**
**and join the Body of God on Earth.**

7. Archangel Michael, I want ultimate freedom. I am willing to look at every illusion, every serpentine lie that has crept into my consciousness. I know this can be done, for I have a Christ Self that is internal to me. And when I connect to that Christ Self, I get the inner recognition that shows me what is real and what is unreal in my being and world.

**Hail Michael**

8. Archangel Michael, I will be alert and true to the inner promptings of my Christ self, so that I can take the steps that are specific to my immediate situation and will help me rise one step higher on my path and attain a greater degree of freedom from the darkness. I know that by taking one doable step at a time, I WILL gradually overcome all of the darkness.

**Hail Michael**

9. Archangel Michael, I understand that one can become used to the illusions, and even the presence of dark forces can become almost an addiction, where the outer mind is so addicted to these dark forces and what they do, that the outer mind cannot let it go. I see that behind any addiction is the outer mind's sense that it cannot do without the darkness. It has so internalized the darkness and made it part of its own being that it literally could not maintain a sense of continuity and identity without it. Yet I also know I am

more than the outer mind and the body. Thus, the conscious self is hereby letting go of all darkness in my being.

**Hail Michael**

## I Choose Life!

**Beloved Archangel Michael, save me or I perish!** (3X)

Archangel Michael, save me from the consciousness of death that causes me to identify myself as a mortal human being who is separated from my God.

Beloved Archangel Michael, thou Defender of my Faith, if people knew better, they would do better, and by the authority of my God-given free will I hereby declare that I am willing to know better. I am willing to be cut free from the lies of anti-christ that have enveloped my soul, so that I am caught in a spider web of lies from which there seems to be no way out.

Archangel Michael, I am willing to rise above the consciousness of death and be free to see the truth of Christ and the shining reality of God. I am willing to see my God and no longer live as a human being but live as the spiritual being that I truly am.

Archangel Michael, I am willing to change my life. I am willing to lose my mortal sense of life, my mortal sense of identity, that is based on the limitations of this world and the duality of the carnal mind. I am willing to let mine eye be single, so that I can see beyond the subtle lies of the serpentine mind and be filled with the Light of Christ. I am willing to surrender my emotional attachments to the things of this world and the limitations that seem so real. I am willing to lose this sense of life to win the immortal life of the Christ consciousness and accept my true identity as a co-creator with God.

Therefore I now say, with the full authority of my free will and the power of the Christ Flame within me:

**I CHOOSE LIFE!** (4X)

I choose the consciousness of life, the Christ consciousness, and I accept that am alive forevermore in the light of Christ. I accept that behind all appearances of this world is the reality of my God, and therefore I vow to nevermore give permanency to any worldly appearances. I affirm that God is everywhere and therefore also in me.

I choose to be one with my God, and therefore I am the Presence of Archangel Michael in this world.

## Archangel Michael, I will keep going to the victory

1. Archangel Michael, I recognize that even if I have a long road ahead of me, you are willing to walk with me every step of the way—as I am willing to keep taking one small step at a time. I do not expect that I can come up to the full freedom in an instant. I know that a journey of a thousand miles is completed only when I keep taking one small step at a time.

**Hail Archangel Michael, Lord of Angels,**
**Your Presence is always with me.**
**Protect me from all forces of darkness,**
**and bind the enemy within me.**
**I take dominion over my mind,**
**and manifest God's kingdom in my life.**

**Holy Michael, Defender of Faith.**
**I invoke your Blue-flame Sword.**
**Cut me free from the lies of anti-christ,**
**so I can pierce the veil of separation.**
**I affirm my oneness with God,**
**and join the Body of God on Earth.**

2. Archangel Michael, I decide right now that I want to be free of this darkness, and I will keep taking one small step at a time. Archangel Michael, I believe your promise that eventually the forces of darkness will lose their grip over my mind. I realize that I can indeed be free, that I WILL indeed be free—if I keep taking one step at a time.

**Hail Michael**

3. Archangel Michael, I recognize that no matter how burdened I might be, I can always take some small step—and I am willing to do so. I recognize that the law of free will mandates that you can only help those who are willing to help themselves by making decisions. I know that God did not create darkness or allowed it to be on Earth, but that it is created through the law of free will, whereby the people on Earth have allowed the darkness to enter this planet and have continued to allow it to maintain a presence here.

**Hail Michael**

4. Archangel Michael, I recognize that my conscious self has the ability to connect to the reality of God and experience that God is beyond duality. I am willing to keep taking one small step at a time and rise in consciousness, until the clouds part and I suddenly see a

glimpse of the non-dualistic reality of God. At that point I will know that what you say is true, even though I cannot know it with the outer mind right now.

**Hail Michael**

5. Archangel Michael, I will continue your program of giving this rosary and listening to your dictation until I have taken back control over my being. I refuse to continue the same old momentums of letting my emotional body and my thoughts run wild because they are taken over by the darkness. Instead, I will remain in your Presence for as long as I need, until I feel that the darkness has receded enough to allow me to make clear decisions and go on with my daily life. I am determined that with your empowerment, I will not be among those who go down in a downward spiral, a black hole of self-destruction. Instead, I am willing to make my own decisions, to help myself come up higher—and to keep taking that one small step at a time.

**Hail Michael**

6. Archangel Michael, with your help I will not expect immediate relief, I will not get discouraged or bored or start doubting that this will work in the end. I recognize that discouragement is the sharpest tool in the devil's toolkit. I know the dark forces will try to discourage me, yet I will keep on keeping on, until I break through to a higher level of consciousness. I will not allow doubt to creep into my mind or become discouraged at the last minute. I will go with you all the way until I experience an entirely new phase in my life.

**Hail Michael**

7. Archangel Michael, I recognize that you have given me the tool to turn my life around. I know I have the potential to come up higher and turn my life into a positive spiral. I will not fall prey to any excuse from my ego or the dark forces to stop. I know that by listening to your words and giving this rosary, they become so uncomfortable that they can barely stand to be in my auric field. And I want nothing more than to see them go so that I can move into oneness with my own Higher Being and attain peace of mind.

**Hail Michael**

8. Archangel Michael, I am willing to let your Presence be with me, and I allow you full and unrestricted access to my being, so that you can shine your light and remove all hiding places for the darkness. I will listen beyond your words to the vibration that you are. I recognize the reality that even though the forces of darkness

that have burdened and controlled me may seem to have power, Archangel Michael does not accept that they have any power over me. Therefore, neither do I accept that they have any power over me.

**Hail Archangel Michael, Lord of Angels,**
**Your Presence is always with me.**
**Protect me from all forces of darkness,**
**and bind the enemy within me.**
**I take dominion over my mind,**
**and manifest God's kingdom in my life.**

**Holy Michael, Defender of Faith.**
**I invoke your Blue-flame Sword.**
**Cut me free from the lies of anti-christ,**
**so I can pierce the veil of separation.**
**I affirm my oneness with God,**
**and join the Body of God on Earth.**

9. Archangel Michael, I recognize that the dark forces and my ego have controlled my ability to make choices to the point where I cannot see the reality that allows me to make free choices. Yet I will no longer allow the forces of darkness to influence my choosing, and I take up your offer to become one with your will power and your reality. I know that I will thereby gain strength to make my own choices by taking back my power of will. I will find the element of peace, comfort, and the sense that there is hope ahead. Thus, I accept that there is still a sun shining above the storm clouds in my forcefield. And that sun is my own I AM Presence, which is my true identity in God. Thus, I know all lower sense of identity is unreal, and I hereby let it go. I am willing to lose my mortal life in order to win the eternal life of Christ.

**Hail Michael**

### I Choose Life!

**Beloved Archangel Michael, save me or I perish!** (3X)

Archangel Michael, save me from the consciousness of death that causes me to identify myself as a mortal human being who is separated from my God.

Beloved Archangel Michael, thou Defender of my Faith, if people knew better, they would do better, and by the authority of my God-given free will I hereby declare that I am willing to know better. I am willing to be cut free from the lies of anti-christ that have enveloped my soul, so that I am caught in a spider web of lies from which there seems to be no way out.

Archangel Michael, I am willing to rise above the consciousness of death and be free to see the truth of Christ and the shining reality of God. I am willing to see my God and no longer live as a human being but live as the spiritual being that I truly am.

Archangel Michael, I am willing to change my life. I am willing to lose my mortal sense of life, my mortal sense of identity, that is based on the limitations of this world and the duality of the carnal mind. I am willing to let mine eye be single, so that I can see beyond the subtle lies of the serpentine mind and be filled with the Light of Christ. I am willing to surrender my emotional attachments to the things of this world and the limitations that seem so real. I am willing to lose this sense of life to win the immortal life of the Christ consciousness and accept my true identity as a co-creator with God.

Therefore I now say, with the full authority of my free will and the power of the Christ Flame within me:

**I CHOOSE LIFE!** (4X)

I choose the consciousness of life, the Christ consciousness, and I accept that am alive forevermore in the light of Christ. I accept that behind all appearances of this world is the reality of my God, and therefore I vow to nevermore give permanency to any worldly appearances. I affirm that God is everywhere and therefore also in me. I choose to be one with my God, and therefore I am the Presence of Archangel Michael in this world.

I affirm that Archangel Michael and his billions of Blue-flame Angels are cutting me free from dark spirits and dark energies.

I affirm that Archangel Michael and his billions of Blue-flame Angels are cutting me free from the lies of anti-christ.

I affirm that Archangel Michael and his billions of Blue-flame Angels are cutting me free from spiritual slavery under the forces of anti-christ.

I affirm that Archangel Michael and his billions of Blue-flame Angels are cutting me free from material slavery under the power elite.

**My being and world is the Lord's and the fullness thereof.** (3X) Amen.

In the name of the unconditional love of the Father, the Son, the Holy Spirit and the Miracle Mother, Amen.

## Sealing

Archangel Michael, I will no longer listen to the demons and the ego that howl their songs incessantly, trying to overwhelm me. I will listen to the voice and absorb the vibration of an archangel. And in your vibration, I am sealed in the inner knowing that no external force can take away. I know there is a God, that God is real and that God is everywhere, including in me. I now find the God within, and I accept the reality of that God and that it is the only reality.

I am sealed in the knowing that all manifestations on this Earth are ultimately illusions that have no power over the real spiritual being that I AM. I am sealed in that reality, and I accept the Presence of an archangel until I can accept the Presence of my own Higher Being.

I am sealed in the God Power of the first ray of the Will of God—the infinite faith that is beyond doubt because it is not faith, it is not belief, it is Oneness with reality, the reality that I AM.

# Taking command over your state of mind

A dictation by Mother Mary

My beloved heart,

I know you are burdened. I know you feel like you have lost control of your life, like you are up against forces, or energies, or an outer situation that seems to be beyond your control. Thus, you feel powerless. You feel stuck. You feel paralyzed. You feel even a sense of anger or resentment against the material world that seems to set these insurmountable obstacles in your path and seems to set so many limits to what you can and cannot do.

My beloved, I can assure you that I feel your pain and I know what you are going through. How can I say this? I can say this, my beloved, because I too have been in embodiment on planet Earth. So there is hardly a shade of pain, of frustration, that I have not personally experienced while in embodiment.

In my last embodiment, which took place 2,000 years ago, I was known as Mary, the mother of Jesus. Yet I can assure you that I am more than the saintly figure revered by Catholics. I have indeed ascended to heaven. And in the ascended realm, I have risen to the rank of holding the spiritual office as representative of the Mother Flame of God for planet Earth.

You might recall, my beloved, that the Bible itself states that "I AM Alpha and Omega, the beginning and the ending, sayeth the Lord, which was and which is and which is to come the Almighty." So my beloved, you see then that God has both a masculine and a feminine side, an Alpha and an Omega, a beginning and an ending. And so, I come in this release to be the ending to the beginning of Archangel Michael in his powerful release, that is designed to make the demons and the dark forces flee from your being because they cannot stand the Presence of an archangel.

Well my beloved, while I choose not to speak with the same power of the masculine force of Archangel Michael, I can assure you that I am no less powerful, and thus no dark force can stand to be in *my* Presence. Yet I come primarily to give you a new sense of comfort, a new sense of hope, a new sense of self-worth, of self-esteem. For my beloved, is it not true that when you face a crises in your life, one of the first things to go is your self-esteem, your sense of self-worth? In fact, my beloved, could we not say that it is precisely the loss of self esteem that is the very essence of the crises, or at least the very factor that prevents you from rising out of the crises? For my beloved, is it not precisely the lack of self-worth that makes you believe the subtle thoughts that you cannot possibly overcome your current situation? Is it not the lack of self-worth that makes you vulnerable to the very subtle belief that – because you have made this or that mistake – you can never again be free of it, you can never be pure, you can never be forgiven.

Is it not the lack of self-esteem, my beloved, that makes you believe in the subtle lie that your past actions prove that you are no good? And therefore, you can never build a better future, you can never overcome your present situation, your present problems. For you simply do not have what it takes to overcome those problems, as is proven, your voice says, by your mistakes of the past.

Well my beloved, I am indeed the representative of the Mother of God for planet Earth. And as that representative of the Mother Flame of God, I can assure you that there is absolutely nothing about the physical, material universe that I do not know. My beloved, I know every aspect of this world. Thus, my beloved, I know every possible problem that a human being on Earth could ever face. And therefore, with that knowledge, I can assure you, my beloved, that there is not one single problem on Earth that does not have a solution.

My beloved, it does not matter how insurmountable your situation may seem at the moment. There is a way out, or rather my beloved, there is a way *up*. It does not matter how big a mistake you have made in the past, how imperfect or impure you might feel. There is absolutely no condition on Earth from which you cannot rise, from which you cannot be purified. My beloved, how can I say this? I can say this because I know something about the material world that you were not taught in school, not even in Sunday school.

For my beloved, there are forces in this world who do not want you to know the truth that I will now tell you. You see my beloved, you might go down to your local sewer treatment plant and watch some of the dirtiest water you can imagine coming into that plant. It might be polluted by chemicals, by human waste or by all manner of foul things. Yet my beloved, if you took a pot of that water, put it on your stove and boiled it, what would happen? Well my beloved, the water would turn into steam, would it not? And the water would then rise above the pot and the water would leave behind all of the impurities. And it would then take on a different form, as the pure molecules of hydrogen and oxygen combine to form vapor that is invisible to the human eye—but nevertheless can be condensed again into water drops that are now pure. In fact so pure that the former state of pollution is no longer in existence. It is as if the water that was in the pot no longer exists. And indeed, it *does* no longer exist but has been transformed into a pure state, the pure state of water that it had before the pollution started.

And so my beloved, the truth that I want you to understand is that everything in the material world is made from one basic substance, namely what I like to call the Ma-ter light, the Mother Light. This is not hard for you to understand, my beloved, when you realize what science has told you that all the matter you see around you is made from smaller building blocks, called molecules. And even those are made from smaller blocks, called atoms. But even the atoms are made from even smaller particles, called subatomic particles. Yet my beloved, even the particles are made from a finer substance, namely energy itself, energy called light.

And so you see, my beloved, even modern science has discovered the reality that you live in a universe where everything is light. And so when you combine this with the statement in the Gospel of John that "without him was not anything made that was made," you see that everything in this world is made from the Light of God, the Ma-ter light that has taken on form. Yet my beloved, the form that the Ma-ter light has taken on is only a temporary manifestation that has not altered the fundamental qualities of the light. It is indeed, my beloved, like the white light that is shined through a movie projector that is colored by the images on the film strip. Yet the light is still the light. And if you remove the film strip, you have again the pure white light hitting the screen.

And so you see, my beloved, without him was not anything made that was made. Without the Light of God was not anything made that was made. And I can assure you that you were made and thus you are made of light. And that means that you are a being of light, a spiritual being. You are not a mortal human being. You are not created as a mortal sinner who can do nothing but sin. You are not created, or evolved, as a sophisticated monkey. And your thoughts are not the products exclusively of processes in your physical brain.

My beloved, you are more than the body, you are more than this Earth, you are more than the material universe itself. You have a spiritual reality, a spiritual identity, that is beyond this world. And my beloved, precisely because it is beyond this world, it cannot be affected by anything that you have experienced or anything you have done in this world. Do you see, my beloved, there is a core of your being that is permanently residing in the spiritual realm. That core contains the blueprint for your identity, for your individuality in God. And it has not been destroyed or altered, or even covered over by anything you have experienced in the material world.

So my beloved, even though you might feel burdened or feel a sense of being stuck in your present situation, I can assure you that there is a higher part of your being which is not in the least affected by your present situation. My beloved, I know you cannot see this given your present state of consciousness. And that is why I have come, as your spiritual mother, to tell you this reality that is beyond your present vision. For my beloved, I can assure you that I know you intimately. I know you personally. I know who you are. I know the higher reality of your being. And I have, from your very first descent into the denser realm of the material realm, been holding the immaculate concept for you. For I see your true reality. I see your true identity. And I see your highest potential for what you can manifest in this world.

So you see, my beloved, beyond your present situation is a deeper reality. And if you could – for one instant – connect to that reality, you would gain an entirely different perspective on your present situation. For my beloved, it is not, as I said, that the reason why you are burdened by your present situation is that you see no way out. You see no solution to your problems. You do not see how you can be purified from your past mistakes.

But my beloved, the reason you see no way out is that you do not see who you are. For if you could see who you truly are, then you would know that you are more than your present situation. And therefore, there *is* a way out, which is to reconnect to the true spiritual being that you are. And so my beloved, who and what is it that can reconnect to your spiritual being, what we call your I AM Presence? Well my beloved, the core of our being is that which is conscious of your own existence here in the material universe. That part of your being I like to call the Conscious You. And I have given much more detailed teachings on it in the book that I have prepared for your use and for your freedom.[15]

Yet my beloved, you will know that you have a conscious self if you will only contemplate the very fact that you are conscious. This should not be difficult. For my beloved if you were not conscious, if you were not conscious of yourself, if you were not self-aware, then how could you possibly suffer from your present situation? You see my beloved, the logic is very simple. You are bur-

---

15 *Master Keys to the Abundant Life.*

dened, you are suffering, and you are very conscious of the fact that you are suffering. Well my beloved, the very fact that you are conscious of your suffering, means that there is a part of you that is self-aware. And that is precisely the part of you that I call the Conscious You or the conscious self. Well, what you need to realize, my beloved, is that your conscious self is more than your present situation, is more than your outer mind, is more than your present sense of identity.

You see, my beloved, your conscious self is an extension of your spiritual being. And your spiritual being, your I AM Presence, is an extension of the very Being of your Creator, of God itself. And therefore, your conscious self is also beyond this world. But you see, my beloved, your conscious self is designed to descend into the material world and experience this world and help co-create this world, eventually manifesting the kingdom of God on Earth. I know you have forgotten this purpose. I know you have forgotten this true identity. And that is why I have come to remind you. For my beloved, the only true source of self-esteem is self-knowledge, the realization of who and what you really are.

For my beloved, as you very well know in your present situation, any self-esteem that is based on the conditions or the things of this world is fragile, is mortal, can easily be taken away from you. That is precisely why the conditions you experience in your present situation have caused you to lose your self-esteem. Is it not so, my beloved? And the reason is clear now, is it not? Your self-esteem was based on the things of this world, it was a house built on sand. And therefore, it could easily be blown over when the winds and the rains descended upon it, when you were hit by "the slings and arrows of outrageous fortune," as Shakespeare used to put it.

And so my beloved, do you now see the simple, yet eminently logical, reality that if you want to build a true sense of self-esteem, a sense of self-esteem that is not vulnerable to the conditions of this world, then you must build a sense of self-esteem that is above and beyond anything in this world. And how can you build this sense of self-esteem? Well my beloved, you can do so by reconnecting to the higher being that you are, to the reality that you are a spiritual being having a material experience. You are not, as the saying goes, a material being trying to have a spiritual experience. You are already a spiritual being. So it is not a matter of becoming something you are not. It is a matter of realizing who and what you already are. Ah my beloved, but in order to realize who you really are, you first have to come to the realization that your present sense of identity – as a mortal human being – is indeed unreal, is nothing but an illusion.

And so my beloved, your present sense of identity is indeed like the polluted water that runs into the sewer plant. Over the course of this lifetime, even over the course of many lifetimes, the pure water of your consciousness has been polluted by all manner of foul and smelly things that have fallen into the stream of consciousness. Thus, the waters of your mind have become so muddy that you can no longer see through them to see the deeper parts of your being—thus you only see the surface, where the dirt and debris is swirling around. Yet my beloved, the water of your consciousness is still the pure water. And by purifying it of the impurities that have accumulated in it, you can come to see clearly who you truly are.

So my beloved, it is only a matter of following the admonition of Archangel Michael—that if you will keep taking one small doable step at a time, then you *will* indeed rise above your present condition, your present circumstance, your present state of consciousness. For you see, my beloved, here is another reality that you were not taught by the powers of this world. That reality is that everything in your outer situation is created by the Ma-ter light that has taken on a certain form. But my beloved, that form was not created by conditions outside of yourself, not by bad luck or fate or even bad karma. It was determined by the images and beliefs that you hold in your mind.

As I said before, the pure stream of your consciousness is like the white light of the movie projector. And the beliefs and images and illusions you hold in your mind, even at subconscious levels, are like the film strip in a movie projector. Thus, what is projected onto the screen of your conscious mind and the screen of your outer material situation is simply a reflection of the images on the film strip of your mind. And thus, my beloved, the reason why you feel you are paralyzed, the reason why you feel like you can never again be cured or regain your self-esteem – why you could never again regain your innocence – is that you have been programmed by the false teachers of this world, even the institutions of your present society, to believe that the world works in the opposite way from the way that it really works.

You see, my beloved, it is simply not true that your state of mind is a product of your outer circumstances. The reality is that your outer circumstances are the products of your state of mind. Therefore, my beloved, one of the most insidious illusions perpetrated upon humankind is the illusion that only when your outer circumstances change, will your state of consciousness change.

Can you not see, my beloved, that from your very early childhood, you have been programmed by well-meaning people, such as your parents, your teachers or the authorities of your society, to believe in a very subtle lie? That subtle lie says that in order for you to be happy, you must have certain outer conditions fulfilled. Some of those conditions might be that you need certain material things. And obviously you can see, my beloved, that this is caused by the fact that there is somebody who wants to sell you something. Other conditions may be that you have to live in a certain society. And again there is somebody who wants to sell you a political belief system.

Perhaps you have even been programmed to believe that you need to be a member of a certain religion and live up to certain outer requirements defined by that religion. But again, my beloved, I must tell you the truth that – again – somebody is trying to sell you something, a religious belief system. So you see, my beloved, there are forces in this world who want to control you, and they do this by programming you to believe in the subtle lie that you cannot be in command of your mind unless you have control over your outer circumstances. And my beloved, this very subtle belief is precisely what has lead to your current crisis and thus has put you in what feels like a catch-22, like an impossible situation for which there is no way out.

For you see, my beloved, you are attempting to put the cart before the horse—to solve the problem in a way that can never lead to a real solution. For my beloved, you will never be happy as a result of outer conditions. Why is this so, my beloved? It is so because happiness, peace of mind, self-worth are *inner* conditions. They are feelings, they are a state of mind, are they not?

So you see, my beloved, it makes no logical sense whatsoever to say that your *inner* condition is a product of your *outer* condition. This is a very subtle lie, my beloved, perpetrated upon you by those who want to control you from without. For they know that if they can make you believe in this lie, then they can control your inner circumstances by controlling your outer circumstances. And certainly, there are many forces in this world who have a certain degree of control over your outer circumstances. Thus, if you believe that your outer circumstances control your inner circumstances, well my beloved, the forces of this world, the prince of this world, will have control over you. For the prince of this world will come and have something in you whereby he can control you. That something in you is indeed the very belief that your inner conditions are the products of outer conditions.

So you see, my beloved, the stark reality – as also explained by archangel Michael – is that everything in the material world is a product of certain mental images that are projected upon the Ma-ter light, thereby causing the Ma-ter light to take on a certain form. And thus, your outer circumstances are the exclusive products of the images that are held in your personal mind and in the collective consciousness of humankind, insofar as you have allowed your personal mind to become open to the collective mind.

You see, my beloved, the forces and energies that have invaded your auric field from without are partly coming from the mass consciousness, the collective consciousness of humankind. But along with these forces and energies are the images and beliefs that they are based upon, the images to which they owe there very existence. So you see, when you are open to the mass consciousness, to the collective mind, well then you take in these images and you are so overwhelmed by the energy and the subtle lies and arguments presented by the dark forces and your own ego, that you come to believe and accept these images as real, as unchangeable, as unavoidable.

Thus, you take them into your mind and then – when the light shines through the film strip of your mind – it is colored by those very images. So you project onto the screen of light, onto the Ma-ter light, images that are illusions, images that can only cause you suffering. So my beloved, it is inevitable that after a certain time these images will manifest themselves as actual material, physical, outer circumstances that you cannot ignore and seemingly cannot escape.

Yet my beloved I am here to tell you the absolute truth that if you will make the effort, a conscious and determined effort, to clear your forcefield, to clear your mind – even the subconscious levels of your mind – from all unreality, then my beloved, you will indeed change your outer situation. You will overcome your current crisis and you will begin to see clearly through the stream of your consciousness. Until you see the very deepest recesses of your being and certainly experience – not a theoretical intellectual knowledge, but as an actual intuitive mystical experience – that you are more than the outer identity, more than the outer self, more than the ego, more that this world. You are a spiritual being. You have a reality in God. And therefore, my beloved, you have the ultimate self-worth that is possible anywhere, namely the absolute knowing that you are an extension of God. You are an individualization of God. And my beloved, would you not say that God is infinitely worthy, has infinite value?

So my beloved, when you realize that you are an extension of God's infinite Being – and thus *you* truly are God's infinite Being manifest as a specific identity – then my beloved, you will know – you will realize, you will experience – the ultimate self-worth of knowing what Jesus knew, what Jesus experienced when Jesus said, "I and my Father are one." Ah my beloved, there is no greater feeling, there is no greater experience on Earth than coming to the realization of who you truly are in God.

My beloved, I can assure you that no matter what pleasure or experience you have had on this Earth, it is as nothing compared to the experience of oneness with your Higher Being, oneness with the reality of your Creator. It is a feeling that is beyond what can be imagined by your outer mind. But I can assure you that if you will keep moving away from the darkness by taking one small step higher every day, then you will eventually break through and have a glimpse of that experience of ultimate self-worth. Thus, you will know that no matter what mistakes you have made or the experiences you have had – no matter how degrading or inhumane or humiliating – well my beloved, they have no part of the reality of your being. They are simply temporary illusions, mirages that are nothing more than flickering images in the distance. Thus, when you know and experience that you are more than this, well my beloved, then you can let it go. I assure you that at that point – when you experience the reality that you are, the reality that I AM – well then you can fully forgive yourself. You can fully forgive all the people with whom you have been involved, all people you may have hurt, all people who may have hurt you. You can forgive yourself, you can forgive them, you can forgive God, you can even forgive the Ma-ter light for causing you to experience limitations and suffering.

My beloved, if you will keep moving on, there will come that point of total release, total forgiveness, total surrender where you give up the mortal sense of identity—where you let it die and you then merge into the greater reality that you are. And you realize that you *are* that greater being, you always were that greater being and you can return to experiencing the reality of that greater being, even while you are still in a physical body. But only, you will now be transformed so you will no longer identify with your body or your outer circumstances, for you will *know,* you will *experience,* that you are more.

Oh my beloved, this is the greatest joy, the greatest freedom, the greatest happiness, the greatest sense of self-worth, the greatest sense of self-esteem that can possibly be experienced by any self-aware being. And my beloved, I have come to tell you or show you that *that* experience is possible for you. Why is is possible? It is possible because you are self-aware. And thus, you have the potential to be more aware than you are right now, and to be aware of a greater self than the self of which you are aware right now. Do you see, my beloved, what I am saying? Do you see the deeper reality here? The very fact that you are suffering with a limited sense of self proves that you can expand your sense of self, expand your awareness and become more than you are right now—by accepting, by merging with, the greater self that you already are.

So my beloved, even if you cannot fully accept this with your outer mind, I ask only one thing of you—be willing to TRY. Be willing to make the effort to move towards that point of inner realization of who you are. So my beloved, when you have given Archangel Michael's rosary and listened to his dictation to the point where you feel that you have taken back some control of your life, then my beloved, use the program that I have designed, of listening to this dictation and giving the rosary based upon it, the rosary for attaining self-esteem. If you will keep doing this for at least thirty-three days, then you will feel a difference. And then after that continue the program, but now do Archangel Michael's rosary one day and my rosary the next, so that you alternate between the vibration of the Alpha and the Omega aspects of God.

And if, my beloved, you will keep doing this until you feel an inner prompting to study other teachings – to give other rosaries of the many I have prepared for you – well then you will indeed turn your life around. And you will experience that your life has become an upward spiral. And when you have experienced this, you can – if you are willing to do so – consciously lock your life permanently in an upward spiral. And once you are locked in an upward spiral, it is only a matter of time before you break through to the inner realization of who you truly are.

Oh my beloved, this is indeed possible for you, and I shall hold that immaculate vision, that immaculate concept, for you as I held for Jesus every day until the very day, where he manifested his Christhood and was resurrected permanently into a higher sense of self. Thus, give the rosaries, but also do not forget to daily make a simple call to me and simply say, "Oh Mother Mary, show me the immaculate concept for myself as I am able to grasp it right now."

My beloved, if you will make this request, I will show you what you are able to see, what you are willing to see. And I can assure you that you and I – together with Archangel Michael, with your Christ self and with other members of the Ascended Host – can indeed walk all the way home, until every part of our beings has achieved oneness with the greater Being that we all are. Because, you see my beloved, in the spiritual realm we know the reality that all life is one because all life is God.

Thus, my beloved, be sealed in the infinite love, the infinite nurturance and the infinite comfort of your Divine Mother's heart that overflows with a very personal love for you, a love that transcends all boundaries of the material world. A love that you can experience right now, if you are only willing to look beyond the outer conditions and accept the love that I AM, the unconditional love that I AM, the unconditional love that I have for you. For my beloved, when my love is unconditional, you do not need to live up to any conditions on Earth in order to receive that love, do you? So forget about the conditions and accept that I love you, that Archangel Michael loves you, that your I AM Presence loves you, that your Christ self loves you, that Jesus loves you and that your Creator loves you, has always loved you and will always love you. Be sealed, my beloved, in the infinite love that I AM, in the infinite love that *you* are.

# Mother Mary's Self-esteem Rosary

In the name of the Unconditional Love of the Father, the Son, the Holy Spirit and the Mother of Light, Amen.

In the name of the I AM THAT I AM, Jesus Christ, I dedicate this rosary to the manifestation of the perfect vision of Christ in . . . (insert personal prayer here).

## God is Father and Mother

God is Father, God is Mother,
never one without the other.

Your balanced union is our source,
your Love will keep us on our course.
You offer us abundant life,
to free us from all sense of strife.
We plunge ourselves into the stream,
awakening from this bad dream.
We see that life is truly one,
and thus our victory is won.
We have returned unto our God,
on the path the saints have trod.
We form God's body on the Earth,
and give our planet its rebirth,
into a Golden Age of Love,
with ample blessings from Above.
We set all people free to see
that oneness is reality,
and in that oneness we will be
whole for all eternity.
And now the Earth is truly healed,
all life in God's perfection sealed.

God is Father, God is Mother,
we see God in each other.

## I am more than the human self

1. Only the human self can feel burdened, can feel it has lost control, can feel powerless, stuck or paralyzed. Only the human self can feel a sense of anger or resentment against the material world and its insurmountable obstacles or limits for what can and cannot be done. I AM MORE than the human self.

Hail Being of Light
**I now surrender all that's less,**
**forever upward I progress.**
**I now accept my sacred worth,**
**as I go through a grand rebirth.**

**I know my true identity,**
**I know my God is real in me.**
**I am a being of God's light,**
**it shines within me ever bright.**

2. In a crisis, one of the first things I lose is self-esteem, the sense of self-worth. The loss of self-esteem is the very essence of the crisis, the very factor that prevents me from rising out of the crisis. Yet only the human self can lose self-esteem. I AM MORE than the human self.

**Hail Being of Light**

3. It is ALWAYS possible to overcome my current situation. Only the human self can believe the subtle lie that because I have made this or that mistake, I can never again be free of it, I can never be pure, I can never be forgiven. I AM MORE than the human self.

**Hail Being of Light**

4. No matter what mistakes I might have made, I am still a good person and I can build a better future, I can overcome my present problems. Only the human self can believe that it does not have what it takes to overcome those problems. I AM MORE than the human self.

**Hail Being of Light**

5. Every single problem on Earth has a solution. No matter how insurmountable a situation may seem to the human self, there is a way up. No matter how big a mistake I have made in the past, how imperfect or impure my human self might feel, there is absolutely

no condition on Earth from which I cannot rise, from which I cannot be purified. I AM MORE than the human self.

**I now surrender all that's less,**
**forever upward I progress.**
**I now accept my sacred worth,**
**as I go through a grand rebirth.**

**I know my true identity,**
**I know my God is real in me.**
**I am a being of God's light,**
**it shines within me ever bright.**

6. Everything in the material world is made from one basic substance, namely the Ma-ter light, the Mother Light. I live in a universe where everything is light. Everything is made from the Light of God, the Ma-ter light that has taken on form. A form is only a temporary manifestation that has not altered the fundamental qualities of the light. Everything in this world is a temporary appearance, and the light can always be returned to its pure state. I AM MORE than the human self.

**Hail Being of Light**

7. Without the Light of God was not anything made that was made. I was made, and thus I am made of light, I am a being of light, a spiritual being. I am not a mortal human being, I was not created as a mortal sinner who can do nothing but sin. I was not created, or evolved, as a sophisticated monkey. My thoughts are more than the processes in my physical brain. I AM MORE than the human self.

**Hail Being of Light**

8. I am more than the body, I am more than this Earth, I am more than the material universe itself. I have a spiritual reality, a spiritual identity, that is beyond this world. Because my true identity is beyond this world, it cannot be affected by anything I have experienced or anything I have done in this world. I AM MORE than the human self.

**Hail Being of Light**

9. There is a core of my being that is permanently residing in the spiritual realm. That core contains the blueprint for my identity, my individuality in God. It has not been destroyed or altered, or even

covered over by anything I have experienced in the material world. I AM MORE than the human self.

**Hail Being of Light**

## 1. Throat, Solar plexus

Hail Mary, we give praise
the Mother Light in all you raise.
In perfect balance light will stream,
in harmony our souls will gleam.

Refrain:
**Oh Mother Mary, we release**
**all thoughts and feelings less than peace,**
**releasing now all patterns old,**
**we leave behind the mortal mold.**

**River of Life, eternal flow,**
**we will to live, we will to grow.**
**We will transcend and be the more,**
**the joy of life we do adore.**

All troubles in the heart now cease,
as Mary's love brings great release.
The rose of twelve in fullest bloom,
the soul is free to meet her groom.

The throat is shining oh so blue,
the will of God is always true.
God's power is released in love
through Christ direction from Above.

The solar center is at peace,
as fear and anger we release.
The sacred ten will now unfold
a glow of purple and of gold.

When Mother Light and Buddha meet,
the force of darkness they defeat,
with Jesus and our Saint Germain,
they bring the Golden Age again.

I feel the Mother's gentle kiss,
as I am in eternal bliss,
floating in a space sublime,
in harmony with sacred chime.

**Oh Mother Mary, we release**
**all thoughts and feelings less than peace,**
**releasing now all patterns old,**
**we leave behind the mortal mold.**

**River of Life, eternal flow,**
**we will to live, we will to grow.**
**We will transcend and be the more,**
**the joy of life we do adore.**

Coda:
By Mother Mary's endless Grace,
we conquer time, we conquer space.
The Buddha Nature is in all
and thus we rise to heed the call
to be the Christed ones on Earth,
the Golden Age is given birth.

## I am more than material conditions

1. My human self might feel burdened and stuck in my present situation, yet there is a higher part of my being which is not affected by my present situation. Beyond my outer situation is a deeper reality. I can connect to that reality and gain an entirely different perspective on my life. I AM MORE than any material conditions.

**I now surrender all that's less,**
**forever upward I progress.**
**I now accept my sacred worth,**
**as I go through a grand rebirth.**

**I know my true identity,**
**I know my God is real in me.**
**I am a being of God's light,**
**it shines within me ever bright.**

2. When I think there is no way out of my present situation, it is because I do not see who I am. When I see who I truly am, I know

that I am more than my present situation. Therefore, there is a way out, which is to reconnect to the true spiritual being that I am. I can reconnect to my spiritual being, my I AM Presence, because the core of my being is my conscious self. I AM MORE than any material conditions.

**Hail Being of Light**

3. The fact that I am suffering proves that I am self-aware. And because I am self-aware, I can become aware that my conscious self is more than my present situation, is more than my outer mind, is more than my present sense of identity. I AM MORE than any material conditions.

**Hail Being of Light**

4. My conscious self is an extension of my spiritual being, and my I AM Presence is an extension of the very Being of my Creator. My conscious self is designed to descend into the material world in order to experience this world and help co-create the kingdom of God on Earth. I AM MORE than any material conditions.

**Hail Being of Light**

5. My outer mind has forgotten this purpose, has forgotten my true identity. Yet I can reconnect to my true identity, and the only true source of self-esteem is self-knowledge, the realization of who and what I really am. I AM MORE than any material conditions.

**Hail Being of Light**

6. Any self-esteem that is based on the conditions or the things of this world is fragile and can easily be lost. The conditions I experience in my present situation have caused me to lose the self-esteem that was based on the things of this world. I AM MORE than any material conditions.

**Hail Being of Light**

7. I will build a sense of self-esteem that is not vulnerable to material conditions by reaching for the self-esteem that is above and beyond anything in this world. I can build this self-esteem by reconnecting to the Higher Being that I am, to the reality that I am a spiritual being having a material experience, not a material being trying to have a spiritual experience. I AM MORE than any material conditions.

**Hail Being of Light**

8. I am already a spiritual being, and thus I am not seeking to become something I am not. I am seeking the realization of who and what I already am. I realize that my sense of identity as a mortal human being is unreal, is only an illusion. I AM MORE than any material conditions.

**I now surrender all that's less,**
**forever upward I progress.**
**I now accept my sacred worth,**
**as I go through a grand rebirth.**

**I know my true identity,**
**I know my God is real in me.**
**I am a being of God's light,**
**it shines within me ever bright.**

9. My present sense of identity is like water that has become polluted, has become so muddy that I can no longer see the deeper parts of my being. Yet the water of my consciousness is still the pure water. And by purifying it of all impurities, I will see clearly who I truly am. I will keep taking one small, doable step at a time, until I see the reality of my I AM Presence. I AM MORE than any material conditions.

**Hail Being of Light**

## 2. Third Eye, Soul

Hail Mary, we give praise
the Mother Light in all you raise.
In perfect balance light will stream,
in harmony our souls will gleam.

Refrain:
**Oh Mother Mary, we release**
**all thoughts and feelings less than peace,**
**releasing now all patterns old,**
**we leave behind the mortal mold.**

**River of Life, eternal flow,**
**we will to live, we will to grow.**
**We will transcend and be the more,**
**the joy of life we do adore.**

All troubles in the heart now cease,
as Mary's love brings great release.
The rose of twelve in fullest bloom,
the soul is free to meet her groom.

The brow emits an emerald hue,
Christ's perfect vision we pursue,
and as we see God's perfect plan,
we feel God's love for every man.

The soul is basking in delight,
as violet flame is shining bright.
The soul is breathing God's pure air,
she feels so free in Mother's care.

When Mother Light and Buddha meet,
the force of darkness they defeat,
with Jesus and our Saint Germain,
they bring the Golden Age again.

I feel the Mother's gentle kiss,
as I am in eternal bliss,
floating in a space sublime,
in harmony with sacred chime.

Coda:
By Mother Mary's endless Grace,
we conquer time, we conquer space.
The Buddha Nature is in all
and thus we rise to heed the call
to be the Christed ones on Earth,
the Golden Age is given birth.

### I am a stream of God's consciousness

1. Everything in my outer situation is created by the Ma-ter light that has taken on a certain form. That form was not created by conditions outside myself. It was determined by the images and beliefs I hold in my mind. I AM a pure stream of God's consciousness.

**I now surrender all that's less,**
**forever upward I progress.**
**I now accept my sacred worth,**
**as I go through a grand rebirth.**

**I know my true identity,**
**I know my God is real in me.**
**I am a being of God's light,**
**it shines within me ever bright.**

2. The stream of my consciousness is like the white light in a movie projector. The beliefs, images and illusions I hold in my mind, even at subconscious levels, are like the film strip in a movie projector. What is projected onto the screen of my conscious mind, and the screen of my material situation, is simply a reflection of the images on the film strip of my mind. I AM a pure stream of God's consciousness.

**Hail Being of Light**

3. My state of mind is not a product of my outer circumstances. Instead, my outer circumstances are the products of my state of mind. It is a lie that in order to be happy, I must have certain outer conditions fulfilled. I do not need material things, political conditions or religious conditions in order to be happy and have peace of mind. I only need to reconnect to my true identity. I AM a pure stream of God's consciousness.

**Hail Being of Light**

4. I no longer accept the subtle lie that I cannot be in command of my mind unless I have control over my outer circumstances. It is this belief that has lead to my current crisis and has put me in a catch-22. I will never be happy as a result of outer conditions. Happiness, peace of mind, self-worth are inner conditions—they are feelings, they are states of mind. I AM a pure stream of God's consciousness.

**Hail Being of Light**

5. I let go of the lie that in order to control my inner circumstances I must control my outer circumstances. I no longer believe that my outer circumstances control my inner circumstances, and thus the forces of this world, the prince of this world, will have no more control over me. For the prince of this world will come and have

nothing in me whereby he can control me. I AM a pure stream of God's consciousness.

**Hail Being of Light**

6. Everything in the material world is a product of mental images that are projected upon the Ma-ter light, thereby causing the light to take on a certain form. My outer circumstances are the exclusive products of the images that are held in my personal mind and in the collective consciousness of humankind. I AM a pure stream of God's consciousness.

**Hail Being of Light**

7. The forces and energies that have invaded my auric field from without are coming from the collective consciousness. Along with them are the images and beliefs to which they owe their existence. I now close my mind to the mass consciousness, to the collective mind. I refuse to take in these images and the subtle lies and arguments presented by the dark forces and my own ego. I no longer accept these images as real, as unchangeable or as unavoidable. I AM a pure stream of God's consciousness.

**Hail Being of Light**

8. I will make a conscious and determined effort to clear my forcefield, to clear the subconscious levels of my mind, from all unreality. I know this will also change my outer situation. I will overcome my current crisis by seeking first the kingdom of God that I know is the real self within me. I AM a pure stream of God's consciousness.

**Hail Being of Light**

9. I will see the deepest recesses of my being and experience, as an actual intuitive mystical experience, that I am more than the outer identity, more than the outer self, more than the ego and more than this world. I AM a pure stream of God's consciousness.

**Hail Being of Light**

## 3. Crown, Base

Hail Mary, we give praise
the Mother Light in all you raise.
In perfect balance light will stream,
in harmony our souls will gleam.

Refrain:
**Oh Mother Mary, we release**
**all thoughts and feelings less than peace,**
**releasing now all patterns old,**
**we leave behind the mortal mold.**

**River of Life, eternal flow,**
**we will to live, we will to grow.**
**We will transcend and be the more,**
**the joy of life we do adore.**

All troubles in the heart now cease,
as Mary's love brings great release.
The rose of twelve in fullest bloom,
the soul is free to meet her groom.

The crown is like a sea of gold,
as thousand petals now unfold.
We see the Buddha in the crown,
arrayed in his celestial gown.

The base is of the purest white,
four petals radiate your light.
The Mother bows in purest love
to God the Father from Above.

When Mother Light and Buddha meet,
the force of darkness they defeat,
with Jesus and our Saint Germain,
they bring the Golden Age again.

I feel the Mother's gentle kiss,
as I am in eternal bliss,
floating in a space sublime,
in harmony with sacred chime.

Coda:
By Mother Mary's endless Grace,
we conquer time, we conquer space.
The Buddha Nature is in all
and thus we rise to heed the call
to be the Christed ones on Earth,
the Golden Age is given birth.

## I am an individualization of my Creator

1. I am a spiritual being, and I have a reality in God. I have the ultimate self-worth, namely the absolute knowing that I am an extension of God, an individualization of God. I know that God has infinite value, and because I am an extension of God's infinite being – I am God's infinite being manifest as a specific identity – I have the ultimate self-worth of knowing what Jesus experienced when he said, "I and my Father are one." I AM an individualization of my Creator.

**I now surrender all that's less,**
**forever upward I progress.**
**I now accept my sacred worth,**
**as I go through a grand rebirth.**

**I know my true identity,**
**I know my God is real in me.**
**I am a being of God's light,**
**it shines within me ever bright.**

2. There is no greater experience on Earth than coming to the realization of who I truly am in God. No matter what pleasure or experience I have had on this Earth, it is as nothing compared to the experience of oneness with my Higher Being, oneness with the reality of my Creator. I AM an individualization of my Creator.

**Hail Being of Light**

3. As I keep moving away from the darkness by taking one step every day, I will eventually break through and have a glimpse of the ultimate self-worth. No matter what mistakes I have made or what experiences I have had, they have no part of the reality of my Being. They are temporary illusions, and I let it all go. I AM an individualization of my Creator.

**Hail Being of Light**

4. Because I know the reality that I AM, I can fully forgive myself. I can fully forgive all people I have hurt, all people who have hurt me. I forgive myself, I forgive others, I forgive God, I even forgive the Ma-ter light for my experiences of limitations and suffering. I AM an individualization of my Creator.

**Hail Being of Light**

5. I will move on to the point of total release, total forgiveness, total surrender. I give up the mortal sense of identity, I let it die and I merge into the greater reality that I am. I realize that I am that greater being, I was always that greater being and I can return to experiencing the reality of that greater being even while I am still in a physical body. I am transformed and I will no longer identify with my body or my outer circumstances, for I know I am more. I AM an individualization of my Creator.

**I now surrender all that's less,**
**forever upward I progress.**
**I now accept my sacred worth,**
**as I go through a grand rebirth.**

**I know my true identity,**
**I know my God is real in me.**
**I am a being of God's light,**
**it shines within me ever bright.**

6. In oneness with my Higher Being, I experience the greatest joy, the greatest freedom, the greatest happiness, the greatest sense of self-worth, the greatest sense of self-esteem that can possibly be experienced by any self-aware being. This experience is possible for me because I am self-aware. I have the potential to be aware of a greater self than the self of which I am aware right now. I AM an individualization of my Creator.

**Hail Being of Light**

7. I can expand my awareness and become more than I am right now by merging with the greater self that I already am. I am willing to try, I am willing to make the effort to move toward that point of inner realization of who I am. I know that as I keep doing this, I will indeed turn my life into an upward spiral. It is only a matter of time before I break through to the inner realization of who I truly am. I AM an individualization of my Creator.

**Hail Being of Light**

8. I accept that this is possible because Mother Mary will hold the immaculate vision, the immaculate concept, for me until the day when I manifest my Christhood and I am resurrected permanently into a higher sense of self. Thus I say, "Oh Mother Mary, show me the immaculate concept for myself, as I am able to grasp it right now." I AM an individualization of my Creator.

**Hail Being of Light**

9. I know that as long as I hold true to my highest vision, I will – together with Archangel Michael, my Christ self and all members of the Ascended Host – walk all the way home, until every part of our beings has achieved oneness with the greater Being that we all are. In the spiritual realm all Beings know the reality that all life is one because all life is God. I AM an individualization of my Creator.

**Hail Being of Light**

## 4. Combined

Hail Mary, we give praise
the Mother Light in all you raise.
In perfect balance light will stream,
in harmony our souls will gleam.

Refrain:
**Oh Mother Mary, we release**
**all thoughts and feelings less than peace,**
**releasing now all patterns old,**
**we leave behind the mortal mold.**

**River of Life, eternal flow,**
**we will to live, we will to grow.**
**We will transcend and be the more,**
**the joy of life we do adore.**

All troubles in the heart now cease,
as Mary's love brings great release.
The rose of twelve in fullest bloom,
the soul is free to meet her groom.

The throat is shining oh so blue,
the will of God is always true.
God's power is released in love
through Christ direction from Above.

The solar center is at peace,
as fear and anger we release.
The sacred ten will now unfold
a glow of purple and of gold.

All troubles in the heart now cease,
as Mary's love brings great release.
The rose of twelve in fullest bloom,
the soul is free to meet her groom.

**Oh Mother Mary, we release**
**all thoughts and feelings less than peace,**
**releasing now all patterns old,**
**we leave behind the mortal mold.**

**River of Life, eternal flow,**
**we will to live, we will to grow.**
**We will transcend and be the more,**
**the joy of life we do adore.**

The brow emits an emerald hue,
Christ's perfect vision we pursue,
and as we see God's perfect plan,
we feel God's love for every man.

The soul is basking in delight,
as violet flame is shining bright.
The soul is breathing God's pure air,
she feels so free in Mother's care.

All troubles in the heart now cease,
as Mary's love brings great release.
The rose of twelve in fullest bloom,
the soul is free to meet her groom.

The crown is like a sea of gold,
as thousand petals now unfold.
We see the Buddha in the crown,
arrayed in his celestial gown.

The base is of the purest white,
four petals radiate your light.
The Mother bows in purest love
to God the Father from Above.

When Mother Light and Buddha meet,
the force of darkness they defeat,
with Jesus and our Saint Germain,
they bring the Golden Age again.

I feel the Mother's gentle kiss,
as I am in eternal bliss,
floating in a space sublime,
in harmony with sacred chime.

Coda:
By Mother Mary's endless Grace,
we conquer time, we conquer space.
The Buddha Nature is in all
and thus we rise to heed the call
to be the Christed ones on Earth,
the Golden Age is given birth.

**The Earth is the Lord's and the fullness of his Love.** (3X)
Amen.

In the name of the Unconditional Love of the Father, the Son, the Holy Spirit and the Mother of Light, Amen.

## Sealing

I AM sealed in the infinite love, the infinite nurturance and the infinite comfort of my Divine Mother's heart, the heart that overflows with a very personal love for me, a love that transcends all boundaries of the material world. I experience that love right now because I am willing to look beyond the outer conditions and accept the love of Mother Mary, the unconditional love of Mother Mary, the unconditional love that Mother Mary has for me.

I accept that when love is unconditional, I do not need to live up to any conditions on Earth in order to receive that love. Thus, I let go of all conditions and accept that Mother Mary loves me, that Archangel Michael loves me, that my I AM Presence loves me, that my Christ self loves me and that Jesus loves me. I accept that my Creator loves me, has always loved me and will always love me. I am sealed in the infinite love that is Mother Mary, in the infinite love that I AM.

18 - seek deep mysteries of life

20 - Performing Miracles



35 - What the 'Kingdom of God' Really means!

39 - Meaning of, "to be born again!!"

44-45 - Spiritual Blindness.

81 - Following Christ by our willingness to see what we cannot, and

81 - our refusal to see what we cannot see, stops us.

82 - The 'beam in your eye is the EGO!!!

82 - Salvation is our own Responsibility!
(by Purifying our own consciousness)

83 - Salvation is gradual - we do our part + Jesus or - an A.M will help us from Their side.

83 - and Christ Consciousness is the kingdom of God!

84 - our Comforter, our Christ Self who is in our Kingdom of God within us - helps each of us.

85 - The Way of Christ!! is to always transcend our selves
《self-examine our self》

88 - Becoming aware of an ability we did not know we had.

91 - communist type system.

96 - How to choose one's Reality of Christ!!

100 - How to access the Christ mind.

101 - (important)

102 - Our Challenge is to descern between Christ Self + ego

106-108 - Jesus' directions for this study course.

110 - The devil's appearance

110-111 - subtlty of What is True.

115 - Buddha's direction on new ideas

115 - importance of Self Examination

121-122 - overcoming limitations and even doing MIRACLES

128 - What the Comforter and Christ Self Really is !!!

130 - How the ego works to cancel spiritual ideas.

131-32 Magnificent Confusion - means confusion can be a good sign

135. Experience Pure awareness.

92 - Miracles - a way to go ~~out~~ beyond human limitations

124 - Important - The 'beginner's mind'

CPSIA information can be obtained at www.ICGtesting.com
Printed in the USA
BVOW02s2018290815

415724BV00013B/157/P

9 780982 574614